CRISIS IN AMERICAN INSTITUTIONS

CRISIS IN AMERICAN INSTITUTIONS

Ninth Edition

Jerome H. Skolnick
Elliott Currie
University of California, Berkeley

■HarperCollins*CollegePublishers*

Senior Editor: Alan McClare
Project Editor: David Nickol
Design Supervisor: Molly Heron
Cover Design: Molly Heron
Production Manager: Willie Lane
Compositor: University Graphics, Inc.
Printer and Binder: R. R. Donnelley & Sons Company
Cover Printer: The Lehigh Press

Crisis in American Institutions, Ninth Edition

Library of Congress Cataloging-in-Publication Data

Crisis in American Institutions / [edited by] Jerome H. Skolnick,
   Elliott Currie.—9th ed.
      p.   cm.
   ISBN 0-673-52321-7
      1. United States—Social conditions—1980– 2. United States—
Social conditions—1980–1990. 3. Social problems—United States.
I. Skolnick, Jerome H. II. Currie, Elliott.
HN65.C684   1994
306'.0973—dc20   93-36617
                                                                 CIP

93   94   95   96   9   8   7   6   5   4   3   2   1

CONTENTS

PART FIVE ❖ SEXISM 197

Institutions in Crisis

PART SIX ❖ THE FAMILY 227

PART SEVEN ❖ THE ENVIRONMENT 265

PART EIGHT ❖ THE WORKPLACE 307

PART NINE ❖ HEALTH AND WELFARE 341

PART TEN ❖ THE SCHOOLS 381

PREFACE

For this ninth edition, the plan of the book remains basically the same as in earlier editions. But we have added new articles and dropped others, reflecting the changing contours of the crisis in American institutions in the 1990s.

We've eliminated our section on National Defense—not because we think there are no longer important issues surrounding our military institutions, but because, with the end of the Cold War, we felt that the most important of those issues, for courses on American social problems, was one we take up in the Epilogue—how to turn the military economy to constructive civilian purposes. At the same time, we've reinstated a section on education—absent from the book for several editions—with three new articles drawn from an impressive crop of recent writing on the crisis in America's schools.

We've also updated and, we think, strengthened several other sections—including adding two new articles on gender issues as well as articles on gun control and the flight of American jobs overseas—two issues at the forefront of public concern in the nineties.

Each edition has offered an opportunity to review the best contemporary writing on American social problems, and with each we have regretted dropping old favorites and being unable to include promising new writings. We invariably find far more worthwhile writing than we are able to use. After all, we survey a range of topics—from corporate power through racism, to the family and the environment—each of which could profitably occupy a lifetime of study and writing.

As always, many people helped us in many ways to make this edition a reality. At HarperCollins, Alan McClare and David Nickol again ably helped to transform manuscript into finished book. The Center for the Study of Law and Society at the University of California, Berkeley, once again offered crucial facilities and a supportive environment. Rod Watanabe, the Center's administrative assistant, as always created order whenever chaos threatened. Indispensable help with the manuscript was also provided by Kara Hatfield and Jennifer Tarleton. We appreciate their assistance and good cheer. Finally, we are most grateful to the students and teachers who have continued to teach us about each edition's strengths and weaknesses.

CRISIS IN AMERICAN INSTITUTIONS

INTRODUCTION: APPROACHES TO SOCIAL PROBLEMS

When we first put this book together in the late 1960s, the American mood was very different than it is today. The United States in those days was the undisputed political and economic leader among the world's countries. American living standards had been steadily rising. Each year brought new technological wonders that seemed to promise still more abundance to come. Small wonder that many social scientists accepted the widely prevailing view that most fundamental economic and political problems had been solved in the United States—or, at least, were well on their way to a solution.

Today, all of that seems like ancient history, even to us—not to mention today's students, many of whom were not yet born when the first edition of this book appeared. Indeed, by the time *Crisis in American Institutions* first appeared, the superficial tranquility of postwar American society had already begun to unravel—hence our choice of title. But by now, Americans are confronted with a range of social problems whose magnitude and visibility would have seemed almost incomprehensible when we first wrote our book.

These changes have had a profound effect on the way social scientists (and other observers of American society) have thought about social problems. The study of social problems, after all—like any other aspect of social science—does not take place in the antiseptic confines of a scientific laboratory. Social theorists, like everyone else, are deeply influenced by broader trends in the

1

society, in the economy, and in the cultural and technological setting of social life. As a way of introducing the articles that follow, of placing the debates of the 1980s and 1990s in some historical and intellectual context, we want to spend a few pages outlining the way in which the study of social problems has developed over time and how those larger social changes have shaped its basic assumptions and its guiding themes.

❖ DEFECTIVES AND DELINQUENTS

The earliest writers on social problems in this country were straightforward moralists, staunch supporters of the virtues of thrift, hard work, sexual purity, and personal discipline. Writing at the end of the nineteenth century, they sought ways of maintaining the values of an earlier, whiter, more Protestant, and more stable America in the face of the new challenges of industrialization, urbanization, and immigration.[1]

This early social science usually concentrated on the problems of what one nineteenth-century textbook described as the "defective, dependent, and delinquent classes."[2] The causes of social problems were located in the physical constitution or the moral "character" of the poor, the criminal, the insane, and other "unfortunates." For these theorists, the solution to nineteenth-century social problems lay in developing means of transforming the character of these "defective" classes, in the hope of equipping them better to succeed within a competitive, hierarchical society whose basic assumptions were never questioned. Social reformers working from these theories created, in the last part of the nineteenth and the first part of the twentieth centuries, much of the modern apparatus of "social control" in the United States: reformatories, modern prisons, institutions for the mentally ill, and the beginnings of the modern welfare system.

❖ THE RISE OF "VALUE-FREE" SOCIAL PROBLEMS

During the first decades of this century, this straightforward moralism was increasingly discarded in favor of a more subtle, ostensibly "neutral" approach to writing about social problems. By the 1930s, the idea that the social sciences were—or could be—purely "objective" or "value-free" had come to be widely accepted. From that point until the present, social problems theory has been characterized by a tortuous attempt to prove that theories and policies that serve to support the status quo are actually scientific judgments arrived at objectively. In this view, social scientists do not try to impose their own values in deciding what kinds of things will be defined and dealt with as social problems. Instead, the "scientific" student of social problems simply accepts "society's" definition of what is a problem and what is not. This approach is apparent in these statements, taken from major textbooks, on what constitutes a social problem:

> Any difficulty or misbehavior of a fairly large number of persons which we wish to remove or correct.[3]

> What people think they are.[4]

> Whenever people begin to say, isn't it awful! Why don't they do something about it?[5]

> Conditions which affect sizable proportions of the population, which are out of harmony with the values of a significant segment of the population, and which people feel can be improved or eliminated.[6]

> Any substantial discrepancy between socially shared standards and actual conditions of social life.[7]

These definitions share the common idea that social problems are popularly defined. No condition is a problem unless a certain number of people in a society say it is. Since we are merely taking, as our starting point, the definitions of the problem that "other people," "society," or "significant segments of the population" provide, we are no longer in the position of moralizing about objective conditions.

The basic flaw in this happy scheme is that it does not make clear *which* segments of the population to consult when defining problems or how to decide between conflicting ideas about what is problematic and what is not. In the real world, societies are divided along class, racial, sexual, and other lines, and the sociologist who proposes to follow "people's" definitions of social problems in fact generally adopts one of several competing ideologies of social problems based on those divisions. In practice, the ideology adopted has usually been not too different from that of the "unscientific" social problems writers of the nineteenth century.

These points are not new; they were raised as early as 1936 in an unusually perceptive paper called "Social Problems and the Mores," by the sociologist Willard Waller. Waller noted, for example, that discussions of poverty in the social problems literature of the 1930s were shaped by the unquestioning acceptance of the ideology of competitive capitalism:

> *A simpleton would suggest that the remedy for poverty in the midst of plenty is to redistribute income. We reject this solution at once because it would interfere with the institution of private property, would destroy the incentive for thrift and hard work and disjoint the entire economic system.*[8]

Waller's question is fundamental: What has been left out in a writer's choice of what are to be considered as problems? What features of society are going to be taken for granted as the framework *within* which problems will be defined and resolved? In this case, the taken-for-granted framework is the principle of private property and individual competition. In general, Waller argued, "social problems are not solved because people do not want to solve them";[9] they *are* problems mainly because of people's unwillingness to alter the basic conditions from which they arise. Thus:

> Venereal disease becomes a social problem in that it arises from our family institutions and also in that the medical means which could be used to prevent it, which would unquestionably be fairly effective, cannot be employed for fear of altering the mores of chastity.[10]

For Waller the definition of social problems was, in the broadest sense, a political issue involving the opposed ideologies of conflicting groups.

Waller's points still ring true. Most social problems writers in the United States still tacitly accept the basic structure of American society and restrict their treatment of social problems to maladjustments *within* that structure.

❖ SOCIAL PROBLEMS IN THE 1950S: GRADUALISM AND ANTICOMMUNISM

This is not to say that the literature on social problems since the 1930s has all been the same. Books on social problems, not surprisingly, tend to reflect the preoccupations of the time when they were written. Those conceived in the 1950s, for example, reflect social and political concerns that now seem bizarre. The shadow of McCarthyism and the general national hysteria over the "Communist menace" pervaded this literature. Consider the discussion of "civil liberties and subversion" in Paul B. Horton and Gerald R. Leslie's textbook, *The Sociology of Social Problems.*[11] Horton and Leslie saw the "American heritage of liberty" being attacked from both left and right, from both "monolithic communism" and overzealous attempts to defend "our" way of life from it. Their position was resolutely "moderate." They claimed a scientific objectivity; yet, they were quite capable of moral condemnation of people whose politics were "extreme," whether right or left:

> Most extremists are deviants. Most extremists show a fanatical preoccupation with their cause, a suspicious distrust of other people in general, a disinterest in normal pursuits, recreations, and small talk, and a strong tendency to divide other people into enemies and allies.[12]

The preference for "normal pursuits," even "small talk," over social criticism and action was common in an age noted for its "silent generation," but it was hardly "scientific." Among the other presumably objective features of the book were the authors' "rational proposals for preserving liberty and security," including these:

> An adequate national defense *is, needless to say, necessary in a world where an international revolutionary movement is joined to an aggressive major power. This is a military problem, not a sociological problem, and is not discussed here.*
>
> Counterespionage is essential. *Highly trained professional agencies such as the FBI and the Central Intelligence Agency can do this efficiently and without endangering personal liberties of citizens. If headline-hunting congressmen, Legion officials, or other amateurs turn G-men, they merely scare off any real spies and destroy the counterespionage efforts of the professionals.*[13]

The military and intelligence services themselves were not considered as problems relevant for social science. Questions about the operation of these agencies were viewed as internal and technical, military rather than sociological, issues.

In a section on "Questions and Projects," the authors asked: "How have conservatives or reactionaries sometimes given unintentional assistance to the Communists? How have liberals sometimes given unintentional assistance to the Communists?"[14]

In the introduction to their book, Horton and Leslie considered the possibilities of social change and the proper role of social scientists in promoting it. They carefully adopted a middle ground between conservatives, to whom social problems were primarily problems of individual character, and "extremists" hoping for sudden or radical changes in social structure. They argued that the resolution of social problems "nearly always involves sweeping institutional changes" but also that such changes are "costly" and "difficult," and that therefore

> it is unrealistic to expect that these problems will be solved easily or quickly.... Basic solutions of social problems will come slowly, if at all. Meanwhile, however, considerable amelioration or "improvement" may be possible.[15]

Social change, according to these authors, must be gradual and realistic; it must also be guided by experts. The authors insisted that their own role, and that of social experts in general, was merely to show the public how to get what they already valued. But in this role it was folly for the "layman" to question the expert. Horton and Leslie wrote that "when experts are *agreed* upon the futility of one policy or the soundness of another, it is sheer stupidity for the layman to disagree."[16]

An elitist, cold-war liberalism and gradualism, a fear of extremism and of an international Communist conspiracy—all these were presented not as moral and political positions but as fundamental social scientific truths. The sturdy entrepreneurial and Protestant values described in Waller's paper of the 1930s gave way, in Horton and Leslie's book of the 1950s, to a general preference for moderation, anticommunism, and "normal pursuits."

❖ THE 1960S: AFFLUENCE AND OPTIMISM

A different imagery dominated the social problems literature of the next decade. Robert K. Merton and Robert M. Nisbet's *Contemporary Social Problems*[17] was a product of the beginning of the 1960s, the period of the "New Frontier," which saw a significant shift, at least on the surface, in the focus of social concern. Americans were becoming aware of an "underdeveloped" world abroad and a "disadvantaged" world at home, both unhappily excluded from the benefits of an age of general "affluence" and well-being. New agencies of social improvement were created at home and abroad. A critique of old-style welfare efforts began to develop, along with the notion of "helping people help themselves," whether in Latin America, Harlem, or Appalachia. The idea of inclusion, of participation, in the American way of life became a political metaphor for the age. From a slightly different vantage, the idea emerged as "development" or "modernization." The social problems of the 1960s would be solved by extending the technological and intellectual resources of established American institutions into excluded, deprived, or underdeveloped places and groups. An intervention-minded government combined with an energetic social science on a scale unprecedented in this country.

In this period—very brief, as it turned out—social problems were often seen as problems of being *left out* of the American mainstream: "left behind," as the people of Appalachia were described; "traditional," like the Mexican-Americans; or "underdeveloped," like most Africans, Asians, and Latin Americans. In social problems theory, these ideas were manifested in a conservative ideology that celebrated American society as a whole, coupled with a liberal critique of the conditions hindering the extension of the American way to all.

One variant of this view was given in Nisbet's introduction to *Contemporary Social Problems*. For Nisbet, social facts become problematic when they "represent interruptions in the expected or desired scheme of things; violations of the right or the proper, as a society defines these qualities; dislocations in the social patterns and relationships that a society cherishes."[18]

Nisbet's assessment of the American situation was in keeping with the exaggerated optimism of the early 1960s:

> In America today we live in what is often called an affluent society. It is a society characterized by imposing command of physical resources, high standards of private consumption, effective maintenance of public order and security, freedom from most of the uncertainties of life that plagued our ancestors, and relatively high levels of humanitarianism. There are also, of course, squalid slums, both urban and rural; occasional epidemics of disease; sudden eruptions of violence or bigotry, even in the most civilized of communities; people for

whom the struggle for food and shelter yet remains obsessing and precarious.
Thus, we are not free of social problems, and some of them seem to grow
almost in direct proportion to our affluence.[19]

Nisbet was aware that America had not yet solved all its problems; indeed,
that some seem to come with the generally glittering package that is America
in the twentieth century. Yet, the problems were viewed as peripheral, as occasional eruptions in the backwaters of society where modern institutions had
not fully penetrated.

Like earlier theorists, Nisbet sharply separated the role of the scientific
student of social problems from that of other concerned people. The social scientist, as a scientist, should not engage in moral exhortation or political action
but should concentrate on understanding. At the same time, the scientist is

> *as interested as the next citizen in making the protection of society his first*
> *responsibility, in seeing society reach higher levels of moral decency, and when*
> *necessary, in promoting such legal actions as are necessary in the short run for*
> *protection or decency.[20]*

Here the scientific stance masked a preference for vaguely defined values—
"societal protection" and "moral decency"—which, in turn, determine what
will be selected as social problems. In this instance, problems were selected
according to whether they offended the values of social stability, that is, values
associated with the conservative tradition in social thought.

Thus, problems were repeatedly equated with "dislocations and deviations";[21] they were problems of "dissensus," as if consensus might not also be a
problem. Indeed, the entire book was divided into two sections, one of which
dealt with "deviant behavior" and the other, with "social disorganization."
The articles in the text were not all of a piece. A paper by Robert S. Weiss and
David Riesman on the problems of work took a different view on what constitutes a problem; the authors declared that "social forms which tend toward the
suppression or frustration of meaning and purpose in life are inferior forms,
whether or not they tend toward disorganization."[22] But many of the articles
simply accepted the purposes of existing institutions and defined problems in
terms of combating disorganization *within* those institutions. Perhaps the
clearest illustration of this tendency appeared in an essay by Morris Janowitz
dealing with problems of the military establishment:

> *It is self-evident that the military establishment, the armed forces, and their*
> *administrative organizations have become and will remain important institu-*
> *tions of United States society. The distinctive forms of military organization*
> *must be analyzed in order to understand the typical sources of personal and*
> *social disorganization found in military life.[23]*

The existence of a large military establishment was defined as outside the critical concern of the sociologist. The focus was not on the effect of the military
on national or international life but on the problems of maladjustment within

the military apparatus. The increasing scope of military activities was noted, but it was simply accepted as a fact of modern life:

> The armed forces have also become involved in a wide variety of logistical, research, and training activities. In the current international scene, they must take on many politico-military duties, including military assistance of allied powers.[24]

The implication was that the militarization of American society is not itself a problem for social analysis. And the acceptance of the place of the military in American society leads to the enlistment of social science in the service of military ends. Thus, in discussing changes in the requirements of military discipline, Janowitz noted that, in the 1960s, instead of employing "shock technique" to assimilate the recruit into the military, the problem had become how to foster "positive incentives and group loyalties through a team concept."[25] Janowitz didn't ask *what* the recruit is being assimilated *into*. The effect of primary-group relations on morale under cold-war conditions was extensively discussed, but the cold war itself was not.

Robert Merton's epilogue to *Contemporary Social Problems*, called "Social Problems and Sociological Theory," represented a major attempt to give theoretical definition to the "field" of social problems. Merton was well aware that different interests are present in society and therefore that definitions of social problems are likely to be contested—"one group's problem will be another group's asset"—and more specifically that "those occupying strategic positions of authority and power of course carry more weight than others in deciding social policy and so, among other things, in identifying for the rest what are to be taken as significant departures from social standards."[26]

According to Merton, however, this diversity of perspectives does not mean that sociologists must succumb to relativism or abandon their position as scientific students of society's problems. The way out of the dilemma is to distinguish between "manifest" and "latent" social problems—the latter are problems also "at odds with the values of the group" but not recognized as such. The task of the sociologist is to uncover the "latent" problems or unrecognized consequences of existing institutions and policies; in this way, "sociological inquiry does make men increasingly accountable for the outcome of their collective and institutionalized actions."[27]

The demand that social science make people accountable for their actions was a healthy departure from the false relativism of some earlier theorists. But the distinction between manifest and latent problems did not do what Merton claimed for it: it did not make the choice of problems a technical or neutral one. Actually, Merton's approach is best seen as providing a rationale for evaluating and criticizing particular policies and structures within a presumably consensual society whose basic values and institutions are not seen as problematic.

We could easily agree with Merton that "to confine the study of social problems to only those circumstances that are expressly defined as problems in the society is arbitrarily to discard a complement of conditions that are also dysfunctional to values held by people in that society."[28] But what about those values themselves? Shouldn't they be examined and, if necessary, criticized? It seems obvious to us, for example, that it is part of the sociologist's task to study and criticize the values held by people in German society during the Nazi era or by slaveholders in the antebellum American South, rather than to confine ourselves to studying those conditions that might be "dysfunctional" in terms of those values. To do otherwise amounts to an acceptance by default; the social scientist becomes an expert at handling problems within the confines of an assumed consensus on basic goals and values.

The division of social problems into the two categories of *deviant behavior* and *social disorganization* reflected this acceptance, for both categories were defined as "disruptions" of an existing social order and did not question the adequacy of that social order itself. Thus:

> *Whereas social disorganization refers to faults in the arrangement and working of social statuses and roles, deviant behavior refers to conduct that departs significantly from the norms set for people in their social statuses.*[29]

It is not, as some critics have suggested, that this kind of analysis suggests that whatever is, is right. But it does imply that whatever *disturbs* the existing social system is the primary problem.

The sociologist's "expert" judgment, of course, may conflict with what people themselves feel to be their problems, and if so, according to Merton, the expert should prevail. Merton argued that

> *we cannot take for granted a reasonably correct public imagery of social problems; of their scale, distribution, causation, consequences and persistence or change. . . . Popular perceptions are no safe guide to the magnitude of a social problem.*[30]

The corollary, presumably, is that the sociologist's imagery of social problems is at least "reasonably correct," even, perhaps, where segments of the public strongly object to having their problems defined, or redefined, for them. We seem to have come back to the same condescending attitude toward the public expressed by Horton and Leslie and other sociologists of the 1950s.

This kind of attitude wasn't, of course, confined to writers on social problems. It was a major theme in the social thought and government policy of the 1960s, a decade characterized by an increasing detachment of governmental action from public knowledge and accountability—as exemplified in the growth of a vast intelligence apparatus, the repeated attempts to overthrow popularly elected governments overseas, and the whole conduct of the Vietnam War. This process was often excused on the ground that political decisions involved technical judgments that were out of the reach of ordinary people.

The conception of social problems as technical, rather than moral and political, issues was explicit in Merton and Nisbet's text. Thus, Merton suggested that "the kind of problem that is dominated by social disorganization results from instrumental and technical flaws in the social system. The system comes to operate less efficiently than it realistically might."[31]

If the problems are technical ones, then it was, of course, reasonable to view social scientists as technicians and to regard their intervention into social life as free from partisan interest. It is this, apparently, that renders the social scientist a responsible citizen, rather than a "mere" social critic or ideologue:

> *Under the philosophy intrinsic to the distinction between manifest and latent social problems, the social scientist neither abdicates his intellectual and professional responsibilities nor usurps the position of sitting in judgment on his fellow men.*[32]

It is apparent, however, that this kind of "philosophy" lends itself all too easily to an alignment of expertise and "professionalism" with dominant values and interests masquerading as societal consensus. This is apparent in the choice of topics offered in most textbooks. Merton and Nisbet—whose widely used textbook has gone through several editions—characteristically dealt with mental disorders, crime and delinquency, drug use, alcoholism, suicide, sexual behavior, the population crisis, race relations, family disorganization, work and automation, poverty, community disorganization, violence, and youth and politics. The book did not deal with (to take some examples from our own table of contents) corporate power, sexism, health care, the criminal justice system, and so on. The pattern of these differences is obvious: Merton and Nisbet focused most heavily on those who have, for one reason or another, failed to "make it" within the American system—delinquents, criminals, the mentally ill, drug users—and on disorganization *within* established institutions. Even when individual authors in their book attempted to analyze the system itself, the effort was usually relegated to a peripheral, or merely symbolic, place.

In spite of its claim to political neutrality, the social science of the 1960s typically focused on the symptoms of social ills, rather than their sources: the culture of the poor, rather than the decisions of the rich; the "pathology" of the ghetto, rather than the problems of the economy. What "socially shared standards" dictated this choice of emphasis? In the introduction to a newer edition of *Contemporary Social Problems*, Nisbet tried to answer this question. "It may well be asked," he writes, "why these problems have been chosen by the editors," rather than others, which "for some persons at least might be regarded as even more pressing to national policy."

> *The answer is that this is a textbook in sociology. Sociology is a special science characterized by concepts and conclusions, which are based on analysis and research, yielding in turn perspectives on society and its central problems. For many decades now, sociologists have worked carefully and patiently on these problems. In other words this book is concerned not only with the presentation*

of major social problems but with the scientific concepts and procedures by which these problems have been, and continue to be, studied.[33]

Nisbet seems to be explaining that these problems were selected by the editors because sociologists have studied them, and not others, in the past. Such an argument is hardly compelling.

Even the Merton and Nisbet view of contemporary social problems has changed somewhat with the times. Their latest editions include some chapters and revisions far more critical of the prevailing social system than was evident in previous editions. Still, as the preface points out, "the fundamental character of this book has remained constant through all editions."

❖ THE 1970S AND 1980S: A HARSHER VISION

Much of the thinking about social problems in the 1960s—and the public policies that flowed from it—tended to assume, at least implicitly, that most of the ills of American society were solvable; that a rich and technologically advanced society should be able to overcome problems like poverty, unemployment, and inadequate health care, if it had the will to do so. And so an active government launched a number of social programs and experiments designed to bring the American reality in closer harmony with the American ideal. In the 1980s it became fashionable to say that government attempted too much in those years, throwing vast amounts of money at social problems. In fact, though we did try a multitude of programs, the amounts we spent on them were never large. Our total federal spending on job training, public job creation, and schooling programs for low-income people, for example, never rose to as much as one-half of 1 percent of our gross national product during the sixties.[34]

But the belief that government had taken on too big a role helped to usher in a harsher, more pessimistic perspective in the seventies—a perspective that has dominated social policy in the United States ever since. In the context of a deeply troubled economy, the stubborn persistence of poverty and joblessness, and frightening levels of social pathology in the cities, the moderate optimism of the sixties began to give way to a new brand of scholarly pessimism that argued that many of these problems were due to "human nature" or defective "culture"—or even genetic deficiencies. The implication was that social concern of the sixties' variety couldn't have much positive impact on social problems—and, in the view of some writers, had probably made them worse.

Writers like Arthur Jensen resurrected long-discredited hereditary theories of racial inferiority in intelligence to explain why blacks still remained at the bottom of the educational and economic ladder, in spite of all the equal-opportunity programs of the sixties. Others, like Harvard's Edward Banfield, explained the persistence of poverty and urban crime as the reflection of a distinctive "lower-class culture" that prevented the poor from thinking ahead or delaying immediate gratification. By the eighties, Charles Murray and other critics were explaining the stubbornness of poverty as the result of the demoralization of the poor through an overly generous welfare system. The growth of urban violence was similarly explained as the result of excessive leniency with criminals; and in the eighties, when years of "getting tough" with criminals left us with still frightful levels of crime and violence, some writers began looking for the roots of crime—and of poverty and other social pathologies as well—in faulty physiology or defective genes.

By the eighties, in other words, American thinking about social problems had just about come full circle; we had returned to something that looked very much like the focus on "defectives, dependents, and delinquents" that characterized late nineteenth-century social science. And the harsh social policies that flowed from this attitude were also strikingly reminiscent of the Social "Darwinism" of the late nineteenth century. The belief that many of our social problems (from school failure to juvenile delinquency to welfare dependency) can be traced to deficiencies in the minds, cultures, or genetic makeup of a hard-core few—and/or to the folly of government intervention—so comforting to the complacent thinkers of the nineteenth century, had returned with a vengeance.

As in the past, this outlook served to explain away some of the most troubling expressions of the crisis in American institutions: swollen prisons, the rapid descent of millions into the ranks of the poor, minority joblessness that persists at near-Depression levels. And it helped to justify sharp cutbacks in many of the programs we had created to address those problems—even successful programs in children's health care, in job training, and in nutrition.

By now, however, this perspective has itself come under growing criticism. Its proponents, after all, have been arguing for a *long* time that the poor, the jobless, and the sick are largely responsible for their own problems and that they—along with the rest of us—would be better off with less help from government. We have, accordingly, been reducing government's role as well for a long time. But the problems haven't gone away; they have grown. And so the job of developing a fresh and creative approach to social problems is once again on the agenda.

By the 1990s, indeed, a new mood of social engagement—reminiscent, in many ways, of the 1960s—began to emerge in America. A new national administration, more favorable to active government, was swept into office with a broad mandate for social change. The cycle of our thinking about social problems seemed to have turned once more.

If so, the change comes not a moment too soon. As many of the articles in this book suggest, we have reached what seems to be a crucial turning point in our policies toward social problems. Technological and economic changes are reshaping the conditions of American life with sometimes dizzying speed, and how we choose to deal with those changes will profoundly affect the character of life in the United States for many years to come.

Consider just one example: the rapidly shifting character of work in America. As suggested by several of the articles in this book (notably those by

Barlett and Steele; Currie, Dunn, and Fogarty; and Leontief), a combination of intense global economic competition and the continuing march of new work-place technology is dramatically affecting the pattern of jobs and incomes in the United States—often for the worse. Whether we can harness these changes to build a more sustaining and fulfilling society will depend on how our social and political institutions respond to them—whether, for example, we are will-ing to make a sufficient investment in worker retraining and job creation to offset the loss of many traditional jobs and livelihoods.

Much the same holds for another dramatic change in the 1990s—the col-lapse of the former Soviet bloc and the end of the cold war. The absence of the traditional superpower antagonisms means that we can, for the first time in many decades, significantly shrink military spending. But if we do not simulta-neously plan for full-scale conversion to meet civilian needs (as outlined in Melman's article in Part XII), the coming of peace could add to our long-standing problems of high unemployment and the economic decline of Ameri-can communities.

These are very big questions, and in this book we can only begin to explore them, not answer them once and for all. But we believe the articles that follow represent some of the best and most searching thinking on American social problems available today. As in earlier editions, they represent a wide range of styles and perspectives. But most of them fit comfortably within a common general vision: a critical, democratically inclined approach to social institutions that emphasizes the potential for constructive change.

Within this very broad perspective, there is plenty of room for controver-sy. Our authors don't necessarily share the same theoretical positions or social or political views. The editors, for that matter, don't always agree—and we think that's as it should be. We frequently argue about many of the issues cov-ered in this book, and this debate has continued through nine editions. But we think this tension is fruitful, and we have tried to capture it in our selection of readings.

We see this book as an introductory work, useful for beginning courses in sociology, social problems, or political science. Its purpose is to raise issues, to provide students with the beginnings of a critical approach to the society they live in and will, it is hoped, help change. It provides few definitive answers, and it leaves unresolved many basic theoretical and practical questions about the sources and solutions of the American crisis. But its purpose will be accomplished if it helps students to begin their own process of confronting those questions.

References

1. C. Wright Mills, "The Professional Ideology of the Social Pathologists," in Irving L. Horowitz, ed., *Power, Politics and People: The Collected Essays of C. Wright Mills* (New York: Ballantine, 1963).

2. Charles Richmond Henderson, *An Introduction to the Study of Defective, Depen-dent and Delinquent Classes* (Boston: Heath, 1906).

3. Lawrence K. Frank, "Social Problems," *American Journal of Sociology*, 30 (January 1925), p. 463.

4. Richard C. Fuller and Richard R. Myers, "The Natural History of a Social Problem," *American Sociological Review*, 6 (June 1941), p. 320.

5. Paul B. Horton and Gerald R. Leslie, *The Sociology of Social Problems* (New York: Appleton-Century-Crofts, 1955), p. 6.

6. Arnold M. Rose, "Theory for the Study of Social Problems," *Social Problems*, 4 (January 1957), p. 190.

7. Robert K. Merton and Robert M. Nisbet, *Contemporary Social Problems* (New York: Harcourt, Brace and World, 1961), p. 702.

8. Willard Waller, "Social Problems and the Mores," *American Sociological Review*, 1 (December 1936), p. 926.

9. Ibid., p. 928.

10. Ibid., p. 927.

11. Horton and Leslie, *Sociology*. We refer here to the original edition in order to place the book in its historical context.

12. Ibid., p. 517.

13. Ibid., p. 520.

14. Ibid., p. 523.

15. Ibid., p. 12.

16. Ibid., p. 19.

17. Merton and Nisbet, *Contemporary Social Problems*. Here, too, we refer to the first edition in order to consider the book in historical perspective. The general theoretical perspective in the book has changed little, if at all, as we will note later; there have been some substantive changes, however—for example, the chapter by Janowitz has been dropped and new chapters added.

18. Robert A. Nisbet, "The Study of Social Problems," in ibid., p. 4.

19. Ibid., p. 5. The reader might compare C. Wright Mills's notion, developed during the same period, that the United States should be seen as an "overdeveloped" society; see Irving L. Horowitz, "Introduction," in Horowitz, *Power, Politics and People*, p. 8.

20. Nisbet, "The Study of Social Problems," p. 9.

21. Ibid., p. 12.

22. Robert S. Weiss and David Riesman, "Social Problems and Disorganization in the World of Work," in Merton and Nisbet, *Contemporary Social Problems*, p. 464.

23. Morris Janowitz, "The Military Establishment: Organization and Disorganization," in Merton and Nisbet, *Contemporary Social Problems*, p. 515.

24. Ibid., p. 516.

25. Ibid., pp. 533–534.

26. Robert K. Merton, "Social Problems and Sociological Theory," in Merton and Nisbet, *Contemporary Social Problems,* p. 706.

27. Ibid., p. 710.

28. Ibid., p. 711.

29. Ibid., p. 723.

30. Ibid., pp. 712–713.

31. Ibid., p. 723.

32. Ibid., p. 712.

33. Robert M. Nisbet, "The Study of Social Problems," in ibid., p. 2.

34. Gary L. Burtless, "Public Spending for the Poor," in Sheldon H. Danziger and Daniel H. Weinberg, *Fighting Poverty: What Works and What Doesn't* (Cambridge, MA: Harvard University Press, 1986), p. 37.

Systemic Problems

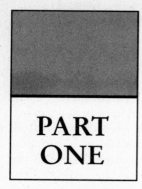

PART ONE

CORPORATE POWER

The myth of American capitalism is individual "free enterprise": the vision of the hard-working, thrifty entrepreneur competing with others and constrained by the forces of the market. But the reality of American capitalism is what Ralph Nader once called "corporate collectivism": the domination of economic life by a relative handful of giant corporations—corporations whose size and power enable them to control markets rather than be controlled by them.

Since the late 1960s, the 500 largest industrial corporations in America have consistently accounted for about two-thirds of all industrial sales, four-fifths of all industrial profits, and three-fourths of all industrial employment. The largest 50 of those corporations alone account for about one-fourth of the value of all manufactured goods in the country and employ about one in five industrial workers. Similar concentration exists in other areas of business as well—banking and finance, transportation, utilities, and communications. All told, about 1,000 corporations now produce roughly one-half of all privately produced goods and services in the United States, and those corporations are deeply entwined with government in a multitude of ways—from long-term defense contracts to massive federal bailouts of big corporations in trouble.

The real issue, then, is not whether we have a "free enterprise" economy. Instead, the important questions have to do with the performance and control of the modern corporate version of capitalism: How has the concentration of corporate power affected such key economic problems as inflation and recession? How has it changed the terms on which business relates to the public and to political authorities? And how, more generally, does the growing power of the giant corporation affect the quality of social and economic life?

Mark Dowie's story of the Ford Motor Company's refusal to make minor changes in its Pinto that could have saved hundreds of lives shows, in stark relief, the ability of the large corporations to insulate themselves from public accountability or social control. When the article was written, Ford was the fifth largest industrial corporation in the world; its total sales exceeded the gross national products of all but 30 of the world's countries. The company's enormous economic power enabled it to operate with militarylike secrecy, open defiance of government safety standards, and near-total disregard for the lives of its consumers. Dowie's article has become something of a classic for our understanding of how the profit motive can lead managers and engineers to ignore the safety of the public in the interests of maximizing the black side of the balance sheet.

Sometimes, the pressures to be profitable edge business executives over the line between efficient production and dangerous production, as in the case of the Pinto. But we rarely, if ever, have serious suggestions that the automobile—when properly designed and manufactured—is not a socially desirable product.

The same claim, however, can scarcely be made for tobacco. As the Surgeon General warns on cigarette packages and advertising, "Smoking causes lung cancer, heart disease, emphysema, and may complicate pregnancy . . . smoking by pregnant women may result in fetal injury, premature birth, and low birth weight." That, in a time of increasing concern over the effects of drugs and a law enforcement "war on drugs," we permit cigarettes to be advertised and sold may be a national scandal. But what of smokeless tobacco— chewing tobacco and snuff? These products do not carry similar warnings. Whether their manufacturer knew that these products also caused cancer is the question in the case of Sean Marsee, who died of cancer at 19, after six years of heavy snuff use. The case involved U.S. Tobacco's liability for Sean's addiction to the Copenhagen brand. Morton Mintz's article shows how the expert witnesses for U.S. Tobacco dissembled on the witness stand about what they knew about the relation between tobacco and cancer.

John Logue's portrait of the steel corporations' destruction of the industry in Youngstown, Ohio, illustrates how the search for fast profits can undermine even a profitable industry and the communities that depend on it. The shutdown of the Mahoning Valley steel mills wasn't primarily the result of foreign competition or declining productivity, two of the problems most often said to be responsible for industrial decline in America. Instead, Logue shows that the mills were deliberately drained of resources by their new owners—conglomerate corporations less interested in making steel than in finding other, more immediately profitable places in which to invest. Since Logue first wrote this article, the self-destruction of the American steel industry has continued; and, while the steel companies increasingly shift their capital into shopping malls and chemical corporations, tens of thousands of steelworkers will never work in their industry again.

When we think of corporate power and concentration, we usually think of major manufacturers of automobiles, cigarettes, and steel. We may not, however, consider the media as a prime area of corporate concentration. But, just as anyone has the legal right to begin a business in America, while few have the resources to do so, so it is with the media. Everyone has the right to freedom of speech under the First Amendment, but increasingly few have the means to participate in the "marketplace of ideas" protected by the Constitution. Here, too, as in the manufacturing businesses, myth and economic reality are at considerable odds. As Ben Bagdikian indicates, the major media are exhibiting "an extraordinary race to monopoly control." This, according to Bagdikian, results in journalistic self-censorship, pressures to support the status quo, and a loss of public knowledge about major and important events.

PINTO MADNESS

MARK DOWIE

One evening in the mid-1960s, Arjay Miller was driving home from his office in Dearborn, Michigan, in the four-door Lincoln Continental that went with his job as president of the Ford Motor Company. On a crowded highway, another car struck his from the rear. The Continental spun around and burst into flames. Because he was wearing a shoulder-strap seat belt, Miller was unharmed by the crash, and because his doors didn't jam he escaped the flaming wreck. But the accident made a vivid impression on him. Several months later, on July 15, 1965, he recounted it to a U.S. Senate subcommittee that was hearing testimony on auto safety legislation. "I still have burning in my mind the image of that gas tank on fire," Miller said. He went on to express an almost passionate interest in controlling fuel-fed fires in cars that crash or roll over. He spoke with excitement about the fabric gas tank Ford was testing at that very moment. "If it proves out," he promised the senators, "it will be a feature you will see in our standard cars."

Almost seven years after Miller's testimony, a woman, whom for legal reasons we will call Sandra Gillespie, pulled onto a Minneapolis highway in her new Ford Pinto. Riding with her was a young boy, whom we'll call Robbie Carlton. As she entered a merge lane, Sandra Gillespie's car stalled. Another

Mark Dowie, "Pinto Madness," from *Mother Jones*, Vol. II, No. VIII, September/October 1977. Reprinted by permission.

car rear-ended hers at an impact speed of 28 miles per hour. The Pinto's gas tank ruptured. Vapors from it mixed quickly with the air in the passenger compartment. A spark ignited the mixture and the car exploded in a ball of fire. Sandra died in agony a few hours later in an emergency hospital. Her passenger, 13-year-old Robbie Carlton, is still alive; he has just come home from another futile operation aimed at grafting a new ear and nose from skin on the few unscarred portions of his badly burned body. (This accident is real; the details are from police reports.)

Why did Sandra Gillespie's Ford Pinto catch fire so easily, seven years after Ford's Arjay Miller made his apparently sincere pronouncements—the same seven years that brought more safety improvements to cars than any other period in automotive history? An extensive investigation by *Mother Jones* over the past six months has found these answers:

> Fighting strong competition from Volkswagen for the lucrative small-car market, the Ford Motor Company rushed the Pinto into production in much less than the usual time.

> Ford engineers discovered in pre-production crash tests that rear-end collisions would rupture the Pinto's fuel system extremely easily.

> Because assembly-line machinery was already tooled when engineers found this defect, top Ford officials decided to manufacture the car anyway—exploding gas tank and all—*even though Ford owned the patent on a much safer gas tank.*

> For more than eight years afterwards, Ford successfully lobbied, with extraordinary vigor and some blatant lies, against a key government safety standard that would have forced the company to change the Pinto's fire-prone gas tank.

By conservative estimates Pinto crashes have caused 500 burn deaths to people who would not have been seriously injured if the car had not burst into flames. Burning Pintos have become such an embarrassment to Ford that its advertising agency, J. Walter Thompson, dropped a line from the end of a radio spot that read, "Pinto leaves you with that warm feeling."

Ford knows the Pinto is a firetrap, yet it has paid out millions to settle damage suits out of court, and it is prepared to spend millions more lobbying against safety standards. With a half million cars rolling off the assembly lines each year, Pinto is the biggest-selling subcompact in America, and the company's operating profit on the car is fantastic. Finally, in 1977, new Pinto models have incorporated a few minor alterations necessary to meet that federal standard Ford managed to hold off for eight years. Why did the company delay so long in making these minimal, inexpensive improvements?

Ford waited eight years because its internal "cost-benefit analysis," *which places a dollar value on human life,* said it wasn't profitable to make the changes sooner.

Before we get to the question of how much Ford thinks your life is worth, let's trace the history of the death trap itself. Although this particular story is about the Pinto, the way in which Ford made its decision is typical of the U.S. auto industry generally. There are plenty of similar stories about other cars made by other companies. But this case is the worst of them all.

The next time you drive behind a Pinto (with over two million of them on the road, you shouldn't have much trouble finding one), take a look at the rear end. That long silver object hanging down under the bumper is the gas tank. The tank begins about six inches forward of the bumper. In late models the bumper is designed to withstand a collision of only about five miles per hour. Earlier bumpers may as well not have been on the car for all the protection they offered the gas tank.

Mother Jones has studied hundreds of reports and documents on rear-end collisions involving Pintos. These reports conclusively reveal that if you ran into that Pinto you were following at over 30 miles per hour, the rear end of the car would buckle like an accordion, right up to the back seat. The tube leading to the gas-tank cap would be ripped away from the tank itself, and gas would immediately begin sloshing onto the road around the car. The buckled gas tank would be jammed up against the differential housing, which contains four sharp protruding bolts likely to gash holes in the tank and spill still more gas. The welded seam between the main body frame and the wheel well would split, allowing gas to enter the interior of the car.

Now all you need is a spark from a cigarette, ignition, or scraping metal, and both cars would be engulfed in flames. If you gave the Pinto a really good whack—say, at 40 mph—chances are excellent that its doors would jam and you would have to stand by and watch its trapped passengers burn to death.

This scenario is no news to Ford. Internal company documents in our possession show that Ford has crash-tested the Pinto at a top-secret site more than 40 times and that *every* test made at over 25 mph without special structural alteration of the car has resulted in a ruptured fuel tank. Despite this, Ford officials denied having crash-tested the Pinto.

Eleven of these tests, averaging a 31-mph impact speed, came before Pintos started rolling out of the factories. Only three cars passed the test with unbroken fuel tanks. In one of them an inexpensive light-weight metal baffle was placed so those bolts would not perforate the tank. (Don't forget about that baffle, which costs about a dollar and weighs about a pound. It plays an important role in our story later on.) In another successful test, a piece of steel was placed between the tank and the bumper. In the third test car the gas tank was lined with a rubber bladder. But none of these protective alterations was used in the mass-produced Pinto.

In preproduction planning, engineers seriously considered using in the Pinto the same kind of gas tank Ford uses in the Capri. The Capri tank rides over the rear axle and differential housing. It has been so successful in over 50 crash tests that Ford used it in its Experimental Safety Vehicle, which withstood rear-end impacts of 60 mph. So why wasn't the Capri tank used in the Pinto? Or, why wasn't that baffle placed between the tank and the axle—

something that would have saved the life of Sandra Gillespie and hundreds like her. Why was a car known to be a serious fire hazard deliberately released to production in August of 1970?

Whether Ford should manufacture subcompacts at all was the subject of a bitter two-year debate at the company's Dearborn headquarters. The principals in the corporate struggle were the then-president Semon "Bunky" Knudsen, whom Henry Ford II had hired away from General Motors, and Lee Iacocca, a spunky young turk who had risen fast within the company on the enormous success of the Mustang. Iacocca argued forcefully that Volkswagen and the Japanese were going to capture the entire American subcompact market unless Ford put out its own alternative to the VW Beetle. Bunky Knudsen said, in effect: let them have the small-car market; Ford makes good money on medium and large models. But he lost the battle and later resigned. Iacocca became president and almost immediately began a rush program to produce the Pinto.

Like the Mustang, the Pinto became known in the company as "Lee's car." Lee Iacocca wanted that little car in the showrooms of America with the 1971 models. So he ordered his engineering vice president, Bob Alexander, to oversee what was probably the shortest production planning period in modern automotive history. The normal time span from conception to production of a new car model is about 43 months. The Pinto schedule was set at just under 25.

Design, styling, product planning, advance engineering and quality assurance all have flexible time frames, and engineers can pretty much carry these on simultaneously. Tooling, on the other hand, has a fixed time frame of about 18 months. Normally, an auto company doesn't begin tooling until the other processes are almost over. *But Iacocca's speed-up meant Pinto tooling went on at the same time as product development.* So when crash tests revealed a serious defect in the gas tank, it was too late. The tooling was well under way.

When it was discovered the gas tank was unsafe, did anyone go to Iacocca and tell him? "Hell no," replied an engineer who worked on the Pinto, a high company official for many years, who, unlike several others at Ford, maintains a necessarily clandestine concern for safety. "That person would have been fired. Safety wasn't a popular subject around Ford in those days. With Lee it was taboo. Whenever a problem was raised that meant a delay on the Pinto, Lee would chomp on his cigar, look out the window and say 'Read the product objectives and get back to work.'"

The product objectives are clearly stated in the Pinto "green book." This is a thick, top-secret manual in green covers containing a step-by-step production plan for the model, detailing the metallurgy, weight, strength and quality of every part in the car. The product objectives for the Pinto are repeated in an article by Ford executive F. G. Olsen published by the Society of Automotive Engineers. He lists these product objectives as follows:

1. TRUE SUBCOMPACT
    Size
    Weight

2. LOW COST OF OWNERSHIP
   Initial price
   Fuel consumption
   Reliability
   Serviceability
3. CLEAR PRODUCT SUPERIORITY
   Appearance
   Comfort
   Features
   Ride and Handling
   Performance

Safety, you will notice, is not there. It is not mentioned in the entire article. As Lee Iacocca was fond of saying, "Safety doesn't sell."

Heightening the anti-safety pressure on Pinto engineers was an important goal set by Iacocca known as "the limits of 2,000." The Pinto was not to weigh an ounce over 2,000 pounds and not to cost a cent over $2,000. "Iacocca enforced these limits with an iron hand," recalls the engineer quoted earlier. So, even when a crash test showed that that one-pound, one-dollar piece of metal stopped the puncture of the gas tank, it was thrown out as extra cost and extra weight.

People shopping for subcompacts are watching every dollar. "You have to keep in mind," the engineer explained, "that the price elasticity on these subcompacts is extremely tight. You can price yourself right out of the market by adding $25 to the production cost of the model. And nobody understands that better than Iacocca."

Dr. Leslie Ball, the retired safety chief for the NASA manned space program and a founder of the International Society of Reliability Engineers, recently made a careful study of the Pinto. "The release to production of the Pinto was the most reprehensible decision in the history of American engineering," he said. Ball can name more than 40 European and Japanese models in the Pinto price and weight range with safer gas-tank positioning. Ironically, many of them, like the Ford Capri, contain a "saddle-type" gas tank riding over the back axle. *The patent on the saddle-type tank is owned by the Ford Motor Co.*

Los Angeles auto safety expert Byron Bloch has made an in-depth study of the Pinto fuel system. "It's a catastrophic blunder," he says. "Ford made an extremely irresponsible decision when they placed such a weak tank in such a ridiculous location in such a soft rear end. It's almost designed to blow up—premeditated."

A Ford engineer, who doesn't want his name used, comments: "This company is run by salesmen, not engineers: so the priority is styling, not safety." He goes on to tell a story about gas-tank safety at Ford:

Lou Tubben is one of the most popular engineers at Ford. He's a friendly, outgoing guy with a genuine concern for safety. By 1971 he had grown so concerned about gas-tank integrity that he asked his boss if he could prepare a presentation on safer tank design. Tubben and his boss had both worked on the Pinto and shared a concern for its safety. His boss gave him the go-ahead, scheduled a date for the presentation and invited all company engineers and key production planning personnel. When time came for the meeting, a total of two people showed up—Lou Tubben and his boss.

"So you see," continued the anonymous Ford engineer, "there *are* a few of us here at Ford who are concerned about fire safety." He adds: "They are mostly engineers who have to study a lot of accident reports and look at pictures of burned people. But we don't talk about it much. It isn't a popular subject. I've never seen safety on the agenda of a product meeting and, except for a brief period in 1956, can't remember seeing the word safety in an advertisement. I really don't think the company wants American consumers to start thinking too much about safety—for fear they might demand it, I suppose."

Asked about the Pinto gas tank, another Ford engineer admitted: "That's all true. But you miss the point entirely. You see, safety isn't the issue, trunk space is. You have no idea how stiff the competition is over trunk space. Do you realize that if we put a Capri-type tank in the Pinto you could only get one set of golf clubs in the trunk?"

Blame for Sandra Gillespie's death, Robbie Carlton's unrecognizable face and all the other injuries and deaths in Pintos since 1970 does not rest on the shoulders of Lee Iacocca alone. For, while he and his associates fought their battle against a safer Pinto in Dearborn, a larger war against safer cars raged in Washington. One skirmish in that war involved Ford's successful eight-year lobbying effort against Federal Motor Vehicle Safety Standard 301, the rear-end provisions of which would have forced Ford to redesign the Pinto.

But first some background:

During the early '60s, auto safety legislation became the *bête-noire* of American big business. The auto industry was the last great unregulated business, and if *it* couldn't reverse the tide of government regulation, the reasoning went, no one could.

People who know him cannot remember Henry Ford taking a stronger stand than the one he took against the regulation of safety design. He spent weeks in Washington calling on members of Congress, holding press conferences and recruiting business cronies like W. B. Murphy of Campbell's Soup to join the anti-regulation battle. Displaying the sophistication for which today's American corporate leaders will be remembered, Murphy publicly called auto safety "a hula hoop, a fad that will pass." He was speaking to a special luncheon of the Business Council, an organization of 100 chief executives who gather periodically in Washington to provide "advice" and "counsel" to government. The target of their wrath in this instance was the Motor Vehicle Safety Bills introduced in both houses of Congress, largely in response to Ralph Nader's *Unsafe at Any Speed*.

By 1965, most pundits and lobbyists saw the handwriting on the wall and prepared to accept government "meddling" in the last bastion of free enterprise. Not Henry. With bulldog tenacity, he held out for defeat of the legislation to the very end, loyal to his grandfather's invention and to the company that makes it. But the Safety Act passed the House and Senate unanimously, and was signed into law by Lyndon Johnson in 1966.

While lobbying for and against legislation is pretty much a process of high-level back-slapping, press-conferencing and speech-making, fighting a regulatory agency is a much subtler matter. Henry headed home to lick his wounds in Grosse Pointe, Michigan, and a planeload of the Ford Motor Company's best brains flew to Washington to start the "education" of the new federal auto safety bureaucrats.

Their job was to implant the official industry ideology in the minds of the new officials regulating auto safety. Briefly summarized, that ideology states that auto accidents are caused not by *cars*, but by people and highway conditions.

It is an experience to hear automotive "safety engineers" talk for hours without ever mentioning cars. They will advocate spending billions educating youngsters, punishing drunks and redesigning street signs. Listening to them, you begin to think that it is easier to control 100 million drivers than a handful of manufacturers. They show movies about guardrail design and advocate the clear-cutting of trees 100 feet back from every highway in the nation. If a car is unsafe, they argue, it is because its owner doesn't maintain it properly.

In light of an annual death rate approaching 50,000, they are forced to admit that driving is hazardous. But the car is, in the words of Arjay Miller, "the safest link in the safety chain."

Before the Ford experts left Washington to return to drafting tables in Dearborn they did one other thing. They managed to informally reach an agreement with the major public servants who would be making auto safety decisions. This agreement was that "cost-benefit" would be an acceptable mode of analysis by Detroit and its new regulators. And, as we shall see, cost-benefit analysis quickly became the basis of Ford's argument against safer car design.

Cost-benefit analysis was used only occasionally in government until President Kennedy appointed Ford Motor Company President Robert McNamara to be Secretary of Defense. McNamara, originally an accountant, preached cost-benefit with all the force of a Biblical zealot. Stated in its simplest terms, cost-benefit analysis says that if the cost is greater than the benefit, the project is not worth it—no matter what the benefit. Examine the cost of every action, decision, contract, part, or change, the doctrine says, then carefully evaluate the benefits (in dollars) to be certain that they exceed the cost before you begin a program or pass a regulation.

As a management tool in a business in which profits count over all else, cost-benefit analysis makes a certain amount of sense. Serious problems arise, however, when public officials who ought to have more than corporate profits at heart apply cost-benefit analysis to every conceivable decision. The inevitable result is that they must place a dollar value on human life.

Ever wonder what your life is worth in dollars? Perhaps $10 million? Ford has a better idea: $200,000.

Remember, Ford had gotten the federal regulators to agree to talk auto

TABLE 1	WHAT'S YOUR LIFE WORTH? SOCIETAL COST COMPONENTS FOR FATALITIES, 1972 NHTSA STUDY

COMPONENT	1971 COSTS
Future productivity losses	
Direct	$132,000
Indirect	41,300
Medical costs	
Hospital	700
Other	425
Property damage	1,500
Insurance administration	4,700
Legal and court	3,000
Employer losses	1,000
Victim's pain and suffering	10,000
Funeral	900
Assets (lost consumption)	5,000
Miscellaneous accident cost	200
Total per fatality: $200,725	

Here is a chart from a federal study showing how the National Highway Traffic Safety Administration has calculated the value of a human life. The estimate was arrived at under pressure from the auto industry. The Ford Motor Company has used it in cost-benefit analyses arguing why certain safety measures are not "worth" the savings in human lives. The calculation above is a breakdown of the estimated cost to society every time someone is killed in a car accident. We were not able to find anyone, either in the government or at Ford, who could explain how the $10,000 figure for "pain and suffering" had been arrived at.

safety in terms of cost-benefit. But in order to be able to argue that various safety costs were greater than their benefits, Ford needed to have a dollar value figure for the "benefit." Rather than coming up with a price tag itself, the auto industry pressured the National Highway Traffic Safety Administration to do so. And in a 1972 report the agency determined that a human life lost on the highway was worth $200,725 [Table 1]. Inflationary forces have recently pushed the figure up to $278,000.

Furnished with this useful tool, Ford immediately went to work using it to prove why various safety improvements were too expensive to make.

Nowhere did the company argue harder that it should make no changes than in the area of rupture-prone fuel tanks. Not long after the government arrived at the $200,725-per-life figure, it surfaced, rounded off to a cleaner $200,000, in an internal Ford memorandum. This cost-benefit analysis argued that Ford should not make an $11-per-car improvement that would prevent 180 fiery deaths a year.

TABLE 1	BENEFITS AND COSTS RELATING TO FUEL LEAKAGE ASSOCIATED WITH THE STATIC ROLLOVER TEST PORTION OF FMVSS 208

BENEFITS
Savings: 180 burn deaths, 180 serious burn injuries, 2,100 burned vehicles. *Unit cost:* $200,000 per death, $67,000 per injury, $700 per vehicle. *Total benefit:* 180 × ($200,000) + 180 × ($67,000) + 2,100 × ($700) = $49.5 million.

COSTS
Sales: 11 million cars, 1.5 million light trucks. *Unit cost:* $11 per car, $11 per truck. *Total cost:* 11,000,000 × ($11) + 1,500,000 × ($11) = $137 million.

This cold calculus [Table 2] is buried in a seven-page company memorandum entitled "Fatalities Associated with Crash-Induced Fuel Leakage and Fires."

The memo goes on to argue that there is no financial benefit in complying with proposed safety standards that would admittedly result in fewer auto fires, fewer burn deaths and fewer burn injuries. Naturally, memoranda that speak so casually of "burn deaths" and "burn injuries" are not released to the public. They are very effective, however, with Department of Transportation officials indoctrinated in McNamarian cost-benefit analysis.

All Ford had to do was convince men like John Volpe, Claude Brinegar and William Coleman (successive Secretaries of Transportation during the Nixon-Ford years) that certain safety standards would add so much to the price of cars that fewer people would buy them. This could damage the auto industry, which was still believed to be the bulwark of the American economy. "Compliance to these standards," Henry Ford II prophesied at more than one press conference, "will shut down the industry."

The Nixon Transportation Secretaries were the kind of regulatory officials big business dreams of. They understood and loved capitalism and thought like businessmen. Yet, best of all, they came into office uninformed on technical automotive matters. And you could talk "burn injuries" and "burn deaths" with these guys, and they didn't seem to envision children crying at funerals and people hiding in their homes with melted faces. Their minds appeared to have leapt right to the bottom line—more safety meant higher prices, higher prices meant lower sales and lower sales meant lower profits.

So when J. C. Echold, Director of Automotive Safety (chief anti-safety lobbyist) for Ford, wrote to the Department of Transportation—which he still does frequently, at great length—he felt secure attaching a memorandum that in effect says it is acceptable to kill 180 people and burn another 180 every year, *even though we have the technology that could save their lives for $11 a car.*

Furthermore, Echold attached this memo, confident, evidently, that the Secretary would question neither his low death/injury statistics nor his high cost estimates. But it turns out, on closer examination, that both these findings were misleading.

First, note that Ford's table shows an equal number of burn deaths and burn injuries. This is false. All independent experts estimate that for each person who dies by an auto fire, many more are left with charred hands, faces and limbs. Andrew McGuire of the Northern California Burn Center estimates the ratio of burn injuries to deaths at ten to one instead of the one to one Ford shows here. Even though Ford values a burn at only a piddling $67,000 instead of the $200,000 price of life, the true ratio obviously throws the company's calculations way off.

The other side of the equation, the alleged $11 cost of a fire-prevention device, is also a misleading estimation. One document that was *not* sent to Washington by Ford was a "Confidential" cost analysis *Mother Jones* has managed to obtain, showing that crash fires could be largely prevented for considerably *less* than $11 a car. The cheapest method involves placing a heavy rubber bladder inside the gas tank to keep the fuel from spilling if the tank ruptures. Goodyear had developed the bladder and had demonstrated it to the automotive industry. We have in our possession crash-test reports showing that the Goodyear bladder worked well. On December 2, 1970 (*two years before* Echold sent his cost-benefit memo to Washington), Ford Motor Company ran a rear-end crash test on a car with the rubber bladder in the gas tank. The tank ruptured, but no fuel leaked. On January 15, 1971, Ford again tested the bladder and again it worked. The total purchase and installation cost of the bladder would have been $5.08 per car. That $5.08 could have saved the lives of Sandra Gillespie and several hundred others.

When a federal regulatory agency like the National Highway Traffic Safety Administration (NHTSA) decides to issue a new standard, the law usually requires it to invite all interested parties to respond before the standard is enforced—a reasonable-enough custom on the surface. However, the auto industry has taken advantage of this process and has used it to delay lifesaving emission and safety standards for years. In the case of the standard that would have corrected that fragile Pinto fuel tank, the delay was for an incredible eight years.

The particular regulation involved here was Federal Motor Vehicle Safety Standard 301. Ford picked portions of Standard 301 for strong opposition back in 1968 when the Pinto was still in the blueprint stage. The intent of 301, and the 300 series that followed it, was to protect drivers and passengers *after* a crash occurs. Without question the worst postcrash hazard is fire. So Standard 301 originally proposed that all cars should be able to withstand a fixed-barrier impact of 20 mph (that is, running into a wall at that speed) without losing fuel.

When the standard was proposed, Ford engineers pulled their crash-test results out of their files. The front ends of most cars were no problem—with minor alterations they could stand the impact without losing fuel. "We were already working on the front end," Ford engineer Dick Kimble admitted. "We knew we could meet the test on the front end." But with the Pinto particularly, a 20-mph rear-end standard meant redesigning the entire rear end of the car. With the Pinto scheduled for production in August of 1970, and with $200 million worth of tools in place, adoption of this standard would have created a minor financial disaster. So Standard 301 was targeted for delay, and, with some assistance from its industry associates, Ford succeeded beyond its wildest expectations: the standard was not adopted until the 1977 model year. Here is how it happened:

There are several main techniques in the art of combating a government safety standard: a) make your arguments in succession, so the feds can be working on disproving only one at a time; b) claim that the real problem is not X but Y (we already saw one instance of this in "the problem is not cars but people"); c) no matter how ridiculous each argument is, accompanying it with thousands of pages of highly technical assertions it will take the government months or, preferably, years to test. Ford's large and active Washington office brought these techniques to new heights and became the envy of the lobbyists' trade.

The Ford people started arguing against Standard 301 way back in 1968 with a strong attack of technique b). Fire, they said, was not the real problem. Sure, cars catch fire and people burn occasionally. But statistically auto fires are such a minor problem that NHTSA should really concern itself with other matters.

Strange as it may seem, the Department of Transportation (NHTSA's parent agency) didn't know whether or not this was true. So it contracted with several independent research groups to study auto fires. The studies took months, often years, which was just what Ford wanted. The completed studies, however, showed auto fires to be more of a problem than Transportation officials ever dreamed of. A Washington research firm found that 400,000 cars were burning up every year, burning more than 3,000 people to death. Furthermore, auto fires were increasing five times as fast as building fires. Another study showed that 35 per cent of all fire deaths in the U.S. occurred in automobiles. Forty per cent of all fire department calls in the 1960s were to vehicle fires—a public cost of $350 million a year, a figure that, incidentally, never shows up in cost-benefit analyses.

Another study was done by the Highway Traffic Research Institute in Ann Arbor, Michigan, a safety think-tank funded primarily by the auto industry (the giveaway there is the words "highway traffic" rather than "automobile" in the group's name). It concluded that 40 per cent of the lives lost in fuel-fed fires could be saved if the manufacturers complied with proposed Standard 301. Finally, a third report was prepared for NHTSA. This report indicated that the Ford Motor Company makes 24 per cent of the cars on the American road, yet these cars account for 42 per cent of the collision-ruptured fuel tanks.

Ford lobbyists then used technique a)—bringing up a new argument.

Their line then became: yes, perhaps burn accidents do happen, but rear-end collisions are relatively rare (note the echo of technique b) here as well). Thus Standard 301 was not needed. This set the NHTSA off on a new round of analyzing accident reports. The government's findings finally were that rear-end collisions were seven and a half times more likely to result in fuel spills than were front-end collisions. So much for that argument.

By now it was 1972; NHTSA had been researching and analyzing for four years to answer Ford's objections. During that time, nearly 9,000 people burned to death in flaming wrecks. Tens of thousands more were badly burned and scarred for life. And the four-year delay meant that well over 10 million new unsafe vehicles went on the road, vehicles that will be crashing, leaking fuel and incinerating people well into the 1980s.

Ford now had to enter its third round of battling the new regulations. On the "the problem is not X but Y" principle, the company had to look around for something new to get itself off the hook. One might have thought that, faced with all the latest statistics on the horrifying number of deaths in flaming accidents, Ford would find the task difficult. But the company's rhetoric was brilliant. The problem was not burns, but . . . impact! Most of the people killed in these fiery accidents, claimed Ford, would have died whether the car burned or not. They were killed by the kinetic force of the impact, not the fire.

And so once again, the ball bounced into the government's court and the absurdly pro-industry NHTSA began another slow-motion response. Once again it began a time-consuming round of test crashes and embarked on a study of accidents. The latter, however, revealed that a large and growing number of corpses taken from burned cars involved in rear-end crashes contained no cuts, bruises or broken bones. They clearly would have survived the accident unharmed if the cars had not caught fire. This pattern was confirmed in careful rear-end crash tests performed by the Insurance Institute for Highway Safety. A University of Miami study found an inordinate number of Pintos burning on rear-end impact and concluded that this demonstrated "a clear and present hazard to all Pinto owners."

Pressure on NHTSA from Ralph Nader and consumer groups began mounting. The industry-agency collusion was so obvious that Senator Joseph Montoya (D-N.M.) introduced legislation about Standard 301. NHTSA waffled some more and again announced its intentions to promulgate a rear-end collision standard.

Waiting, as it normally does, until the last day allowed for response, Ford filed with NHTSA a gargantuan batch of letters, studies and charts now arguing that the federal testing criteria were unfair. Ford also argued that design changes required to meet the standard would take 43 months, which seemed like a rather long time in light of the fact that the entire Pinto was designed in about two years. Specifically new complaints about the standard involved the weight of the test vehicle, whether or not the brakes should be engaged at the moment of impact and the claim that the standard should only apply to cars, not trucks or buses. Perhaps the most amusing argument was that the engine should not be idling during crash tests, the rationale being that an idling engine meant that the gas tank had to contain gasoline and that the hot lights needed to film the crash might ignite the gasoline and cause a fire.

Some of these complaints were accepted, others rejected. But they all required examination and testing by a weak-kneed NHTSA, meaning more of those 18-month studies the industry loves so much. So the complaints served their real purpose—delay; all told, an eight-year delay, while Ford manufactured more than three million profitable, dangerously incendiary Pintos. To justify this delay, Henry Ford II called more press conferences to predict the demise of American civilization. "If we can't meet the standards when they are published," he warned, "we will have to close down. And if we have to close down some production because we don't meet standards we're in for real trouble in this country."

While government bureaucrats dragged their feet on lifesaving Standard 301, a different kind of expert was taking a close look at the Pinto—the "recon man." "Recon" stands for reconstruction; recon men reconstruct accidents for police departments, insurance companies and lawyers who want to know exactly who or what caused an accident. It didn't take many rear-end Pinto accidents to demonstrate the weakness of the car. Recon men began encouraging lawyers to look beyond one driver or another to the manufacturer in their search for fault, particularly in the growing number of accidents where passengers were uninjured by collision but were badly burned by fire.

Pinto lawsuits began mounting fast against Ford. Says John Versace, executive safety engineer at Ford's Safety Research Center, "Ulcers are running pretty high among the engineers who worked on the Pinto. Every lawyer in the country seems to want to take their depositions." (The Safety Research Center is an impressive glass and concrete building standing by itself about a mile from Ford World Headquarters in Dearborn. Looking at it, one imagines its large staff protects consumers from burned and broken limbs. Not so. The Center is the technical support arm of Jack Echold's 14-person anti-regulatory lobbying team in World Headquarters.)

When the Pinto liability suits began, Ford strategy was to go to a jury. Confident it could hide the Pinto crash tests, Ford thought that juries of solid American registered voters would buy the industry doctrine that drivers, not cars, cause accidents. It didn't work. It seems that citizens are much quicker to see the truth than bureaucracies. Juries began ruling against the company, granting million-dollar awards to plaintiffs.

"We'll never go to a jury again," says Al Slechter in Ford's Washington office. "Not in a fire case. Juries are just too sentimental. They see those charred remains and forget the evidence. No sir, we'll settle."

Settlement involves less cash, smaller legal fees and less publicity, but it is an indication of the weakness of their case. Nevertheless, Ford has been offering to settle when it is clear that the company can't pin the blame on the driver of the other car. But, since the company carries $2 million deductible product-liability insurance, these settlements have a direct impact on the bottom line. They must therefore be considered a factor in determining the net operating profit on the Pinto. It's impossible to get a straight answer from Ford on the profitability of the Pinto and the impact of lawsuit settlements on it—even when you have a curious and mildly irate shareholder call to inquire, as we did. However, financial officer Charles Matthews did admit that the company establishes a reserve for large dollar settlements. He would not divulge the amount of the reserve and had no explanation for its absence from the annual report.

Until recently, it was clear that, whatever the cost of these settlements, it was not enough to seriously cut into the Pinto's enormous profits. The cost of retooling Pinto assembly lines and of equipping each car with a safety gadget like that $5.08 Goodyear bladder was, company accountants calculated, greater than that of paying out millions to survivors like Robbie Carlton or to widows and widowers of victims like Sandra Gillespie. The bottom line ruled, and inflammable Pintos kept rolling out of the factories.

In 1977, however, an incredibly sluggish government has at last instituted Standard 301. Now Pintos will have to have rupture-proof gas tanks. Or will they?

To everyone's surprise, the 1977 Pinto recently passed a rear-end crash test in Phoenix, Arizona, for NHTSA. The agency was so convinced the Pinto would fail that it was the first car tested. Amazingly, it did not burst into flame.

"We have had so many Ford failures in the past," explained agency engineer Tom Grubbs, "I felt sure the Pinto would fail."

How did it pass?

Remember that one-dollar, one-pound metal baffle that was on one of the three modified Pintos that passed the pre-production crash tests nearly ten years ago? Well, it is a standard feature on the 1977 Pinto. In the Phoenix test it protected the gas tank from being perforated by those four bolts on the differential housing.

We asked Grubbs if he noticed any other substantial alterations in the rear-end structure of the car. "No," he replied, "the [baffle] seems to be the only noticeable change over the 1976 model."

But was it? What Tom Grubbs and the Department of Transportation didn't know when they tested the car was that it was manufactured in St. Thomas, Ontario. Ontario? The significance of that becomes clear when you learn that Canada has for years had extremely strict rear-end collision standards.

Tom Irwin is the business manager of Charlie Rossi Ford, the Scottsdale, Arizona dealership that sold the Pinto to Tom Grubbs. He refused to explain why he was selling Fords made in Canada when there is a huge Pinto assembly plant much closer by in California. "I know why you're asking that question, and I'm not going to answer it," he blurted out. "You'll have to ask the company."

But Ford's regional office in Phoenix has "no explanation" for the presence of Canadian cars in their local dealerships. Farther up the line in Dearborn, Ford people claim there is absolutely no difference between American and Canadian Pintos. They say cars are shipped back and forth across the border as a matter of course. But they were hard pressed to explain why some Canadian Pintos were shipped all the way to Scottsdale, Arizona. Significantly, one engineer at the St. Thomas plant did admit that the existence of strict rear-end collision standards in Canada "might encourage us to pay a little more attention to quality control on that part of the car."

The Department of Transportation is considering buying an American Pinto and running the test again. For now, it will only say that the situation is under investigation.

Whether the new American Pinto fails or passes the test, Standard 301 will never force the company to test or recall the more than two million pre-1977 Pintos still on the highway. Seventy or more people will burn to death in those cars every year for many years to come. If the past is any indication, Ford will continue to accept the deaths.

According to safety expert Byron Bloch, the older cars could quite easily be retrofitted with gas tanks containing fuel cells. "These improved tanks would add at least 10 mph improved safety performance to the rear end," he estimated, "but it would cost Ford $20 to $30 a car so they won't do it unless they are forced to." Dr. Kenneth Saczalski, safety engineer with the Office of Naval Research in Washington, agrees. "The Defense Department has developed virtually fail-safe fuel systems and retrofitted them into existing vehicles. We have shown them to the auto industry and they have ignored them."

Unfortunately, the Pinto is not an isolated case of corporate malpractice in the auto industry. Neither is Ford a lone sinner. There probably isn't a car on the road without a safety hazard known to its manufacturer. And though Ford may have the best auto lobbyists in Washington, it is not alone. The anti-emission control lobby and the anti-safety lobby usually work in chorus form, presenting a well-harmonized message from the country's richest industry, spoken through the voices of individual companies—the Motor Vehicle Manufacturers Association, the Business Council and the U.S. Chamber of Commerce.

Furthermore, cost-valuing human life is not used by Ford alone. Ford was just the only company careless enough to let such an embarrassing calculation slip into public records. The process of willfully trading lives for profits goes back at least as far as Commodore Vanderbilt, who publicly scorned George Westinghouse and his "foolish" air brakes while people died by the hundreds in accidents on Vanderbilt's railroads.

The original draft of the Motor Vehicle Safety Act provided for criminal sanction against a manufacturer who willfully placed an unsafe car on the market. Early in the proceedings the auto industry lobbied the provision out of the bill. Since then, there have been those damage settlements, of course, but the only government punishment meted out to auto companies for non-compliance to standards has been a minuscule fine, usually $5,000 to $10,000. One wonders how long the Ford Motor Company would continue to market lethal cars were Henry Ford II and Lee Iacocca serving 20-year terms in Leavenworth for consumer homicide.

This article was published in September of 1977, and in February 1978 a jury awarded a sixteen-year-old boy, badly burned in a rear-end Pinto accident, $128 million in damages (the accident occurred in 1973 in Santa Ana, Calif.). That was the largest single personal injury judgment in history.

On May 8, 1978, the Department of Transportation announced that tests conducted in response to this article showed conclusively that the Pinto was defective in all respects described in the article and called for a recall of all 1971 to 1976 Pintos—the most expensive recall in automotive history.

2

THE ARTFUL DODGERS

MORTON MINTZ

The story of Sean Marsee is familiar to millions of Americans. They saw it on "60 Minutes," and read about it in *Reader's Digest* and newspapers around the country. Marsee was the 12-year-old closet "snuff dipper" from Oklahoma. He was habituated or addicted to the Copenhagen brand, which is made from moist smokeless tobacco and which has very high levels of nicotine. His mother, a nurse, discovered what he was doing, but he told her that smokeless tobacco couldn't hurt his lungs as cigarettes would. It mattered very much to him that he not damage his lungs because he wanted to, and did, become a medal-winning high school track star. Besides, if snuff weren't safe, the cans would carry warnings, as do cigarette packs, and professional athletes wouldn't promote it.

In 1983, when Sean was 18, he was found to have cancer in the middle third of his tongue near the groove on the right side of his mouth where he had kept his quid of Copenhagen. He underwent three increasingly mutilating rounds of surgery, and in February 1984, when he was 19, he died.

Later when Sean's mother, Betty Marsee, was living in Ada, Oklahoma, she told her son's story to Dania Deschamps-Braly, a local attorney. The result

Morton Mintz, "The Artful Dodgers," reprinted with permission from *The Washington Monthly,* October 1986. Copyright 1986 by The Washington Monthly Co., 1711 Connecticut Avenue, NW, Washington, DC 20009. (202) 462-0128.

was a David-and-Goliath product-liability lawsuit that pitted Betty Marsee against United States Tobacco Company, the 476th-largest industrial corporation in America.

In previous smoking lawsuits, judges have sealed documents obtained in pretrial discovery that showed that cigarette executives knew about tobacco-related disease, marketing strategies, and other major issues, and when they knew it. The Marsee trial was different. Dania Deschamps-Braly and her husband and legal partner George Braly not only obtained and reviewed an estimated 800,000 pages of documents from U.S. Tobacco, which had also once manufactured cigarettes, but also exposed the papers—many of them devastating—to public scrutiny.

A jury of four women and two men tried the case for 22 days last May and June in the U.S. District Court in Oklahoma City. The Bralys argued that Copenhagen is far richer than any other consumer product in nitrosamines, extremely potent carcinogens that have caused cancer—including tongue cancer—in about 40 separate species of laboratory animals. Defense counsel Alston Jennings Sr., a famed trial attorney from Little Rock, Arkansas, countered that it hasn't been "scientifically established" that tobacco, whether smoked or held in the mouth, causes disease. Moreover, he pointed out, no abnormality at all was found in the tip of Sean's tongue, which he used to position the quid, nor in the cheek and gum tissue that were directly and almost constantly exposed to the quid. The plaintiff's experts, including world-renowned scientists, blamed Sean's cancer on his use of snuff; the defense experts, some of them equipped with minor-league credentials and suspect motives, tried to exonerate tobacco.

Goliath won. On June 20, the jury found for U.S. Tobacco, deciding that a preponderance of the evidence did not show that Sean's six-year, heavy use of Copenhagen had caused his tongue cancer. Having made that decision, the jury, as instructed, did not consider other issues, such as the conduct of the company and the credibility of some of its witnesses, particularly Louis F. Bantle, chairman and chief executive officer of U.S. Tobacco, and Dr. Richard A. Manning, vice president for research and development.

Moreover, in numerous pretrial and trial rulings, U.S. District Judge David L. Russell barred important plaintiff's evidence, and these rulings will be the foundation of an appeal. Had the jury considered such issues and evidence, it might have severely jolted U.S. Tobacco because, for the first time in a tobacco product-liability case, the jury was allowed to set punitive damages.

Did Bantle, Manning, or others testifying on behalf of U.S. Tobacco commit perjury by hiding behind a wall of alleged ignorance despite overwhelming evidence that the product they produce kills people? Does their testimony say something about our own cynicism, about our tolerance for disingenuousness and our willingness to accept it from top corporate officials hoping to guard the bottom line? The jury couldn't rule on these questions. You can.

❖ ROBINSPEAK

U.S. Tobacco manufactures Copenhagen and Skoal, the world's best-selling brands of snuff. In 1985, in this country alone, U.S. Tobacco sold 480.8 million cans of these and other brands of snuff—17.3 million more than in 1984 and 54.9 million more than in 1983. Sales were $480 million, with smokeless tobacco, cigars, and pipe tobacco accounting for 86 percent of the total. In four years profits had more than doubled to $93.5 million, or 19.5 percent of sales—the highest rate among the Fortune 500. For this financial performance, chairman and CEO Bantle received compensation of more than $1.1 million. He, his wife, and their children own about 172,000 shares of company stock worth about $7 million.

Such data provide a context for troubling questions. Suppose snuff causes mouth cancer, gum disease, and tooth loss. Suppose also that these sales increases and high profits are significantly attributable to marketing techniques that were intended to, and do, hook children and youths. Suppose, too, that a U.S. Tobacco official is realistic enough to know the suppositions to be truths. Finally, suppose he knows that admitting what he knows would probably ruin U.S. Tobacco, causing the loss of investment, of thousands of jobs, and of his executive compensation. Would you expect him, under oath, to tell the whole truth?

In Oklahoma City, issues of this very kind confronted Bantle, Manning, other U.S. Tobacco executives, and several well-paid scientific experts. All swore the answers they gave were the whole truth.

Louis Bantle swore that "I am not aware that anyone has said that snuff causes cancer." Like a number of company officials, Bantle refused to attend the trial and, under court rules, he couldn't be compelled to do so. George Braly managed to get, instead, Bantle's testimony in a sworn deposition that he videotaped and played before the jury in Oklahoma. In the deposition Bantle testified that he didn't know of a statement by the National Cancer Advisory Board in February 1985 that "there is sufficient evidence for a cause-and-effect relationship between smokeless-tobacco use and human cancer." He said that "I have not heard of" the International Agency for Research on Cancer, which is funded by the World Health Organization, and which, in September 1985, found "sufficient evidence that oral use of snuff . . . is carcinogenic to humans."

An advisory panel on smokeless tobacco appointed by the Surgeon General said in a much-publicized report last March: "The scientific evidence is strong that the use of snuff can cause cancer in humans." Bantle said he did know of this report, but hadn't read it. He gave this testimony ten days after the report was issued and five weeks after President Reagan signed legislation that requires rotating warnings on smokeless tobacco products.

One of Bantle's partners in sworn ignorance was Hugh W. Foley, the company spokesman to whom all health inquiries about smokeless tobacco were referred from February 1981 to the spring of 1985, when he was promoted to vice president for corporate affairs. The National Cancer Advisory Board resolution that found "sufficient evidence for a cause and effect relationship between smokeless tobacco use and human cancer" had been adopted in February 1985 during his watch. Was he even aware that the International Agency for Research on Cancer had considered the issue? "No sir, I am not." Like Bantle, Foley gave his videotaped deposition a few days after the press reported that the Surgeon General's advisory panel had found strong scientific evidence "that the use of snuff can cause cancer in humans." Did Foley know of this? "No sir, I was not aware of that statement."

Why should a U.S. Tobacco executive bother himself with such matters when, as Bantle told George Braly, he doesn't believe the scientific evidence warrants a health warning on the cans, or even a statement that a controversy exists about the safety of smokeless tobacco? Besides, he pointed out in testimony, he subscribes even today to a joint statement, which his own and other tobacco companies published as an advertisement in 1954, that "an interest in public health is a basic responsibility paramount to every other consideration in our business." Had it ever "entered your mind?" that a health warning might have hurt U.S. Tobacco's soaring sales, Braly asked. "No, sir," Bantle replied. "Not at all?" "No, sir." For some years, the smokeless tobacco U.S. Tobacco has shipped to Sweden has carried a warning saying in part that it "contains nicotine causing a strong dependency equal to that of tobacco smoking. Mucous membranes and gums may be damaged and require medical attention." Asked about why his company warned Swedes but not Americans, Bantle said, "Well, it's the law in Sweden."

In May 1974, T.C. Tso, a tobacco scientist with the Agricultural Research Service, sent W.B. Bennett, then U.S. Tobacco's director of research and development, a copy of a report that one might expect to have set off alarm bells, a report that *Science* would publish the following October. The report, mainly by Drs. Dietrich Hoffman and Stephen S. Hecht, stated that N-Nitrosomornicotine (NNN), a "potential carcinogen, has been positively identified" in smokeless tobacco at levels of "between 1.9 to 88.6 parts per million, one of the highest values of an environmental nitrosamine yet reported. The amount in food and drink rarely exceeds 0.1 part per million. This compound is the first example of a potential organic carcinogen isolated from tobacco."

When Silence Is Golden

Frequently, a corporation or trade association dumps an executive or hireling, but buys his silence with a wad of cash. Only rarely do the terms of the deal surface. But surface they did in the Marsee case concerning the eternal silence about smokeless tobacco of one Gerald V. Gilmartin.

In 1957, Gilmartin went to work in Peekskill, New York, for Allied Public Relations, Inc., which represented U.S. Tobacco and three other snuff makers. In 1965, he shifted those accounts to his own company, Prudential Public Relations, Inc. Fifteen years later these accounts were again shifted, this time to the Smokeless Tobacco Council (STC), which shared offices with Prudential and employed Gilmartin as its executive vice president and secretary-treasurer. After some undisclosed disagreements developed, the STC asked Gilmartin to leave. He did so in June 1984.

Under the termination agreement, signed by James W. Chapin, chairman of the STC and general counsel of U.S. Tobacco, the STC bought a $257,000 annuity for Gilmartin. The owner of the annuity was listed as the STC, c/o Jacob, Medinger & Finnegan. The annuity might be viewed as generosity, because Gilmartin did not have an ongoing contract that had to be bought out; he served at will and could be let go at any time. "I was told," Gilmartin testified, that the annuity "was in payment for many years of faithful and productive service."

But, as Braly showed, the termination agreement provided for "forfeiture of all amounts payable" under the agreement and the $257,000 annuity if "Gilmartin shall at any time make any statement (written or oral) which is disparaging or inimical to the STC, its member companies, or any tobacco products."

". . . have you ever made any statements that were disparaging or inimical to the Smokeless Tobacco Council?" Braly asked.

"No," Gilmartin answered.

—M. M.

The company's reaction was, and remained, cool. "Our initial approach was to attempt to discredit the claims," according to a September 1975 memo by Richard Manning, who would succeed Bennett in 1980 before becoming vice president for R&D. U.S. Tobacco "made a judgment" that no action be taken, Bantle testified a decade later.

A major concern about smokeless tobacco is its promotion to children under 18, who commonly start with a low-nicotine brand, become hooked, and are "graduated" to Copenhagen, the richest in nicotine. In answers to interrogatories, Vice President Wuchiski said: ". . . defendant has always maintained a strict and explicit company policy forbidding the giving of free samples of smokeless tobacco to minors." Similarly, Bantle swore that under "written policies dating way back into the thirties, we never have—and we never will—market tobacco to persons under 18."

However, in January 1968, when Bantle was vice president for marketing, he attended a two-day meeting in New York on "the future of the company's orally utilized tobacco products." The minutes quote him as having said: "We must sell the use of tobacco in the mouth and appeal to young people . . . we hope to start a fad." Confronted with the quote by Braly, Bantle did not dispute it. Braly also quoted from a 1977 *Chicago Tribune* article in which Bantle said, "We've gotten excellent sales growth from young people." "I don't remember that statement," Bantle testified. "But I don't deny it."

Bantle also conceded that certain U.S. Tobacco marketing methods could reach boys. An example cited by Braly was an offer of free snuff samples to anyone who mailed in a coupon in advertisements in magazines such as *Sports Illustrated*, which, Bantle acknowledged, are read by those under 18. But the people who processed the coupons "reviewed the signatures," Bantle testified. "If they looked like they were coming from young people, they were not answered."

S. David Schiller, an assistant United States attorney in Richmond, Virginia, has described the evasive testimony about blatant violations of court bankruptcy orders by several executives of the A.H. Robins Company as "Robinspeak," which he defined as: "I don't know," "I don't recall," "I have no present recollection," "We had no definitive discussion," "I probably said," "I would have said." Were the answers of Louis Bantle the whole truth and nothing but? Or were the answers of the professedly ignorant CEO merely Robinspeak on tobacco road?

❖ WHAT CARCINOGENS?

Dr. Richard Manning, vice president for R&D, joined U.S. Tobacco in 1969 as a senior research chemist. Because of his position, his testimony left many courtroom observers incredulous. It's easy to see why. For starters, he and George Braly had this exchange:

Q. "What is the range of nicotine found in tobacco?"
A. "I don't know."
Q. "Did you tell the jury you are a tobacco chemist?"
A. "Yes, sir. . . ."
Q. "No information on that subject?"
A. "No."

Per Erik Lindqvist, senior vice president for worldwide marketing, followed Manning's lead in obscuring the importance of nicotine in hooking snuff dippers. Looking toward the development of new smokeless tobacco products, Lindqvist wrote the president of the tobacco division in June 1981: "Flavorwise we should try for innovation, taste, and strength. Nicotine should be medium, *recognizing the fact that virtually all tobacco usage is based upon nicotine, 'the kick,' satisfaction.*" (My emphasis.) Was this a recognition by Lindqvist "that virtually all tobacco usage is based upon nicotine?" George Braly asked. "No," the executive swore. "What I am saying in this paragraph is that it is important that the consumer can feel the tobacco satisfaction."

Q. "Don't you, in fact, use the following precise words, 'recognizing the fact that virtually all tobacco usage is based upon nicotine'?"
A. "Satisfaction."
Q. "Yes."
A. "Nicotine satisfaction."
Q. "Yes."
A. "That is what I am saying."
Q. "Virtually all tobacco usage is based upon nicotine satisfaction; is that what you are telling the jury?"
A. "That's what this document says. . . ."
Q. "The United States Tobacco Company had for years planned different

tobacco products around different levels of nicotine satisfaction; isn't that correct?"

A. "No, I can't answer that question. I don't know what you refer to here."

Q. "Do you deny that that is true?"

A. "I don't deny it and I don't admit it. I don't recall."

The next exchange with Manning led more eyebrows to rise:

Q. "What are carcinogens?"

A. "What do you mean by carcinogens?"

Timothy M. Finnegan of Jacob, Medinger & Finnegan in New York, U.S. Tobacco's principal law firm, interjected: "The witness is entitled to have a question that he understands. I ask you to clarify."

Q. "Doctor, my question is what are carcinogens?"

A. "I really don't know what you mean by carcinogens."

After Manning gave the same answer a third time:

Q. "I will tell you that what I understand the word carcinogen to mean is something that causes cancer. Do you understand it any differently?"

A. "It causes cancer in what, sir?"

Q. "Animals."

A. "What is cancer in animals? I am an organic chemist. I am not a pathologist. I am not an oncologist. I am not a medical doctor and, no, I cannot answer that question because I don't know."

Three times Braly asked: "Is there anybody that works for the United States Tobacco Company that knows more about this particular subject of carcinogens than you do?" Manning's first answer was, "I didn't say I knew about this particular subject of carcinogens." His second answer was, "Is your question is there somebody that knows more than nothing?"

Q. "About carcinogens."

A. "I don't know."

Q. "So if there is such a person that works for the U.S. Tobacco Company, you don't have any idea who it is?"

A. "Correct."

Q. "And you admit to this jury that you know nothing about that subject?"

Immediately, there followed exchanges, twice interrupted by Finnegan, in which Manning tried to deny his admission that he was a total ignoramus about carcinogens. Finally:

Q. "My question was didn't you just tell the jury that you didn't know of anybody in the company that knew more than nothing about carcinogens?"

A. "I think you are telling me I just said that."
Q. "I am asking you. Didn't you just say that a few minutes ago?"
A. "Right now, I don't remember."

Later:

Q. "What research has been carried out by the United States Tobacco Company in connection with the safety of snuff used by human beings?"
A. "I don't know what you mean by the use of the word safety in that context, either."
Q. "Has the United States Tobacco Company ever carried out any research to determine whether or not its snuff products are dangerous for human beings to use?"
A. "I don't know what you mean by dangerous in that concept—or context."

There was much more of the same kind of grappling over issues such as whether the company has researched or hired others to research whether snuff is carcinogenic or mutagenic. And, to end, there was this:

Q. "What is a low concentration of nitrosamines?"
A. "I do not know what a low concentration of nitrosamines is."

Braly told the jury he had a word for Manning's testimony: "Snuff-speak."

After the verdict, a juror told me this about the executives' testimony: "They stonewalled it. It was very obvious to everybody. Dr. Manning pretended he didn't know anything at all. The chairman was even worse than Manning." But the same juror, asking not to be identified, said that deposition testimony taken in advance of a trial is like "a game plan" in sports, i.e., a strategy to be held close to the vest, is therefore not taken as seriously as live testimony in the courtroom. It didn't faze the juror, who spoke as if this notion was widely shared in this buckle of the Bible Belt, when I pointed out that both kinds of testimony are given under an identical oath.

❖ ARRANT EXPERTS

It's easy for cash-rich corporate law firms to find academicians to provide helpful testimony. It was particularly easy in the Marsee case because of the foresightedness of U.S. Tobacco. In August 1974, R&D chief Bennett wrote a letter, with a copy to Bantle, in which he said that "cigarette companies have built up quite a stable of experts in these fields related to their products, but we are not in too good a shape in this respect." How they got in shape is exemplified by their recruitment of Dr. William H. Binnie, chairman of pathology at Baylor College of Dentistry in Dallas.

In early 1984, Binnie went to an oral pathology meeting in Holland. So did Janet S. McClendon of Jacob, Medinger, the U.S. Tobacco law firm, which for several years also represented R.J. Reynolds Tobacco Company, the big cigarette maker. Within a few minutes in the trial, Binnie gave George Braly two differing accounts of the origin of his availability to Jacob, Medinger and the smokeless tobacco industry.

Initially, he said "I was approached" by McClendon. Then he said he had "sought out" the lawyer. "Here was this lady sitting in our meeting and I was just curious to find out who she was," Binnie said. "I didn't even know she was an attorney." Braly asked Binnie whether McClendon "travels around to all these medical meetings hunting for doctors that will testify for the tobacco industry?" The doctor replied, "No comment."

Braly asked Binnie if he had "testified on behalf of the smokeless tobacco industry before Congress about a year ago?" "No," he said, "I submitted a document." In it, he expressed the belief that smokeless tobacco does not cause oral cancer. At whose request had he given his opinion to Congress? "I had seen the proposed bill [to require health warnings on smokeless tobacco products] and the law firm asked if I wanted to see what I thought of it."

Q. "And, I take it, you think that tobacco doesn't cause oral cancer?"
A. "Correct."

Braly reminded him that at least 90 percent of the victims of head and neck cancers are tobacco users and asked if this had "any significance to you?" "No," Binnie said. Indeed, he was so protective of all tobacco use that, when asked whether cigarette smoking is "a cause of lung cancer," he replied, "I don't know that."

Then Braly asked the witness if he was the same W.H. Binnie who had published an article in the *Journal of Oral Pathology* in 1983—a year before the McClendon recruitment in Holland. Binnie said he was. In the article he had written: "The method of smoking notwithstanding, there is ample evidence to support the premises of tobacco consumption as a dose/time related entity in the etiology of intra-oral cancer."

Q. "But have you changed your mind now?"
A. "No, I haven't."

On January 10, 1983, ABC television aired a piece on snuff that disturbed the peace of Chairman Bantle. Two days later, he sent a memo to Executive Vice President Barry Nova: "What is the downside of Monday's broadcast? 'The Surgeon General warning snuff dipping may cause cancer'? It's possible it could trigger such a suggestion. We should develop a strategy for such a possibility, or better, for seeing that it does not happen." A few days later the company's Task Force on Regulatory/Political Environment came up with an unsigned memo listing numerous "preliminary strategy recommendations." One of them was only three words, the second word of which is an adjective that, dictionaries say, often modifies "knave": "Develop arrant doctors." Braly inquired, "Are you one of the arrant doctors that they have recruited?" Binnie said he was not.

❖ YOU DIRTY RAT

So, how, with all this dubious testimony, could the jury rule in favor of U.S. Tobacco? The witness who decisively influenced them to conclude that snuff hadn't been shown to have killed Sean Marsee was Dr. Arthur Furst, immediate past president of the American College of Toxicology. Although an organic chemist, the impressively credentialed Furst is a full professor in the pharmacology department at Stanford University Medical School and is the author of about 220 professional papers in the fields of cancer research, chemistry, and toxicology.

From 1965 to 1969, while he was at the University of San Francisco, Furst conducted smoking studies paid for in full or in part by the Council for Tobacco Research U.S.A., which is funded by the cigarette industry. In 1981, when the Smokeless Tobacco Research Council was formed, Furst became a member of its scientific advisory board. He testified that the 1974 "stable of experts" letter was "news to me." "Isn't the Council the 'stable' for the smokeless tobacco industry?" George Braly asked. "Absolutely not," Furst replied.

Furst acknowledged at the trial that he hadn't published an article on the subject of tobacco and cancer for probably 20 years. He testified that he was aware that the Surgeon General, on the advice of a large number of the country's most prestigious scientists, had listed five criteria to be taken into account in determining whether there is "a sufficient basis to form a judgment of causality." But when asked "if you have any recollection of what they are?" he replied, "At the moment, no." He went on to "disagree, absolutely," with the criteria and claim that "the scientists" do not agree either.

As one would expect, the positions Furst took on the relationship between tobacco and disease were echoes of the views of the cigarette and smokeless tobacco industries, and rejections of views of the majority of the medical and scientific community. "[A]re cigarettes a cause of lung cancer in human beings?" Braly asked. "[T]he answer would be no because it has not been proven," Furst said. Similarly, he dismissed all of the authoritative warnings by the Surgeon General and others that snuff can cause mouth cancer.

Furst's testimony was seductive. Yes, he said, nitrosamines are carcinogens in animals. But he had happy news: in snuff, they are counteracted by "anti-cancer agents." In asserting this, he relied heavily on an experiment in which snuff components caused cancer in rats, while snuff itself did not. "There must be some anti-cancer activity in that snuff," he testified.

Once again, George Braly's cross-examination was shattering, even if it didn't strike the jury that way. Furst admitted he had not made the simple calculations that would have established the comparative exposures to NNN, in terms of body weight, of the rats in the experiment on which he relied, and of Sean Marsee. These calculations, which Braly did on the spot, showed that Sean, by consuming four cans of Copenhagen a week for six years, had been exposed to nine to ten times as much NNN as the rats.

Moreover, Furst said he believed it to be "absolutely" important to have hands-on experience in scientific experiments, but admitted he had never test-ed nitrosamines in animals. Few, if any, scientists know more about or have more hands-on experience with nitrosamines than Dr. William Lijinsky of the Cancer Research Center in Frederick, Maryland. Lijinsky had done his own study in which NNN caused tongue cancer in animals, and U.S. Tobacco attorney Jennings had told Furst of this. But, Furst testified, Jennings had not told him (or other defense experts) of the most salient fact, revealed in this exchange:

Q. "Did they tell you that this was the experiment that had been done at the lowest dose levels ever tested on nitrosamines?"
A. "Obviously not, no, sir."

Furst also disclosed that he had not been told that Lijinsky had testified at the trial about the dose levels in his tongue-cancer study. "I just learned about this today," Furst told Braly during cross-examination. "I won't argue with that."

He did not, however, change his position.

❖ SILENT OATHS

If, in 1986, the chairman and CEO of the leading snuff company is "not aware that anyone has said that snuff causes cancer," and if the vice president for R&D doesn't know what a "carcinogen" is, or what "safe" or "dangerous" are, do they know what an oath is? What the "whole truth" is? I believe they do.

Probably I'm naive, but I have to say I'm repelled by the sight of platoons of corporate executives, on Capitol Hill as well as in the courts, who swear to tell—but who tell nothing like—the truth, the whole truth, and nothing but the truth. And I'm appalled when they tell nothing like the truth about con-duct that has exposed dozens, hundreds, or even tens of thousands of human beings to avoidable disease, injury, and death.

To be blunt, I am talking about conduct that, when engaged in on the street, is universally recognized as manslaughter, or, if the conduct was know-ing and willful, as murder. Maybe it's also naive to wonder why it is that when corporate executives who engage in such conduct violate a solemn oath to tell the truth, "so help you God," they rarely, if ever, elicit even a tut-tut from mainline editorialists and columnists, or the wrath of mainline clergymen, or such telegenic hellfire preachers as Jerry Falwell and Jimmy Swaggart.

But maybe the public oath these executives mouth is not the silent oath they obey. The silent oath, as I imagine it, would run like this: "I do solemnly swear to tell the truth, the whole truth, and nothing but the truth, so long as I reveal no truth that could hurt my corporation or me, so help me CEO."

3

WHEN THEY CLOSE THE FACTORY GATES: HOW BIG STEEL SCRAPPED A COMMUNITY

JOHN LOGUE

Just west of the Pennsylvania border lies the Mahoning Valley, once the second-leading steel producing area in the United States. In Youngstown and in its industrial suburbs, mills line both sides of the river. For genera tions their noise has muted the Mahoning, but in recent times the furnaces have gradually been banked, and one by one the mills have closed. In a matter of months, the sounds of the river will be audible again.

Youngstown is a microcosm of the problems of the aging industrial towns of the Northeast: the predatory conglomerate, systematic disinvestment, the flight south, the trained labor force suddenly unemployed, the collapse of the community tax base, and the obsolescence of the saving their plants and jobs depended on increasing production. They succeeded, but the gates still closed.

In the long run, labor force dedication cannot replace modernization. And modernization simply did not occur in Youngstown. The steel companies took millions out of the valley over the last decades and returned little to the plants.

The lack of reinvestment in the Mahoning Valley had a variety of causes. One is geographic: Inland mills lack cheap water transportation, a notable handicap for traditional mills (though not for those with modern electric furnaces which use a higher proportion of scrap). More crucial was the changing industrial structure. Merger activity hit steel—and Youngstown—hard. Lykes, the New Orleans-based shipping conglomerate, acquired Youngstown Sheet and Tube in the late 1960s. Sheet and Tube was more than six times the size of Lykes at the time of acquisition but the smaller fish swallowed the bigger. Lykes was less interested in Sheet and Tube's dies and presses than in its large cash flow, which could be diverted into financing other acquisitions. Plant maintenance diminished from the day Lykes took over, and investment in modernizing steel facilities slowed notably. Similarly, Jones and Laughlin Steel (J & L) was absorbed by the LTV corporation, a Dallas-based conglomerate.

Systematic disinvestment by the conglomerates is a symptom of the deeper problem: International competition in steel is intense, and profits are lower than in other industries. Emerging from World War II with its facilities intact, the American steel industry prospered while its foreign competition was prostrate. In time, the German and Japanese mills were reconstructed with more advanced technology, but American management rested on its laurels, in large measure because of the conviction that the new technology being pioneered abroad (derived, ironically, from foreign studies of American plants) was inappropriate for the huge scale of the American domestic market. New investment went instead into advanced versions of technologically antiquated production processes. By the late 1960s, foreign steel companies were making major inroads into the American market, while American investment had lagged so far behind the growth in demand that American producers were no longer able to meet peak domestic requirements.

Wages play a subsidiary role to investment. American steelworkers are among the best-paid industrial workers in the country, but the same can be said of Western European steelworkers. Japanese wage rates, long below those in other industrial countries, have moved up rapidly. But new plants now coming on line in such Third World countries as Brazil and South Korea will benefit not only from a low-wage labor force but also from the anti-union policies of those governments.

The obvious answer is to encourage unionization, and efforts to aid union organizers in Third World countries have met limited success. The principal problem is pressuring Third World governments to permit union organizing. Unions in western nations have had occasional successes: The threat of a boycott on unloading Chilean exports wrung a few concessions from that government in allowing union activity in Chile. But what is really needed is governmental pressure, and for all the human rights campaign, the Carter Administration has done little in this area.

Not all American steel firms have been slow to modernize. Some smaller companies, like Armco's Western Steel division, which has installed electric furnaces in all its plants, are fully modern, highly competitive, and profitable. But the industry giant, U.S. Steel—which last year grossed $12 billion, equal to the gross national product of Egypt—has lagged so far behind that cynical outsiders suspect it of deferring capital spending and allowing foreign inroads into its markets in order to compel the Government to provide tax breaks for the industry.

Instead of modernizing their mills, many American steel firms are diversifying—diverting profits from steel into investment in other areas. The conglomerates that now own Youngstown Sheet and Tube and J & L do this as a matter of course. But even U.S. Steel is turning its back on the industry, channeling an increasing portion of its investment dollars into the chemical industry, oil, gas, and uranium exploration, and real estate development. U.S. Steel's latest annual report is illustrated with pictures of a company-developed shopping mall.

If Youngstown's problems were typical of the industry's, its response was not: Workers and community have fought stubbornly and imaginatively to save the valley's economic backbone. It is this struggle that has projected Youngstown into the national consciousness.

The fight began with Lykes's surprise shutdown of Sheet and Tube's Campbell works. Campbell local union presidents first learned of the impending disaster when they were called into management offices one Monday morning in September 1977 to receive the press release announcing the closure; the first layoffs began three days later. Initially accepting management's explanation that the plant was a victim of pollution control rules and Japanese imports, ten of thousands signed petitions asking the Government to invoke import restrictions and relax environmental protection standards.

But public outrage grew as the real reasons for the closure became clear: New Orleans executives had plundered Sheet and Tube to invest elsewhere, leaving Youngstown with a silent mill and 5,000 unemployed. The formation by religious leaders of the Ecumenical Coalition of the Mahoning Valley provided a focal point for organization. Its goal quickly became a worker–community-run steel mill—a suggestion first made by Gerald Dickey, a steelworker at the Brier Hill works and recording secretary of the union local. The proposal called for a community corporation that would combine worker, community, and private investment. After a study by Gar Alperovitz and the Center for Economic Alternatives established that a community mill was potentially viable, the Ecumenical Coalition asked the Federal Government for $245 million in loan guarantees—guarantees of the sort provided to other steel producers, such as Wheeling-Pittsburgh, for modernizing aging plants. Reaction was initially favorable, but in March 1979 the Government rejected the request, killing the Campbell plan. (See "Must Youngstown Roll Over and Die? How 'Big Steel' Got to Jimmy Carter," *The Progressive*, October 1979.)

By this time, the Justice Department had compounded Youngstown's problems by suspending antitrust rules that would probably have prevented the merger of Lykes, the owner of Youngstown Sheet and Tube (the nation's eighth-largest steel producer), and LTV, which owned Jones and Laughlin (the seventh-largest). Overruling staff recommendations, Attorney General Griffin Bell approved the merger under an imaginative application of the "failing business doctrine," otherwise reserved for firms in or near bankruptcy. Bell cited a desire to save jobs at Sheet and Tube, but that wasn't one of the results of the merger. Sheet and Tube's Brier Hill mill was superfluous to the integrated company and was closed in December 1979.

The U.S. Steel shutdown, announced November 27, 1979, was less surprising than the earlier closures. The Ohio and McDonald works were among the most marginal facilities the company owned; they had been close to getting the ax before. Yet to a community organized on the issue of plant closings, the shutdown was the final straw: Keeping the plants open or selling them to the employes was an issue to be pushed in the streets as well as in the courts. Irate steelworkers seized U.S. Steel's district headquarters on January 28 to underline their view.

The aborted plan for a community takeover of the Campbell works was readily adapted to U.S. Steel's Youngstown works. This time the plan called for a small infusion of local capital, a $60 million Federally guaranteed loan, and a substantial reduction in labor costs by deferring incentive payments and writing off accumulated pension and vacation benefits. Plans called for running the mills "as is" until the regular capital market could be tapped—possibly with Government loan guarantees—for modernization funds. The plan called for cutting labor costs by 21 per cent, but this time it was hoped that labor's sacrifice would save the mill jobs permanently.

"We have a much better chance than ever existed for reviving the Campbell works," said Bob Vasquez, chairman of the Ohio Works local. "The labor force is in place. The management is in place. Our customers have not turned to other suppliers yet."

There was just one problem: U.S. Steel refused to sell the mills to any group which sought Federal loan guarantees—a proviso that would exclude sales to several of U.S. Steel's competitors as well as to former employes. Ironically, the company's stand was announced at a press conference in conjunction with the steel industry's request for new tax deductions which would cost other taxpayers some tens of billions of dollars.

The leadership of the steelworkers' locals at U.S. Steel's McDonald and Ohio Works in Youngstown are not radicals. They seemed more discomfited than the company itself by the temporary occupation of U.S. Steel's Youngstown headquarters, preferring to place their hopes in reviving the mills under community ownership. That required the cooperation of the Carter Administration, not notable for its enthusiasm for plant occupations. They sought redress in the courts, suing U.S. Steel for breaking what they alleged was an oral agreement to keep the mills open as long as they broke even, and for anti-trust violations in refusing to sell the mills to Community Steel.

"We are not talking about a local bakery shop, a grocery store, a tool-and-die shop, or a body shop in Youngstown that is planning to close and move out," Federal District Judge Thomas Lambros declared in granting the restraining order that prevented the planned March 10 shutdown. "U.S. Steel cannot leave the Mahoning Valley and the Youngstown area in a state of waste." In agreeing to hear the case, the judge said he chose to "view the law not as something static but in terms of the modern-day conditions." And he moved the trial to Youngstown to enable the plaintiffs to subpoena U.S. Steel executives from Pittsburgh.

William Roesch, president of U.S. Steel since April 1979, told the crowded courtroom of studies that had been undertaken to determine whether there was a "viable fit" between Jones and Laughlin and Youngstown Sheet and Tube, and whether a merger would improve the profitability of the two.

What about the "fit" between Sheet and Tube's Brier Hill works in Youngstown and J&L's seamless operation at Aliquippa, Pennsylvania? asked Staughton Lynd, attorney for the steelworkers.

"I didn't see that as a problem," Roesch responded. There were murmurs from the audience, most of whom were free to attend the trial because of what the "fit" had done to the Brier Hill works in December.

David Roderick, chairman and former president of U.S. Steel, making his first trip to Youngstown since 1977, testified that when the decision was made to shut down the Youngstown works on November 27, 1979, U.S. Steel officials had performance figures for Youngstown showing profitable operation on the first half of the year and a cumulative loss of only $300,000 for the first ten months (Roderick's salary in 1979 was $360,000). It was on the basis of future projections that U.S. Steel acted, Roderick said.

What projections? Lynd demanded. He said U.S. Steel's own figures, from plant management, showed a projected 1980 *profit* on fixed expenses. Roderick said he had no knowledge of that report.

Roderick's answers seemed surprisingly thin on facts, but he spoke categorically on policy topics. U.S. Steel would not sell the plants to its employes or any other group with a Government-guaranteed loan.

"Are you closing the door?" Lynd asked. Roderick affirmed his belief in free enterprise and the market place.

"Is there anything that the USW locals and the community can do to reopen U.S. Steel's consideration of the closures?" Lynd asked. "I cannot foresee such circumstances," the company chairman replied. His answer had a ring of finality.

The judge also heard from William Kirwan, general superintendent of the Youngstown works. Kirwan did not talk of free enterprise but of producing steel profitably—of the fact that the Youngstown works turned a $10 million profit on fixed expenses in 1978 and $4 million in 1979, with the projection of a tiny profit in 1980. He recalled how, in February 1979, Youngstown had produced half the profits in U.S. Steel's Eastern Division, and how production records were broken time and time again despite the antiquity of the equipment.

Kirwan spelled out the details of his "Kirwan plan," which he had pushed on the unreceptive U.S. Steel hierarchy, for massive new investment in the Youngstown works, and for building a new mill on the site of the old works. The audience applauded this glimpse of what community control is all about.

Judge Lambros's decision favored the company. The last heat of iron was tapped at the Ohio works within hours after the decision was handed down. Judge Lambros dismissed the employes' antitrust case three weeks later, ruling that despite Community Steel's offer of $20 million for the Youngstown works, the steelworkers had not demonstrated "any ability to purchase, [and] therefore no one has denied them anything."

A legal victory by the steelworkers might have brought a delay of one or two years in the shutdown. But the Youngstown issue goes deeper than that: What is a corporation's responsibility to employes and the community and what influence should employes have on investment decisions?

The Youngstown shutdowns and community opposition to them have drawn national attention. The United Steel Workers, whose national leaders have done little to help save the Youngstown mills, have now introduced plant shutdowns as a national bargaining issue.

Pending before the Ohio legislature is a bill requiring advance notification, severance pay, and payment to a community readjustment fund in the event of closures of major plants. Similar legislation has been proposed in Oregon, Michigan, Massachusetts, Pennsylvania, and New York, and in Congress. Milder plant closing laws are already on the books in Maine and Wisconsin.

Such moves deal with effects, not causes. Employe influence on investment decisions is more crucial; it was the decision not to reinvest in Youngstown, made in the 1960s and early 1970s, that led to the shutdown. Employes now have some influence in other countries—in Sweden and in Germany, for example—and few would maintain that the plants are the worse run for it. Swedish employers are required to provide full information to their employes and to negotiate all major investment decisions with the union. Full disclosure requirements would probably improve the quality of information in the hands of managers when they make important decisions. Perhaps the most astonishing point in Roderick's testimony in the Youngstown trial was the paucity of his company's knowledge of the profitability of the Youngstown works when the decision was made to shut them. He had never heard of the "Kirwan plan" to modernize the works.

Though the plant closing legislation under consideration confers no powers on employes or communities, it does raise the cost of shutting marginal facilities rather than modernizing them. Currently the tax law weights the balance on the other side. The economics of massive closures are more attractive to corporate executives because the public pays most of the tab. The company takes a one-year bath of tax losses (which can be written off against future income) and ends the drain on current earnings. Its executives gain a reputation for acting decisively to "turn the company's profits around."

But the cost to the taxpaying public for shutting marginal mills is heavy. Of the roughly $200 million loss, charged against future taxable income, that U.S. Steel took in the Youngstown shutdown, other taxpayers will eventually pick up 46 per cent, or almost $100 million. In addition, the direct cost in unemployment compensation, retraining, and other benefits for workers idled by the shutdown is estimated at $70 million over the next three years. Add in the state and Federal governments' losses in taxes, the waste in underutilization of Youngstown schools, roads, water and sewage plants, and the sum of losses absorbed by the public would far exceed $200 million—about the cost of Kirwan's modernization program.

Perhaps the greatest irony is that Youngstown employes were unable to use their considerable financial clout. The assets of U.S. Steel's manual employes pension plan are *double* the value of the corporation's stock. Were the equity of the fund subdivided, Youngstown workers would be entitled to about $100 million. But far from following the interests of its normal owners, the company-controlled pension fund has sunk (as of 1976) a half billion dollars into the stock of predominantly non-union and, in some cases, blatantly anti-union firms. Conceivably, many of the beneficiaries would have preferred to see some of that fund invested in saving jobs by modernizing the mills instead of being pumped into non-union companies investing in the South or farther afield in Taiwan, South Korea, or Brazil. But the company controls the fund.

At issue in Youngstown, then, was the question of economic power. Do the rights of property ownership include the right to scrap jobs, mills, an entire town? The answer of the Youngstown community was a resounding No. While community control has been invoked as a last resort, Community Steel could have provided the vehicle to save Youngstown's steel industry by taking over the mills as Sheet and Tube, J&L, and U.S. Steel shut them down. Stabilizing the Youngstown steel industry under community control would also have cost jobs, but nothing like the 10,000 that now have disappeared.

The decision was not up to Youngstown. It rested with the steel companies and the courts, which ruled, albeit reluctantly, that the privileges of ownership included the right to scrap a community and its people.

From Family Firm to Mini-Conglomerate

Small, family-owned companies have been hit hard by the merger wave of the 1960s and 1970s, with countless hundreds of locally owned firms falling into new hands. The A. C. Williams Company in Ravenna, Ohio, about thirty miles west of Youngstown, is a case in point.

Founded in 1844, A. C. Williams is among the oldest foundries in the country, and until 1976 it was still owned and managed by the family that founded it. The firm's two plants in Ravenna—together the town's second-largest private employer—had been unionized since the mid-1930s, and while wages were hardly munificent, the atmosphere was decent, the work steady, and the stress less than at the higher-paid assembly line jobs in the region. Union local president Jim Boyle described labor relations as average to good; in the twenty-one years he had worked at A. C. Williams, there had been only one strike, and that had lasted less than a day.

Four years ago, a group of investors bought the firm, and quickly used the assets to acquire three other Ohio foundries. As it happened, two of the new plants were non-union. So it was hardly surprising that the new management was willing to take a strike at A. C. Williams when the old contract expired in January 1980. Management did not even appear at the bargaining table; it sent only its attorney.

In the third week of the strike, the company bought a non-union foundry in Tennessee and announced its intention to move machinery from one of the struck plants to the new one, where production could be resumed. What followed could have been a scene out of a Grade B 1930s strike film.

Shortly after midnight on Thursday, February 14, a convoy of eleven trucks drove full speed through the picket line, along with a car and a van carrying twelve men equipped with pistols, shotguns, mace, nightsticks, and riot helmets. The pickets were forewarned of the arrival of the "movers" (who, according to Boyle's queries, specialize in such operations and have moved 192 plants under comparable circumstances) because the convoy got lost and radioed the police for directions. The police charged the eight pickets with aggravated riot, but they did not search the trucks for armaments. Only after the trucks were on the road did the police have a look in the remaining vehicle—the van—to find some disassembled shotguns and a fully assembled pistol.

The story has a happy ending. Although production did begin at the Tennessee plant, a decent contract was finally signed in Ravenna, raising wages, improving pensions, and leading to the rehiring of three employes previously fired. The old machinery stayed in Tennessee, but new machinery was brought in from yet another plant bought during the strike. The union chalked it up as a victory.

But the nature of the company and its relations with the employes had been fundamentally changed. Four years ago, A. C. Williams was part of the community; today, it is free to shift work among union and non-union plants, or even out of state.

"When I went to work there twenty-one years ago," Boyle says, "the manager was Harry Beck. He knew the wife's name, the names of your children, whether they played baseball or football, when they were sick. All that's gone now. This president don't give a damn whether he operates in Ravenna or someplace else."

A few months after the end of the strike, the company proved Boyle right by shutting one of its two Ravenna plants indefinitely for economic reasons and laying off half the work force. It was the first shutdown within memory; A. C. Williams had weathered other recessions and the Great Depression by reducing the work week rather than shutting down.

As in Youngstown, the power has moved out of the community, and with it has gone the old sense of security. Community loyalty and 130 years of tradition mean little in the new world of the mini-conglomerate.

4

MISSING FROM THE NEWS

BEN H. BAGDIKIAN

Almost weekly we read of yet another great media merger. Time-Warner attempts to form the largest media conglomerate in the world, or Rupert Murdoch adds another major segment to his global empire. We are witnessing an extraordinary race toward monopoly control. In 1982, fifty corporations had half or more of all the business in the major media of the United States. Today, that number is less than twenty-five and shrinking.

Among our 1,600 daily newspapers, for example, about a dozen corporations now control more than half the circulation. Among our 11,000 individual magazine titles, a half dozen corporations have most of the revenue. Among our four television networks and 900 commercial stations, three corporations have most of the audience and revenue. There are at least 2,500 book-publishing companies, but a half dozen corporations have most of the sales in the book industry. Three major studios have most of the movie business.

What these giants seek is control or market domination not just in one medium, but in all the media. The aim is to control the entire process from an original manuscript to its use in as many forms as possible. A magazine article owned by the company becomes a book owned by the company, then becomes a television program owned by the company, then becomes a movie owned by the company. The movie is then shown in theaters owned by the company, and the movie's sound track is issued by a record label owned by the company. Obviously, the company will not be enthusiastic about outside ideas and productions that it does not own. More and more, we will be dealing with closed circuits.

The leading owners of our daily newspapers include Gannett, which owns *USA Today* and eighty-eight other dailies, or about six million in total daily circulation; International Thomson, with 116 papers and two million circulation; Knight-Ridder, with three million; Newhouse, and about eight others.

The chief owners of magazines dealing with the general news will be dominated by Time-Warner, which will control more than 40 per cent of the country's magazine business. Other major owners are Rupert Murdoch, Hearst, and Newhouse, though not all issue general news. *Newsweek,* which does carry news, is owned by the Washington Post Company.

In broadcasting, despite some loss of audience, the three networks, ABC, CBS, and NBC, still have most of the television viewers and business. In books, some of the major owners are Gulf + Western, owners of Simon & Schuster; Time-Warner; Reader's Digest Association; Bertelsmann, a German firm; Maxwell, a British firm; Hachette, a French firm; and Thomson, a Canadian firm.

How well do these major owners of the news and knowledge serve the public?

The good news about American reporting is that in some technical matters, it is the best in the world. Its journalists are the best educated, far better educated than any earlier generation of American journalists. They operate under higher professional ethics than journalists elsewhere and higher than at any time in the past. They lie less than journalists elsewhere, fictionalize less, and, on the whole, take seriously their individual duty to provide the public with accurate information. Collectively, they issue an extraordinary volume of news every day.

But if things are so good, why are they so bad? The problem lies with the institutions and the conventions of standard American journalism. Most reporters in the standard media can say, truthfully, "No editor tells me to lie." But most reporters are told every day what to write *about.*

There are 50,000 print reporters and 50,000 broadcast reporters in the country, and each day, each week, each month they are pointed toward particular tasks, particular stories, particular personalities, particular government activities, particular foreign scenes, particular series. In the resulting mass of stories, there are often articles of importance and distinction, and there is a daily volume of routine, factual, essential local and national information.

The problem lies in something beyond the mass of useful items.

Each day, editors necessarily select some stories for emphasis, some for deemphasis, and some for the waste basket. Certain kinds of stories, certain public figures, certain social data, certain analysts of social and political events are regularly on the network evening news and the front page, while other stories, spokespersons, and analysts are mentioned obscurely if at all. The main problem in the news today is not what is false, but what is missing.

The pattern begins when owners appoint executive editors and producers. Owners seldom appoint someone who is likely to be interested in emphasizing those events and interpretations that undermine the owners' political and economic interests. Some editors do so, and there is a steady record of their being fired or resigning to protest restrictions.

In 1980, members of the American Society of Newspaper Editors were asked whether they would feel free to publish news harmful to the parent corporation of their newspaper. One-third said they would not feel free to do so. Given how offensive the very idea is to professional journalists, I think we're safe in assuming that 33 per cent is a conservative figure.

The consequences, I believe, are clear. In foreign affairs, the main news of the country follows the official national policy. This does not mean that there is never any reporting contrary to officialdom. But it does mean that information that contradicts governmental versions gets into the news with greater difficulty and only briefly compared to the official view. It is not done by official censorship, but by self-censorship.

If journalists are as much improved as I think they are, it's fair to ask what causes this self-censorship. One reason is the awareness by the top editors and executive producers that stories seriously affecting their owners' interests will cause the editor problems. Such stories do appear, but infrequently. And they usually focus on those developments that are, in effect, unavoidable.

The recent departure of William Kovach as editor of the *Atlanta Constitution & Journal* illustrates the editor's dilemma. He had been told to be fearless and make his paper the best in the country. He took this literally, and his paper began publishing stories about problems in Atlanta—problems of race, of commercial development, and of flaws in the establishment. He was squeezed out, and it took no memorandum from the publisher to let the staff know that stories of that kind will get reporters and their editors in trouble with the owners.

Several years ago, a reporter and editor at the *Dallas Morning News* did a documented story about a bank in serious trouble. The reporter was fired, and so was the editor who passed the story. The bank did fail, and the story was confirmed. But no memorandum has to instruct that news staff or others around the country that stories disclosing flaws in specific banks will get them into trouble. As we all know, there are no problems with banks and savings-and-loan associations in the state of Texas, or anyplace else.

Self-censorship also comes from a basic strategy of American news. Since most of the revenues of the news media are derived from advertising and there is an incentive to maintain an audience of as many affluent people as possible, news policies are designed not to offend the political sensibilities of the advertising target-audience.

This is done in two ways. One is to attribute every fact and judgment to as high an authority as possible, so that no one can accuse a journalist of selective reporting. The other method is to give the news a kind of political tone-deafness, an appearance of neutrality without political, social, or economic context. When you give the context of events, you begin to be political. Accurate reports of events, with interpretation by high officials, is much safer.

But the result is not neutral. If you strain out independent political and economic contexts, if you do not pursue the likely causes and consequences of events, if you emphasize or rely exclusively on the words and ideas of the highest officials, public and private, you have presented a picture of an uncontested and inevitable status quo. When you add to that the Cold War and the nature of anticommunism in American politics, it is always safer to swing to the Right than to the Left. The status quo, in politics and in corporate life is, of course, sharply skewed to the conservative side. It resists significant change in society.

Finally, self-censorship in the standard news media comes from twenty years of accusations against American journalists by neoconservative intellectuals and academics and conservative political leaders who have branded journalists, individually and as a group, for being biased against the established order and conservative politics.

These charges, when they are based on anything at all, are based on surveys of journalists who, when asked whether they tend to be Democrats or Republicans, say they tend more to be Democrats than Republicans, or tend to be more liberal than conservative. That this is precisely the pattern of the American electorate seems not to make any difference. While recent Presidential elections have gone Republican, countrywide voting for Congress and for state and local office continues to be heavily Democratic. But the accusations by conservatives have had the effect of making many journalists lean over backward to favor conservatives to show that they are not biased.

These pressures to support the status quo happen to conform with the politics and economics of the major media owners. If the breaking news is noticeably embarrassing for conservatives, the question regularly asked within news organizations is whether the reporting is really being fair to the conservatives. I have never heard of similar questions of fairness being raised in regard to the treatment of Ralph Nader, Common Cause, labor unions, and other forces on the other side.

Public knowledge of events in Nicaragua and El Salvador has suffered from an astonishing failure of the mainstream news media to do continuous reporting from the field, though Central America remains the center of White House attention and activities, and the closest we have been to a new war. The main body of news coverage has never checked out assertions about events in those countries in any systematic way. For years the news media took official declarations at face value, often when there was overwhelming evidence to the contrary.

Recent examples include the case of Raymond Bonner, a correspondent for *The New York Times,* who was withdrawn from El Salvador because he reported that a real civil war existed in that country, and that atrocities were committed on both sides, including the side supported by American aid. His recall did not require a printed order to other correspondents warning them that departing from the official line in Washington or at the American embassies can get them in trouble with their editors.

The Iran-contra exercise, in violation of the Constitution and contrary to the word of our highest officials, was exposed fairly early by the alternative press in this country and finally was blown open by an obscure publication in Beirut, not a mainstream American news organization.

In domestic affairs, there is a steady pattern of looking the other way, of avoiding obvious causes and consequences, so as not to disturb or threaten the status quo.

President Reagan's program of supply-side economics, with huge military spending accompanied by large tax cuts, had enormous support in corporate America. But people with perfectly respectable expert credentials saw it from the start as a formula for disaster. Nevertheless, for years, most of the judgments reported in the news came from organizations and individuals who were beneficiaries of those economic policies. Even after David Stockman, one of the architects of the idea, went on record to say it was all really a cover to shift wealth from the poor to the rich, the mainstream media continued to quote almost exclusively these same beneficiaries, as though Stockman and serious economists had never spoken. If criticism ever was aired, it was in the seventeenth paragraph.

We have had massive deregulation of our economy, with some good results and some bad. But for more than ten years, the news media were close to silent on the bad results. One is tempted to say that some of the serious negative effects of deregulation finally broke into the standard news only when corporate officials themselves began to worry about the safety of the airplanes they were riding in. To this day, there is a zone of silence on the negative effects of mergers, acquisitions, leveraged buyouts, ominous levels of corporate debt, and monopolistic levels of market domination, including those in the news business.

We have turned our economy on its head by eliminating the progressive income tax, the only sane and fair way to build our public institutions, but the media have turned a deaf ear to those who say so.

The causes and consequences of some public acts are seldom made clear. For example, in the miles of newsprint and hours of television reporting on fantastically high real-estate prices for the middle class and the millions of homeless, how often has this been placed in the context of a number of rather clear causes: (1) in the 1970s, 200,000 low-cost housing units were built each year with Federal help, and in the 1980s only 17,000 a year; (2) the increase in the homeless population can be directly related to that reduction and to cuts in Social Security and other benefits during the 1980s; (3) it is clearly connected to the growing separation in this country between the rich and the poor, thanks to changes in tax and welfare policies; (4) it comes from tax advantages to the builders of commercial property even if it remains empty and has replaced urban residential housing.

A regular story on the economy is the need for greater productivity in the workplace. This has been accompanied by dramatic coverage of strikes and union activities, with corporate sources regularly citing unions as the problem. How often have you seen in such stories the established data, true for years, that show productivity has increased in unionized activities and decreased at managerial and administrative levels?

The whole society, including government and corporations, suffers in the long run because accountability and correction of faulty policies require good information that simply isn't available. Damaging or ineffective policies continue longer than they should. Positive opportunities are lost.

The spectrum of allowable context in the news runs vaguely from right to center. One of the major networks recently had a brief announcement of proposed economic policy and followed it with three commentaries: fifteen seconds from the chair of a House committee, twelve seconds from a spokesperson for the American Enterprise Institute, a conservative think tank, and eleven seconds from a spokesperson from the Heritage Foundation, a right-wing group. By keeping the news tone-deaf, but weighted heavily toward facts and spokespersons from the centers of power, the media render the national discourse more sterile each year. Ideas for solution to problems are not aired, alternatives to present policies fade, and the status quo seems unchangeable.

The effect of the homogenized, narrow spectrum of information and context in American news is profound. A country whose major news media are oriented around the centers of power will soon have national politics also homogenized around centers of power. That is what we have today. Our national political discourse is sterile in ideas for necessary change, deficient in its confrontation with the realities of social injustice, and therefore narrow in plausible alternatives held out to the public.

When masses of people are bedeviled by problems but see no possibility of significant change, the result is hopelessness and apathy. Many who have no hope become destructive. It is not surprising that each year since 1960, the percentage of eligible voters who go to the polls has declined. And when the cause of suffering remains mysterious, people find scapegoats. When we look for scapegoats, we move to the Right and we move to race hatred.

Our mainstream news media have fine figures to prove what the world looks like from the standpoint of policymakers in Washington, from the interplay of lawyer-lobbyists and legislators, from the opinions of conservative think tanks, the board rooms of corporations, and the floors of stock exchanges. But that is a long way from the compelling realities in which most of our citizens live.

There is another reality, in our streets where millions sleep in doorways; where most children can no longer expect to live in families with one income or buy a house or go to a university; where the poor are getting poorer and the rich richer; where ever-more-lavish skyscrapers and luxury hotels cast shadows on deteriorating schools and libraries; where air and water are increasingly unhealthy; where thirty-seven million people have no health-insurance coverage; where millions of children in hopeless neighborhoods with hopeless schools and no hopes for good jobs are killing themselves with drugs—drugs often imported from countries we favor because their governments call themselves anticommunist.

All this in a rich society, still full of vitality and with millions willing to work for policies that will improve their lives. But the ideas for plausible policies to take advantage of this vitality, the ideas to produce change, must enter the national discussion. And this cannot happen unless these ideas and possible solutions enter our mainstream news media, not as abstracted verbiage in the dialogue between Wall Street and Washington and the ten-second television slogans of election campaigns, but in the reporting about our whole society, directed clearly and primarily to the realities in our cities and towns.

That, in essence, is what is missing in our main media, and, therefore, in our politics.

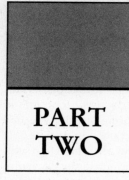

PART TWO

ECONOMIC CRISIS

conomic troubles remain a harsh fact of life in America in the last years of the twentieth century. The specific form they take changes rapidly, often confusingly; inflation waxes and wanes in severity, and the unemployment rate rises and falls as we oscillate giddily between recession and "recovery." But some things seem to have changed, perhaps irrevocably, from the days when the American economy was thought to be a virtually invincible source of abundance, stability, and material well-being. The level of unemployment we consider to be "normal" is far higher than it used to be; our status as the undisputed leader of the world's economies has been shattered by the performance of Japan and other competitors; and some of our largest, most traditional industries are declining with brutal speed, taking with them hundreds of thousands of jobs and the livelihoods of whole communities.

Today, there isn't much serious disagreement that what we once described as the "affluent" society is facing an economic crisis of unprecedented proportions—and one that has changed the face of American society in fundamental ways. The articles in this part explore some of the dimensions, causes, and impacts of that crisis.

One of the most devastating aspects of the economic crisis has been the loss of vast numbers of jobs that once supported a "middle-class" lifestyle for millions of Americans. No one disputes that the jobs have disappeared. But where have they gone—and *why* have they disappeared? In "Losing Out to Mexico," Donald Barlett and James Steele offer some revealing answers. In the face of escalating worldwide economic competition—and of financial manipulations that have loaded many American businesses with huge amounts of debt—companies have shut down their U.S. operations in droves, often relocating to poorer countries where they can pay far lower wages and benefits (and can avoid many health, safety, and environmental regulations). This process is often defended on the ground that it is good for *both* economies in the long run—making America more competitive while bringing much-needed jobs and income to Third World countries, whose workers will in turn be able to buy American products. But as Barlett and Steele show, the only clear winners in this economic game are the wealthy investors who make the decisions. The American workers whose jobs disappear after a lifetime of hard work are obviously among the losers. But so, the authors suggest, are the workers in the poor countries—who do indeed get the jobs, but who also must subsist in grim shantytowns on $59 a week.

Thomas Cottle's article drives home the savage personal impact of the massive job losses in recent years. In a society where having a steady job is critical to establishing a sense of worth, to be out of work for years at a time—and to face the prospect of never working again—can be, quite literally, like dying. Perhaps the cruelest effect of long-term unemployment, for the men Cottle interviewed, is that after awhile they come to blame their situation on their own inadequacies—not on the corporate machinations described by writers like Barlett and Steele.

Barry Bluestone and Bennett Harrison's article, "Boomtown and Busttown," looks at the other side of the economic crisis—the costs and pains of economic growth or, at any rate, of the kind of growth that the American economy has undergone in recent years. Focusing on the problems emerging in the Sunbelt of the southern and southwestern states, Bluestone and Harrison show that unregulated growth has had highly disruptive consequences for American communities—ranging from urban sprawl and congestion to high rates of crime and frustratingly unyielding levels of poverty and unemployment. The implication of their analysis is that simply trying to spur "growth," of whatever kind and by whatever means, is—by itself—no real answer to the human and social problems of the American economy.

By the late 1980s, indeed, many of the "boomtowns" described by Bluestone and Harrison had "gone bust," especially in Texas and other states of the Southwest. The collapse of that shaky economic "boom" is part of the backdrop for what, by all accounts, is the most massive single financial disaster in American history—the scandal-ridden collapse of a large part of the savings and loan industry. Though that collapse may cost Americans half a *trillion dollars* in the coming decades, its growth and causes have been hard for most Americans to comprehend—in part because its financial roots are so complex, but also because the depth of the impending crisis was systematically covered up by a complaisant government. Some of the roots of the savings and loan crisis are described in "Bonfire of the S and Ls," written by staff reporters of *Newsweek* magazine. The causes are diverse, but at bottom the savings and loan debacle is a reflection of the same freewheeling climate of heedless economic deregulation that Bluestone and Harrison describe.

5

LOSING OUT TO MEXICO

DONALD L. BARLETT AND JAMES B. STEELE

Rosa Vasquez and Mollie James share a common interest. Vasquez works for the company that once employed Mollie James. That is where similarities end. James earned $7.91 an hour. Vasquez earns $1.45 an hour.

James lives in a six-room, two-story house on a paved street in a working-class neighborhood of Paterson, New Jersey. Vasquez lives in a one-room shack in a Mexican shantytown reachable only by foot along a dirt path. James's house has electricity and indoor plumbing. Vasquez's house has neither. When Mollie James wants to watch television, she turns on the set in her living room. When Rosa Vasquez wants to watch television, she connects a car battery to a thirteen-inch black-and-white set.

For thirty-three years, Mollie James worked for a company that manufactured electrical components for fluorescent lights in New Jersey. Now Rosa Vasquez works for the same company, making the same kinds of products at a new plant in Mexico.

Mollie James's story is that of many Americans in the 1980s. After decades of working for one employer, they suddenly found themselves out of work— unable to secure another job and deprived of benefits they had counted on for their later years.

Universal Manufacturing Company, the company that employed James, was founded in 1947 as a recent invention—fluorescent lights—grew in popularity. Universal manufactured a mechanism called a ballast that regulated the flow of electricity to the light.

Mollie James went to work at Universal's Paterson plant in 1955 for ninety-five cents an hour. She worked as a laminator, a tester, a machine operator and finally a press operator. "I could do any job in the plant," she said proudly. Although there was usually abundant overtime, James held a second full-time job for eighteen years to bring in more money to raise and educate her four children. Universal's original owners knew the workers and routinely walked through the plant talking to them, James recalled. "We were more or less like a family," she said. "The owner would come out and talk to us and would help us in any way that he could. He saw that many of us got homes through their help, by speaking to a bank or even making you a personal loan. They were concerned about the welfare of the workers." If something didn't work, James said, the owners wanted to know so they could make adjustments and produce a better product. "We were number one," she said.

In 1986, Universal was acquired by MagneTek, Inc. of Los Angeles. MagneTek had been formed in 1984 by a Los Angeles investment company, the Spectrum Group, headed by Andrew G. Galef, a business consultant who specialized in advising troubled businesses. The company was an early beneficiary of Michael Milken's junk bond machine. Drexel Burnham Lambert, Inc. served as MagneTek's investment adviser, underwriting millions of dollars in high-yield bonds that enabled the company to acquire Universal and other businesses.

Although Drexel is operating under United States Bankruptcy Court supervision and Milken is in prison for securities law violations, Drexel is still very much a part of MagneTek. Two limited partnerships made up of former Drexel employees and a Drexel subsidiary own 37 percent of the corporation's stock, according to reports filed with the United States Securities and Exchange Commission (SEC).

MagneTek went public in 1989 with investment analysts predicting a bright future. "We think this stock has above average intermediate term prospects," Merrill Lynch said in 1989, "[and] looks even more reasonably priced on prospects in the period beyond, which accounts for our buy, long term rating."

While it achieved record sales of $1.1 billion and record earnings of $34.6 million in 1991, MagneTek faces challenges in coming years to manage its huge debt. Starting in 1992, the corporation must make a series of steep principal payments. All told, $400 million will have to be repaid or refinanced by the year 2000. Galef, MagneTek's chairman, received $272,852 in bonuses from the company in the fiscal year ended June 30, 1991.

More important, the Spectrum Group—of which Galef is the sole stockholder—collects an annual fee to provide "management services" to MagneTek, according to SEC reports. In 1991, those fees totaled $678,000, and since 1986, MagneTek has paid Spectrum $3.6 million in such fees. Spectrum has similar arrangements with other companies that Galef reorganized, including the Warnaco Group, Inc., a textile manufacturer, and Exide Corporation, a maker of automotive and industrial batteries. Over all, Spectrum has collected millions of dollars in fees to advise these companies and assist in acquisitions.

Galef and his third wife live in the fashionable Bel Air section of Los Angeles, popular with entertainers and movie executives. Peter Bogdanovich, the film director, and Terry S. Semel, president of Warner Brothers, are among their neighbors. Their house on Copa de Oro (Cup of Gold) Road is valued at $3.9 million by the Los Angeles County assessor.

The flavor of Galef's lifestyle emerged in court papers filed in 1987 during a divorce action initiated by his second wife, Billie: "At Christmas we always had a large dinner party with at least 200 guests. . . . Travel was also extensive. Last July, we went to Australia, Hong Kong, China and Japan for approximately three weeks. We stayed, as we always do, in first-class hotels, ate at the best restaurants, and generally traveled by limousine.

"In September, we took the Concorde to Paris and London, where we spent a week, again staying at the best hotels and eating in the best restaurants."

While Galef and his wife were jetting about the world, his managers at the Paterson plant where Mollie James worked were assuring employees that nothing would change under MagneTek, the new owner. "They came through the plant and talked to each worker and told us we wouldn't have anything to worry about because they would always have operations in Paterson," James said. "They gave us the impression that we had great prospects here. They told us they were going to get us new equipment, new machinery."

All the promises notwithstanding, the new equipment failed to materialize. Instead, the existing equipment began to disappear. Mollie James and her co-workers would leave the factory one day, and a piece of equipment, such as a large stamping machine, would be in place, bolted to the floor. And then, she remembered: "You'd come in the next morning and it would be gone. There'd be a bare space on the floor."

Employees discovered later that the equipment had been shipped to other MagneTek plants. The company subsequently sent Paterson workers to those plants to train other persons to use the machines that had once provided work in Paterson. Incidents like that made employees wonder if the plant's days were numbered. Nonetheless, MagneTek continued to say it would never close Paterson. "They told us we were doing a great job," James remembered.

But one day a notice went up on the plant bulletin board. Effective June 30, 1989, Universal's thirty-eight-year-old Paterson plant would be shut. "It was very devastating," James said. "People asked, 'What are we going to do now?' We just always thought we would have a job." In July 1989, the plant that had once employed 500 people became a distribution center, receiving products made at other MagneTek facilities. James was offered a job in the shipping department. But at fifty-eight, she was unable to lift the heavy boxes. She was out of work.

❖ RUSH TO THE BORDER

As MagneTek stopped manufacturing in Paterson, the company reached full production at a 150,000-square-foot plant in Matamoros, Mexico, a burgeoning border town across the Rio Grande from Brownsville, Texas.

While Galef declined to discuss MagneTek's move to Mexico—"Mr. Galef usually doesn't do interviews," a secretary said—another company official explained the transfer. Robert W. Murray, vice president of communications and public relations, said that production operations at Paterson were transferred to a plant in Blytheville, Arkansas, and that part of the Blytheville operation was, in turn, moved to Matamoros.

Commenting on the shutdown of production in Paterson, Murray said, "On a local basis, it can be a tragedy. That, we regret. But to keep our 16,000 people employed, we need to stay in business. . . . But the market—the labor market that was once called the United States—is now North America, and I include in that Central America. . . . Regions rather than countries are now competing on a world scale. We've got to cooperate with both our neighbors to the north, Canada, and with Mexico to the south to put together the kind of competitive package that can really compete on a world scale."

The MagneTek plant is part of Mexico's Maquiladora program, a venture started to persuade United States companies to establish assembly plants there. The government encourages such plants by setting a low tariff on finished goods shipped back to the United States. Originally, Maquiladoras assembled components shipped in from the United States by American corporations. Now many of these so-called assembly plants are full-scale manufacturing facilities performing the same type of work that was once done by American workers, but at much lower wages.

United States government agencies, notably the Commerce Department and State Department, have encouraged America's corporate flight to the border. In testimony before a Congressional subcommittee in December 1986, Alexander H. Good, director general of the United States and Foreign Commercial Service, summed up the government's position: "We are convinced the program has important economic benefits for both the U.S. and Mexican economies. . . . The Commerce Department supports participation in the Maquiladora program by U.S. industry because it helps U.S. companies to remain healthy in the face of intense international competition and it keeps U.S. employment as high as possible."

With this kind of backing from government rule makers, Maquiladora plants have blossomed along the border. The strip of land that runs for 1,500 miles from California to Texas has become a highway of *Fortune* 500 companies. All along the Mexican side of the border are names long associated with the other side—General Motors, Fisher-Price, Trico, Parker-Hannifin, Xerox, Ford, Kimberly-Clark, IBM, Samsonite, General Electric and Rockwell. All told, there are more than 1,800 plants employing more than 500,000 workers in Mexico—all since 1965.

With few exceptions, the new plants are replacing facilities that once provided jobs for United States workers. Like the Zenith Electronics Corporation plant in Reynosa, across the Rio Grande from McAllen, Texas. As recently as 1965, every color television set purchased in the United States was made by an American-owned company in a domestic plant. In that year, Americans purchased 2.6 million sets manufactured by companies such as Sylvania, Motorola, Admiral, Philco, Sunbeam, RCA, Quasar, Magnavox and Wizard.

Twenty-six years later, in 1991, sales of television sets to United States consumers soared to twenty-one million. But only one company was still making the sets in the United States—Zenith Corporation, at a lone domestic plant in Springfield, Missouri. By 1992, there were none. In October 1991 Zenith announced that it was ending production in Springfield in 1992 and shifting the jobs to a Zenith plant in Reynosa, Mexico.

For the American television industry, the end came with a swiftness that would have seemed inconceivable a generation ago, when more than two dozen American-owned plants were turning out all the television sets purchased in this country. That was before Japanese television manufacturers began dumping huge quantities of low-priced receivers on the American market.

When American manufacturers objected to what they called unfair trade practices, the Japanese claimed they were able to undersell American makers because their products resulted from greater cost efficiencies. But American television makers said there was no evidence to support that assertion. As proof, they pointed to the fact that the Japanese were selling television sets to Americans at much lower prices than they were selling them in Japan.

Zenith asserted in a 1977 report: "The fact that the Japanese manufacturers, whose lowest-priced nineteen-inch offerings in Japan are priced at about $500, are selling similar receivers to American private brand retailers at prices that permit resale in the United States at under $300, provides substantial support for the premise that those receivers are being dumped in the United States."

The United States Tariff Commission had agreed, saying in a 1971 ruling that the television "industry in the United States is being injured by reason of the importation of television receivers from Japan, which are being sold at less than fair value." Fines and duties totaling several hundred million dollars were later assessed against the Japanese television makers. But years of legal wrangling and diplomatic maneuvering followed, with the Japanese companies ultimately paying only nominal amounts.

Zenith also filed a lawsuit against the major Japanese manufacturers, charging them with violating United States antitrust and antidumping laws. The case found its way to the United States Supreme Court, which ruled in favor of the Japanese. By the time litigation and the regulatory proceedings were over, the American television industry was history.

Every American-owned company had either shut down its television production line or been sold to the Japanese. Except Zenith. The company known for innovation and quality—"The quality goes in before the name goes on"—

continued to maintain one production plant. Zenith's sprawling Springfield plant—it covers an area the size of twenty-nine football fields—was the town's largest private employer and a steady source of earnings for 1,750 local residents.

Until 1992. Having lost $500 million in revenue over the previous five years, the company announced that it had to cut costs. When labor contracts expired in 1992, a total of 1,350 employees would be let go and the work shifted to Mexico. In a statement that has become all too familiar to middle-class Americans, Jerry K. Pearlman, Zenith's chairman and president, explained that the Springfield shutdown, while "painful," was necessary for Zenith to remain competitive: "This further consolidation of our operations is a necessary component of Zenith's programs to reduce costs and improve profitability."

The chief reason, Zenith officials emphasized, was Mexico's low wage rate. Wages ranged from $5 to $11 an hour at Springfield; in Mexico they were $1.60 an hour. Actually, the average wage rate at Springfield was $7 an hour. That translated into an annual income of under $15,000, meaning that, by national standards, that the work force in Springfield was, on average, at the low end of the pay scale for the American middle class.

Robert W. Mingus, president of Local 1453 of the International Brotherhood of Electrical Workers, which represents the Zenith workers, does not blame the company for the shutdown. He blames the last four presidents, the Commerce Department and members of Congress, both for not doing more to counter Japanese moves, and for making it possible for United States industry to relocate to Mexico. "We're encouraging our industrial base right out of this country," he said.

In Matamoros, where Mollie James's company relocated, Maquiladora operations are similar to those found in Tijuana, Mexicali, Juarez, Nuevo Laredo and other border towns. Plants make everything from cosmetic brushes to auto flashers. Rosa Vasquez, twenty-six, one of 1,500 employees—mostly female—at the MagneTek facility in Matamoros, began working the 4:30 P.M.-to-1:30 A.M. shift in July 1988, the year the plant opened. She earns 179,000 pesos, or about $59, a week.

In 1989, MagneTek, in a report filed with the Securities and Exchange Commission, cited the benefits of this low-wage haven: "The company has consolidated manufacturing and relocated product lines to facilities having lower per-unit labor and overhead costs. For example, the company has established a full-scale manufacturing facility in Mexico, where it benefits from lower wage rates."

Mollie James doesn't understand. "The company said we were hurt by foreign trade," she said. "But this company has plants in Mexico. Why isn't that foreign trade?" Rosa Vasquez does understand. She needs the money from the plant—even if it is only enough to buy essentials. Asked how she spends her earnings, she answered, "The children, food, clothing for the children, clothing for us."

To get to and from work, most MagneTek workers must ride crowded, stuffy yellow vans called Maxi-Taxis that were designed for twelve passengers, but that carry twice that many in cramped, often sweltering conditions for journeys that take up to an hour. In this sense Vasquez is fortunate. She walks to work.

Her home is one of about 200 primitive dwellings in a colony of poor people called "Vista Hermosa" bordering the MagneTek plant. Vista Hermosa (which means "beautiful view" in Spanish) is a collection of ramshackle dwellings, made of wood or cement blocks, in varying stages of disrepair. Wooden outhouses serve as toilets. People light their houses with kerosene lamps. Chickens and pigs wander about.

Vasquez and her husband live behind the plant, where the roar of MagneTek's air-conditioning system can be heard twenty-four hours a day. She describes her home as a "small wooden house." It is actually one room, twelve feet long and ten feet wide, with a tin, peaked roof. It contains a double bed, two small dressers, a table, a cupboard, clothes hamper, two chairs and a propane stove.

Vasquez and her husband, Alberto, a carpenter, live at the house during the week while their two children stay nearby with her parents. Although she works until 1:30 A.M., she rises early to take her small boys to preschool each morning, riding thirty minutes by bus each way. She and her husband believe in education. The only object on the walls of their modest home is a poster showing a child bent intently over a desk with the slogan above, *Total Principio es Dificil.* An ode to hard work, the expression translates roughly as, "Starting all over is difficult."

For entertainment, the family watches television at the house of Rosa Vasquez's parents, using a car battery to power the set. Every two weeks a brother puts the battery in an old car and drives around to charge it up.

President Bush and other promoters of free trade with Mexico are fond of pointing to Mexico's large population as a potential market for American-made products under a hemispheric free trade agreement. They see finished products moving back and forth across the border. Items once made in the United States would be manufactured instead in Mexico and shipped north for sale to American consumers. Other products would continue to be manufactured in the United States and shipped south for sale to Mexican consumers.

American workers, they say, have nothing to fear from such an arrangement because it would open the door for United States products in Mexico's vast domestic market. The president cited the benefits of an unrestricted trade policy during a speech in Houston in April 1991: "I don't have to tell anyone in this room about Mexico's market potential: eighty-five million consumers who want to buy our goods. Nor do I have to tell you that as Mexico grows and prospers, it will need even more of the goods we're best at producing: computers, manufacturing equipment, high-tech and high-value products."

That is the theory. Reality is quite different.

There is no doubt that under a free trade agreement more United States companies would rush to establish plants in Mexico to take advantage of low wage rates. But there is little likelihood that the Mexican masses would be able to buy many goods made in the United States in return.

That is because their wages—even those earned by the Rosa Vasquezes, which are at the high end of the Mexican wage scale—do not translate into a standard of living comparable to that enjoyed by Rosa's counterpart, Mollie James. As a result, the material goods that are common features of middle-class American households are beyond the reach of the Vasquezes.

Like refrigerators. Even if Vista Hermosa had electric power, and even if the Vasquezes could afford electricity, they still couldn't afford a refrigerator. In Matamoros, refrigerators sell for $450, or about two months' wages. Even so, Rosa Vasquez feels fortunate. She has a job, which is more than Mollie James can say.

After the Paterson plant closed in 1989, Mollie James collected unemployment benefits for six months and then went back to school. She learned how to repair computers but has yet to find anyone who will hire her. "When you are . . . going on fifty-nine, it is very hard to get a job," she said. "Any time you put your age down, they say nicely, 'We will contact you.'" For eighteen months she paid for her own health benefits, but it became too expensive at $114 a month. "I hope for the best," she said.

Mollie James liked her job and took pride in her work. In the 1970s, she had to overcome management's reluctance to allow a woman to operate a large metal stamping machine. But she passed the thirty-day tryout and ran the machine until the plant closed. "I've seen men lose fingers," she recalled, "but thank God I never lost anything."

Except, in the end, her job.

6

WHEN YOU STOP, YOU DIE: THE HUMAN TOLL OF UNEMPLOYMENT

THOMAS J. COTTLE

It goes without saying that a man's work is essential to his identity. The little boy grows up knowing that someday he will have a job like his daddy or mommy. It is expected, moreover, that he will make something of his life, which he will do by working. It all begins with adults asking him that fateful question: What are you going to be when you grow up?

Because it is only "natural" that men work, there can be no preparation for unemployment; it overtakes the entire being of a man. Indeed, it is this seemingly "inbred" assumption of working that makes long-term unemployment so drastic and traumatic for many men. Accordingly, it is not merely that a man assumes he will work until retirement, or that he trembles at the sound of the numbers describing a gloomy economic landscape. Rather, he believes that no matter what the personal exigencies and national statistics, no matter what the talk in the bars or the reports on television, he will be going to work the next morning.

Americans presently confront a dismal employment scene. In every quarter of the economy, small businesses and individuals are filing for bankruptcy in record numbers, large corporations are announcing unprecedented quarterly losses and laying off thousands of workers. Men who once ran six-figure businesses stand in unemployment lines alongside people who, two months earlier,

From *Commonweal*, June 19, 1992. Reprinted by permission.

were in their employ. Where unemployment hasn't hit, the threat of it fills the air.

For more than fifteen years I have been meeting with the families of the hard-core unemployed. These are people where the main provider has been out of work for at least six months, and usually much longer. The stories of these families inevitably are saddening since the longer a man goes without a job, the greater the likelihood he gives up hope of ever being re-employed. The government calls people out of work longer than six months "discouraged workers." In truth, most of them have moved far beyond anything resembling mere discouragement.

One of the more painful aspects of the unemployed man's existence is the daily obligation to answer a host of questions, each one, surely, feeling like a knife to the ribs: "Hey, Fred, how come you're home? What'd you do, take an early retirement? Somebody in your house hit the lottery?"

"Sam, would you be insulted if I gave you a little something? Come on, I've always got a little extra around the house. You'd do it for me."

"What are you going to do, Brian, sit there doing nothing? The worst thing, believe me, is to sit there not moving. I know. I had an uncle once, didn't work for a helluva lot longer than you've been out of commission. Believe me, you don't move, you'll die sitting there in that chair."

Hearing this last remark, Brian McShane, fifty-one years old and out of work thirty-nine months—and don't think he ever stopped keeping track— looked at me and grinned. It was as if he wanted to say, You see, Doc, what I have to put up with every day. In fact he did reply:

"Toonie O'Neill, meet Dr. Tom Cottle." Brian looked at me. "I've known Toonie forty years, if I've known him a day. We were working pretty regular in those days. Hell, I was twelve years old. Life was filled with possibilities.

"Dr. Tom's studying guys like me, out-of-work guys, you know what I mean? Not like you, Toones. And he's got something important to tell you." Brian winked in my direction and grinned.

I rose from my chair to shake Toonie O'Neill's hand, which was broad and rough. "Tell him what, Mac?" I asked.

"Come on, you know. Tell him." Brian McShane was neither an old or close friend, but I knew him well enough to know how furious he had been made to feel by the suggestion that he should just get up out of his chair. "You're the doctor, so you tell him. Tell him he hit the nail right on the head. Tell him the reason I don't get out of this chair is because there isn't a reason in the world good enough to get me out of this chair. And if he's worried that I might die sitting here, tell him he ain't more worried about it than I am. I know I'm going to die in this chair. Tell him I wanna die in this chair. Tell him that's the way I'm coping with being unemployed for forever now. Go ahead, Doc, tell him. He'll listen to you. Tell him this is the way I'm coping with a story that's got a lousy ending."

Driving home that afternoon, I found myself thinking about the death of my father. I recalled a family friend visiting him in the hospital months before my father actually died. The friend, a psychiatrist, was upset by my father's weakening condition. My mother was eager to get a psychological reading on my father. "He's very depressed, isn't he?" she asked, almost rhetorically. "Not at all," the friend answered with uncharacteristic sternness, as if he wished to protect my father's reputation. "He's not depressed at all; he's dying!"

Suddenly, my visits with unemployed men began coalescing around that single theme. People like Brian McShane weren't feeling sorry for themselves. Technically, probably, many of them could have been diagnosed as depressed, but that wasn't the point. They were dying men, they even spoke of it. Forty-seven-year-old George Wilkinson had said it this way: "There's only two worlds: Either you work every day in a normal nine-to-five job with a couple weeks vacation, or you're dead! There's no in-between. . . . Working is breathing. It's something you don't think about; you just do it and it keeps you alive. When you stop you die." A year after uttering these words, George Wilkinson, once a manager of a small tool company, killed himself with a shotgun.

Each man I spoke with knew it as clearly as a man knows it when a doctor tells him he has only a few weeks to live. It also struck me that the ones who had disappeared, usually after years of being unemployed—and there were many of them—went away to die. They were like weary elephants looking for the burial ground. In almost atavistic fashion, they knew it was not meant for them to die at home.

Gradually, I began to see my research on unemployed families in a wholly different light. I hadn't been speaking with so-called discouraged workers only; I had been speaking with people mourning their deaths, and lives. For me to ask them about their childhoods, their remembrances of early career aspirations and evaluations of their lives, had become an opportunity for them to write their memoirs, to compose their own obituaries. Their discussions of educational and employment experiences and philosophies of living were all part of this final self-assessment and remembrance. The longer my final account of them, the more they believed I had found their life to have merit.

Although it sounds melodramatic, I had come to feel there was little difference between my visits to the homes of unemployed families and the visits one pays to terminally-ill people. They know why we come, and still it is always they who help us through the ordeal of conversing. "You want to know how much time they're giving me?" dying friends have asked me. I want to respond, I do, and I don't. I don't know what we should be talking about. And they're saying, "We should be talking about you and me and about living and dying." The unemployed men were telling me this same thing: We should be talking about you and me; about working and not working; about living and dying.

I recall something thirty-one-year-old Johnnie Nobles said when we were trying to reconstruct his father's life. John Nobles, Sr., had spent the last years of his life unemployed: "There are things, Tom, that make you an expert. But you aren't an expert on this. No one would have called my father an expert, but he was. Every man's an expert on what not working does to him. The priest tells you about death? He doesn't know about death. He's just heard about death. He may give last rites to the dying, but that's as close as he'll ever come. He hasn't touched anything there; he's just present at the dying. That's his job, right?

"My father and his friends, they could tell you about death. They could tell you about jobs, too. They could tell you about the last bits of life seeping out of your body when you don't have a job. Because you know how you know if a man's an expert? You listen to him, and you watch him, and something inside you says, this guy knows what he's talking about. He's not making this stuff up. He hasn't just heard about this; he's lived this. He's telling you the truth as he lived it, and never forgot it. That's what makes a guy an expert."

I thought of Johnnie's words months later when I listened to Gerry Murphy's description of himself. Fifty-six years old, Gerry is one of America's atomic veterans. He once took pride in his ability to sell almost any product: "I want to work. I don't think I'm unable to do anything. . . . [But] I'm told that I'm unemployable. . . . I don't seem to have any concentration. . . . I couldn't sit in one place at one thing for an hour. . . . I've been lost in the general scheme of things. . . . I don't even know what I'm doing, you know? I'm just what they call 'free falling.' There's no plans or anything. I used to try to make plans; there's no concentration. I feel like I'm in a fog. I have been called a vegetable. I don't read the newspaper. I try. It's just that I can't really concentrate. I used to."

In the first months following their layoffs, I heard any number of protestations, particularly in conversations while in line at unemployment offices. The men spewed vitriol at the state and federal governments for letting them down and abandoning them. America's workers were innocent victims. They had worked regular shifts, rarely taken days off, rarely came late; no question about it. It was the government or the company or the economy that was at fault. Like a chorus, the other men shouted out: "Damn straight," "You got that right," "Better believe it."

I recall a morning when Jack Blum, a man who had held numerous jobs in his forty-six years, looked about at the unemployment lines and observed: "I'm at the bottom and nobody likes it at the bottom. But okay, somebody's got to be at the bottom. Poor people, all walks of life, ethnic types, black, white: you don't make money, down to the bottom! Here's the real melting pot of this country."

Then there was that refrain about the government "taking my taxes for thirty years, and now they claim they've run out of benefits at twenty-six or thirty weeks!" More recently, I have heard: "The government bailed the S and L boys out of trouble with our money, but bail us out when we didn't break a single law, didn't make one wrong decision, how do you explain that one!"

Men like forty-nine-year-old Amos Payton, an unemployed cement worker, rode their anger as though life itself drew electricity from it: "'Fraid of getting angry, and getting angry 'cause I get afraid. Hell, man, afraid of not being angry no more. . . . Anger and fear, they're gonna keep you alert, like an animal. Got to keep on the prowl." (During one of his many angry moods, Jack Blum had told me: "The day that anger stops, like a motor, I'm dead. Kaput. Good-bye.")

Somewhere around the first anniversary of their unemployment, as it became clear that they might never again locate steady work, the tone of the men's conversations shifted. Rather than direct their anger outward at former bosses or the government, they turned it inward, portraying themselves as wrongdoers, transgressors, people who had committed grievous offenses. In this regard, no one could assault Amos Payton as he himself did. Whatever the topic, Payton could turn it back on himself in devastating terms: "But some black men found work. Even if they have 20 percent unemployed, they still have 80 percent employed, and a lot of that 80 percent is black, ain't they? So lots of men living right in this community may be in the same boat I am, but most of 'em ain't! There is someone to blame, and you don't need the police to find him. . . . A man like me wants to yell out, it's somebody else's fault. But it's my fault."

In time the men's anger receded, as though their bodies could no longer supply the strength that anger requires. Whereas anger once may have been a life force, it now made them weary. In its place was born an intensity of shame I hadn't before witnessed. Men with whom I had established close friendships suddenly were afraid to be seen. Men who had spoken with a characteristic toughness months before, now seemed embarrassed by my visits. They began hiding, masking feelings, running away from it all, and not surprisingly, canceling our appointments more frequently.

They turned away from their families as well. Their masculinity and strength sapped, they appeared shameful, childlike, as if they deserved to be the invisible, reclusive people they in fact had become. Covering their faces, their tracks, their own life stories, they acted out the parts of men ashamed of themselves and of the utter mess they insisted they had made of their lives. Jack Blum joked that shame and guilt were his middle names: "I'm the captain of the ship, right? I drown, it's my fault. That woman and those two kids upstairs. . . , they drown, that's also my fault. So maybe I'm also a murderer, huh? You want to think about this thing that way? I kill me, my wife, and kids, and they don't even know they're being murdered."

The men's shame often emerged as anger directed at their children: "What the hell you looking at? If you want a show, go watch television!" And early on, the children learned not to talk about the unemployment situation, and never to question their dads about it.

The origin of these emotions is obvious. A man is supposed to hold down a steady job. According to traditional values, this is all a man is meant to do. George Wilkinson said it this way: "Men leave in the morning and come back at night with a pay check in their hand. Makes me old-fashioned? Then I'm old-fashioned!" Believing this, it is understandable that a man would come home at the end of a day expecting dinner to be waiting for him, and the children, already bathed, ready for a little play and their nightly bedtime routine. The pattern, I suppose, bespeaks a form of chauvinism. But for centuries, men have been taught that eight or ten hours of steady work entitles them to this form of human compensation.

Similarly, when a man loses his job he loses his status in his home. He feels he has no right to be there. He cannot face his wife without a job; he hasn't earned his keep or his place. And there is no longer reason for his child to feel proud of him. "I'm sick of looking at you, sitting there," Dorie McShane yelled at Brian one afternoon, unaffected by my presence in their home. "You're a miserable sight. . . . I don't want to come home anymore and have you be the first thing I see."

There were no more painful words than those of Rosemary Mullen, desperate to vent her frustration with her husband: "He should have taken me somewhere, thrown me down, slapped me if that was the only thing that would have quieted me, and made love to me. I mean pull my clothes off and rape me, if he had to. Anything to show me he wasn't scared, that he was alive, that he had some energy left; something, some little bit of life. I mean it. I wanted to be roughed up that night and feel that he was really a man. But he was dead."

At times the men did fight back, hardly valiantly, but they tried. Still, their shame, guilt, and depression precluded much of a battle. To their wives they said, if you can't stand the sight of me you can always leave. But the words were the antithesis of what they all knew to be the truth: They feared being abandoned by their families, despite the belief that they deserved no less a punishment.

In writing about the nature of work, sociologist Kai Erikson has remarked: "High rates of unemployment are thought to be not only inevitable but *natural*" [my emphasis]. Indeed, throughout the literature of economic theory, one finds the terms, "natural rates" of unemployment and "noninflationary full-employment rates," terms all meant to disguise an ideological bias: namely, that for our economy to work well, a certain number of people must be out of work. These unemployed are the people André Gorz called the "nonclass of nonworkers."

As much as the men with whom I visited struggled to maintain control of their lives and destinies, in the end, economic and market forces, along with human decisions, combined to break them down, and in some instances to kill them. Nothing hurt Brian McShane, George Wilkinson, or Amos Payton as much as experts debating the pros and cons of unemployment policies, arguing for the necessity of a certain base rate of unemployment. Nothing disturbed them more than experts rejoicing in the downturn of unemployment rates when each one knew that even 2 percent or 3 percent unemployment means that millions of human beings may be suffering as they were.

Like sociologists, the unemployed understand the implications of government work policies. Reading labor reports and newspaper accounts, they hunt for the humanity that often gets lost in discussions of unemployment, for something they themselves long ago had lost, and now are convinced they may never regain. How many times did I find myself listening to the lamentations and expressions of incredulity of strong, articulate, even eloquent people who believed fiercely in the goodness of America, but who now could neither fathom nor reconcile the idea of their country forsaking them, given the dues—in all meanings of that word—they had paid?

Ultimately, the men hunted for a single reason to keep going, and despaired over the fact that the existence of the wives and children they so adored no longer sufficed as that reason. They remained keenly aware of the huge numbers of unemployed Americans, a network one imagines they found to be a rather sacred congregation. "Lost sheep," Jack Blum had called them. "And all of them," George Wilkinson used to say, shaking his head so that his yellow silver hair fell over his forehead, "could be saved."

7

BOOMTOWN AND BUST-TOWN

BARRY BLUESTONE AND BENNETT HARRISON

Few people, and certainly not those who have spent any time in cities like Youngstown and Detroit, or in towns like Anaconda, Montana, would deny that deindustrialization is an agonizing experience for the families and communities that must contend with it. Yet the belief lingers that disinvestment is somehow a necessary precondition for the constant renewal and reinvigoration of the economy. It is part of the grand scheme of creative destruction—a reminder that omelettes can be made only by cracking eggs.

The omelettes, in this case, are presumably cities like Houston, the southern metropolis that *U.S. News & World Report* claims is "bursting out all over." Houston is not a city, it declared,

> *It's a phenomenon—an explosive, roaring urban juggernaut that's shattering traditions as it expands outward and upward with an energy that surprises even its residents. . . . Absorbing capital, people and new corporations like a sponge, Houston is constantly being reshaped—physically by the wrecking ball and new construction and culturally by newcomers with fresh ideas and philosophies.*

In a twenty-page special advertisement in *Fortune,* Houston recently paid tribute to itself as the new international city of America. The statistics are indeed impressive. By the end of 1980, Houston led the nation in "almost every economic indicator," including growth in population, employment, retail sales, and per capita income. It was first among the nation's cities in residential construction, and in the latter part of the 1970s, in overall construction. Office space tripled during the decade; bank deposits quadrupled. Office towers went up by the dozen, while millionaires were turned out as though on an assembly line. The spirit of prosperity lost elsewhere in the country seems to be incarnate in Houston. As one leading Texas architect put it, "People still think big and act big here. They have the confidence that the rest of the country seems to lack."

❖ THE QUINTESSENTIAL BOOMTOWN

In part, Houston is what *reindustrialization* is all about. This exploding metropolis and cities like it have been able to attract billions of dollars of investment in practically no time at all. Between 1971 and 1978 alone, ninety-nine large firms moved into the city followed by thousands of smaller supplier establishments. This created so many jobs that despite population growth of more than half a million residents during the 1970s, unemployment rates have generally remained below 4 percent. In 1979 the area's economy generated 79,000 new jobs, driving the jobless rate down to an extraordinary 2.6 percent. The nationwide unemployment rate was nearly three times larger.

By the middle of this decade, Houston will surpass Philadelphia in population, making it the nation's fourth largest city. Only New York, Los Angeles, and Chicago will be bigger; this will give each of the four census regions of the country its own natural "capital city." Houston's 45 percent population boom during the last ten years contrasts with Frostbelt declines of 27 percent in St. Louis, 24 percent in Cleveland, and 23 percent in Buffalo. More than 1,000 new residents arrive every week, many making the same cross-country trek as Houston's founders—the Allen brothers from New York who bought the land site for $10,000 in 1836.

Houston is perhaps not exactly typical of all the new boomtowns in America, but its evolution illustrates how reindustrialization is supposed to work. What has attracted capital and people to the city is its energy industry. It is a city built on oil. Thirty-four of the thirty-five largest U.S. petroleum companies have their headquarters there, or have major divisions for exploration, production, research, and marketing. Four hundred other oil companies and more than 1,600 suppliers and manufacturers of oil-related equipment have settled in the surrounding area, as have hundreds of marine service enterprises, drilling contractors, seismic companies, and pipeline installers. About 40 percent of the nation's oil is refined in Houston and the nearby Texas Gulf Coast. Altogether the area manufactures about 60 percent of the country's basic petrochemicals. Based on this incredible wealth, the financial community has attracted foreign bankers from Germany, England, France, Saudi Arabia, Switzerland, Brazil, and Hong Kong. More than forty-five foreign banks are represented in the city.

Unabashedly the city boasts that "it is not just lukewarm towards business, it is *pro-business*" (emphasis theirs). Its advertisements placed in business journals to attract even more capital remind potential investors that "Texas is virtually a tax haven." It is one of only four states in the nation without an income tax on corporate earnings and is one of just six states with no personal income tax. As a result, according to the U.S. Census Bureau, Houston's per capita tax burden is a mere $175 compared with New York City's $841 and Boston's $695. To add to its attractiveness, its workers' compensation costs are among the lowest in the nation, and it is one of the so-called right-to-work states that have outlawed the union shop.

With a pro-business climate to attract investment, the city's public relations office has only the job of convincing corporate executives—those who manage these investment dollars—that, despite the heat and humidity, Houston is a charming place to live. One advertisement, aimed particularly at those in the North, claims "everything is dehumidified and air conditioned" with a housing selection to meet every need. With ballet, opera, concerts, and theater, seven four-year colleges, and the largest medical complex in the world, the city's backers believe they have rounded up everything necessary to create "the good life" and to continue to attract capital and labor.

Houston is not alone in the burgeoning Sunbelt. Rapid economic growth has meant that family incomes in the South are quickly catching up with those in the rest of the country. Between 1953 and 1978 median family income, adjusted for inflation, rose by two thirds in the Northeast, the North Central states, and the West. But in the South, family incomes nearly doubled. Whereas southern incomes averaged only 73 percent of those elsewhere in the country in 1953, by the dawn of the 1980s, they approached 90 percent. Moreover, between 1973 and 1978 while real incomes were actually falling outside the South, they were rising in the Sunbelt. The median family in the Northeast received 3.5 percent *less* real income in 1978 while the average southern family—despite double digit inflation—was able to enjoy a modest (2.3 percent) improvement over its 1973 income.

The standard of living in the South is actually better than these numbers indicate because living costs are so much lower. The Bureau of Labor Statistics estimates that in 1979 a family of four needed $19,025 to maintain an "intermediate" standard of living in Houston. To maintain the same standard in Boston cost $24,381 and in New York, $23,856. The median family income in the South is 14.6 percent lower than that in the Northeast, but the budget requirement is 22 percent less in Houston. As a result, the typical family in this Sunbelt metropolis—despite its lower *money* income—enjoys 7.4 percent more real purchasing power than the median family in Beantown and 5.6 percent more than the same family in the Big Apple. For the wealthy in cities like Houston, the cost of living differential is even greater, proving what many boomtown residents already know—that it is cheaper to live high off the hog in Texas than in New York, Boston, or other northern cities. Excluding Anchorage and Honolulu, the cities of New York, Boston, and Washington, D.C. are the most expensive to live in (if you can afford an intermediate- or higher-budget standard of living) while three of the leading Sunbelt cities, Dallas, Atlanta, and Houston, are the cheapest. At an intermediate budget level, food costs in Houston are 8 percent lower, transportation costs are 13 percent lower, and housing costs and personal income taxes are less than half what they are in Boston. Boomtown growth seems to be the yellow brick road in the nation's otherwise gloomy economic landscape.

❖ THE "DOWNSIDE" OF THE BOOMTOWN STORY

Indeed the economic juices of the nation seem to be flowing swiftly to areas like Houston, and millions of transient families are following the flow. Youngstown's loss seems to be Houston's gain, so that on average the nation prospers.

But does it? A closer look at America's new boomtowns suggests that not all is well there either. The movement of capital imposes enormous social costs on the "winners" just as it does on the "losers." Like the boomtowns of the nineteenth-century Wild West, much of the glitter is true gold, but not everyone in town is overjoyed with the social conditions that accompany its discovery.

No one can deny the fact that explosive economic growth in the Sunbelt has brought "the good life" to many of the region's residents and to those who have migrated to the area. Yet this is only one side of the Sunbelt story. To leave off here would be to totally ignore the other side of the "boomtown syndrome"—the often-destructive consequences of unplanned rapid development.

With a deliberate policy of enacting no zoning laws and doing practically no planning, Houston and other boomtown cities have been virtually overrun by the influx of capital. Growth has occurred so rapidly and haphazardly that boomtown metropolises now paradoxically exhibit many of the same urban woes that plague northern central cities. To most city planners, "Houston's sprawling growth represents how not to do it. In Houston, developers can build what they want, when they want, where they want. While such laissez faire certainly engenders boomtown vitality, it also creates boom-town problems."

Among these are highway congestion, air pollution, water shortages, overcrowded schools, and a housing crisis marked by some real estate prices that have tripled in a matter of a few years. Twenty-five percent of the city's streets remained unlighted, 400 miles were unpaved, and 29 percent of the poor lived in substandard housing—even as recently as 1978. Every day nearly 200 newly registered cars join the armada that clog Houston's freeways. As a result, a commute that took thirty minutes five years ago takes an hour today. And there is no alternative way to get to work. What passes for the bus system, according to *Newsweek,* is "a joke"; the more charitable *Wall Street Journal* calls it merely "decrepit." Only eighty-two buses—four fifths of them paid for by the federal government—serve Houston's 400,000 residents. This situation is typical of many Sunbelt cities built during the age of the internal-combustion engine. In neighboring Albuquerque, New Mexico, 95 percent of all trips in and around the metropolitan area are done by car.

Other city services suffer as well. Annexation of suburban communities, combined with successful attempts at limiting property-tax levies to lure yet more industry, leave many a boomtown with inadequate revenues for even the most basic social services. This is certainly true in Houston where there is only one policeman for every 600 people and the average police response time to an emergency call is twenty-six minutes. (This amounts to one third of the police protection of Philadelphia and less than half of that found in other big cities.) The frighteningly slow emergency response time in Houston is almost surely due to the fact that a total of only seven police stations service the city's 556 square miles!

Yet perhaps the worst legacy of uncontrollable boomtown expansion is not in poor social services but in the violence done to a community's social fabric. As a consequence of the hyper-investment boom, the disparity between rich and poor is becoming increasingly evident throughout the Sunbelt, creating a dualism reminiscent of the pre-Civil War South. In 1978 the richest 5 percent of the Sunbelt population enjoyed a far larger share (16.4 percent) of income than the top 5 percent in any other region, and the bottom 20 percent have less (only 4.8 percent) than anywhere else. The wealthiest one fifth of the southern population has nearly nine times the aggregate income of the poorest fifth. Outside the South, that differential is 7.4 to 1.

Reflecting on these data, Georgia State Senator Julian Bond fears "the creation of a permanent underclass in the new South." *Fortune* magazine, a champion of Sunbelt development, admits that the black population (16 percent of the Sunbelt) has "scarcely shared in the economic upsurge." Again the statistics tell a gloomy story. In spite of boom conditions all around them, over *one third* (35.1 percent) of all blacks in the South—more than 4.8 million—were still below the official poverty line in 1980. More than a quarter (27.3 percent) of what the Census Bureau calls the "Spanish origin" population shared the same fate. In Houston the poverty has been described in particularly graphic terms:

> *Left behind in Houston's headlong flight toward growth and economic success are an estimated 400,000 people who live in a 73-square-mile slum that, says a college professor, has an infant mortality rate "that would have embarrassed the Belgian Congo."*

As a partial consequence of extreme income inequality, acutely visible in the juxtaposition of new industrial wealth and old rural squalor, the new boomtowns are experiencing a crime wave. In 1979, reports the FBI, Houston distinguished itself with one of the highest murder rates in the country: 40.4 killings per 100,000 residents, two thirds higher than New York City's homicide record. It is at least partly for this reason that the Commission on the Future of the South—made up of bankers, a judge, college presidents, and regional politicians—concluded that the South is a "time bomb" ready to go off. The unmet need for services for new residents is so staggering that the whole urban system may be on the brink of an explosion. The Fantus Company, which helps businesses select new plant locations, has even gone so far as to lower its official assessment of Houston's business climate, precisely because of poor public services. The city's own residents agree. In a recent University of Houston survey, only 26 percent of those who live in the city now think the impact of rapid growth has been "good."

Houston's problems are not unique. In many ways, they can be found in all of the boomtowns that have become the victims of too much unplanned development too fast. Atlanta has even sorrier stories to tell. And so do many of the cities in Florida. Every six minutes, the equivalent of a family of four moves to the Sunshine State seeking jobs or a retirement home. The new residents require housing, roads, schools, sewers, and water. Given the extremely fragile ecology of Florida, fresh water is a real problem—as it is in the booming Southwest. The Florida aquifer, the water table underlying the state, is down to its lowest level in recorded history. Fresh-water wells are being destroyed by salt-water seepage and some lakes are down by as much as 12 feet. Air pollution is killing Dade Country's palm trees, while the state's rivers are dying of chemicals, sewer waste, and algae. The water and sewage system is simply overloaded and many experts fear a real environmental calamity. A leading Florida newspaper editor summed up his assessment of the situation to a group of state planners saying, "[Florida] is going to die of thirst or choke to death on a glut of people, exhaust fumes, concrete, and sewage unless the public wakes up."

Silicon Valley, California, the bustling home of the computer "chip" in Santa Clara County, suffers from the same boomtown syndrome. At the end of World War II, Santa Clara County was known for its fruit orchards and Stanford University. Today, it is blanketed with 500 electronics firms that make components for everything from the cruise missile to Space Invader computer games. Between 1960 and 1975, employment in the valley grew by 156 percent—three times the national rate and twice that of California. High-tech workers flocked into the area the way that retirees headed for Florida. And with the influx came the same problems.

By 1980 there were over 670,000 jobs, but only 480,000 housing units in the county. As a result the *average* price for a house soared to well over $100,000. Cheaper houses were bid up in price so rapidly that low-income families were displaced in the process. With no viable mass transit, the freeways became jammed and the average commuting time reached three hours or more for workers living in the southern parts of the county. Federal air-quality standards are now violated at least 10 percent of the time. With land prices out of control and the air spoiled, the fruit orchards have entirely disappeared.

This drama of industrialization that has gone haywire seems quite ubiquitous across the Sunbelt. University of California regional economist Ann Markusen estimates that between 5 and 15 million Americans are now involved in rapid-growth boomtowns in the Southwest and Mountain states alone. In many of the thousands of smaller communities, particularly where new capital-intensive energy investment is leading to exaggerated boom-bust cycles, long-time residents are finding themselves evicted from their homes, and the competition for land is resulting in the direct displacement of agricultural and tourist related jobs. The newly introduced production techniques and skill requirements often mean that the higher-wage jobs created in the capital-intensive sector are not available to those who lose their jobs in more traditional lines of work. Indeed, . . . much of this high-tech development often leads to job creation for technicians and managers brought into the area by the companies, *not* for local residents. This population influx places added stress on a city or town's existing school, water, and sanitation services—usually at the expense of those same local citizens who could not obtain the jobs.

There has never been a comprehensive or systematic cost-benefit analysis of the boomtown syndrome. But economists and sociologists have at least devoted some attention to particular case studies of economic expansion. From these we can hazard some generalizations about the costs of rapid economic development. One group of sociologists, led by Gene Summers of the University of Wisconsin, has recently compiled evidence from 186 case studies of what they term the "industrial invasion of nonmetropolitan America." They found that the net gains from boomtown development are not anywhere near as great as most people imagine. In the majority of cases only a small proportion of the new jobs created are filled by previously unemployed persons. In thirteen studies that examined this specific question (excluding one special case in which the Area Redevelopment Administration stipulated the hiring of unemployed workers as a *quid pro quo* for federal grant support), the proportion of jobs filled by the previously unemployed was less than 11 percent. What employment opportunities are created by the establishment of a new plant are often taken by workers from outside the immediate area, both commuters and immigrants. "Possessing more education, better skills, or the 'right' racial heritage, these newcomers intervene between the jobs and the local residents, especially the disadvantaged."

Of course, other jobs are created in the process of new plant location through the ripple effect. . . . These are mostly in wholesale and retail trade and in services. But even there the net gain is not as great as normally imagined, for in half of all the case studies of new industrial development, the estimated employment multiplier is below 1.2. That is, ten new jobs in a new manufacturing firm generate, in the majority of cases, less than two new *local* jobs in other sectors. Part of the reason for the low local multiplier effect is that new establishments that are part of a larger firm or conglomerate tend to use the services of suppliers that are already doing business with the home office rather than ones from the local community. Another reason is that commuters tend to patronize retail establishments in their home towns rather than where they work. Moreover, in many communities where the process of industrialization is just beginning, there is surplus capacity in the retail trade and service sector that can absorb some of the new growth.

One surprising finding is how often new industrial development fails to reduce measured unemployment at all. To be sure, in two thirds of the case studies unemployment rates declined after new industry came to town. But in most cases the impact on unemployment was less than 1 percentage point. Regional experts believe this is due to the fact that the perceived promise of new jobs slows the rate of outmigration, causes local labor-force participation to increase, and attracts immigrants who take a disproportionate share of the new opportunities.

In light of these private sector impacts, it is useful to consider the net gain to the public sector. Here the sociologists are in near agreement. New industry clearly is associated with an increase in the public sector costs of delivering basic services to residents. Utilities, especially water and sewage, appear to be the primary source of increased local cost. The need for new roads, schools, and police and fire protection is also important. What makes matters worse is that since industry is often attracted through the provision of tax holidays and other incentives, the revenue generated by new establishments is often not sufficient to pay for the increased service needs. As a result, the overall net gain of boomtown growth is often small, and sometimes even negative.

The unrealized burden of boomtown expansion goes beyond that which is easily measured. Paradoxically, both the physical and emotional health consequences of boomtown developments turn out to be similar to those found in communities like Youngstown and Akron that experience acute capital loss. El Dean V. Kohrs, for example, finds that unplanned expansions

> *always seem to leave in their wake the grim statistics of mental depression, family disorganization, emotional damage, alcoholism, delinquency, and dissipation. These boomtown crises are not new to rural America, but the social consequences are becoming clearer today, and they are being felt in more parts of the country . . .*

A growing segment of the population in the Sunbelt now recognizes the immense social costs that accompany unplanned and anarchic hyperinvestment. They are being forced to pay for some of these costs through rapidly rising tax rates, although until recently they were getting the federal government to pick up a large share. With the new Reagan "federalism" forcing local communities to shoulder more of the fiscal burden, the contradictions of boomtown growth are becoming more evident. "Deep inside," notes Juan de Torres, an economist for the Conference Board, "the people of the South simply don't want their areas to grow any larger." The boomtown expansion has simply been too rapid for the city's public services, the environment, and the people themselves.

8

BONFIRE OF THE S AND Ls: HOW DID IT HAPPEN?

STEVEN WALDMAN AND RICH THOMAS

Like a huge storm in the financial stratosphere, the great savings and loan scandal has been raging for years without really touching most Americans. Rogues and swindlers paraded across the business pages and through the courts, accused of looting astronomical sums. Inept state and federal regulators fumbled to figure out what was going on, and bumbling politicians resolutely looked the other way, all the while accepting millions in campaign contributions. Like the sums involved, the scandal was too big and abstract for most people to grasp. But in recent weeks, the storm has dipped down to blast the earth—or at least to bring an uneasy chill. Does the spreading slump in housing prices have something to do with the S&L problem? Is the bailout, so painfully crafted last year, itself in trouble? What does the huge loss mean in real money, and how can it be repaid? What's all this talk of a credit crunch, maybe a recession? How is it going to affect *me*?

The answers are depressing, and getting worse as the price tag ratchets up. The scandal was by any measure the worst in U.S. history, a 10-year loss estimated by *Newsweek* at $250 billion that was stolen or wasted and must be repaid. That's $1,000 for every man, woman and child in America, not count-

WHAT $250 B COULD BUY

The huge sums destined to be sucked down the drain by the S&L crisis could easily fund some of the country's biggest wish lists.

Defense: Cover cuts slated for the next five years or buy 132 B-2 bombers, 40 Aegis cruisers and 100 Seawolf submarines.

Education: Fully fund every existing government program—from preschool through college—for the next four years.

Health care: Provide universal insurance *and* long-term care for the elderly and disabled for nearly four years.

Environment: Fund a 20-year coast-to-coast project to tackle the country's mounting hazardous-waste problem.

Infrastructure: Overhaul the nation's water systems, repair all bridges and have money left over to start fixing the highways.

ing the interest that we will go on paying for the next 40 years. It is an unfair drain on honest citizens to pay the piper for knaves and fools, and it will hit the young and poor harder than the old and rich. We will almost surely avoid financial disaster, but the bill is a drag on the economy and could trigger recession. Recession or no, it will curb our standard of living. We will feel it most in choices we must forgo: roads and clinics unbuilt, educational programs untried, job retraining that won't happen. And the victims are all of us, from the low-income residents evicted from a Phoenix housing project to the unborn children who will still be paying the tax bill four decades hence.

Worse yet may be to come: the S&L scandal is only part of a mountain of bad debt that lawmakers have allowed to pile up in recent decades. There is an additional $100 billion to $150 billion to be written off in government-guaranteed loans to millions of private interests. . . . Worst of all, the nation's commercial banks may be next in line. Like the $945 billion in S&L deposits, their $2.5 trillion deposits are unconditionally guaranteed by Uncle Sam. Many banks are playing out a script remarkably like the follies of the S&Ls, to much the same official indifference. If their watchdog, the Federal Deposit Insurance Corp., were to close all the ailing banks it is now permitting to operate, its $14 billion insurance fund might be exhausted overnight. Official Washington scoffs there's nothing to worry about—"The FDIC is not in question," a Treasury aide told *Newsweek*—but outside experts dispute that. "The administration and Congress just don't want to acknowledge the problem," says R. Dan Brumbaugh, the Stanford economist who first predicted the S&L collapse. "This is *déjà vu* all over again. You can't believe it's happening, but there it is." . . .

How could the savings and loan crisis *possibly* have happened? How could the government inadvertently lose $250 billion—an amount approaching the cost of the Vietnam War? "This is the single most grievous legislative error of judgment this century," says Republican Rep. Jim Leach of Iowa, a House Banking Committee member who warned in vain about the problem for years. "It's the single greatest accounting misjudgment this century. It's the largest lapse on the part of the press. It's the single greatest regulatory lapse of this century. It's the single greatest indicator of the defer-at-all-costs approach to government in this century."

It would be comforting to think the scandal occurred because of a conspiracy of unusual forces, the political equivalent of a rare planetary alignment. But actually the forces that caused the S&L problems to fester for so long are familiar parts of American political culture. The warped campaign-finance system, failures to police white-collar crime, ethical permissiveness—all contributed to the S&L crisis and all could, without dramatic reform, cause the next scandal.

❖ A FAILURE OF (DE)REGULATION

Before the 1980s, S&Ls were the most boring businesses in America. They loaned money to individuals to buy houses. Period. No loans for office buildings, none for breathtaking shopping malls or brash oil ventures. The motto was 3-6-3: offer 3 percent on savings, lend at 6 percent, and hit the golf course by 3 o'clock. The staid life changed with the high inflation of the late '70s as depositors pulled funds out of S&Ls to take advantage of higher-yield possibilities like money-market funds. The S&Ls were left holding long-term mortgages that paid them little. That left Congress with a choice: shrink the industry or let it fly free in the winds of deregulation. They chose the latter course—and the industry quickly became a lot more aggressive.

Congress took three key steps to revitalize the industry, all of which contributed to the fiasco. In 1980 it allowed S&Ls to pay much higher interest rates. The effect: S&Ls competed by offering savings-account rates as high as 13 percent. But to make up for the money they lost by paying more interest, they needed to generate extra income from investments. So in the early 1980s, Congress and many states allowed thrifts to invest in anything they wished. Effect: the thrifts bought everything from palatial estates for their owners to an Iowa plant that converted manure to methane. The government also permitted investors to open an unlimited number of accounts, each insured up to $100,000. That brought in more deposits—and gave irresponsible S&L managers more Monopoly money to spend. Together, these steps gave the industry the money and the freedom to fly high. "All in all," said Ronald Reagan when signing the 1982 deregulation act, "I think we've hit the jackpot."

Unfortunately, that "we" included a lot of high rollers with vivid imaginations. Don Dixon, head of Vernon Savings and Loan in Vernon, Texas, took his wife on a "gastronomique fantastique" tour of fancy European restaurants. But he defended the junket as a scouting trip for investments. "You think it's easy eating in three-star restaurants twice a day six days a week?" he protested.

Such behavior was allowed to persist because of a profound flaw in the Reagan administration's thinking about deregulation: that markets should be liberated not only by writing new laws but by weakly enforcing existing ones. Officials did this at other agencies, like the Occupational Safety and Health Administration, but the financial cost was greatest at the Federal Home Loan Bank Board, which regulated S&Ls. The three other regulatory bodies that oversee banks hired more examiners to monitor commercial banks, which had been partially deregulated in the early 1980s to compete with other financial markets. But while those agencies could pay for new cops by increasing fees on banks, S&L regulators had to go cup in hand to ask the White House budget office. The White House turned them down flat.

Adding insult to bureaucratic injury, the other financial agencies then picked off some of the Bank Board's most talented examiners. That wasn't hard: in 1983 the starting salary for an accountant at the Comptroller of the Currency, which regulates federally chartered banks, was $26,000; at the Bank Board it was $14,000. In the early '80s, the S&L overseer lost about half of its veteran examiner staff. Those who remained were told by Reagan's first S&L regulator, Richard Pratt, to adopt new accounting procedures that let thrifts pretend to be solvent until they worked their way back—or so they hoped—to real health. These gimmicks made things seem better, but in the same way a doctor can make a patient appear better by whiting out a tumor on an X-ray.

❖ THE IMPACT OF POLITICAL MONEY

Debates about the role of money in politics often make the need for reform seem either abstractly moralistic ("an affront to democratic values") or oddly trivial ("we're trying to eliminate not wrongdoing but the *appearance* of impropriety"). The S&L scandal shows clearly the dangers of having legislators depend so heavily on campaign funds from interest groups and businessmen with dealings before the federal government. Quid pro quos can rarely be proven but we do know this: never has so much money gone to such key legislators who worked so hard for measures that cost taxpayers so dearly.

The biggest politician to fall was Jim Wright, who resigned as speaker of the House in 1989 as the House Ethics Committee zeroed in on his attempts to bully regulators on behalf of thrift operators. Tony Coelho, the House majority whip who raised hundreds of thousands of dollars from thrift owners for the Democratic Congressional Campaign Committee, also retired that year under fire for a deal with Columbia S&L. Fernand St. Germain, former chairman of the House Banking Committee, lost his bid for reelection after disclosures he was using the credit card of the U.S. League of Savings Institutions for his personal entertainment. Now the Senate Ethics Committee is investigating the Keating Five, a group of powerful senators (Alan Cranston, John Glenn, Donald Riegle, John McCain and Dennis DeConcini) who received a total of $1.4 million in contributions from Charles Keating, head of the Lincoln S&L.

That's not to mention the $131,000 Keating gave to Arizona state politicians and the $255,000 he gave to politicians in the Phoenix area, according to a PBS "Frontline" documentary. Near Phoenix, Keating built the Phoenician, a lavish hotel with gold-leaf ceilings and $12 million in Italian marble.

Mostly what the S&Ls got from these politicians was delay. In 1986 Wright sat on a key piece of reform legislation that would have raised $15 billion in desperately needed bailout funds. During the ensuing delay, the bailout's price tag rose several billion dollars. The Keating Five helped push regulators into putting off action against the Lincoln S&L. The senators deny wrongdoing, but after their intervention the Bank Board waited another two years before shutting down Lincoln—a postponement that may have cost taxpayers millions more.

Responding to questions about whether his money had influenced the senators, Keating said, "I want to say in the most forceful way that I can, I certainly hope so." All five senators denied the money swayed them and Cranston said, "I never did anything to derail any investigation of anybody." Glenn argues that there's a difference between pressure and questioning: "I learned very quickly that as a senator I can ask any question that I want. How [the regulators] answer is their decision." The senators also say part of their job is to help constituents—whether it's Aunt Sally with her social-security check or Keating with his S&L. Yet as William Black, a top Bank Board enforcer, puts it, "there were lots of constituents that needed protecting. But the one constituent who put up more than a million bucks in contributions to the five senators is the only one that got the protection." The pressures of the campaign-finance system tempt legislators to define the "public interest" as the sum of narrow special interests—too often the special interests with the most money.

❖ THE HIRED-GUN SYNDROME

Follow the bouncing buck. Regulators eased off Charles Keating after intervention from the senators. The senators say that they interceded on behalf of Keating because they were persuaded by a letter written by Alan Greenspan, now chairman of the Federal Reserve and then a private consultant, vouching for Lincoln's health. And Greenspan was paid to write the letter by a law firm that was representing . . . Charles Keating.

Greenspan claims he genuinely thought, as he wrote, that Lincoln's management was "seasoned and expert" and that the S&L itself was "a financially strong institution that presents no foreseeable risk." He says Lincoln was regarded as a sound thrift when he wrote his endorsement and he is now "surprised and distressed" by the S&L's demise. Financial consultant Bert Ely, who has studied the case, says that if Greenspan had objectively studied the existing data "there's no way he could have reached those conclusions. It was clearly an inappropriate letter."

Keating was also helped because Arthur Young, a big-eight accounting firm, diagnosed his S&L as sound and accused the government of harassment. DeConcini cited the Arthur Young study in his meeting with regulators, asking, "You believe they'd prostitute themselves for a client?" Michael Patriarca, chief thrift regulator in San Francisco, answered: "Absolutely; it happens all the time." Jack Atchison, the accountant who gave Lincoln a glowing report, soon afterward joined Keating's firm at a salary of more than $900,000. Atchison declined to comment. Arthur Young officials say the firm carefully considered regulators' arguments at the time but concluded they were wrong.

Other hired guns contributed to the mess. "Professional" real-estate appraisers valued a parcel of California land at $30 million even though most of it was on a sloped, completely undevelopable piece of mountainside. Margery Waxman, a lawyer in the Washington law offices of Sidley & Austin, helped get the Bank Board to take the Keating investigation out of the hands of the San Francisco office, which was leading the charge. "As you know," she wrote Keating, "I have put pressure on [then Bank Board chairman M. Danny] Wall to work toward meeting your demands and he has so instructed his staff." Waxman declined to comment last week, but a Sidley & Austin spokesman told Legal Times that the firm holds her "in high regard."

Lobbyists, corporate lawyers and consultants often compare their work to that of the noble public defender toiling in a grimy municipal court. Their point: society doesn't chastise a criminal-defense lawyer for representing a murderer—it's part of our adversary system, after all—so it shouldn't blame an advocate for representing an unpopular business client. But campaigning for government benefits should not enjoy the same moral standing as protecting constitutional rights. When professionals become, in effect, political lobbyists, they should be held accountable if their efforts succeed. That would force them to make some independent judgments about what they're advocating and provide an important check on irresponsible behavior.

❖ SUICIDE BY FOUNTAIN PEN

Cosigning someone else's loan is known in private business as "suicide by fountain pen." It is a simple problem of human nature: people are less careful if they know someone else will pick up the pieces after the crash. If Uncle Sam pays off any deposits if an S&L goes under, the depositors may be less careful about where they put their money. That is why the government's decision to allow large investors to open unlimited numbers of guaranteed $100,000 accounts is considered one cause of the catastrophe. Savvy investors started putting money in the S&Ls with the highest interest rates, which gave men like Charles Keating the money with which to build their dreams. Meanwhile, "the gamblers at least could reassure themselves that depositors wouldn't suffer," says Northwestern University economist Haskel Benishay. And the deeper in trouble the owners became, the less they had to lose by gambling some more.

This "moral hazard," as economists call the effect of government guarantees, has plagued other programs as well. Congress will soon have to spend $100 billion to $150 billion *on top of* the S&L bailout to cover losses from programs ranging from student loans to flood insurance to commercial banking. Ironically, Congress loves these programs because they seem so cheap. The cost becomes clear only years later, when the loan goes bad or the disaster happens.

Even though these programs often cover bad risks, they get lax scrutiny because they are off-budget. "Nobody dreamed we'd have to raise $120 billion to bail out savings and loan depositors," say Rep. J. J. Pickle. "Nobody dreamed we'd have to put up $4 billion for the Farm Credit System. Nobody dreamed. Why, all of a sudden we realize that there's a tremendous risk. We've handed credit cards to these folks without ever watching what happened."

❖ THE CULTURE OF FINANCIAL CRIME

Picture the following scene: five senators sit in a room with a local district attorney who is prosecuting an accused bank robber. The senators charge the D.A. with harassing the bank robber and a few help a Senate employee, friendly with the accused, to be appointed the new D.A. Even the most cynical observer cannot fathom this happening. Yet five senators didn't view inquiries on behalf of Keating to be improper—even though the Bank Board's investigation was attempting to protect taxpayers from huge losses and, as it turns out, alleged fraud.

In the private sector, people who would be outraged to see a thief snatch an old woman's purse become numb to the implications of a senior being ripped off through fraud. Such a double standard is reinforced by the criminal-justice system: an unarmed bank robber who steals $100,000 will get a sentence between 51 and 63 months. Someone who commits a $100,000 fraud gets between 15 and 21 months.

Political and corporate culture can include pockets of permissiveness about crime just as ghetto subcultures can incubate violent crime. Until the insider-trading crackdown, Wall Street financial crime often went unpunished because it was so complicated—and in some cases so routine. The same sort of lapse in ethical standards lay at the heart of the HUD scandal, as Housing and Urban Development officials gave out grants on the basis of political ties instead of merit. People seem to forget that their gain comes at someone else's expense.

As part of his reform efforts, Rep. Henry Gonzalez, chairman of the House Banking Committee, required that regulators log contacts from congressmen. The S&L meddling suggests a further step: a ban on lawmakers privately lobbying regulators about the solvency problems of an individual bank or company.

❖ THE BIG DENIAL

Adolf Hitler theorized that "the big lie" would work because human beings have a limited capacity to fathom deception on a grand scale. The S&L scandal provides a corollary that might be called "the big denial." When the facts present a situation so extraordinarily bad, human beings will devise brilliant ways to avoid reality. Congress and the regulators didn't face the S&L crisis early in part because they just couldn't believe it was as bad as people thought. The same has been true with problems like nuclear-waste disposal at the Department of Energy facilities, which will require an additional $150 billion in taxpayer funds to correct.

Facts weren't faced for more mundane reasons as well. To do so would have meant paying for a bailout earlier, which might have required an unpopular tax increase. Thrift watchers charge that Wall continually downplayed the size of the thrift problem to keep it from becoming an issue in the 1988 presidential election campaign, a claim Wall denies. Examiners within the Home Loan Bank Board feared that if they pushed too hard they would incur the wrath of their bosses who, in turn, were being browbeaten by the politicians.

The failure to confront the S&L crisis made a bad problem into the worst financial scandal in American history. The sicker S&Ls became, the more their managers threw good money after bad. If Congress had confronted the problem in 1984 it would have cost $40 billion, estimates consultant Bert Ely—a lot of money but a small fraction of what we'll end up paying. "It's like the government has been borrowing from a loan shark," Ely says. So if it depresses you to think of how much we'll be paying now that we're confronting the problem, think of how much we're saving by dealing with it now instead of in 1995.

PART THREE

INEQUALITY

In the 1950s and 1960s many social scientists described the United States as an "affluent" society—one in which most people could expect a steady improvement in their standard of living, great disparities in income and wealth were fast disappearing, and true poverty was soon to be a thing of the past. These perceptions were based on some undeniable facts. On average, Americans' incomes did rise substantially after World War II, and during the 1960s millions of the poor were lifted above the official poverty line. It was natural to believe that these trends would continue.

But even in the expanding economy of the 1950s and 1960s, there were important limits to what some believed was a steady march toward greater equality. For one thing, even the progress in raising the overall standard of living had virtually no impact on the *distribution* of income and wealth in America—the gap between rich and poor. Throughout most of the period since World War II, the upper one-fifth of income earners received roughly 40 percent of the country's total personal income; the bottom fifth, about 5 percent. And, although poverty was sharply reduced in many rural areas, it proved to be much more stubborn in the inner cities.

More recently the trends have become much more discouraging: the limited postwar progress toward economic equality has been reversed. By the early 1980s, the spread of income inequality in the United States had begun to increase as the share of the most affluent began a slow but perceptible shift upward and the share of the poor fell correspondingly: At the beginning of the 1990s, income inequality had reached its most extreme level since World War II. Poverty, too, rose sharply from the late 1970s onward. And, under the impact of recession, inflation, and slower economic growth, the living standards of many American families began a steady decline.

As the article by Elliott Currie, Robert Dunn, and David Fogarty shows, that decline has struck unevenly among different sectors of the population, creating new and complex patterns of inequality. Broad changes in the economy have deeply affected living standards, work, and family life in the United States and have profoundly altered what many Americans can expect from the future. Currie, Dunn, and Fogarty argue that currently fashionable policies designed to boost the overall economy will not restore the American dream of equality in abundance. If anything, they may aggravate existing inequalities and contribute to the impoverishment and desperation of millions of Americans. For this edition of *Crisis in American Institutions,* Currie, Dunn, and Fogarty have added a new postscript describing the changes—and similarities—in the "New Inequality" in the early 1990s.

Currie, Dunn, and Fogarty see new kinds of poverty emerging in the United States along with new kinds of affluence. Unfortunately, recent events bear out their prediction. In an earlier edition of this book, we wrote that "the size of the poverty population has remained depressingly unchanged for a decade." Today we cannot make that statement, for things are even more depressing. The proportion of Americans living below the poverty line has increased dramatically since the end of the 1970s. There were over 9 million more poor people in America in 1990 than in 1978—two-thirds of them white and 3.5 million of them children.

Perhaps the most tragic aspect of the rise in poverty, indeed, is that it has been fastest among children. Today more than one child in five in the United States lives below the federal government's poverty line—which stood at about $14,000 for a family of four in 1992. Many people are aware that poverty among children is widespread in America, but fewer realize that it is *much* more prevalent here than in other industrial societies. Recent data from the Luxemburg Income Study, an international comparison of levels of inequality and poverty begun in the 1980s, illustrate just how stark those differences are. Isaac Shapiro and Robert Greenstein's summary of this evidence shows a disturbing pattern. Not only are more Americans condemned to poverty because of their disadvantaged position in the economy, but also our government policies do less to help than those of other countries. The result is that the U.S. rate of child poverty after taxes and social benefits are figured in is 4 times as high, on average, as those of the other industrial countries—and a stunning 25 times the rate in Sweden.

Poverty is more than a matter of income alone. One of the most devastating, and most visible, consequences of rising poverty (among other causes) has been the growth of homelessness in the United States. Peter Rossi's article, which is based on original research on Chicago's homeless population, carefully disentangles the multiple roots of homelessness. Though many forces contribute to the problem—including high levels of mental and physical disability—Rossi reminds us that in the final analysis, the spread of homelessness means that our housing market is simply failing to provide sufficient shelter that the poor can afford.

The final article in this part, "Hunger in America: The Growing Epidemic," written by a group of physicians who recently toured the country to witness the problem firsthand, illustrates even more starkly the real-life consequences of rising poverty. In this except from their report, the doctors describe some of the shocking conditions they discovered—ironically enough—in America's traditional "breadbasket," the Midwest. They found people in Chicago living on dog food, mothers watering down their babies' formula so it would last through the month, elderly people so inured to starvation that they no longer felt hungry. In the Declaration of Independence, "life" is enshrined as one of the three "inalienable rights" that flow to Americans by virtue of having been "created equal." The threat of starvation in the midst of great wealth surely violates that right—and mocks the most basic American ideals.

9

THE FADING DREAM: ECONOMIC CRISIS AND THE NEW INEQUALITY

ELLIOTT CURRIE, ROBERT DUNN, AND DAVID FOGARTY

In the 1980s, no one any longer doubts that the United States is in the midst of a deep crisis in expectations. In the 1950s and 1960s, most Americans were led to believe in a future of indefinite economic expansion. Rising living standards, it was said, had made most people feel part of the "middle class." Real economic deprivation, to the extent that it was acknowledged at all, was presumed to be confined to the margins of the "affluent" society.

The combination of economic stagnation and high inflation—"stagflation"—in the 1970s replaced that rosy vision with the sense that the United States was slipping rapidly into economic decline. Suddenly the celebrated American standard of living seemed to be falling precipitously, and the easy optimism was quickly displaced by gloom and anxiety about the future. Faith in the "American Dream" disintegrated with dizzying speed, bringing fear, resentment, and a widespread demand to "turn the country around" at whatever cost. Today, some variant of a program for economic "revitalization" is on everyone's agenda, at all points on the political spectrum.

But beyond the sense of crisis and the urgent call for change, there is remarkably little agreement about the degree to which the era of "stagflation" has actually damaged American standards of living or clouded the prospects

Elliott Currie, Robert Dunn, and David Fogarty, "The Fading Dream" from *Socialist Review*, No. 54, November/December 1980. Reprinted by permission.

for the future. *Fortune* magazine recently described, with considerable accuracy, the national pessimism about the state of the economy:

> *Of all the changes in American society during the Seventies, none was more fundamental than the erosion of faith in the future. By the end of the decade, the conviction that the material aspects of life will get a little bit better each year had given way to the bleakness of spirit known as diminishing expectations. It seems that most people nowadays aspire to little more than holding on to what they've already got, and many become downright despondent when they contemplate the world their children will inherit.*

Fortune hastened to assure us, however, that such "dour resignation" was "out of phase" with the "upbeat outlook" for family income in the 1980s and also exaggerated what really happened during the 1970s. Many groups "did a lot better in the 1970s than is generally appreciated." The real problem, *Fortune* insisted, was psychological; people's expectations had been too high to begin with, so they "didn't *think* they were doing particularly well."

The disagreement has been sharpest over the impact of inflation. The business-oriented Committee for Economic Development, for example, describing inflation as a "pernicious addiction," declared that "the damage inflation does to the fabric of both our economic system and our society is so great that it must not be allowed to proceed unchecked." On the other hand, others have argued, with the economist Robert Heilbroner, that whatever dangers inflation may hold for the future, its impact on current living standards has been "much less than we commonly believe." "Despite our sense of being impoverished by inflation," Heilbroner writes, inflation has not "substantially" affected the "national standard of well-being and comfort."

Which of these views is accurate? As with so many social issues, the answers we get depend greatly on the kinds of questions we ask. In what follows, we want to delve beneath the conventional statistics on income and earnings to ask a different, and broader, set of questions about the way the economic crisis has affected social life and living standards in the United States.

In particular, we want to address two crucial problems in the usual statistics and the debates based on them: (1) They tell us nothing about the measures people have had to take in order to cope with recession and inflation, and (2) they are *averages* that tell us nothing about how *different groups* have fared under the impact of economic crisis.

The answers to these questions are crucial to an understanding of the social impact of the current economic crisis and, consequently, for evaluating policies that claim to confront it. We will look at the way inflation and recession have affected work and family life, patterns of saving and debt, and the availability of housing and jobs, and will argue that neither the relatively optimistic view—that the crisis has had only a mild effect on living standards—nor the more drastic vision of a massive economic decline adequately conveys what has happened to American life under the impact of "stagflation."

The real picture is more complicated. Developments in the economy have brought a complex sorting of the population into "winners" and "losers"—a recomposition, or reshuffling of the deck, rather than a uniform decline. On the one hand, many American families have maintained living standards, if at all, only by working harder, sacrificing leisure and family life, and/or mortgaging their futures and those of their children. Those hardest hit by the economic crisis, and with the least resources to cope with it, have suffered real decline; poverty-level styles of life have appeared among people who once thought of themselves as part of the "middle class." Some of the basics of the "American Dream"—the home of one's own, the successful job as the reward for education and effort—have moved, for all practical purposes, beyond their reach. At the same time, at the other end of the scale is a new affluence for the relative "winners" in the restructuring of social and economic life in America.

Increasingly, one's chances of affluence or poverty, comfort or insecurity, are crucially determined by a complex web of conditions that includes not only one's sex, color, and age, but also family composition, position in the housing market, and much more. One implication of this complex trend—as we will see—is that policies of economic "renewal" designed to stimulate the economy as a whole through such means as cuts in taxes and social spending may only accelerate the re-sorting of the American population into affluent "winners" and impoverished "losers." And the destruction of the social programs that have traditionally cushioned the blows suffered by those "losers" can only hasten the process.

❖ THE PLIGHT OF THE THREE-JOB FAMILY

How we define the contours of a problem depends crucially on the way we choose to measure it. Measured in terms of overall family income, the rapid growth in living standards that fed rising expectations throughout postwar America came to an abrupt halt in the early 1970s. The median income for all American families approximately doubled (in constant dollars) between 1950 and 1973. But it fell—by over a thousand dollars—during the recession of the mid-1970s and by 1979 had inched back no further than its level of six years before.

Some economists dispute the relevance of these figures, arguing that real living standards actually *rose* even at the height of the mid-1970s "stagflation." This view is based on the argument that *per capita* income—total personal income divided by the number of people—is a much better measure, since it allows us to take account of the statistical impact of population changes. For example, since families are smaller, on the average, than they used to be, measures of overall family income will give a misleading picture of trends in how well-off families are: What we need to know is the income available per person, which may have increased even while total family income has stagnated. As Lester Thurow argues, "from 1972 to 1978, real per capita disposable income rose 16%. After accounting for inflation, taxes, and population growth, real incomes have gone up, not down. The average American is better off, not worse off."

What this argument ignores is that behind the soothing figures on per capita income is the grinding reality that, for many families, that income has been achieved only by sending more people to work. The clearest evidence of this fact comes when we look not simply at income per family or per person, but per *worker*. Thus discretionary income—basically, disposable income minus expenditures for necessities and transfer payments—declined by about 5 percent between 1973 and 1979. But this figure ignores one of the most striking features of the 1970s—the great increase in the number of people working. As *Business Week* points out, "Adjusting discretionary income for the huge recent increases in employment, to reflect the sweat that goes into producing that income, shows that discretionary income per worker over the past six years declined by 16%." These figures show that families increasingly need two—or more—workers just to keep up, much less to "get ahead." Statistics on the trend of family incomes in the 1970s bear this out: the incomes of families with only one earner fell about 7 percent behind the cost of living from 1969 to 1978; those of two- (and three-) earner families came out about 6 percent above it.

This trend has given the family a crucial—and somewhat paradoxical—role in the contemporary economy. On the one hand, the material support of other family members is often all-important as a protection against the erosion of living standards. Such support is especially crucial for women, given the pervasive discrimination they face in the labor market. This difference is most apparent in what has been called the "feminization of poverty"; single women, especially those with young children, have become the most predictably impoverished group in America. But at the same time, increased labor places severe strains on many dual-earner families. The need for two incomes in such families means that three jobs are now being done for the price of one—two in the paid labor force, one unpaid—the household and child-rearing tasks done in the home. As the work time needed to keep up with living costs increases, something has to give. And there is considerable evidence that often what is "giving" is the quality of family life.

On the one hand, the tasks of child-rearing and housework are often being pushed out of the home—usually to the private sector—as working people, if they can afford to, consume more and more day care, fast food, and even paid housekeeping. (One result is the rapid growth of low-wage, quasi-domestic "service" occupations that both cater to the needs of the multiearner household and often supply what passes for job opportunities for the second earner.) On the other hand, especially for those who cannot afford outside services, modern family life often means a decline in the possibility of real leisure—or, what amounts to the same thing, an increase in the pace of life, a kind of social "speedup" resembling the deliberately increased pace of an industrial assembly line. With an extra job to do and little public provision for domestic services, many people wind up routinely cutting corners, compressing their lives, and feeling "hassled" much of the time they are supposedly "off the job." While this situation has always been the fate of many lower-income working families, it is now becoming a predictable aspect of the lives of many who once saw themselves as part of the "middle class."

But—like other effects of the rising cost of living—the burden of this "social speedup" has not been evenly distributed among working people. Instead, it has served to widen the gap between men and women and between income groups, in ways that are obscured by the conventional statistics on income and earnings.

Most of the extra work brought by the "speedup" has fallen on women— both because they are most of the second earners in the paid labor force and because paid work has not freed most women from unpaid work in the home. Instead, the extra job that women do has most often been coupled with continuing responsibility for running the household. As Willard Wirtz, head of the National Commission on Working Women, puts it,

> For a great many women, taking a job outside the home isn't a matter of substituting one kind of work for another; what it means is double duty. . . . If limited opportunities on the new job away from home are part of the problem, the rest of it is the unchanging terms and conditions of the job at home. When all the old duties still have to be performed, body and mind sag under the double burden.

Much of that burden involves child care. A 1978 study by the University of Michigan's Survey Research Center found that nearly half of women working in the paid labor force, versus only 13 percent of men, reported spending $3^{1}/_{2}$ hours or more—on working days—with their children. Forty-four percent also reported spending an additional $3^{1}/_{2}$ hours on other household chores.

It is remarkable, in fact, how closely the overall working time of typical two-earner families matches the time requirements of three full-time jobs— and what a large proportion of the "third job" falls to women. Another recent study found that among working couples, the men spent an average of about 9 hours a week on family care, the women an average of about 29 hours. At the same time, the men averaged 44, to the women's 40, hours of paid work (because men were more often in jobs with frequent overtime). Put together, this amounts to an average of 69 hours of work a week for women, 53 for men, or 122 altogether for a family—the equivalent of three full-time jobs.

For many women, then, entering the labor force to keep the family standard of living intact has meant more work, less leisure, and a more harried family life. What one critic has called the "overwhelming poverty of time" in these families is given abundant testimony in a national survey of women wage-earners undertaken by the National Commission on Working Women. An astonishing 55 percent of the women surveyed reported having *no* leisure time; 39 percent had no time to pursue education. Only 14 percent were able to say that job and family life did not seriously interfere with each other.

There is, of course, another side to this increase in women's work. It is doubtless true that moving into the paid labor force has provided many women with wider options and may have helped undermine the traditional subordination of women in many families. But because of the persistence of the sexual division of labor in the home and the lack of adequate public support services, it has also meant that women have shouldered a disproportionate—though often hidden—share of the burdens imposed by the economic crisis. And the potential benefits in greater independence for women have also been constrained by the rising cost of living—especially in housing—which, in some areas, has made "coupling" almost an economic requirement.

Obviously, the effects of entering the labor force are different for the grocery clerk's wife who gets a job as a telephone operator than for the lawyer's wife who becomes a stockbroker or psychotherapist. And this difference illustrates one of the most striking trends of the stagflation era. For women who have the resources to enter well-paying and rewarding jobs, and to afford the costs of the private-sector "industrialization" of domestic services, the "two-paycheck" family can represent an enviable and liberating way of life. At the other end of the scale, it can mean a virtually unrelieved round of dull, rote work, in and out of the home. And the distance between these two ways of life is growing—in part because an increasing proportion of the wives entering the paid labor force comes from more affluent families, with the result that, as a Labor Department study puts it, "the gap between above-average income families and below-average income families will widen" in the coming years.

As access to extra work becomes more and more important in maintaining or improving standards of living, we can expect this gap to widen for another reason as well. Not everyone has the *opportunity* to take on more work—even relatively unrewarding work—in response to threats to their living standards. In a survey of how different kinds of families coped with recession and inflation, David Caplovitz found that about two out of five tried to handle inflation by working more—either sending more family members to work or taking on overtime or an extra job. But poorer people, often lacking access to even *one* job, were less often able to exercise those options.

The "new impoverishment"—of time as well as income—of many American families, then, is only one side of the coin; the other is the growing affluence of some families. Between 1970 and 1977, when average family incomes barely improved at all and many families' living standards fell sharply, the proportion of families with incomes above $25,000 (in constant dollars) jumped by about 23 percent. The rise in the number of relatively affluent families was even sharper for blacks, at the same time as many blacks suffered even greater stagnation or decline in living standards.

At one end of the new scale of living standards is what *Fortune* has gushingly termed the "superclass"; those two-income families with the additional "formidable advantages of connections, intelligence, and education," whose incomes may reach six figures. At the other end is a broad stratum of the poor and nearly poor—single parents, one-earner families with low incomes, and people on fixed incomes. Somewhere in the middle are the broad ranks of two-earner families with middling incomes who must cope with the escalated costs of necessities and the increased need for domestic services, for whom even two paychecks barely cover expenses from one week to the next.

✦ MORTGAGING THE FUTURE

Conventional data on living standards, then, obscure the enormous increases in labor—and the resulting changes in family life—that have gone into keeping up with the rising cost of living. Something similar happens with the conventional picture of working people's consumption. The fact that levels of buying and spending have, on the whole, remained remarkably high in the stagflation era is often taken as evidence that things can't be as bad as we might think. Again, though, this conclusion ignores what working people have *done* in order to maintain consumption. For many families, stagflation has meant sacrificing the future to pay for the present, making the future a source of anxiety and dread—a situation most clearly visible in the changing patterns of savings and debt.

As recently as the fourth quarter of 1975, the rate of personal saving—the proportion of people's income put away for the future—stood at 7.1 percent. By the fourth quarter of 1979, it had dropped to 3.3 percent, less than half its level only four years before. This general figure masks much lower rates of saving at the lower levels of the income ladder and among younger people, but the inability to save afflicts even many middle-class families that have otherwise been able to weather inflation's attack fairly well. As Caplovitz's survey discovered, "Even if they are able to maintain their standard of living within limits, many white collar families find for the first time that they are unable to save money."

Along with reduced saving has come rising consumer debt. The average American consumer now holds only about $3 in assets for every dollar of debt owed, compared with about $5 in the 1950s. Installment credit as a proportion of disposable income rose by about 42 percent between 1960 and 1978.

Like the increase in labor, the growth of debt has struck some people much more severely than others—in this case, particularly lower-income and younger people. Debt repayments as a percentage of disposable income were 25 percent for the lowest income fifth in 1977, only 6 percent for the highest fifth. And that disparity has been increasing steadily; the proportion rose from 19 percent for the lowest-income fifth since 1970, while it dropped slightly for the most affluent.

The result is that low-to-moderate income families have become even more highly "leveraged," in financial jargon, and hence ever more precarious financially. As a leading student of debt patterns in the United States notes, "As measured by the ratio of debt payment commitments to income, vulnerability to recession has increased, especially among the lowest 20 percent of the income distribution." Debt use is also most frequent among the young—especially younger families.

Why has debt grown—and savings evaporated—so rapidly while average family incomes have remained relatively stable? Part of the answer is that, as research by the National Center for Economic Alternatives has shown, costs for the necessities—food, energy, housing, health care—have risen much faster than the Consumer Price Index as a whole in the past few years. This rise in the cost of necessities seriously undermines the value of income even when it is measured in "real" terms—that is, adjusted for rises in the overall cost of living. Hence the sharp rise in the debt burden of families at the lower end of the income scale, where necessity costs already take a larger chunk of total income.

But there is a more subtle and less measurable reason for the growth of debt: more expenses become necessary as inflation creates its own set of escalated needs. Thus sharply rising housing prices may force a family out of easy commuting range to jobs and services, raising transportation and energy costs, perhaps requiring a second car. Paying for the extra car and the extra gas may require a second job. The second job in turn increases transportation costs still further; it may also create the need for more paid day care, and probably changes eating habits in a vastly more expensive direction—more eating out, less careful food shopping, and less economical food preparation. Thus the changes in family living patterns we noted above lead not only to increased labor, but to escalating expenses as well. At the extreme, the new expenses may cancel out most of the benefits of increased work, in an inflationary "Catch 22."

Greater "leveraging" of family income to cope with these inflation-induced "needs," as well as the rising cost of necessities, is hard to avoid, given the insufficiency of public services that could cushion the need for ever-higher individual expenditures. But this "leveraging" means that some families—again, especially younger and poorer ones—may not be able to provide for a reasonably secure future. They won't be able to send their kids to college, cope with emergencies like major illnesses or deaths, or add savings to their pensions to help ensure a decent retirement.

These issues have become especially keen because of the specter of disintegration of the traditional systems of support for old age. Although Social Security benefits have so far kept up with inflation, the entire system's funding is increasingly in jeopardy—and reduction in benefits is now on the political agenda. Living on Social Security benefits alone, in any case, is a sure ticket to poverty; and private pensions, the most common alternative support, are rarely adjusted for increases in the cost of living.

The need to sacrifice security to keep up with essentials can only have a devastating psychological impact on the quality of life. It not only makes the present more frightening, but is one reason why many can no longer look forward to the ideal of a decent old age as the reward for a lifetime of labor—and why opinion polls show that Americans, for the first time in memory, think that their children will live in conditions worse than the present. In 1979, according to a *Washington Post*/ABC News poll, 66 percent of respondents still believed that their children would be "better off" than they were, whereas 18 percent thought their children would be worse off. By March 1981, only 47 percent thought their children would be better off, and 43 percent now believed their children would lead worse lives than their own.

❖ THE VANISHING PROSPECT FOR HOME OWNERSHIP

Coping with "stagflation," then, has meant cutting deeply into savings and going further into debt, as well as greatly increasing labor—for some people much more than others. But even with these adaptations, there are aspects of the traditional American Dream that many working people—especially the young—may never achieve, given the peculiar contours of the economic crisis. One of them, as we'll see in a moment, is the good job with reasonable chances for achievement—or at least good pay. Another is a home of one's own.

What has happened to housing represents a drastic change from traditional expectations. Decent housing, even rental housing, is fast becoming an unrealistic goal for all but a dwindling fraction of young Americans. Between 1972 and 1978, the price of an average one-family new home increased 72 percent nationally, 86 percent in the West, and much more in some high-demand metropolitan areas, while median family income increased only 40 percent. The Department of Housing and Urban Development estimates that in 1970 half of the American people could have afforded a median-priced new house (then costing $23,400), using the standard rule of thumb that no more than a fourth of pretax income should be spent on mortgage costs. In 1979, by the same standard, only 13 percent could afford new-home ownership (the median price then being $62,000), and 38 percent of all actual new-home buyers were ignoring the prudent rule of thumb.

The "affordability crisis" has hit renters as well, and today both owners and renters are overspending in order to put a roof over their heads. American families are now paying an average of almost 36 percent of disposable income for housing and housing-related expenses, double the average of only ten years ago. For low-income households the situation is much worse; by 1977, some 5.8 million households—4.2 million renters and 1.6 million owners—were paying over half of their incomes for shelter, and the problem has worsened considerably since then.

For many of these families, the cost of housing has meant stretching their budgets beyond the point where they can pay for other necessities and has made them terribly vulnerable to recession-caused disasters—either forced sale, default, or learning to live with poverty-level habits in all other realms of life.

Rising housing costs, moreover, have priced some groups out of the housing market altogether—notably low-income families, young couples, singles, and minorities. In 1975, a couple earning $16,650 could have bought a median-priced California home for $41,000; They would have made a 20 percent down payment of $8,000, and their monthly mortgage payment—including insurance, interest and taxes—would have been $347. By the end of 1979, the same home cost $88,300. A buyer had to earn over $35,000 to qualify for a loan, put down $17,750 as a 20 percent down payment, and pay out $878.42 per month.

At those rates, a broad segment of American working people—especially those now coming of age and those who, for whatever reasons, have delayed entry into the housing market for too long—may never have a chance to own a home. The fading dream of home ownership represents a crucial change in living standards—not only because it condemns some people to inferior housing, but perhaps even more importantly, because it eliminates one of the only tangible assets traditionally available to people without high incomes. The fact that roughly two-thirds of American families own their own homes today suggests how far down the income scale home ownership has extended in postwar America. Without the home as asset, the material security of these people will drop precipitously, again suggesting that ordinary income and wealth data greatly underestimate the real "losses" stagflation has caused for some groups.

Meanwhile, those who already have a strong foothold in the housing market have seen their homes appreciate wildly in value and their relative mortgage costs decline, often dramatically, because of inflation. The benefits of inflation for people who already own their homes should not be exaggerated, however, for other costs—maintenance and taxes, particularly—have risen dramatically in the decade. For people with limited or fixed incomes, these costs can tip the balance between being able to keep a home or being forced back into the rental market. Still, the crisis in housing has created one of the deepest and most powerful divisions between "winners" and "losers" in the stagflation era.

❖ THE OUTLOOK FOR JOBS

The divisions between winners and losers multiply and deepen when we look at what recent changes in the American economy have meant in terms of the kinds of jobs that will be available in the future. For, like housing, the job outlook is changing—in ways that will mean intensified competition for a shrinking proportion of good jobs. The losers in that competition may face a lifetime of poorly paid, dull, and unstable work.

Some point to the rapid growth of overall employment, even during the recessionary 1970s, as evidence of the fundamental health of the economy. Nearly 13 million new jobs were created between 1973 and 1979. The American economy, in fact, produced new jobs at a rate much faster than its chief economic competitors, West Germany and Japan. What is striking, however, is that the economy stagnated, and living conditions flattened, in *spite* of all those new jobs. Why, with all those people newly at work, did only a minority of families see their standard of living rise?

The answer lies partly in the nature of the new jobs themselves—and it bodes ill for the future. For the new jobs have overwhelmingly been in those parts of the economy that offer the poorest pay, the fewest chances for advancement, and the least possibility of providing an adequate livelihood. And it is precisely these jobs that are expected to continue to grow in the future, while those that have traditionally offered a ticket to higher living standards will correspondingly decline.

By the end of the 1970s, well over two-fifths of all American workers in the private, nonagricultural economy were employed in just two sectors: retail trade and "services." More significantly, over 70 percent of all *new* jobs created in the private economy between 1973 and 1980 were in those two sectors. What kinds of jobs are these? Labor Department economists estimate that by 1990 there will be over 4 million new jobs in various private medical-care services—nursing homes, hospitals, blood banks, and medical laboratories. Another fast-growing sector is "miscellaneous business services," including janitorial, photocopying, and temporary office help. Over 5 million new jobs are expected in retail trade, mainly in fast-food restaurants, department stores, and food stores.

The jobs in these expanding fields are notoriously low-paying. In 1979, workers in manufacturing industries averaged about $232 a week in spendable earnings. Workers in service industries averaged $162, and in wholesale and retail trade, $155. Part of the reason for these low average earnings is that these jobs are often part-time, as is illustrated by the short—and declining—work weeks in service and retail trade. The average work week in retail trade was almost 40 hours in 1959, had dropped to 33 hours by 1977, and is expected to drop to 30 hours by 1990. Workers in manufacturing, as Emma Rothschild points out, had an average work week (in 1979) of about 40 hours, while workers in eating and drinking places, one of the fastest-growing sectors of the economy, averaged just 26 hours a week.

In the 1950s and 1960s social critics often worried that technological changes in the economy were on the verge of eliminating work. A whole literature about the "postindustrial" society emerged, in which the problem of what to do with the predicted increase in leisure was a primary concern. But the reality today is not quite what these critics expected. Technological change has not so much eliminated jobs, in the aggregate, as it has changed the mix of jobs available—and with it, the relative chances that work will bring economic security. The prediction of a "postindustrial" or "service" economy has been partly realized—and will become even more so during the remainder of this century. But—as we've already seen—the rise of the "service society" has not brought greater leisure—but, in many cases, the opposite; not increased freedom from toil—but, often, an ever-faster race to stay in one place.

The impact of these changes is already ensuring that youth are one of the greatest casualties of the economic crisis. Men and women under twenty-four are earning less today, in real terms, than their counterparts did in 1967. Even *Fortune* magazine, in its generally "upbeat" rendering of the income picture during the 1970s, notes that the combination of the "bulge" of baby-boom workers and a declining job market has played havoc with youth's life chances. Men aged fifty-five to sixty-four, the magazine points out, enjoyed a real income increase of nearly 18 percent between 1969 and 1977; those twenty-five to thirty-four saw their incomes rise less than 3 percent, while men eighteen to twenty-four suffered a slight decline. The cumulative effect has been dramatic: "By the end of the Seventies," *Fortune* notes, "the baby boomers had effectively lost about ten years' income growth relative to the group just ahead of them. One of the biggest uncertainties about income in the Eighties is whether they will be able to make up that lost ground." The division between those with a clear shot at the dwindling proportion of good jobs, and those who may never rise out of the poorly paid, unstable work force in the spreading retail and service sectors will become increasingly important in the coming years.

That division will probably be intensified by the wholesale destruction of many blue-collar jobs under the impact of the decline and restructuring of key industries like auto, steel, and rubber. Traditionally, these industries provided high-wage jobs that often offered a path into relative affluence (though that affluence was always threatened by job instability). Until the late 1970s workers in these industries (as well as certain others, like coal mining) fared best in terms of real income. By 1977, nearly a third of all American families making between $25,000 and $50,000 a year were officially classified as "blue collar." But these jobs, of course, are threatened with elimination as those industries either shut down, move away, or automate in response to intense competition. According to recent estimates, for example, by late 1980 the crisis in the American auto industry had cost the jobs of close to 300,000 workers in the industry itself and another 600,000 in related industries. And it is clear that—even if the industry does ever regain its past level of production—it will do so with a work force that is considerably smaller, replaced as much as possible by new, superefficient "robots."

To the extent that these and other well-paying blue-collar jobs are obliterated, the result will be a still greater split between a relatively few high-level professional and technical jobs on the one hand, and a growing array of poorly paid, rote jobs on the other. This split will strike hardest at younger workers' expectations for a decent job in the future, especially young minority workers, for whom industrial blue-collar jobs have long been a main route to a decent standard of living.

❖ THE NEW INEQUALITY AND ECONOMIC POLICY

Two themes stand out most strongly from the strands of evidence on changes in work and family life, expectations for jobs and housing, and patterns of spending, saving, and debt.

First, it is true that—as *Business Week* magazine puts it—"the American credo that each generation can look forward to a better life than its predecessor has been shattered." What's more, it has been shattered in particularly threatening ways, for what have been most powerfully assaulted by the changes in the economy are the most fundamental expectations and most basic courses of stability and security—the quality and character of home and family life, the security of one's future, and the fate of one's children.

At the same time, these burdens have been felt very differently by different groups. The lineup of "winners" and "losers" in this redistribution of life-chances is complicated and sometimes unexpected. Traditional differences, like sex, race, and age, have been widened and redefined, while newer ones based on family composition, position in the housing market, or—increasingly—participation in specific industries have arisen or become more important. The brunt of stagflation's impact on living standards, patterns of labor and family life, and job prospects has been borne by a few especially hard-hit groups. Others, better endowed with the appropriate resources, have coped more than adequately, carving out new kinds of affluence in the midst of economic "decline."

What do these trends tell us about the social and economic policies that could reverse the harshest effects of the new inequality? It would take another article to do justice to such a large, and freighted, question. But a few general points seem clear.

Most importantly, our analysis suggests that the kind of economic "revitalization" so fashionable among the legions of the "New Right"—and given political momentum by the Reagan administration—is more likely to aggravate the trends we've outlined than to alter them. At the core of the "conservative" program is a set of incentives designed to fuel economic expansion by stimulating private investment. These incentives include across-the-board tax cuts, "deregulation" of industry, and drastic reductions in public spending on social programs (coupled, of course, with massively increased spending for defense). According to the new conventional wisdom of "supply-side" economics, these policies would both fight high inflation and "get America moving again" by "unleashing" private enterprise.

At bottom, the "supply-side" vision is the most recent (and most drastic) variant of the longstanding argument that the way to increase jobs, income, and well-being throughout the society is to allow them to "trickle down" from an expanding private economy. By shifting the balance of social resources upward and improving the "business climate," society as a whole—including its poorest members—should benefit.

Whether such a program can, in fact, cause a spurt of economic growth—

as measured by a rising Gross National Product or a higher rate of productivi-ty—is a question we won't venture to answer. For our purposes, it is the wrong question. The more important one is not whether we can generate *some* kind of economic growth—but whether the growth we produce will be trans-lated into better lives and greater opportunities across all sectors of society. And this is where the "supply-side" program seems badly out of touch with the reality of modern society.

The "supply-side" program assumes, at least implicitly, that the problem we face is a general economic decline—a decline that can be reversed by pro-viding sufficient lures to ever-greater investment. But the notion of a *general* economic decline, as we've demonstrated, is misleading. Something far more complex has been taking place. Rather than a simple, overall stagnation, we are witnessing a complicated process of recomposition and "restratification," bringing new sources of affluence along with new forms of poverty. Economic shifts have been translated into complex changes in work, family, and other social institutions. Policies of "revitalization" that fail to take account of those changes—of the institutional structure that necessarily forms the context of economic life—will only deepen present inequalities, worsening the situation of those "losing" and accelerating the advance of those already "winning" in the social and economic reshuffling we've described.

Illustrations are not hard to come by. How will an economic "boom," fueled by tax cuts for the wealthy, help an unskilled single mother find eco-nomic security—especially when the same policies are, with the other hand, taking away public funds for child care that would enable her to take a job—if a job were there? How will growth in nursing homes and hamburger stands help a skilled blue-collar worker whose $20,000-a-year job has been lost to a more "productive" industrial robot? How will the expansion of defense industries in the Southwest help a young minority couple facing the runaway housing market in New York? Or an unemployed 18-year-old in Chicago's ghetto?

Dealing effectively with the new forms of impoverishment will require policies targeted directly to those groups most at risk in the modern econo-my—and to those sectors of the economy where inflation and recession have taken their worst toll. A program to confront the new inequality cannot sim-ply bank on the "trickling down" of jobs and income from expanding private investment, but must involve active intervention in economic life toward explicit social goals.

Addressing these problems will require *more* "government intervention," not less; a larger (if more efficient) public sector, not a diminished one; more "planning," not less. We know that these strategies go strongly against the stream. But we believe that without them the alternative scenario is clear: a sharper division between the newly affluent and the newly poor; for the young, fast-vanishing opportunities for good jobs and decent housing; and continued inflation with its devastating pressures on home and family. The choice is clear. We will either decide to engage in serious, democratic public planning to redress the social imbalances generated by economic development or we will watch helplessly as an uncontrolled "revitalization" brings greater insecurity, desperation, and misery in its train.

❖ STAGFLATION, INEQUALITY, AND THE POLITICAL CULTURE

What are the prospects for that kind of democratic social planning? At first glance, the outlook seems less than hopeful. In the face of the injuries inflicted by the economic crisis, there have been some encouraging expressions of public mobilization and concern. But, at least as often, the crisis has seemed to generate cynicism and political withdrawal, epitomized by the fact that the winner of the 1980 presidential election came into office on only 26 percent of the potential popular vote. Contemporary politics—and contemporary American culture as a whole—often seem mired in narrow interest-group concerns and a spirit of individual indulgence.

And these responses—negativism, cynicism, withdrawal from social concern—are themselves partly rooted in the changes we have already described. The heightened insecurity that economic crisis has brought to personal life in America—the receding prospects for decent jobs and housing, the looming threat of downward mobility and of a pauperized old age—helps explain the resurgence of broader cultural themes of competition and individual survival. ("Tomorrow only the fit will survive," declares an ad for a new magazine for "entrepreneurs," "and only the *very* fit will flourish.") And it also offers fertile soil for the desperate focus on the "self" that Barbara Ehrenreich has aptly called a "psychological version of the 'lifeboat ethic'"—the "me-first" character of life lived mainly in the present because the future seems less and less certain or worth building toward. Given the particularly harsh effects of the economic crisis on family life, it isn't surprising that political campaigns narrowly focused on the "defense" of the traditional family—like the campaign against the Equal Rights Amendment—have enjoyed especially wide appeal in the era of "stagflation."

All of these tendencies have been reinforced by the increasing *fragmentation* we have described. When relative prosperity or impoverishment may hang on the timing of a house purchase or the fact of working in (say) the aerospace rather than the auto industry or having been born in 1940 rather than 1950, the sense of commonality of experience and needs disintegrates. Individual (or, at best, familial) solutions to social and economic problems can easily come to seem the only alternatives available, the only visible avenues to security and well-being.

This individualization is aggravated by the growing split between the newly affluent and other working people—what we might call the "Brazilianization" of the American class structure. Working people see some enjoying considerable success—"making it" in highly visible ways—while others sink; some buying second homes in the mountains, speedboats, and Cuisinarts, while others descend into the ranks of the welfare poor. Those differences act both as a spur to individual striving and as a demonstration that the proper management of personal life can bring significant rewards—that it can put you, as *Fortune* pants, on "a fast track to the good life." And for those at the upper reaches of the scale, it provides a sharp and nagging incentive to hold on more tightly to what they have.

These trends—fragmentation, individualization, the narrowing of political concern to family and personal life—are not the only ones now evident in the United States. As Michael Harrington has pointed out, the American people seem to be moving in several different ideological directions at once. There is a new theme of narrow self-seeking in American culture; but there is also—as public opinion polls reveal—a growing support for guaranteeing jobs through public programs and for accepting wage and price controls in response to runaway inflation. There is, in some quarters, a new reverence for private gain and the forces of the "market"; but there is also evidence of a growing concern for what the psychologist Urie Bronfenbrenner has called the "human ecology"— a recognition of the connectedness of the fabric of social life and a rejection of the periodically fashionable idea that human life should be left to the not-so-tender mercies of the "free market." Which trend will prevail depends crucially on the seriousness and energy with which we build a broad movement for democratic planning and control of economic life.

❖ POSTSCRIPT—1990

When we wrote this article in the late 1970s, we associated the decline in American living standards, and the sense of diminished expectations that went with it, with the effects of "stagflation"—the unprecedented combination of high inflation with high unemployement—which so preoccupied both economists and the American public at that time. Today, the effect of falling oil prices rippling through the economy combined with the tight money policies of the Reagan and Bush administrations has brought the overall rate of inflation down considerably. But that overall drop masks continuing rises in the costs of housing, medical care, and college tuition—among other expenses. And it has not affected the main economic and social trends we discussed: the loss of well-paying industrial jobs and the multiplication of low-paying ones in the service sector; the stagnation of average family income even with more and more families having two earners to support them; an increasingly unequal income distribution, leading to more of the very rich and many more of the very poor; a declining rate of homeownership combined with greater housing costs for both renters and owners; and a level of public and private indebtedness that threatens the very basis for future economic growth. A great deal of research published since we first wrote has shown that these trends have continued and even intensified in the 1980s.

The continued weakening of America's international economic position has steadily aggravated the loss of jobs in industries like steel, auto, and now even semiconductors. As recently as 1979, for example, the United States steel industry accounted for 400,000 production workers; by 1986 it employed only 200,000. Severe job losses have affected many white-collar and service industries as well, as companies have "restructured" and "downsized" in an increasingly tough economic environment.

By the end of the 1980s the spread of income inequality was wider than at any point since World War Two. After taxes, between 1977 and 1990, the poorest fifth of American families suffered a drop in income of 14 percent. The next-poorest fifth lost 10 percent, and the middle fifth lost 7 percent. The top one percent of families enjoyed an increase of 110 *percent* in after-tax income. The ranks of the rich, according to the economists Sheldon Danziger, Peter Gottschalk, and Eugene Smolensky, have more than doubled since the early 1970s (their study defined the rich as earning more than $95,000 a year in 1987). In the past, as Danziger and his colleagues point out, economic inequality has generally increased in periods of recession but *diminished* in times of economic recovery. What is perhaps most troubling about the "new" inequality of the eighties and nineties is that it has continued to rise during a several-year-long recovery.

The sources of the continuing growth of inequality are, as we suggested, complex. Some of it is attributable to government policies that have reduced spending for low-income people while simultaneously reducing taxes for the affluent—resulting, as Barbara Ehrenreich has put it, in the government's "first major upward distribution of wealth since World War Two." Despite the much-touted tax reform of 1986, ostensibly designed to make the tax structure more progressive, the wealthy now pay a proportionately lower share of their income in taxes than they did in the late 1970s. Between 1977 and 1990, according to the House Ways and Means Committee, the most affluent one percent of the population enjoyed a startling 85 percent rise in real pretax income—and a 23 percent *drop* in their tax rate. The poorest fifth of Americans, meanwhile, suffered a 12 percent loss in income and saw *their* tax rate increase by 3 percent. Overall, as the Congressional Budget Office has shown, nine out of ten American families now pay a larger proportion of their incomes in federal taxes than they did before the "tax cuts" of the late 1970s and early 1980s. Only the wealthiest tenth has actually seen their rates go down as a proportion of income. These shifts are due in part to reductions in personal income tax rates and large cuts in corporate income taxes for the wealthy, on the one hand, and steady increases in Social Security taxes for working people on the other.

Other causes were underway well before President Reagan took office in 1981, and are therefore probably rooted in a longer-term decline in the competitive position of the American economy and the way this has affected the labor market.

Barry Bluestone, Bennett Harrison, and Chris Tilly have recently shown that this "sharp U-turn" toward inequality can be dated to sometime in the years 1975 to 1978, with the distribution of wage and salary income becoming steadily more unequal ever since. They conclude that "the sense of relative deprivation, of frustrated expectations, of falling behind, of being badly-paid—this is becoming the common experience of a growing number of Americans. They are white as well as persons of color. They are men as well as women. Having a full-time, year-round job is no longer a guarantee of being sheltered from this experience."

Nor, as we suggested, does the future look any brighter, since most of the new jobs now being created in the "service" economy are low-paying and often unstable. Other research by Bluestone and Harrison shows that, between 1963 and 1978, only about a fourth of all new jobs paid poverty- or near-poverty-level wages; but of the new jobs created between 1978 and 1984, almost half did so.

Research by the Senate Budget Committee has shown that the burden of the shifting job market has fallen heaviest on the young. Between 1979 and 1987, the quality of jobs available to workers under 35 dropped sharply; the number of jobs for younger workers that paid middle-level wages fell by more than 1.5 million, while the proportion paying low wages correspondingly rose. For workers over thirty-five, the proportion of high-level jobs actually increased slightly in those years. In our original article, we noted that the young were already among the "greatest casualties" of the emerging economic crisis. As we'll see, that has become even more true since we wrote.

Other writers, notably Robert Kuttner and Lester Thurow, have called this erosion in the number of people earning middle-level wages a "decline of the middle class" in the United States. If we take the "middle class" to be those families earning between $20,000 and $49,999, in 1984 dollars, then the middle class did indeed decline in recent years, while the proportion of both low- and high-income families increased. According to Katharine Bradbury, an economist for the Federal Reserve Board of Boston, the proportion of American families earning less than $20,000 increased by over 4 percent between 1973 and 1984, while the proportion earning $20,000 to $50,000 dropped by more than 5 percent.

Although these numbers don't sound very dramatic, before 1973 the income distribution pattern in this country had changed only glacially since the Census Bureau began collecting statistics in 1947; so this is a remarkable shift. Taken in combination with the stagnation of real incomes over the same period, it means that millions of American families have been unable to achieve the living standards they had expected to attain at their current stage in life.

The only real disagreement about the "decline of the middle class" is over *why* it is occurring. Some economists, notably Robert Lawrence of the Brookings Institution, say that the problem isn't economics, but demographics. He thinks that the baby-boom generation made up of people born between 1946 and 1964 has flooded the labor market, temporarily increasing the competition for jobs and bringing down wage levels. As fewer young workers enter the labor market, and as the baby boomers reach prime earning age, wage levels will increase and the "middle class" will expand again. In other words, we don't need any change in social or economic policy, because the problem will correct itself in good time.

But Katharine Bradbury recently tested this theory and found it to be incorrect. Using Census data, she demonstrated that "the fraction of families with middle-class incomes declined within virtually all demographic groups." It declined within all regions, within all age ranges, and within all family types except families in which the head was 65 or over. But not surprisingly, given the declining job opportunities for younger workers we've just noted, the decline in living standards has struck hardest at younger families, especially those with young children. Between 1973 and 1987, according to the Children's Defense Fund, those families suffered an average income decline of almost 25 percent.

That decline has been concentrated at the lower end of the income scale. But even for middle-income people, relatively stagnant wages combined with rising housing costs have meant (as we predicted) that fewer young families can afford to buy their own home, the major single element of the American Dream. In a 1985 study for the Joint Economic Committee, Frank Levy and Richard Michel showed that in 1973 the typical 30-year-old man could make the payments required to purchase a median-priced house with only 21 percent of his salary. By 1984, he would need to spend 44 percent of his salary for the house, since the cost of housing had risen much more rapidly than the average salary for that age group. Similarly, a 1986 study by the Joint Center for Housing Studies of MIT and Harvard concluded that "unless young adults achieve substantial income growth or unless the cost of homeownership declines to more traditional levels, many more young families than in the past will find themselves unable to purchase a home." The study found that in the period 1981 to 1985 alone, the percentage of homeowners dropped from 20.7 to 17.4 among those under 25; from 41.7 to 37.7 in the 25–29 age bracket; and from 59.3 to 54.7 in the 30–34 age group. And the shrinking chances for homeownership are only one aspect of the housing pressure on young families, many of which are trapped in a rental housing market that is itself escalating drastically. The median rent burden for young lower-income households— that is, rent payments as a proportion of income—went up by 50 percent between 1974 and 1987, and there is no relief in sight.

With their income stretched precariously to meet stratospheric mortgage payments, and most or all of their assests locked into housing, young families are now terribly vulnerable to catastrophe if their income falls. In parts of the country now undergoing economic slowdowns after the long housing "boom" of the eighties, disaster has already struck many overextended families.

According to the *New York Times,* for example, in New Jersey, Connecticut, and on Long Island, "housing foreclosures, delinquent mortgage payments and personal bankruptcy filings are rising." The economic crunch is taking its toll on personal and family life; "As a result of financial pressures caused largely by high housing costs . . . psychologists and social workers say they are treating many more cases of stress, depression, spouse and child abuse and marital strife."

Our article pointed out that, squeezed between stagnant wages and rising outlays for housing and other costs, families had two main methods to maintain their living standards: sending an additional family member to work (usually the wife), and buying more things on credit. But, as Frank Levy has pointed out, the potential of the first method is nearly exhausted because more than two-thirds of young married couples now rely on two earners, and "there is no third earner in reserve to keep consumption growing." There is also evidence that American households can no longer continue to support the rising burden of consumer debt.

Consumer installment credit outstanding has more than *tripled* since 1976 and didn't stop growing even during the 1981–1982 recession. With almost one-third of average monthly cash household income now allocated to debt payments, many economists fear that this burden will inevitably put a brake on consumer spending and sharply limit future economic growth.

Two groups are already suffering noticeable effects from indebtedness: small farmers and college students. In large part because of farmers' inability to meet debt payments, the number of farms with less than $20,000 in annual sales fell by 60 percent between 1975 and 1985. Thirty percent of all farms are now owned by people over 65, and only 6 percent by people under 35, indicating a severe erosion in the number of future farm families. And student loan programs that originated in the 1960s as a convenience to the middle class have turned into a necessity for millions of college students as a result of sharply rising tuition costs and simultaneously declining federal grants for tuition aid.

By 1986, borrowing under the Federal Guaranteed Student Loan Program had soared to nearly $10 billion a year, with the total amount of loans outstanding exceeding $50 billion. The College Board estimates that about half of the nation's 10 million undergraduates are now leaving school with some debts, but for those who go on to graduate or professional school, the amount owed easily grows so large that it inevitably shapes personal and professional decisions. With new doctors now owing an average of $30,000 on graduation, few can afford to become rural general practitioners; and new lawyers, who now owe an average of $25,000, will think twice before deciding to practice public interest law.

The rise in debt and decline in homeownership are part of a major trend toward concentration of wealth in the United States, as shown by a study for the Joint Economic Committee released in July 1986 and based on data collected in 1983 for the Federal Reserve Board and other government agencies. The report defined wealth as "stored-up purchasing power . . . measured by the value of what could be purchased if all a family's debts were paid off and the remaining assets turned into cash." By this measure of net assets, the group the report called the "Super Rich"—the top one-half of 1 percent of the population—held an astonishing 35.1 percent of the nation's total wealth in 1983. Between 1963 and 1983, the share owned by the top one-half of 1 percent of the population increased by 38 percent while the share owned by every other group declined. The "Everyone Else" category, which includes 90 percent of the population, suffered the greatest decline. By 1983 the 419,590 households classified as "Super Rich" owned average holdings worth $8.9 million, and some held many times more than that. The 75 million households in the "Everyone Else" category had average holdings worth $39,598. The disparities would be even greater if the JEC study had broken down the Everyone Else category into the lower 50 percent of the population or the lowest 20 percent. Unless they own substantial equity in their home, most families have little or no net wealth.

Just how thin the financial safety net is for many American families is illustrated in a more recent study by the sociologists Thomas Shapiro and Melvin Oliver. If we subtract equity in homes and cars, for example, 67 percent of black and 30 percent of white households have zero or negative "net financial assets"; that is, what they owe is equal to or greater than what they have saved in cash, stocks and bonds, or other assets. What this means is that almost any sudden economic misfortune—loss of a job, a big medical expense—could put the assets they do have, especially their homes, in jeopardy. Again, the financial safety net is thinnest for younger families; over half of households headed by someone under 35, versus 30 percent of those between 35 and 64, have no or negative financial assets.

But perhaps even more than the new pressures on the middle and the rising fortunes of the rich, it is the precipitous decline at the bottom that has most transformed the social and economic landscape in America. Writing in the late 1970s, we anticipated that the adverse shifts in jobs and income would bring new kinds of poverty to the United States. We did not anticipate how massive and rapid the impoverishment of lower-income Americans would be. About 8 million people have joined the ranks of the poor since we wrote, 3 million of them children. And while poverty widened its grip on Americans, it also deepened; about 2 out of 5 of the poor had less than *half* the poverty-level income in 1987, the highest proportion in a decade. Poverty has also "hardened" in the United States over the last several years; according to the University of Michigan's Panel Study of Income Dynamics, the chances of "exiting" from poverty decreased substantially after the early 1970s.

Nor do the official poverty figures alone adequately capture the disaster that has afflicted the low-income population since the start of the 1980s. The deepening income poverty has been brutally compounded by the erosion of public services—including health and mental health care, subsidized housing, and resources for the public schools. In many inner cities and hard-hit rural areas, the most basic human needs are now routinely unmet in the 1990s. It's no exaggeration to say that we may be witnessing the emergence of two distinct classes of citizenship in America, based not only on growing differences

in income but on sharply diverging access to the fundamental means of participation in economic, social and political life.

That widening gap may help to shed light on the perplexing *political* question we noted in the original article. If living standards have declined since the
early 1970s, and if the country has moved much further toward inequality in
income and wealth, why haven't the victims of this process demanded more
egalitarian social and economic policies? Voters have, of course, shown some
discontent around economic issues, but on the whole, unrest around "pocket-
book" concerns has been mobilized much more successfully by the right than
the left. In particular, the right has offered voters some economic relief
through property tax "revolts" and President Reagan's cuts in the personal
income tax, although the right's traditional constituency, the wealthy, has been
the main beneficiary of these reductions.

In our original article we suggested the troubling possibility that the
trends toward greater inequality and insecurity might be self-perpetuating.
The growing fragmentation of experience and the gnawing sense of an unsure
future seemed, to us, to be pitting Americans against each other in an individu-
alistic struggle for constricting rewards—not spurring them toward common
action in pursuit of larger social and economic goals. The decline of the sense
of commonality is surely exacerbated by the very real deterioration at the bottom—the resurgence of violent crime and hard drugs, the abrasive visibility of
the homeless.

That kind of individualism, of course, isn't new to the United States; as
Robert Bellah and his coauthors remind us, in their noted book *Habits of the
Heart,* "it is individualism, and not equality, as Tocqueville thought, that has
marched inexorably through our history." But we think that a number of
recent institutional changes may have exacerbated the atomization of American political culture and further eroded the potential for a strong, unifying
movement built around egalitarian concerns.

Historically, for example, two of the most important channels for the
political expression of those concerns have been the labor movement and the
Democratic party. But many of the same forces that have fostered the new
inequality have also weakened the influence of organized labor: the shift from
traditional blue-collar industry to services, the displacement of jobs overseas,
the resulting growing power of management to wring concessions on pay and
working conditions from labor. In 1984, according to the AFL-CIO, the
labor movement organized about 350,000 new workers—but *lost* about
700,000 members from plant closings, layoffs, and decertification elections.
Just to maintain their current membership, then, unions would have to double
their rate of organizing victories. At the same time, as the *Washington Post*
political reporter Thomas Edsall has shown, *both* political parties have come
to be increasingly dominated by the affluent—to the detriment of the concerns of the other 60 percent of the American population. In both cases, the
result has been a vacuum of leadership and organizational support for a more
genuinely democratic political and economic agenda. Whether that vacuum

can be filled and a new, more cohesive political vision created, in the face of increasing pressures toward social fragmentation, is one of the most important social questions of our time—and one we cannot yet answer. As we said over a decade ago, the quality of our collective future will depend on the "seriousness and energy" with which we work to build a movement for social change.

❖ POSTSCRIPT: THE VIEW FROM 1993

Since our last postscript, the trends underlying the "new inequality" have continued undiminished. The real changes since 1990 have been in the realm of politics—as the spread of inequality and the continuing assaults on the well-being of ordinary Americans effectively brought down one administration and ushered in another with a new mandate for social and economic change.

Despite ever weaker efforts at denial by the Bush administration, by the 1990s it was increasingly apparent that the tenuous "prosperity" of the Reagan/Bush years, such as it was, had unravelled. Indeed, the trends we charted in the late 1970s had now become so pervasive that they were the staple of public discourse about the precarious state of America. Even conservative pundits rushed to publish analyses of how adverse changes in jobs, income, and the quality of life generally had brought the great American middle class to the *Boiling Point,* as Kevin Phillips titled a best-selling account. *Fortune* magazine, which at the close of the 1970s had insisted that the outlook for the future was much more "upbeat" than most (presumably befuddled) Americans realized, published a cover story in 1993—"Fortune's Survival Guide to the 90s"—exhorting white-collar Americans to toughen their reflexes to cope with the "wrenching" changes in what it described as a "new Darwinian workplace." (The story even featured a cartoon showing nattily suited executives being flattened to pancakes by a steamroller).

An ever-growing body of evidence helped to make these grim trends increasingly visible. The continuing decline of that part of the American income spectrum that could reasonably be defined as "middle class" was affirmed in several studies. The University of Michigan's Panel Study of Income Dynamics found a drop of 15 percentage points in the proportion of Americans with "middle" incomes between 1978 and 1989; a Census Bureau study in 1992 similarly found that the percentage with incomes somewhere between half the national median and twice the median fell from 71 to 63 percent from 1969 to 1989—with more falling downward than moving upward.

The special impact of these income shifts on the young, which we noted in 1990, was disturbingly reaffirmed in more recent research. The Census Bureau found that whereas in 1969 only about 19 percent of people under 18 had incomes less than half the median for all Americans, by 1989 the figure had climbed to nearly 30 percent—and had risen fastest for youth who had *finished* high school but not gone on to college. As this suggested, one particularly baneful shift has been that the economic rewards of education have stagnated or fallen for vast numbers of the young. Sheldon Danziger and Gregory Acs, for example, have shown that men with a high school education were more than twice as likely to be working in a low-wage job than their counterparts had been in 1973.

Indeed, what became most clear in the early 1990s was the extraordinary degree to which any gains from the economic growth of the past 15 years had accrued to a *very* narrow slice of the American population. That was perhaps most dramatically revealed in a widely discussed calculation by the MIT economist Paul Krugman that a stunning 70 percent of all the growth in average family income from 1977 to 1990 had been "siphoned off" by the top *one* percent of income earners. It was often said during the 1980s that we were becoming a society divided between a successful "mainstream" majority and a relatively small, but floundering and troublesome, "underclass." But the reality was very different: *Most* Americans were hurting, often badly, as a result of both deep economic trends since the early seventies and the antiegalitarian policies of the Reagan and Bush administrations. The "mainstream" was in deep trouble, if indeed it could still be said to exist in any meaningful sense.

That "democratization of decline," as we might call it, was more responsible than anything else for the swift collapse of the dominance of the Republican Party after 12 years of what had begun to look like invincibility. Bill Clinton's campaign wisely, and successfully, sought to unite that aggrieved majority around broad economic issues. Happily, that appeal overcame—at least for a time—the tendencies toward fragmentation and atomization that we worried might make the new inequality self-perpetuating. In our original article we wrote that "a program to confront the new inequality cannot simply bank on the 'trickling down' of jobs and income," but "must involve active intervention in economic life toward explicit social goals." A similar critique of "trickle-down economics" was a central theme of Clinton's campaign, and in its first months of office his administration moved swiftly to address several of the issues we thought were most urgent—signing a family leave bill to reduce stresses on what we called the "three-job family," establishing a task force to bring decent health care within the reach of all Americans, proposing substantial spending on infrastructure to create good jobs at good wages.

We think these are important steps—not only because of the relief they may bring to hard-pressed Americans, but perhaps more importantly because of the deeper message that they send about the values of mutual responsibility and the legitimacy of active government. They are a signal that the era of the heedless obeisance to "market forces" may be waning and that one more attuned to what we called the "connectedness of the fabric of social life" may be dawning. Clearly, the national mood has shifted in important ways since we last wrote. A new spirit of common concern and engagement has begun to emerge, both in Washington and across the country. How far these changes will go, and how long they will last—against what will surely be considerable resistance—we cannot say. But we are hopeful.

10

POVERTY AND INEQUALITY IN INTERNATIONAL PERSPECTIVE

ISAAC SHAPIRO AND ROBERT GREENSTEIN

The Luxembourg Income Study—one of the most comprehensive studies of its sort ever undertaken—compares income levels, poverty rates, and government policies in selected Western nations, including the United States. Data from the study show that income is distributed more unevenly in the United States than in any of the comparison nations.

- In the United States, 24.2 percent of the population had incomes much lower than the median income. In the average comparison country, 16.9 percent of the population had incomes that were low relative to the country's median. (In this comparison, an unweighted average was calculated for Australia, Canada, Germany, Israel, Netherlands, Norway, Sweden, Switzerland, and the United Kingdom.)

- In the U.S., 53.7 percent of the population had incomes at or near the median. The middle class was much larger in the comparison countries, equaling 64.4 percent of the population, on average.

From Isaac Shapiro and Robert Greenstein, *Selective Prosperity: Increasing Income Disparities Since 1977*, Washington, DC, Center on Budget and Policy Priorities, 1991, pp. 22–24. Reprinted by permission.

- At the same time, the U.S. had a larger share of the population with incomes well above the median income. Some 22.1 percent of the U.S. population fell into this category, compared to an average of 18.8 percent in the comparison countries.*

The Luxembourg Income Study also examined child poverty rates in various countries, as well as the degree to which government policies reduced these rates. In each country, children living in families with incomes below 40 percent of that country's median disposable income, as adjusted by family size, were considered poor.† (This yields a poverty line for the United States that is extremely close to the official poverty line.) The study's findings show:

- In 1986, the U.S. child poverty rate before taxes and government benefits stood at 22.3 percent. The next closest rate was 18.7 percent in France, while the average rate for all of the countries compared to the U.S. was 13.2 percent. (See Table I.)

- When the effects of taxes and benefits were considered, the U.S. child poverty rate barely budged, dropping to 20.4 percent. U.S. policies directly reduced child poverty by less than one-tenth. In sharp contrast, policies in other countries reduced child poverty by nearly two-thirds, to an average of 4.8 percent.

- The study showed that the child poverty rate in the U.S., after taxes and benefits are considered, was *more than twice that in Canada and four times the average child poverty rate in the other nations in the study.* It also showed that the poverty rate just among white children in the U.S. was higher than the poverty rate among *all* children in all other countries in the study except Australia.

In short, the private economy in the United State generates more relative poverty among children than the private economies of many other western, industrialized nations—and the U.S. then does far less than the other nations to address this problem.

A recent study comparing family poverty trends from 1970 to 1986 in the United States and Canada also is illuminating. During the period examined, the

---

*The source for these data is Timothy M. Smeeding, "Income Inequality: Cross-National and Comprehensive Perspectives," Statement prepared for the Joint Economic Committee, May 11, 1989, using Luxembourg Income Study database.

For each country, people with incomes considered to be low relative to the median income are those people whose family incomes are less than 62.5 percent of their country's median income, adjusted for family size. Middle-income people are those with family incomes between 62.5 percent and 150 percent of median adjusted income. Upper-income people are considered to be those living in families with incomes above 150 percent of median adjusted income.

†Because this relative poverty measure is based on each country's median income, it is, to some degree, a comparative measure of income distribution. It estimates what share of children in a country live in families with very low incomes relative to the median income in that country.

TABLE 1 CHILD POVERTY RATES IN SELECTED NATIONS			
	YEAR	POVERTY RATE BEFORE BENEFITS AND TAXES	POVERTY RATES AFTER BENEFITS AND TAXES	NET CHANGE DUE TO BENEFIT AND TAX POLICIES

	YEAR	POVERTY RATE BEFORE BENEFITS AND TAXES	POVERTY RATES AFTER BENEFITS AND TAXES	NET CHANGE DUE TO BENEFIT AND TAX POLICIES
Australia	1985	16.4%	9.0%	−45%
Canada	1987	15.7	9.3	−41%
France	1979	18.7	4.7	−75%
Netherlands	1983	15.2	4.0	−74%
Sweden	1987	7.7	0.8	−90%
United Kingdom	1979	10.5	3.3	−69%
West Germany	1984	8.4	2.8	−67%
Average*		13.2	4.8	−64%
United States	1986	22.3	20.4	−9%

Source: Timothy M. Smeeding, "Cross National Perspectives on Trends in Child Poverty and the Effectiveness of Government Policies in Preventing Poverty among Families with Children in the 1980's: The First Evidence from LIS," Unpublished manuscript.
*This reflects an unweighted average of the most recent data provided for the seven comparison nations.

poverty rate among non-elderly families increased in the U.S., while falling by 60 percent in Canada. The study found that faster economic growth in Canada during the 1970s explained our northern neighbor's better progress against poverty in that decade, but that "virtually all of the [large] difference in U.S. and Canadian poverty rates between 1979 and 1986 is attributable to changes in the number of families moved out of poverty by [government benefit programs]."

The study found that from 1979 to 1986, benefits were made more generous in Canada, but cut in the U.S. As a result, even though the recession was deeper and more protracted in Canada—and the unemployment rate was higher there in 1986 than in the U.S.—family poverty declined in Canada during this period while rising significantly in the U.S.[†]

Alternative government policies, it appears, can help yield different poverty and income distribution outcomes than those experienced in the United States in recent years.

[†]Maria J. Hanratty and Rebecca M. Blank, "Down and Out in North America: Recent Trends in Poverty Rates in the U.S. and Canada," National Bureau of Economic Research, Inc., Working Paper No. 3462, October 1990.

WHY WE HAVE HOMELESSNESS

PETER H. ROSSI

❖ HOUSING AND HOMELESSNESS

In discussing the distinguishing characteristics of homeless Americans, it is easy to lose sight of the fact that the essential and defining symptom of homelessness is lack of access to conventional housing. Clearly, if conventional housing were both everywhere abundant and without cost, there would be no homelessness except for those who preferred to sleep in the streets and in public places.* That there are homeless people in fairly large numbers means that our housing market is not providing appropriate housing abundantly at prices the homeless can afford. Nor is it providing affordable housing for the extremely poor, who must double up with others.

To be sure, there is no way any housing market dominated by private providers can offer housing at an "affordable price" for those who have close to zero income. But market-offered housing is not the only option. Most of

---

*Many commentators and researchers on homelessness claim they have talked to homeless people who said they preferred homelessness to conventional housing. I have no doubt that such statements have been made. I also have little doubt that when offered an option under realistic conditions, few homeless people would make such a choice.

From Peter H. Rossi, *Down and Out in America: The Origins of Homelessness,* University of Chicago Press, 1988.

the extremely poor are domiciled, and their housing chances are affected by the supply of low-cost housing generally, a market factor that affects the households they live with. There is abundant evidence that homelessness is related both directly and indirectly to the shortage of inexpensive housing for poor families and poor unattached persons that began in the 1970s and has accelerated in the 1980s.

The decline in the inexpensive segment of our housing stock has been precipitous in the largest cities, such as New York and Los Angeles, but it also has characterized cities of all sizes (Wright and Lam 1987). The Annual Housing Survey, conducted by the Census Bureau for the Department of Housing and Urban Development, has recorded in city after city declines in the proportion of housing renting for 40% or less of poverty-level incomes. These declines ranged from 12% in Baltimore between 1978 and 1983 to 40% in Washington D.C. for 1977 to 1981 and 58% in Anaheim, California, in the same period. In twelve large cities surveyed between 1978 and 1983, the amount of inexpensive rental housing available to poor families dropped precipitously, averaging 30%. At the same time, the number of households living at or below the poverty level in the same cities increased by 36%. The consequence of these two trends is that in the early 1980s a severe shortage occurred in housing that poor households could afford without bearing an excessive rent burden. Note that these calculations assume that such affordable housing rents for 40% or less of the poverty level, a larger proportion of income than the customary prudent 25% for rent.

Most of the housing I have discussed so far consists of multiroom units appropriate to families. If we restrict our attention to that portion of the housing stock that is ordinarily occupied by poor unattached single persons, then the decline is even more precipitous. Chicago's Planning Department estimated that between 1973 and 1984, 18,000 single-person dwelling units in SRO hotels and small apartment buildings—amounting to 19% of the stock existing in 1973—were demolished or transformed for other uses (Chicago Department of Planning 1985).* In Los Angeles a recent report (Hamilton, Rabinowitz and Alschuler, Inc. 1987) indicated that between 1970 and 1985 more than half of the SRO units in downtown Los Angeles had been demolished. Of course there is nothing wrong per se with the demolition of SROs; most were certainly not historical landmarks or examples of any notable architectural style. Nor can they be said to have been of high quality. The problem is that units comparable in function or price were not built or converted in sufficient volume to replace them. . . .

In 1958 about 8,000 homeless men were accommodated in such units in Chicago; by 1980 all the cubicle hotels had been removed.[†] In New York, by

---

*At the same time, 11,000 subsidized senior citizens' units had been added to the stock, and 8,500 section 8 senior citizens' housing vouchers were issued. Provision was made for replacing housing stock, but only for a portion of the single-person housing, that used by persons sixty-five and over.

†In 1980 the last two Chicago cubicle hotels, the Star and the Major, were demolished to be replaced by Presidential Towers, a 1,200-unit luxury apartment complex.

1987 only one of the cheap hotels that dominated the Bowery in the 1960s remained (Jackson 1987).* Similar changes have occurred in other large cities. Of course it is difficult to mourn the passing of the often dirty and always inadequate cubicle hotels. Like the SROs, they had little or no symbolic or aesthetic value. But only the emergency dormitory shelters have replaced the housing stock they represented. There are virtually no rooms in Chicago today that can be rented for $1.80 to $2.70 a night, today's dollar equivalent of the 1958 rents. The emergency dormitory shelters are arguably cleaner than the cubicle hotels, but they are certainly not much closer to decent housing. Indeed, the old Skid Row residents regarded the mission dormitory shelters as considerably inferior to the cubicle hotels, lacking in privacy and personal safety (Bogue 1963).†

The decline in inexpensive housing influences homelessness both directly and indirectly. Indirectly, the effect can be felt through the increased financial housing burden placed on poor families, whose generosity toward their dependent adult members becomes more difficult to extend or maintain. Housing prices partially reflect the amount of housing involved, with larger units commanding higher prices. Faced with declining real income, poor families may have had to opt for smaller dwellings, restricting their ability to shelter adult children.

The direct effects are upon the homeless themselves, putting inexpensive housing, such as SRO accommodations, beyond the reach of most of the new homeless. For example, in a study of SROs in Chicago, Hoch (1985) found that the average monthly rental for SRO hotels in Chicago in 1984 was $195 if rented by the month or $240 ($8 a day), if rented day to day. For most of the homeless, with median monthly incomes of $100, renting an SRO room steadily was out of the question.

Because rents were so high relative to income, the tenants of Chicago's SROs were forced to spend a very large proportion of their income on housing. When some out of the ordinary expense occurred, many had to resort to the shelters and the streets. According to Hoch, about one in ten of the SRO tenants had been homeless for some period during the previous year, apparently too short of funds to pay the rent. Hoch does not tell us whether these SRO tenants lived in shelters or on the streets when they became homeless. But in our survey of the Chicago homeless, both the shelter and the street samples claimed they spent about 10% of their nights in rented rooms, presumably in SRO hotels.

Some of the homeless people we interviewed on the streets or in the shelters ordinarily spent most nights in SRO hotels and were just temporarily homeless.‡ Others occasionally spent a night or two in an SRO, perhaps when

---

*Jackson's essay on the history of the Bowery relates that by 1987 gentrification had begun to convert land to upscale condominiums.

†The dormitory shelters in the old Skid Rows were those offered by the religious missions. At least part of the old Skid Row men's dislike for the shelters centered on the typical requirement that they attend religious services in return for access to the dormitory beds.

‡This information comes from interviewers' comments on the filled-out questionnaires. Unfortunately, we did not ask shelter residents for enough detailed information to estimate the prevalence of this pattern of intermittent homelessness.

they received a windfall. Apparently there is a considerable interchange between the homeless and the SRO populations, the latter being a cut above the former in income. Similarly, Piliavin and Sosin (1987–88) found that homeless people in Minneapolis typically moved between having homes and being homeless several times a year.

High rents relative to income also forced some of the SRO tenants to overspend on housing and, accordingly, to skimp on other expenditures. Hoch reports that many SRO residents resorted to the food kitchens, to the medical clinics set up for homeless persons, and to the clothing depots. In a study of the homeless in downtown Los Angeles, one out of every three persons in the soup-kitchen lines was renting a room in an SRO (Farr, Koegel, and Burnham 1986). Further confirmation can be found in Sosin's 1986 study of persons using Chicago food kitchens and day centers (Sosin, Colson, and Grossman 1988), which found that about half were living in SROs and apartments.

The impact of the housing market on homelessness in the aggregate was shown dramatically in a recent analysis by Tucker (1987). There are several deficiencies in Tucker's procedures; nevertheless, some of his findings are both useful and relevant. Using the HUD estimates[*] of the number of homeless in each of fifty cities to compute a homelessness rate for each city,[†] Tucker was able to show a fairly strong negative correlation, –.39, between housing vacancy rates in 1980 and homelessness rates in 1984 across cities. In other words, the higher the vacancy rate in a city, the lower its homelessness rate. Tucker also showed that the vacancy rate is highly sensitive to the presence of rent control measures, but that need not concern us here. The point Tucker's analysis drives home is that the tighter the housing market from the buyer's (or renter's) point of view, the greater the housing burden on poor families and the more difficult it becomes for the extremely poor to obtain housing, and consequently the easier it is to become homeless.

In a perfect unrestricted housing market, the range of housing offered by sellers at equilibrium would supply all buyers who can enter bids. But this statement is more a matter of faith than of fact. The American housing market is neither unfettered nor perfect. Nor would we have it any other way. Our building codes are designed to ensure that the housing industry provides accommodations that meet minimum standards of public health and safety. Zoning laws attempt to regulate the externalities surrounding existing structures. Occupancy laws discourage overcrowding of dwelling units. These regulations also accomplish other ends, some undesirable to many citizens: for

---

[*]These estimates are simply averages of what informed persons in the cities studied thought were the total number of homeless people there. Although no one can gauge their accuracy, it is likely that they reflect well the differences among cities in amount of homelessness. Note that these intercity differences in homelessness are the focus of Tucker's analysis.

[†]HUD analysts related the number of homeless people in each city to the population for the Rand McNally metropolitan area in which the city was situated, a strategy that was heavily criticized. Tucker computed his rates by using only the populations for the central cities.

example, zoning laws designed to ensure that structures occupy no more than some given proportion of urban land plots, a desirable aesthetic amenity, also make neighborhoods socioeconomically homogeneous. In some cities rent control is an additional restriction whose burden falls heavily on households entering the market and provides a bonus in the form of cheaper rents to long-term residents. These regulations are not the only factors restricting the amount of "affordable housing" available to the poor, but they certainly drive up the prices of even minimum standard housing.

However, there can be no market where there is no effective demand. The market cannot provide affordable housing for the homeless because their incomes are so low and variable that their demand is too weak to stimulate housing providers. The housing market was not always unresponsive to the demand of poor people. The Skid Rows of the nation were such responses, but the old cubicle hotels of the 1950s and 1960s were responding to a much stronger demand. Recall that the constant-dollar income of the Skid Row residents in 1958 was at least three times the income of the current homeless. Even so, as Bogue and the other social researchers observed in the 1950s and 1960s, the cubicle hotels were experiencing high vacancy rates.

The records are silent on whether the cubicle hotel owners and operators welcomed or fought the exercise of eminent domain in the urban renewal of Skid Row areas. Perhaps they welcomed the bulldozers as a way to recover some of the equity they had sunk into an increasingly unprofitable business.

In the past, when the housing industry was unable (or unwilling) to provide homes for the extremely poor they sometimes built their own. In the Great Depression of the 1930s, "shantytowns" consisting of shacks cobbled together out of scrap materials were built on New York's riverfronts and even in Central Park. Similar settlements were erected on Chicago's lakefront, in Washington's Anacostia Flats, and on vacant sites in other cities. In the 1980s no comparable settlements have appeared, unless one counts the cardboard and wooden packing cases used as living quarters by a few of the homeless. It may be that vacant land is not as available now or that law enforcement officials are quicker to respond.* Whatever has caused the difference, the self-help response of the homeless to market failure has not been as strong as in the past.

As the rents the homeless could afford declined with their incomes during the 1970s and 1980s, housing providers found them an increasingly unattractive set of customers, especially in contrast to others. There is no mystery about why no housing is offered on the unsubsidized market that is affordable to the homeless. If there is a question, it is why local, state, and federal government have not intervened in the market to ensure that such housing is supplied. . . .

---

*Indeed, in 1987 when homeless people in Los Angeles built a "tent city" on a vacant downtown parcel, the mayor ordered the police to tear it down. Temporary shacks and tents have been built in Washington's Lafayette Park, but they must be removed every evening.

❖ THE LABOR MARKET AND HOMELESSNESS

A major factor in the 1960s and 1970s decline of the Skid Rows was the shrinkage of the casual labor market in urban economies. This decline in labor demand is carefully documented in Barrett Lee's (1980) analysis of the trends in Skid Row populations in forty-one cities from 1950 to 1970, showing that as the proportion of each city's labor force employed in unskilled labor and unskilled service occupations declined in that period, so did the population of its Skid Row.

In earlier decades, urban employers needing muscle power to wrestle cargo apparently put up with the low productivity of the Skid Row inhabitants because they could hire them as needed for low pay. Apparently, materials-handling equipment such as forklifts put both the homeless and Skid Row out of business. Cause and effect are almost hopelessly muddled here. As Skid Row populations declined, employers may have been motivated to invest in equipment that lowered their need for casual labor, and at the same time the lowered need for such labor meant that Skid Rows were populated more and more by persons out of the labor force (e.g., pensioners either retired or disabled).

The lack of demand for unskilled labor contributes to contemporary homelessness and helps account for the poor employment and earnings records of the extremely poor and the homeless. Labor market factors are especially important in understanding the sharp decline in the average age of the extremely poor and the homeless over the past three decades. Between 1955 and 1985 there was a drastic increase in unemployment among young males in general and blacks in particular. Unemployment reached catastrophic proportions in 1985 with 40% rates among black males under twenty-five (Freeman and Holzer 1986). Freeman and Holzer showed that young black males were considerably more likely to be employed only for short periods and were more likely to be fired.

The demographic processes at work during the post—World War II period also help explain the declining average age of the homeless. Recent decades have seen a bulge in the proportion of persons in our population who are between twenty and thirty-five, an outcome of the postwar baby boom. This excess of young people, especially males, depressed the earnings level for young adults and elevated the unemployment rate. As Easterlin (1987) has shown, the earnings of workers under thirty-five declined between 1968 and 1984 to about 80% of the 1968 level, computed in constant dollars. In contrast, the real wages of workers forty-five to fifty-five rose in the same period to 125% of their 1968 levels. Easterlin showed similar trends in the unemployment rate. At the beginning of the period under study, unemployment rates for young men below thirty-five were under 5% and rose to a high of 15% in 1980, declining to 13% in 1984. Older workers did not show such fluctuations.

The point of this analysis of the labor market is to show that the employment opportunities for young men has been extremely poor over the same period when the homeless population has increased and its composition has changed, with a time lag of five to ten years. As usual, the burdens of a poor labor market fall disproportionately upon precisely those groups we find over-respresented among the homeless—the disabled and minorities.

The impact on females of labor market and demographic trends since 1965 is a little more subtle. Easterlin's analysis shows that young women did not suffer as much from increased unemployment and decreased earnings as young men, although their positions on the labor market certainly showed no improvement over time. In comparison with those of young men, their earnings did not show as radical a decline in real dollars, and unemployment rates did not rise as dramatically.

But there is also an indirect effect on household formation that did affect the proportion of women with children who are married and thus contributed to what has been called the feminization of poverty. . . . Homeless women are younger than homeless men—on the average five to ten years younger. Almost all the homeless heads of households were female. The abrupt rise in female-headed households from 1968 to 1984 in part reflects the uncertain economic fate of young men, who thereby become less attractive as mates, less willing to become household heads, and less able to fulfill the economic role of husband and father when marriage does take place.* In this respect it is significant that almost all the families housed in New York's welfare hotels are black or Hispanic female-headed households. Likewise, almost all the young homeless women we studied in Chicago were black, and almost all the homeless families were headed by black females.

In short, the uncertain labor market and earnings fates of young black men jeopardized family formation among young blacks. The consequence is that young black women became heads of extremely poor households with high risk of becoming periodically homeless. In his analysis of poverty among blacks in Chicago, Wilson (1987) attributes much of the rise in female-headed households to the lack of marriageable black males. Owing to their catastrophically high unemployment rates, few young black men were able to make economic contributions to the households formed by the mothers of their children, let alone be the major providers.

❖ THE LIMITS OF KINSHIP OBLIGATIONS

It is an easy wager that there are few if any readers of this book whose families and kin would allow them to sink into literal homelessness. It is another easy wager that few if any readers would allow a family member or a near relative to become homeless. At least that would be our initial reaction to someone

---

*Although few of the homeless men had married and those that had were divorced or separated, a majority (60%) claimed to be fathers. It is tempting to speculate how many of the fathers of the children in the homeless female-headed households are to be found among the homeless men.

close to us who had become destitute through disabling illness, severe alcoholism, or an episode of mental disturbance. We would certainly offer financial help and even make room in our homes. American norms concerning obligations owed to kin support strongly such actions.* But how long could we keep it up? One would not begrudge support over a few weeks or months or even a year, but imagine having to supply maintenance and food for several years and, in addition, to share crowded housing.

Sharing might not be too hard for those of us who have room to spare in our houses and apartments and who have some discretionary income left after we finance a reasonably good standard of living. The generous impulse would be harder to extinguish if the dependent family member or kin was well behaved and did nothing bizarre or in poor taste. Even so, it would be hard to put up with. Doubtless we all know, and admire, people in our circles of kin, friends, and acquaintances who have made such sacrifices for fairly long periods. . . .

In 1987 2.6 million extremely poor adult children aged twenty-two to fifty-nine were living in their parents' homes, and an additional 677,000 were living with siblings or grandparents. Of course many, if not most, of their families could sustain the additional burden: the household incomes of the supportive families were slightly above average. In addition, some families subsidized their impoverished adult members without taking them into their homes. Unfortunately, the Current Population Survey does not provide enough information so we can estimate the extent of such cash subsidies: we do know that there are at least 3.5 million impoverished dependent adults who are being subsidized by their parents and possibly as many as 6.5 million.

But now imagine the situation of poor parents, living at the poverty level or below in cramped quarters, on whom the responsibility for supporting an impoverished unemployed adult family member has fallen. How long could they keep it up? Imagine, in addition, that this dependent adult child has a serious alcohol or drug problem or has been in prison or exhibits the bizarre thinking or behavior of the chronically mentally ill.

It appears from our . . . data that the average life of tolerance and help under such conditions is about four years, the period that the homeless were without steady work before becoming homeless. For that length of time they were presumably supported by their families' and friends' sharing housing, food, and maintenance. In addition, keep in mind that the families and friends are also poor and all those necessities are in short supply. Indeed, it is also a euphemism to talk about families, since many of the homeless come from single-parent households: their mothers and siblings may have been all there was

---

*In a recent study of kinship norms, Alice Rossi and I found that almost all of a sample of metropolitan Boston adults acknowledged strong obligations to provide financial help to primary kin (parents, children, and siblings) who were suffering from the effects of illness, psychological difficulties, or unemployment.

to the "family" they relied on for support.[*] Piliavin and Sosin (1987) and Sosin, Colson, and Grossman (1988) comment that many of the homeless grew up in foster homes and may have had no parents at all or ones who were unable to fulfill their parental responsibilities.

There is good evidence that many of the homeless have worn out their welcome as dependents of their parents or as recipients of aid and funds from their friends. . . . striking differences [exist] between the extremely poor unattached persons in the General Assistance population and the homeless. . . . the groups are almost equally destitute, but most of the GA recipients are not living in shelters or out on the streets.

There are other important differences between the two groups that go along with their living arrangements. First, the levels of disability among GA clients are much lower on every indicator we can find in the data. Chronic mental illness, alcoholism, serious criminal records, and physical illnesses are far less prevalent among the domiciled. Second, the GA recipients largely manage to get by because their family and friendship support networks subsidize them, either by providing housing and maintenance or by supplementing their income.

Recall also that the GA recipients are on the average six years younger than the homeless men, suggesting that they have not yet worn out their welcome in their parents' households. Their much lower levels of alcoholism and chronic mental illness may also mean it is more acceptable to share housing with them. At least some of the GA recipients may thus simply be younger versions of the homeless and may wear out their acceptance if their dependence goes on too long. The demoralizing and debilitating effects of long-term unemployment undoubtedly also play a role: the longer a person goes unemployed, the more likely it is that the disabilities of depression, mental illness, and even alcoholism will take their toll.

I suggest that the poverty of the families the homeless come from and their levels of disability both contribute heavily to their being homeless. Generosity may come up against the constraints of poverty when disability makes it difficult to exercise that virtue.

❖ THE EROSION OF PUBLIC WELFARE BENEFITS

We have seen that at least part of the burden of supporting extremely poor unattached persons is borne by poverty-stricken households who stretch their meager resources to house and maintain dependent adult children and sometimes friends. We can see national trends in young people living with their parents, especially among the poor. Indeed, black young men are especially likely

---

[*]Many of the mothers may also have been on AFDC during much of the time the sons were growing up and in their late teens or early adulthood. The Chicago AFDC study showed that 10% of AFDC recipients had children over eighteen living in their households.

to live in their parents' households. According to the census, in 1970, 39% of both black and white young men aged eighteen to twenty-nine lived with their parents. By 1984, 54% of black young men lived with their parents while only 41% of white men of comparable age did so.

Evidence for the extent of the burden on poor families is difficult to come by, since we do not know much about the households the homeless come from. But we do know that those households are poor and that many are supported by welfare—in particular, AFDC payments. Strong indicators of the declining positions of poor families can be found in the downward trends of transfer payments from 1968 to 1985. The level of welfare benefits also directly affects the capacity of the extremely poor to take care of themselves without the help of their parents. It is obvious that at the heart of homelessness and extreme poverty are the extremely low incomes of those groups. Among those states that have programs of income support to unattached persons, none provides enough to reach $4,000 a year. In addition, there are many states—for example, Texas, Alabama, and Tennessee—that have no income support programs at all for this segment of the population.

The importance of income support in alleviating extreme poverty is obvious. What is not obvious is that income support programs that cover unattached people below retirement age have undergone a severe deterioration in value over the past decade and a half, exacerbating the erosion of the life chances of the poor caused by labor and housing market trends. . . .

On the national level, in 1985 AFDC payments declined to 63% of their 1968 value. Illinois AFDC payments declined to 53% of 1968 value in the same period. An even more drastic decline occurred in Illinois's General Assistance payments, the program most often available to homeless persons and to unattached persons generally: 1985 General Assistance payments in Illinois were only 48% of 1968 payments in constant dollars. The major drop in value of these two transfer programs occurred in the five years between 1975 and 1980, reflecting the ravages of inflationary trends that were not sufficiently compensated for by raising payment levels.* As the burden of supporting unemployed adults fell upon families who in turn were dependent on AFDC or GA payments, such poor families entered the 1980s with considerably diminished financial capability and hence reduced capacity to help.

In addition, the reduction in the real value of AFDC payments contributed directly to the appearance of female-headed households among the homeless. Female-headed households dependent on AFDC surely must have had a hard time meeting housing and other expenses on payments that barely covered average rents for small apartments. Living so close to the edge of

---

*Of course there were some compensatory increases in other programs for which unemployed persons became eligible. Food stamps in 1985 could provide an additional $70 in food purchases, a benefit of dubious value to the homeless. Medicaid coverage was also extended in some states (Illinois, for example) and provided for most medical needs. Although food stamps and housing subsidies compensate in a very direct way for low income, Medicare or Medicaid is more questionable: you cannot pay the rent or eat with Medicaid coverage.

financial disaster and often slipping into crisis, households headed by young females understandably often become literally homeless. Indeed, it is difficult to understand how the typical Illinois AFDC household composed of a mother and her 1.5 children managed to get by on $4,014 a year in direct cash payments and $798 in food stamps. More than a third of the AFDC households received help from other persons (presumably relatives) over a year's time. The Chicago AFDC study provides considerable evidence that AFDC families had a tenuous hold on their housing, with close to one in four experiencing problems over the previous year.

Illinois's AFDC payment schedule in 1985 and 1986 was among the ten most generous state plans. AFDC households in Illinois fared much better than comparable households in, say, Alabama or Texas, where payments averaged under $2,000 a year. Indeed, a major reason the extremely poor female-headed households were concentrated in the southern regions was that even with AFDC payments total annual income rarely reached $2,000.

The similar drop in the dollar value of General Assistance payments also influenced homelessness. General Assistance payments in 1968 were generous enough to cover SRO rent, with a bit left over for other types of consumption. In addition, in 1968 unattached adults on General Assistance had enough income from their benefits to make significant contributions to the income of a household, possibly making their dependence more palatable to their hosts. By 1985, with General Assistance payments more than cut in half, GA clients could neither make large contributions to host households nor get by on their own.*

The low levels of GA benefits may help explain why so few homeless applied for and received them. Such benefits were not enough to allow recipients to leave the homeless state and were difficult to obtain. Applying for GA benefits in 1984, as described by Stagner and Richman (1986), involved at least three interviews with Illinois Department of Public Aid caseworkers, a determination of employability, and an assignment either to an unemployable class or to a "jobs" program in which a person had to sustain eligibility by applying for work to at least eight employers a month. A person assigned to the jobs program who did not find employment within sixty days was assigned either to the unemployable class or to a public service workfare task. Keeping to the complex schedule of interviews and reporting requirements must have been difficult for the homeless.

---

*Contributions toward rent reported by the GA recipients were more than half of the benefit level received, as shown below:

Living Arrangements	Average Monthly Rent or Contribution
Living alone	$159
Living with nonrelatives	$122
Living with relatives	$ 97

Note that GA recipients living alone paid more in rent, on the average, than they received in GA payments. Most (84%) GA recipients living alone also received help from their relatives. (Unfortunately the survey did not ascertain either the kind or the amount of help received. It is a fair presumption, however, that financial help must have loomed large.)

Table 1 also contains clues to why so few aged persons are found among the homeless and the extremely poor in the 1980s. Fewer than 2% of the Chicago homeless were sixty-five or over. Only 500,000 of the extremely poor persons in the 1987 Current Population Survey were sixty-one or older with incomes under $4,000. Old age Social Security retirement benefits increased by 162% from 1968 to 1985, thanks to favorable changes in the benefit levels in 1972 plus the indexing of such benefits by tying them to the consumer price index. The constant-dollar value of the average old age pension in Illinois in 1968 was slightly below the value of General Assistance payments, but by 1985 it had increased by 164% and was 3.3 times the value of General Assistance.

Note also that the absolute amount of Illinois average monthly old age pension payments in 1985, $511, was enough to rent accommodations at the bottom portion of the conventional housing market and certainly sufficient for the subsidized senior citizens' housing developments.

The sharply enhanced economic well-being of the elderly is one of the great program success stories of the twentieth century. Throughout the century, until the 1970s, the elderly were greatly overrepresented among the poor; today, for the first time in our history, the poverty rate for persons aged sixty-five and over is less than that for the rest of the population. How this was accomplished says a lot about how the problem of homelessness will have to be solved, if indeed it ever is. We virtually wiped out poverty among the aged by providing generous benefits. Public spending on the elderly, through Social Security pensions, Medicare, and housing subsidies, dwarfs every other item in the federal human services budget.*

There are two main lessons to be drawn from the past decade's decline in welfare. First, our policies have undermined the income positions of the extremely poor and the capacity of poor families to care for their dependent adult members. In every state, income support programs for unattached persons are not generous enough to support minimum standard housing and diet. In addition, by allowing welfare payments to be eaten away by inflation, we have reduced the capacity of families to care for their dependent adult members. Second, we have not sufficiently assimilated the lessons of the recent history of the Social Security retirement program. By providing decent payment levels, this program has virtually wiped out homelessness and extreme poverty among the aged.

❖ AN INTERPRETATION OF HOMELESSNESS

Throughout this book I have described the characteristics of the current homeless, highlighting those that mark off this population from that of the old Skid

---

*In 1984 the total federal social welfare expenditure was $419 billion. Social Security pensions and Medicare expenditures alone amounted to $302 billion, 72% of the total social welfare expenditure. See *Statistical Abstract of the United States: 1987* (Washington, D.C.: U.S. Department of Commerce, 1986, table 574).

Rows and from the current domiciled poor. Drawing these various threads together, we can now begin to weave an explanation both of why some people are more likely to be found among the homeless and of why homelessness has apparently increased over the past decade.

First of all, it is important to distinguish between the short-term (episodic) homeless, and the long-term (chronic) homeless who appear likely to remain so. Most of what I have to say . . . concerns the latter group; the former consists primarily of people in the lower ranks of the income distribution who meet short-term reversals of fortune. This is not to deemphasize the problems of the short-term homeless but simply to say that their problems are different.

The "dynamics" of episodic homelessness are distressingly straightforward. So long as there is a poverty population whose incomes put them at the economic edge, there will always be people who fall over that edge into homelessness. Small setbacks that those above the poverty line can absorb may become major disruptions to the very poor. Several homely examples illustrate this point. The failure of an old refrigerator or stove and a subsequent repair bill of $50 can make the nonpoor grumble about bad luck, but for someone whose monthly income is under $500 and whose rent is $300, the bill represents one-fourth of the monthly resources used to buy food, clothing, and other necessities. For a poor person who depends on a car to travel to work, a car repair bill of a few hundred dollars may mean months of deprivation. Renting an apartment increasingly means paying one month's rent in advance and perhaps a security deposit as well and is often why poor people remain in substandard housing. In many states welfare programs make provision for such emergency expenses, but the unattached person who is not eligible for welfare may experience wide swings of fortune, with the downsides spent among the homeless.

The solution is to be found in extending the coverage of the social welfare system and incorporating provisions that would cushion against short-term economic difficulties.

What about the long-term or chronic homeless? Their critical characteristic is the high level of disabilities that both impair their earning capacity and reduce their acceptance by their families, kin, and friends. These are the people who are most strongly affected by shortages of unskilled positions in the labor force, lack of inexpensive housing, and declines in the economic fortunes of their families, kin, and friends. Under these unfavorable conditions, unattached persons with disabilities have increasing difficulty in getting along on their own. And as the living conditions of poor households decline, those disabled by chronic mental or physical illnesses or by chronic substance abuse are no longer tolerated as dependents.

Note that I am using the term disabled in this context to mark any condition that appreciably impairs the ability to make minimally successful connections with the labor market and to form mutually satisfactory relationships with family, kin, and friends. This definition goes beyond the usual meaning of disability to include a much wider set of conditions—for example, criminal records that interfere with employment chances or chronic problems with drinking, as well as physical and psychiatric impairments.

Let me emphasize that this interpretation is not "blaming the victim." It is an attempt to explain who become the victims of perverse macrolevel social forces. If there is any blame, it should be placed on the failure of the housing market, labor market, and welfare system, which forces some people—the most vulnerable—to become victims by undermining their ability to get along by themselves and weakening the ability of family, kin, and friends to help them. . . .

The resurgence of extreme poverty and homelessness in the past two decades should remind us that the safety nets we initiated during the Great Depression and augmented in the 1960s are failing to prevent destitution. The Reagan administration did not succeed in dismantling any significant portion of the net, but it made the mesh so coarse and weak that many fall through. Those who are disabled by minority status, chronic mental illness, physical illness, or substance abuse are especially vulnerable. All the very poor suffer, but it is the most vulnerable who fall to the very bottom—homelessness.

The social welfare system has never been very attentive to unattached, disaffiliated men, and now it appears to be as unresponsive to unattached females. Likewise, the social welfare system does little to help families support their dependent adult members. Many of the homeless of the 1950s and early 1960s were pushed out or thrown away by their families when they passed the peak of adulthood; many of the new homeless are products of a similar process, but this one commences at age twenty-five or thirty rather than at fifty or sixty.

As a consequence, homelessness now looms large on our political agenda, and there is anxious concern about what can be done. I have suggested a number of measures to reduce homelessness to a more acceptable level. These include compensating for the failure of our housing market by fostering the retention and enlargement of our urban low-income housing stock, especially that appropriate for unattached persons; reversing the policy that has put personal choice above institutionalization for those so severely disabled that they are unable to make decisions that will preserve their physical well-being; enlarging our conception of disability to include conditions not purely physical in character and, in particular, recognizing that chronic mental illness and chronic substance abuse are often profound disabilities; restoring the real value of welfare payments to the purchasing power they had in the late 1960s; and extending the coverage of welfare benefits to include long-term unemployed, unattached persons.

There is considerable public support in the United States for a social welfare system that guarantees a minimally decent standard of living to all. Homelessness on the scale currently being experienced is clear evidence that such a system is not yet in place. That homelessness exists amid national prosperity without parallel in the history of the world is likewise clear evidence that we can do something about the problem if we choose to. I have stressed that public policy decisions have in large measure created the problem of homelessness; they can solve the problem as well.

12

HUNGER IN AMERICA: THE GROWING EPIDEMIC

PHYSICIAN TASK FORCE ON HUNGER IN AMERICA

One cannot help but appreciate the special irony of hunger in America's breadbasket. The prolific crops which spring from the fertile land produce hundreds of thousands of tons of grains and other food products, so much that each year millions of excess tons are stored in underground caves. Yet American citizens living within a short distance of this productive system are hungry.

The huge, overwhelming complex of buildings known as Cook County Hospital is located right in the middle of Chicago, the nation's third-largest city. It is an unlikely place to find kwashiorkor and marasmus, the Third World diseases of advanced malnutrition and starvation, which were reported to us in south Texas. As our team of doctors listened, joined by the Administrator of the hospital and the Chief of Internal Medicine, Dr. Stephen Nightingale, we learned that these conditions do exist in urban America: "They say we don't see kwashiorkor and marasmus in this country, but we do. I see 15–20 cases every year in my hospital."

The person speaking was Dr. Katherine K. Christoffel, Chair of the Committee on Nutrition of the Illinois Chapter of the American Academy of Pediatrics. The hospital about which she spoke is Children's Memorial Hospital, where she is Attending Pediatrician in the Division of Ambulatory Services.

Despite her impressive credentials, members of the visiting team of physicians remained skeptical until her report was corroborated by yet another Chicago doctor with his own impressive credentials and experience.

Dr. Howard B. Levy is Chairman of Pediatrics at Mount Sinai Hospital, and previously was Chief of Pediatric Nephrology at the Walter Reed Army Medical Center in Washington, D.C. A member of the American Academy of Pediatrics and the American Medical Association, Dr. Levy joined us to express concern about what he is seeing: "We too are seeing kwashiorkor and marasmus, problems which I have not seen since I was overseas. Malnutrition has clearly gone up in the last few years. We have more low-birth-weight babies. We are seeing so much TB that my house staff is no longer excited by it; it excites me that they are not excited by this trend."

Dr. Levy underscored the significance of what he was reporting: "clear, measurable, methodological phenomena" which demonstrate that the health of the patients is getting worse. More and more patients, Dr. Levy observed, have inadequate money to purchase food necessary to prevent growth failure and other nutrition-related problems among the pediatric population.

Well-known Chicago pediatrician Effie Ellis concurred with this observation: "We have a problem here of serious proportions. Social service agencies are having to provide medicines, and hospitals and clinics are having to give out food."

Cook County Hospital gives out food itself and is asked regularly for more by hungry patients. Dr. Nightingale, the Internal Medicine Chief, said that he admits 20 people a day whose problems stem from inadequate nutrition. Pediatric social worker Brenda Chandler has patients come to her saying, "Do you have anything I could eat?" Dietitian Mary Jo Davis sees hunger among "patients" who are not really admitted to the hospital. "Almost every day we have people looking around trying to find out where the hospital leaves its garbage," she reported. Elaborating, she added: "Our hospital patients can't worry about special diets; they do well just to have food in their homes. Sometimes we do dietary recalls over the past three to four days for patients and find that the pages are entirely blank!"

The Chicago Department of Human Services reported that applicants for emergency food have increased 900% in the last two years, a phenomenon seen by social service and religious organizations in the city. The Salvation Army presented statistics showing hunger up significantly for 1984 over 1983, and other agencies, such as the Association House, state that hunger is their number one problem.

Betty Williams of Chicago United Charities placed the mounting hunger problem in a unique perspective: "Our agency is over 100 years old, and this period is as bad as many of us can recall." According to Joel Carp, Chairman of the Mayor's Task Force on Hunger, at least 600,000 Chicago residents are hungry or likely to be hungry every month. These are people of all ages living well below the federal poverty line: people, he said, "like the old folks on the North Side whom we found living on dog food."

Later that day, some of our team of doctors would confirm this report during their visit to the Marillac House, a large Catholic settlement house in the city. In discussions with the director and her staff, as well as home visits conducted in a housing project, we learned that it is not uncommon for elderly people, living alone in apartments with no cooking facilities, to consume an evening meal of a tin of cat food and a raw egg.

The mayor's office reported that at least 224,000 residents seek emergency food assistance each month, and that the actual number may be twice as high. To respond to the increasing demand, the number of soup kitchens in the city jumped over 80% in the last two years, and now serve 11,500 meals a week. The number of church-related food pantries increased 45% in the same period of time. . . .

The Chicago Health Systems Agency presented survey data to the mayor's office showing food distribution in the city between 1981 and 1983, as part of the city's Emergency Food Program. Approved requests for food assistance rose from 19,312 the first year to 223,500 the last year.

Another barometer of food assistance to the hungry is the Greater Chicago Food Depository, which distributes 400% more food today than it did two years ago. . . . Increasing need is one variable at which we looked. Another is the profile of the hungry and the impact of hunger on their lives. In southwest Chicago our inquiry into the situation faced by laid-off steelworkers at the Wisconsin Plant could have taken place at the Armco Plant in Houston. Frustrated and angry, unemployed workers and their families stand in line for a 5-pound block of cheese and a loaf of bread. Frank Lumkin, president of the Save Our Jobs Committee, explained the dimensions of the problem. "It's having 100 bags of food to give to the families and finding 500 people show up, already in line, at 7:00 A.M."

The hungry are also the elderly. There are 8,000 poor elderly in need of food who are not being served, according to Chicago Office for Senior Citizens. Director Robert Ahrens points out that it is believed that this figure is considerably under the number who are in need of food.

The hungry in Chicago are the families seen by the Visiting Nurse Association, whose district offices have been forced to open food pantries to respond to the lack of food among their patients. "These babies are hungry," implored executive director Margaret Ahern. But, according to her, not only babies. She cited many instances of parents and the elderly also going hungry, some whose caloric intake is as low as 550 calories and 24 grams of protein. "In the prison camps of Germany," she noted, "the daily ration was 800 calories and 40 grams of protein."

The hungry are the patients at the South Lawndale Health Center. The medical director, Dr. Alvarez, and the clinic staff report that health problems related to poor nutrition are not uncommon. Some 10% of their pediatric patients have iron-deficiency anemia, and pulmonary tuberculosis is seen in young people they serve, itself often a result of compromised nutrition. Health workers note that, when they do home visits, they find families unable to purchase adequate food. Children often consume only coffee and an egg for a meal.

The hungry, according to other Chicago agencies, are the undocumented workers whose fear of being deported prevents their even standing in line for cheese. Hector Hernandez sees the realities faced by these families, who come through the Immigrant Services branch of the Traveler's Aid office. Hernandez says that the families often have very little to eat and receive no help as a general rule. Many of them, he explained, have children born in the United States. Yet, if parents seek help such as emergency food assistance, they stand the risk of being reported to Immigration. Immigration may well attempt to deport the parents of the children who are U.S. citizens, thereby breaking apart the family. In this fundamental sense, he explained, the ability of some American children to eat brings with it the likelihood that they will lose their parents.

Hunger in Chicago is the faces, young and old, black and white, of people living on the margins, and many who live beyond the margins of a full stomach:

- The 81-year-old man and his wife who come for a meal at the Uptown Ministries, who live on $293 monthly in social security benefits and $24 in food stamps. They eat mostly grits and oatmeal, sometimes rice and beans.

- The 30-year-old woman whose acknowledged racism was turned around when she saw more people suffering who are white, as she is, than blacks and Spanish. "I used to go without food just so my kids could eat, but now they often go without also."

- The patient in a hospital who, along with her three children, stuffed food into their mouths by hand. They had had nothing to eat for three days.

- The mothers whom doctors find diluting their infant's formula in order to make it last the month.

These American citizens are hungry. They are the "anecdotes" which together reflect and comprise a large problem in this city—people without adequate food to eat. They are the individuals behind the numbers which Dr. Howard Levy and his medical colleagues in the city tabulate: increasing low-birth-weight rates, 50% anemia rates, and the high proportion of children failing to grow, which other doctors noted in a recent study.

"These people are human beings," Charles Betcher reminded us when we visited the soup kitchen at the Uptown Baptist Church. "You can't live long on two pieces of bread a day." Both the center at which Betcher works and this church are among the many agencies in the area trying to feed the hungry, a task that is getting bigger, not smaller.

It is perhaps what Jack Ramsey, director of Second Harvest, umbrella organization for food banks around the nation, had in mind when he observed: "When you see government agencies making referrals to small food pantries that are running out of resources, that's an American tragedy."

Ramsey was not the only person to see the extent of hunger in this major city as a tragedy. Psychiatrist Gordon Harper, a physician who has examined hunger in other regions of the nation, visited a soup kitchen run by the Missionaries of Charity, the order started by Mother Teresa in Calcutta. Reported Dr. Harper: "We observed the spectacle and the tragedy of Missionaries of Charity coming from Calcutta to the West Side of Chicago to provide food for the hungry in America." . . .

Throughout the breadbasket region of southern Illinois, agencies feeding the hungry report increasing need. In June, 1984, the Salvation Army conducted a telephone survey of ten food pantries located in various counties in downstate Illinois. . . . Selected randomly to present a representative picture of pantry experience, the agencies were asked to compare caseloads (however they maintained their records) this year and last. Only one pantry, the Salvation Army in West Frankfort, reported a slight decline in need, a factor attributed to a union and other churches in the town opening food facilities. All the rest report increasing hunger.

The Salvation Army survey reflects the data reported by others whose records we examined. The Friendship House in Peoria, which went from feeding 400 families in 1982 to 2,400 in 1984, perhaps depicts the dimensions of the problem in that city, where hunger is of unusual proportions. Zack Monroe, Peoria welfare director for some 32 years, sat before statistical tables piled on his desk as he analyzed trends over recent years: "Things are getting worse, not better. Even in the Depression there weren't as many people in need of help as now."

"I grew up in the Depression," reported a woman at an elderly feeding site. "I never thought I'd see this again." But there is evidence of Depression-like hunger and suffering in this area. At the Labor Temple in Peoria, we met with unemployed workers and their families. "Thank you for coming," the business manager said as he welcomed our group of doctors, "and for trying to understand the pain and suffering in our lives."

A 30-year-old woman, neatly dressed and self-confident, spoke first. Employed until her factory closed, she and her son now live on AFDC and food stamps, a total income of $368 monthly. "I don't like coming here to reveal my personal life in front of everyone," she admitted, "but I got to because of my son. I'm willing to work, I always have. Just try me."

Among numerous others speaking was a 53-year-old Army veteran, a painter out of work for two years. A tanned, lined face and light hair reflected the features of many in this region of the nation. Now with no income, no car insurance, and his children studying by candlelight since his electricity was shut off, he and his family frequently go hungry. "I was reluctant to apply for food stamps," he says. "The politicians keep saying there aren't enough to go around, so you think someone else needs them more than you. You keep hoping the phone will ring."

Another worker, sitting silently until prodded by his wife, who reported that her husband is a good man and tries hard to provide for his family, told his plight. He can't find work, and his family cannot live on what income he does receive. "You keep thinking you'll progress to middle-class, but instead you get poorer. My mother got us through the last Depression, and now I somehow got to get us through this one."

Peoria, Illinois, the all-American city. Southern Illinois, heart of American agricultural production. We found substantial hunger in this region of the nation, suffering reminiscent, as so many of the residents reminded us, of the Depression some 50 years ago.

In the 1930s, American farms produced more inconsistently. Today, they produce enough, some say, to feed the world. Yet many people who used to work those farms, and the workers who once built the machinery by which others farm, are now hungry.

Eighty-six-year-old Effie Alsop is hungry, but only sometimes. As the doctors talked to her in the living room of her modest home in the southern Missouri town of Caruthersville, Mrs. Alsop was a picture of emaciation:

Q: What did you eat today?
A: Nothing.
Q: You've had nothing all day?
A: No.
Q: You must get hungry.
A: I get hungry when food is in the house, but when I don't have any I'm not hungry. Isn't that funny, doctor?

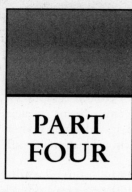

PART
FOUR

RACISM

During the 1960s, the successful struggle for legislation to enforce equal opportunity for minorities—in jobs, housing, and education—created the hope that government action would effectively remove the most important barriers to racial equality in American society. This sense of optimism was enhanced by the expectation of an ever-expanding economy, which seemed to promise that there would be room for everyone to have a chance at the good life in America.

To some extent, these expectations were borne out—for a while. Blacks and other minorities made significant social and economic progress, particularly in the 1960s, as a result of civil rights protest, government action, and an expanding economy. But the urban riots of the sixties also showed a more ominous side of the racial picture and revealed that some aspects of racial disadvantage in the United States were relatively impervious to both economic growth and the expansion of civil rights. And during the 1970s and early 1980s, some of the gains made by minorities in earlier years began to be reversed. Minority income fell behind as a proportion of white income, and minority poverty—especially in the inner cities—increased sharply. A combination of unfavorable economic trends, a less generous public policy, and a waning commitment to the vigorous enforcement of civil rights laws have taken their toll on minority progress in the past several years. The depth of the disaster for many inner-city minorities was brutally revealed in the explosion of rioting in Los Angeles in 1992—the worst single urban civil disorder in America in this century.

At the same time, a series of ugly and tragic incidents—at Bensonhurst and Howard Beach in New York City, and on a number of college campuses—revealed all too clearly that the most virulent and dangerous forms of racial animosity were still deeply entrenched in America. Race, in short, still matters very much in the United States, as the articles in this section illustrate in various ways.

In 1989, the government-funded National Research Council pulled together much of what social scientists had learned about the progress of black Americans in recent decades. In this excerpt from their report, "Blacks and American Society," the council shows that in every area of American life—from education to jobs to housing and more—blacks remain disadvantaged relative to whites 25 years after the passage of the Civil Rights Act. There has been considerable improvement, to be sure—a good part of it resulting from strong antidiscrimination measures. But the historic gap between black and white Americans "has only been narowed; it has not closed." And the recent crisis of the American economy means that the future, for many African-Americans, is even more uncertain.

The 20 million Hispanic residents in the United States, according to Rafael Valdivieso and Cary Davis in "U.S. Hispanics: Challenging Issues for the 1990s," suffer not only from high rates of poverty, underemployment, and dropping out of school but also from a kind of invisibility that hobbles effective policies to deal with those problems. Even the term "Hispanic" itself is a kind of catchall that blurs important distinctions among different groups. But, as Hispanics move into the schools and the labor force in ever-greater numbers, the need to address the causes of their disadvantage, especially through better education and job training and attacking discrimination in hiring and promotion at work, becomes ever more urgent.

Americans of Asian descent often confront their own kind of invisibility, as Ronald Takaki shows in "Asian-Americans: The Myth of the Model Minority." According to the 1990 census, the "Asian or Pacific Islander" population in the United States nearly doubled during the 1980s, to over 7 million people divided among a wide range of groups from very different countries and very different traditions—from the more than 1.6 million Chinese to over 800,000 Asian Indians to the 90,000 Hmong immigrants from rural Southeast Asia. But Americans from other origins often know little about them, and what they think they know is often wrong. Part of the problem is that the very real educational and economic successes of some Asian-American groups mask the difficulties faced by others—especially the growing Southeast Asian population—who face high rates of poverty, unemployment, school problems, and preventable diseases. Nor does the success of some Asian-Americans mean that discrimination against them has disappeared. Despite considerable upward mobility, Asians often run into a "glass ceiling" in the job hierarchy—and, especially in a time of economic crisis, often face brutal, overt racism in the streets as well.

As Takaki notes, Asian-American success has also sometimes been used to disparage others who haven't moved as far up the economic ladder. In the face of the continuing—and in some ways worsening—situation of some American minority groups, there has been a resurgence of theories attempting to blame this outcome on some deficiency of culture or motivation in the groups themselves rather than on adverse forces in the larger society. If other groups have "made it" in America despite obstacles, the typical refrain goes, "why can't they?" But, as Stanley Lieberson shows in "A Piece of the Pie," what this rather self-righteous argument ignores is that the experience of different groups can't be so simply equated. Though some other ethnic groups faced considerable discrimination and prejudice in the American past, the barriers faced by blacks have been uniquely formidable, and we won't understand the current situation of different groups without taking that difference into account.

BLACKS AND AMERICAN SOCIETY

NATIONAL RESEARCH COUNCIL

Just five decades ago, most black Americans could not work, live, shop, eat, seek entertainment, or travel where they chose. Even a quarter century ago—100 years after the Emancipation Proclamation of 1863—most blacks were effectively denied the right to vote. A large majority of blacks lived in poverty, and very few black children had the opportunity to receive a basic education; indeed, black children were still forced to attend inferior and separate schools in jurisdictions that had not accepted the 1954 decision of the Supreme Court declaring segregated schools unconstitutional.

Today the situation is very different. In education, many blacks have received college degrees from universities that formerly excluded them. In the workplace, blacks frequently hold professional and managerial jobs in desegregated settings. In politics, most blacks now participate in elections, and blacks have been elected to all but the highest political offices. Overall, many blacks have achieved middle-class status.

Yet the great gulf that existed between black and white Americans in 1939 has only been narrowed; it has not closed. One of three blacks still live in households with incomes below the poverty line. Even more blacks live in areas where ineffective schools, high rates of dependence on public assistance,

From National Research Council, *Blacks and American Society,* Washington, DC, National Academy of Sciences Press, 1989. Reprinted by permission. Portions of the original have been omitted.

severe problems of crime and drug use, and low and declining employment prevail. Race relations, as they affect the lives of inhabitants of these areas, differ considerably from black-white relations involving middle-class blacks. Lower status blacks have less access to desegregated schools, neighborhoods, and other institutions and public facilities. Their interactions with whites frequently emphasize their subordinate status—as low-skilled employees, public agency clients, and marginally performing pupils.

The status of black Americans today can be characterized as a glass that is half full—if measured by progress since 1939—or as a glass that is half empty—if measured by the persisting disparities between black and white Americans since the early 1970s. Any assessment of the quality of life for blacks is also complicated by the contrast between blacks who have achieved middle-class status and those who have not.

The progress occurred because sustained struggles by blacks and their allies changed American law and politics, moving all governments and most private institutions from support of principles of racial inequality to support of principles of racial equality. Gradually, and often with much resistance, the behaviors and attitudes of individual whites moved in the same direction. Over the 50-year span covered by this study, the social status of American blacks has *on average* improved dramatically, both in absolute terms and relative to whites. The growth of the economy and public policies promoting racial equality led to an erosion of segregation and discrimination, making it possible for a substantial fraction of blacks to enter the mainstream of American life.

The reasons for the continuing distress of large numbers of black Americans are complex. Racial discrimination continues despite the victories of the civil rights movement. Yet, the problems faced today by blacks who are isolated from economic and social progress are less directly open to political amelioration than were the problems of legal segregation and the widely practiced overt discrimination of a few decades past. Slow overall growth of the economy during the 1970s and 1980s has been an important impediment to black progress; in the three previous decades economic prosperity and rapid growth had been a great help to most blacks. Educational institutions and government policies have not successfully responded to underlying changes in the society. Opportunities for upward mobility have been reduced for all lower status Americans, but especially for those who are black. If all racial discrimination were abolished today, the life prospects facing many poor blacks would still constitute major challenges for public policy. . . .

■ Blacks and Whites in a Changing Society

Two general developments in the status of black Americans stand out; each is reflective of a near-identical development in the population at large. First, for the period 1940–1973, real earnings of Americans improved steadily, but they stagnated and declined after 1973. Similarly, over these same periods, there was a clear record of improving average material status of blacks relative to whites followed by stagnation and decline. Second, during the post-1973 period, inequality increased among Americans as the lowest income and least skilled people were hurt most by changes in the overall economy. Similarly, there were increasing differences in material well-being and opportunities among blacks, and they have been extremely pronounced.

These developments may be understood as consequences of four interdependent events that have altered the status of blacks, relative black-white status, and race relations in the United States. These events were the urbanization and northern movement of the black population from 1940 to 1970; the civil rights movement that forced the nation to open its major institutions to black participation during the same three decades; the unprecedented high and sustained rate of national economic growth for roughly the same period; and the significant slowdown in the U.S. economy since the early 1970s.

The civil rights movement, blacks' more proximate location near centers of industrial activity, and high economic growth enabled those blacks best prepared to take advantage of new opportunities to respond with initiative and success. Increases in educational opportunities were seized by many blacks who were then able to translate better educations into higher status occupations than most blacks had ever enjoyed. Black incomes and earnings rose generally, with many individuals and families reaching middle-class and even upper middle income status. . . . The new black middle class moved into better housing, frequently in the suburbs, and sometimes in desegregated neighborhoods. Despite much confrontation between whites and blacks as blacks abandoned traditional approaches to black-white relations, race relations eventually advanced closer to equal treatment.

At the same time, many blacks were not able to take advantage of the new conditions that developed: some were still located in areas relatively untouched by the changes; some lacked the family support networks to provide assistance; for some, better opportunities simply did not arise. Those who were left behind during the 1960s and 1970s faced and still face very different situations than poor blacks immediately before that period.

A major reason is the performance of the economy. Real weekly earnings (in constant 1984 dollars) of all American men, on average, fell from $488 in 1969 to $414 in 1984; real weekly earnings of women fell from $266 in 1969 to $230 in 1984. For the first time since the Great Depression of the 1930s, American men born in one year (e.g., 1960) may face lower lifetime real earnings than men born 10 years earlier. . . . Among the myriad and complex responses to these economic conditions have been rising employment rates among women, but falling rates among men, while the unemployment rates of both men and women have been on an upward trend for three decades. . . .

A generation ago, a low-skilled man had relatively abundant opportunity to obtain a blue-collar job with a wage adequate to support a family at a lower middle class level or better. Today the jobs available to such men—and women—are often below or just barely above the official poverty line for a family of four. For example, black males aged 25–34, with some high school but no diploma, earned on average $268 weekly in 1986; in 1969, black male dropouts of that age had averaged $334 weekly (in constant 1984 dollars). For white men of the same age and education, work conditions have been better, but changes over time cannot be said to have been good: in the years 1969 and 1986, mean weekly earnings were $447 and $381. Thus, among men who did not complete high school, blacks and whites had lower real earnings in 1986 than in 1969.

Obtaining a well-paying job increasingly requires a good education or a specific skill. Many young blacks and whites do not obtain such training, and the educational system in many locations is apparently not equipped to provide them. Recent reports on the state of American education sound great alarm about the future status of today's students. One in six youths dropped out of high school in 1985, and levels of scholastic achievement are disturbingly low by many measures. Young men with poor credentials, finding themselves facing low-wage job offers and high unemployment rates, frequently abandon the labor force intermittently or completely. Some choose criminal activity as an alternative to the labor market.

Greater numbers of people are today susceptible to poverty than in the recent past. With some year-to-year variation, the percentage of Americans living in poverty has been on an upward trend: from 11.2 percent in 1974 to 13.5 percent in 1986. In addition, the poor may be getting poorer in the 1980s: the average poor family has persistently had a yearly income further below the poverty line than any year since 1963.

More and more of the poor are working family heads, men and women who are employed or seeking employment but who cannot find a job that pays enough to prevent their families from sliding into or near poverty. For the more fortunate, reasonably secure from the fear of poverty, such middle-class advantages as a home in the suburbs and the ability to send their children to the best college for which they qualify are goals that were reached by their parents but may be unattainable for many of them.

Perhaps the most important consequences of the stagnating U.S. economy have been the effects on the status of children. Many members of the next generation of young adults live in conditions ill suited to prepare them to contribute to the nation's future. In 1987, 1 of 5 (20 percent) American children under age 18—white, black, Hispanic, Native American, and Asian-American—were being raised in families with incomes below official poverty standards. Among minorities the conditions were worse: for example, 45 percent of black children and 39 percent of Hispanic children were living in poverty. During the 1970s, approximately 2 of every 3 black children could expect to live in poverty for at least 1 of the first 10 years of their childhood, while an astounding 1 of 3 could expect at least 7 of those 10 years to be lived in poverty.

We cannot emphasize too much the gravity of the fact that in any given year more than two-fifths of all black children live under conditions of poverty as the 1980s draw to a close. As fertility rates decrease, the total youth population of the United States will contain a larger proportion of comparatively disadvantaged youths from minority ethnic and racial groups. This change may in turn lead to major changes in labor markets, childbearing, the armed forces, and education.

Under conditions of increasing economic hardship for the least prosperous members of society, blacks, because of their special legacy of poverty and discrimination, are afflicted sooner, more deeply, and longer. But the signs of distress that are most visible in parts of the black population are becoming more discernible within the entire population. This distress should be viewed in the context of the underlying changes within American society that affect not only black-white differences, but all disadvantaged blacks and whites who face the difficult economic conditions of the late 1980s. . . .

■ Attitudes, Participation, Identity, and Institutions

Large majorities of blacks and whites accept the principles of equal access to public institutions and equal treatment in race relations. For whites this is the result of a long upward trend from a low base in the 1940s; blacks have favored equality since survey data have been collected. Yet there remain important signs of continuing resistance to full equality of black Americans. Principles of equality are endorsed less when they would result in close, frequent, or prolonged social contact, and whites are much less prone to endorse policies meant to implement equal participation of blacks in important social institutions. In practice, many whites refuse or are reluctant to participate in social settings (e.g., neighborhoods and schools) in which significant numbers of blacks are present; see Figures S.1, S.2, and S.3.

Whether one considers arts and entertainment, religious institutions, public schools, or a number of other major institutions, black participation has increased significantly since 1940 and since 1960. Yet increased black participation has not produced substantial integration. An exception is the U.S. Army, where a true modicum of integration—significant numerical participation on terms of equal treatment—has been accomplished. The other three military services, although generally ahead of the civilian sector, have not attained the level of equality found in the Army. Although large-scale desegregation of public schools occurred in the South during the late 1960s and early 1970s— and has been substantial in many small and medium-sized cities elsewhere— the pace of school desegregation has slowed, and racial separation in education is significant, especially outside the South. And residential separation of whites and blacks in large metropolitan areas remains nearly as high in the 1980s as it was in the 1960s.

These findings suggest that a considerable amount of remaining black-white inequality is due to continuing discriminatory treatment of blacks. The clearest evidence is in housing. Discrimination against blacks seeking housing has been conclusively demonstrated. In employment and public accommodations, discrimination, although greatly reduced, is still a problem. . . .

The long history of discrimination and segregation produced among blacks a heightened sense of group consciousness and a stronger orientation

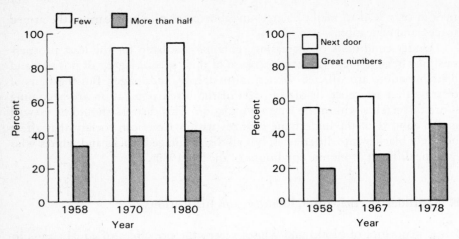

Figure S.1 left Whites with *no* objection to sending their children to a school in which a few or more than half of the children are black. Figure S.2 right Whites who would *not* move if black peolple came to live next door or in great numbers in the neighborhood.

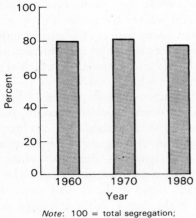

Note: 100 = total segregation;
0 = no segregation.

Figure S.3 Median residential segregation in 29 metropolitan areas with the largest black populations.

toward collective values and behavior than exists generally among Americans, and group consciousness remains strong among blacks today.... Contemporary conditions in the United States reinforce a recognition of group identity and position among blacks, who continue to be conspicuously separated from the white majority. This separation is manifested in a range of specific findings: two findings of special importance are separation of blacks and whites in residential areas and public schools. The residential separation of blacks and whites is nearly twice the rate of white and Asian-Americans, and it is often much greater than residential separation between Hispanic Americans and whites in many cities. . . .

These past experiences and current conditions have important consequences for the status of blacks and the manner in which they attempt to improve their status. Blacks overwhelmingly believe in values such as individual responsibility and free competition, but they are more likely to disapprove of the ubiquity of individualism and market autonomy throughout American society than are whites. This disapproval has appeared primarily in black support, at levels higher than whites, of such federal policies as guaranteed full employment, guaranteed income floors, and national health care. . . .

Given blacks' history, the sources of this desire for change are not difficult to identify. Data show that blacks generally believe that basic social institutions are biased in favor of whites and against blacks. . . . Many blacks believe that their relative position in society cannot be improved without government policies to intervene with social institutions on behalf of minorities and the disadvantaged. In contrast with whites, blacks have highly favorable views of the high activity years of government policy intervention of the 1960s.

As a consequence of their heightened group consciousness, their belief that racial discrimination remains a major deterrent to black progress, and their history of collective social expression, black Americans vote at the same or higher rates than whites of comparable socioeconomic status, support redistributive policies more often than do whites, and participate in a wider variety of political activity.

This political participation has had some important effects on American politics. After the legislative and judicial successes of the civil rights movement during the 1960s, there have been continuous struggles to enforce laws and administrative measures aimed at eliminating discrimination and improving opportunities. As a result, blacks' right of access to public facilities and accommodations is now widely accepted. Arbitrary harassment and intimidation of blacks by legal authorities, by organized antiblack organizations, and by unorganized individuals have greatly diminished, although there are regular reports of such incidents.

The changes since 1940—and particularly since the 1960s—have had important effects on the nature of black communities. The organizations and institutions created by blacks, as well as changing concepts of black identity, were two crucial foundations on which the achievement of sweeping improvements in blacks' legal and political status were attained. Changes in black social structure have resulted from the rising incomes, occupations, and educations of many blacks. The exit of higher status blacks from inner cities has accentuated problems of increasing social stratification among blacks. The service needs of poorer blacks have placed strains on many black institutions, including schools, churches, and voluntary service organizations. These strains have resulted in a proliferation of activities devoted to the material needs of poor blacks by black organizations. . . .

Other effects on black institutions and organizations have been produced by the civil rights movement. Greater access to majority white institutions by higher status blacks has led to alterations in black leadership structure, problems of recruitment and retention of black talent by black organizations, and reduced participation in many spheres of black life by those blacks. As a result, the often well-knit, if poor and underserviced, black communities of the past have lost some of their cultural cohesion and distinct identity. However, most blacks retain a high degree of racial pride and a conscious need to retain aspects of black culture as a significant component of their American identity. Because of these desires and needs, black institutions continue to play important roles in the lives of most blacks.

■ Political Participation

Until the 1960s, black political activity was primarily directed toward the attainment of basic democratic rights. Exclusion of black Americans from voting and office holding meant that blacks had to seek political and civil rights through protest and litigation. The civil rights movement arose out of long-standing grievances and aspirations. It was based on strong networks of local organizations and given a clear focus and direction by articulate leadership. Because most blacks were unable to vote, move freely, or buy and sell property as they wished, their efforts were directed to the objective of attaining these basic rights of citizenship. During the civil rights movement, civic equality and political liberty came to be viewed by increasing percentages of Americans as basic human rights that blacks should enjoy. By the 1960s, the federal executive branch and a congressional coalition backed by a sufficient public opinion was finally able to legislate black civil equality.

Active participation by blacks in American political life has had a major impact on their role in the society. Figures S.4 to S.7 highlight some of the effects. The number of black elected officials has risen from a few dozen in 1940 to over 6,800 in 1988. However, blacks comprise only about 1.5 percent of all elected officials. The election of black officials does result in additional hiring and higher salaries for blacks in public-sector jobs and more senior positions for blacks in appointive public office. The black proportion of federal, state, and local public administrators rose from less than 1 percent in 1940 to 8 percent in 1980; even so, it was less than blacks' 13 percent proportion of the U.S. population. As measured by the proportion of delegates to the national party conventions, black participation in the political party organizations has increased dramatically among Democrats since 1940, while black participation in Republican party affairs, after declining during the 1960s and 1970s, has returned to be about the same level as in 1940.

Blacks' desires for political rights were not merely based on abstract principles of equality, but also on the practical fruits of political participation. Blacks sought democratic rights because they believed that direct access to political institutions through voting, lobbying, and office holding would lead to greater material equality between themselves and the rest of society. How-

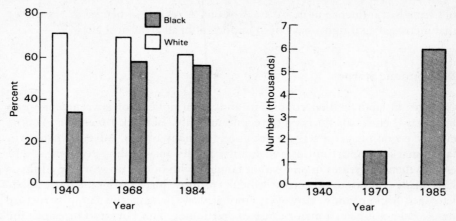

Figure S.4 left Reported voter participation as a percentage of the voting-age population, by race. Figure S.5 right Black elected officials.

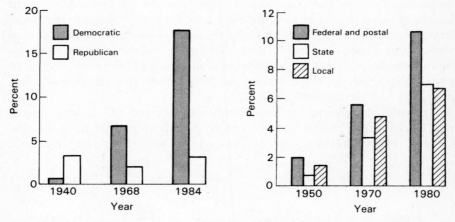

Figure S.6 left Black national convention delegates, by party. Figure S.7 right Black officials and administrators, by level of government.

ever, changes in blacks' socioeconomic status, although complex, have not attained levels commensurate to black-white equality with respect to civil rights. But black influence in the political sector has been an important factor in determining many of the important gains that have occurred. In particular, the extensive development of equal opportunity law has improved the status of blacks (as well as that of women and other minorities) in the areas of education, occupations, health care, criminal justice, and business enterprise. Blacks have also benefited from increased public-sector provision of job training, health care, Social Security, and other cash and in-kind benefit programs.

Although political participation has not been the only important determinant of changes in black opportunities, resulting alterations in American politics have had influence in many areas of life. A review of blacks' status shows that increased civil rights have been important in all areas of society.

■ Economic Status

Changes in labor market conditions and social policies of governments have had many beneficial effects on the economic status of black Americans. Yet the current economic prospects are not good for many blacks. Adverse changes in labor market opportunities and family conditions—falling real wages and employment, increases in one-parent families with one or no working adults— have made conditions especially difficult for those blacks from the most disadvantaged backgrounds. However, among blacks, changes in family structure per se have not been a major cause of continuing high poverty rates since the early 1970s.

Black-white differences are large despite significant improvements in the absolute and relative positions of blacks over the past 50 years. After initial decades of rising relative black economic status, black gains stagnated on many measures after the early 1970s. Lack of progress in important indicators of economic status during the past two decades is largely a consequence of two conflicting trends: while blacks' weekly and hourly wages have risen relative to whites, blacks' relative employment rates have deteriorated significantly. Figures S.8 to S.11 present some key data.

In terms of per capita incomes, family incomes, and male workers' earnings, blacks gained relative to whites fairly steadily from 1939 to 1969; measures of relative status peaked in the early to mid-1970s and since have

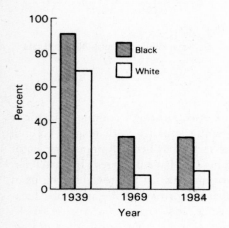
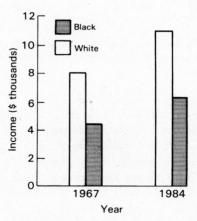

Note: Per capita income is calculated in 1984 constant dollars.

Figure S.8 left Persons below the poverty level, by race. Figure S.9 right Per capita income, by race.

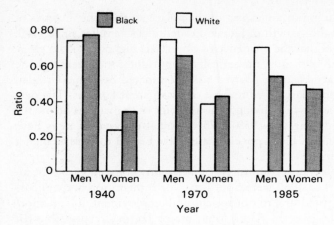

Figure S.10 Employment to population ratios, by race.

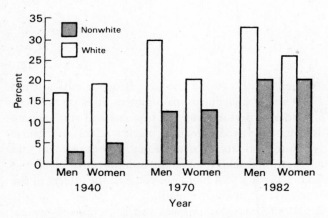

Figure S.11 Employed workers holding professional or managerial jobs, by race.

remained stagnant or declined. Women earn much less than men, but the gap
between black and white women decreased steadily throughout the period
until, by 1984, black women had earnings very close to those of white women.
Employment rates of adult black men and women have been falling relative to
those of white men and women throughout the period; black unemployment
rates remain approximately twice those of white rates. The proportion of
working black men and women in white-collar occupations and in managerial
and professional positions increased throughout the period, but these gains
show signs of slowing in the 1980s.

Uneven change in the average economic position of blacks has been
accompanied, especially during the past 25 years, by accentuated differences in

status among blacks. An important aspect of the polarization in the incomes of black families has been the growth of female-headed black families since 1960. It is among such families that the incidence of poverty is highest. It is no exaggeration to say that the two most numerically important components of the black class structure have become a lower class dominated by female-headed families and a middle class largely composed of two-parent families. The percentage of both blacks and whites living in households with incomes below the poverty line declined during the 1939–1975 period. But poverty rates have risen in the past decade, and black poverty rates have been 2 to 3 times higher than white rates at all times.

The major developments accounting for black gains in earnings and occupation status from 1939 to 1969 were South-to-North migration and concurrent movement from agricultural to nonagricultural employment, job creation, and national economic growth. After 1965, major factors responsible for improvements in blacks' status have been government policies against discrimination, government incentives for the equal employment opportunity of minorities, general changes in race relations, and higher educational attainment.

■ Schooling

Substantial progress has been made toward the provision of educational resources to blacks. Yet black and white educational opportunities are not generally equal. Standards of academic performance for teachers and students are not equivalent in schools that serve predominantly black students and those that serve predominantly white students. Nor are equal encouragement and support provided for the educational achievement and attainment of black and white students. Figures S.12, S.13, and S.14 highlight some of the effects of the progress that has been made and the gaps that remain.

Measures of educational outcomes—attainment and achievement—reveal substantial gaps between blacks and whites. Blacks, on average, enter the schools with substantial disadvantages in socioeconomic backgrounds and tested achievement. American schools do not compensate for these disadvantages in background: on average, students leave the schools with black-white gaps not having been appreciably diminished.

There remain persistent and large gaps in the schooling quality and achievement outcomes of education for blacks and whites. At the pinnacle of the educational process, blacks' life opportunities relative to whites' are demonstrated by the fact that the odds that a black high school graduate will enter college within a year of graduation are less than one-half the odds that a white high school graduate will do so. College enrollment rates of high school graduates, after rising sharply since the late 1960s, declined in the mid-1970s; while white enrollment rates have recovered, black rates in the 1980s remain well below those of the 1970s. The proportion of advanced degrees awarded to blacks has also decreased. While we cannot conclude with certainty that the

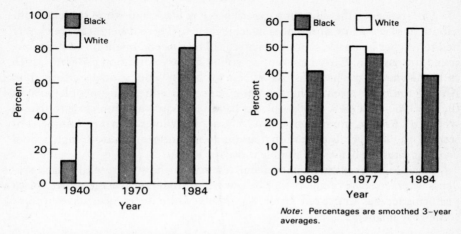

Figure S.12 left High school graduates aged 25–29, by race. Figure S.13 right High school graduates enrolled in college, by race.

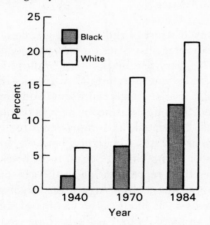

Figure S.14 College graduates aged 25–29, by race.

cause has been the decline in (real) financial aid grants to students, other reasonable hypotheses can explain only a negligible component of this change.

Segregation and differential treatment of blacks continue to be widespread in the elementary and secondary schools. We find that school desegregation does not substantially affect the academic performance of white students, but it does modestly improve black performance (in particular, reading). When several key conditions are met, intergroup attitudes and relations improve after schools are desegregated. And desegregation is most likely to reduce racial isolation as well as improve academic and social outcomes for blacks when it is part of a comprehensive and rapid desegregation plan.

Differences in the schooling experienced by black and white students contribute to black-white differences in achievement. These differences are closely tied to teacher behavior; school climate; and the content, quality, and organization of instruction. Early intervention compensatory education programs, such as Head Start, have had positive effects on blacks' educational performance. Among the most recent cohorts to complete their education—people born in the late 1950s and early 1960s—blacks have a median education close to that of whites, 12.6 years, compared with 12.9 years for whites. But a remaining substantial gap in overall educational attainment is noncompletion: high school dropout rates for blacks are double those for whites.

Changes in academic achievement test scores show that, while black students' average scores remain well below white students' average scores, black performance has improved faster, and black-white differences have become somewhat smaller. . . .

■ Crime and Criminal Justice

Among black Americans, distrust of the criminal justice system is widespread. Historically, discrimination against blacks in arrests and sentencing was ubiquitous. Prior to the 1970s, very few blacks were employed as law enforcement officials, but in the 1980s, the percentage of blacks in police forces has increased to substantial levels. Black representation among attorneys and judges has also increased, although it is not as high as that in the police.

Blacks are arrested, convicted, and imprisoned for criminal offenses at rates much higher than are whites. Currently, blacks account for nearly one-half of all prison inmates in the United States; thus, blacks' representation in prisons is about 4 times their representation in the general population. Compared with the total population, black Americans are disproportionately victims of crime: they are twice as likely to be victims of robbery, vehicle theft, and aggravated assault, and 6 to 7 times as likely to be victims of homicide, the leading cause of death among young black males. Blacks also suffer disproportionately from injuries and economic losses due to criminal actions.

Most black offenders victimize other blacks. But offenders and victims are often in different socioeconomic strata: most offenders are poor; many victims are not. Consequently, middle-income and near-poor blacks have greater economic losses due to criminal acts than the black poor or than whites at any income level.

The role of discrimination in criminal justice has apparently varied substantially from place to place and over time. Some part of the unexplained differences in black-white arrest rates may be due to racial bias and the resulting differential treatment. Current black-white differences in sentencing appear to be due less to overt racial bias than to socioeconomic differences between blacks and whites: people of lower socioeconomic status—regardless of race—receive more severe sentences than people of higher status. An important exception may be bias in sentencing that is related to the race of the victim:

criminals whose victims are white are on average punished more severely than those whose victims are black.

As long as there are great disparities in the socioeconomic status of blacks and whites, blacks will continue to be overrepresented in the criminal justice system as victims and offenders. And because of these disparities, the precise degree to which the overrepresentation reflects racial bias cannot be determined.

■ Children and Families

Changes since the mid-1960s among both blacks and whites have brought higher rates of marital breakup, decreased rates of marriage, rapidly rising proportions of female-headed households, and increasing proportions of children being reared in single-parent families. The changes have been much greater among blacks than among whites. Some characteristics of families are shown in Figures S.15, S.16, and S.17.

Birthrates for both the white and black populations have fallen since the baby boom of the 1950s, and fertility rates have declined for women of all ages. By the mid-1980s, the lifetime fertility rates were similar for black and white women. Contrary to popular myth, birthrates among black teenagers— although still an important problem—have declined significantly during the past two decades.

In 1970, about 18 percent of black families had incomes over $35,000 (1987 constant dollars); by 1986 this proportion had grown to 22 percent. The increase in well-to-do families was matched by an increase in low-income families. During the same 1970–1980 period, the proportion of black families with incomes of less than $10,000 grew from about 26 to 30 percent. After declining during earlier decades, the percentage of black and white children in poverty began to increase in the 1970s. In 1986, 43 percent of black children and 16 percent of white children under age 18 lived in households below the poverty line.

Black and white children are increasingly different with regard to their living arrangements. As we noted above, a majority of black children under age 18 live in families that include their mothers but not their fathers; in contrast, four of every five white children live with both parents. (Although some fathers who are not counted as household members may actually aid in child rearing, there are no data to estimate the number, and it is believed to be small.) In the course of their childhood, 86 percent of black children and 42 percent of white children are likely to spend some time in a single-parent household.

The greater inequality between family types among blacks has important consequences for the welfare of future generations. Black female-headed families were 50 percent of all black families with children in 1985, but had 25 percent of total black family income, while 70 percent of black family income was received by black husband-wife families.

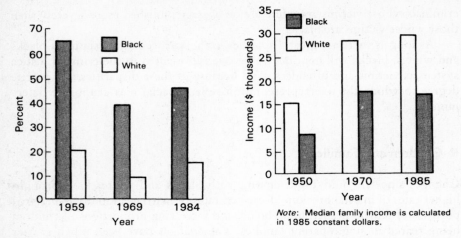

Figure S.15 left Children in poverty, by race. Figure S.16 right Median family income, by race.

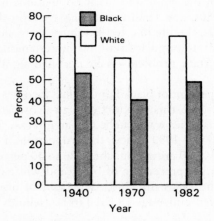

Figure S.17 Childless women aged 20–24, by race.

The data and analyses we have examined throw doubt on the validity of the thesis that a culture of poverty is a major cause of long-term poverty. Although cultural factors are important in social behavior, arguments for the existence of unalterable behaviors among the poor are not supported by empirical research. The behaviors that are detrimental to success are often responses to existing social barriers to opportunity. The primary correlates of poverty are macroeconomic conditions of prosperity or recession and changes in family composition. However, increases in female-headed families have had only negligible effects on increasing black poverty rates since the mid-1970s.

Importantly, attitudes toward work and the desire to succeed are not very different among the poor and the nonpoor.

Black-white differences in family structures result from a complex set of interrelated factors. The most salient are black-white differences in income and employment, greater (relative) economic independence of black women, and a more limited pool of black men who are good marriage prospects.

❖ THE FUTURE: ALTERNATIVES AND POLICY IMPLICATIONS

▪ Blacks' Status in the Near Future

In assessing the status of black Americans, we have asked what roles blacks play in the nation today and what role they are likely to play in the near future. Our conclusion is largely positive, but it is mixed. The great majority of black Americans contribute to the political, economic, and social health of the nation. The typical black adult—like the typical white adult—is a full-time employee or homemaker who pays taxes, votes in public elections, and sends children to school. Blacks make important contributions to all forms of American life, from the sciences and health care, to politics and education, to arts and entertainment.

However, this role is not available to a sizable minority of black—and of a small but growing group of white—Americans. The evidence for this assessment is clear. High school dropout rates among young black adults have risen, and attaining high standards of academic competence seems unavailable to millions of poor black youths attending school systems that are not able to teach them. During the 1980s, thousands of young black men who were not enrolled in school have also not been active participants in the labor market. Many of these men are incarcerated or have dropped out of society into the escape offered by alcohol and drug addiction. And, on the basis of the fertility rates of 1986, 170 of 1,000 black females become mothers before the age of 20, often disrupting or discontinuing their secondary educations. These young mothers are likely to be poor as they establish households, and they will frequently have to receive family assistance benefits. These alarming developments are mirrored by similar, if more modest, trends among whites.

Barring unforeseen events or changes in present conditions—that is, no changes in educational policies and opportunities, no increased income and employment opportunities, and no major national programs to deal directly with the problems of economic dependency—our findings imply several negative developments for blacks in the near future, developments that in turn do not bode well for American society:

- A substantial majority of black Americans will remain contributors to the nation, but improvements in their status relative to whites are likely to slow even more as the rate of increase of the black middle class is likely to decline.

- Approximately one-third of the black population will continue to be poor, and the relative employment and earnings status of black men is likely to deteriorate further.

- Drugs and crime, teenage parenthood, poor educational opportunities, and joblessness will maintain their grip on large numbers of poor and near-poor blacks.

- High rates of residential segregation between blacks and whites will continue.

- The United States is faced with the prospect of continued great inequality between whites and blacks and a continuing division of social status within the black population.

- A growing population of poor and undereducated citizens, disproportionately black and minority, will pose challenges to the nation's abilities to solve the emerging economic and social problems of the twenty-first century.

14

U.S. HISPANICS: CHALLENGING ISSUES FOR THE 1990S

RAFAEL VALDIVIESO AND CARY DAVIS

The number of Hispanic residents in the United States reached 20 million in 1988. After blacks, they are the nation's largest minority. Most Americans know that the number of Hispanics is increasing rapidly, but few really know much about the Hispanic community or appreciate the diversity among Latino groups. Nor do they realize the impact the Hispanic population will have on the nation's schools and labor force in the future.

The very term "Hispanic" is a label with a nebulous meaning, applied by the general population to an ever-changing group of U.S. residents. The terms Hispanic or Latino generally refer to individuals whose cultural heritage traces back to a Spanish-speaking country in Latin America, but also include those persons with links to Spain, or from the southwestern region of the U.S., once under Spanish or Mexican control.

Hispanics are found in every U.S. state, in every type of profession, and may be of any race—but the tendency to generalize about them as a group is fueled by the fact that the majority speak Spanish, live in the Southwest, and occupy the lower end of the social hierarchy.

Many Hispanics face similar problems which—because of their increasing numbers—U.S. policymakers must address. High dropout rates, low salaries,

Rafael Valdivieso and Cary Davis, "U.S. Hispanics: Challenging Issues for the 1990s," Population Reference Bureau, Inc., Washington, DC, 1988. Reprinted by permission.

and job discrimination have plagued many Latinos, ensnaring them in a cycle of poverty, alienation, and underachievement. Public policies and programs dealing with education, welfare, and labor relations can help Hispanics lead more productive, independent lives. In addition, because at least one-third of U.S. immigrants in the 1980s are from Latin America, federal immigration laws and enforcement guidelines affect the Hispanic community.

❖ HOW MANY HISPANICS?

Since the first European settlers arrived in the New World in the 17th century, the composition of the U.S. population has never remained stable for very long. While most of the U.S. population growth has been due to natural increase (the excess of births over deaths) immigration has always been an important component. During the late 1980s, nearly one-third of annual U.S. population increase has been due to immigration.

The Western European settlers to the continental United States were superseded by Northern and then Southern and Eastern Europeans in the late 19th and early 20th centuries. As the centuries of origin for immigration shift over time, with new immigration streams opening while older ones wither away, our self-image as a nation is transformed. This process continues today. In the late 20th century, the "new immigrants" come from Asian, African, and Latin American countries.

Using U.S. Census Bureau definitions, which have evolved over time, the Hispanic population grew from 4 million in 1950, when they were 2.7 percent of the total population, to 14.6 million in 1980, 6.4 percent of the total. In March 1988, there were an estimated 19.4 million U.S. Hispanics, accounting for 8.1 percent of the total U.S. population. . . . The number of Hispanics increased 34 percent between 1980 and 1988, compared to only a 7 percent increase in the general population.

The key factors responsible for this impressive growth are heavy immigration to the U.S. from Latin America and relatively high birth rates among U.S. Hispanic residents. These two factors contributed equally to the 5 million increase in the U.S. Hispanic population between 1980 and 1988.

❖ YOUTHFUL AGE STRUCTURE

Immigration and high birth rates contribute to the young age structure of Hispanics, relative to the U.S. as a whole. In 1988, the median age in the U.S. was 32.2 years, compared to only 25.5 years of age among Hispanics.

High fertility keeps a population young because of the continuous influx of increasing numbers of births. Immigration also leads to a low average age because migrants are likely to be young adults, just entering the ages for starting a family.

What is the significance of a young age structure? From a public policy perspective, a young population will require day care, education, and jobs, for example, rather than pensions, retirement planning, and geriatric health care. To the extent that Hispanic and non-Hispanic populations differ in age structure, there may be conflicting priorities for public and private spending.

From a strictly demographic perspective, the Hispanics' young age structure means that Latino youth form a greater proportion of U.S. young people. Latinos accounted for 8 percent of the total U.S. population in 1988, but 11 percent of those under age 15. Society's effort to educate and nurture the next generation will be directed increasingly at an Hispanic audience.

The young age structure also contains a built-in momentum for further growth because a greater percentage of the population has yet to reach childbearing age. Even without additional immigration the Hispanics would grow relative to non-Hispanics. With high fertility and low mortality rates, Hispanics contribute an increasing proportion of the natural increase of the U.S. population.

International immigration is the second major factor in the remarkable growth of the Hispanic population. The Immigration and Naturalization Service (INS) recorded 2.7 million Latin American immigrants to the U.S. between 1960 and 1970, and many have remained here. (Puerto Ricans, who are U.S. citizens, are not included in this count.) According to Census Bureau estimates, a net figure of over 2 million Hispanic immigrants (including undocumented) entered between 1980 and 1988.

The immigration of Latinos to the U.S. is expected to remain high for the foreseeable future. In many sending countries in Latin America, the high international debt and economic disarray combined with an unprecedented number of new job seekers guarantees a growing pool of potential migrants. Continuing political unrest in countries such as El Salvador and Nicaragua will augment the flow. No provision in existing INS regulations or in recently proposed legislation is likely to seriously slow the flow of Hispanics into the U.S.

❖ STARK CONTRASTS: HISPANIC POPULATION GROUPS

The growing Hispanic presence in the U.S. has blinded many Americans to the real diversity that exists within this community. The categories of "Hispanics" used by the Census Bureau largely reflect the countries of origin for recent migration streams: Mexicans; Puerto Ricans; Cubans; Central and South Americans; along with the catchall "Other Hispanics."

Latinos of Mexican ancestry have long been the largest U.S. group covered by the umbrella term Hispanic. In 1988, Mexicans accounted for 62 percent of all Hispanic Americans. About 13 percent of U.S. mainland Hispanics were Puerto Rican in 1988; 5 percent were Cuban; 12 percent Central and South American; and 8 percent "Other Hispanic." Except for the "Other" category, all the groups have made their major numerical impact on the U.S. since World War II.

The point of entry for each Hispanic group has largely determined its current geographic distribution. Mexican Americans are concentrated in the Southwest, particularly in California and Texas. In 1980, only about one-quarter of them were foreign-born, underscoring the fact that they are among the oldest Hispanic groups residing in the United States.

Puerto Ricans, the second largest subgroup, are clustered heavily in the New York metropolitan area. Waves of Puerto Ricans entered the U.S. when inexpensive air traffic opened up between Puerto Rico and New York in the 1950s. As natives of a U.S. Commonwealth, Puerto Ricans may enter or leave the U.S. mainland at will. In 1980, about one-half of those residing on the U.S. mainland had been born on the island of Puerto Rico.

The Cuban migration stream has flowed primarily into Florida, the point of entry for Cuban refugees fleeing the Fidel Castro regime in the 1950s and 1960s. Remarkably, Dade County, Florida, still contains about one-half of the 1 million Cuban Americans. According to the 1980 Census, three-fourths of U.S. Cubans were foreign-born. However, this number does not reflect the influx of 125,000 Cuban refugees during the 1980 Mariel Sealift.

The Central and South Americans are among the most recent of the major immigrant streams. In 1980, about 80 percent were foreign-born. The majority live in California, a favorite entry point, but large communities also exist in large eastern urban areas. New York contains sizable communities of Dominicans and Colombians, for example, and many Central Americans have flocked to the Boston and Washington, D.C. metropolitan areas.

"Other Hispanics" are heavily concentrated in the Southwest, particularly New Mexico and Arizona. The group includes some Americans who immigrated recently from Spain, and others who came centuries ago. Many are from families that have been here so many generations they no longer identify themselves with Spain or a specific Latin American country but still consider themselves to be "of Hispanic origin." The vast majority (80 percent) were born in the U.S., according to 1980 Census figures.

Although Latinos reside in every state, 89 percent live in one of nine states, five of these in the Southwest. Because most immigrants enter the U.S. through California or Texas, the Hispanic presence in these states has grown. More than one-half of U.S. Hispanics live in California and Texas; another 8 percent live in the neighboring states of Arizona, New Mexico, and Colorado. Over 14 percent of all Hispanics reside in New York and New Jersey, 8 percent in Florida, and 4 percent in Illinois. . . . Only 11 percent of the total live in the other 41 states.

❖ DISADVANTAGED MINORITY

Latinos have many characteristics that set them apart from other Americans, but which are also common to other disadvantaged minorities and to earlier immigrant groups. In general, Hispanics have less education, lower incomes, and higher rates of unemployment and poverty than the general population.

They have been painted with a broad brush of ethnic stereotyping—hated for their differences and feared because of their growing presence.

Because many Hispanics have darker skin than the average non-Hispanic, and because most speak Spanish, they are an easy target for discrimination. Public concern and misinformation about illegal immigration has tarnished the image of all Hispanics because most illegals are from Latin America. Many blame Hispanics for the flow of illegal drugs from Latin America.

Hispanics have faced discrimination in schools and housing, and in obtaining jobs and promotions. They have suffered harassment by police and been discouraged from political participation. Many earlier immigrant groups suffered from similar injustices. However, in part because substantial immigration from Latin America is still occurring, Hispanics continue to experience ethnic discrimination.

■ Slow Educational Progress

Low educational achievement has been a major barrier to the advancement of Hispanics in U.S. society. Hispanics have made modest gains in educational attainment since 1970, yet education still stands out as one of the quality-of-life indicators most at odds with the non-Hispanic population. More than 3 out of 5 (62 percent) Latinos age 25 to 34 had completed four years of high school by March 1988, but a much higher proportion (89 percent) of non-Hispanics had completed high school. . . .

Although good schools can break the cycle, research consistently shows that the success of children in school can usually be predicted from the educational status of their parents. The Latino adults most likely to have school-age children are in the 25-to-34 age bracket. In 1988, this group was over three times as likely to have not completed high school as other Americans.

Some U.S. Latino groups are more likely than others to have high school diplomas. In 1988, nearly 83 percent of Cuban Americans age 25 to 34 had completed high school compared to only 67 percent of Puerto Ricans and 54 percent of Mexican Americans.

Only 12 percent of Hispanics in the 25-to-34 age bracket had completed four or more years of college, less than half the percentage of non-Hispanics. The range within Hispanic groups is even more striking, from a low of 8 percent of Mexican Americans to a high of 24 percent of Cuban Americans with four or more years of college.

Although many Hispanic students are handicapped by a limited knowledge of English, this alone does not explain poor academic performance. Among Hispanics, Cuban students are the most likely to speak Spanish at home, yet have the highest educational levels. Clearly, for these students the benefits of the middle class, professional background of the majority of U.S. Cuban parents outweigh the "disadvantage" of having to learn English as a second language.

While college attendance is crucial for overall advancement of Hispanics, increasing the percentage who finish high school is a necessary first step. The high dropout rate not only hurts Hispanics, it constitutes a massive waste of human resources sorely needed in this era of keen international economic competition. Moreover, because educational attainment is strongly associated with social and economic status, the high dropout rate is certain to contribute to Latino poverty in the future.

■ Low-paying Jobs

In 1988, Hispanics made up only 7 percent of the U.S. civilian labor force. The Hispanic share, however, is likely to increase as the non-Hispanic population ages and the number of working-age Hispanics continues to grow.

Hispanic men, indeed, are more likely to be employed or seeking work than other American men, 79 percent versus 74 percent, although only about 71 percent of Puerto Rican and Other Hispanic males are in the labor force.

Hispanic women, and Puerto Ricans in particular, are less likely to be working than other women. Only 51 percent of female Hispanics, and 40 percent of Puerto Rican women, were in the labor force in 1988 compared to 56 percent of non-Hispanic women. Some observers feel that this difference reflects the traditional Latin American disapproval of women working outside the home. However, this gap may be closing: The percentage of younger Hispanic women who are working exceeds that of young non-Hispanics.

Because of their relatively low educational levels and language problems, Hispanics tend to enter poorly-paid jobs with little chance of advancement. In 1988, only 28 percent of Hispanic men were in the upper-level managerial, technical, and administrative categories compared to 48 percent of non-Hispanic men. Cuban men are an exception to this; 51 percent held higher-status positions.

Not only are Hispanics overrepresented in low-paying, semi-skilled jobs but they work in economic sectors vulnerable to cyclical unemployment and in some industries, like manufacturing, that are threatened with a long-term decline. Hispanics are as likely as non-Hispanics to be in the labor force, yet they are more likely to be unemployed. In 1988, 8.5 percent of Hispanics were out of work compared to only 5.8 percent of other Americans.

■ High Poverty Rates

The low-status occupations and high unemployment among Hispanics translate into low incomes and high poverty rates. Median family income for Hispanics in 1987 was only $20,300, two-thirds of the non-Hispanic median income of $31,600. In real dollars, this income gap between Hispanics and other Americans actually grew between 1978 and 1987, primarily because Hispanics still have not recovered from the economic recession of 1980 and 1981.

Within the Hispanic community, income levels reveal marked differences. Cuban family income in 1987, at $27,300, approached the non-Hispanic median. Puerto Rican families, at the other extreme, had average annual incomes of only $15,200, one-half of the non-Hispanic median and more than $5,000 less than the next highest Hispanic group.

Since Hispanic families are relatively large, these incomes must support more household members. The average family size for non-Hispanics in 1988 was 3.1, compared to 3.8 for all Hispanics and 4.1 persons for Mexican Americans.

Also, Hispanic families are less likely than others to be headed by a married couple and much more likely to be headed by a single parent, usually the mother. Consequently, fewer Hispanic families have the potential earning power provided by two working parents. Married-couple families account for only 70 percent of all Hispanic families, compared to 80 percent of non-Hispanic families. Nearly one-quarter, 23 percent, are headed by an unmarried or separated woman, while 16 percent of non-Hispanic families are female-headed. A whopping 44 percent of Puerto Rican families are headed by single females, double the Hispanic and almost triple the non-Hispanic average.

These statistics highlight the handicaps faced by many Latino children. With large families, low incomes, and a high proportion of single-parent families, the success of a significant proportion of the next generation is at risk. In 1987, 26 percent of all Hispanic families had incomes below the poverty threshold, compared to only 10 percent of non-Hispanic families. In single-parent families headed by an Hispanic female, over half (52 percent) were below the poverty line, exactly equal to the proportion of black families headed by a single female in poverty. . . .

Within Hispanic groups, poverty rates range from a high of 38 percent for Puerto Rican families to a low of 14 percent for Cuban. Perhaps most discouraging, two-thirds of female-headed Puerto Rican families were poor in 1987.

Poverty rates for Hispanics actually increased between 1978 and 1987, while rates for white and black Americans have decreased. The number of poor Hispanics grew from 2.9 million in 1979 to 5.5 million in 1987, a 90 percent increase.

Poor Hispanics are less likely to benefit from federal welfare programs than poor black Americans, but more likely than non-Hispanic whites. The percentage of poor Hispanics served by federal welfare programs fell slightly between 1980 and 1988, partly as a result of federal budget cuts. The only major program that reaches a majority of poor Hispanics is the subsidized school lunch program, received by 92 percent of poor Hispanic children in 1988. In the same year, only 30 percent of poor Hispanics received cash assistance; 13 percent lived in public housing; 49 percent received food stamps; and 42 percent received Medicaid. . . .

High poverty rates are likely to persist among Hispanics in the 1990s. Actions to curb the high poverty levels must deal primarily with:

- Education and job training;

- Discrimination in hiring and promotion; and

- Access to welfare programs by the Hispanic poor, especially single-parent families.

Each of these issues requires the attention of policymakers and community leaders from the national to the local level. . . .

As we enter the 1990s, U.S. Hispanics constitute an increasing share of our school children and entry-level job seekers; yet they remain a disadvantaged minority. The Latinos' growing presence suggests that policymakers should seek ways to:

- Ease their transition into mainstream society;

- Ensure their maximum productivity through improved education and training; and

- Encourage their participation in the decision-making and political processes.

Perhaps the recognition that improving the position of Hispanics is in the best interest of all Americans offers policymakers the best incentive to focus more attention on Hispanic concerns.

ASIAN AMERICANS: THE MYTH OF THE MODEL MINORITY

RONALD TAKAKI

Today Asian Americans are celebrated as America's "model minority." In 1986, *NBC Nightly News* and the *McNeil/Lehrer Report* aired special news segments on Asian Americans and their success, and a year later, CBS's *60 Minutes* presented a glowing report on their stunning achievements in the academy. "Why are Asian Americans doing so exceptionally well in school?" Mike Wallace asked, and quickly added, "They must be doing something right. Let's bottle it." Meanwhile, *U.S. News & World Report* featured Asian-American advances in a cover story, and *Time* devoted an entire section on this meteoric minority in its special immigrants issue, "The Changing Face of America." Not to be outdone by its competitors, *Newsweek* titled the cover story of its college-campus magazine "Asian-Americans: The Drive to Excel" and a lead article of its weekly edition "Asian Americans: A 'Model Minority.'" *Fortune* went even further, applauding them as "America's Super Minority," and the *New Republic* extolled "The Triumph of Asian-Americans" as "America's greatest success story."

The celebration of Asian-American achievements in the press has been echoed in the political realm. Congratulations have come even from the White House. In a speech presented to Asian and Pacific Americans in the chief exec-

From Ronald Takaki, *Strangers from a Different Shore: A History of Asian-Americans*, Boston, Little, Brown, 1989, pp. 474–482. Reprinted by permission.

utive's mansion in 1984, President Ronald Reagan explained the significance of their success. America has a rich and diverse heritage, Reagan declared, and Americans are all descendants of immigrants in search of the "American dream." He praised Asian and Pacific Americans for helping to "preserve that dream by living up to the bedrock values" of America—the principles of "the sacred worth of human life, religious faith, community spirit and the responsibility of parents and schools to be teachers of tolerance, hard work, fiscal responsibility, cooperation, and love." "It's no wonder," Reagan emphatically noted, "that the median incomes of Asian and Pacific-American families are much higher than the total American average." Hailing Asian and Pacific Americans as an example for all Americans, Reagan conveyed his gratitude to them: we need "your values, your hard work" expressed within "our political system."

But in their celebration of this "model minority," the pundits and the politicians have exaggerated Asian-American "success" and have created a new myth. Their comparisons of incomes between Asians and whites fail to recognize the regional location of the Asian-American population. Concentrated in California, Hawaii, and New York, Asian Americans reside largely in states with higher incomes but also higher costs of living than the national average: 59 percent of all Asian Americans lived in these three states in 1980, compared to only 19 percent of the general population. The use of "family incomes" by Reagan and others has been very misleading, for Asian-American families have more persons working per family than white families. In 1980, white nuclear families in California had only 1.6 workers per family, compared to 2.1 for Japanese, 2.0 for immigrant Chinese, 2.2 for immigrant Filipino, and 1.8 for immigrant Korean (this last figure is actually higher, for many Korean women are unpaid family workers). Thus the family incomes of Asian Americans indicate the presence of more workers in each family, rather than higher incomes.

Actually, in terms of personal incomes, Asian Americans have not reached equality. In 1980 the mean personal income for white men in California was $23,400. While Japanese men earned a comparable income, they did so only by acquiring more education (17.7 years compared to 16.8 years for white men twenty-five to forty-four years old) and by working more hours (2,160 hours compared to 2,120 hours for white men in the same age category). In reality, then, Japanese men were still behind Caucasian men. Income inequalities for other men were more evident: Korean men earned only $19,200, or 82 percent of the income of white men, Chinese men only $15,900 or 68 percent, and Filipino men only $14,500 or 62 percent. In New York the mean personal income for white men was $21,600, compared to only $18,900 or 88 percent for Korean men, $16,500 or 76 percent for Filipino men, and only $11,200 or 52 percent for Chinese men. In the San Francisco Bay Area, Chinese-immigrant men earned only 72 percent of what their white counterparts earned, Filipino-immigrant men 68 percent, Korean-immigrant men 69 percent, and Vietnamese-immigrant men 52 percent. The incomes of Asian-American men were close to and sometimes even below those of black men (68 percent) and Mexican-American men (71 percent).

The patterns of income inequality for Asian men reflect a structural problem: Asians tend to be located in the labor market's secondary sector, where wages are low and promotional prospects minimal. Asian men are clustered as janitors, machinists, postal clerks, technicians, waiters, cooks, gardeners, and computer programmers; they can also be found in the primary sector, but here they are found mostly in the lower-tier levels as architects, engineers, computer-systems analysts, pharmacists, and schoolteachers, rather than in the upper-tier levels of management and decision making. "Labor market segmentation and restricted mobility between sectors," observed social scientists Amado Cabezas and Gary Kawaguchi, "help promote the economic interest and privilege of those with capital or those in the primary sector, who mostly are white men."

This pattern of Asian absence from the higher levels of administration is characterized as "a glass ceiling"—a barrier through which top management positions can only be seen, but not reached, by Asian Americans. While they are increasing in numbers on university campuses as students, they are virtually nonexistent as administrators: at Berkeley's University of California campus where 25 percent of the students were Asian in 1987, only one out of 102 top-level administrators was an Asian. In the United States as a whole, only 8 percent of Asian Americans in 1988 were "officials" and "managers," as compared to 12 percent for all groups. Asian Americans are even more scarce in the upper strata of the corporate hierarchy: they constituted less than half of one percent of the 29,000 officers and directors of the nation's thousand largest companies. Though they are highly educated, Asian Americans are generally not present in positions of executive leadership and decision making. "Many Asian Americans hoping to climb the corporate ladder face an arduous ascent," the *Wall Street Journal* observed. "Ironically, the same companies that pursue them for technical jobs often shun them when filling managerial and executive positions."

Asian Americans complain that they are often stereotyped as passive and told they lack the aggressiveness required in administration. The problem is not whether their culture encourages a reserved manner, they argue, but whether they have opportunities for social activities that have traditionally been the exclusive preserve of elite white men. "How do you get invited to the cocktail party and talk to the chairman?" asked Landy Eng, a former assistant vice president of Citibank. "It's a lot easier if your father or your uncle or his friend puts his arm around you at the party and says, 'Landy, let me introduce you to Walt.'" Excluded from the "old boy" network, Asian Americans are also told they are inarticulate and have an accent. Edwin Wong, a junior manager at Acurex, said: "I was given the equivalent of an ultimatum: 'Either you improve your accent or your future in getting promoted to senior management is in jeopardy.'" The accent was a perceived problem at work. "I felt that just because I had an accent a lot of Caucasians thought I was stupid." But whites with German, French, or English accents do not seem to be similarly handicapped. Asian Americans are frequently viewed as technicians rather than administrators. Thomas Campbell, a general manager at Westinghouse Electric

Corp., said that Asian Americans would be happier staying in technical fields and that few of them are adept at sorting through the complexities of large-scale business. This very image can produce a reinforcing pattern: Asian-American professionals often find they "top out," reaching a promotional ceiling early in their careers. "The only jobs we could get were based on merit," explained Kumar Patel, head of the material science division at AT&T. "That is why you find most [Asian-Indian] professionals in technical rather than administrative or managerial positions." Similarly an Asian-Indian engineer who had worked for Kaiser for some twenty years told a friend: "They [management] never ever give you [Asian Indians] an executive position in the company. You can only go up so high and no more."

Asian-American "success" has emerged as the new stereotype for this ethnic minority. While this image has led many teachers and employers to view Asians as intelligent and hardworking and has opened some opportunities, it has also been harmful. Asian Americans find their diversity as individuals denied: many feel forced to conform to the "model minority" mold and want more freedom to be their individual selves, to be "extravagant." Asian university students are concentrated in the sciences and technical fields, but many of them wish they had greater opportunities to major in the social sciences and humanities. "We are educating a generation of Asian technicians," observed an Asian-American professor at Berkeley, "but the communities also need their historians and poets." Asian Americans find themselves all lumped together and their diversity as groups overlooked. Groups that are not doing well, such as the unemployed Hmong, the Downtown Chinese, the elderly Japanese, the old Filipino farm laborers, and others, have been rendered invisible. To be out of sight is also to be without social services. Thinking Asian Americans have succeeded, government officials have sometimes denied funding for social service programs designed to help Asian Americans learn English and find employment. Failing to realize that there are poor Asian families, college administrators have sometimes excluded Asian-American students from Educational Opportunity Programs (EOP), which are intended for *all* students from low-income families. Asian Americans also find themselves pitted against and resented by other racial minorities and even whites. If Asian Americans can make it on their own, pundits are asking, why can't poor blacks and whites on welfare? Even middle-class whites, who are experiencing economic difficulties because of plant closures in a deindustrializing America and the expansion of low-wage service employment, have been urged to emulate the Asian-American "model minority" and to work harder.

Indeed, the story of the Asian-American triumph offers ideological affirmation of the American Dream in an era anxiously witnessing the decline of the United States in the international economy (due to its trade imbalance and its transformation from a creditor to a debtor nation), the emergence of a new black underclass (the percentage of black female-headed families having almost doubled from 22 percent in 1960 to 40 percent in 1980), and a collapsing white middle class (the percentage of households earning a "middle-class" income falling from 28.7 percent in 1967 to 23.2 percent in 1983). Intellectually, it has

been used to explain "losing ground"—why the situation of the poor has deteriorated during the last two decades of expanded government social services.
According to this view, advanced by pundits like Charles Murray, the inter-
ventionist federal state, operating on the "misguided wisdom" of the 1960s,
made matters worse: it created a web of welfare dependency. But this analysis
has overlooked the structural problems in society and our economy, and it has
led to easy cultural explanations and quick-fix prescriptions. Our difficulties,
we are sternly told, stem from our waywardness: Americans have strayed from
the Puritan "errand into the wilderness." They have abandoned the old American "habits of the heart." Praise for Asian-American success is America's most
recent jeremiad—a renewed commitment to make America number one again
and a call for a rededication to the bedrock values of hard work, thrift, and
industry. Like many congratulations, this one may veil a spirit of competition,
even jealousy.

Significantly, Asian-American "success" has been accompanied by the rise
of a new wave of anti-Asian sentiment. On college campuses, racial slurs have
surfaced in conversations on the quad: "Look out for the Asian Invasion."
"M.I.T. means Made in Taiwan." "U.C.L.A. stands for University of Caucasians Living among Asians." Nasty anti-Asian graffiti have suddenly
appeared on the walls of college dormitories and in the elevators of classroom
buildings: "Chink, chink, cheating chink!" "Stop the Yellow Hordes." "Stop
the Chinese before they flunk you out." Ugly racial incidents have broken out
on college campuses. At the University of Connecticut, for example, eight
Asian-American students experienced a nightmare of abuse in 1987. Four couples had boarded a college bus to attend a dance. "The dance was a formal and
so we were wearing gowns," said Marta Ho, recalling the horrible evening
with tears. "The bus was packed, and there was a rowdy bunch of white guys
in the back of the bus. Suddenly I felt this warm sticky stuff on my hair. They
were spitting on us! My friend was sitting sidewise and got hit on her face and
she started screaming. Our boy friends turned around, and one of the white
guys, a football player, shouted: 'You want to make something out of this, you
Oriental faggots!'"

Asian-American students at the University of Connecticut and other colleges are angry, arguing that there should be no place for racism on campus
and that they have as much right as anyone else to be in the university. Many
of them are children of recent immigrants who had been college-educated professionals in Asia. They see how their parents had to become greengrocers,
restaurant operators, and storekeepers in America, and they want to have
greater career choices for themselves. Hopeful a college education can help
them overcome racial obstacles, they realize the need to be serious about their
studies. But white college students complain: "Asian students are nerds." This
very stereotype betrays nervousness—fears that Asian-American students are
raising class grade curves. White parents, especially alumni, express concern
about how Asian-American students are taking away "their" slots—admission
places that should have gone to their children. "Legacy" admission slots
reserved for children of alumni have come to function as a kind of invisible

affirmative-action program for whites. A college education has always represented a valuable economic resource, credentialing individuals for high income and status employment, and the university has recently become a contested terrain of competition between whites and Asians. In paneled offices, university administrators meet to discuss the "problem" of Asian-American "over-representation" in enrollments.

Paralleling the complaint about the rising numbers of Asian-American students in the university is a growing worry that there are also "too many" immigrants coming from Asia. Recent efforts to "reform" the 1965 Immigration Act seem reminiscent of the nativism prevalent in the 1880s and the 1920s. Senator Alan K. Simpson of Wyoming, for example, noted how the great majority of the new immigrants were from Latin America and Asia, and how "a substantial portion" of them did not "integrate fully" into American society. "If language and cultural separatism rise above a certain level," he warned, "the unity and political stability of the Nation will—in time—be seriously eroded. Pluralism within a united American nation has been our greatest strength. The unity comes from a common language and a core public culture of certain shared values, beliefs, and customs, which make us distinctly 'Americans.'" In the view of many supporters of immigration reform, the post-1965 immigration from Asia and Latin America threatens the traditional unity and identity of the American people. "The immigration from the turn of the century was largely a continuation of immigration from previous years in that the European stock of Americans was being maintained," explained Steve Rosen, a member of an organization lobbying for changes in the current law. "Now, we are having a large influx of third-world people, which could be potentially disruptive of our whole Judeo-Christian heritage." Significantly, in March 1988, the Senate passed a bill that would limit the entry of family members and that would provide 55,000 new visas to be awarded to "independent immigrants" on the basis of education, work experience, occupations, and "English language skills."

Political concerns usually have cultural representations. The entertainment media have begun marketing Asian stereotypes again: where Hollywood had earlier portrayed Asians as Charlie Chan displaying his wit and wisdom in his fortune cookie Confucian quotes and as the evil Fu Manchu threatening white women, the film industry has recently been presenting images of comic Asians (in *Sixteen Candles*) and criminal Asian aliens (in *Year of the Dragon*). Hollywood has entered the realm of foreign affairs. *The Deer Hunter* explained why the United States lost the war in Vietnam. In this story, young American men are sent to fight in Vietnam, but they are not psychologically prepared for the utter cruelty of physically disfigured Viet Cong clad in black pajamas. Shocked and disoriented, they collapse morally into a world of corruption, drugs, gambling, and Russian roulette. There seems to be something sinister in Asia and the people there that is beyond the capability of civilized Americans to comprehend. Upset after seeing this movie, refugee Thu-Thuy Truong exclaimed: "We didn't play Russian roulette games in Saigon! The whole thing was made up." Similarly *Apocalypse Now* portrayed lost innocence: Americans enter the heart of darkness in Vietnam and become possessed by madness (in the persona played by Marlon Brando) but are saved in the end by their own technology and violence (represented by Martin Sheen). Finally, in movies celebrating the exploits of Rambo, Hollywood has allowed Americans to win in fantasy the Vietnam War they had lost in reality. "Do we get to win this time?" snarls Rambo, our modern Natty Bumppo, a hero of limited conversation and immense patriotic rage.

Meanwhile, anti-Asian feelings and misunderstandings have been exploding violently in communities across the country, from Philadelphia, Boston, and New York to Denver and Galveston, Seattle, Portland, Monterey, and San Francisco. In Jersey City, the home of 15,000 Asian Indians, a hate letter published in a local newspaper warned: "We will go to any extreme to get Indians to move out of Jersey City. If I'm walking down the street and I see a Hindu and the setting is right, I will just hit him or her. We plan some of our more extreme attacks such as breaking windows, breaking car windows and crashing family parties. We use the phone book and look up the name Patel. Have you seen how many there are?" The letter was reportedly written by the "Dotbusters," a cruel reference to the *bindi* some Indian women wear as a sign of sanctity. Actual attacks have taken place, ranging from verbal harassments and egg throwing to serious beatings. Outside a Hoboken restaurant on September 27, 1987, a gang of youths changing "Hindu, Hindu" beat Navroz Mody to death. A grand jury has indicted four teenagers for the murder.

Five years earlier a similarly brutal incident occurred in Detroit. There, in July, Vincent Chin, a young Chinese American, and two friends went to a bar in the late afternoon to celebrate his upcoming wedding. Two white autoworkers, Ronald Ebens and Michael Nitz, called Chin a "Jap" and cursed: "It's because of you motherfuckers that we're out of work." A fistfight broke out, and Chin then quickly left the bar. But Ebens and Nitz took out a baseball bat from the trunk of their car and chased Chin through the streets. They finally cornered him in front of a McDonald's restaurant. Nitz held Chin while Ebens swung the bat across the victim's shins and then bludgeoned Chin to death by shattering his skull. Allowed to plead guilty to manslaughter, Ebens and Nitz were sentenced to three years' probation and fined $3,780 each. But they have not spent a single night in jail for their bloody deed. "Three thousand dollars can't even buy a good used car these days," snapped a Chinese American, "and this was the price of a life." "What kind of law is this? What kind of justice?" cried Mrs. Lily Chin, the slain man's mother. "This happened because my son is Chinese. If two Chinese killed a white person, they must go to jail, maybe for their whole lives. . . . Something is wrong with this country."

16

A PIECE OF THE PIE

STANLEY LIEBERSON

The source of European migrants to the United States shifted radically toward the end of the last century; Northwestern Europe declined in relative importance, thanks to the unheralded numbers arriving from the Southern, Central, and Eastern parts of Europe. These "new" sources, which had contributed less than one-tenth of all immigrants as late as 1880, were soon sending the vast majority of newcomers, until large-scale immigration was permanently cut off in the 1920s. For example, less than 1 percent of all immigrants in the 1860s had come from Italy, but in the first two decades of the twentieth century more migrants arrived from this one nation than from all of the Northwestern European countries combined. These new European groups piled up in the slums of the great urban centers of the East and Midwest, as well as in the factory towns of those regions, and in the coal-mining districts of Pennsylvania and elsewhere. They were largely unskilled, minimally educated, poor, relegated to undesirable jobs and residences, and life was harsh.

The descendants of these South-Central-Eastern (SCE) European groups have done relatively well in the United States. By all accounts, their education, occupations, and incomes are presently close to—or even in excess of—white

Americans from the earlier Northwestern European sources. To be sure, there are still areas where they have not quite "made it." Americans of Italian and Slavic origin are underrepresented in *Who's Who in America,* although their numbers are growing. Every president of the United States has thus far been of old European origin. Likewise, a study of the 106 largest Chicago-area corporations found Poles and Italians grossly underrepresented on the boards or as officers when compared with their proportion in the population in the metropolitan area. There is also evidence of discrimination in the upper echelons of banking directed at Roman Catholics and Jews, to say nothing of nonwhites and women generally. For example, as of a few years ago there were only a handful of Jews employed as senior officers in all of New York City's eight giant banks and there were *no* Jews employed as senior officers in any of the nation's 50 largest non-New York banks.

Nevertheless, it is clear that the new Europeans have "made it" to a degree far in excess of that which would have been expected or predicted at the time of their arrival here. It is also equally apparent that blacks have not. Whether it be income, education, occupation, self-employment, power, position in major corporations, residential location, health, or living conditions, the average black status is distinctly below that held by the average white of SCE European origin. Numerous exceptions exist, of course, and progress has occurred: There are many blacks who have made it. But if these exceptions should not be overlooked, it is also the case that blacks and new Europeans occupy radically different average positions in society.

Since the end of slavery occurred about 20 years before the new Europeans started their massive move to the United States and because the latter groups seem to have done so well in this nation, there are numerous speculations as to why the groups have experienced such radically different outcomes. Most of these end up in one of two camps: either blacks were placed under greater disadvantages by the society and other forces outside of their control; or, by contrast, the new Europeans had more going for them in terms of their basic characteristics. Examples of the former explanation include: the race and skin color markers faced by blacks but not by SCE Europeans; greater discrimination against blacks in institutions ranging from courts to unions to schools; the preference that dominant whites had for other whites over blacks; and the decline in opportunities by the time blacks moved to the North in sizable numbers. Interpretations based on the assumption that the differences in success reflect superior new European attributes include speculations regarding family cohesion, work ethic, intelligence, acceptance of demeaning work, and a different outlook toward education as a means of mobility. Not only is it possible for both types of forces to be operating but that their relative role could easily change over time, since a period of about 100 years is long enough to permit all sorts of feedback processes as well as broad societal changes which have consequences for the groups involved. Hence the problem is extremely complex. As one might expect, those sympathetic to the difficulties faced by blacks tend to emphasize the first factor; those emphasizing the second set of forces tend to be less sympathetic.

The answer to this issue is relevant to current social policies because an understanding of the causes would affect the ways proposed for dealing with the present black-white gap. In addition, there is the related issue of whether the SCE groups provide an analogy or a model for blacks. Finally, the historical causes of present-day circumstances are of grave concern to all those who are enmeshed in these events. Is the relatively favorable position enjoyed by the descendants of new European immigrants to be seen as purely a function of more blood, sweat, and tears such that easy access to the same goodies will in some sense desecrate all of these earlier struggles—let alone mean sharing future opportunities with blacks? If, on the other hand, the position held by blacks vis-à-vis the new Europeans is due to their skin color and the fact that blacks experience more severe forms of discrimination, then the present-day position of blacks is proof of the injustices that exist and the need to redress them.

Because there is a big stake in the answer, not surprisingly a number of scholars have addressed the question already. But as we will see, many of the answers have been highly speculative. It is one thing to note the sharp present-day differences between the new European groups and blacks and then to speculate about the causes of these differences. A far different task is the search for data that might help one determine in at least a moderately rigorous way what was going on earlier in this century and at the tail end of the last. Indeed, there are moments when I empathize with both the frustrations and challenges archaeologists must feel as they try to piece together events from some ancient society.

❖ RACE AND DISCRIMINATION

The obstacles faced by the new Europeans were enormous and in some cases, such as the development of political power . . . , comparable to the black experience in the North. However, a massive body of evidence indicates that blacks were discriminated against far more intensely in many domains of life than were the new Europeans. Witness, for example, the disposition of both employers and labor unions . . . This fact cannot be glossed over as it is central to any explanation of group differences in outcome. This raises two questions about race. If blacks did have greater obstacles, to what degree were these due to race? Second, if race did play an important role, how does one reconcile this interpretation with the fact that such other nonwhite groups as the Chinese and Japanese have done so well in the United States (to be sure only after a rocky start)?

Among those recognizing the fact that other nonwhite groups did better in the United States, there are several variations of the same basic theme, namely, that these other groups had certain characteristics that blacks lacked. For example, there may have been special institutional forces and advantages that these groups had. Or, we return to the speculations about norms, values dispositions, and the like. Another variation of this emphasizes the heritage of slavery and the damaging effects of slavery, obstacles that did not exist for the other nonwhite groups. In any case, it leads to conclusions that the gaps were not really due to race after all, at least as an immediate cause as other nonwhite groups did alright.

There is another way of thinking about these racial gaps, one that emphasizes differences in the social context of contact. This perspective leads one to conclude that much of the black disadvantage was due to neither race nor certain personality characteristics. Rather, it is the structure of the situation that was so radically different for blacks and these other groups.

Let us recognize at the outset that there are certain disadvantages that blacks and any other nonwhite group would suffer in a society where the dominant white population has a preference for whites over nonwhites. This disadvantage is one blacks share with Japanese, Chinese, Filipinos, American Indians, and any other nonwhite group. These groups were more visible and more sharply discriminated against than were various white ethnic groups. The disposition to apply the same levels of legal protection and rights was weaker than that directed toward white populations. (This is possibly due to white predispositions stemming from the earlier slavery period as well as the fact that the SCE groups were at least European.) However, it is not impossible that whites have a hierarchy with respect to nonwhites such that blacks and Africans generally rank lower than Asian groups. In the early 1930s 100 Princeton University undergraduates were asked to characterize various racial and ethnic groups. Consider how radically different were the characterizations of blacks, Chinese, and Japanese shown in Table 1. Particularly impressive is the list of characteristics listed for the Japanese, almost all of which would be considered "desirable" by most Americans. By contrast, the list of black characteristics is striking both because of its almost uniform lack of any favorable attributes and also because, I suspect, the emphasis would be quite different now.

To be sure, one might argue that these stereotypes reflect real differences between these groups and hence serve to prove that the Japanese and Chinese levels of success were a reflection of important personality differences. However, given the relatively small number of Japanese in the United States and their concentration on the Pacific Coast during the 1930s, it is unlikely that the responses of these Princeton students reflect much in the way of actual contact experience. Hence these results show radical differences in the way nonwhite groups were perceived by whites.

The reader may wonder if all of this is a bit too pat; rather than simply concluding that blacks had less of the necessary characteristics for making it in the United States, it is claimed that they did not do as well as other nonwhite groups because they faced even more severe disadvantages. Why would blacks suffer more? This is the heart of the matter. In my estimation, there are two key features that distinguish blacks from other nonwhite groups in the United States and which help explain their different outcomes. First, an exceptionally unfavorable disposition toward blacks existed on the part of the dominant

Table 1   Characteristics Most Commonly Used by 100 Princeton Students [to Describe Various Ethnic and Racial Groups], 1932

CHINESE		JAPANESE		NEGROES	
CHARACTERISTIC	*NUMBER OF RESPONDENTS AGREEING*	*CHARACTERISTIC*	*NUMBER OF RESPONDENTS AGREEING*	*CHARACTERISTIC*	*NUMBER OF RESPONDENTS AGREEING*
Superstitious	34	Intelligent	45	Superstitious	84
Sly	29	Industrious	43	Lazy	75
Conservative	29	Progressive	24	Happy-go-lucky	38
Tradition-loving	26	Shrewd	22	Ignorant	38
Loyal to family ties	22	Sly	20	Musical	26
Industrious	18	Quiet	19	Ostentatious	26
Meditative	18	Imitative	17	Very religious	24
Reserved	17	Alert	16	Stupid	22
Very religious	15	Suave	16	Physically dirty	17
Ignorant	15	Neat	16	Naive	14
Deceitful	14	Treacherous	13	Slovenly	13
Quiet	13	Aggressive	13	Unreliable	12

Source: Daniel Katz and Kenneth W. Braly, "Verbal Stereotypes and Racial Prejudice," in Guy E. Swanson, Theodore Newcomb, and Eugene L. Hartley (eds.), *Readings in Social Psychology* (2nd edition). New York: Holt, Rinehart & Winston, 1952.

white society due to the slave period and the initial contact with Africans. Blacks enter into competition as free people, but they are unable to shake off easily the derogatory notions about them and the negative dispositions toward blacks which go back to the slavery era. Of course, this was not a problem for the other nonwhite groups. Second, the threat of Asian groups was not anywhere as severe because migration was cut off before their numbers were very large. The response of whites to Chinese and Japanese was of the same violent and savage character in areas where they were concentrated, but the threat was quickly stopped through changes in immigration policy. This meant that Asian groups had more time to develop special mobility niches (see the discussion below) and that they have been of less *actual* (as opposed to *potential*) threat to whites than blacks. The cessation of sizable migration from Asia for a number of decades on the one hand indicates how quickly threatened whites were by Asian groups. On the other hand, this very cessation made it possible for those who were here to avoid eventually some of the disadvantages that would occur if there were as many of their compatriots in the country as there were blacks.

For those unconvinced, have patience because the problem is too complicated to be quickly resolved by a simple data set. Rather the answer must rest on satisfactorily weaving together the various threads of evidence and theory so that they make sense from a single perspective. Later, after analyzing the consequences that follow from a cessation of immigration, it will be possible to consider further whether the main source of black disadvantage was neither race nor their internal characteristics. At the moment, one can speculate that the comparison between Asian groups and blacks in the United States, although unfavorable to the latter in recent decades, may be due to the distinctive context of their contact with whites and the incredible threat that blacks posed. However, the contrast with other nonwhites does show that being a nonwhite was not an insurmountable obstacle.

❖ OCCUPATIONAL OPPORTUNITIES

It is difficult to overstate the direct importance of occupation and income as well as their indirect consequences for other long-run gaps between blacks and the new Europeans. Thanks to an excellent set of 1900 occupational data from the Census Bureau, one can draw some important conclusions about the situation these groups faced in the urban North at the beginning of the century. As one might guess, neither the new Europeans nor blacks held many of the specially desirable jobs at that time so there were not sharp differences at the upper end of the scale. But there were substantial differences in some areas, particularly in the service jobs where blacks were more concentrated and in the manufacturing jobs where the new Europeans held the edge. There was some evidence, even in 1900, that the new Europeans were in a more favorable position, even if they were still lower on the queue than were the older white groups. There is also strong evidence that the black pattern in the North resembled very much the same pattern found in the urban South after compositional differences are taken into account. . . .

Other data . . . also indicate that earlier in this century blacks were disadvantaged in the urban North relative to the new Europeans. The antipathy toward blacks among labor unions displayed a striking interaction between discrimination by employers, employees, and customers, lower-wage levels among blacks, and strike breaking. However, the net effect is to see much more severe discriminatory forces operating against blacks in the labor market, with important feedback consequences on other domains of black-new European differences. As noted earlier, there is just no way of avoiding the fact that blacks were more severely discriminated against in the labor market and elsewhere. By contrast, there is strong evidence that new European participation in the labor market was not greatly affected by ethnic membership after one takes into account their lower origins. At least this is the case for a number of recent generations. Hence, the new Europeans were close enough to the intergenerational mobility rates for whites generally, and the rates were sufficiently open, that the SCE groups could do very well in relatively short order whereas this was not the case for blacks.

❖ FURTHER ANALYSIS OF RACE

Returning to a theme suggested earlier . . . , I believe there is further reason for speculating that race was not as crucial an issue as is commonly supposed for understanding the black outcome relative to the new Europeans. In order to avoid being misunderstood by the casual reader, let me reiterate that such a conclusion does not mean that other nonwhite groups or the new Europeans possessed certain favorable characteristics to a greater degree than did blacks. There is an alternative way of interpreting these events, namely, a substantial source of the disadvantage faced by blacks is due to their position with respect to certain structural conditions that affect race relations generally. Having been reviewed in this chapter, one should now make sense of black-new European gaps, but what about comparisons of blacks with other nonwhites? There are eight important factors to consider.

1. Although hard quantitative data are not available, there is every reason to believe that the response to Chinese and Japanese in the United States was every bit as severe and as violent initially as that toward blacks when the latter moved outside of their traditional niches.

2. There was a cessation of sizable immigration from Japan and China for a number of decades before these groups were able to advance in the society.

3. The cessation was due to the intense pressures within the United States against Asian migration, particularly by those whites who were threatened by these potential competitors.

4. This meant that the number of these groups in the nation is quite small relative to blacks. In the 1970 census there were 22,580,000 blacks recorded compared with 591,000 Japanese and 435,000 Chinese.

5. Because of factors 2 and 4 above, the opportunity for these Asian groups to occupy special niches was far greater than for blacks. Imagine more than 22 million Japanese Americans trying to carve out initial niches through truck farming!

6. Because of factor 2 there has been less negative effect on the general position of these groups due to recent immigrants (a situation that is now beginning to change somewhat for the Chinese).

7. Ignoring situations generated by direct competition between Asians and whites such as existed in the West earlier, there is some evidence that the white disposition toward blacks was otherwise even more unfavorable than that toward Asians. This is due to the ideologies that developed in connection with slavery as well as perhaps the images of Africa and its people stemming from exploration of the continent. Whatever the reason, one has the impression that whites have strikingly different attitudes toward the cultures of China and Japan than toward those of blacks or of Africa.

8. The massive economic threat blacks posed for whites earlier in the century in both the South and North was not duplicated by the Asians except in certain parts of the West.

I am suggesting a general process that occurs when racial and ethnic groups have an inherent conflict—and certainly competition for jobs, power, position, maintenance of different subcultural systems, and the like are such conflicts. Under the circumstances, there is a tendency for the competitors to focus on differences between themselves. The observers (in this case the sociologists) may then assume that these differences are the sources of conflict. In point of fact, the rhetoric involving such differences may indeed inflame them, but we can be reasonably certain that the conflict would have occurred in their absence. To use a contemporary example, if Protestants in Northern Ireland had orange skin color and if the skin color of Roman Catholics in that country was green, then very likely these physical differences would be emphasized by observers seeking to explain the sharp conflict between these groups. Indeed, very likely such racial differences would be emphasized by the combatants themselves. No doubt such physical differences would enter into the situation as a secondary cause because the rhetoric would inflame that difference, but we can be reasonably certain that the conflict would occur in their absence. In the same fashion, differences between blacks and whites—real ones, imaginary ones, and those that are the product of earlier race relations—enter into the rhetoric of race and ethnic relations, but they are ultimately secondary to the conflict for society's goodies.

This certainly is the conclusion that can be generated from the classic experiment . . . in which a homogeneous group of children at camp were randomly sorted into two groups and then competition and conflict between the groups was stimulated. The experiment resulted in each of the groups developing all sorts of images about themselves and the other group. Yet, unknown to them, the groups were identical in their initial distribution of characteristics.

In order to avoid a misunderstanding of a position that is radically different from that held by most observers, whether they be black or white, oriented toward one group or the other, let me restate this part of my thesis. There is powerful evidence that blacks were victims of more severe forms of discrimination than were the new Europeans—although the latter also suffered from intense discrimination. Much of the antagonism toward blacks was based on racial features, but one should not interpret this as the ultimate cause. Rather the racial emphasis resulted from the use of the most obvious feature(s) of the group to support the intergroup conflict generated by a fear of blacks based on their threat as economic competitors. If this analysis is correct, it also means that were the present-day conflict between blacks and dominant white groups to be resolved, then the race issue could rapidly disintegrate as a crucial barrier between the groups just as a very profound and deep distaste for Roman Catholics on the part of the dominant Protestants has diminished rather substantially (albeit not disappeared).

❖ THE GREAT NON SEQUITUR

The data comparing blacks and the new Europeans earlier in this century lead one to a rather clear conclusion about the initial question. The early living conditions of the new Europeans after their migration to the United States were extremely harsh and their point of entry into the socioeconomic system was quite low. However, it is a non sequitur to assume that new Europeans had it as bad as did blacks or that the failure of blacks to move upward as rapidly reflected some ethnic deficiencies. The situation for new Europeans in the United States, bad as it may have been, was not as bad as that experienced by blacks at the same time. Witness, for example, the differences in the disposition to ban openly blacks from unions at the turn of the century . . . , the greater concentration of blacks in 1900 in service occupations and their smaller numbers in manufacturing and mechanical jobs . . . , the higher black death rates in the North . . . and even the greater segregation of blacks with respect to the avenues of eminence open to them. It is a serious mistake to underestimate how far the new Europeans have come in the nation and how hard it all was, but it is equally erroneous to assume that the obstacles were as great as those faced by blacks or that the starting point was the same.

PART FIVE

SEXISM

The 1960s were known as a decade of civil rights struggles, black militancy, antiwar protests, and campus disturbances. It seemed unlikely that yet another social movement could take hold and grow, but the consciousness of women's oppression could, and did, grow, with enormous impact over remarkably few years.

Black militancy, the student movement, the antiwar movement, youth militancy, and radicalism all affirmed freedom, equality, and liberation, but none of these was thought to be particularly necessary or applicable to women, especially by radical men. Ironically, it was political experience with radical men that led radical women to the consciousness of women as a distinctly oppressed group and, therefore, a group with distinctive interests.

The feminism that emerged in the 1970s was in fact both novel and part of a long and often painful series of movements for the liberation of women. Women's rights proposals were first heard over a century ago. According to Peter Gabriel Filene, the movement for the equality of women ground to a halt around 1932, the darkest year of the Depression, beginning a period he calls "The Long Amnesia," when the emergencies of the Depression and World War II pushed aside feminist concerns. With victory, both sexes gratefully resumed the middle-class dream of family, security, and upward mobility. These years of the late 1940s and early 1950s were the years of "The Feminine Mystique," when the *domestic* role of women dominated American culture.

When women began, in the 1970s, once again to reassert themselves and claimed to be able to be doctors and lawyers and bankers and pilots, they were met with derision. The "Long Amnesia" had taken hold and stereotyped woman's roles into those of the 1940s and 1950s. People, especially men, had come to regard female domesticity almost as a natural phenomenon. Nevertheless, women persevered, and, in what was historically a brief period, it became inconceivable to see no female faces broadcasting the news, granting loans, and training to be jet pilots at the U.S. Air Force Academy.

The idea of sexual equality has surely made progress since the 1950s, but the struggle is hard, for reasons suggested by the readings. Although the idea of male supremacy may be on the way out in industrialized nations, female equality is not necessarily a social reality—in part because conceptions of equality vary, and in part because of the persistence of sexist norms and attitudes. As journalist Susan Faludi demonstrates in the section of her book reprinted here, the backlash against women's equality, especially during the Reagan and Bush administrations, perpetuated a significant wage gap between women and men. In addition, far more lower-echelon jobs fell to women than is commonly believed, along with sex discrimination and harassment on the job.

Although harassment of women at work has become fairly well known and studied, legal scholar Cynthia Grant Bowman argues that lawyers and social scientists have virtually ignored the issue of *street* harassment of women. This occurs when a man or men intrude on a woman's privacy through unwanted looks, gestures, or words. Bownman maintains that street harassment, however unwelcome and painful, is so universal that it has become virtually normal and accepted. It is consequently not perceived as a social problem although it should be considered a form of assault.

The idea of "fetal rights" raises another set of potentially troubling issues about how we define womens' position in contemporary society. Should a woman be required to undertake unwanted medical procedures—for example, a Caesarean section—in the interest of the health of the fetus? Assuming that a woman wishes to have a child, rather than to abort a pregnancy, how much should the state "police" her pregnancy? Suppose she smokes, drinks alcohol, or uses drugs? Should she be monitored or imprisoned? Katha Pollitt argues in "'Fetal Rights': A New Assault on Feminism," that the new "fetal-rights" movement offers yet another illustration of, and opportunity for, the subordination of women.

17

THE WAGES OF THE BACKLASH: THE TOLL ON WORKING WOMEN

SUSAN FALUDI

Many myths about working women's "improving" circumstances made the rounds in the '80s—while some discouraging and *real* trends that working women faced didn't get much press. Here are just a few examples.

The trend story we all read about women's wages:
PAY GAP BETWEEN THE SEXES CLOSING!
The difference between the average man's and woman's paycheck, we learned in 1986, had suddenly narrowed. Women who work full-time were now said to make an unprecedented 70 cents to a man's dollar. Newspaper editorials applauded and advised feminists to retire their "obsolete" buttons protesting female pay of 59 cents to a man's dollar.
The trend story we should have seen:
IT'S BACK! THE '50s PAY GAP
The pay gap did *not* suddenly improve to 70 cents in 1986. Women working full-time made only 64 cents to a man's dollar that year, actually slightly *worse* than the year before—and exactly the same gap that working women had faced in *1955*.

From Susan Faludi, *Backlash: The Undeclared War Against American Women*, New York, Crown Publishers, 1991, pp. 363–367. Reprinted by permission.

The press got the 70-cent figure from a onetime Census Bureau report that was actually based on data from another year and that departed from the bureau's standard method for computing the gap. This report artificially inflated women's earnings by using weekly instead of the standard yearly wages—thus grossly exaggerating the salary of part-time workers, a predominantly female group, who don't work a full year. Later, the Census Bureau calculated the pay gap for 1986 using its standard formula and came up with 64 cents. This report, however, managed to elude media notice.

By that year, in fact, the pay gap had only "improved" for women by less than five percentage points since 1979. And as much as half of that improvement was due to men's falling wages, not women's improving earnings. Take out men's declining pay as a factor and the gap had closed only three percentage points.

By 1988, women with a college diploma could still wear the famous 59-cent buttons. They were still making 59 cents to their male counterparts' dollar. In fact, the pay gap for them was now a bit worse than five years earlier. Black women, who had made almost no progress in the decade, could wear the 59-cent buttons, too. Older and Hispanic women couldn't—but only because their pay gap was even worse now than 59 cents. Older working women had actually fared better in *1968,* when they had made hourly wages of 61 cents to a man's dollar; by 1986, they were down to 58 cents. And Hispanic women, by 1988, found their wages backsliding; they were now making an abysmal 54 cents to a white man's dollar.

The pay gap was also getting worse in many occupations, from social work to screenwriting to real estate management, as U.S. Labor Department data detail. By 1989, the pay gap for women in all full-time managerial jobs was growing worse again; that year, while the average male manager enjoyed a four-percent income boost, his average female counterpart received none. And the gap was widening most in the very fields where female employment was growing most, a list that includes food-preparation and service supervisory jobs, waiting tables, and cleaning services. In public relations, where women doubled their ranks in the decade, the pay gap grew so massively that communications professor Elizabeth Lance Toth, who tracks women's status in this profession, reported, "In a forty-year career, a woman will lose $1 million on gender alone."

The trend story we all read about integrating the workplace:
WOMEN INVADE MAN'S WORLD!
Women, we learned, charged into traditional "male" occupations. A sea of women in their dress-for-success suits and stride-to-work sneakers abandoned the "pink-collar" ghettos and descended on Wall Street, law firms, and corporate suites. Still other women laced up army boots, slapped on hard hats, and barged into the all-male military and blue-collar factories.

The trend story we should have seen:
MORE AND MORE, WOMEN STUCK IN SECRETARIAL POOL
While the level of occupational segregation between the sexes eased by 9 percent in the 1970s—the first time it had improved in the century—that progress stalled in the '80s. The Bureau of Labor Statistics soon began project-

ing a more sex-segregated work force. This was a bitter financial pill for women: as much as 45 percent of the pay gap is caused by sex segregation in the work force. (By one estimate, for every 10 percent rise in the number of women in an occupation, the annual wage for women drops by roughly $700.) A resegregating work force was one reason why women's wages fell in the '80s; by 1986, more working women would be taking home poverty-level wages than in 1973.

Women were pouring into many low-paid female work ghettos. The already huge proportion of working women holding down menial clerical jobs climbed to nearly 40 percent by the early '80s, higher than it had been in 1970. By the late '80s, the proportion of women consigned to the traditionally female service industries had grown, too. A long list of traditionally "female" jobs became *more* female-dominated, including salesclerking, cleaning services, food preparation, and secretarial, administrative, and reception work. The proportion of bookkeepers who were women, for example, rose from 88 to 93 percent between 1979 and 1986. Black women, especially, were resegregated into such traditional female jobs as nursing, teaching, and secretarial and social work. And the story was the same at the office of the nation's largest employer, the federal government. Between 1976 and 1986, the lowest job rungs in the civil service ladder went from 67 to 71 percent female. (At the same time at the top of the ladder, the proportion of women in senior executive services had not improved since 1979—it was still a paltry 8 percent. And the rate of women appointed to top posts had declined to the point that, by the early '80s, less than 1 percent of the G.S. 13 and 14 grade office holders were women.)

In the few cases where working women did make substantial inroads into male enclaves, they were only admitted by default. As a job-integration study by sociologist Barbara Reskin found, in the dozen occupations where women had made the most progress entering "male" jobs—a list that ranged from typesetting to insurance adjustment to pharmaceuticals—women succeeded only because the pay and status of these jobs had fallen dramatically and men were bailing out. Computerization, for example, had demoted male typesetters to typists; the retail chaining of drugstores had turned independent pharmacists into poorly paid clerks. Other studies of women's "progress" in bank management found that women were largely just inheriting branch-manager jobs that men didn't want anymore because their pay, power, and status had declined dramatically. And still another analysis of occupational shifts concluded that one-third of the growth of female employment in transportation and half of the growth in financial services could be attributed simply to a loss of status in the jobs that women were getting in these two professions.

In many of the higher-paying white-collar occupations, where women's successes have been most heavily publicized, the rate of progress slowed to a trickle or stopped altogether by the end of the decade. The proportion of women in some of the more elite or glamorous fields actually shrank slightly in the last half of the '80s. Professional athletes, screenwriters, commercial voice-overs, producers and orchestra musicians, economists, geologists, biological and life scientists were all a little *less* likely to be female by the late '80s than earlier in the decade.

The breathless reports about droves of female "careerists" crashing the legal, medical, and other elite professions were inflated. Between 1972 and 1988, women increased their share of such professional jobs by only 5 percent. In fact, only 2 percent more of all working women were in professional specialties in 1988 than fifteen years earlier—and that increase had been largely achieved by the early '80s and barely budged since.

Hardly any progress occurred in the upper echelons of corporations. In fact, according to scattered studies, in the top executive suites in many industries, from advertising to retailing, women's already tiny numbers were beginning to fall once more by the end of the decade. The rate of growth in numbers of women appointed to Fortune 1000 boards slacked off by the late '80s, after women's share of the director chairs had reached only 6.8 percent. Even the many reports of the rise of female "entrepreneurs" founding their own companies masked the nickel-and-dime reality: the majority of white female-owned businesses had sales of less than $5,000 a year.

Under Reagan, women's progress in the military soon came under fire. In the mid-'70s, after quota ceilings on female recruits had been lifted and combat classifications rewritten to open more jobs to women, women's ranks in the armed services had soared—by 800 percent by 1980. But shortly after Reagan's election, the new army chief of staff declared, "I have called a pause to further increases in the number of army women"—and by 1982, the army had revised combat classifications to bar women from an additional twenty-three career occupations. All the services reined in their recruitment efforts, subsequently slowing female employment growth in the military throughout the '80s.

The blue-collar working world offered no better news. After 1983, as a Labor Department study quietly reported to no fanfare, women made *no* progress breaking into the blue-collar work force with its better salaries. By 1988, the tiny proportions of women who had squeezed into the trades were shrinking in a long list of job categories from electricians and plumbers to automotive mechanics and machine operators. The already tiny ranks of female carpenters, for example, fell by half, to 0.5 percent, between 1979 and 1986. Higher up the ladder, women's share of construction inspector jobs fell from 7 to 5.4 percent between 1983 and 1988.

Where women did improve their toeholds in blue-collar jobs, the increments were pretty insubstantial. The proportion of women in construction, for example, rose from 1.1 to 1.4 percent between 1978 and 1988. Women made the most progress in the blue-collar professions as motor vehicle operators—more than doubling their numbers between 1972 and 1985—but that was only because women were being hired to drive school buses, typically a part-time job with the worst pay and benefits of any transportation position.

The trend story we all read about equal opportunity:
DISCRIMINATION ON THE JOB: FADING FAST!
Corporations, we read, were now welcoming women. "Virtually all large employers are now on [women's] side," *Working Woman* assured female readers in 1986. Discrimination was dropping, mistreatment of female workers was

on the wane—and any reports to the contrary were just "propaganda from self-interested parties," as *Forbes* asserted in 1989—in its story on the "decline" of sexual harassment on the job.

The trend story we should have seen:

Now MORE THAN EVER! INEQUITY AND INTIMIDATION

Reports of sex discrimination and sexual harassment reached record highs in the decade—by both private and federal employees. Women's sex discrimination complaints to the Equal Employment Opportunity Commission climbed by nearly 25 percent in the Reagan years—and by 40 percent among federally employed women just in the first half of the '80s. Complaints of exclusion, demotions, and discharges on the basis of sex rose 30 percent. General harassment of women, excluding sexual harassment, more than doubled. And while the EEOC's public relations office issued statements claiming that sexual harassment in corporate America was falling, its own figures showed that annual charges of sexual harassment nearly doubled in the decade.

Throughout much of the '80s, women were also far more likely than men to lose their jobs or get their wages cut—and legal challenges to remedy the imbalance went nowhere in the courts. Press accounts to the contrary, the mass layoffs of the '80s actually took a greater toll on female service workers than male manufacturing workers—the service sector accounted for almost half of the job displacement in the decade, nearly 10 percentage points more than manufacturing. And even among blue-collar workers, women suffered higher unemployment rates than men. In the federal "reductions in force" in the early '80s, too, women who held higher-paid civil-service jobs (G.S. 12 and above) got laid off at more than twice the average rate. Far more working women than men were also forced into the part-time work force and expanding "temp" pools of the '80s, where women faced an extraordinary pay gap of 52 cents to a man's dollar and labored with little to no job security, insurance, benefits, or pension. Even among displaced workers who managed to get rehired, women had it worse. Women in service jobs who were reemployed had to settle for pay reductions of 16 percent, nearly double the reductions borne by their male counterparts.

If we heard less about discrimination in the '80s workplace, that was partly because the federal government had muzzled, or fired, its equal-employment investigators. At the same time that the EEOC's sex discrimination files were overflowing, the Reagan administration was cutting the agency's budget in half and jettisoning its caseload. The year Reagan came into office, the EEOC had twenty-five active class-action cases; a year later, it had none. The agency scaled back the number of suits it pursued by more than 300 percent. A House Education and Labor Committee report found that in the first half of the '80s, the number of discrimination victims receiving compensation fell by two-thirds. By 1987, a General Accounting Office study found that EEOC district offices and state equal-employment agencies were closing 40 to 80 percent of their cases without proper, or any, investigation.

A similar process was taking place in the other federal agencies charged with enforcing equal opportunity for women and minorities. At the Office of

Federal Contract Compliance, for example, back-pay awards fell from $9.3 million in 1980 to $600,000 in 1983; the number of government contractors that this agency barred from federal work because of discrimination fell from five in the year before Reagan took office to none a year after his inauguration. In fact, in a 1982 study, every OFCC staff member interviewed said that they had never found a company *not* to be in compliance. This wasn't because American corporations had suddenly reformed: the majority of federal contractors polled in the same study said they just felt no pressure to comply with the agency's affirmative action requirements anymore.

18

STREET HARASSMENT AND THE INFORMAL GHETTOIZATION OF WOMEN

CYNTHIA GRANT BOWMAN

The literature of law and social science is largely silent about the harassment of women in public places. The legal academy has not viewed street harassment as an issue worthy of attention, despite Robin West's repeated depiction of it as a disempowering injury to women that is virtually unrecognized by the law:

> [W]omen suffer unpunished and uncompensated sexual assaults continually. Women who live in urban areas and walk rather than drive or take taxis endure tortious or criminal sexual assaults daily. Although we have a trivializing phrase for these encounters—"street hassling"—these assaults are not at all trivial. They are frightening and threatening whispered messages of power and subjection. They are, in short, assaults. Yet, men who harass women on the street are not apprehended, they are not punished, the victims are not compensated, and no damages are paid. The entire transaction is entirely invisible to the state.

With the exception of one sociological discussion written in English and one survey by two Austrian sociologists, the study of street harassment has been carried out by a handful of scholars in the fields of speech, language, and com-

From *Harvard Law Review*, January 1993. Reprinted by permission. Portions of the original have been omitted.

munication. In the face of this relative silence, any student of street harassment must supplement the academic literature with sources less typical of legal scholarship—popular magazines directed at female audiences, literature, movies, plays, and letters to the editor in large city newspapers—in which women have related their experiences with street harassment. From these studies and stories, it is possible to construct an account of the harms of street harassment by describing the impact it has on its individual targets and to assess the impact of street harassment upon women as a group, upon relations between the sexes, and upon society as a whole.

❖ A. TOWARD A WORKING DEFINITION OF STREET HARASSMENT

A wide variety of behavior is included within the conduct generally considered by targets, survey respondents, and commentators to constitute street harassment. It includes both verbal and nonverbal behavior, such as "wolf-whistles, leers, winks, grabs, pinches, catcalls and street remarks"; the remarks are frequently sexual in nature and comment evaluatively on a woman's physical appearance or on her presence in public. The comments range from "Hello, baby" to vulgar suggestions and outright threats, such as "fucking bitch, fucking cunt," "[w]hite whore," or "you're just a piece of meat to me, bitch." Although street harassment encompasses a wide variety of behaviors, gestures, and comments, it has some defining characteristics: (1) the targets of street harassment are female; (2) the harassers are male; (3) the harassers are unacquainted with their targets; (4) the encounter is face to face; (5) the forum is a public one, such as a street, sidewalk, bus, bus station, taxi, or other place to which the public generally has access; but (6) the content of the speech, if any, is not intended as public discourse. Rather, the remarks are aimed at the individual (although the harasser may intend that they be overheard by comrades or passers-by), and they are objectively degrading, objectifying, humiliating, and frequently threatening in nature.

Anthropologist Micaela di Leonardo has offered the best working definition of street harassment:

> Street harassment occurs when one or more strange men accost one or more women . . . in a public place which is not the woman's/women's worksite. Through looks, words, or gestures the man asserts his right to intrude on the woman's attention, defining her as a sexual object, and forcing her to interact with him.

Although I will attempt to improve upon this definition by making it more specific and in some ways narrower when I define street harassment as a legal term, di Leonardo's definition is excellent for its descriptive value. It offers an objective rather than subjective standard by which to define street harassment; it focusses upon the harasser's actions rather than upon his intentions or perceptions; and it captures the experience of street harassment as intrusion.

One must turn to first-person accounts and to literature to get a sense of the experience of street harassment. The following description appeared in *Mademoiselle* magazine in 1984. It recounts the experiences of a woman who had been inclined as a girl to regard remarks from strange men or boys on the streets as complimentary:

> The shift in [my] thinking started when I moved to Manhattan and discovered that the relatively innocuous "Hey, good-looking" of my suburban girlhood was the exception rather than the rule. For the most part, men simply approached me with crude propositions. The first time a man walked toward me, opened his mouth, began panting and jerked his crotch, I didn't feel the least bit affirmed or desirable. I did feel embarrassed, humiliated, furious— and helpless. . . . It made me feel vulnerable and defenseless, as if I didn't really have control over my own flesh.

Another woman reported the following interchange, which occurred when she was out walking, absorbed in serious thought, and passed two men on the sidewalk:

> "Hey, why so serious, honey? Give us a little smile." My sense of humor, he didn't know, was temporarily out of service, so of course I didn't give him a little smile. But in not smiling, I had again violated the code, provoking another seizure of silent suffering that became verbal. As I passed the sleeve on the street, it hissed a word at me, with the edge of anger to it, with a sharp rebuke in it: "Bitch."

This account describes a common pattern, in which the target's failure to respond results in escalation and a superficially friendly interaction is transformed into one that is transparently hostile.

Finally, an example from a novel by Joyce Carol Oates:

> False facts.
> The detour around the construction, the mud, the planks, Elena walking carefully on one of the planks, and one of the men yelling at her. Cupping his hands to his mouth, yelling. Another man laughing. Another man laughing. Another man, stocky in his workclothes, throwing something at her that hadn't enough weight to carry itself to her—just a crumpled-up paper bag, a lunch bag.
> False facts: they didn't really want to hurt her.
> Didn't hate her.
> Didn't want her dead.
> False facts: the recitation of the weather around the country, the temperature recorded at all the airports. You believe it must mean something but it will not.
> False facts: blood on instruments, no proof of pain. Proof only of blood.

One cannot help but note the thinly concealed violence underlying each of these encounters.

The interactions described above also reflect major deviations from what sociologists refer to as the norm of civil inattention among strangers in public places. Typically, unacquainted persons passing on a public street, particularly in large cities, do not address one another, but instead perform an avoidance ritual: they make eye contact briefly from a distance of eight to ten feet, then avert their eyes and raise them again with a mid-distance focus on a point to the side of the passerby. Staring at a stranger is a well-established cultural taboo. Indeed, Erving Goffman noted, "'[t]he act of staring is a thing which one does not ordinarily do to another human being; it seems to put the object stared at in a class apart. One does not talk to a monkey in a zoo, or to a freak in a sideshow—one only stares.'"

Breaches of civil inattention that include a spoken component typically occur only when one encounters a person who is either very unusual (such as an individual carrying a couch, hopping on one foot, or dressed in costume) or unusually similar to oneself in some respect (for example, someone wearing the same college sweatshirt or driving the same make of car), or who is accompanied by someone or something in an "open" category, such as dogs or children. Men seem to regard women generally as such "open persons." Unlike men, women passing through public areas are subject to "markers of passage" that imply either that women are acting out of role simply by their presence in public or that a part of their role is in fact to be open to the public. These "markers" emphasize that women, unlike men, belong in the private sphere, the sphere of domestic rather than public responsibility. Ironically, men convey this message by intruding upon a woman's privacy as she enters the public sphere.

Central to the freedom to be at ease in public spaces is the capacity to pass through them while retaining a certain zone of privacy and autonomy—a zone of interpersonal distance that is crossed only by mutual consent. If, by contrast, women are subject to violation of that zone of personal privacy when they enter public areas, that very invasion of privacy effectively drives women back into the private sphere, where they may avoid such violations. Thus, by turning women into objects of public attention when they are in public, harassers drive home the message that women belong only in the world of the private.

❖ C. THE GEOGRAPHY OF STREET HARASSMENT

Street harassment is a common occurrence in large urban areas. News articles and commentators report that street harassment is particularly frequent, intense, and sexually explicit in Washington, D.C. Street harassment occurs both in the South of the United States and in the North. Florence King described her encounter with some "Good Ole Boys," whom she described as a "Southern Wasp phenomenon" with a facility for double entendre:

> Benches always draw the Good Ole Boys; any long seating arrangement in the South is bound to be full of them. Courthouse railings are their favorite hangout but a row of anything will do.

As I walked past them [in a bus station waiting room] it began.
"Shore would like to have that swing in my backyard."
"You want me to help you with your box, li'l lady?"
"Hesh up, Alvin, that ain't nice. Don't you talk to her like that."
"I just want to help her with her box, thass all."

Indeed, street harassment is a worldwide phenomenon, apparently absent only in small villages and under fundamentalist regimes in which women are literally veiled and seldom seen in public. One graduate student from India told me, for example, that, in the more than one year during which she worked as a lawyer in New Delhi, she was harassed at least once every day; she attributed this harassment to the fact that she was wearing Western clothes and engaging in non-traditional pursuits. Newspaper reports support her account of the pervasiveness of this conduct, which is called "Eve teasing" in India.

Within American cities, harassment is more common in certain places than others. Construction sites are perennial problems, and the presence of street pornography in an area seems to increase the likelihood of hassling, perhaps by symbolically condoning sexist attitudes and behavior. Some women report that they are spared stares and comments when they are in public places traditionally associated with the home, such as department stores, grocery stores, and churches; but others write of unpleasant encounters in these places as well. In addition, both personal and shared experiences reveal that men in trucks often harass women in cars. The 1991 movie *Thelma and Louise* graphically depicted this particular form of harassment. (The movie's two female protagonists ultimately confront their harasser and blow up his truck, usually to the cheers of the audience.) Case law and recent news articles show that taxicabs are also a common venue for harassment.

Benard and Schlaffer's empirical study indicates that there are some places, such as small villages, in which street harassment does *not* occur. This discovery led the authors to conclude that harassment is confined to the "genuinely *public* world," where people are strangers to one another. Apparently if someone exists for you as an individual, you are less likely to harass her—a fact reflected in the prototypical question used to confront harassers: "Would you want someone to treat your sister (or wife, or mother) this way?"

❖ D. HARASSERS AND THEIR TARGETS: WHO ARE THEY?

As should be clear from these accounts, the men who harass women in the street are not just construction workers; they include bus and taxi drivers, train conductors, males congregated on the streets, "Good Ole Boys," and passers-by. The activity crosses lines of geography, religion, race, age, and class. As one observer has suggested, the only reason street harassment superficially appears to be an institution of working-class men is that their place of business is more often the street. Benard and Schlaffer, who personally tested their hypotheses by acting as "testers" on the streets, reported that age, education, and income bore little relation to harassing behavior (although younger men tended to be more aggressive, and older men tended to lower their voices).

The target of street harassment is literally every woman between the age when her body begins to develop sexually and that undefined point when she is no longer assumed to be a sexual being because she is "too old." Different women may experience street harassment in different ways, though. For a very young girl, it is one of her first lessons in what it means to be a sexual being—a confusing and shame-producing experience. According to Robin West:

> *Street hassling is also the earliest—and therefore the* defining—*lesson in the source of a girl's disempowerment. If they haven't learned it anywhere else, street hassling teaches girls that their sexuality implies their vulnerability. It is damaging to be pointed at, jeered at, and laughed at for one's sexuality, and it is infantilizing to know you have to take it.*

Lesbians are subjected to a uniquely offensive experience, as they are both "punished" for being women and assumed to be what they are not—heterosexual. On the other hand, if it is obvious that they are lesbian, men harass them for that status as well.

The experience of street harassment may also differ with the race, class, or ethnicity of the targeted woman and the history of gender interactions to which she has become accustomed. Although it would be impossible adequately to describe all of these disparate reactions, it is useful to note some differences between the harassment experience of African-American women and of European-American women. In many African-American communities, men and women engage in sexually oriented banter in public; several writers have pointed to similarities between street harassment and these forms of repartee. Others conclude that African-American women are therefore not harmed by street remarks. Yet, although "rapping" may resemble some forms of street harassment in some respects, this custom is also distinguishable from street harassment, because women are not ratified speakers in the typical harassment context, but are merely intended overhearers. Furthermore, badinage, or humorous banter, is a mutually agreed-upon interaction, whereas street harassment takes place and persists even when the woman actively avoids interaction. Finally, it should be noted that, although many African-American women respond assertively to rapping, they typically do not initiate it. Thus, even in this context, speech rights are asymmetrical.

Although African-American women may be familiar with forms of interaction similar to street harassment and thus may experience harassment as something akin to a familiar gender interaction, it does not necessarily follow that they like it. I have not located any accounts in which Black women stated that they enjoyed street harassment. Rather, it is clear from newspaper stories that African-American women suffer great pain from street harassment and that in many large cities such harassment can be both more frequent and more intense for them than for other women. One African-American woman described the difference between the interactions to which she was accustomed and those that she encountered upon moving to Washington from the South:

> *I come from . . . the South. Where I'm from, black men and women address each other on the street. Those who don't are considered rude, ill-bred and hateful of black tradition. So I once had no qualms about speaking to men on the street.*
>
> *But in the past few months of living in Washington, I have lost the ability to discriminate between men who are being friendly and those who wish to do me harm. Now I view all gestures from men on the street as potential threats. All the car honks and "hey-baby" comments that I once considered just annoying are now ominous and alarming.*

In short, despite familiarity with forms of interaction superficially similar to street harassment, African-American women are also offended by it.

Moreover, Black women are harassed by both white and Black men—experiences that evoke different historical associations. Historically, African-American women have been subjected to particularly virulent and degrading forms of harassment by white men. They were treated as the sexual property of their masters during slavery, and this attitude survived emancipation. A typical modern interchange is described in a scene in Lorraine Hansberry's *To Be Young, Gifted and Black*:

> *In these streets out there, any little white boy from Long Island or Westchester sees me and leans out of his car and yells—"Hey there, hot chocolate! Say there, Jezebel! Hey you—'Hundred Dollar Misunderstanding'! YOU! Bet you know where there's a good time tonight. . . ."*

bell hooks has accurately explained this exchange as premised upon the assumption that all Black women, regardless of their class, are prostitutes and are available as sex objects. Thus, when African-American women are harassed on the street, the experience evokes a long history of disrespect, degradation, and inhumane sexual mistreatment to which Black women have been subjected over the years. One woman has tried to convey this message to African-American men who engage in street harassment:

> *I would like to address a special concern to those black men who are making the District a living hell for their sisters.*
>
> *. . . Your lewd invitations and crude commands may seem funny to you, but the truth is that nothing comes closer to the slave-era mentality of white men toward black women.*
>
> *Young black men yell at women who are mothers, "Come here, girl!" They whistle at women as if calling dogs. Even black children are not immune. I heard a grown man tell a 12-year-old, "I'll be back when you get a little older, baby."*

Hence, despite familiarity with sexual repartee on the streets, Black women may in fact suffer more intensely from street harassment than other women, because it resonates with remnants of a slave-era mentality.

In sum, although women from different backgrounds may experience street harassment through the lens of different historical and personal experiences, at base it remains an unwelcome and painful event for us all. In this sense, it is also a universalizing experience—one that virtually all women share. Indeed, its near-universality denotes the extent to which such harassment is simply accepted as normal and thus becomes invisible as a social problem.

19

"FETAL RIGHTS": A NEW ASSAULT ON FEMINISM

KATHA POLLITT

Some scenes from the way we live now:

In New York City, a pregnant woman orders a glass of wine with her restaurant meal. A stranger comes over to her table. "Don't you know you're poisoning your baby?" he says angrily, pointing to a city-mandated sign warning women that drinking during pregnancy can cause birth defects.

In California, Pamela Rae Stewart is advised by her obstetrician to stay off her feet, to eschew sex and "street drugs," and to go to the hospital immediately if she starts to bleed. She fails to follow this advice and delivers a brain-damaged baby who soon dies. She is charged with failing to deliver support to a child under an old criminal statute that was intended to force men to provide for women they have made pregnant.

In Washington, D.C., a hospital administration asks a court whether it should intervene and perform a Caesarean section on Angela Carder, seriously ill with cancer, against her wishes and those of her husband, her

parents and her doctors. Acknowledging that the operation would probably shorten her life without necessarily saving the life of her 25-week-
old fetus, the judge nonetheless provides the order. The Caesarean is performed immediately, before her lawyers can appeal. Angela Carder dies;
so does her unviable fetus. That incident is subsequently dramatized on
L.A. Law, with postfeminist softy Ann Kelsey arguing for the hospital;
on TV the baby lives.

In the Midwest, the U.S. Court of Appeals for the Seventh Circuit, ruling
in *UAW v. Johnson Controls,* upholds an automotive battery plant's
seven-year-old "fetal protection policy" barring fertile women (in effect,
all women) from jobs that would expose them to lead [see Carolyn Marshall, "An Excuse for Workplace Hazard," April 25, 1987]. The court
discounts testimony about the individual reproductive lives and plans of
female employees (many in their late 40s, celibate and/or with completed
families), testimony showing that no child born to female employees had
shown ill effects traceable to lead exposure and testimony showing that
lead poses a comparable danger to male reproductive health. The court
accepts testimony that says making the workplace safe would be too
expensive.

All over the country, pregnant women who use illegal drugs and/or alcohol are targeted by the criminal justice system. They are "preventively
detained" by judges who mete out jail sentences for minor crimes that would
ordinarily result in probation or a fine; charged with child abuse or neglect
(although by law the fetus is not a child) and threatened with manslaughter
charges should they miscarry; and placed under court orders not to drink,
although drinking is not a crime and does not invariably (or even usually)
result in birth defects. While state legislatures ponder bills that would authorize these questionable practices by criminalizing drug use or "excessive" alcohol use during pregnancy (California Senator Pete Wilson is pushing a similar
bill at the federal level), mothers are arrested in their hospital beds when their
newborns test positive for drugs. Social workers increasingly remove positive-
testing babies into foster care on the presumption that even a single use of
drugs during pregnancy renders a mother ipso facto an unfit parent.

What's going on here? Right now the hot area in the developing issue of "fetal
rights" is the use of drugs and alcohol during pregnancy. We've all seen the
nightly news reports of inner-city intensive care units overflowing with crack
babies, of Indian reservations where one in four children is said to be born
physically and mentally stunted by fetal alcohol syndrome (F.A.S.) or the
milder, but still serious, fetal alcohol effect. We've read the front-page stories
reporting studies that suggest staggering rates of drug use during pregnancy
(11 percent, according to *The New York Times,* or 375,000 women per year)
and the dangers of even moderate drinking during pregnancy.

But drugs and alcohol are only the latest focus of a preoccupation with the fetus and its "rights" that has been wandering around the *Zeitgeist* for the past decade. A few years ago, the big issue was forced Caesareans. (It was, in fact, largely thanks to the horrific Angela Carder case—one of the few involving a white, middle-class woman—that the American College of Obstetricians and Gynecologists condemned the practice, which nonetheless has not entirely ceased.) If the Supreme Court upholds the *Johnson Controls* decision, the next battleground may be the workplace. The "save the babies" mentality may look like a necessary, if troubling, approach when it's a matter of keeping a drug addict away from a substance that is, after all, illegal. What happens if the same mentality is applied to some 15 million to 20 million highly paid unionized jobs in heavy industry to "protect" fetuses that do not even exist? Or if the list of things women are put on legal notice to avoid expands to match medical findings on the dangers to the fetus posed by junk food, salt, aspirin, air travel and cigarettes?

Critics of the punitive approach to pregnant drug and alcohol users point out the ironies inherent in treating a public-health concern as a matter for the criminal justice system: the contradiction, for instance, of punishing addicted women when most drug treatment programs refuse to accept pregnant women. Indeed, Jennifer Johnson, a Florida woman who was the first person convicted after giving birth to a baby who tested positive for cocaine, had sought treatment and been turned away. (In her case the charge was delivering drugs to a minor.) The critics point out that threats of jail or the loss of their kids may drive women away from prenatal care and hospital deliveries, and that almost all the women affected so far have been poor and black or Latino, without private doctors to protect them (in Florida, nonwhite women are ten times as likely to be reported for substance abuse as white women, although rates of drug use are actually higher for whites).

These are all important points. But they leave unchallenged the notion of fetal rights itself. What we really ought to be asking is, How have we come to see women as the major threat to the health of their newborns, and the womb as the most dangerous place a child will ever inhabit? Why is our basic model "innocent" fetuses that would be fine if only presumably "guilty" women refrained from indulging their "whims"? The list of dangers to the fetus is, after all, very long; the list of dangers to children even longer. Why does maternal behavior, a relatively small piece of the total picture, seem such an urgent matter, while much more important factors—that one in five pregnant women receive no prenatal care at all, for instance—attract so little attention? Here are some of the strands that make up the current tangle that is fetal rights.

❖ THE ASSAULT ON THE POOR

It would be pleasant to report that the aura of crisis surrounding crack and F.A.S. babies—the urge to do *something*, however unconstitutional or cruel, that suddenly pervades society, from judge's bench to chic dinner party to 7 o'clock news—was part of a massive national campaign to help women have healthy, wanted pregnancies and healthy babies. But significantly, the current wave of concern is not occurring in that context. Judges order pregnant addicts to jail, but they don't order drug treatment programs to accept them, or Medicaid, which pays for heroin treatment, to cover crack addiction—let alone order landlords not to evict them, or obstetricians to take uninsured women as patients, or the federal government to fund fully the Women, Infants, and Children supplemental feeding program, which reaches only two-thirds of those who are eligible. The policies that have underwritten maternal and infant health in most of the industrialized West since World War II—a national health service, paid maternity leave, direct payments to mothers, government-funded day care, home health visitors for new mothers, welfare payments that reflect the cost of living—are still regarded in the United States by even the most liberal as hopeless causes, and by everyone else as budget-breaking give-aways to the undeserving, pie-in-the-sky items from a mad socialist's wish list.

The focus on maternal behavior allows the government to appear to be concerned about babies without having to spend any money, change any priorities or challenge any vested interests. As with crime, as with poverty, a complicated, multifaceted problem is construed as a matter of freely chosen individual behavior. We have crime because we have lots of bad people, poverty because we have lots of lazy people (Republican version) or lots of pathological people (Democratic version), and tiny, sickly, impaired babies because we have lots of women who just don't give a damn.

Once the problem has been defined as original sin, coercion and punishment start to look like hardheaded and common-sensical answers. Thus, syndicated columnist and *New Republic* intellectual Charles Krauthammer proposes locking up pregnant drug users en masse. Never mind the impracticality of the notion—suddenly the same Administration that refuses to pay for drug treatment and prenatal care is supposed to finance all that plus nine months of detention for hundreds of thousands of women a year. Or its disregard of real life—what, for example, about the children those women already have? Do they go to jail, too, like Little Dorrit? Or join the rolls of the notorious foster care system? The satisfactions of the punitive mind-set sweep all such considerations aside. (Nor are liberal pundits immune from its spell. Around the same time Krauthammer was calling for mass incarceration, Mary McGrory was suggesting that we stop wasting resources—*what* resources?—on addicted women and simply put their babies in orphanages.)

❖ THE NEW TEMPERANCE

While rightly sounding the alarm about the health risks and social costs of drugs, alcohol and nicotine, the various "just say no" crusades have so upped the moral ante across the board that it is now difficult to distinguish between levels and kinds of substance use and abuse and even rather suspect to try. A joint on the weekend is the moral equivalent of a twenty-four-hour-a-day crack habit; wine with meals is next door to a daily quart of rotgut. The stigmatizing of addicts, casual users, alcoholics, social drinkers and smokers makes punitive measures against them palatable. It also helps us avoid uncomfortable questions about why we are having all these "substance abuse" epidemics in the first place. Finally, it lets us assume, not always correctly, that drugs and alcohol, all by themselves, cause harm during pregnancy, and ignore the role of malnutrition, violence, chaotic lives, serious maternal health problems and lack of medical care.

✥ SCIENCE MARCHES ON

We know a lot more about fetal development than we did twenty years ago. But how much of what we know will we continue to know in ten years? As recently as the early 1970s, pregnant women were harassed by their doctors to keep their weight down. They were urged to take tranquilizers and other prescription drugs, to drink in moderation (liquor was routinely used to stop premature labor), to deliver under anesthesia and not bother to breast-feed. Then too, studies examined contemporary wisdom and found it good. Today, those precepts seem the obvious expression of social forces: the wish of doctors to control pregnancy and delivery, a lack of respect for women and a distaste for female physiological processes. It was not the disinterested progress of science that outmoded these practices. It was another set of social forces: the women's movement, the prepared-childbirth movement and the natural-health movement.

What about today's precepts? At the very least, the history of scientific research into pregnancy and childbirth ought to make us skeptical. Instead, we leap to embrace tentative findings and outright bad science because they fit current social prejudices. Those who argue for total abstinence during pregnancy have made much, for example, of a recent study in *The New England Journal of Medicine* that claimed women are more vulnerable than men to alcohol because they have less of a stomach enzyme that neutralizes it before it enters the bloodstream. Universally unreported, however, was the fact that the study included alcoholics and patients with gastrointestinal disease. It is a basic rule of medical research that results cannot be generalized from the sick to the healthy.

In a 1989 article in *The Lancet*, "Bias Against the Null Hypothesis: The Reproductive Hazards of Cocaine," Canadian researchers reported that studies that found a connection between cocaine use and poor pregnancy outcome had a better than even chance of being accepted for presentation at the annual meeting of the Society for Pediatric Research, while studies that found no connection had a negligible chance—although the latter were better designed. While it's hard to imagine that anyone will ever show that heavy drug use or alcohol consumption is good for fetal development, studies like this one suggest that when the dust settles (because the drug war is officially "won"? because someone finally looks at the newborns of Italy, where everyone drinks moderate amounts of wine with food, and finds them to be perfectly fine?) the current scientific wisdom will look alarmist.

❖ MEDIA BIAS

The assumptions that shape the way researchers frame their studies and the questions they choose to investigate are magnified by bias in the news media. Studies that show the bad effects of maternal behavior make the headlines, studies that show no bad effects don't get reported and studies that show the bad effects of paternal behavior (alcoholic males, and males who drink at conception, have been linked to lower I.Q. and a propensity to alcoholism in offspring) get two paragraphs in the science section. So did the study, briefly mentioned in a recent issue of *The New York Times,* suggesting that housewives run a higher risk than working women of having premature babies, stillbirths, underweight babies and babies who die in the first week of life. Imagine the publicity had it come out the other way around! Numbers that back up the feeling of crisis (those 375,000 drug-taking pregnant women) are presented as monolithic, although they cover a wide range of behavior (from daily use of cocaine to marijuana use during delivery, which some midwives recommend, and for which one Long Island woman lost custody of her newborn for eight months), and are illustrated by dire examples of harm that properly apply only to the most hard-core cases.

❖ THE "PRO-LIFE MOVEMENT"

Antichoicers have not succeeded in criminalizing abortion but they have made it inaccessible to millions of women (only sixteen states pay for poor women's abortions, and only 18 percent of counties have even one abortion provider) and made it a badge of sin and failure for millions more. In Sweden, where heavy drinking is common, relatively few F.A.S. babies are born, because alcoholic women have ready access to abortion and it is not a stigmatized choice. In America antichoice sentiment makes it impossible to suggest to a homeless, malnourished, venereally diseased crack addict that her first priority ought to be getting well: Get help, then have a baby. While the possibility of coerced abortions is something to be wary of, the current policy of regulation and punishment in the name of the fetus ironically risks the same end. Faced with criminal charges, pregnant women may seek abortions in order to stay out of jail (a Washington, D.C., women who "miscarried" a few days before sentencing may have done just that).

As lobbyists, antichoicers have sought to bolster their cause by interjecting the fetus-as-person argument into a wide variety of situations that would seem to have nothing to do with abortion. They have fought to exclude pregnant women from proposed legislation recognizing the validity of "living wills" that reject the use of life support systems (coma baby lives!), and have campaigned to classify as homicides assaults on pregnant women that result in fetal death or miscarriage. Arcane as such proposals may seem, they have the effect of broadening little by little the areas of the law in which the fetus is regarded as a person, and in which the woman is regarded as its container.

At a deeper level, the "pro-life" movement has polluted the way we think about pregnancy. It has promoted a model of pregnancy as a condition that by its very nature pits women and fetuses against each other, with the fetus invariably taking precedence, and a model of women as selfish, confused, potentially violent and incapable of making responsible choices. As the "rights" of the fetus grow and respect for the capacities and rights of women declines, it becomes harder and harder to explain why drug addiction is a crime if it produces an addicted baby, but not if it produces a miscarriage, and why a woman can choose abortion but not vodka. And that is just what the "pro-lifers" want.

❖ THE PRIVILEGED STATUS OF THE FETUS

Pro-choice activists rightly argue that antiabortion and fetal-rights advocates grant fetuses more rights than women. A point less often made is that they grant fetuses more rights than 2-year-olds—the right, for example, to a safe, healthy place to live. No court in this country would ever rule that a parent must undergo a medical procedure in order to benefit a child, even if that procedure is as riskless as a blood donation and the child is sure to die without it. (A Seattle woman is currently suing the father of her leukemic child to force him to donate bone marrow, but she is sure to lose, and her mere attempt roused *Newsday* science writer B.D. Colen to heights of choler unusual even for him.) Nor would a court force someone who had promised to donate a kidney and then changed his mind to keep his date with the organ bank. Yet, as the forced-Caesarean issue shows, we seem willing to deny the basic right of bodily integrity to pregnant women and to give the fetus rights we deny children.

Although concern for the fetus may look like a way of helping children, it is actually, in a funny way, a substitute for it. It is an illusion to think that by "protecting" the fetus from its mother's behavior we have insured a healthy birth, a healthy infancy or a healthy childhood, and that the only insurmountable obstacle for crack babies is prenatal exposure to crack.

It is no coincidence that we are obsessed with pregnant women's behavior at the same time that children's health is declining, by virtually any yardstick one chooses. Take general well-being: In constant dollars, welfare payments are now about two-thirds the 1965 level. Take housing: Thousands of children are now growing up in homeless shelters and welfare hotels. Even desperately alcoholic women bear healthy babies two-thirds of the time. Will two-thirds of today's homeless kids emerge unscathed from their dangerous and lead-permeated environments? Take access to medical care: Inner-city hospitals are closing all over the country, millions of kids have no health insurance and most doctors refuse uninsured or Medicaid patients. Even immunization rates are down: Whooping cough and measles are on the rise.

❖ THE "DUTY OF CARE"

Not everyone who favors legal intervention to protect the fetus is anti-choice. Some pro-choicers support the coercion and punishment of addicts and alcoholics—uneasily, like some of my liberal women friends, or gleefully, like Alan Dershowitz, who dismisses as absurd the "slippery slope" argument (crack today, cigarettes tomorrow) he finds so persuasive when applied to First Amendment issues. For some years now bioethicists have been fascinated by the doctrine of "duty of care," expounded most rigorously by Margery Shaw and John Robertson. In this view, a woman can abort, but once she has decided to bear a child she has a moral, and should have a legal, responsibility to insure a healthy birth. It's an attractive notion because it seems to combine an acceptance of abortion with intuitive feelings shared by just about everyone, including this writer, that pregnancy is a serious undertaking, that society has an interest in the health of babies, that the fetus, although not a person, is also not property.

Whatever its merits as a sentiment, though, the duty of care is a legal disaster. Exactly when, for instance, does the decision to keep a pregnancy take place? For the most desperately addicted—the crack addicts who live on the subway or prostitute themselves for drugs—one may ask if they ever form any idea ordinary people would call a decision, or indeed know they are pregnant until they are practically in labor. Certainly the inaccessibility of abortion denies millions of women the ability to decide.

But for almost all women the decision to carry a pregnancy to term has important, if usually unstated, qualifications. What one owes the fetus is balanced against other considerations, such as serious health risks to oneself (taking chemotherapy or other crucial medication), or the need to feed one's family (keeping a job that may pose risks) or to care for the children one already has (not getting the bed rest the doctor says you need). Why should pregnant women be barred from considering their own interests? It is, after all, what parents do all the time. The model of women's relation to the fetus proposed by the duty of care ethicists is an abstraction that ignores the realities of life even when they affect the fetus itself. In real life, for instance, to quit one's dangerous job means to lose one's health insurance, thus exposing the fetus to another set of risks.

It is also, even as an abstraction, a false picture. Try as she might, a woman cannot insure a healthy newborn; nor can statistical studies of probability (even well-designed ones) be related in an airtight way to individual cases. We know that cigarettes cause lung cancer, but try proving in a court of law that cigarettes and not air pollution, your job, your genes or causes unknown caused *your* lung cancer.

Yet far from shrinking from the slippery slope, duty of care theorists positively hurl themselves down it. Margery Shaw, for instance, believes that the production of an imperfect newborn should make a woman liable to criminal charges and "wrongful life" suits if she knows, or should have known, the risk involved in her behavior, whether it's drinking when her period is late (she has a duty to keep track of her cycle), delivering at home when her doctor advises her not to (what doctor doesn't?) or failing to abort a genetically damaged fetus (which she has a duty to find out about). So much for that "decision" to bear a child—a woman can't qualify it in her own interests but the state can revoke it for her on eugenic grounds.

As these examples show, there is no way to limit the duty of care to cases of flagrant or illegal misbehavior—duty is duty, and risk is risk. Thus, there is no way to enshrine duty of care in law without creating the sort of Romania-style fetal-police state whose possibility Dershowitz, among others, pooh-poohs. For there is no way to define the limits of what a pregnant woman must sacrifice for fetal benefit, or what she "should have known," or at what point a trivial risk becomes significant. My aunt advised me to get rid of my cats while I was pregnant because of the risk of toxoplasmosis. My doctor and I thought this rather extreme, and my husband simply took charge of the litter box. What if my doctor had backed up my aunt instead of me? If the worst had happened (and it always does to someone, somewhere), would I have been charged with the crime of not sending my cats to the Bide-A-Wee?

Although duty of care theorists would impose upon women a virtually limitless obligation to put the fetus first, they impose that responsibility *only* on women. Philosophy being what it is, perhaps it should not surprise us that they place no corresponding duty upon society as a whole. But what about Dad? It's his kid too, after all. His drug and alcohol use, his prescription medications, his workplace exposure and general habits of health not only play a part in determining the quality of his sperm but affect the course of pregnancy as well. Cocaine dust and smoke from crack, marijuana and tobacco present dangers to others who breathe them; his alcoholism often bolsters hers. Does he have a duty of care to make it possible for his pregnant partner to obey those judge's orders and that doctor's advice that now has the force of law? To quit his job to mind the children so that she can get the bed rest without which her fetus may be harmed? Apparently not.

The sexist bias of duty of care has already had alarming legal consequences. In the Pamela Rae Stewart case cited at the beginning of this article, Stewart's husband, who had heard the doctor's advice, ignored it all and beat his wife into the bargain. Everything she did, he did—they had sex together, smoked pot together, delayed getting to the hospital together—but he was not charged with a crime, not even with wife-beating, although no one can say that his assaults were not a contributing cause of the infant's injury and death. In Tennessee, a husband succeeded in getting a court order forbidding his wife to drink or take drugs, although he himself had lost his driver's license for driving while intoxicated. In Wyoming, a pregnant woman was arrested for drinking when she presented herself at the hospital for treatment of injuries inflicted by her husband. Those charges were dropped (to be reinstated, should her baby be born with defects), but none were instituted against her spouse.

It is interesting to note in this regard that approximately one in twelve women are beaten during pregnancy, a time when many previously nonviolent men become brutal. We do not know how many miscarriages, stillbirths and damaged newborns are due, or partly due, to male violence—this is itself a comment on the skewed nature of supposedly objective scientific research. But if it ever does come to be an officially recognized factor in fetal health, the duty of care would probably take yet another ironic twist and hold battered pregnant women liable for their partner's assaults.

The Broken Cord, Michael Dorris's much-praised memoir of his adopted F.A.S. child, Adam, is a textbook example of the way in which all these social trends come together—and the largely uncritical attention the book has received shows how seductive a pattern they make. Dorris has nothing but contempt for Adam's birth mother. Perhaps it is asking too much of human nature to expect him to feel much sympathy for her. He has witnessed, in the most intimate and heartbreaking way, the damage her alcoholism did, and seen the ruin of his every hope for Adam, who is deeply retarded. But why is his anger directed only at her? Here was a seriously alcoholic woman, living on an Indian reservation where heavy drinking is a way of life, along with poverty, squalor, violence, despair and powerlessness, where, one might even say, a kind of racial suicide is taking place, with liquor as the weapon of choice. Adam's mother, in fact, died two years after his birth from drinking antifreeze.

Dorris dismisses any consideration of these facts as bleeding-heart fuzzy-mindedness. Like Hope on *thirtysomething*, Adam's mother "decides" to have a baby; like the martini-sipping pregnant woman Dorris badgers in an airport bar, she "chooses" to drink out of "weakness" and "self-indulgence."

Dorris proposes preventive detention of alcoholic pregnant women and quotes sympathetically a social worker who thinks the real answer is sterilization. Why do alcoholic Indian women have so many children? To up their government checks. (In fact, Bureau of Indian Affairs hospitals are prohibited by law from performing abortions, even if women can pay for them.) And why, according to Dorris, do they drink so much in the first place? Because of the feminist movement, which has undermined the traditional temperance of reservation women.

The women's movement has had about as much effect on impoverished reservation dwellers as it had on the slum women of eighteenth-century London, whose heavy binge drinking—and stunted babies—appalled contemporary observers. That Dorris pins the blame on such an improbable villain points to what fetal rights is really about—controlling women. It's a reaction to legalized abortion and contraception, which have given women, for the first time in history, real reproductive power. They can have a baby, they can "kill" a baby, they can refuse to conceive at all, without asking permission from anyone. More broadly, it's an index of deep discomfort with the notion of women as self-directed social beings, for whom parenthood is only one aspect of life, as it has always been for men. Never mind that in the real world, women still want children, have children and take care of children, often under the most discouraging circumstances and at tremendous emotional, economic and physical cost. There is still a vague but powerful cultural fear that one of these days, women will just walk out on the whole business of motherhood and the large helpings of humble pie we have, as a society, built into that task. And *then* where will we be?

Looked at in this light, the inconsistent and fitful nature of our concern about the health of babies forms a pattern. The threat to newborns is interesting when and only when it can, accurately or fancifully, be laid at women's doorstep. Babies "possibly" impaired by maternal drinking? Front-page stories, a national wave of alarm. A *New England Journal of Medicine* report that 16 percent of American children have been mentally and neurologically damaged because of exposure to lead, mostly from flaking lead paint in substandard housing? Peter Jennings looks mournful and suggests that "all parents can do" is to have their children tested frequently. If the mother isn't to blame, no one is to blame.

In its various aspects "fetal rights" attacks virtually all the gains of the women's movement. Forced medical treatment attacks women's increased control over pregnancy and delivery by putting doctors back in the driver's seat, with judges to back them up. The *Johnson Controls* decision reverses the entry of women into high-paying, unionized, traditionally male jobs. In the female ghetto, where women can hardly be dispensed with, the growing practice of laying off or shifting pregnant women around transforms women, whose rates of labor-force participation are approaching those of men, into casual laborers with reduced access to benefits, pensions, seniority and promotions. In a particularly vicious twist of the knife, "fetal rights" makes legal abortion—which makes all the other gains possible—the trigger for a loss of human rights. Like the divorce-court judges who tell middle-aged housewives to go out and get a job, or who favor fathers in custody disputes because to recognize the primary-caretaker role of mothers would be "sexist," protectors of the fetus enlist the rhetoric of feminism to punish women.

There are lots of things wrong with the concept of fetal rights. It posits a world in which women will be held accountable, on sketchy or no evidence, for birth defects; in which all fertile women will be treated as potentially pregnant all the time; in which courts, employers, social workers and doctors—not to mention nosy neighbors and vengeful male partners—will monitor women's behavior. It imposes responsibilities without giving women the wherewithal to fulfill them, and places upon women alone duties that belong to both parents and to the community.

But the worst thing about fetal rights is that it portrays a woman as having only contingent value. Her work, her health, her choices and needs and beliefs, can all be set aside in an instant because, next to maternity, they are all perceived as trivial. For the middle class, fetal rights is mostly symbolic, the gateway to a view of motherhood as self-sacrifice and endless guilty soul-searching. It ties in neatly with the currently fashionable suspicion of working mothers, day care and (now that wives are more likely than husbands to sue for it) divorce. For the poor, for whom it means jail and the loss of custody, it becomes a way of saying that women can't even be mothers. They can only be potting soil.

The plight of addicted and alcohol-impaired babies is indeed a tragedy. Finally, we are forced to look at the results of our harsh neglect of the welfare and working poor, and it's only natural that we don't like what we see. We are indeed in danger of losing a generation. But what about the generation we already have? Why is it so hard for us to see that the tragedy of Adam Dorris is inextricable from the tragedy of his mother? Why is her loss—to society, to herself—so easy to dismiss?

"People are always talking about women's duties to others," said Lynn Paltrow, the A.C.L.U. lawyer who successfully led the Pamela Rae Stewart defense, "as though women were not the chief caregivers in this society. But no one talks about women's duty of care to *themselves.* A pregnant addict or alcoholic needs to get help for *herself.* She's not just potentially ruining someone else's life. She's ruining her own life.

"Why isn't her own life important? Why don't we care about her?"

Institutions in Crisis

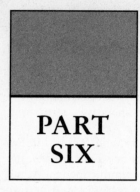

PART SIX

THE FAMILY

Is there a crisis in the American family? Certainly it is a time of change for the family, and many believe it is also a time of trouble. Over the past two decades, the divorce rate has risen and the birthrate has decreased. The "traditional" family, with the husband as the sole source of financial support and the wife as a full-time homebody, still exists, of course, but it is now a statistical minority. Increasingly large numbers of women, married or not, have entered the labor force. Others live in unconventional intimate arrangements and contribute to the increasing diversity of American family lifestyles. All of this diversity, this permissiveness, if you will, seems to many to be menacing the integrity and stability of the American family.

Still, the American family will doubtless remain with us for a long time. It may look less and less like the conventional family of suburbia in the 1950s—with its traditional male and female roles—but the family will nevertheless continue, with accompanying transformations, readjustments, and problems.

These changes do not, however, necessarily signal decline or decay—just difference. To conclude that the family is declining, one must point to a historical era when things were rosier. Certainly the ideal of home, motherhood, and apple pie is part of our romantic mythology, but the myth did not always match the experience. As one historian concludes, "There is no Golden Age of the Family gleaming at us from far back in the historical past."

Still, because of change, many Americans—men and women, husbands and wives, parents and children—are experiencing marked uncertainties and anxieties. We have known deep changes in family life and in society. But our understanding of how to interpret these changes—and to deal with them—has been impaired by lack of knowledge about the relationship between family life and society, particularly about the impact of societal imperatives, structures, and constraints upon the everyday workings of family life.

America has become a high-risk, high-stress society, and family life has been feeling the strain. Economic recessions produce major strains for families and those living within them. This is especially true as economic inequality and homelessness have hardened into stubbornly persistent features of American life. But the middle-class family has also been hit uncommonly hard by economic decline. Layoffs among blue- and white-collar workers have resulted in downward social mobility for suburban as well as inner-city families. Private family troubles have become controversial public issues as the holes in the social safety net have widened throughout American society.

During the 1980s, conservative arguments stressing the moral irresponsibility of the poor dominated the national debate about the family. During the 1990s, under the Clinton administration, public and private policies regarding family leave and child care may help in supporting the underpinnings of family life and reducing its most evident pathologies.

Of all the pathologies of the family, none is more destructive than domestic violence against women and children. Male violence against women, as Nancy Gibbs reports in her article on domestic violence, is nothing new. As one of those she interviewed stated, "It is at least as old an institution as marriage." Recently, however, reports of domestic violence have escalated. That is probably because women in battered relationships have come to understand that there is no shame in reporting their victimization.

At the same time, a new and troubling issue has arisen. What of women who kill their tormenters, not "imminently" as the criminal law of self-defense requires, but with planning and forethought? As Nancy Gibbs's article suggests, this crisis of domestic violence has no easy answers, although mercy and understanding are increasingly being offered to battered women who murder their batterers.

As economic inequality grows in the United States, increasing numbers of children, particularly black and minority children, are being consigned to a life of poverty. In part, this is related to high teenage pregnancy rates. As Marian Wright Edelman points out in "Children at Risk," adolescent parents are generally not affluent parents. They are typically unskilled, and it is their lack of marketable skills that keeps them and their children from rising out of poverty. As Edelman concludes, a disproportionate number of children will grow up unskilled and poor just when our society desperately requires healthy, educated, and productive people. This, as a recent report by a national commission concluded, is "a staggering national tragedy" facing America's future.

Is family poverty an economic or a moral problem? Does family disintegration lead to poverty, or does poverty lead to family disintegration? Which is the cause, and which the effect? More to the point, does it much matter?

Obviously, poverty and family disintegration are correlated. Those who stress traditional "family values" rarely consider the need for a social system in which it is possible for family values to be generated and nurtured. We do know how to help children. We know that Head Start works—not every time, nor in every instance—but on the whole. We know that prenatal care works. We know that affordable housing works. The more economic and social neglect of families and children our society tolerates, the more it must be prepared to accept the unwelcome consequences of such neglect.

In thinking about the family and its relation to society, we also need to ask a deeper question: What *is* this social formation we call the "family"? During the 1950s, sociologists studying the family entertained a vision of the nuclear family as a breadwinner father, a homemaker mother, and two or three children living in the suburbs. That vision was already becoming outdated and would become seriously so as social conceptions of gender roles shifted in the 1960s and 1970s. As we look toward the twenty-first century, it is expected that 80 percent of women will be in the work force. Today the proportion is roughly 70 percent. Two women, Zoe Baird and Kimba Wood, were disqualified to be U.S. attorney general because they had hired illegal immigrants as caretakers for their children.

But since 1970, when the White House Conference on Children declared child care to be the most serious problem facing American families, little has been done to reach a solution to this problem, a predicament that Edward F. Zigler calls a "crisis" as increasing numbers of women flock to the job market. In "Addressing the Nation's Child Care Crisis," Zigler compares child care to education and argues that we will have to develop the same sort of commitment to universal child care that we do to education. We have learned that education is fundamental to our conception of a free society. It is both a public good and public responsibility; so, Zigler argues, is child care.

20

'TIL DEATH DO US PART

NANCY GIBBS

The law has always made room for killers. Soldiers kill the nation's enemies, executioners kill its killers, police officers under fire may fire back. Even a murder is measured in degrees, depending on the mind of the criminal and the character of the crime. And sometime this spring, in a triumph of pity over punishment, the law may just find room for Rita Collins.

"They all cried, didn't they? But not me," she starts out, to distinguish herself from her fellow inmates in a Florida prison, who also have stories to tell. "No one will help me. No one will write about me. I don't have a dirty story. I wasn't abused as a child. I was a respectable government employee, employed by the Navy in a high position in Washington."

Her husband John was a military recruiter, a solid man who had a way with words. "He said I was old, fat, crazy and had no friends that were real friends. He said I needed him and he would take care of me." She says his care included threats with a knife, punches, a kick to the stomach that caused a hemorrhage. Navy doctors treated her for injuries to her neck and arm. "He'd slam me up against doors. He gave me black eyes, bruises. Winter and summer,

I'd go to work like a Puritan, with long sleeves. Afterward he'd soothe me, and I'd think, He's a good man. What did I do wrong?"

The bravado dissolves, and she starts to cry.

"I was envied by other wives. I felt ashamed because I didn't appreciate him." After each beating came apologies and offerings, gifts, a trip. "It's like blackmail. You think it's going to stop, but it doesn't." Collins never told any-one—not her friends in the church choir, not even a son by her first marriage. "I should have, but it was the humiliation of it all. I'm a professional woman. I didn't want people to think I was crazy." But some of them knew anyway; they had seen the bruises, the black eye behind the dark glasses.

She tried to get out. She filed for divorce, got a restraining order, filed an assault-and-battery charge against him, forced him from the house they had bought with a large chunk of her money when they retired to Florida. But still, she says, he came, night after night, banging on windows and doors, trying to break the locks.

It wasn't her idea to buy a weapon. "The police did all they could, but they had no control. They felt sorry for me. They told me to get a gun." She still doesn't remember firing it. She says she remembers her husband's face, the glassy eyes, a knife in his hands. "To this day, I don't remember pulling the trigger."

The jury couldn't figure it out either. At Collins' first trial, for first-degree murder, her friends, a minister, her doctors and several experts testified about her character and the violence she had suffered. The prosecution played tapes of her threatening her husband over the phone and portrayed her as a bitter, unstable woman who had bought a gun, lured him to the house and murdered him out of jealousy and anger over the divorce. That trial ended with a hung jury. At her second, nine men and three women debated just two hours before finding her guilty of the lesser charge, second-degree murder Collins' appeals were denied, and the parole board last year recommended against clemency. Orlando prosecutor Dorothy Sedgwick is certain that justice was done. "Rita Collins is a classic example of how a woman can decide to kill her husband and use the battered woman's syndrome as a fake defense," she says. "She lured him to his death. He was trying to escape her." Collins says her lawyers got everything: the $125,000 three-bedroom house with a pool, $98,000 in cash. "I've worked since I was 15, and I have nothing," she says. "The Bible says, 'Thou shalt not kill,' and everybody figures if you're in here, you're guilty. But I'm not a criminal. Nobody cares if I die in here, but if I live, I tell you one thing: I'm not going to keep quiet."

If in the next round of clemency hearings on March 10, Governor Lawton Chiles grants Collins or any other battered woman clemency, Florida will join 26 other states in a national movement to take another look at the cases of abuse victims who kill their abusers. Just before Christmas, Missouri's conserva-tive Republican Governor John Ashcroft commuted the life sentences of two women who claimed they had killed their husbands in self-defense. After 20 years of trying, these women have made a Darwinian claim for mercy: Vic-tims of perpetual violence should be forgiven if they turn violent themselves.

More American women—rich and poor alike—are injured by the men in their life than by car accidents, muggings and rape combined. Advocates and experts liken the effect over time to a slow-acting poison. "Most battered women aren't killing to protect themselves from being killed that very moment," observes Charles Ewing, a law professor at SUNY Buffalo. "What they're protecting themselves from is slow but certain destruction, psychologically and physically. There's no place in the law for that."

As the clemency movement grows, it challenges a legal system that does not always distinguish between a crime and a tragedy. What special claims should victims of fate, poverty, violence, addiction be able to make upon the sympathies of juries and the boundaries of the law? In cases of domestic assaults, some women who suffered terrible abuse resorted to terrible means to escape it. Now the juries, and ultimately the society they speak for, have to find some way to express outrage at the brutality that women and children face every day, without accepting murder as a reasonable response to it.

But until America finds a better way to keep people safe in their own homes or offers them some means of surviving if they flee, it will be hard to answer the defendants who ask their judges, "What choice did I really have?"

❖ HOME IS WHERE THE HURT IS

Last year the A.M.A., backed by the Surgeon General, declared that violent men constitute a major threat to women's health. The National League of Cities estimates that as many as half of all women will experience violence at some time in their marriage. Between 22% and 35% of all visits by females to emergency rooms are for injuries from domestic assaults. Though some studies have found that women are just as likely to start a fight as men, others indicate they are six times as likely to be seriously injured in one. Especially grotesque is the brutality reserved for pregnant women: the March of Dimes has concluded that the battering of women during pregnancy causes more birth defects than all the diseases put together for which children are usually immunized. Anywhere from one-third to as many as half of all female murder victims are killed by their spouses or lovers, compared with 4% of male victims.

"Male violence against women is at least as old an institution as marriage," says clinical psychologist Gus Kaufman Jr., cofounder of Men Stopping Violence, an Atlanta clinic established to help men face their battering problems. So long as a woman was considered her husband's legal property, police and the courts were unable to prevent—and unwilling to punish—domestic assaults. Notes N.Y.U. law professor Holly Maguigan: "We talk about the notion of the rule of thumb, forgetting that it had to do with the restriction on a man's right to use a weapon against his wife: he couldn't use a rod that was larger than his thumb." In 1874 North Carolina became one of the first states to limit a man's right to beat his wife, but lawmakers noted that unless he beat her nearly to death "it is better to draw the curtain, shut out the public gaze and leave the parties to forget and forgive."

Out of that old reluctance grew the modern double standard. Until the first wave of legal reform in the 1970s, an aggravated assault against a stranger was a felony, but assaulting a spouse was considered a misdemeanor, which rarely landed the attacker in court, much less in jail. That distinction, which still exists in most states, does not reflect the danger involved: a study by the Boston Bar Association found that the domestic attacks were at least as dangerous as 90% of felony assaults. "Police seldom arrest, even when there are injuries serious enough to require hospitalization of the victim," declared the Florida Supreme Court in a 1990 gender-bias study, which also noted the tendency of prosecutors to drop domestic-violence cases.

Police have always hated answering complaints about domestic disputes. Experts acknowledge that such situations are often particularly dangerous, but suspect that there are other reasons for holding back. "This issue pushes buttons, summons up personal emotions, that almost no other issue does for police and judges," says Linda Osmundson, who co-chairs a battered wives' task force for the National Coalition Against Domestic Violence. "Domestic violence is not seen as a crime. A man's home is still his castle. There is a system that really believes that women should be passive in every circumstance." And it persists despite a 20-year effort by advocates to transform attitudes toward domestic violence.

While most of the effort has been directed at helping women survive, and escape abusive homes, much of the publicity has fallen on those rare cases when women resort to violence themselves. Researcher and author Angela Browne points out that a woman is much more likely to be killed by her partner than to kill him. In 1991, when some 4 million women were beaten and 1,320 murdered in domestic attacks, 622 women killed their husbands or boyfriends. Yet the women have become the lightning rods for debate, since their circumstances, and their response, were most extreme.

❖ WHAT CHOICE DID SHE HAVE?

"There is an appropriate means to deal with one's marital problems—legal recourse. Not a .357 Magnum," argues former Florida prosecutor Bill Catto. "If you choose to use a gun to end a problem, then you must suffer the consequences of your act." Defense lawyers call it legitimate self-protection when a victim of abuse fights back—even if she shoots her husband in his sleep. Prosecutors call it an act of vengeance, and in the past, juries have usually agreed and sent the killer to jail. Michael Dowd, director of the Pace University Battered Women's Justice Center, has found that the average sentence for a woman who kills her mate is 15 to 20 years; for a man, 2 to 6.

The punishment is not surprising, since many judges insist that evidence of past abuse, even if it went on for years, is not relevant in court unless it occurred around the time of the killing. It is not the dead husband who is on trial, they note, but the wife who pulled the trigger. "Frankly, I feel changing the law would be authorizing preventive murder," argued Los Angeles Superior Court Judge Lillian Stevens in the Los Angeles *Times.* "The only thing that really matters is, Was there an immediate danger? There can't be an old grievance." And even if a woman is allowed to testify about past violence, the jury may still condemn her response to it. If he was really so savage, the prosecutor typically asks, why didn't she leave, seek shelter, call the police, file a complaint?

"The question presumes she has good options," says Julie Blackman, a New Jersey–based social psychologist who has testified as an expert witness in abuse and murder cases. "Sometimes, they don't leave because they have young children and no other way to support them, or because they grow up in cultures that are so immersed in violence that they don't figure there's any place better to go, or because they can't get apartments." The shelter facilities around the country are uniformly inadequate: New York has about 1,300 beds for a state with 18 million people. In 1990 the Baltimore zoo spent twice as much money to care for animals as the state of Maryland spent on shelters for victims of domestic violence.

Last July, even as reports of violence continued to multiply, the National Domestic Violence Hotline was disconnected. The 800 number had received as many as 10,000 calls a month from across the country. Now, says Mary Ann Bohrer, founder of the New York City–based Council for Safe Families, "there is no number, no national resource, for people seeking information about domestic violence."

The other reason women don't flee is because, ironically, they are afraid for their life. Law-enforcement experts agree that running away greatly increases the danger a woman faces. Angered at the loss of power and control, violent men often try to track down their wives and threaten them, or their children, if they don't come home. James Cox III, an unemployed dishwasher in Jacksonville, Florida, was determined to find his ex-girlfriend, despite a court order to stay away from her. Two weeks ago, he forced her mother at gunpoint to tell him the location of the battered women's shelter where her daughter had fled, and stormed the building, firing a shotgun. Police shot him dead. "This case illustrates the extent to which men go to pursue their victims," said executive director Rita DeYoung. "It creates a catch-22 for all battered women. Some will choose to return to their abusers, thinking they can control their behavior."

"After the law turns you away, society closes its doors on you, and you find yourself trapped in a life with someone capable of homicide. What choice in the end was I given?" asks Shalanda Burt, 21, who is serving 17 years for shooting her boyfriend James Fairley two years ago in Bradenton, Florida. She was three months pregnant at the time. A week after she delivered their first baby, James raped her and ripped her stitches. Several times she tried to leave or get help. "I would have a bloody mouth and a swollen face. All the police would do is give me a card with a deputy's name on it and tell me it was a 'lovers' quarrel.' The battered women's shelter was full. All they could offer was a counselor on the phone."

Two weeks before the shooting, the police arrested them both: him for aggravated assault because she was pregnant, her for assault with a deadly missile and violently resisting arrest. She had thrown a bottle at his truck. Her bail was $10,000; his was $3,000. He was back home before she was, so she sent the baby to stay with relatives while she tried to raise bail. The end came on a Christmas weekend. After a particularly vicious beating, he followed her to her aunt's house. When he came at her again, she shot him. "They say I'm a violent person, but I'm not. I didn't want revenge. I just wanted out." Facing 25 years, she was told by a female public defender to take a plea bargain and 17 years. "I wanted to fight. But she said I'd get life or the electric chair. I was in a no-win situation."

It is hard for juries to understand why women like Burt do not turn to the courts for orders of protection. But these are a makeshift shield at best, often violated and hard to enforce. Olympic skier Patricia Kastle had a restraining order when her former husband shot her. Lisa Bianco in Indiana remained terrified of her husband even after he was sent to jail for eight years. When prison officials granted Alan Matheney an eight-hour pass in March 1989, he drove directly to Bianco's home, broke in and beat her to death with the butt of a shotgun. Last March, Shirley Lowery, a grandmother of 11, was stabbed 19 times with a butcher knife by her former boyfriend in the hallway of the courthouse where she had gone to get an order of protection.

❖ THE MIND OF THE VICTIM

Defense lawyers have a hard time explaining to juries the shame, isolation and emotional dependency that bind victims to their abusers. Many women are too proud to admit to their family or friends that their marriage is not working and blame themselves for its failure even as they cling to the faith that their violent lover will change. "People confuse the woman's love for the man with love of abuse," says Pace's Dowd. "It's not the same thing. Which of us hasn't been involved in a romantic relationship where people say this is no good for you?"

It was Denver psychologist Lenore Walker, writing in 1984, who coined the term battered-woman syndrome to explain the behavior of abuse victims. Her study discussed the cycle of violence in shattering households: first a period of growing tension; then a violent explosion, often unleashed by drugs or alcohol; and finally a stage of remorse and kindness. A violent man, she argues, typically acts out of a powerful need for control—physical, emotional, even financial. He may keep his wife under close surveillance, isolating her from family and friends, forbidding her to work or calling constantly to check on her whereabouts. Woven into the scrutiny are insults and threats that in the end can destroy a woman's confidence and leave her feeling trapped between her fear of staying in a violent home—and her fear of fleeing it.

Many lawyers say it is virtually impossible to defend a battered woman without some expert testimony about the effect of that syndrome over time. Such testimony allows attorneys to stretch the rules governing self-defense, which were designed to deal with two men caught in a bar fight, not a woman caught in a violent relationship with a stronger man.

In a traditional case of self-defense, a jury is presented a "snapshot" of a crime: the mugger threatens a subway rider with a knife; the rider pulls a gun and shoots his attacker. It is up to the jurors to decide whether the danger was real and immediate and whether the response was reasonable. A woman who shoots her husband while he lunges at her with a knife should have little trouble claiming that she acted in self-defense. Yet lawyers still find jurors to be very uncomfortable with female violence under any circumstances, especially violence directed at a man she may have lived with for years.

Given that bias, it is even harder for a lawyer to call it self-defense when a woman shoots a sleeping husband. The danger was hardly immediate, prosecutors argue, nor was the lethal response reasonable. Evidence about battered-woman syndrome may be the only way to persuade a jury to identify with a killer. "Battered women are extraordinarily sensitive to cues of danger, and that's how they survive," says Walker. "That is why many battered women kill, not during what looks like the middle of a fight, but when the man is more vulnerable or the violence is just beginning."

A classic self-defense plea also demands a fair fight. A person who is punched can punch back, but if he shoots, he runs the risk of being charged with murder or manslaughter. This leaves women and children, who are almost always smaller and weaker than their attackers, in a bind. They often see no way to escape an assault without using a weapon and the element of surprise—arguing, in essence, that their best hope of self-defense was a preemptive strike. "Morally and legally a woman should not be expected to wait until his hands are around her neck," argues Los Angeles defense attorney Leslie Abramson. "Say a husband says, 'When I get up tomorrow morning, I'm going to beat the living daylights out of you,'" says Joshua Dressler, a law professor at Wayne State University who specializes in criminal procedures. "If you use the word imminent, the woman would have to wait until the next morning and, just as he's about to kill her, then use self-defense."

That argument, prosecutors retort, is an invitation to anarchy. If a woman has survived past beatings, what persuaded her that this time was different, that she had no choice but to kill or be killed? The real catalyst, they suggest, was not her fear but her fury. Prosecutors often turn a woman's history of abuse into a motive for murder. "What some clemency advocates are really saying is that that s.o.b. deserved to die and why should she be punished for what she did," argues Dressler. Unless the killing came in the midst of a violent attack, it amounts to a personal death-penalty sentence. "I find it very hard to say that killing the most rotten human being in the world when he's not currently threatening the individual is the right thing to do."

Those who oppose changes in the laws point out that many domestic disputes are much more complicated than the clemency movement would suggest. "We've got to stop perpetuating the myth that men are all vicious and that women are all Snow White," says Sonny Burmeister, a divorced father of three children who, as president of the Georgia Council for Children's Rights in Marietta, lobbies for equal treatment of men involved in custody battles. He recently sheltered a husband whose wife had pulled a gun on him. When police were called, their response was "So?" Says Burmeister: "We perpetuate this macho, chauvinistic, paternalistic attitude for men. We are taught to be protective of the weaker sex. We encourage women to report domestic violence. We believe men are guilty. But women are just as guilty."

He charges that feminists are trying to write a customized set of laws. "If Mom gets mad and shoots Dad, we call it PMS and point out that he hit her six months ago," he complains. "If Dad gets mad and shoots Mom, we call it domestic violence and charge him with murder. We paint men as violent and we paint women as victims, removing them from the social and legal consequences of their actions. I don't care how oppressed a woman is; should we condone premeditated murder?"

Only nine states have passed laws permitting expert testimony on battered-woman syndrome and spousal violence. In most cases it remains a matter of judicial discretion. One Pennsylvania judge ruled that testimony presented by a prosecutor showed that the defendant had not been beaten badly enough to qualify as a battered woman and therefore could not have that standard applied to her case. President Bush signed legislation in October urging states to accept expert testimony in criminal cases involving battered women. The law calls for development of training materials to assist defendants and their attorneys in using such testimony in appropriate cases.

Judge Lillian Stevens instructed the jury on the rules governing self-defense at the 1983 trial of Brenda Clubine, who claimed that she killed her police-informant husband because he was going to kill her. Clubine says that during an 11-year relationship, she was kicked, punched, stabbed, had the skin on one side of her face torn off, a lung pierced, ribs broken. She had a judge's order protecting her and had pressed charges to have her husband arrested for felony battery. But six weeks later, she agreed to meet him in a motel, where Clubine alleges that she felt her life was in danger and hit him over the head with a wine bottle, causing a fatal brain hemorrhage, "I didn't mean to kill him," she says. "He had hit me several times. Something inside me snapped; I grabbed the bottle and swung." The jury found Clubine guilty of second-degree manslaughter, and Judge Stevens sentenced her to 15 years to life. She says Clubine drugged her husband into lethargy before fatally hitting him. "It seemed to me [the beatings] were some time ago," Stevens told the Los Angeles *Times.* Furthermore, she added, "there was evidence that a lot of it was mutual."

It is interesting that within the legal community there are eloquent opponents of battered-woman syndrome—on feminist grounds—who dislike the label's implication that all battered women are helpless victims of some shared mental disability that prevents them from acting rationally. Social liberals, says N.Y.U.'s Maguigan, typically explain male violence in terms of social or economic pressures. Female violence, on the other hand, is examined in psychological terms. "They look to what's wrong with her and reinforce a notion that women who use violence are, per se, unreasonable, that something must be wrong with her because she's not acting like a good woman, in the way that women are socialized to behave."

Researcher Charles Ewing compared a group of 100 battered women who had killed their partners with 100 battered women who hadn't taken that fatal step. Women who resorted to violence were usually those who were most isolated, socially and economically; they had been the most badly beaten, their children had been abused, and their husbands were drug or alcohol abusers. That is, the common bond was circumstantial, not psychological. "They're not pathological," says social psychologist Blackman. "They don't have personality disorders. They're just beat up worse."

Women who have endured years of beatings without fighting back may reach the breaking point once the abuse spreads to others they love. Arlene Caris is serving a 25-year sentence in New York for killing her husband. He had tormented her for years, both physically and psychologically. Then she reportedly learned that he was sexually abusing her granddaughter. On the night she finally decided to leave him, he came at her in a rage. She took a rifle, shot him, wrapped him in bedsheets and then hid the body in the attic for five months.

Offering such women clemency, the advocates note, is not precisely the same as amnesty; the punishment is reduced, though the act is not excused. Clemency may be most appropriate in cases where all the circumstances of the crime were not heard in court. The higher courts have certainly sent the message that justice is not uniform in domestic-violence cases. One study found that 40% of women who appeal their murder convictions get the sentence thrown out, compared with an 8.5% reversal rate for homicides as a whole. "I've worked on cases involving battered women who have talked only briefly to their lawyers in the courtroom for 15 or 20 minutes and then they take a plea and do 15 to life," recalls Blackman. "I see women who are Hispanic and don't speak English well, or women who are very quickly moved through the system, who take pleas and do substantial chunks of time, often without getting any real attention paid to the circumstances of their case."

The first mass release in the U.S. came at Christmas in 1990, when Ohio Governor Richard Celeste commuted the sentences of 27 battered women serving time for killing or assaulting male companions. His initiative was born of long-held convictions. As a legislator in the early '70s, he and his wife helped open a women's center in Cleveland and held hearings on domestic violence. When he became lieutenant governor in 1974 and moved to Columbus, he and his wife rented out their home in Cleveland as emergency shelter for battered women. He and the parole board reviewed 107 cases, looking at evidence of past abuse, criminal record, adjustment to prison life and participation in postrelease programs before granting the clemencies. "The system of justice had not really worked in their cases," he says. "They had not had the opportunity for a fair trial because vitally important evidence affecting their circumstances and the terrible things done to them was not presented to the jury."

The impending reviews in other states have caused some prosecutors and judges to sound an alarm. They are worried that Governors' second-guessing the courts undermines the judicial system and invites manipulation by prisoners. "Anybody in the penitentiary, if they see a possible out, will be claiming, 'Oh, I was a battered woman,'" says Dallas assistant district attorney Norman Kinne. "They can't take every female who says she's a battered woman and say, 'Oh, we're sorry, we'll let you out.' If they're going to do it right, it's an exhaustive study."

Clemency critics point to one woman released in Maryland who soon afterward boasted about having committed the crime. Especially controversial are women who have been granted clemency for crimes that were undeniably premeditated. Delia Alaniz hired a contract killer to pretend to rob her home and murder her husband in the process. He had beaten her and their children for years, sexually abusing their 14-year-old daughter. The prosecutor from Skagit County, Washington, was sufficiently impressed by the evidence of abuse that he reduced the charge from first-degree murder and life imprisonment to second-degree manslaughter with a sentence of 10 to 14 years. In October 1989, Governor Booth Gardner granted her clemency. "Delia was driven to extremes. The situation was desperate, and she viewed it that way," says Skagit County public defender Robert Jones. "The harm to those kids having a mom in prison was too much considering the suffering they went through. As a state, we don't condone what she did, but we understand and have compassion."

❖ THE ALTERNATIVES TO MURDER

There is always a risk that the debate over clemency will continue to obscure the missing debate over violence. "I grew up in a society that really tolerated a lot of injustice when it came to women," says Pace University's Dowd. "It was ingrained as a part of society. This isn't a woman's issue. It's a human-rights issue. Men should have as much to offer fighting sexism as they do racism because the reality is that it's our hands that strike the blows." The best way to keep battered women out of jail is to keep them from being battered in the first place.

In a sense, a society's priorities can be measured by whom it punishes. A survey of the population of a typical prison suggests that violent husbands and fathers are still not viewed as criminals. In New York State about half the inmates are drug offenders, the result of a decade-long War on Drugs that demanded mandatory sentences. A War on Violence would send the same message, that society genuinely abhors parents who beat children and spouses who batter each other, and is willing to punish the behavior rather than dismiss it.

Minnesota serves as a model for other states. In 1981 Duluth was the first U.S. city to institute mandatory arrests in domestic disputes. Since then about half the states have done the same, which means that even if a victim does not wish to press charges, the police are obliged to make an arrest if they see evidence of abuse. Advocates in some Minnesota jurisdictions track cases from the first call to police through prosecution and sentencing, to try to spot where the system is falling. Prosecutors are increasingly reluctant to plea-bargain assault down to disorderly conduct. They have also found it helpful to use the arresting officer as complainant, so that their case does not depend on a frightened victim's testifying.

Better training of police officers, judges, emergency-room personnel and other professionals is having an impact in many cities. "We used to train police to be counselors in domestic-abuse cases," says Osumndson. "No longer. We teach them to go make arrests." In Jacksonville, Florida, new procedures helped raise the arrest rate from 25% to 40%. "Arrests send a message to the woman that help is available and to men that abuse is not accepted," says shelter executive director DeYoung, who also serves as president of the Florida Coalition Against Domestic Violence. "Children too see that it's not accepted and are more likely to grow up not accepting abuse in the home."

Since 1990 at least 28 states have passed "stalking laws" that make it a crime to threaten, follow or harass someone. Congress this month may take up the Violence Against Women bill, which would increase penalties for federal sex crimes; provide $300 million to police, prosecutors and courts to combat violent crimes against women; and reinforce state domestic-violence laws. Most women, of course, are not looking to put their partners in jail; they just want the violence to stop.

A Minneapolis project was founded in 1979 at the prompting of women in shelters who said they wanted to go back to their partners if they would stop battering. Counselors have found that men resort to violence because they want to control their partners, and they know they can get away with it—unlike in other relationships. "A lot of people experience low impulse control, fear of abandonment, alcohol and drug addiction, all the characteristics of a batterer," says Ellen Pence, training coordinator for the Domestic Abuse Intervention Project in Duluth. "However, the same guy is not beating up his boss."

Most men come to the program either by order of the courts or as a condition set by their partners. The counselors start with the assumption that battering is learned behavior. Eighty percent of the participants grew up in a home where they saw or were victims of physical, sexual or other abuse. Once imprinted with that model, they must be taught to recognize warning signs and redirect their anger. "We don't say, 'Never get angry,'" says Carol Arthur, the Minneapolis project's executive director. "Anger is a normal, healthy emotion. What we work with is a way to express it." Men describe to the group their most violent incident. One man told about throwing food in his wife's face at dinner and then beating her to the floor—only to turn and see his two small children huddled terrified under the table. Arthur remembers his self-assessment at that moment: "My God, what must they be thinking about me? I didn't want to be like that."

If the police and the courts crack down on abusers, and programs exist to help change violent behavior, victims will be less likely to take—and less justified in taking—the law into their own hands. And once the cycle of violence winds down in this generation, it is less likely to poison the next. That would be a family value worth fighting for.

21

CHILDREN AT RISK

MARIAN WRIGHT EDELMAN

arents generally accept and even cherish the fact that each child has his or her unique personality, likes and dislikes, strengths and weaknesses, and needs. Within the family these individual differences are accepted. Most parents attempt to respond to each child's needs and welcome the child's special contributions to the life of the family. At the broader level of public policy, however, the uniqueness of each child is not recognized. Public policies, to a large degree, have yet to acknowledge that every child is special and important, not just to his or her family but also to the country. Both individual children and groups of children—by virtue of their race, family income, or other circumstances—have special needs that society must recognize and address.

Despite the inadequacy of existing public policies to meet the varied needs of children at risk, there has been some progress in defining the characteristics of children with special needs and in devising strategies for helping them. More than two decades of research, data collection, judicial activity, and restructuring state and national legislation and budgets have at least helped identify the types of children who are special and who, without a national commitment to help them, are likely to fall through the cracks to a life of poverty. The list of

From *Proceedings of the Academy of Political Science,* Vol. 37, No. 2, 1989. Reprinted by permission.

children at risk includes minority children, poor children, teenage parents and their children, the physically or emotionally handicapped, abused and neglected children and others in the child welfare system, and the homeless.

As society changes and analyses become more sophisticated and more perceptive, the list both changes and grows. Twenty-five years ago it would probably not have included abused and neglected children. And although the child welfare system has long targeted orphans and young vagrants among those with special needs, as recently as 1985 the list would probably not have included homeless children in the sense that they are defined now—those who are still with their parents but in family units that are consigned to a nomadic, often squalid existence on the streets and in shelters that can never be a substitute for a stable family home.

But one must not oversimplify. The problem with making lists is that many children belong to several categories, increasing their jeopardy of falling into the group that has become a synonym for hopelessness—the underclass.

❖ THE IMPORTANCE OF EVERY CHILD

The first high-school graduating class of the twenty-first century entered the first grade in September 1988. They are the country's future workers, parents, college students, taxpayers, soldiers, and leaders. Yet millions of them are already beginning to lose hope:

- One in five of them (a total of 12.4 million) is poor.
- One in five is at risk of becoming a teenage parent.
- One in five is nonwhite; among nonwhites, two in five are poor.
- One in six has no health insurance.
- One in seven is at risk of dropping out of school.
- One in two has a mother in the labor force, but only a minority have safe, affordable, quality child care.

No society that considers itself civilized or moral can condone the victimization of millions of children by discrimination, poverty, and neglect. Help should be extended to children not only because of moral obligations but also because of faith in the future of society, its progress, its values, and its traditions and because children should have every possible opportunity, as they mature, to participate in the society and contribute to it. But as the last decade of the twentieth century approaches, there are also compelling demographic reasons to reject and reverse these trends. In addition to the moral motivation of alleviating human suffering, one must add the motivation of national economic self-interest.

Because of dramatic social changes in the past century, parents no longer expect their own children to support them directly when they are elderly. Rather, they rely on Social Security, Medicaid and Medicare, tax-supported pensions, and retirement benefits financed by employers. Many will require contributions to these programs from the next generation as a whole and from that generation's children. It is therefore in everyone's self-interest that today's children—and their children—are healthy, educated, productive, and compassionate. Yet the society is aging, and the number of children and youths in relation to other age groups in the population is declining.

The William T. Grant Foundation Commission on Work, Family and Citizenship, which is examining the status and future of American youth, documented these trends in its June 1987 publication, "American Youth: A Statistical Snapshot." Among the points made by the commission:

> *The number of American youth is shrinking dramatically. Between 1980 and 1996, our youth population, ages 15–25, is expected to fall 21 percent, from 43 to 34 million. Young people as a percentage of the nation's population will also decline from 18.8 to 13 percent. . . .*
>
> *These falling numbers will drastically alter the characteristics of the nation's labor pool, higher education enrollments. . . .*
>
> *The problems facing minority youth will take on even greater importance as they account for larger and larger proportions of America's youth population. . . .*

Children are not only a precious resource, then, but an increasingly scarce one. Until recently, America's youth population has been relatively plentiful, allowing the society to survive and the economy to grow, despite the waste of many young lives through society's neglect. That margin for error no longer exists. The ratio of workers to retirees has shrunk and will continue to shrink in the coming decades. And one in three of the new potential workers is a member of a minority group.

❖ MINORITY CHILDREN

For many blacks, recent years have been good. Black per-capita income is at an all-time high, black purchasing power—now at $200 billion a year—exceeds the gross national product of Australia and New Zealand combined, and there are more black elected officials than ever. Blacks head the House Budget Committee of the U.S. Congress, the Ford Foundation, and the marketing activities of the Xerox Corporation, and they represent the United States on the Olympic Committee. These are important, tangible gains of the civil rights movement. But there is another black community for which these have not been good years—a community, in fact, where life is getting worse.

Today, black children are more likely than in 1980 to be born into poverty, to have been deprived of early prenatal care, to have a single mother or no employed parent, to be unemployed as teenagers, and not to go to college. They are twice as likely as white children to be born prematurely, to suffer low birth weights, to live in substandard housing, or to die in the first year of life. Black children are three times as likely as white children to be poor, to live in a female-headed family, to have no parent employed, or to be murdered between five and nine years of age. They are five times as likely as white children to rely on welfare and nine times as likely to live with a parent who has never married.

While black children's plight is the worst, the fast-growing population of Hispanic children in this country also suffers much higher rates of poverty than their white counterparts. The U.S. Bureau of the Census reported the following poverty rates for 1987: for all American children, 20.6 percent; for white children, 15.6 percent; for Hispanic children, 39.8 percent; and for black children, 48.8 percent.

Some other key indicators further tell the story of problems faced by minority children. For example, National Center for Health Statistics data on infant mortality in 1985 reveal that for all races, per 1,000 live births, there are 10.6 deaths; for whites, 9.3; for blacks, 18.2; and for nonwhite infants, 15.8. Other data show that Hispanic youths as well as blacks are less likely to be employed than whites and are more likely to become teenage parents than their white counterparts.

❖ THE SPREAD OF POVERTY

The tide of misery that poverty breeds and that blacks have borne disproportionately throughout history has now enveloped a critical mass of white American families and children. Thirty-three million individuals—one-seventh of all Americans—are now poor as a result of economic recession, followed by slow growth, structural changes in the economy, declining real wage rates, federal tax and budget policies that favor the rich at the expense of the poor, and changing family demographics. One in every five American children lives in a female-headed household, and one in four will be dependent on welfare at some point in his or her lifetime.

Most Americans now realize that poverty is not just the result of personal inadequacy, laziness, and unworthiness, despite some national leaders' attempts to portray the poor as culpable. Iowa farmers, Detroit autoworkers, Youngstown steel workers, South Carolina textile workers, and small-business people have lost their livelihoods as a result of the economic dislocations afflicting the United States. They have been surprised to find themselves in unemployment lines or bread lines or new jobs paying a fraction of their former earnings. Of those 32.5 million poor, more than 13 million are children. Children make up the poorest age group in America. Nearly half of black children, almost two-fifths of Hispanic children, and nearly one-seventh of white children in the United States are poor. These figures are appalling.

For a growing number of Americans, moreover, working does not mean escaping poverty. The ranks of the working poor have also grown. In 1979 a parent working full-time at the minimum wage earned enough to lift a family of three above the poverty line. By 1986, a full-time, minimum-wage job yielded a paycheck equivalent to only 75 percent of the poverty-level income for a family of three and 61 percent of the poverty-level income for a family of four. (The poverty-level income for a family of four in 1986 was $11,203.) In 1986 more than a million Americans supported families on full-time, year-round jobs that did not raise them out of poverty. And fully half of the country's 7 million heads of poor households worked at least part-time in 1986.

Young parents and their children have been squeezed by changes in the economy and the job market in the past decade and a half. Young families have borne almost all of the income losses caused by the resulting turmoil. The median income for all American families declined by only 1 percent between 1973 and 1986. Among young families (those headed by persons under age thirty), however, median income dropped by 14 percent during this period. Young families with children suffered the greatest income loss—nearly 26 percent.

Not surprisingly, poverty among young families and their children has also increased far more rapidly than for older American families. The poverty rate for all young families nearly doubled between 1973 and 1986, rising from 12 percent to 22 percent. The chances of being poor are even greater for young families with children—their poverty rate jumped from 16 percent in 1973 to 30 percent in 1986. In contrast, the poverty rate for older families with children increased more gradually, from 9 percent to 13 percent. As a result of the growing economic plight of young families, one-third of all poor children in the United States now live in young families. And among the youngest families—those headed by persons under age twenty-five—a staggering 54 percent of all children are poor.

For a child of poverty, the most ordinary needs—from health care to housing—become extraordinary. Testifying in April 1988 before the U.S. House of Representatives' Select Committee on Children, Youth, and Families, twelve-year-old Yvette Diaz of New York City painted a vivid picture of the assaults on mind and body that are an integral part of daily life for her and other residents of the Hotel Martinique for homeless families. She, her mother, her sisters ages seven and nine, and her brother age three went to live in the Martinique "because my aunt's house burned down and we didn't have any place to live," she testified. "I don't like the hotel because there is always a lot of trouble there. I don't go down into the street to play because there is no place to play. . . . The streets are dangerous, with all kinds of sick people who are on drugs or crazy. My mother is afraid to let me go downstairs. Only this Saturday, my friend, the security guard at the hotel, Mr. Santiago, was killed on my floor. The blood is still on the walls and on the floor. . . . We can't cook in the apartment. The hotel warned us that if we are caught cooking in the rooms, we could be sent to a shelter."

❖ ADOLESCENT PARENTS

Teenage pregnancy is both a cause and a consequence of poverty. In recent years a huge new group of children has been added to the list of those with special needs—adolescent parents.

A young woman testified before the House Select Committee about her life: "I would like for you to meet Robin. She is 15 years old and alone, out of school and married at 16. By the age of 21 she has no friends or family, no education, no skills. . . . She is basically alone. I guess Robin never would have been able to have seen the grave mistakes she made, if she had not been seeing her children reliving her own mistakes. . . . I am Robin." She described as eloquently as anyone could the frustrating viciousness of the cycle of teenage pregnancy, poverty, and dependency.

Adolescent pregnancy is a crisis among all races and classes of American youth today. Each day almost 2,700 girls under the age of twenty get pregnant and 1,300 give birth. Every year a million teenage girls—one in ten—get pregnant. Although these statistics include a disproportionate number of poor, minority, and urban teenagers, two-thirds of those who give birth each year are white, two-thirds do not live in big cities, and two-thirds come from families with above-poverty incomes.

Adolescent pregnancy is a crisis not because teenage birthrates are rising, as is widely believed. (In fact, both the proportion and number of adolescents giving birth generally have fallen since 1970.) It is a crisis because the society is changing and young parents are tragically unprepared to deal with the consequences of early birth in contemporary America. Both the number and rate of births to teenagers who are unmarried are rising, thereby increasing the likelihood of poverty for two generations of children—young mothers and their children. In 1950, 15.4 percent of these births were to unmarried teenagers. By 1970, the proportion had doubled. By 1986, it had doubled again—to 60.8 percent.

The costs of adolescent parenthood are enormous, and they are magnified if the mother is unmarried. Forty percent of teenage girls who drop out of school do so because of pregnancy or marriage. Only half of the young women who become parents before the age of eighteen complete high school by the time they reach their midtwenties. Furthermore, the average lifetime earnings of a woman who has dropped out of school are roughly half those of a woman who has graduated from college. In 1986, more than four out of five children living in families headed by young females were poor.

An eighteen- or nineteen-year-old man can no longer earn enough to support a family, and the average single mother of any age has never earned a decent wage in this country. Yet the birth of a child to a teenager often means that the mother will not complete her education and will be unable to secure any employment at all, let alone a job that pays well enough to support the family.

Often the father of a child born to a teenage girl is in his early twenties. As discussed in the previous section, the erosion of employment opportunities and wage levels makes it impossible for even the young men who find work to earn enough to support their families.

This trend is particularly disturbing because earnings losses among young men reduce the likelihood that young Americans will marry and form two-parent families. Research indicates a connection between unemployment or low earnings and marital instability and between joblessness and delayed marriage. The decline in real earnings and the resulting drop in marriage rates have been most severe among high-school dropouts and graduates who do not go on to college—the young people who have tended to marry and bear children earliest. While a reversal of recent earnings losses would not restore marriage rates to their previous levels, more adequate earnings would substantially increase the proportion of young adults who would be willing and able to form stable families.

❖ CHILDREN OF ADOLESCENT PARENTS

As Robin suggested in her congressional testimony, the babies born to adolescent parents often seem condemned to repeat the mistakes and suffering of their parents. Shawn Grant, a member of a gang in Philadelphia, grew up in a single-parent household. When he testified before the House Select Committee on Children, Youth and Families, he was on intensive probation for committing a robbery. "My father has had little contact with me since I was one year old," he told the committee. "In my neighborhood, a lot of negative things go on. People sell drugs; a lot of the gang members' parents use drugs and often these guys do not see their parents. . . . When I was young I use [sic] to worry about my father. I also resented his not being involved in my life. Now I do not care. However, I think that I would not have become involved in a gang if I had had a job and if my father had had a relationship with me."

Babies born to adolescent, single parents have two strikes against them. First, they enter life with particularly high risks to their health and well-being. Babies born to single mothers are five times more likely to be poor than those born to two-parent families. Only 53 percent of all infants born to teenagers in 1985 had mothers who began prenatal care in the first three months of pregnancy. More than one in eight—twice the national average—had a mother who received either no prenatal care at all or none until the last trimester. Babies born to women who receive no prenatal care are three times more likely to die in their first year of life than infants whose mothers received comprehensive care. Children born to teenagers are also more likely than other children to grow up in poverty. Young families are two and a half times more likely than the average American family to have incomes below the poverty line.

Children who grow up in persistently poor families are far more likely to face inadequate nutrition, housing, and health care, not to be enrolled in preschool programs, to enter school less prepared than their more advantaged peers, and to be held back one or more grades. They are also more likely to drop out of school with seriously deficient academic skills that prevent them from competing in the labor market and gaining access to postsecondary education and training programs. Like Shawn, children of poor single parents may end up in a gang, committing crimes, feeling that they would prefer another kind of life but having no idea how to find it. In this way the cycle of poverty that begins with limited employment opportunities, low wages, too-early pregnancies, and low marriage rates among today's teenagers and young adults will—if society fails to intervene—be repeated and perhaps amplified in the next generation.

❖ CHILDREN WITH OTHER SPECIAL NEEDS

While most children grow up safe, secure, and emotionally sound, a sizable minority do not. Millions of American children and adolescents endure abuse or neglect in their parental homes; others are awaiting permanent homes while in foster care; and many have unmet emotional needs. Judicial decisions and federal statutes have given handicapped children a right to education and provided a framework for state efforts to address the complex needs of children who are abused, neglected, emotionally disturbed, or in foster care. Current resources and systems, however, remain grossly inadequate to meet their growing needs.

Reports of child abuse and neglect have increased steadily since 1976, with more than a 90 percent national increase between 1981 and 1986. More than three-fifths of the states reported to the House Select Committee on Children, Youth, and Families in 1986 that the deteriorating economic conditions faced by many families were a primary contributor to the increases in child abuse and neglect since 1981. While reports of abuse and neglect escalated between 1981 and 1985, federal resources for prevention and treatment fell further and further behind, and child protective service agencies have been overwhelmed.

About 275,000 children and adolescents live in foster-family homes, group homes, residential treatment centers, and other institutions. While some have been abused or neglected, others enter care because their parents are unable to meet the demands of their disabilities or behavior problems. Still others enter because their families are homeless or too poor to support their children.

The group is varied in age and background. About one-half are minority children, who are represented disproportionately in care in many states and who tend to be in care longer, waiting for permanent homes. While youths thirteen and older account for about 46 percent of the children in foster care, very young children are also entering the system in greater numbers in some communities. Moreover, children in foster care are increasingly reported to have more special needs, such as serious medical and emotional problems, compared with the foster-care population in the past.

The foster-care system is severely challenged by increasing poverty and homelessness; the use of crack, which results in births of infants at high risk of medical and development problems; and the spread of acquired immune deficiency syndrome (AIDS), which requires more intensive supports for the children and families who are affected. Although many states report fewer children in foster care, several states—particularly those with large urban centers—report that the number of children in care is going up, not down. And virtually every state and region agrees that children in care today pose greater challenges to the foster-care system's resources. Shortages of foster homes (partly due to inadequate community support and low reimbursement rates) have propelled some states to increase out-of-state placements, a practice that impedes the reuniting of families and hampers the home state's ability to monitor the quality of care. The foster-care system also lacks the necessary resources to help children make a successful transition when they leave care. Of special concern are the tens of thousands of youths who "age out" of the system in their late teens and have no family members or friends to whom they can turn.

An estimated 7.5 million to 9.5 million children in this country have emotional or other problems that require mental-health services. Of this group, 70 to 80 percent do not receive the care they need. Even among the approximately 3 million children who suffer from serious emotional disturbances, the majority go without proper treatment. Today many of these children are being helped in a piecemeal fashion, or not at all.

Various state mental-health systems have cited growing demands and continuing deficiencies similar to those facing child-welfare agencies: the increasing severity of the problems presented by disturbed children and their families, overreliance on institutional settings and a lack of sufficient in-home and community-based support programs, the transition needs of youths aging out of mental-health programs, and the inadequate number of professionals trained to address the mental-health needs of children and adolescents.

❖ SAVING THE CHILDREN

If it is to save itself, America must save its children. Millions of children are not safe physically, educationally, economically, or spiritually. Many of the special children described in this essay are poor or members of minority groups. On average, they are less safe than their white, more affluent counterparts. But all are at risk spiritually. The common good, truth-telling, and moral example have become devalued commodities in the United States. And all children are in danger of being corrupted by their exposure to the values reflected by the Michael Deavers, Ivan Boeskys, and Jim and Tammy Bakkers of the world. The poor black youths who shoot up drugs on street corners and the rich white youths who do the same thing in their mansions share a common disconnectedness from any hope and purpose, sense of community, and shared strivings. What one social observer has called the bug of "affluenza" has indeed bitten thousands of youths who are growing up in families that offer everything that money can buy but somehow not enough to create a purpose in life. What is done collectively to save this generation will have a major impact on how today's children and youths perform as tomorrow's adults.

❖ SOLUTIONS DO EXIST

Despite the length and dreariness of the litany of special children and their problems, solutions are at hand. One absolutely essential avenue to pursue to save the next generation—and a generation yet unborn—is to launch a full-scale campaign to prevent teenage pregnancy.

This essay has shown how poverty and lack of education reinforce a cycle that results in underemployment or unemployment and a declining rate of marriage among young people, even when they have children. A society in which growing up with a single parent—and, worse, one who does not have the maturity, education, or resources to cope—is dangerously close to becoming the norm.

The Children's Defense Fund has been engaged since 1983 in a major initiative to prevent adolescent pregnancy. Its top priority is to prevent a teenager's first pregnancy. The second is to ensure that teenagers who have already had a child do not have a second one. The third priority is to make sure that teenage mothers get adequate prenatal care so that prematurity, low birth weight, and birth defects are not added to the hurdles already awaiting their babies as they enter this world. More specifically, it has identified six areas that are extremely important in bolstering the motivation and capacity of teenagers to prevent too-early pregnancy:

1. Education and strong basic skills. Youths who are behind a grade or have poor basic skills or poor attendance are at high risk of early parenthood. Low-income and minority teenagers have higher rates of school failure.

2. Work-related skills and exposure to work. Teenagers who perform poorly in school and become parents often have poor work-related skills and, because of lack of exposure to workplace norms, behave in ways unacceptable to employers.

3. Community service, sports, and other nonacademic opportunities for success. The potential for self-sufficiency is related to self-esteem and self-perception. For youths who are not doing well in school, nonacademic avenues for success are crucial.

4. Family life education and life planning.

5. Comprehensive adolescent health services.

6. A national and community climate that makes the prevention of teenage pregnancy a leading priority.

A decent society cannot condone any increase in child poverty, let alone the increase from 10 million to more than 12 million children between 1979 and 1987. And child poverty is not just a widening problem—it is a rapidly deepening one, as poor children become poorer.

An effective national effort must be launched to address the root cause of child poverty—inadequate family incomes. This effort requires progress on several fronts:

- Restore a strong economic base by continuing to pursue full employment, investing in productivity improvements for young workers, raising the federal minimum wage, and expanding the earned income tax credit.

- Respond more effectively to the new realities of a rapidly changing labor market by enacting the Act for Better Child Care Services, extending basic health-insurance coverage to all low-income families, and strengthening child-support enforcement and safety-net programs for poor families.

- Prepare today's children and youths for productive roles in tomorrow's economy by expanding the successful Head Start, Chapter 1, and Job Corps programs, increasing investments to help youths who are not college-bound enter the job market, and bolstering college enrollments among poor and minority youth. Only these things will provide the strong foundation that will make it possible for any child—no matter how special, no matter how many problems he or she may have—to become a proud, productive member of society.

In the long term, a service system must be established that can respond to the individual needs of children and families, regardless of the label assigned them by particular public agencies. The goal should be to develop a single system that serves vulnerable children and adolescents and has the capacity to assess, mobilize, and utilize all the resources necessary to meet their multiple needs. Such a system must have a staff that is appropriately qualified and compensated. The staff must have a system for fully addressing the needs of children and youths who need help as well as a continuum of services and other resources that can meet needs as they are identified.

❖ A CALL FOR ACTION

If current trends continue, a disproportionate number of children will grow up poor, uneducated, and untrained at the very time that society will need all of our young to be healthy, educated, and productive. Despite a national debt of $2.7 trillion (which children did not cause) and despite uncertainties in the national and international economies, now is the time to invest in building healthy children, self-sufficient youth and economically secure families.

Children are poor because the country has lost its moral bearings. Perverse national values, hidden behind profamily, "traditional values" rhetoric, have been manifested in budget decisions that have cut billions of dollars each year since 1980 from survival programs for poor children and families. They are creating a new American apartheid between rich and poor, white and black, old and young, corporation and individual, military and domestic needs—and abandoned millions of poor children to the furies of hunger, homelessness, abuse, and even death.

What has been missing is the moral and political urgency required to make children and families a leading national priority. The willingness to protect children is a moral litmus test of a compassionate society.

22

ADDRESSING THE NATION'S CHILD CARE CRISIS: THE SCHOOL OF THE TWENTY-FIRST CENTURY

EDWARD F. ZIGLER

In 1970, the White House Conference on Children voted child care as the most serious problem facing America's families. That was two decades ago. Despite some noble attempts to deal with the matter (namely the 1971 Comprehensive Child Development Act, the Child Care Act of 1979, and the 100-plus child care bills considered by the 100th Session of Congress in 1988), our nation has not come a single step closer to providing a solution. This "serious problem" has grown so pervasive that it is now called America's child care crisis.

And a crisis it is. One brief look at current demographics will demonstrate the magnitude of the child care problem. Today in America, roughly 70% of the mothers of school-age children are in the out-of-home work force; among preschoolers, that number is approximately 60% (*Shank, 1988*). Most startling is the fact that slightly over half of the mothers of infants under one year of age hold jobs outside the home (*Bureau of Labor Statistics, 1987*). Our best prognostication is that by the year 1995, about three-quarters of all children will have a working mother (*Hofferth & Phillips, 1987*). What does this mean in

From *The American Journal of Orthopsychiatry*, Vol. 59, No. 4, October, 1989.

terms of the numbers of children? If current trends continue, in 1995 there will be 14.6 million preschool children and 37.4 million school-age children who have mothers working outside the home (*Hofferth & Phillips*).

Social scientists and economists have offered much discussion and analysis as to why women are flocking to the job market. Still, there is no question that the majority of women work primarily for economic reasons. In 1989, the Select Committee on Children, Youth, and Families reported that in two-parent homes, 68% of employed mothers had husbands who earned $15–19,000 annually. Of the working mothers of preschoolers, 60% were married to men earning less than $25,000. Clearly, both husband and wife must now work to provide their family a decent standard of living.

For single-parent families, which are almost always headed by women, the situation is even more desperate. In 1986, approximately one-fifth of all single mothers had incomes below *half* the adjusted poverty line (i.e., below $3,974 for a family of three). Some 40% of these families had incomes below the adjusted poverty line (*Select Committee on Children, Youth, and Families, 1988*). Today in the United States, approximately one in four children live with only one parent (*U.S. Bureau of the Census, 1986*); among our black citizens, that number is more than half. These single mothers have no choice other than go to work, go on welfare, or starve. For them, child care is a particularly pressing need that will determine their children's security and future. One final statistic: it is estimated that 80% of women in the work force are of childbearing age, and that 93% of these women will become pregnant sometime during their careers (*Select Committee on Children, Youth, and Families, 1984*).

These numbers leave no doubt that child care is a real or potential problem for the majority of American parents. From the point of view of a developmentalist, the most worrisome aspect of the problem is the impact of such widespread nonparental care on the development of our nation's children. By now researchers have reached a general consensus that child care of high quality does not harm children. (They are not so sure when it comes to infants, as reflected in the diverse range of viewpoints presented in issues 3 and 4 of the *Early Childhood Research Quarterly* in 1988.) But quality is not guaranteed in the vast nonsystem of child care in place in this country. There is little doubt that hundreds of thousands of American children are currently experiencing child care environments that are compromising their optimal development.

❖ STANDARDS OF QUALITY

When parents select a child care setting, they are not purchasing a service that permits them to work. Rather, they are purchasing an environment where part of the rearing of their child will take place. This environment will help to shape the course of development of the child. Child-rearing environments can be arranged on a continuum of quality from good to bad. If the environment experienced by the child falls below a certain point on this continuum, optimal development will be threatened. Standards and their expression in licensing codes represent our efforts to define objectively this threshold. Actually "standards" is another misnomer because the quality of child care environments available in America is anything but standard.

Of special concern are the hundreds of thousands of settings called family day care homes. These are private homes in which a provider (usually a woman) takes care of three to nine children. Several states do not require that these homes be licensed or monitored. Even in those states that do mandate some form of registration, the vast majority of family day care providers operate underground. Estimates range up to 90% or more (*Corsini, Wisensale, & Caruso, 1988*). Some of these settings are excellent, but there are horror stories as well (*Keyserling, 1972*). What is most frightening about the diversity of care in the family day care system is that this is the most popular choice of parents with children under three years of age who need full-time care (*Hofferth & Phillips, 1987*). Many parents feel that family day care is more home-like than center care, and it is often more affordable. Yet we have no assurances that these very young children are receiving care that meets the quality threshold required for healthy development.

Further evidence substantiating these concerns is presented in a recent state-by-state analysis of staff/child ratios in infant and toddler settings in this country (*Young & Zigler, 1986*). Most experts agree that there should be no more than three infants per adult caregiver; yet in 1986 only three states met this standard. Six to one, and even eight to one, was not uncommon. No adult, no matter how well trained, can provide proper stimulation and care to six or eight infants, much less be able to evacuate them in an emergency. A staff/child ratio such as this constitutes prima facie evidence that the development of many children in child care settings is being compromised.

Allowing a caregiver to be responsible for too many children does help to keep the cost to parents down, which highlights another aspect of our current child care crisis: quality care is expensive. What has developed in America is a two-tiered system of child care. Economically advantaged families can purchase quality caregiving environments for their children. Poor, working-class, and many lower-middle-class families cannot afford quality and must settle for marginal or inadequate care. Children whose development is at risk because of economically disadvantaged life circumstances are put at even greater risk when placed in poor child care settings.

❖ THE EDUCATION PARADIGM

There are many similarities between this two-tiered system of child care and the history of our nation's educational system. Before the advent of universal public schooling, only rich children received an extensive education. When free common schools began, children from wealthy families remained in their expensive private schools and went on to expensive universities. Gradually these inequities ended, as taxpayers and educators improved the offerings of the common school, extended free education through the high school years, and began to subsidize higher education to some extent. While students in some private schools may still receive superior educational benefits, those who go through the public school system have comparable opportunities to learn. They too may become leaders and productive members of the society. The child in a quality caregiving setting, like the educated elite of yesteryear, is likely to have his or her developmental path secured. For the child in poor quality care, however, the society may pay the price in increased social services and an unprepared labor force in the not too distant future.

We have today the knowledge to provide good quality care to every child who needs it. What is lacking in our country is the commitment and the will to do so. This is best demonstrated by a consideration of the cost of a child care system in America. No one in or out of government wishes to deal with the true dollar cost of providing good quality child care to all the children in our nation who require it. The best estimate we have been able to produce is that it will cost this country $75–100 billion a year to solve the child care problem. The fact that our federal government has no firm figure to give to policy analysts and decision makers indicates the vacuum of leadership at the national level that we have witnessed for over a decade, as the child care problem has worsened. How can anyone even begin to develop approaches to the problem until there is some sense of the dollar outlay involved in the solution? In the absence of a reasonable cost estimate, the proposals that have been put forth have tended to be unrealistic and unworkable; they include help from the private sector and from charitable organizations, and the resurrection of old child care bills.

The private sector solution was favored by the Reagan administration. That is, private business should provide or underwrite the cost of employees' child care. This has simply not happened. While some employers have moved in this direction, the fact is that out of six million U.S. employers, only 3,500 (six-hundredths of one per cent) offer some form of child care assistance (*Reisman, Moore, & Fitzgerald, 1988*). Usually this assistance is in the form of information and referral services, which may help parents find child care but does not help them afford it. We should do all we can to get private employers to do more, but the nature of our private enterprise system guarantees the failure of this approach as a real solution. We do not directly ask business to provide children's education; why should we ask business to provide child care?

Others have suggested that we give the task of child care to a conglomeration of caring institutions: churches, YMCAs, and some other non-profit settings. While those who run these institutions have their hearts in the right places, they have neither the money nor the personnel for such an undertaking. Some have proposed that we resurrect the 1971 Child Development Act and put into place a national network of child care settings available to all citizens (along the lines of the Swedish model). Given our federal government's precarious financial condition, this solution is unrealistic; its pursuit would likely be a waste of energy. Some have suggested expanding the Head Start program. But Head Start is designed for preschoolers, not infants and school-age children, who need quite different types of programs. Furthermore, today Head Start serves only 16% of the children who are eligible for it (*Children's Defense Fund, 1987*), so any expansion should begin with this target population.

Recently many other possible solutions have been presented in Congress. Legislators considered more than 100 of them in 1988, and that number will certainly be topped by the end of the current session. Yet even the most ambitious of these proposals, the ABC bill sponsored by Sen. Christopher Dodd with many cosponsors in both houses, provides only $2.5 billion for child care services throughout the entire country. This amount would not begin to address the magnitude of our child care problem. If the money is provided, we still do not have a coherent child care system that would enable us to put even these small funds to best advantage.

❖ DEVELOPING A SOLUTION

Over the past years, I have developed my own plan for addressing America's child care crisis. This plan was presented before the last session of Congress, and is now being considered again in the form of two bills (one sponsored by Sen. Dodd of Connecticut and the other by Rep. Augustus Hawkins of California). My plan has taken me over a lot of intellectual terrain. I relied primarily on my own knowledge about the nature of children and their developmental needs. In the process of evolving this plan, I decided to be explicit and unwavering about certain principles and criteria that must be met for a satisfactory child care system to come about. If it does not meet these principles, then I would consider it inadequate.

The very first principle is that the child care system we create, and the child care services in that system, must be reliable and stable. We cannot wait each year to see if the federal government will appropriate the required monies. Otherwise, parents will find themselves in the same predicament they face today. The rate of caregiver turnover is very high, and providers go in and out of business frequently. This leaves parents frantic to find new arrangements, and insecure about the longevity of the setting they do find. Children suffer the most in this situation, since an important developmental need is for a consistent caregiving environment. Thus the child care system we provide must be permanent and become part of the very structure of our society. It must be tied to a major societal institution.

Child care, like education, is not mentioned in the U.S. Constitution. Therefore, like education, child care must be primarily a state-based system. There is an important federal role, however. The federal government should be funding the research that is necessary to create adequate child care and to determine its effects on children of various ages and life circumstances. The nation should also subsidize care for the most needy and the handicapped (as it currently does for education with Chapter 1 in the *Elementary and Secondary School Act and Public Law 94–142*). Through most of this decade the executive branch has been slow to provide the kind of leadership that can only come with what Theodore Roosevelt called the "Bully Pulpit."

Another principle is that there should be equal access to child care for every child who needs it. At the same time, the various ethnic and socioeconomic groups should be integrated as fully as possible. Let us not repeat the one great mistake of our nation's Head Start program, where we send poor children to one set of centers and affluent children to another.

The primary goal of the new child care system is to insure the optimal development of the children using the system, not to enable parents to work. In the past, child care has always been an adjunct to welfare reform plans, with the purpose of reducing welfare rolls by allowing recipients to enter training or gain employment. The proposed child care system must stand on its own. It must be built upon policies to meet the needs of children, not upon the politics of social services. This means we must, once and for all, mandate child care of good quality. A solid model is provided by the Federal Inter-Agency Day Care Requirements, revised in 1980 and sent to Congress by the Carter Administration.

Of course, helping parents to be able to work can contribute to the child's optimal development. Children stand to benefit when the financial status of their family improves. Yet working families may be so busy that this produces stress, which in turn may be aggravated by undependable and inadequate child care. The child care system must be sensitive to the varying needs of the children and families it serves. Thus we must appreciate the great heterogeneity of our populace. While all children will be in the same system, that system must be flexible enough to adapt to requirements of each individual child and parent.

The child care solution must be available to the child throughout all of the years of dependency. This means as early in pregnancy as possible through at least the first 12 years of life. Let us not again fall into the trap of magic periods. We are now hearing much about the first five years of life. While these are truly important years, the next five years are also important. We must remember that half the need for child care is represented by children ages 6 to 12. We must remember also that the developing child is growing from stage to stage, and that each stage requires particular environmental nutrients. These nutrients must be provided for the entire range of human development, not just for cognitive growth. We must optimize physical and mental health, and be just as concerned with the child's personality development as we are with the child's IQ. Child care programs must be committed to the optimal development of the whole child.

Another principle we have learned is that child care must be predicated on a true partnership between parents and the children's caregivers. This lesson was taught by our nation's Head Start program and by successful school programs such as the Comer project in New Haven (Comer, 1980). The key ingredient in our child care plan is an adult who cares for the children while parents work. The system will never be of good quality unless the adult caregivers are skilled and dedicated. We must do everything we can to train, upgrade the pay, and increase the status of those individuals who help parents raise our nation's children. Does it make any sense that today in America, 60% of all child care workers earn less than five dollars an hour *(Reisman et al., 1988)?* In 1984, 90% of licensed family day care mothers earned less than the poverty level *(Children's Defense Fund, 1987).* We are paying to the caregivers of our next generation about what we pay to zoo keepers, and less than we pay to janitors.

The program outlined here is a child care system of the highest quality. Although such a system will carry a high price tag, we can work to make it as cost-effective as possible without sacrificing quality. The best route toward this goal is to implement the system within the established educational structure. We will enhance already existing elementary school buildings, where formal education takes place, and create the school of the 21st century. The child care component will operate in an on-site center and provide care for children from about the age of three. The system will also have three outreach programs: (1) a family support system for first-time parents; (2) support for family day care homes within the neighborhood; and (3) information and referral services.

❖ IMPLEMENTING THE MODEL

To start at the very beginning, the earliest child care takes place at home in the form of an infant care leave. There is a consensus today among all experts that parents should care for their children during the first few months of life. In 1983, the Yale Bush Center in Child Development and Social Policy convened a national panel of experts to study the problem and make formal recommendations to Congress. The committee recommended the provision of six months of leave, three months paid at 75% of salary. The infant care leave bills that have since been proposed have not provided this length of time or level of pay. Still, it behooves advocates for children and families to support *any* national legislation regarding infant leaves. Once a law is in place, it can be adapted over time to reach the desired length and economic benefit. In the meantime, babies will at least be guaranteed a time to begin life with the nurturance of their own parent and family.

The child care system conceptualized here would reach out to new parents through child care workers in the school. They would work with the parents of infants up to age three. This is taking place in Missouri as part of the "Parents as First Teachers" program. In this program, parents receive guidance beginning in the third trimester of pregnancy and wise counsel and support to help promote the child's development thereafter. There is an outreach program from the school building to provide this support service for all parents in the district.

Next, all family day care homes in the neighborhood of the school would be combined into a network, with the school's child care system as the hub. The school's child care staff would monitor, train, and generally support the family day care mothers. They would also connect these providers with parents of infants and toddlers who are considering going back to work. There would also be a general information/referral system to help meet other needs such as night care for children. Clearly, I am incorporating here much that has been learned from American family support groups.

Now let us look at what will happen in the school building. The on-site program will offer quality child care for preschoolers. School-age children could also receive care both before and after regular school hours, and on a full-time basis during vacations. For 3–4-year-olds, there will be developmentally appropriate child care within the school building, not formal schooling. Five-year-olds would receive one half-day of kindergarten in the formal school system; then, those children who require it could move over to the child care system for the other half of the day. The school buildings we are talking about would open two hours before formal schooling begins and remain open two or three hours after the school day.

Who would run the school of the 21st century? Formal schooling today is in the able hands of professional educators, principals and teachers. These educators are already overburdened and are working tirelessly to upgrade the quality of the American schools. It is not appropriate to ask them to take over child care as well. Also, most school personnel do not have the training or expertise necessary to work with very young children and their families. Finally, if this child care system were in the hands of formal educators, the cost to this nation would be prohibitive.

Rather, the child care system within the school building would be headed by someone with a Master's or Bachelor's degree and training in early childhood education. This person would be in charge of the overall child care system, including the outreach functions and the program in the on-site center. The day-to-day care of children would then be in the hands of Child Development Associates, fully qualified for such a role. This would require expansion of the CDA program, including subsidized tuition for those who need it. Our nation has done much to help prospective teachers gain the education they require; child care workers deserve no less.

The big question in the minds of most taxpayers is who will pay the huge cost of this system? When the percentage of working women reaches a critical mass, that is, when some 80% of all women are in the work force in the 21st century, this cost should be absorbed primarily through property taxes. Today, education is paid for by taxes; when most women are employed, we can expect that this nation will not be opposed to a tax for child care. However, during the interim period, in order to absorb costs and to keep quiescent the vocal and active minority of taxpayers who do not wish to see public monies expended to aid women's entry into the labor force, I suggest a fee system. Each family that voluntarily chooses to use a child care system in the school will be asked to pay a fee calibrated to family income. The high cost of good quality child care will demand subsidization by all levels of government, particularly in the case of the working poor who most need this service. To further offset the costs, private businesses should be induced to include child care as a conventional fringe benefit for employees.

The first step in implementing this plan would be the development of demonstration schools throughout the country (at least one in each state). The demonstration schools should be funded initially by the federal government. Then, the role of the federal government should be to help states move as quickly as possible to open more schools of this type. Bills proposing demonstration schools that encompass this model are presently before Congress. Some states have already acted on their own initiatives, however; and many others are considering similar action. The state of Missouri has implemented the 21st century school plan, and Connecticut has funded its own demonstration schools. The experiences of these states will be invaluable to our national plan.

This plan is the fruit of almost a quarter of a century of thought on this matter. The child care problem in the United States today is so massive and has been ignored for so long that it is too late to rely on Band-Aid approaches. We must institutionalize high quality child care for each and every child who requires substitute care. Our society and our place in the world depend upon the degree to which we optimize the development of every American child. We must provide our future citizens with not just a quality education, but with quality child care as well.

REFERENCES

Bureau of Labor Statistics, U.S. Department of Labor. (1987). *Employment in perspective: Women in the labor force.* Fourth Quarter, Report 749.

Children's Defense Fund. (1987). *A children's defense budget: FY 1988.* Washington, DC: Author.

Comer, J.P. (1980). *School power: Implications of an intervention project.* New York: Free Press.

Corsini, D.A., Wisensale, S.K., & Caruso, G.L. (1988, September). Family day care: System issues and regulatory models. *Young Children.* 17–19.

Hofferth, S.L., & Phillips, D.A. (1987). Child care in the United States: 1970–1995. *Journal of Marriage and the Family, 49,* 559–571.

Keyserling, M.D. (1972). *Windows on day care.* New York: National Council of Jewish Women.

Reisman, B., Moore, A.J., & Fitzgerald, K. (1988). *Child care: The bottom line.* New York: Child Care Action Campaign.

Select Committee on Children, Youth, and Families. (1984). *Families and child care: Improving the options.* Washington, DC: U.S. Government Printing Office.

Select Committee on Children, Youth, and Families. (1988). *Children and families in poverty: The struggle to survive.* Washington, DC: U.S. Government Printing Office.

Select Committee on Children, Youth, and Families. (1989). *Children and families: Key trends in the 1980s.* Washington, DC: U.S. Government Printing Office.

Shank, S.E. (1988). Women and the labor market: The link grows stronger. *Monthly Labor Review, 111* (3), 3–8.

U.S. Bureau of the Census. (1986, March). *Current population reports* (Series P-20, No. 419, Household and family characteristics).

Young, K.T., & Zigler, E. (1986). Infant and toddler day care: Regulations and policy implications. *American Journal of Orthopsychiatry, 56,* 43–55.

PART SEVEN

THE ENVIRONMENT

The tragedy of environmental destruction is all around us—a part of our daily lives that we can't ignore. In recent years, there has been growing concern over the state of the environment from all quarters. But there is little agreement on the causes or cures of the environmental crisis.

One approach regards environmental destruction as a necessary, if unfortunate, "trade-off" for economic growth. In this view, the greatest danger is that, in our concern for environmental issues, we'll hobble the economy with needless regulations and weaken our ability to compete economically with other industrial countries.

A second approach takes environmental problems more seriously, arguing that they are the inevitable result of a high level of industrialization, growing population, and our craving for more and more consumer goods. From this perspective, the basic problem is *people*—too many of them, consuming too much, and making extravagant demands on the earth's limited resources. The solution is often cast in individual terms: We should recycle more, use bicycles instead of our cars, and in other ways change our lifestyles to mesh better with the needs of a fragile environment.

A third approach agrees that individual change has an important place in securing our environmental future. But it also calls attention to the larger social, political, and economic forces that shape the crisis of the environment. It acknowledges that the sheer number of people, the growth of industry, and the limits of energy resources would create formidable environmental issues in any society. But it also points to such more specific forces as the nature of our economic institutions, the decisions of powerful corporations, and the frequent failure of governmental regulatory agencies as contributors to the current crisis of the environment. It views the environmental crisis, in short, not just as an individual problem or a technical, scientific one, but as a *social* problem as well. The articles in this part explore several of the social aspects of the environmental crisis.

In the selection from his book *The Closing Circle,* Barry Commoner develops an argument explaining the frequent connection between pollution and the uncontrolled quest for profit. According to Commoner, the key problem is the profitability of introducing new technologies—technologies that may have a devastating impact on the natural environment and ultimately even on the functioning of the industry itself but that provide a very high rate of profit for the corporations, at least in the short run. In Commoner's view, the dramatic destruction of the environment in the years since World War II has been primarily the result of the explosion of these new technologies, which enriched the large corporations while impoverishing everyone else.

In his case study of the history of American transportation, Bradford Curie Snell further explores the links between pollution and profit, offering a shocking story of corporate complicity in the destruction of the environment. It is well known that the automobile has been the source of much of our air pollution problem—not to mention the more general distortion of the urban and rural landscape produced by freeways, parking lots, and the other artifacts of automotive civilization. Snell shows that the rise of the private automobile and the decline of other, more efficient and less polluting means of transportation was, in large part, the result of a conscious policy by the auto and oil corporations—especially General Motors—to destroy other forms of ground transportation in order to create dependency on the automobile. His study speaks volumes about the relation between the irresponsible exercise of corporate power and the deepening destruction of the natural and social environment in the twentieth century.

The next two selections describe some of the most troubling results of our heedless approach to the natural environment. In "The Toxic Cloud," Michael H. Brown, the reporter who uncovered the massive toxic contamination at Love Canal in New York State during the 1970s, turns his attention to the growing problem of toxic chemicals in America's air. A government study estimates that roughly 20 pounds of some of the most dangerous substances known are released into the air over the United States each year for every man, woman, and child in the country. For some of these chemicals, there is *no* safe level of exposure; even the tiniest amount can bring cancer or other diseases. As Brown points out, one of the most disturbing aspects of this new toxic pollution is how easily these chemicals can drift from their point of origin to anywhere in the United States; no part of the country, even the most pristine, is now safe from this chemical fallout.

As frightening as it is, the pouring of carcinogenic chemicals into the air may not be our most urgent environmental problem. Even more troubling is that a range of human activities—from the production of industrial chemicals to the burning of forests in the name of economic development—is changing the basic composition of the earth's atmosphere itself. As Thomas E. Graedel and Paul J. Crutzen show, the consequences range from acid rain and the stubborn persistence of urban smog to the longer-range threats of global warming and the depletion of the ozone layer, which protects us from the extremes of ultraviolet radiation. We are learning that tampering with the chemical balance of the atmosphere may have momentous consequences, all the more worrisome because they are still "incompletely understood." Short of a global effort to alter our approach to economic development, they warn, we may face more "unwelcome surprises" further down the road.

23

THE ECONOMIC MEANING OF ECOLOGY

BARRY COMMONER

What is the connection between pollution and profit in a private enterprise economic system such as the United States? Let us recall that in the United States, intense environmental pollution is closely associated with the technological transformation of the productive system since World War II. Much of our pollution problem can be traced to a series of large scale technological displacements in industry and agriculture since 1946. A number of the new, rapidly growing productive activities are much more prone to pollute than the older ones they have displaced.

Thus, since World War II, in the United States, private business has chosen to invest its capital preferentially in a series of new productive enterprises that are closely related to the intensification of environmental pollution. What has motivated this pattern of investment? According to Heilbroner:

> Whether the investment is for the replacement of old capital or for the installation of new capital, the ruling consideration is virtually never the personal use or satisfaction that the investment yields to the owners of the firm. Instead, the touchstone of investment decisions is profit.

The introduction of new technology has clearly played an important role in the profitability of postwar business enterprise. The economic factor that links profit to technology is *productivity,* which is usually defined as the output of product per unit input of labor. Productivity has grown rapidly since World War II and, according to Heilbroner, this is largely due to the introduction of new technologies in that period of time. The following relationship seems to be at work: new investment in the postwar economy, as expected, has moved in directions that appeared to promise, and in fact yielded, increased profit; these investments have been heavily based on the introduction of new technology, which is a major factor in the notable increase in productivity, the major source of profit.

If these relationships have been operative in the technological displacements that, as we have seen, have played such an important role in generating the environment crisis in the United States, then we would expect to find, in the appropriate statistics, that production based on the new technology has been more profitable than production based on the old technology it has replaced. That is, the new, more polluting technologies should yield higher profits than the older, less polluting technologies they have displaced.

The available data seem to bear out this expectation. A good example is the pervasive displacement of soap by synthetic detergents. As it happens, United States government statistics report economic data on the combined soap and detergent industry. In 1947, when the industry produced essentially no detergents, the profit was 30 per cent of sales. In 1967, when the industry produced about one-third per cent soap and two-thirds per cent detergents, the profit from sales was 42 per cent. From the data for intervening years it can be computed that the profit on pure detergent sales is about 52 per cent, considerably higher than that of pure soap sales. Significantly, the industry has experienced a considerable increase in productivity, labor input relative to output in sales having declined by about 25 per cent. Clearly, if profitability is a powerful motivation, the rapid displacement of soap by detergents—and the resultant environmental pollution—has a rational explanation. This helps to explain why, despite its continued usefulness for most cleaning purposes, soap has been driven off the market by detergents. It has benefitted the investor, if not society.

The synthetic chemical industry is another example that illustrates some of the reasons for the profitability of such technological innovations. This is readily documented from an informative volume on the economics of the chemical industry published by the Manufacturing Chemists' Association. The chemical industry, particularly the manufacturers of synthetic organic chemicals, during the 1946–66 period recorded an unusually high rate of profit. During that period, while the average return on net worth for all manufacturing industries was 13.1 per cent, the chemical industry averaged 14.7 per cent. The MCA volume offers an explanation for this exceptionally high rate of profit. This is largely based on the introduction of newly developed materials, especially synthetic ones. For about from four to five years after a new, innovative chemical product reaches the market, profits are well above the average (innovative firms enjoy about twice the rate of profit of noninnovative firms). This is due to the effective monopoly enjoyed by the firm that developed the materials, that permits the establishment of a high sales price. After four to five years, smaller competitors are able to develop their own methods of manufacture; as they enter the market, the supply increases, competition intensifies, the price drops, and profits decline. At this point the large innovative firm, through its extensive research and development effort, is ready to introduce a new synthetic substance and can recover a high rate of profit. And so on. As the MCA volume points out: "The maintenance of above average profit margins requires the continuous discovery of new products and specialties on which high profit margins may be earned while the former products in that category evolve into commodity chemicals with lower margins." It is therefore no accident that the synthetic organic chemical industry has one of the highest rates of investment in research and development (in 1967, 3.7 per cent of sales, as compared with an average of 2.1 per cent for all manufacturing industries).

Thus, the extraordinarily high rate of profit of this industry appears to be a direct result of the development and production at rapid intervals of new, usually unnatural, synthetic materials—which, entering the environment, for reasons already given, often pollute it. This situation is an ecologist's nightmare, for in the four to five year period in which a new synthetic substance, such as a detergent or pesticide, is massively moved into the market—and into the environment—there is literally not enough time to work out its ecological effects. Inevitably, by the time the effects are known, the damage is done and the inertia of the heavy investment in a new productive technology makes a retreat extraordinarily difficult. The very system of enhancing profit in this industry is precisely the cause of its intense, detrimental impact on the environment.

It is significant that since 1966, the profit position of the chemical industry has declined sharply. Industry spokesmen have themselves described environmental concern as an important reason for this decline. For example, at recent congressional hearings, an industry official pointed out that a number of chemical companies had found pesticide manufacturing decreasingly profitable because of the need to meet new environmental demands. Because of these demands, costs of developing new pesticides and of testing their environmental effects have risen sharply. At the same time, cancellation or suspension of official pesticide registrations increased from 25 in 1967 to 123 in 1970. As a result, a number of companies have abandoned production of pesticides, although over-all production continues to increase. One company reported that it had dropped pesticide production "because investments in other areas promised better business."

Another explicit example of the impact of environmental concern on the profitability of new chemicals is NTA, a supposedly nonpolluting substitute for phosphate in detergents. Under the pressure of intense public concern over water pollution due to detergent phosphates, the industry developed NTA as a replacement. Two large firms then proceeded to construct plants for the manufacture of NTA—at a cost of about $100 million each. When the plants were partially built, the United States Public Health Service advised against the use of NTA, because of evidence that birth defects occur in laboratory animals exposed to NTA. The new plants had to be abandoned, at considerable cost to these firms. As a result of such hazards, research and development expenditures in the chemical industry have recently declined—a process which is likely to reduce the industry's profit position even more.

Nitrogen fertilizer provides another informative example of the link between pollution and profits. In a typical United States Corn Belt farm, a yield that is more than from 25 to 30 bushels per acre below present averages may mean no profit for the farmer. . . . [P]resent corn yields depend on a high rate of nitrogen applications. Under these conditions, the uptake of nitrogen by the crop is approaching saturation, so that an appreciable fraction of the fertilizer drains from the land and pollutes surface waters. In other words, under present conditions, it appears that the farmer *must* use sufficient fertilizer to pollute the water if he is to make a profit. Perhaps the simplest way to exemplify this tragic connection between economic survival and environmental pollution is in the words of one thoughtful farmer in recent testimony before the Illinois State Pollution Control Board:

> *Money spent on fertilizer year in and year out is the best investment a farmer can make. It is one of our production tools that hasn't nearly priced itself out of all realm of possibility as is the case with machinery and other farm inputs. Fertilizer expense in my case exceeds $20 per acre, but I feel I get back one to three dollars for every dollar spent on fertilizer. . . . I doubt that I could operate if I lost the use of fertilizers and chemicals as I know them today. I hope adequate substitutes are developed and researched if the government decides our production tools are a danger to society.*

National statistics support this farmer's view of the economic importance of fertilizers or pesticides. These statistics show that, whereas such chemicals yield three or four dollars per dollar spent, other inputs—labor and machinery, for example—yield much lower returns.

This is evidence that a high rate of profit is associated with practices that are particularly stressful toward the environment and that when these practices are restricted, profits decline.

Another important example is provided by the auto industry where the displacement of small, low-powered cars by large, high-powered ones is a major cause of environmental pollution. Although specific data on the relationship between profitability and crucial engineering factors such as horsepower do not appear to be available, some more general evidence is at hand. According to a recent article in *Fortune* magazine:

> *As the size and selling price of a car are reduced, then, the profit margin tends to drop even faster. A standard United States sedan with a basic price of $3,000, for example, yields something like $250 to $300 in profit to its manufacturer. But when the price falls by a third, to $2,000, the factory profit drops by about half. Below $2,000, the decline grows even more precipitous.*

Clearly, the introduction of a car of reduced environmental impact, which would necessarily have a relatively low-powered, low-compression engine and a low over-all weight, would sell at a relatively low price. It would therefore yield a smaller profit relative to sales price than the standard heavy, high-powered, high-polluting vehicle. This may explain the recent remark by Henry Ford II, that "minicars make miniprofits."

. . . [P]rominent among the large-scale technological displacements that have increased environmental impacts are certain construction materials: steel, aluminum, lumber, cement, and plastics. In construction and other uses, steel and lumber have been increasingly displaced by aluminum, cement (in the form of concrete), and plastics. In 1969 the profits (in terms of profit as per cent of total sales) from steel production (by blast furnaces) and lumber production were 12.5 per cent and 15.4 per cent, respectively. In contrast, the products that have displaced steel and lumber yielded significantly higher profits: aluminum, 25.7 per cent; cement, 37.4 per cent; plastics and resins, 21.4 per cent. Again, displacement of technologies with relatively weak environmental impacts by technologies with more intensive impacts is accompanied by a significant increase in profitability.

A similar situation is evident in the displacement of railroad freight haulage (relatively weak environmental impact) and truck freight haulage (intense environmental impact). In this case, economic data are somewhat equivocal because of the relatively large capital investment in railroads as compared to trucks (the trucks' right-of-way being provided by government-supported roads). Nevertheless, truck freight appears to yield significantly more profit than railroad freight; the ratio of net income to shareholders' and proprietors' equity in the case of railroads is 2.61 per cent, and for trucks, 8.84 per cent (in 1969).

In connection with the foregoing examples, in which profitability appears to increase when a new, more environmentally intense technology displaces an older one, it should be noted that not all new technologies share this characteristic. For example, the displacement of coal-burning locomotives by diesel engines *improved* the environmental impact of railroads between 1946 and 1950, for diesel engines burn considerably less fuel per ton-mile of freight than do coal-burning engines. Unfortunately, this improvement has been vitiated by the subsequent displacement of railroad freight haulage by truck freight, and at the same time made no lasting improvement in the railroads' economic position. It is also evident that certain new technologies, which are wholly novel, rather than displacing older ones—for example, television sets and other consumer electronics—may well be highly profitable without incurring an unusually intense environmental impact. The point of the foregoing observations is not that they establish the rule that increased profitability inevitably means increased pollution, but only that many of the heavily polluting new technologies have brought with them a higher rate of profit than the less polluting technologies they have displaced.

Nor is this to say that the relationship is intentional on the part of the entrepreneur. Indeed, there is considerable evidence, some of which has been cited earlier, that the producers are typically unaware of the potential environmental effects of their operation until the effects become manifest, after the limits of biological accommodation have been exceeded, in ecological collapse or human illness. Nevertheless, despite these limitations, these examples of the relationship between pollution and profit-taking in a private enterprise economic system need to be taken seriously, I believe, because they relate to important segments of the economic system of the world's largest capitalist power.

In response to such evidence, some will argue that such a connection between pollution and profit-taking is irrational because pollution degrades the quality of the environment on which the future success of even the most voracious capitalist enterprise depends. In general, this argument has a considerable force, for it is certainly true that industrial pollution tends to destroy the very "biological capital" that the ecosystem provides and on which production depends. A good example is the potential effect of mercury pollution from chloralkali plants on the successful operation of these plants. Every ton of chlorine produced by such a plant requires about 15,000 gallons of water, which must meet rigorous standards of purity. This water is obtained from nearby rivers or lakes, in which purity is achieved by ecological cycles, driven by the metabolic activities of a number of microorganisms. Since mercury compounds are highly toxic to most living organisms, the release of mercury by chloralkali plants must be regarded as a serious threat to the source of pure water on which these plants depend. Nevertheless, it is a fact that in this and other instances, the industrial operation—until constrained by outside forces—has proceeded on the seemingly irrational, self-destructive course of polluting the environment on which it depends.

A statistician, Daniel Fife, has recently made an interesting observation that helps to explain this paradoxical relationship between the profitability of a business and its tendency to destroy its own environmental base. His example is the whaling industry, which has been driving itself out of business by killing whales so fast as to ensure that they will soon become extinct. Fife refers to this kind of business operation as "irresponsible," in contrast with a "responsible" operation, which would only kill whales as fast as they can reproduce. He points out that even though the irresponsible business will eventually wipe itself out, it *may be profitable to do so*—at least for the entrepreneur, if not for society—if the extra profit derived from the irresponsible operation is high enough to yield a return on investment elsewhere that outweighs the ultimate effect of killing off the whaling business. To paraphrase Fife, the "irresponsible" entrepreneur finds it profitable to kill the goose that lays the golden eggs, so long as the goose lives long enough to provide him with sufficient eggs to pay for the purchase of a new goose. Ecological irresponsibility can pay—for the entrepreneur, but not for society as a whole.

The crucial link between pollution and profits appears to be modern technology, which is both the main source of recent increases in productivity—and therefore of profits—and of recent assaults on the environment. Driven by an inherent tendency to maximize profits, modern private enterprise has seized upon those massive technological innovations that promise to gratify this need, usually unaware that these same innovations are often also instruments of environmental destruction. Nor is this surprising, for ... technologies tend to be designed at present as single-purpose instruments. Apparently, this purpose is, unfortunately, too often dominated by the desire to enhance productivity—and therefore profit.

Obviously, we need to know a great deal more about the connection between pollution and profits in private enterprise economies. Meanwhile, it would be prudent to give some thought to the meaning of the functional connection between pollution and profits, which is at least suggested by the present information.

The general proposition that emerges from these considerations is that environmental pollution is connected to the economics of the private enterprise system in two ways. First, pollution tends to become intensified by the displacement of older productive techniques by new, ecologically faulty, but more profitable technologies. Thus, in these cases, pollution is an intended concomitant of the natural drive of the economic system to introduce new technologies that increase productivity. Second, the cost[s] of environmental degradation are chiefly borne not by the producer, but by society as a whole, in the form of "externalities." A business enterprise that pollutes the environment is therefore being subsidized by society; to this extent, the enterprise, though free, is not wholly private.

24

AMERICAN GROUND TRANSPORT

BRADFORD CURIE SNELL

The manufacture of ground transportation equipment is one of this nation's least competitive industrial activities. . . .

Ground transport is dominated by a single, diversified firm to an extent possibly without parallel in the American economy. General Motors, the world's largest producer of cars and trucks, has also achieved monopoly control of buses and locomotives which compete with motor vehicles for passengers and freight. Its dominance of the bus and locomotive industries, moreover, would seem to constitute a classic monopoly. Although GM technically accounts for 75 percent of current city bus production, its only remaining competitor, the Flxible Co., relies on it for diesel propulsion systems, major engine components, technical assistance, and financing. In short, Flxible is more a distributor for GM than a viable competitor; virtually its sole function is the assembly of General Motors' bus parts for sale under the Flxible trade name. Likewise, in the production of intercity buses, its only remaining competitor, Motor Coach Industries, is wholly dependent upon GM for diesel propulsion systems and major mechanical components. In addition, General Motors accounts for 100 percent of all passenger and 80 percent of all freight locomotives manufactured in the United States. Such concentration in a single firm of control over three rival transportation equipment industries all but precludes the existence of competitive conduct and performance.

The distribution of economic power in this sector is remarkably asymmetrical. . . . [E]conomic power is fundamentally a function of concentration and size. In terms of concentration, the ground transport sector is virtually controlled by the Big Three auto companies. General Motors, Ford, and Chrysler account for 97 percent of automobile and 84 percent of truck production: GM alone dominates the bus and rail locomotive industries. Accordingly, the automakers have the power to impose a tax, in the form of a price increase, on purchasers of new cars to underwrite political campaigns against bus and rail systems.

In terms of size, there is an enormous divergence between the competing automotive and nonautomotive industries. Moreover, General Motors' diversification program has left only a small portion of the bus and rail industries in the hands of independent producers. As measured by aggregate sales, employment, and financial resources, therefore, the independent bus and rail firms are no match for the automakers. The Big Three's aggregate sales of motor vehicles and parts amount to about $52 billion each year, or more than 25 times the combined sales of trains, buses, subway and rapid transit cars by the four largest firms other than GM which produce bus and rail vehicles: Pullman and Budd (railway freight and passenger cars, subway and rapid transit cars); Rohr (buses and rapid transit cars); General Electric (commuter railcars and locomotives). The Big Three automakers employ nearly 1½ million workers, or more than three times as many as their four principal rivals: General Motors alone maintains plants in 19 different states. The Big Three also excel in their ability to finance lobbying and related political activities. GM, Ford, and Chrysler annually contribute more than an estimated $14 million to trade associations which lobby for the promotion of automotive transportation. By contrast, their four leading rivals contribute not more than $1 million, or less than one-tenth this amount, to rail transit lobbies. The magnitude of their sales, employment, and financial resources, therefore, affords the automakers overwhelming political influence.

It may be argued, moreover, that due to their conflicting interlocks with the motor vehicle manufacturers, these bus and rail firms would be reluctant to set their economic and political resources against them. Eighty percent of Budd's sales, for example, consist of automotive components purchased by the Big Three; Rohr, which also owns the Flxible Co., is wholly dependent upon GM for major bus components; Pullman derives more income from manufacturing trailers for highway trucks than from selling freight cars to the railroads; and General Electric manufactures a vast range of automotive electrical equipment, including about 80 percent of all automotive lamps. In sum, the independent bus and rail equipment manufacturers are probably unable and possibly unwilling to oppose the Big Three automakers effectively in political struggles over transportation policy.

Lacking a competitive structure, the group of industries responsible for providing us with ground transportation equipment fail to behave competitively. Diversification by General Motors into bus and rail production may have contributed to the displacement of these alternatives by automobiles and trucks. In addition, the asymmetrical distribution of economic and political power may have enabled the automakers to divert Government funds from rail transit to highways.

The Big Three automakers' efforts to restrain nonautomotive forms of passenger and freight transport have been perfectly consistent with profit maximization. One trolley coach or bus can eliminate 35 automobiles; 1 streetcar, subway, or rapid transit vehicle can supplant 50 passenger cars; an interurban railway or railroad train can displace 1,000 cars or a fleet of 150 cargo-laden trucks. Given the Big Three automakers' shared monopoly control of motor vehicle production and GM's diversified control of nonautomotive transport, it was inevitable that cars and trucks would eventually displace every other competing form of ground transportation.

The demise of nonautomotive transport is a matter of historical record. By 1973 viable alternatives to cars and trucks had all but ceased to exist. No producers of electric streetcars, trolley coaches, or interurban electric trains remained; only two established railcar builders (Pullman and Rohr) were definitely planning to continue production; a single firm (General Electric) still manufactured a handful of electric locomotives; and General Motors accounted for virtually all of an ever-shrinking number of diesel buses and locomotives.

There were, of course, a number of factors involved in this decline. For example, the popularity of motor vehicles, due in large part to their initial flexibility, most certainly affected public demand for competing methods of travel. On the other hand, the demise of bus and rail forms of transport cannot, as some have suggested, be attributed to the public's desire to travel exclusively by automobile. Rather, much of the growth in autos as well as trucks may have proceeded from the decline of rail and bus systems. In short, as alternatives ceased to be viable, automobiles and trucks became indispensable.

The sections which immediately follow relate in considerable detail how General Motors' diversification into bus and rail production generated conflicts of interest which necessarily contributed to the displacement of alternatives to motor vehicle transportation. A subsequent section will consider how asymmetry in the ground transport sector led to the political restraint of urban rail transit.

Before considering the displacement of bus and rail transportation, however, a distinction between intent and effect should be carefully drawn. This study contends that certain adverse effects flow inevitably from concentrated multi-industry structures regardless of whether these effects were actually intended. Specifically, it argues that structural concentration of auto, truck, bus, and rail production in one firm necessarily resulted in the promotion of motor vehicles and the displacement of competing alternatives. Whether that firm's executives in the 1920's actually intended to construct a society wholly dependent on automobiles and trucks is unlikely and, in any case, irrelevant.

That such a society developed in part as the result of General Motors' common control of competing ground transport industries is both relevant and demonstrable.

❖ 1. THE SUBSTITUTION OF BUS FOR RAIL PASSENGER TRANSPORTATION

By the mid-1920's, the automobile market had become saturated. Those who desired to own automobiles had already purchased them; most new car sales had to be to old car owners. Largely as a result, General Motors diversified into alternative modes of transportation. It undertook the production of city and intercity motor buses. It also became involved in the operation of bus and rail passenger services. As a necessary consequence, it was confronted with fundamental conflicts of interest regarding which of these several competing methods of transport it might promote most profitably and effectively. Its natural economic incentives and prior business experience strongly favored the manufacture and sale of cars and trucks rather than bus, and particularly rail, vehicles. In the course of events, it became committed to the displacement of rail transportation by diesel buses and, ultimately, to their displacement by automobiles.

In 1925, General Motors entered bus production by acquiring Yellow Coach, which at that time was the Nation's largest manufacturer of city and intercity buses. One year later, it integrated forward into intercity bus operation by assisting in the formation of the Greyhound Corp., and soon became involved in that company's attempt to convert passenger rail operations to intercity bus service. Beginning in 1932, it undertook the direct operation and conversion of interurban electric railways and local electric streetcar and trolleybus systems to city bus operations. By the mid-1950's, it could lay claim to having played a prominent role in the complete replacement of electric street transportation with diesel buses. Due to their high cost of operation and slow speed on congested streets, however, these buses ultimately contributed to the collapse of several hundred public transit systems and to the diversion of hundreds of thousands of patrons to automobiles. In sum, the effect of General Motors' diversification program was threefold: substitution of buses for passenger trains, streetcars and trolleybuses; monopolization of bus production; and diversion of riders to automobiles.

Immediately after acquiring Yellow Coach, General Motors integrated forward into intercity bus operation. In 1926, interests allied with GM organized and then combined with the Greyhound Corp. for the purpose of replacing rail passenger service with a GM-equipped and Greyhound-operated nationwide system of intercity bus transportation. By mutual arrangement, Greyhound agreed to purchase virtually all of its buses from GM, which agreed in turn to refrain from selling intercity buses to any of Greyhound's bus operating competitors. In 1928, Greyhound announced its intention of converting commuter rail operations to intercity bus service. By 1939, six major railroads had agreed under pressure from Greyhound to replace substantial portions of their commuter rail service with Greyhound bus systems: Pennsylvania RR (Pennsylvania Greyhound Lines), New York Central RR (Central Greyhound Lines), Southern Pacific RR (Pacific Greyhound Lines), New York, New Haven & Hartford RR (New England Greyhound Lines), Great Northern RR (Northland Greyhound Lines), and St. Louis Southwestern Railway (Southwestern Greyhound Lines). By 1950, Greyhound carried roughly half as many intercity passengers as all the Nation's railroads combined.

During this period, General Motors played a prominent role in Greyhound management. In 1929, for example, it was responsible for the formation, direct operation, and financing of Atlantic Greyhound, which later became Greyhound's southeastern affiliate. Three years later, in 1932, when Greyhound was in serious financial trouble, it arranged for a million dollar cash loan. In addition, I. B. Babcock, the president of GM's bus division, served on Greyhound's board of directors until 1938, when he was replaced by his successor at GM, John A. Ritchie. Until 1948, GM was also the largest single shareholder in the Greyhound Corp. In short, through its interlocking interests in and promotion of Greyhound, General Motors acquired a not insignificant amount of influence over the shape of this nation's intercity passenger transportation. As the largest manufacturer of buses, it inevitably pursued a policy which would divert intercity traffic from rails to the intercity buses which it produced and Greyhound operated. Although this policy was perfectly compatible with GM's legitimate interest in maximizing returns on its stockholders' investments, it was not necessarily in the best interest of the riding public. In effect, the public was substantially deprived of access to an alternative form of intercity travel which, regardless of its merits, was apparently curtailed as a result of corporate rather than public determination.

After its successful experience with intercity buses, General Motors diversified into city bus and rail operations. At first, its procedure consisted of directly acquiring and scrapping local electric transit systems in favor of GM buses. In this fashion, it created a market for its city buses. As GM general Counsel Henry Hogan would observe later, the corporation "decided that the only way this new market for (city) buses could be created was for it to finance the conversion from streetcars to buses in some small cities." On June 29, 1932, the GM-bus executive committee formally resolved that "to develop motorized transportation, our company should initiate a program of this nature and authorize the incorporation of a holding company with a capital of $300,000." Thus was formed United Cities Motor Transit (UCMT) as a subsidiary of GM's bus division. Its sole function was to acquire electric streetcar companies, convert them to GM motorbus operation, and then resell the properties to local concerns which agreed to purchase GM bus replacements. The electric streetcar lines of Kalamazoo and Saginaw, Mich., and Springfield, Ohio, were UCMT's first targets. "In each case," Hogan stated, GM "successfully motorized the city, turned the management over to other interests and liquidated its investment." The program ceased, however, in 1935 when GM was censured by the American Transit Association (ATA) for its self-serving role, as a bus manufacturer, in apparently attempting to motorize Portland's electric streetcar system.

As a result of the ATA censure, GM dissolved UCMT and embarked upon a nationwide plan to accomplish the same result indirectly. In 1936 it combined with the Omnibus Corp. in engineering the tremendous conversion of New York City's electric streetcar system to GM buses. At that time, as a result of stock and management interlocks, GM was able to exert substantial influence over Omnibus. John A. Ritchie, for example, served simultaneously as chairman of GM's bus division and president of Omnibus from 1926 until well after the motorization was completed. The massive conversion within a period of only 18 months of the New York system, then the world's largest streetcar network, has been recognized subsequently as the turning point in the electric railway industry.

Meanwhile, General Motors had organized another holding company to convert the remainder of the Nation's electric transportation system to GM buses. In 1936, it caused its officers and employees, I. B. Babcock, E. J. Stone, E. P. Crenshaw, and several Greyhound executives to form National City Lines, Inc. (NCL). During the following 14 years General Motors, together with Standard Oil of California, Firestone Tire, and two other suppliers of bus-related products, contributed more than $9 million to this holding company for the purpose of converting electric transit systems in 16 states to GM bus operations. The method of operation was basically the same as that which GM employed successfully in its United Cities Motor Transit program: acquisition, motorization, resale. By having NCL resell the properties after conversion was completed, GM and its allied companies were assured that their capital was continually reinvested in the motorization of additional systems. There was, moreover, little possibility of reconversion. To preclude the return of electric vehicles to the dozens of cities it motorized, GM extracted from the local transit companies contracts which prohibited their purchase of ". . . any new equipment using any fuel or means of propulsion other than gas."

The National City Lines campaign had a devastating impact on the quality of urban transportation and urban living in America. Nowhere was the ruin more apparent than in the Greater Los Angeles metropolitan area. Thirty-five years ago it was a beautiful region of lush palm trees, fragrant orange groves, and clean, ocean-enriched air. It was served then by the world's largest interurban electric railway system. The Pacific Electric system branched out from Los Angeles for a radius of more than 75 miles, reaching north to San Fernando, east to San Bernardino, and south to Santa Ana. Its 3,000 quiet, pollution-free, electric trains annually transported 80 million people throughout the sprawling region's 56 separately incorporated cities. Contrary to popular belief, the Pacific Electric, not the automobile, was responsible for the area's geographical development. First constructed in 1911, it established traditions of suburban living long before the automobile had arrived.

In 1938, General Motors and Standard Oil of California organized Pacific

City Lines (PCL) as an affiliate of NCL to motorize west coast electric railways. The following year PCL acquired, scrapped, and substituted bus lines for three northern California electric rail systems in Fresno, San Jose, and Stockton. In 1940 GM, Standard Oil, and Firestone "assumed the active management of Pacific (City Lines)" in order to supervise its California operations more directly. That year, PCL began to acquire and scrap portions of the $100 million Pacific Electric system including rail lines from Los Angeles to Glendale, Burbank, Pasadena, and San Bernardino. Subsequently, in December 1944, another NCL affiliate (American City Lines) was financed by GM and Standard Oil to motorize downtown Los Angeles. At the time, the Pacific Electric shared downtown Los Angeles trackage with a local electric streetcar company, the Los Angeles Railway. American City Lines purchased the local system, scrapped its electric transit cars, tore down its power transmission lines, ripped up the tracks, and placed GM diesel buses fueled by Standard Oil on Los Angeles' crowded streets. In sum, GM and its auto-industrial allies severed Los Angeles' rail links and then motorized its downtown heart.

Motorization drastically altered the quality of life in southern California. Today, Los Angeles is an ecological wasteland: The palm trees are dying from petrochemical smog; the orange groves have been paved over by 300 miles of freeways; the air is a septic tank into which 4 million cars, half of them built by General Motors, pump 13,000 tons of pollutants daily. With the destruction of the efficient Pacific Electric rail system, Los Angeles may have lost its best hope for rapid rail transit and a smog-free metropolitan area. "The Pacific Electric," wrote UCLA Professor Hilton, "could have comprised the nucleus of a highly efficient rapid transit system, which would have contributed greatly to lessening the tremendous traffic and smog problems that developed from population growth." The substitution of GM diesel buses, which were forced to compete with automobiles for space on congested freeways, apparently benefited GM, Standard Oil, and Firestone considerably more than the riding public. Hilton added: "the (Pacific Electric) system, with its extensive private right of way, was far superior to a system consisting solely of buses on the crowded streets." As early as 1963, the city already was seeking ways of raising $500 million to rebuild a rail system "to supersede its present inadequate network of bus lines." A decade later, the estimated cost of constructing a 116-mile rail system, less than one-sixth the size of the earlier Pacific Electric, had escalated to more than $6.6 billion.

By 1949, General Motors had been involved in this replacement of more than 100 electric transit systems with GM buses in 45 cities including New York, Philadelphia, Baltimore, St. Louis, Oakland, Salt Lake City, and Los Angeles. In April of that year, a Chicago Federal jury convicted GM of having criminally conspired with Standard Oil of California, Firestone Tire and others to replace electric transportation with gas- or diesel-powered buses and to monopolize the sale of buses and related products to local transportation companies throughout the country. The court imposed a sanction of $5,000 on GM. In addition, the jury convicted H. C. Grossman, who was then treasurer of General Motors. Grossman had played a key role in the motorization campaigns and had served as a director of PCL when that company undertook the dismantlement of the $100 million Pacific Electric system. The court fined Grossman the magnanimous sum of $1.

Despite its criminal conviction, General Motors continued to acquire and dieselize electric transit properties through September of 1955. By then, approximately 88 percent of the nation's electric streetcar network had been eliminated. In 1936, when GM organized National City Lines, 40,000 street-cars were operating in the United States; at the end of 1955, only 5,000 remained. In December of that year, GM bus chief Roger M. Kyes correctly observed: "The motor coach has supplanted the inter-urban systems and has for all practical purposes eliminated the trolley (streetcar)."

The effect of General Motor's diversification into city transportation sys-tems was substantially to curtail yet another alternative to motor vehicle trans-portation. Electric street railways and electric trolley buses were eliminated without regard to their relative merit as a mode of transport. Their displace-ment by oil-powered buses maximized the earnings of GM stockholders; but it deprived the riding public of a competing method of travel. Moreover, there is some evidence that in terms of air pollution and energy consumption these electric systems were superior to diesel buses. In any event, GM and its oil and tire co-conspirators used National City Lines as a device to force the sale of their products regardless of the public interest. As Professor Smerk, an author-ity on urban transportation, has written, "Street railways and trolley bus oper-ations, even if better suited to traffic needs and the public interest, were doomed in favor of the vehicles and material produced by the conspirators."

General Motors' substitution of buses for city streetcar lines may also have contributed in an indirect manner to the abandonment of electric railway freight service. During the 1930's merchants relied extensively on interurban electric railways to deliver local goods and to interchange distant freight ship-ments with mainline railroads. The Pacific Electric, for example, was once the third largest freight railroad in California; it interchanged freight with the Southern Pacific, the Union Pacific and the Santa Fe. In urban areas, these rail-ways often ran on local streetcar trackage. The conversion of city streetcars to buses, therefore, deprived them of city trackage and hastened their replacement by motor trucks, many of which, incidentally, were produced by GM.

General Motors also stood to profit from its interests in highway freight transport. Until the early 1950's, it maintained sizable stock interests in two of the Nation's largest trucking firms, Associated Transport and Consolidated Freightways, which enjoyed the freight traffic diverted for the electric rail-ways. By 1951, these two companies had established more than 100 freight ter-minals in 29 states coast-to-coast and, more than likely, had invested in a sub-stantial number of GM diesel-powered trucks.

GM's diversification into bus and rail operations would appear not only to have had the effect of foreclosing transport alternatives regardless of their comparative advantages but also to have contributed at least in part to urban air pollution problems. There were in fact some early warnings that GM's replacement of electric-driven vehicles with diesel-powered buses and trucks

was increasing air pollution. On January 26, 1954, for instance, E. P. Crenshaw, GM bus general sales manager, sent the following memorandum to F. J.
Limback, another GM executive:

> There has developed in a number of cities "smog" conditions which has result-
> ed in Anti-Air Pollution committees, who immediately take issue with bus and
> truck operations, and especially Diesel engine exhaust. In many cases, efforts
> are being made to stop further substitution of Diesel buses for electric-driven
> vehicles. . . .

Three months later, in April 1954, the American Conference of Governmental Industrial Hygienists adopted a limit of 5 parts per million for human
exposure to nitrogen oxides. Diesel buses, according to another report by two
GM engineers, emitted "oxides of nitrogen concentrations over 200 times the
recommended" exposure limit. Nevertheless, the dieselization program continued. Crenshaw reported to Limback in 1954:

> The elimination of street-cars and trolley-buses and their replacement by our
> large GM 51-passenger Diesel Hydraulic coaches continues steadily . . . in Den-
> ver, Omaha, Kansas City, San Francisco, Los Angeles, New Orleans, Honolu-
> lu, Baltimore, Milwaukee, Akron, Youngstown, Columbus, etc.

❖ 2. THE DISPLACEMENT OF BUS TRANSIT BY AUTOMOBILES

Diversification into bus production and, subsequently, into bus and rail operation inevitably encouraged General Motors to supplant trains, streetcars and
trolleybuses with first gasoline and then diesel buses. It also contributed to this
firm's monopolization of city and intercity bus production. The effect of
GM's mutually exclusive dealing arrangement with Greyhound, for example,
was to foreclose all other bus manufacturers and bus operating concerns from
a substantial segment of the intercity market. At least by 1952, both companies
had achieved their respective monopolies: GM dominated intercity bus production and Greyhound dominated intercity bus operation. By 1973, GM's
only competitor, Motor Coach Industries (established in 1962 by Greyhound
as the result of a Government antitrust decree) was wholly dependent on it for
major components; and Greyhound's only operating competitor, Trailways,
had been forced to purchase its buses from overseas. In the process, a number
of innovative bus builders and potential manufacturers, including General
Dynamics' predecessor (Consolidated Vultee) and the Douglas Aircraft Co.,
had been driven from the industry.

Likewise, in the city bus market, GM's exclusive bus replacement contracts with National City Lines, American City Lines, Pacific City Lines, the
Omnibus Corporation, Public Transport of New Jersey and practically every
other major bus operating company foreclosed competing city bus manufacturers from all but a handful of cities in the country and assured GM monop-

oly control of this market as well. Since 1925 more than 50 firms have withdrawn from city bus manufacturing including Ford, ACF-Brill, Marmon-Herrington, Mack Trucks, White Motor, International Harvester, Studebaker Twin Coach, Fifth Avenue Coach, Chrysler (Dodge), and Reo Motors. By 1973, only the Flxible Company, which had been established and controlled until 1958 by C. F. Kettering, a GM vice-president, remained as effectively a competitor-assembler of GM city buses. One other firm, AM General (American Motors), had announced its intention to assemble GM-powered city buses for delivery in late 1973. The ability of this firm, or for that matter Flxible and Motor Coach Industries, to survive beyond 1975, however, was seriously doubted by industry observers. That year a Government antitrust decree compelling GM to supply bus assemblers with diesel engines, transmissions and other major components will expire.

Monopolization of bus production and the elimination of electric street transportation has brought an end to price and technological competition in these industries. In this regard, several cities led by New York have filed a lawsuit charging that General Motors sets higher-than-competitive prices for its diesel buses and receives millions of dollars annually in monopoly profits. The suit also alleges that GM may be disregarding technological innovations in propulsion, pollution control and coach design, which would help attract patrons out of their automobiles.

In light of our dwindling petroleum supplies and mounting concerns about air pollution, the decline of technological competition in bus manufacturing is particularly unfortunate. ACF-Brill, Marmon-Herrington, Pullman-Standard, Twin Coach, and St. Louis Car once built electric buses and electric streetcars. Other firms manufactured steam-driven buses. According to a number of studies, these alternative forms of motive power would be preferable in terms of energy consumption, efficiency, pollution, noise, and durability to the diesel engine. Exclusion of these innovative firms, however, and GM's apparent disinterest in steam- or electric-powered vehicles (whose longer life, fewer parts, and easier repair would drastically reduce her placement sales) have precluded the availability of these technological alternatives today. Moreover, domination of domestic bus manufacturing by the world's largest industrial concern tends to deter entry by smaller, innovative firms. Lear Motors, for example, has developed quiet, low-pollution steam turbine buses; Mercedes-Benz, which sells buses in 160 countries, has produced low-pollution electric buses. Neither these nor any other firms, however, have been able to break into the GM-dominated American bus market. Furthermore, GM's conversion of much of this country's streetcar and interurban trackage to bus routes has precluded the survival of domestic streetcar builders and deterred entry by foreign railcar manufacturers. As a result, there remain few transit alternatives to GM diesel buses. None of the early White or Doble steam buses are still in operation. The last electric streetcars were built in 1953; only one electric bus (built in Canada) has been delivered since 1955. In 1973, only five American cities continued to operate electric buses, and eight ran a handful of ancient streetcars.

General Motors' gross revenues are 10 times greater if it sells cars rather than buses. In theory, therefore, GM has every economic incentive to discourage that effect. Engineering studies strongly suggest that conversion from electric transit to diesel buses results in higher operating costs, loss of patronage, and eventual bankruptcy. They demonstrate, for example, that diesel buses have 28 percent shorter economic lives, 40 percent higher operating costs, and 9 percent lower productivity than electric buses. They also conclude that the diesel's foul smoke, ear-splitting noise, and slow acceleration may discourage ridership. In short, by increasing the costs, reducing the revenues, and contributing to the collapse of hundreds of transit systems, GM's dieselization program may have had the long-term effect of selling GM cars.

Today, automobiles have completely replaced bus transportation in many areas of the country. Since 1952, the year GM achieved monopoly control of bus production, ridership has declined by 3 billion passengers and bus sales have fallen by about 60 percent. During that same period, GM automobile sales have risen from 1.7 million to more than 4.8 million units per year. By 1972, in a move which possibly signified the passing of bus transportation in this country, General Motors had begun converting its bus plants to motor home production. . . .

❖ 5. CURRENT PERFORMANCE OF THE GROUND TRANSPORTATION SECTOR

Due to its anticompetitive structure and behavior, this country's ground transport sector can no longer perform satisfactorily. It has become seriously imbalanced in favor of the unlimited production of motor vehicles. Unlike every other industrialized country in the world, America has come to rely almost exclusively on cars and trucks for the land transportation of its people and goods. Cars are used for 90 percent of city and intercity travel; trucks are the only method of intracity freight delivery and account for 78 percent of all freight revenues. This substitution of more than 100 million petroleum-consuming cars and trucks for competing forms of alternately powered ground transportation is a significant factor in this sector's unacceptable level of inefficient and nonprogressive performance.

Efficiency in terms of market performance may be defined as a comparison of actual prices or costs with those that would [be obtained] in a competitively structured market. Currently, Americans pay $181 billion per year for motor vehicle transportation. In terms of high energy consumption, accident rates, contribution to pollution, and displacement of urban amenities, however, motor vehicle travel is possibly the most inefficient method of transportation devised by modern man.

More specifically, the diversion of traffic from energy-efficient electric rails to fuel-guzzling highway transport has resulted in an enormous consumption of energy. Rails can move passengers and freight for less than one-fifth the amount of energy required by cars and trucks. The displacement of rails by highways, therefore, has seriously depleted our scarce supplies of energy and has increased by several billion dollars a year the amount consumers must pay for ground transportation. It has been estimated, for example, that the diversion of passengers in urban areas from energy-efficient electric rail to gasoline automobiles results in their paying $18 billion a year more in energy cost alone. In addition, economists have found that the inefficient diversion of intercity freight from rail to trucks costs consumers $5 billion per year in higher prices for goods.

The substitution of highways for rails has also reduced efficiency by imposing higher indirect costs on the public in the form of accidents, pollution, and land consumption. Rail travel is 23 times as safe as travel by motor vehicles. The diversion to highways has cost the public an estimated $17 billion each year in economic damages attributable to motor vehicle accidents. This figure, however, cannot reflect the incalculable human costs of motor vehicle accidents: the violent deaths each year by car and truck of 55,000 Americans, more than all who died in the entire 12 years of our involvement in Vietnam, and the serious injuries to an additional 5 million of our citizens.

Likewise, the costs of urban air pollution have been greatly accentuated by the imbalance in favor of cars and trucks. Motor vehicles annually consume 42 billion gallons of petroleum within the densely populated 2 percent of the U.S. geographic area classified as urban. The consumption of this enormous quantity of fuel in urban areas produces in excess of 60 million tons of toxic pollutants, which in turn cost urban residents more than $4 billion in economic damages.

The presence of high concentrations of these motor vehicle pollutants, particularly oxides of nitrogen, in densely populated areas has also generated smog. The hazards of carbon monoxide and hydrocarbon emissions from automobiles have been widely acknowledged. Less well known are the potentially more serious effects of oxides of nitrogen produced primarily by diesel trucks and buses in high concentrations on congested city streets. When inhaled, these oxides combine with moisture in the lungs to form corrosive nitric acid which permanently damages lung tissues and accelerates death by slowly destroying the body's ability to resist heart and lung diseases. By contrast, if electric rail transportation were substituted in cities for motor vehicles, urban air pollution might be reduced substantially. Although the burning of fuels to generate this increased electrical energy would produce some pollution, it would pose a substantially less serious hazard to public health. Electric power plants can often be located in areas remote from population centers. Moreover, the increased pollution by generating facilities would be offset by a reduction in pollution due to oil refinery operations. Furthermore, the abatement of air pollution at a relatively small number of stationary power plants would represent a far easier task than attempting to install and monitor devices on 100 million transient motor vehicles.

The diversion of traffic from rail to highways has imposed a third cost on consumers—the consumption of vast amounts of taxable urban landscapes.

From 60 to 65 percent of our cities' land area is devoted to highways, parking facilities, and other auto- and truck-related uses. In downtown Los Angeles, the figure approaches 85 percent. This has led to an erosion in the cities' tax base and, concomitantly, to a decline in their ability to finance the delivery of vital municipal services. Electric rail transportation, by comparison, requires less than one-thirteenth as much space as highways to move a comparable amount of passengers or goods, and in many cases can be located underground.

Progressiveness in terms of market performance is generally understood as a comparison of the number and importance of actual innovations with those which optimally could have been developed and introduced. The substitution of highways for rails has resulted in the decrease in mobility and has precluded important innovations in high-speed urban and intercity ground transportation. The decrease in mobility is most acute in urban areas. The average speed of rush hour traffic in cities dependent on motor vehicles, for example, is 12 miles per hour. Studies indicate that city traffic moved more quickly in 1890. Moreover, 20 percent of our urban population (the aged, youth, disabled, and poor) lack access to automobiles and, due to the nonexistence of adequate public transportation, are effectively isolated from employment or educational opportunities and other urban amenities. Substitution of highways for rails has also retarded innovations in high-speed urban and intercity transport. Technologically advanced rail transit systems, which currently operate in the major cities of Europe and Japan, would relieve congestion and contribute to urban mobility. High-speed intercity rail systems, such as Japan's 150-mile-per-hour electric Tokaido Express, would help to relieve mounting air traffic congestion and offer a practical alternative to slower and more tedious travel by car or truck. But the political predilections of the automakers have become the guidelines for American transportation policy. In contrast to the advanced rail transport emphasis of Europe and Japan, this country has persisted in the expansion of highway transport. As a result, America has become a second-rate nation in transportation.

There are strong indications, moreover, that due to mounting concerns about air pollution and a worldwide shortage of petroleum, our motor-vehicle-dominated transportation system will perform even worse in the future. The Environmental Protection Agency has warned that by 1977 motor vehicle emissions in major urban areas may compel a cutback in automobile, truck, and diesel bus use of as much as 60 percent. In addition, the Department of the Interior has forecast that the current petroleum crisis might cripple transportation and cause "serious economic and social disruptions." More precisely, an excessive reliance in the past on fuel-guzzling motor vehicles for transport has contributed to a crisis in energy which now threatens to shut down industries, curb air and ground travel, and deprive our homes of heating oil for winter.

Despite these adverse trends, the automakers appear bent on further motorization. Henry Ford II, for instance, has noted that notwithstanding "the energy crisis, the environmental crisis, and the urban crisis" new car sales in the United States "have increased by more than a million during the past 2 model years." General Motors' chief operating executive has predicted that soon each American will own a "family of cars" for every conceivable travel activity including small cars for trips, recreational vehicles for leisure, and motor homes for mobile living. GM is also engaged in the displacement of what little remains of this Nation's rail systems. To that end, it is developing 750-horsepower diesel engines to haul multiple trailers at speeds of 70 miles per hour along the nearly completed Interstate Highway System. These "truck trains" are slated to replace rail freight service. As substitutes for regional subway systems, GM is also advocating 1,400-unit diesel "bus trains," which would operate on exclusive busways outside cities and in bus tunnels under downtown areas. Both diesel truck trains and underground bus trains, however, would seem grossly incompatible with public concerns about petroleum shortages and suffocating air pollution.

The automakers' motorization program, moreover, is worldwide in scope. The superior bus and rail systems which flourish in the rest of the industrialized world interfere with the sale of cars and trucks by the Big Three's foreign subsidiaries. "The automobile industry put America on wheels," said GM Chairman Gerstenberg in September of 1972. "Today," he added, "expanding markets all around the world give us the historic opportunity to put the whole world on wheels."

25

THE TOXIC CLOUD

MICHAEL H. BROWN

A warning sign could be hung somewhere in every city: Danger, Toxic Air Contamination. The poisons once thought to be a serious concern only near a place such as Love Canal are now known to be everywhere. They appear in the air of an alpine forest, or over a Pacific island. They are also in the cabinet under the kitchen sink. . . .

We live in an era during which life expectancy as a whole has increased because of better health care for conventional types of physical distress. While the majority of cancers are induced by factors other than environmental toxics, we are also at the point where cancer is contracted by 30 percent of the population. Of Americans now living, 74 million will contract the disease. The cancer death rate has increased 26 percent in just two decades. Birth defects are also on the rise. Between 1970 and 1980 there was a 300 percent increase in reported cases of displaced hips and a 240 percent increase in babies with ventricular septal defects—a hole between chambers of the heart.

Dave Haas Ewell, who used to hunt the swamps that surround his home in Louisiana, knows first-hand what pollution means to local communities. "It's unreal what they have done," he said, nodding to the refineries and chemical plants that crowd the Mississippi's banks. "And ya know what? It's our children who'll pay for it. They will."

Adapted from Michael H. Brown, *The Toxic Cloud*, New York, Harper & Row, 1989. Reprinted by permission.

Dave Ewell's herd of cows was poisoned by chlorinated hydrocarbons, solvents, and metals which had deluged the area years ago, scalding the cypresses and turning alligators belly-up. They came from a chemical plant next to his family's plantation, and I remembered that upon my first visit there, in 1979, shiny globules of mercury oozed from the indentations my foot made in the muck near a bayou.

When the sun was hot, a thick, black sludge surfaced down by the bayou, sending an oil slick toward the Mississippi, which supplies drinking water to the city of New Orleans. There, the environment and cancer rates are such that Dr. Velma L. Campbell, a physician at the Ochsner Clinic, describes the toxic poisoning of the region as "a massive human experiment conducted without the consent of the experimental subjects."

Beginning two decades ago, the way we understand air pollution—indeed all forms of pollution—changed radically. In the 1960s and 1970s, scientists equipped with new analytical tools began identifying an array of mysterious synthetic compounds in the flesh of trout and other fish caught in the largest of the Great Lakes, that 31,700 square miles of fresh water known, with due respect, as Lake Superior. PCBs and DDT were among those found. So was another potent chlorinated insecticide called toxaphene.

In Superior's Whitefish Bay, infant birds began suffering from cataracts and edema. Their necks and heads became so swollen they could not open their eyes. Nor could some of them eat. They suffered from a defect, called "cross beak syndrome," that prevented their upper and lower bills from meeting.

In other parts of the Great Lakes, especially near Green Bay, the problem was more acute. In some spots, terns soon would be observed with club foot-like deformities that prevented the birds from being able to stand. Mink and river otters were disappearing from the south shore of Lake Ontario and around Lake Michigan. Though they had been making a comeback, by the mid-1980s bald eagles would have trouble nesting along Lake Superior. The problem, it was suspected, was their diet of chemically contaminated gulls.

There was also concern about human infants along the lakes. In one part of Michigan, some babies tested seemed to have lower birth weights and smaller head circumferences than children born to women who ate no fish. Some of the babies had what appeared to be abnormally jerky and unbalanced movements, weak reflexes, and general sluggishness.

While Lake Superior's vast shoreline could be expected to receive some chemical runoff from farms and scattered industry, the levels and character of its toxicants did not quite fit with what would be expected to enter the lake through the sewers, creeks, and rivers that drain into her.

Located at a relatively remote region between northern Michigan and southern Canada, Superior had not been plagued by the same problems that historically befell its little sister, Lake Erie. Erie's water had been starved of oxygen by phosphates which formed suds at outfall pipes and provoked wild overgrowths of algae—causing bloated fish to wash ashore. That pollution had taken no modern technical gear to detect: on Cleveland's Cuyahoga River, fires had ignited the oil slicks into a biblical spectacle of flames shooting up from the water itself.

But several hundred miles to the northwest, Lake Superior still had the aura of purity. Nearly the size of Indiana, the lake serves as headwaters for the greatest freshwater system on earth, a system that contains 20 percent of the planet's fresh surface water.

Yet suddenly, in the 1970s, its unsullied image was compromised. The compounds being found in Superior were mostly invisible and odorless in nature, but they posed much more of a danger than the more familiar sulfides, raw sewage and oil. Among them, toxaphene—a pesticide that possesses the widely recognized capability of causing thyroid carcinomas in rodents. Though not quite as persistent as DDT, it too accumulates in the ecosystem, it too is biomagnified in animal flesh and it is every bit as toxic as DDT, if not more so. Its concentrations in the lake approached levels at which consumption of fish is banned.

The pressing question: Where was the toxaphene coming from?

In Canada it had been closely restricted, and on the American side its major use was not near the Great Lakes nor anywhere else in the Midwest—it was in two impossibly distant areas: California and the Deep South.

Had it somehow become a constituent of ambient air? Had it descended like acid rain or nuclear fallout? Looking to test an even more isolated ecosystem, scientists began journeying to Siskiwit Lake in a national park called Isle Royale. The island is situated in the northern part of Lake Superior, more than thirty miles from Ontario's Thunder Bay, the nearest community of any real proportion.

The only means of access from one part of Isle Royale to another is by foot trails. There were no outfalls, no farm runoff, no toxic dumps. Nor did any of the tainted water of Superior flow into Siskiwit Lake, for Siskiwit's elevation, propped as it is on the island, is nearly sixty feet higher than Lake Superior's. All things considered, it seemed, there was no way at all for toxaphene to get to Siskiwit.

Yet to the shock of the investigating scientists, fish netted from Siskiwit had nearly double the PCBs that had been found in Lake Superior, and nearly ten times as much DDE—a breakdown product of DDT. One might rationalize certain levels in Lake Superior, with its vast shore and its exposure to at least some modern effluents. But, now, how did the stuff get to the isolated environs of Isle Royale in such high concentrations?

Scientists hauled up their gas chromatographs to various parts of the country and began searching for clues. One big hint was found when rain was tested at an estuary in South Carolina. Toxaphene was found in more than 75 percent of the samples. High levels also turned up in Greenville, on the lower Mississippi River. It was apparently lifting off the fields and into the wind. Tracking it northward, air samples also documented its presence in St. Louis and up in Michigan.

For those who thought such compounds remain firmly earthbound, or that what little bit does become airborne would simply disappear in the troposphere, the numbers were startling ones indeed. By the time it was 825 miles from Greenville and approaching the neighborhood of Lake Superior, the toxaphene was still at 4 percent of the Greenville level. At the same time, toxaphene was also being tracked over Bermuda and the North Atlantic, in the fish and water birds from Swedish lakes, in the North and Baltic seas, in the Tyrolean Alps and in Antarctic cod.

The conclusion seemed as obvious as it was momentous: we were no longer talking about the long-range transport of just sulphur and nitrogen but of the dreaded chlorinated pesticides—thought previously to be a crisis only in lake and river sediments. Chlorinateds, the compounds Rachel Carson worried about in her classic work, *Silent Spring,* were taking wing—in quantities great enough to threaten distant wildlife and people.

Soon, chemists tapping their computers at the University of Minnesota would start making somber estimates that would have seemed like sheer nonsense just a few years before. Perhaps 85, perhaps 90 percent of the total PCB input to Lakes Michigan and Superior was not from sewers but through the air, they said.

Whatever the number, it was a bad signal not just for cormorants and herons but also, perhaps, for the 26 million people who drink from the lakes. One 1981 estimate said about a million pounds of polycyclic aromatic hydrocarbons, a dangerous chemical produced in the generation and use of complex synthetic chemicals, were falling into the lakes each year. Also found in the lakes are substantial quantities of benzene hexachloride, a common synthetic chemical sometimes used as a fungicide, and DDT. Since it had been banned in the U.S. for a decade, the DDT, scientists conjectured, must have come over the poles from Europe and Asia, or from Mexico and parts south.

In tests in places like California, the results showed that the insecticides vaporized in great quantities right off the plants themselves. One study reported a 59 percent loss of toxaphene from a cotton field within twenty-eight days. Other experiments in closed chambers indicated that 24 percent of toxaphene turned into gas within ninety days of the last application, meaning that, in 1974, at least 142.5 million pounds of it vaporized into the American atmosphere.

That meant we were directly breathing chlorinated pesticides and PCBs, not just eating them with contaminated fish. Once the emotional reaction subsided, more questions arose. For example: If toxaphene and PCBs are so airworthy, what else is in the wild blue yonder?

With this line of study came a new understanding of airborne transport of toxic chemicals. We now know that pollution can fly in the form of tiny droplets, small pieces—or particles—of solid matter, invisible gases, or as a sort of mix of them known as the aerosol. The particulates may be washed to earth by the falling rain, or fall by simple gravity.

The gases, depending on how easily they dissolve in water, may become part of airborne moisture, moving wherever it moves, permeate vegetation, or condense into fine particulates that can be seen only with an electron microscope. Many chemicals, including chlorinated pesticides, travel both as passengers on a particle and in a gaseous state. Solvents such as benzene or toluene, by definition "volatile" compounds that easily evaporate, frequently find themselves in vapor states or dissolved in other substances. Even metals, under the right conditions, can turn vaporous. Others, such as the deadly dioxins, are not water soluble and prefer to cling to a particle.

Most large particulates remain within five or ten miles of their origin, but the smaller they are the farther they fly, and if they are small enough they can remain aloft for days or weeks. At times, if they get caught in the stratosphere, the weeks may turn to months, the months to a year. Gases, if they decay slowly enough, can travel still farther.

The question of atmospheric transport, once keen during atmospheric nuclear bomb-testing, has found greatly heightened currency in recent years with the introduction into public consciousness of acid rain. The recent specter of lake fish in Canada and upstate New York dying from acid that originates in coal-fired plants along the Ohio Valley and other parts of the industrialized Midwest has awakened us to the idea that our atmosphere is not infinite. What you place into it does not just disappear.

In the words of meteorologist and textbook author C. Donald Ahrens of California's Modesto Junior College, the atmosphere "is a thin, gaseous envelope comprised mostly of nitrogen and oxygen, with clouds of condensed water vapor and ice particles. Almost 99 percent of the atmosphere lies within eighteen miles of the surface. In fact, if the earth were to shrink to the size of a beach ball, its inhabitable atmosphere would be thinner than a piece of paper." Referring to the radioactivity tracked around the globe from the damaged reactor at Chernobyl, Dr. Kenneth A. Rahn, an atmospheric physicist at the University of Rhode Island said "It was only eleven days from Chernobyl to here. In terms of transport, this is a quite small planet."

It was in the 1950s and the 1960s that medical researchers began tracking blips that turned out to be sharp and steady upward lines on the cancer graphs of Louisiana. Since cancer is believed to take up to two decades to surface in the body, that takes us back to the 1940s when, coincidentally, the petrochemical industry was taking deep root along the lower Mississippi, drawn there by cheap feedstock gas from the oil fields, easy water transport, and lucrative tax incentives.

The government of Louisiana serviced the chemical makers as no other government did—especially those that were offshoots of the revered petroleum industry. As the older industrial states in the North began controlling the wanton pollution there, corporations looked to the South for relief from such costly regulations. Down at the mouth of the Mississippi, a manufacturing company could obtain up to ten years of exemptions from property taxes.

Soon, companies making pesticides, chlorine, rubber, antifreeze, detergents, plastics and a variety of chemical products sprouted along the river and in the swamps. Virtually every major American chemical corporation and several foreign ones have an outpost along the river. By 1986 Louisiana was ranked third nationally in chemical production, behind New Jersey and Texas.

Today, the biggest splotches of black on the nation's maps of lung cancer rates are in the south, allowing the lower Mississippi to borrow from New Jersey the nickname "Cancer Alley." While several Northeastern states still had higher rates for cancer in general in the 1970s (reflecting, perhaps, a longer exposure to industry), Louisiana lost 7,636 people to cancer in 1983 alone, and the decade before, it led the nation in lung cancer deaths with a rate of about eighty per 100,000 people—about 10 percent more than runners-up Maryland, Delaware, and Mississippi.

In one study of lung cancer among white males in three thousand American counties, thirty-eight of Louisiana's sixty-four counties (or parishes) were in the top 10 percent. In one recent period, figures showed that 30 percent of state residents could expect to develop cancer over a lifetime, including 33.1 percent of those living in New Orleans. Noted a special report to the governor in 1984, "Nearly one cancer death per hour in Louisiana is reason to be gravely concerned." The reason: There were only 4.4 million people in the state.

There are dozens of other kinds of industries that contribute to cancer, and by one estimate only 4 percent of the cancer incidents caused by airborne toxics can be laid onto the lap of chemical processors or the combination of toxics emitted by the rubber and petroleum industries. The emissions of road vehicles account for the most cases of toxicant-induced cancer.

But, for the most part, it is chemical firms that release the most troubling types of molecules into the environment. In Baton Rouge, according to company data, an Exxon Chemical plant was leaking 560,000 pounds of benzene yearly, while just south of there, according to a survey by the Sierra Club, eighteen plants in and around St. Gabriel and Geismar dumped about 400 billion pounds of toxic chemicals into the air during the first nine months of 1986. (*Editor's note: State health and environmental agencies are investigating an alarmingly high number of stillbirths in the St. Gabriel area. On August 5, Louisiana Governor Edwin Edwards, who has been criticized for gutting state environmental programs, called it "an emergency situation."*)

Add together the evaporation from oil-field pits, the volatilization from ponds of waste liquids and from storage tanks, the miasma rising from places such as Devil's Swamp, the steaming, hissing valves at petrochemical plants all the way down the Mississippi and the plumes of refinery smoke that form their own cumulus strata across the horizon—and the picture in southern Louisiana becomes one not of a low, lingering smog but more that of a toxic tornado.

How can our society deal with the threat posed by toxic pollution? Much can be accomplished, as the last decade of environmental reforms suggests, through legislation, lobbying and grassroots organizing to stem the tide of toxic pollution. In the end, however, the solution must be pronounced at a philosophical level. In the end highly toxic chemicals must be treated with wary respect—and isolated handling—not unlike what is practiced with radioactive elements.

Since industry has shown itself to be indifferent to public risks it creates, we must move toward a policy by which no company will be allowed to make or use any compound until the firm proves that it can either disassemble that compound into harmless, natural compounds—destroy it completely, with no toxic residues—or proves that the compound has absolutely no health repercussions whatsoever. Those compounds that fail the test but already exist must be gradually phased out, if not outright withdrawn.

Our society has two basic choices: to barter its health for modern conveniences and stop worrying about this at all; or to begin ridding the environment of compounds that threaten our immune systems, that threaten ecosystems, that threaten the very planet itself because of their potential to ruin protective layers of the upper atmosphere. In other words, we must prepare to ban a great many more chemicals than have so far been banned. And we must wean ourselves from certain conveniences—especially plastic—that cannot be made from biodegradable products. Our selfishness, our uncaring, threaten to unravel us all.

26

THE CHANGING ATMOSPHERE

THOMAS E. GRAEDEL AND PAUL J. CRUTZEN

The earth's atmosphere has never been free of change: its composition, temperature and self-cleansing ability have all varied since the planet first formed. Yet the pace in the past two centuries has been remarkable: the atmosphere's composition in particular has changed significantly faster than it has at any time in human history.

The increasingly evident effects of the ongoing changes include acid deposition by rain and other processes, corrosion of materials, urban smog and a thinning of the stratospheric ozone (O_3) shield that protects the earth from harmful ultraviolet radiation. Atmospheric scientists expect also that the planet will soon warm rapidly (causing potentially dramatic climatic shifts) through enhancement of the greenhouse effect—the heating of the earth by gases that absorb infrared radiation from the sun-warmed surface of the planet and then return the radiation to the earth.

Surprisingly, these important phenomena do not stem from modifications in the atmosphere's major constituents. Excluding the widely varying content of water vapor, the concentrations of the gases that make up more than 99.9 percent of the atmosphere—nitrogen (N_2), oxygen (O_2) and totally unreactive noble gases—have been nearly constant for much longer than human beings have been on the earth. Rather, the effects are caused in large part by changes,

From *Scientific American*, September 1989. Reprinted by permission.

mainly increases, in the levels of several of the atmosphere's minor constituents, or trace gases. Such gases include sulfur dioxide (SO_2), two nitrogen oxides known collectively as NO_x—nitric oxide (NO) and nitrogen dioxide (NO_2)—and several chlorofluorocarbons (compounds that contain chlorine, fluorine, carbon and sometimes hydrogen).

Sulfur dioxide, for example, rarely constitutes as much as 50 parts per billion of the atmosphere, even where its emissions are highest, and yet it contributes to acid deposition, to the corrosion of stone and metal and to the aesthetic nuisance of decreased visibility. The NO_x compounds, which are similarly scarce, are important in the formation of both acid deposition and what is called photochemical smog, a product of solar-driven chemical reactions in the atmosphere. The chloroflurocarbons, which as a group account for just one part per billion or so of the atmosphere, are the agents primarily responsible for depleting the stratospheric ozone layer. In addition, rising levels of chlorofluorocarbons, together with methane (CH_4), nitrous oxide (N_2O) and carbon dioxide (CO_2)—by far the most abundant trace gas at 350 parts per million—are enhancing the greenhouse effect.

The hydroxyl radical (OH), a highly reactive molecular fragment, also influences atmospheric activity even though it is much scarcer than the other gases, with a concentration of less than .00001 part per billion. Hydroxyl plays a different role, however: it contributes to the cleansing of the atmosphere. Its abundance in the atmosphere may diminish in the future.

Certainly some fluctuation in the concentrations of atmospheric constituents can derive from variations in rates of emission by natural sources. Volcanoes, for instance, can release sulfur- and chlorine-containing gases into the troposphere (the lower 10 to 15 kilometers of the atmosphere) and the stratosphere (extending roughly from 10 to 50 kilometers above the surface). The fact remains, however, that the activities of human beings account for most of the rapid changes of the past 200 years. Such activities include the combustion of fossil fuels (coal and petroleum) for energy, other industrial and agricultural practices, biomass burning (the burning of vegetation) and deforestation.

So much is clear, but which human activities generate which emissions? How do altered concentrations of trace gases give rise to such an array of effects? How much have the problems grown, and what are their consequences for the planet? Although complete answers to these questions are still forthcoming, multidisciplinary efforts by chemists, meteorologists, solar and space physicists, geophysicists, biologists, ecologists and others are making good headway.

Multidisciplinary collaboration is crucial because the factors influencing the fates of the gases in the atmosphere and their interactions with the biosphere are complex and incompletely understood. For instance, the chemical reactions a gas undergoes in the atmosphere can vary depending on the local mixture of gases and particles, the temperature, the intensity of the sun, the presence of different kinds of clouds or precipitation and patterns of airflow (which move chemicals horizontally and vertically). The reactions, in turn, influence how long a gas remains in the atmosphere and hence whether the gas or its end products have global or more localized effects on the environment.

Among the fruits of the investigations has been an improved understanding of the emissions produced by specific human activities. The combustion of fossil fuels for energy is known to yield substantial amounts of sulfur dioxide (particularly from coal), nitrogen oxides (which form when nitrogen and oxygen in the air are heated) and carbon dioxide. If the burning is incomplete, it also yields carbon monoxide (CO), a variety of hydrocarbons (including methane) and soot (carbon particles). Other industrial activities release additional sulfur dioxide (smelting is an example) or inject such substances as chlorofluorocarbons or toxic metals into the air.

Agricultural practices lead to the emissions of several gases as well. The burning of forests and savanna grasses in tropical and subtropical regions to create pastures and cropland yields additional large amounts of carbon monoxide, methane and nitrogen oxides. Moreover, soil exposed after forests are cleared emits nitrous oxide, as do nitrogen-rich fertilizers spread over fields. The breeding of domestic animals is another major source of methane (from oxygen-shunning bacteria in the digestive tract of cattle and other cud-chewing animals), as is the cultivation of rice, which is a staple food for many people in the tropics and subtropics.

Recent investigations have also led to a better understanding of the effects produced by increased anthropogenic emissions. For example, the much studied phenomenon of "acid rain" (by which we mean also acid snow, fog and dew) is now known to develop mainly as a by-product of atmospheric interactions involving the NO_x gases and sulfur dioxide. Through various reactions, such as combination with the hydroxyl radical, these gases can be converted within days into nitric acid (HNO_3) and sulfuric acid (H_2SO_4), both of which are dissolved readily in water. When the acidified droplets fall to the earth's surface, they constitute acid rain.

Because water droplets are removed from the atmosphere rapidly, acid rain is a regional or continental, rather than global, phenomenon. In contrast, the atmospheric lifetimes of several other trace gases, including methane, carbon dioxide, the chlorofluorocarbons and nitrous oxide, are much longer . . . and so the gases spread rather evenly throughout the atmosphere, causing global effects.

Since the beginning of the Industrial Revolution in the mid-18th century, the acidity of precipitation (as measured by the concentration of hydrogen ions) has increased in many places. For example, it has roughly quadrupled in the northeastern U.S. since 1900, paralleling increased emissions of sulfur dioxide and the NO_x gases. Similar increases have been found elsewhere in the industrialized parts of the world. Acid rain has also been detected in the virtually unindustrialized tropics, where it stems mainly from the release of the NO_x gases and hydrocarbons by biomass burning.

Wet deposition is not the only way sulfuric and nitric acids in the troposphere find their way to the earth's surface. The acids can also be deposited "dry," as gases or as constituents of microscopic particles. Indeed, a growing body of evidence indicates that dry deposition can cause the same environmental problems as the wet form.

Acid deposition clearly places severe stress on many ecosystems. Although the specific interactions of such deposition with lake fauna, soils and different vegetation types are still incompletely understood, acid deposition is known to have strongly increased the acidity of lakes in Scandinavia, the northeastern U.S. and southeastern Canada, thereby leading to reductions in the size and diversity of fish populations. Such deposition also appears to play some role in the forest damage that has been discovered in parts of the northeastern U.S. and Europe.

There is little doubt that acids deposited from the troposphere also contribute to the corrosion of outdoor equipment, buildings and works of art, particularly in urban areas—costing tens of billions of dollars each year for repairs and equipment replacement in the U.S. alone. Particles containing sulfate (SO_4^{2-}) have other effects as well. By scattering light efficiently, they decrease visibility; by influencing cloud albedo, they may have important implications for climate. . . .

In and around cities photochemical smog is another negative consequence of modern life. The term technically refers to the undesirable mixture of gases formed in the lower troposphere when solar radiation acts on anthropogenic emissions (particularly the NO_x gases and hydrocarbons from vehicle exhaust) to produce reactive gases that can be destructive to living organisms.

Ozone is a major product of such photochemical reactions and is itself the main cause of smog-induced eye irritation, impaired lung function and damage to trees and crops. The severity of smog is therefore generally assessed on the basis of ground-level ozone concentrations. In other words, the same three-oxygen molecule that is critically important for absorbing ultraviolet radiation in the stratosphere, where some 90 percent of atmospheric ozone is concentrated, is a problem when it accumulates in excess near the earth's surface.

Investigators have measured ozone levels in the atmosphere since the late 19th century, first from the ground and then within the atmosphere, aided by sophisticated airborne devices. Some of the earliest data showed that the "natural" level of ozone close to the ground at one measuring post in Europe roughly a century ago was about 10 parts per billion. Today the typical ground-level concentrations in Western Europe are from two to four times higher. Abundances more than 10 times higher than the natural level are now often recorded in Western Europe, California, the eastern U.S. and Australia.

Photochemical smog is also appearing in broad regions of the tropics and subtropics, particularly because of the periodic burning of savanna grasses; the same territories may be set afire as often as once a year. This practice releases large amounts of precursors to smog. Because solar radiation is plentiful and strong in those regions and photochemical reactions occur quickly, ozone levels can readily climb to perhaps five times higher than normal. As the populations in the tropics and subtropics grow, unhealthy air should become even more widespread there. Such a prospect is particularly worrisome because the properties of the soil in those regions may make the ecosystems there more vulnerable than the ecosystems in the middle latitudes to smog's effects.

Although a decrease in ozone near the ground would benefit polluted regions, any decrease in stratospheric ozone is disturbing, because the resulting increase in ultraviolet radiation reaching the earth could have many serious effects. It could elevate the incidence of skin cancer and cataracts in human beings, and it might damage crops and phytoplankton, the microscopic plants that are the basis of the food chain in the ocean.

So far, the extent of stratospheric ozone depletion has been most dramatic over Antarctica, where an ozone "hole," a region of increasingly severe ozone loss, has appeared each southern spring since about 1975. In the past decade springtime ozone levels over Antarctica have diminished by about 50 percent. . . . A more global assessment of the stratospheric ozone layer is still in a preliminary stage, but in the past 20 years depletions of from 2 to 10 percent have apparently begun to occur during the winter and early spring in the middle-to-high latitudes of the Northern Hemisphere, with the greatest declines in the higher latitudes.

It is now quite evident that chlorofluorocarbons, particularly CFC-11 ($CFCl_3$) and CFC-12 (CF_2Cl_2), are the major culprits responsible for ozone depletion. These anthropogenic chemicals, whose emissions and atmospheric concentrations have grown rapidly since their introduction several decades ago, are widespread as refrigerants, aerosol propellants, solvents and blowing agents for foam production, in part because they have what initially seemed to be a wonderful property: they are virtually unreactive in the lower atmosphere, and so they pose no direct toxic threat to living organisms.

Unfortunately, the very same characteristics that render chlorofluorocarbons rather inert enable them to reach the stratosphere unchanged. There they are exposed to strong ultraviolet radiation, which breaks them apart and liberates chlorine atoms that can destroy ozone by catalyzing its conversion to molecular oxygen. (Catalysts accelerate chemical reactions but are freed unaltered at the end.) Indeed, every chlorine atom ultimately eliminates many thousands of ozone molecules. Primarily because of the emission of chlorofluorocarbons, the level of ozone-destroying chlorinated compounds in the stratosphere is now four to five times higher than normal and is increasing at a rate of approximately 5 percent a year—developments that highlight the profound effect human activity can have on the stratosphere. . . .

Even if chlorofluorocarbon emissions stopped today, chemical reactions causing the destruction of stratospheric ozone would continue for at least a century. The reason is simple: the compounds remain that long in the atmosphere and would continue to diffuse into the stratosphere from the tropospheric reservoir long after emissions had ceased.

The depletion of global stratospheric ozone seems to be the handiwork primarily of a single class of industrial products—the chlorofluorocarbons—but several different emissions combine to raise the specter of a rapid greenhouse warming of the earth. Exactly how high global temperatures might climb in the years ahead is not yet clear. What is clear is that the levels of such infrared-absorbing trace gases as carbon dioxide, methane, the chlorofluorocarbons and nitrous oxide have mounted dramatically in the past decades, making added heating inevitable.

The trapping of heat near the surface of the planet by naturally emitted trace gases is a vital process: without it the planet would be too cold for habitation. Yet the prospect of a sudden temperature increase of even a few degrees Celsius is disquieting because no one can accurately predict its environmental effects, such as what the precise changes will be in precipitation around the world and in sea level. Any effects will probably be rapid, however, making it extremely difficult or impossible for the world's ecosystems and for human societies to adapt.

The extraordinary pace of the recent increases in greenhouse gases becomes strikingly evident when modern levels are compared with those of the distant past. Such comparisons have been made for several gases, including carbon dioxide—which alone accounts for more than half of the heat trapped by trace species—and methane, which is a more efficient infrared absorber than carbon dioxide but is significantly less abundant.

The histories of carbon dioxide and methane can be reconstructed on the basis of their concentrations in bubbles of air trapped in ice in such perpetually cold places as Antarctica and Greenland. Because the gases are long-lived and hence are spread fairly evenly throughout the atmosphere, the polar samples reveal the approximate global average concentrations of previous eras.

Analyses of the bubbles in ice samples indicate that carbon dioxide and methane concentrations held steady from the end of the last ice age some 10,000 years ago until roughly 300 years ago, at close to 260 parts per million and 700 parts per billion, respectively. Some 300 years ago the methane levels began to climb, and roughly 100 years ago the levels of both gases began to soar to their current levels of 350 parts per million for carbon dioxide and 1,700 parts per billion for methane. Moreover, direct worldwide measurements made by several investigators during the past decade have shown that atmospheric methane levels are growing more rapidly than those of carbon dioxide, at the remarkably high rate of about 1 percent a year.

The increases of both gases in the 20th century must be attributed in large part to the many expanding human influences on emissions. For carbon dioxide the sources are mainly fossil-fuel combustion and deforestation in the tropics; for methane, mainly rice cultivation, cattle breeding, biomass burning in tropical forests and savannas, microbial activity in municipal landfills and leakage of gas during the recovery and distribution of coal, oil and natural gas. As the world's population grows during the next century—and with it the demand for more energy, rice and meat products—the atmospheric concentration of methane could double. The climatic warming caused by methane and other trace gases could well approach that caused by carbon dioxide.

What are the expected trends for other trace gases? We as well as several other workers have extrapolated from the past and the present to make projections for the future, taking into account such factors as estimated increases both in population and in energy consumption. The estimates indicate that increases can be expected in the atmospheric concentrations of virtually all trace species in the next 100 years if new technologies and major energy-conservation efforts are not instituted to diminish the expected dependence on high-sulfur coal, an environmentally disadvantageous fuel, as the world's major energy source.

For example, as part of a multicenter collaboration, we have looked at past sulfur dioxide concentrations over the eastern U.S. and Europe (estimated prior to the mid-1960's on the basis of emission rates) and have speculated about future levels there and over the little-industrialized Gangetic Plain of India. . . . The historical assessment for the U.S. shows a marked increase in sulfur dioxide concentrations between 1890 and 1940, paralleling the buildup of "smokestack" industries and the construction of many new power plants. The amount of sulfur dioxide then leveled off and decreased in the 1960's and early 1970's. To a great extent, the decrease reflects the increased exploitation of oil (which is low in sulfur) for energy as well as the success of clean-air legislation in curbing sulfur emissions.

The concentrations of sulfur dioxide increased over Europe between 1890 and the mid-1900's but then leveled off; they did not decline appreciably, because until recently emission-control efforts were less vigorous than in the U.S. For the Gangetic Plain, where industrialization is rather recent, sulfur dioxide concentrations over some places have climbed from almost nothing in 1890 to levels that are now approaching those over the northeastern U.S.

The average sulfur dioxide concentrations over all three large regions are expected to increase, in part because low-sulfur fuels will probably become scarcer (although extremely stringent emission controls could stabilize levels over the U.S. and Europe for a few decades). The increases could be most marked over India and other developing countries that have rapidly growing populations and access to abundant supplies of high-sulfur coal, which is relatively inexpensive. Clearly, major measures must be introduced in the energy sector to prevent sulfur dioxide concentrations from rising extremely high.

Increases may also occur in a gas we have not yet discussed in detail: carbon monoxide, which has the power to decrease the self-cleansing ability of the atmosphere. A rise in carbon monoxide concentrations is likely because its sources—fossil-fuel combustion, biomass burning and atmospheric reactions involving methane—are all expected to increase. On the other hand, a significant (but still not well-quantified) amount of the gas is formed in the atmosphere over the tropics from the breakdown of hydrocarbons emitted by vegetation, a source that human activities are removing. The future concentrations of carbon monoxide are therefore uncertain, although on balance many workers foresee a rise over the Northern Hemisphere.

Carbon monoxide undermines the self-cleansing ability of the atmosphere by lowering the concentration of the hydroxyl radical, which is an important "detergent" because it reacts with nearly every trace-gas molecule in the atmosphere, including substances that would otherwise be inert. Without hydroxyl, the concentrations of most trace gases would become much higher than those of today, and the atmosphere as a whole would have totally different chemical, physical and climatic properties.

Our projections for the future are discouraging, then, if one assumes that human activities will continue to emit large quantities of undesirable trace gases into the atmosphere. Humanity's unremitting growth and development not only are changing the chemistry of the atmosphere but also are driving the earth rapidly toward a climatic warming of unprecedented magnitude. This climatic change, in combination with increased concentrations of various gases, constitutes a potentially hazardous experiment in which everyone on the earth is taking part.

What is particularly troubling is the possibility of unwelcome surprises, as human activities continue to tax an atmosphere whose inner workings and interactions with organisms and nonliving materials are incompletely understood. The Antarctic ozone hole is a particularly ominous example of the surprises that may be lurking ahead. Its unexpected severity has demonstrated beyond doubt that the atmosphere can be exquisitely sensitive to what seem to be small chemical perturbations and that the manifestations of such perturbations can arise much faster than even the most astute scientists could expect.

Nevertheless, some steps can be taken to counteract rapid atmospheric change, perhaps lessening the known and unknown threats. For example, evidence indicates that a major decrease in the rate of fossil-fuel combustion would slow the greenhouse warming, reduce smog, improve visibility and minimize acid deposition. Other steps could be targeted against particular gases, such as methane. Its emission could be reduced by instituting landfill operations that prevent its release and possibly by adopting less wasteful methods of fossil-fuel production. Methane emission from cattle might even be diminished by novel feeding procedures.

Perhaps more encouraging is the fact that many people and institutions are now aware that their actions can have not only local but also global consequences for the atmosphere and the habitability of the planet. A few recent events exemplify this awareness: in the Montreal protocol of 1987, dozens of nations agreed to halve their chlorofluorocarbon emissions by the end of the century, and several countries and the major chlorofluorocarbon manufacturers have more recently announced their intention to eliminate the chemicals by that deadline. Some of the same nations that have been involved in the Montreal protocol are now discussing the possibility of an international "law of the atmosphere." It would be directed at limiting the release of several greenhouse and chemically active trace gases, including carbon dioxide, methane and nitrous oxide, as well as sulfur dioxide and the NO_x gases.

We and many others think the solution to the earth's environmental problems lies in a truly global effort, involving unprecedented collaboration by scientists, citizens and world leaders. The most technologically developed nations have to reduce their disproportionate use of the earth's resources. Moreover, the developing countries must be helped to adopt environmentally sound technologies and planning strategies as they elevate the standard of living for their populations, whose rapid growth and need for increased energy are a major cause for environmental concern. With proper attention devoted to maintaining the atmosphere's stability, perhaps the chemical changes that are now occurring can be kept within limits that will sustain the physical processes and the ecological balance of the planet.

PART EIGHT

THE WORKPLACE

Americans pride themselves on their commitment to the "work ethic." And despite predictions in the 1950s and 1960s that we were on the verge of becoming a "leisure" society, work remains central to the lives of most of us. It is how, as adults, we make a living, define our identities, find our place in the scheme of things. Ideally, work is one of the most important ways in which we are enabled to participate in a larger human community.

But the reality of work, for all too many people, has always fallen short of the ideal. In the nineteenth century, many social theorists and social critics argued that for the great bulk of people in the emerging industrial societies, work had become a source of torment and exploitation rather than fulfillment. Karl Marx, one of the most influential of those critics, put it this way:

> *What constitutes the alienation of labour? First, that the work is external to the worker, that it is not part of his nature; and that, consequently, he does not fulfill himself in his work but denies himself, has a feeling of misery rather than well-being, does not develop freely his mental and physical energies but is physically exhausted and mentally debased. The worker, therefore, feels himself at home only during his leisure time, whereas at work he feels homeless. His work is not voluntary but imposed, forced labour. It is not satisfaction of a need, but only a means for satisfying other needs. Its alien character is clearly shown by the fact that as soon as there is no physical or other compulsion it is avoided like the plague.[1]*

Today, as we come to the close of the twentieth century, the concerns of the nineteenth-century critics have become, if anything, more urgent. An array of rapid economic and technological changes has made the link between work and well-being more and more problematic. The increasingly competitive global economy has put new strains on the institution of work—radically reshaping the workplace, eliminating jobs, and lowering incomes and benefits for many of those who do work steadily. The three articles in this part explore these themes in detail.

In the first, Nobel Prize-winning economist Wassily Leontief examines the ways in which advancing technology has traditionally eliminated jobs—from the nineteenth century to the present. He argues that the tendency to replace human workers with technology is both long-term and inevitable and that if it is not addressed by creative social policies, it could result in massive social problems as more and more people are steadily excluded from regular work and the income it brings. Avoiding that scenario, Leontief suggests, will require bold economic strategies, including new ways of distributing work more equitably and supplementing the incomes of those who must necessarily work less.

One result of the changes Leontief describes has been the massive loss of industrial jobs—with consequences we explored in Parts One and Three. A more subtle effect has been the replacement of those lost industrial jobs with others that pay much less—often far too little to support a family in present-day America. We are often told that the United States has become a "high-tech" society in which most jobs now require considerable education and skill and are rewarded accordingly. But the reality is less bright. Our economy has indeed produced many high-skill, high-paying jobs in recent years. But it has produced a far greater number of low-level jobs paying only the minimum wage or slightly above it. Morris Thompson and Cass Peterson describe what life is like for the growing numbers of "near-poor" Americans who, unlike the much discussed urban "underclass," work year in and year out but barely rise above mere economic survival.

Another reason for the decline in well-paying jobs in the United States—in addition to the technological changes in industry described by Leontief—is that many American employers have set up plants in Third World countries, where labor is far cheaper and less often unionized than it is at home. Barbara Ehrenreich and Annette Fuentes describe the harsh and dismal working conditions prevailing in some of those overseas factories. Most of the hard-working locals on the "global assembly line" are young women, who face not only wages lower than an 11-year-old in the United States can earn with a paper route but also the increased health hazards that come with the near absence of health and safety regulations in many of these countries.

Reference

1. Quoted in Shlomo Avineri, *The Social and Political Thought of Karl Marx* (Cambridge, Eng.: Cambridge University Press, 1971), p. 106.

27

THE DISTRIBUTION OF WORK AND INCOME

WASSILY W. LEONTIEF

> *My Lords: During the short time I recently passed in Nottinghamshire not twelve hours elapsed without some fresh act of violence;... I was informed that forty Frames had been broken the preceding evening. These machines ... superseded the necessity of employing a number of workmen, who were left in consequence to starve. By the adoption of one species of Frame in particular, one man performed the work of many, and the superfluous labourers were thrown out of employment.... The rejected workmen in the blindness of their ignorance, instead of rejoicing at these improvements in art so beneficial to mankind, conceived themselves to be sacrificed to improvements in mechanism.*

With these words Lord Byron in his maiden speech to the House of Lords in February, 1812, sought to explain, and by explaining to excuse, the renewal of the Luddite protest that was shaking the English social order. Nearly a generation earlier Ned Ludd had led his fellow workers in destroying the "frames": the knitting machines that employers had begun to install in the workshops of the country's growing textile industry. The House had before it legislation to exact the death penalty for such acts of sabotage. The Earl of

Wassily Leontief, "The Distribution of Work and Income," in *Scientific American*, Volume 247, September 1982, pp. 188–90. Reprinted by permission of W. H. Freeman and Company, Publishers.

Lauderdale sharpened Byron's thesis that the misled workers were acting against their own interests: "Nothing could be more certain than the fact that every improvement in machinery contributed to the improvement in the condition of persons manufacturing the machines, there being in a very short time after such improvements were introduced a greater demand for labour than ever before."

History has apparently sustained the optimistic outlook of the early exponents of modern industrial society. The specter of involuntary technological unemployment seems to remain no more than a specter. Beginning with the invention of the steam engine, successive waves of technological innovation have brought in the now industrial, or "developed," countries a spectacular growth of both employment and real wages, a combination that spells prosperity and social peace. Thanks as well to technological innovation, more than half of the labor force in all these countries—70 percent of the U.S. labor force—has been relieved from labor in agriculture and other goods-production that employed substantially everyone before the Industrial Revolution. It is true that the less developed countries are still waiting in line. If the outlook for the future can be based on the experience of the past 200 years, those countries too can expect to move up, provided their governments can succeed in reducing their high rate of population growth and desist from interfering with the budding of the spirit of free private enterprise.

There are signs today, however, that past experience cannot serve as a reliable guide for the future of technological change. With the advent of solid-state electronics, machines that have been displacing human muscle from the production of goods are being succeeded by machines that take over the functions of the human nervous system not only in production but in the service industries as well. . . . The relation between man and machine is being radically transformed.

The beneficence of that relationship is usually measured by the "productivity" of labor. This is the total output divided by the number of workers or, even better, by the number of man-hours required for its production. Thus 30 years ago it took several thousand switchboard operators to handle a million long-distance telephone calls; 10 years later it took several hundred operators, and now, with automatic switchboards linked automatically to other automatic switchboards, only a few dozen are needed. Plainly the productivity of labor—that is, the number of calls completed per operator—has been increasing by leaps and bounds. Simple arithmetic shows that it will reach its highest level when only one operator remains and will become incalculable on the day that operator is discharged.

The inadequacy of this conventional measure is perhaps better illustrated if it is applied to assess the effects of the progressive replacement of horses by tractors in agriculture. Dividing the successive annual harvest figures first by the gradually increasing number of tractors and then by the reciprocally falling number of horses yields the paradoxical conclusion that throughout this time of transition the relative productivity of tractors tended to fall while the productivity of the horses they were replacing was rising. In fact, of course, the cost-effectiveness of horses diminished steadily compared with that of the increasingly efficient tractors.

In the place of such uncertain abstractions it is more productive to try to bring the underlying facts into consideration and analysis. Technological change can be visualized conveniently as change in the cooking recipes—the specific combinations of inputs—followed by different industries to produce their respective outputs. Progress in electromechanical technology enabled the telephone company to replace the old technological recipe calling for a large number of manual switchboards having many operators with a new recipe combining more expensive automatic switchboards having fewer operators. In agriculture technological progress brought the introduction of successive input combinations with smaller inputs of animal and human labor and larger and more diversified inputs of other kinds—not only mechanical equipment but also pesticides, herbicides, vaccines, antibiotics, hormones and hybrid seed.

New recipes come into service in every industry by a constant process of "costing out." Some inputs included in a new recipe are at the outset too expensive, and it takes some time before improvements in their design or in the method of their manufacture bring sufficient reduction in their price and consequently in the total cost of the recipe to allow the adoption of the new technology. The decline, at the nearly constant rate of 30 percent per year for many years, in the cost per memory bit on the integrated-circuit chip has brought solid-state electronics technology first into expensive capital equipment such as telephone switchboards, automatic pilots, machine tools and computers, then into radio and television sets and powerful, low-cost computers as an entirely new category of consumer goods, then into the control systems of automobiles and household appliances and even into such expendable goods as toys. Thus the adoption of a new recipe in one industry often depends on replacement of the old by a new technology in another industry, as the vacuum tube was replaced by the transistor and its descendants in the transformed electronics industry.

Stepping back and contemplating the flow of raw materials and intermediate products through the input-output structure of an industrial system and the corresponding price structure, one can see that prices more or less faithfully reflect the state of technology in the system. With the passage of time price changes can be expected to reflect long-run technological changes going on in the various sectors. In this perspective, human labor of a specific kind appears as one, but only one, of the many different inputs, the price of which must be reckoned in the costing out of a given technological recipe. Its price, the wage rate, enters into the cost comparisons between competing technologies in the same way as the price of any other input.

In the succession of technological changes that have accompanied economic development and growth, new goods and services come on the stage and old ones, having played their role, step off. Such changes proceed at different rates and on different scales, affecting some sectors of economic activity more than

others. Some types of labor are replaced faster than others. Less skilled workers in many instances, but not always, go first, more skilled workers later.
Computers are now taking on the jobs of white-collar workers, performing
first simple and then increasingly complex mental tasks.

Human labor from time immemorial played the role of principal factor of
production. There are reasons to believe human labor will not retain this status
in the future.

Over the past two centuries technological innovation has brought an
exponential growth of total output in the industrial economies, accompanied
by rising per capita consumption. At the same time, until the middle 1940's the
easing of man's labor was enjoyed in the progressive shortening of the working day, working week and working year. Increased leisure (and for that matter cleaner air and purer water) is not counted in the official adding up of
goods and services in the gross national product. It has nonetheless contributed greatly to the well-being of blue-collar workers and salaried employees. Without increase in leisure time the popularization of education and cultural advantages that has distinguished the industrial societies in the first 80
years of this century would not have been possible.

The reduction of the average work week in manufacturing from 67 hours
in 1870 to somewhat less than 42 hours must also be recognized as the withdrawal of many millions of working hours from the labor market. Since the
end of World War II, however, the work week has remained almost constant.
Waves of technological innovation have continued to overtake each other as
before. The real wage rate, discounted for inflation, has continued to go up.
Yet the length of the normal work week today is practically the same as it was
35 years ago. In 1977 the work week in the U.S. manufacturing industries,
adjusted for the growth in vacations and holidays, was still 41.8 hours.

Concurrently the U.S. economy has seen a chronic increase in unemployment from one oscillation of the business cycle to the next. The 2 percent
accepted as the irreducible unemployment rate by proponents of full-employment legislation in 1945 became the 4 percent of New Frontier economic managers in the 1960's. The country's unemployment problem today exceeds 9
percent. How can this be explained?

Without technological change there could, of course, be no technological
unemployment. Nor would there be such unemployment if the total population and the labor force, instead of growing, were to shrink. Workers might
also hang on to their jobs if they would agree to accept lower wages. Those
who are concerned with population growth are likely to proclaim that "too
many workers" is the actual cause of unemployment. Libertarians of the "Keep
your hands off the free market" school urge the remedy of wage cuts brought
about by the systematic curtailment of the power of trade unions and the
reduction of unemployment and welfare benefits. Advocates of full employment have been heard to propose that labor-intensive technologies be given
preference over labor-saving ones. A more familiar medicine is prescribed by
those who advocate stepped-up investment in accelerated economic growth.

Each of these diagnoses has its shortcomings, and the remedies they prescribe can be no more than palliative at best. A drastic general wage cut might temporarily arrest the adoption of laborsaving technology, even though dirt-cheap labor could not compete in many operations with very powerful or very sophisticated machines. The old trend would be bound to resume, however, unless special barriers were erected against laborsaving devices. Even the most principled libertarian must hesitate to have wage questions settled by cutthroat competition among workers under the pressure of steadily advancing technology. The erection of Luddite barriers to technological progress would, on the other hand, bring more menace to the health of the economic and social system than the disease it is intended to cure.

Increased investment can certainly provide jobs for people who would otherwise be unemployed. Given the rate of technological advance, the creation of one additional job that 20 years ago might have required an investment of $50,000 now demands $100,000 and in 20 years will demand $500,000, even with inflation discounted. A high rate of investment is, of course, indispensable to the expanding needs of a growing economy. It can make only a limited contribution to alleviating involuntary technological unemployment, however, because the greater the rate of capital investment, the higher the rate of introduction of new laborsaving technology. The latest copper smelter to go into service in the U.S. cost $450 million and employs fewer than 50 men per shift.

Americans might have continued to absorb potential technological unemployment by voluntary shortening of the work week if real wages had risen over the past 40 years faster than they actually have, allowing the expectation of increase not only of total annual pay but also of total lifetime take-home pay. Because of the greatly expanded opportunities to replace labor by increasingly sophisticated technology it appears that the impersonal forces of the market no longer favor that possibility. Government policies directed at encouraging a steady rise in real wages sufficiently large to induce workers to resume continuous voluntary reduction in the work week could once have been considered. Under present conditions such policies would require such a large increase in the share of total national income going to wages that it would bring decline in productive investment, which is financed largely by undistributed corporate earnings and the savings of the upper income group. This would result in an unacceptable slowdown of economic growth. There remains the alternative of direct action to promote a progressive shortening of the work week combined with income policies, designed to maintain and to increase, as increases in total output allow, the real family income of wage earners and salaried employees.

Recent studies sponsored by the U.S. Department of Labor seem to indicate that the total number of working hours offered by the existing labor force might be reduced in exchange for a more flexible scheduling of work time. Indeed, some workers, depending on their age group, family status, occupation and so on, would even be prepared to forgo a certain fraction of their current income, some by extension of their annual vacation, some by earlier retirement or sabbatical leave and some by working four and a half days per week instead of five. Reducing the work day by 15 minutes proves, incidentally, to be one of the less desirable alternatives. Tentative and obviously somewhat speculative computations based on the most desirable trade-off choices for different groups developed in these studies indicate that the average U.S. worker would be willing to forgo some 4.7 percent of earnings in exchange for free time. On the basis of the 1978 work year the average employee's work time would be reduced from 1,910 work hours to 1,821, or by more than two working weeks in a year.

Although such measures certainly deserve serious consideration and, if at all possible, practical implementation, they cannot provide a final answer to the long-run question of how to enable a modern industrial society to derive the benefits of continued technological progress without experiencing involuntary technological unemployment and resulting social disruption. Sooner or later, and quite probably sooner, the increasingly mechanized society must face another problem: the problem of income distribution.

Adam and Eve enjoyed, before they were expelled from Paradise, a high standard of living without working. After their expulsion they and their successors were condemned to eke out a miserable existence, working from dawn to dusk. The history of technological progress over the past 200 years is essentially the story of the human species working its way slowly and steadily back into Paradise. What would happen, however, if we suddenly found ourselves in it? With all goods and services provided without work, no one would be gainfully employed. Being unemployed means receiving no wages. As a result until appropriate new income policies were formulated to fit the changed technological conditions everyone would starve in Paradise.

The income policies I have in mind do not turn simply on an increase in the legally fixed minimum wage or in the hourly wage or other benefits negotiated by the usual collective bargaining between trade unions and employers. In the long run increases in the direct and indirect hourly labor costs would be bound to accelerate laborsaving mechanization. This, incidentally, is the explicitly stated explanation of the wage policies currently pursued by the benevolently authoritarian government of Singapore. It encourages a rapid rise in real wages in order to induce free domestic enterprise to upgrade the already remarkably efficient production facilities of this city-state. It is perhaps needless to add that these policies are accompanied by strict control of immigration and encouragement of birth control.

What I have in mind is a complex of social and economic measures to supplement by transfer from other income shares the income received by blue- and white-collar workers from the sale of their services on the labor market. A striking example of an income transfer of this kind attained automatically without government intervention is there to be studied in the long-run effects of the mechanization of agriculture on the mode of operation and the income of, say, a prosperous Iowa farm. Half a century ago the farmer and the members of his family worked from early morning until late at night assisted by a team of horses, possibly a tractor and a standard set of simple agricultural implements. Their income consisted of what essentially amounted to wages for a 75- or 80-hour work week, supplemented by a small profit on their modest investment.

Today the farm is fully mechanized and even has some sophisticated electronic equipment. The average work week is much shorter, and from time to time the family can take a real vacation. Their total wage income, if one computes it at the going hourly rate for a much smaller number of manual-labor hours, is probably not much higher than it was 50 years ago and may even be lower. Their standard of living, however, is certainly much higher: the shrinkage of their wage income is more than fully offset by the income earned on their massive capital investment in the rapidly changing technology of agriculture. The shift from the old income structure to the new one was smooth and practically painless. It involved no more than a simple bookkeeping transaction because now, as 50 years ago, both the wage income and the capital income are earned by the same family.

The effect of technological progress on manufacturing and other nonagricultural sectors of the economy is essentially the same as it is on agriculture. So also should be its repercussions with respect to the shortening of the work day and the allocation of income. Because of differences in the institutional setup, however, those repercussions cannot be expected to work through the system automatically. That must be brought about by carefully designed income policies. The accommodation of existing institutions to the demands and to the effects of laborsaving mechanization will not be easy. The setting aside of the Puritan "work ethic," to which Max Weber so convincingly ascribed the success of early industrial society, is bound to prove even more difficult and long drawn out. In popular and political discourse on employment, full employment and unemployment, with its emphasis on the provision of incomes rather than the production of goods, it can be seen that the revision of values has already begun.

The evolution of institutions is under way as well. In the structure of the tax system and through Social Security, medical insurance, unemployment benefits and welfare payments the country is finding its way toward necessary income policies. A desirable near-term step is to reduce the contrast between those who are fully employed and those who are out of work. This is the effect of the widespread European practice of paying supplemental benefits to those who work fewer than the normal number of hours per week. In the long run, responding to the incipient threat of technological unemployment, public policy should aim at securing equitable distribution of work and income, taking care not to obstruct technological progress even indirectly.

Implementation of such policy calls for close and systematic cooperation between management and labor carried on with government support. Large-scale financial transfers inevitably generate inflationary pressure. The inflation that dogs all the market economies, some more than others, does not arise from mere technical economic causes but is the symptom of deep-seated social problems. In this country it is basically the incessant wrangling between management and labor that keeps the cost-price spiral climbing.

West Germany, a country celebrated for its successful stabilization policies, is touted also as an example of the unregulated enterprise economy. In reality the success of the Schmidt government's anti-inflation measures rests on the firm foundation of institutionalized labor-capital cooperation in the management of German industry. The "codetermination" law requires that half of the board of directors of each large corporation be elected by labor, with the stockholders represented by the other half. Among the labor members some are "outside" directors representing the national trade unions. Since wage and employment questions constitute only one problem in the broad range of problems on the agenda of these boards, their deliberations bring employers and employees into working contact at the grass roots of German industry. That relationship cannot but be of crucial importance in determining the nature of agreements reached in collective bargaining conducted between the parties at the national level.

Austria is another country that has up to now successfully resisted inflationary pressure. Relations between management and labor are mediated by institutional arrangements very similar to those in Germany. The government plays a larger and more active role in the national across-the-board wage negotiations. It does so by contributing projections, drawn from the input-output data bank of the country's bookkeeping system, that link decisions affecting the industry in question to the situation of the country as a whole. This approach was employed, for example, to model and project the impact of the new text-processing and printing technologies on the Austrian newspaper industry. That technological revolution, the occasion for months-long disputes and work stoppages in Britain, the U.S. and other countries, was carried out smoothly and expeditiously in Austria by close cooperation between management and labor in accordance with detailed plans developed by the government. Until 1980, when the tidal wave of the second oil crisis, reinforced by the recession in the U.S. economy, reached Austria, the annual rate of inflation had been held below 4 percent and unemployment below 2 percent.

Although current business publications, trade papers and the popular press abound with articles about "automation" and "robotics" and speculation on the economic impact of these developments, only the governmental and scientific agencies of Austria have produced a systematic assessment of the prospective consequences of the present revolution in laborsaving technology in a modern industrial economy and society. . . .

History, even recent history, shows that societies have responded to such challenge with revision of their economic institutions and values conducive to the efficient use of changing technology and to securing its advantages for popular well-being. History shows also societies that have failed to respond and have succumbed to economic stagnation and increasing social disorder.

28

WORKING HARD,
GETTING NOWHERE

MORRIS S. THOMPSON AND CASS PETERSON

Almost everybody knows somebody, by sight or name, like Charlie Luker. Luker, 37, a car washer in Lawrenceburg, Tenn., works long and hard. He relaxes in front of the television with a beer most evenings, goes to bed early, gets up early and does it all over again. He is part of the backbone of the U.S. economy and society, one of the many Americans who make enough to survive but not much more.

They are little noticed by politicians and policy-makers because they do not vote in large numbers or qualify for most forms of government aid. And more affluent Americans rarely consider the life, needs or thoughts of a Charlie Luker, who shined their new cars before they drove them off the lot.

The Washington Post went looking for the one-fifth of Americans, more pervasive than visible, who live above the official poverty line but below the middle-income bracket. These are the Americans who buy used cars or no cars, take few vacations, shop for clothes at discount stores, often go without health insurance and hope for the best.

According to data in the Census Bureau's 1986 Current Population Survey (CPS) of nearly 65,000 households nationwide, this group lives in households where the annual income is $9,941 to $18,700. In two-thirds of those households, it takes two wage-earners to reach that range. The members of this group are demographically so diverse that income is one of the main statistical characteristics they share.

The other is education. Except for the senior citizens, they have less of it than the average for their age group. Throughout their lives, people with less education tend to be paid less and to be unemployed more.

But in interviews, another unquantifiable similarity emerges: Those of the same age, with about the same responsibilities, expressed remarkably similar views about the future despite vast differences in their backgrounds.

The demographic analysis suggests that the members of this nearly-poor quintile are white and black and Hispanic; married, single and divorced; working, retired or between jobs; old, young and in between.

Some, young and on their way up, may belong to the group temporarily. Others, ill or laid-off or on strike, are here suddenly and accidentally. Still others have wittingly chosen professions that will make them happy but not financially comfortable. And some, whose needs outstrip their skills, may be stuck here permanently.

Because living costs vary with family responsibilities, all of these people have to budget carefully, but some more carefully than others.

For example, the largest category of householders in the group (29 percent) is made up of persons over age 65, whose children are likely to be grown and gone.

And because the incomes of most people drop when they retire, senior citizens in this group tend to have done better during their working lives than the wage-earners now in the group. Many have accumulated such valuable assets as a paid-for house.

In fact, only 3 percent of householders older than 65 in the group list Social Security as their sole source of income. But when the workers in the group stop working, their incomes are likely to place them among the poorest of the poor.

The second-largest number of householders in the group (24 percent) are those between 25 and 34. If they are parents, they have learned that the price of children's shoes is out of proportion to their size, but those children's appetites have not yet become the black holes of adolescence.

Of the 15 percent of householders in the group between 35 and 44, many are facing the near certainty that they will never be rich and the probability that they will not be able to pay for their children's education after high school. Many others are divorced; surveys consistently find that money problems are among the leading causes of failed marriages.

The 10 percent between ages 45 and 54 are in the peak earning years for most Americans, but they find it increasingly difficult to get or keep a job, especially one that would allow them to plan for retirement.

The 14 percent between the ages of 55 and 64 have reached the stage at which persons with below-average educations who have unskilled and semi-skilled jobs begin to drop out of the work force. Sometimes the years of unaffordable, and therefore neglected, health care play a role. For white-collar workers in the group, it is the age for hanging in there for their pensions.

Since more than 80 percent of the U.S. population is white, it is not surprising that most households in this group also are headed by white men like Luker, Census data show. But this group has a greater proportion of households headed by someone who is black, Hispanic, female, over 65 or unmarried than any other quintile of the population, except the poorest.

While whites in the group are worse off financially than most other U.S. whites, the median income for all black and Hispanic households in the United States falls in this $9,941 to $18,700 range. So a group often known as "working poor" is, in this land of plenty, the middle class for blacks and Hispanics.

Ray Salinas, Democrat and Roman Catholic and Chicano, a barber in teeming Houston, might seem to have little in common with Tom Price, Republican and Southern Baptist and white, a box-factory worker in tiny Lawrenceburg, Tenn.

But both are men who work hard without getting ahead, and as they speak, the differences between their backgrounds dissolve. What stands out is the similarity in their experiences of the world and the dreams they dream for their children.

Both meet life with limited means as part of America's working poor, the 17.6 million households between poverty and the middle class with incomes of $9,941 to $18,700 a year. As such, Salinas and Price seem to share an unarticulated class consciousness forged by the choices that scarcity has imposed. They struggle to feed their families, hope no one gets sick, try to figure out where the money will come from to educate the children, try not to think about what will happen when they can't work anymore.

On the threshold of middle age, they seem to accept their struggle for economic survival as a routine necessity and the world as an uncaring place in which people like them have little influence. For the sake of the children, they worry about war and hope their babies don't find the world so hard a place as they have.

In 1986, Tom Price, 37, earned about $12,000 as day manager at a local restaurant. In 1987, he earned a bit more working third shift on the gluer at a nearby box factory. Maria, his wife of almost 18 years, did not work in 1986, but was expecting to earn $6,000 or $7,000 in 1987 at a local garment factory.

Ray and Hilda Salinas each earned about $5,500 in 1986. He works six days a week on 70 percent commission as a barber, which for years was merely his moonlighting job. Hilda is paid minimum wage for a four-day week at a shirt factory. They were expecting to make an equal amount in 1986.

Theirs are families that make too much money to qualify for more than token help from the government, but too little to avoid constant financial problems.

"If I'm lucky to keep $20 in a week, I'm lucky," says Salinas, a stocky man with an easy smile. "But most, it's going to food or the car, utilities, the house note. We try, we try, but it's still a little rough."

Their personal finances have gotten worse, not better, over the past decade, an experience shared by many Americans whose raises usually come through increases in the minimum wage, which has been $3.35 an hour for nearly eight years. "Even though my wife and I are working, we're making what we were back in '77 when it was just me working," Salinas says.

Price concurs. "Right after I got out of school, around '74, I was making $10,000, $11,000 a year," he says. "Compared to what things cost, that's more than I'm making now."

In the tales Salinas and Price tell, one sees good men whose lives are constantly buffeted by forces beyond their control. As they look at the events of their time, from Vietnam to the Iran-contra scandal, their experience leads them to focus on consequences, not intentions.

Salinas looks around him and wonders how he, a high school graduate and Air Force veteran trained as a mechanical draftsman and barber, has come to live on the economic brink. "Years ago, I never thought that we were going to hit a situation like what we're in now," he says. "I thought I was always going to have a job and that I'd always be able to provide for my family."

The Salinases live in a two-bedroom house with aluminum siding in a Houston neighborhood with trees but no sidewalks. Reynol Jr., 12, and Rosa Maria, 9, occupy the other bedroom now. Fernando, 21, joined the Air Force after he finished high school in June 1986.

Like many of the working poor, Salinas has a history of jobs rather than a career. He trained as a barber after finishing high school, earning a diploma that few Hispanic men his age have received. He joined the Air Force, in 1966. At the end of his four-year hitch, Salinas took a course in mechanical drawing but couldn't find a job as a draftsman, so he worked nights at a brokerage house, processing the day's stock sales and purchases for $5 an hour.

Salinas helped support his parents and send his brother to college and law school. "Of all the family, he's the only one who got an opportunity to get a good education," Salinas says of his brother, who went on to become a U.S. Justice Department lawyer and served briefly as a judge.

Shortly after Ray Salinas' discharge, he met Hilda, an articulate, Catholic-educated Mexican woman with a young son. They were married in 1972.

Salinas supported his new family by working at anything he could get until finally landing a drafting job. He drew custom ventilators for fast-food grills for the next six years until, just before Christmas 1978, he was laid off.

At one point, jobless and facing foreclosure on the mortgage, he swallowed his pride and applied for food stamps. The application was denied because the house he was about to lose made him too wealthy. "I needed the food for my family," he says. "I ask myself, how many people are there now who get rejected who need it?" The next day, he recalls gratefully, he found a job as a janitor.

Eventually, Salinas was laid off again. He has been a full-time barber ever since. He now wistfully recalls his days as a draftsman. "I really enjoyed that kind of work," he says. "But it seems like when you get a certain age, people want a younger person."

Salinas sees signs all around him that times are hard. "I never thought in my life that I'd see Anglo kids come in the barbershop barefooted with dirty clothes," he says. "We go out and help other countries and provide for them, and it's good. But I think our government should look to the American people first."

The Prices and their children, Thomas Jr., 16, Maria, 14, Theresa, 10, and Charles 8, live on a quiet circle in quiet Lawrenceburg, population about 15,000, 50 miles northwest of Huntsville, Ala., in the rolling farmland of central Tennessee.

Price, a licensed Baptist preacher who believes that creation occurred in six days, taught mathematics and science in Christian academies after college and wishes he still could. The low pay, scant job security, skimpy fringe benefits and his family's growing needs forced him to seek a better-paying job.

"If I could find a situation where I could teach and make enough to live on, I'd do it," he says.

But Price, like Salinas, has been diverted from his druthers by his needs. "My oldest son will be graduating from high school this year," he observes. "He wants to go into engineering, with computers and robots and things like that. Maybe he'll go to Columbia State," which is nearby.

The summer after Price finished high school in 1968 in Lawrenceburg, his home town, he met his future wife, Maria, then 15 years old, at church. They were married that November and lived with Price's parents.

Tom dropped out of college before the second semester and worked for his father, a construction jobber, "digging footings, putting in septic tanks, putting in water lines."

But grief changed the direction of the Prices' lives. "We had one child who died in '75, lived a day," he says. "It sort of made us decide to devote some more to church work, because that's where we found comfort."

So the Prices moved to Chattanooga, about 130 miles to the east, where he majored in Bible at Tennessee Temple College and went on to spend a semester at Temple's seminary. He dropped out when he ran out of money, taking a job teaching junior- and senior-high school math at a Christian academy in Fort Pierce, Fla., 90 miles north of Palm Beach. It paid $8,000 a year.

There, Maria earned her high-school equivalency diploma and decided that one day she would go to college. Over the years, she has done three semesters' course work in hopes of becoming a psychologist.

Tom Price held a succession of teaching jobs. In Tallahassee, Fla., he managed to make $10,000 in 1984 by operating a backhoe on Saturdays when he was teaching seventh-grade math during the week at North Florida Christian School. He left his last teaching job in west Tennessee because he thought the principal used corporal punishment too much, including on Price's son, Tom Jr.

Price took a management-training job with Shoney's Big Boy, a regional restaurant chain. He spent four months in nearby Columbia, then was day manager in Lawrenceburg for two years.

"I got as much as $390 a week, counting the bonus, but I was working 55 to 60 hours a week," he says. "So it was fairly good money, but by the hour it wasn't a lot."

Earlier this year, the Coors Packaging plant in Lawrenceburg was hiring, and friends put in a good word for him. "I'm getting paid $7.75 an hour," he says. "I started at $5 an hour. I'll top out at $9 an hour as I get more skilled on the machines and can do more things." Free health insurance there for his family, he says, is "worth a whole lot to me."

What preoccupies these men, like many others, is not politics but their families' futures. Each speaks of his children with unequivocal pride. "That cuckoo clock?" Salinas says. "My boy Fernando sent it to us from Germany. Sometimes the cuckoo goes, 'Oh, Fernando! Oh, Fernando!'"

Says Price, "Tom Jr. is getting mostly As and Bs. You know that book 'Who's Who in American High Schools'? He's in it."

Salinas gave some advice to his elder son, Fernando. "I said to my boy, 'Take care of yourself and try to save money. Put your money into savings so the day you get married, you don't have to go through what we're struggling with.'"

In normal times, Daryl Kratochvil makes $8.20 an hour working in a Nebraska meatpacking plant, good wages by rural Midwestern standards. Janet Erks does even better—$9.25 an hour at a similar plant in South Dakota.

But Kratochvil spent most of this year doing odd jobs for whatever pay he could get—a few dollars, a bushel of sweet corn. Erks didn't draw a paycheck from the meatpacking plant from May until November. Part of that time she worked part time at a Sioux Falls, S.D., grocery store for $3.75 an hour.

Kratochvil and Erks were on strike in 1987, walking the picket line, surviving on slender checks from their union and trying not to sink deeper into the ranks of the working poor.

When the paychecks are coming in, their wages at the meatpacking plants put their families on the cusp of the second economic quintile, hovering at the $18,700-a-year cutoff that marks the entry point to the middle class. But the issue in the industry is wage concessions, not increases, and for Kratochvil and Erks the battle has an edge of desperation.

Daryl Kratochvil is 50 years old; Janet Erks, 49. Both are in what statisticians consider the peak earning years, the time when most workers are enjoying the best financial health of their lives. Too young to retire, too old to start over, Kratochvil and Erks are tied to their jobs and fighting uphill. "You never figure on going backwards," says Erks, who took a $2.44-an-hour pay cut four years ago and is trying to avoid another.

At a time when many in their age group are buying a few luxuries, planning for retirement and enjoying the economic freedom that comes of financially independent children, Kratochvil and Erks are still worrying about buying food, paying utilities and keeping the car running another year.

And there is another, constant worry: their health. As a group, they are more vulnerable to the income loss that results from an extended or debilitating illness and often lack adequate insurance against the expense of medical care.

The concern is heightened for Kratochvil and Erks, because of their age and because they work in an industry that has one of the nation's highest worker-injury rates. In a given year, three of 10 meatpacking employees can expect to be injured on the job. "That worries me all the time," says Kratochvil, who has come home twice with stitches where a steer kicked a gate into his head.

Janet Erks, a diabetic, could not afford the $216 a month it would have cost to maintain her health insurance while she was on strike. She had to cancel doctor's appointments, because she couldn't afford to go. Back then, she says, she just had to hope "the good Lord" would "take care of me."

Trust in providence is one of two recurring themes in conversations with Kratochvil and Erks. Neither wears religion on a sleeve, but it is there—an undercurrent of faith stressing perseverance more than hope, the gospel of hanging on.

The other theme is betrayal. The immediate villain is The Company, but the frustration goes deeper. Both grew up in homes with strong work ethics, guided by parents who taught them loyalty to the job and assured them that hard work would pay off. It hasn't. "The hardest part is that my father gave them 38 years of his life, and my brother gave 23," Erks says. "I gave them 30 years of my life. You work damned hard. And they have no respect for us at all."

For Kratochvil and Erks, the new watchwords of "competitiveness" and "technology" translate into lower wages, less job security and increasing despair. He is resigned; she feels duped. "When the company cut our pay last time, people believed them," she says. "We thought they needed concessions. Now they're making $28 million a year and they're paying the top man $375,000. And the politicians are saying 'Come to South Dakota, we'll give you the cheapest labor in the country.'"

Hilda Kratochvil, Daryl's wife, sits at the dinette in her small, immaculate kitchen and laughs at the question. "How would I describe us?" she says, with a merry twinkle in her eye. "We're dull."

"Dull," to Daryl and Hilda Kratochvil, means a life without credit cards, spontaneous spending or debt. Supper out is a rare treat. Vacations are planned—and paid for—months in advance. Their modest frame house in Hawarden, Iowa, a community of 2,800 about 40 miles north of Sioux City, is mortgage-free. The cars are old but wholly owned.

The television set is new, replacing the old one that lost its picture tube after 13 years. But there isn't much time to watch it. Kratochvil rises at 3 a.m. for the hour-long drive that will get him to work at the IBP meatpacking plant in Dakota City, Neb., by 5:15. Hilda spends her day babysitting for six small children. ("I've had as many as 10 at one time," she says.) From 4 p.m. to 6 p.m., both work as janitors at a local church, a job that often occupies much of their weekend as well. By 8:30 or 9 on any given night, it's lights out at the Kratochvils.

It is a regimented life, but it keeps the Kratochvils financially afloat. Rigorous frugality allows them to save for the occasional major purchase—a new television, a lower-mileage used car. More important, it allows them to put something aside for the event that keeps the Kratochvils in the stratum of the working poor: the strike.

Working 40 hours a week, Kratochvil earns just over $17,000 annually. Hilda's child-care earnings add about $2,000, and the recently acquired janitorial work contributes $4,000. It would be enough to put the Kratochvils narrowly into the middle class, except that Kratochvil is out of work for extended periods at least once every four years, when the United Food and Commercial Workers contract at IBP expires. There is always a strike.

The most recent strike started two weeks before Christmas in 1986. Kratochvil returned to work in August.

Kratochvil has worked in the stockyards at IBP for 17 years, herding cattle into the chute that leads to the killing area. The couple can accept the periodic strikes. They can be planned for. They end, sooner or later. What makes the Kratochvils apprehensive is the thought of the unexpected: an extended illness, for example, or a disabling injury.

So profound are their concerns about the cost of medical care that the Kratochvils strained their budget to take out a $160-a-month health-insurance policy while he was on strike. When the strike ended, they decided to keep the policy to supplement the coverage offered by IBP.

Retirement isn't even a topic of discussion. The union's most recent contract includes a pension plan for the first time, but Kratochvil isn't confident that it provides much for him. The plan won't become effective until 1990, by which time Kratochvil will be 53, and the size of his pension will then depend on how much profit the company makes. "I won't be able to retire at 65 because I won't be able to afford it," he says. "At the plant, they work you until they carry you out."

Janet Erks went to work at the John Morrell meatpacking plant in Sioux Falls, S.D., a week before she graduated from high school. "My father wanted me to go on to school. I wanted to go into nursing or interior decorating," she says. "But you get down there and start making what is good money for this town. . . ." Her voice trails off.

For a time, it seemed like the right decision. By the late 1970s, Erks and her husband, Don, were bringing home nearly $50,000 a year, Don working as a truck driver and Janet working in the shipping department at Morrells.

With seven children to raise—two hers from a previous marriage, four his and one theirs together—it was an adequate living but not an affluent one. They bought an old house in Lennox, S.D., and fixed it up themselves.

But in 1980, Don had to stop working because of a pulmonary ailment and arthritis. With four children still at home, Janet became the sole breadwinner. Three years later, the union's contract with Morrell expired and the company announced that it would close the plant unless workers accepted lower wages. The union conceded, and the Erkses joined the ranks of the working poor.

When meatpackers went on strike at nearby Sioux City, Iowa, Janet Erks' local walked out in a sympathy strike, fearing that their plant would be the next target for more pay cuts. For six months, the family lived on Don's disability check, her $40-a-week strike benefit from the union, and the income from a part-time job that she spent four months searching for. "Nobody would hire a Morrell striker," she says. But she says she would return to Morrell when the picket lines came down. Her pension is at stake—$15 a month for every year of service—and she is at least a year shy of qualifying for it.

Only 13-year-old Angela lives at home now. One son was killed during flight training in the Air Force. Two sons are working in Sioux Falls. Three daughters have moved away—to western South Dakota, to Michigan, to Montana.

Erks understands why her children have left. Entry-level wages for most jobs in Sioux Falls start at the minimum wage and rarely get higher than $6 an hour. To stay in Sioux Falls is to accept membership in the ranks of the working poor. "Things are so high, and wages are so low," she says. "How can you make it?"

29

LIFE ON THE GLOBAL ASSEMBLY LINE

BARBARA EHRENREICH AND ANNETTE FUENTES

In Ciudad Juárez, Mexico, Anna M. rises at 5 A.M. to feed her son before start-
ing on the two-hour bus trip to the maquiladora (factory). He will spend the
day along with four other children in a neighbor's one-room home. Anna's
husband, frustrated by being unable to find work for himself, left for the Unit-
ed States six months ago. She wonders, as she carefully applies her new lip gloss,
whether she ought to consider herself still married. It might be good to take a
night course, become a secretary. But she seldom gets home before eight at
night, and the factory, where she stitches brassieres that will be sold in the
United States through J.C. Penney, pays only $48 a week.

In Penang, Malaysia, Julie K. is up before the three other young women
with whom she shares a room, and starts heating the leftover rice from last
night's supper. She looks good in the company's green-trimmed uniform, and
she's proud to work in a modern, American-owned factory. Only not quite so
proud as when she started working three years ago—she thinks as she squints
out the door at a passing group of women. Her job involves peering all day
through a microscope, bonding hair-thin gold wires to a silicon chip destined to
end up inside a pocket calculator, and at 21, she is afraid she can no longer see
very clearly.

Barbara Ehrenreich and Annette Fuentes, "Life on the Global Assembly Line," from *Ms* Magazine, January, 1981. Reprinted by permission of the authors.

Every morning, between four and seven, thousands of women like Anna and Julie head out for the day shift. In Ciudad Juárez, they crowd into *ruteras* (run-down vans) for the trip from the slum neighborhoods to the industrial parks on the outskirts of the city. In Penang they squeeze, 60 or more at a time, into buses for the trip from the village to the low, modern factory buildings of the Bayan Lepas free trade zone. In Taiwan, they walk from the dormitories—where the night shift is already asleep in the still-warm beds—through the checkpoints in the high fence surrounding the factory zone.

This is the world's new industrial proletariat: young, female, Third World. Viewed from the "first world," they are still faceless, genderless "cheap labor," signaling their existence only through a label or tiny imprint—"made in Hong Kong," or Taiwan, Korea, the Dominican Republic, Mexico, the Philippines. But they may be one of the most strategic blocs of womanpower in the world of the 1980s. Conservatively, there are 2 million Third World female industrial workers employed now, millions more looking for work, and their numbers are rising every year. Anyone whose image of Third World women features picturesque peasants with babies slung on their backs should be prepared to update it. Just in the last decade, Third World women have become a critical element in the global economy and a key "resource" for expanding multinational corporations.

It doesn't take more than second-grade arithmetic to understand what's happening. In the United States, an assembly-line worker is likely to earn, depending on her length of employment, between $3.10 and $5 an hour. In many Third World countries, a woman doing the same work will earn $3 to $5 a *day*. According to the magazine *Business Asia,* in 1976 the average hourly wage for unskilled work (male or female) was 55 cents in Hong Kong, 52 cents in South Korea, 32 cents in the Philippines, and 17 cents in Indonesia. The logic of the situation is compelling: why pay someone in Massachusetts $5 an hour to do what someone in Manila will do for $2.50 a day? Or, as a corollary, why pay a male worker anywhere to do what a female worker will do for 40 to 60 percent less?

And so, almost everything that can be packed up is being moved out to the Third World; not heavy industry, but just about anything light enough to travel—garment manufacture, textiles, toys, footwear, pharmaceuticals, wigs, appliance parts, tape decks, computer components, plastic goods. In some industries, like garment and textile, American jobs are lost in the process, and the biggest losers are women, often black and Hispanic. But what's going on is much more than a matter of runaway shops. Economists are talking about a "new international division of labor," in which the process of production is broken down and the fragments are dispersed to different parts of the world. In general, the low-skilled jobs are farmed out to the Third World, where labor costs are minuscule, while control over the overall process and technology remains safely at company headquarters in "first world" countries like the United States and Japan.

The American electronics industry provides a classic example: circuits are printed on silicon wafers and tested in California; then the wafers are shipped to Asia for the labor-intensive process by which they are cut into tiny chips and bonded to circuit boards; final assembly into products such as calculators or military equipment usually takes place in the United States. Garment manufacture too is often broken into geographically separated steps, with the most repetitive, labor-intensive jobs going to the poor countries of the southern hemisphere. Most Third World countries welcome whatever jobs come their way in the new division of labor, and the major international development agencies—like the World Bank and the United States Agency for International Development (AID)—encourage them to take what they can get.

So much any economist could tell you. What is less often noted is the *gender* breakdown of the emerging international division of labor. Eighty to 90 percent of the low-skilled assembly jobs that go to the Third World are performed by women—in a remarkable switch from earlier patterns of foreign-dominated industrialization. Until now, "development" under the aegis of foreign corporations has usually meant more jobs for men and—compared to traditional agricultural society—a diminished economic status for women. But multinational corporations and Third World governments alike consider assembly-line work—whether the product is Barbie dolls or missile parts—to be "women's work."

One reason is that women can, in many countries, still be legally paid less than men. But the sheer tedium of the jobs adds to the multinationals' preference for women workers—a preference made clear, for example, by this ad from a Mexican newspaper: *We need female workers; older than 17, younger than 30; single and without children: minimum education primary school, maximum education one year of preparatory school [high school]: available for all shifts.*

It's an article of faith with management that only women can do, or will do, the monotonous, painstaking work that American business is exporting to the Third World. Bill Mitchell, whose job is to attract United States businesses to the Bermudez Industrial Park in Ciudad Juárez told us with a certain macho pride: "A man just won't stay in this tedious kind of work. He'd walk out in a couple of hours." The personnel manager of a light assembly plant in Taiwan told anthropologist Linda Gail Arrigo: "Young male workers are too restless and impatient to do monotonous work with no career value. If displeased, they sabotage the machines and even threaten the foreman. But girls? At most, they cry a little."

In fact, the American businessmen we talked to claimed that Third World women genuinely enjoy doing the very things that would drive a man to assault and sabotage. "You should watch these kids going into work," Bill Mitchell told us. "You don't have any sullenness here. They smile." A top-level management consultant who specializes in advising American companies on where to relocate their factories gave us this global generalization: "The [factory] girls genuinely enjoy themselves. They're away from their families. They have spending money. They can buy motorbikes, whatever. Of course it's a regulated experience too—with dormitories to live in—so it's healthful experience."

What is the real experience of the women in the emerging Third World industrial work force? The conventional Western stereotypes leap to mind: You can't really compare, the standards are so different. . . . Everything's easier in warm countries. . . . They really don't have any alternatives. . . . Commenting on the low wages his company pays its women workers in Singapore, a Hewlett-Packard vice-president said, "They live much differently here than we do. . . ." But the differences are ultimately very simple. To start with, they have less money.

The great majority of the women in the new Third World work force live at or near the subsistence level for one person, whether they work for a multinational corporation or a locally owned factory. In the Philippines, for example, starting wages in U.S.-owned electronics plants are between $34 to $46 a month, compared to a cost of living of $37 a month; in Indonesia the starting wages are actually about $7 a month less than the cost of living. "Living," in these cases, should be interpreted minimally: a diet of rice, dried fish, and water—a Coke might cost a half-day's wages—lodging in a room occupied by four or more other people. Rachael Grossman, a researcher with the Southeast Asia Resource Center, found women employees of U.S. multinational firms in Malaysia and the Philippines living four to eight in a room in boardinghouses, or squeezing into tiny extensions built onto squatter huts near the factory. Where companies do provide dormitories for their employees, they are not of the "healthful," collegiate variety implied by our corporate informant. Staff from the American Friends Service Committee report that dormitory space is "likely to be crowded, with bed rotation paralleling shift rotation—while one shift works, another sleeps, as many as twenty to a room." In one case in Thailand, they found the dormitory "filthy," with workers forced to find their own place to sleep among "splintered floor-boards, rusting sheets of metal, and scraps of dirty cloth."

Wages do increase with seniority, but the money does not go to pay for studio apartments or, very likely, motorbikes. A 1970 study of young women factory workers in Hong Kong found that 88 percent of them were turning more than half their earnings over to their parents. In areas that are still largely agricultural (such as parts of the Philippines and Malaysia), or places where male unemployment runs high (such as northern Mexico), a woman factory worker may be the sole source of cash income for an entire extended family.

But wages on a par with what an 11-year-old American could earn on a paper route, and living conditions resembling what Engels found in 19th-century Manchester are only part of the story. The rest begins at the factory gate. The work that multinational corporations export to the Third World is not only the most tedious, but often the most hazardous part of the production process. The countries they go to are, for the most part, those that will guarantee no interference from health and safety inspectors, trade unions, or even free-lance reformers. As a result, most Third World factory women work under conditions that already have broken or will break their health—or their nerves—within a few years, and often before they've worked long enough to earn any more than a subsistence wage.

"Mass hysteria" as job action?

Hysteria was supposed to have gone out with the 19th century, but it's making a comeback in today's ultramodern, high-tech electronics industry. For Malaysian women employed in the painstaking work of assembling microcircuits, mass hysteria has become a form of resistance. It starts when one young woman sees a hantu or jin, which are particularly hideous varieties of ghosts. She falls to the floor in convulsions, screaming, and within minutes the hysteria spreads up and down the assembly line. Sometimes the plant has to be closed for a week or more to exorcise the spirits.

Western managers have tried Valium, smelling salts, and traditional healers to combat hysteria before it paralyzes production. But Malaysian academics who have studied the phenomenon point out that attacks are likely to be preceded by a speedup or a tightening of plant discipline. Since the Malaysian government does not permit labor unions, more conventional forms of protest are hard to organize. Besides, eight or ten hours a day spent peering through a microscope at tiny wires—for about $2 a day pay—is enough to make anyone hysterical.

Consider first the electronics industry, which is generally thought to be the safest and cleanest of the exported industries. The factory buildings are low and modern, like those one might find in a suburban American industrial park. Inside, rows of young women, neatly dressed in the company uniform or T-shirt, work quietly at their stations. There is air conditioning (not for the women's comfort, but to protect the delicate semiconductor parts they work with), and high-volume piped-in Bee Gees hits (not so much for entertainment, as to prevent talking).

For many Third World women, electronics is a prestige occupation, at least compared to other kinds of factory work. They are unlikely to know that in the United States the National Institute on Occupational Safety and Health (NIOSH) has placed electronics on its select list of "high health-risk industries using the greatest number of toxic substances." If electronics assembly work is risky here, it is doubly so in countries where there is no equivalent of NIOSH to even issue warnings. In many plants toxic chemicals and solvents sit in open containers, filling the work area with fumes that can literally knock you out. "We have been told of cases where ten to twelve women passed out at once," and AFSC field worker in northern Mexico told us, "and the newspapers report this as 'mass hysteria.'"

In one stage of the electronics assembly process, the workers have to dip the circuits into open vats of acid. According to Irene Johnson and Carol Bragg, who toured the National Semiconductor plant in Penang, Malaysia, the women who do the dipping "wear rubber gloves and boots, but these sometimes leak, and burns are common." Occasionally, whole fingers are lost. More commonly, what electronics workers lose is the 20/20 vision they are required to have when they are hired. Most electronics workers spend seven to nine hours a day peering through microscopes, straining to meet their quotas.

One study in South Korea found that most electronics assembly workers developed severe eye problems after only one year of employment: 88 percent had chronic conjunctivitis; 44 percent became near-sighted; and 19 percent developed astigmatism. A manager for Hewlett-Packard's Malaysia plant, in an interview with Rachael Grossman, denied that there were any eye problems: "These girls are used to working with 'scopes.' We've found no eye problems. But it sure makes me dizzy to look through those things."

Electronics, recall, is the "cleanest" of the exported industries. Conditions in the garment and textile industry rival those of any 19th-century (or 20th— see below) sweatshop. The firms, generally local subcontractors to large American chains such as J.C. Penney and Sears, as well as smaller manufacturers, are usually even more indifferent to the health of their employees than the multinationals. Some of the worst conditions have been documented in South Korea, where the garment and textile industries have helped spark that country's "economic miracle." Workers are packed into poorly lit rooms, where summer temperatures rise above 100 degrees. Textile dust, which can cause permanent lung damage, fills the air. When there are rush orders, management may require forced overtime of as much as 48 hours at a stretch, and if that seems to go beyond the limits of human endurance, pep pills and amphetamine injections are thoughtfully provided. In her diary (originally published in a magazine now banned by the South Korean government) Min Chong Suk, 30, a sewing-machine operator, wrote of working from 7 A.M. to 11:30 P.M. in a garment factory: "When [the apprentices] shake the waste threads from the clothes, the whole room fills with dust, and it is hard to breathe. Since we've been working in such dusty air, there have been increasing numbers of people getting tuberculosis, bronchitis, and eye diseases. Since we are women, it makes us so sad when we have pale, unhealthy, wrinkled faces like dried-up spinach. . . . It seems to me that no one knows our blood dissolves into the threads and seams, with sighs and sorrow."

In all the exported industries, the most invidious, inescapable health hazard is stress. On their home ground United States corporations are not likely to sacrifice productivity for human comfort. On someone else's home ground, however, anything goes. Lunch breaks may be barely long enough for a woman to stand in line at the canteen or hawkers' stalls. Visits to the bathroom are treated as privilege; in some cases, workers must raise their hands for permission to use the toilet, and waits up to a half hour are common. Rotating shifts—the day shift one week, the night shift the next—wreak havoc with sleep patterns. Because inaccuracies or failure to meet production quotas can mean substantial pay losses, the pressures are quickly internalized; stomach ailments and nervous problems are not unusual in the multinationals' Third World female work force. In some situations, good work is as likely to be punished as slow or shoddy work. Correspondent Michael Flannery, writing for the AFLCIO's *American Federationist*, tells the story of 23-year-old Basilia Altagracia, a seamstress who stitched collars onto ladies' blouses in the La Romana (Dominican Republic) free trade zone (a heavily guarded industrial zone owned by Gulf & Western Industries, Inc.):

> *A nimble veteran seamstress, Miss Altagracia eventually began to earn as much as $5.75 a day. . . . "I was exceeding my piecework quota by a lot." . . . But then, Altagracia said, her plant supervisor, a Cuban emigré, called her into his*

office. "He said I was doing a fine job, but that I and some other of the women
were making too much money, and he was being forced to lower what we
earned for each piece we sewed." On the best days, she now can clear barely
$3, she said. "I was earning less, so I started working six and seven days a
week. But I was tired and I could not work as fast as before."

Within a few months, she was too ill to work at all.

As if poor health and the stress of factory life weren't enough to drive
women into early retirement, management actually encourages a high turnover
in many industries. "As you know, when seniority rises, wages rise," the management consultant to U.S. multinationals told us. He explained that it's
cheaper to train a fresh supply of teenagers than to pay experienced women
higher wages. "Older" women, aged 23 or 24, are likely to be laid off and not
rehired.

We estimate, based on fragmentary data from several sources, that the
multinational corporations may already have used up (cast off) as many as 6
million Third World workers—women who are too ill, too old (30 is over the
hill in most industries), or too exhausted to be useful any more. Few "retire"
with any transferable skills or savings. The lucky ones find husbands.

Sweatshops—Made in USA

Not every manufacturer has the resources to run away to the cheap labor reser-
voirs of the Southern Hemisphere. An alternative is to try to duplicate in the
United States the conditions that give the Third World its business appeal—
substandard wages, controlled unions (if any), and the kind of no-frills work
conditions that you might expect to find in Seoul or Taiwan. In the fiercely
competitive light-manufacturing industries (toys, garments, artificial flowers),
companies are turning to the sweatshop.

In Los Angeles, Chicago, Boston, New York, cities in New Jersey—any-
place where garment production has roots, sweatshops are springing up by the
hundreds. Exact numbers are hard to come by since the shops are, by and large,
unlicensed and illegal. Anyone with a few thousand dollars can start up a gar-
ment shop. All you need is a dozen sewing machines, a low-rent building, and
people, usually immigrants, desperate for work. Manufacturers ("jobbers") ship
out bundles of precut clothes to the shop owners ("contractors") who hire
workers to stitch the pieces together. A contractor in New York's South Bronx
blames the jobbers for exploitation: "Do they pay enough? You got to be kid-
ding. I pay the girls $1.25 a dress. All I get is $2.60, and I've got to run the
shop, rent machines, pay for electricity."

Women are 90 percent of the sweatshop work force in this country. Here
or in the Third World, women are industry's best bargain. A union organizer
in Los Angeles says: "One woman I talked to this year put in a sixty-hour
week and made fifty dollars." A year ago, the Department of Labor cited 85
garment shops in New York's Chinatown for violations of minimum-wage,
child-labor, and overtime regulations. In many cases, a boss would punch time
cards in and out for employees.

Sweatshop workers are heads of households, needing a steady, if meager,
income to support their families. They are mothers without access to day-care
centers who can bring their children with them to the "informal" setting of the

sweatshop. Some are women who need an extra, but unreported, income to survive on welfare. And others are older women supplementing inadequate pensions.

Jobs in these garment shops are easy to get, and require little or no experience. Walk down 149th Street in the South Bronx and see one sign after another—se necesita operadoras (operators wanted), many with the dubious promise of Buena Paga (good pay). A visit to Damak Sportswear in the Bronx revealed a typical neighborhood garment operation. Thirteen Puerto Rican women were bent over sewing machines in a poorly lit room. The shop, on the third floor of an old tenement building with wooden stairs and floors, lacked fire alarms and a sprinkler system. But that's par for the course, according to Louis Berthold at the South Bronx Working Center, an ILGWU community outreach program. "One building on 161st Street had more than forty health and fire violations, and housed four shops. It wouldn't surprise me if there was another Triangle fire," he remarked.

"Homework" is another abuse spawned by the demands of industry. Women carry bundles of precut garments from the shops to stitch them at home, using their own sewing machines, paying for their own electricity, and often enlisting the help of their children to meet deadlines.

Undocumented workers, known as illegal aliens in the media, are especially vulnerable, because of their fear of discovery and deportation. Ironically, unions, industry, and the government concur in blaming "illegals" for the existence and spread of sweatshops—as if the immigrants bring the miserable conditions into this country along with their family photographs. Kurt Barnard of the Federation of Apparel Manufacturers claims that "the illegals are the cause of sweatshops and the government helps by failing to enforce immigration laws."

A study of undocumented workers in New York done by the North American Congress on Latin America (NACLA . . .) found that labor abuse was not restricted to the undocumented, but that "these are the conditions of labor that now prevail in the sectors of industry where new immigrant workers, legal or not, come to dwell." The study confirms the connection between runaway industry in the Third World and the deterioration of labor conditions at home. Charles Wang, director of New York's Chinatown Planning Council, calls on unions to become "watchdogs and take a militant stand against these conditions."

Despite their vulnerable position, women in sweatshops are beginning to organize. In 1975, 125 Chinese women at the Jung Sai garment shop in San Francisco began the longest strike in Chinese-American history; it ended nearly a year later with an ILGWU contract. In 1977, 250 workers struck the W and W Knitting Mill in Brooklyn for six months; 75 were undocumented and risked deportation to march on the picket lines. From Taiwan to New York, female labor may still be cheap, but it can't be counted on to be docile.

—A.F.

The unlucky ones find themselves at the margins of society—as bar girls, "hostesses," or prostitutes.

At 21, Julie's greatest fear is that she will never be able to find a husband. She knows that just being a "factory girl" is enough to give anyone a bad reputa-

tion. When she first started working at the electronics company, her father refused to speak to her for three months. Now every time she leaves Penang to go back to visit her home village she has to put up with a lecture on morality from her older brother—not to mention a barrage of lewd remarks from men outside her family. If they knew that she had actually gone out on a few dates, that she had been to a discotheque, that she had once kissed a young man who said he was a student . . . Julie's stomach tightens as she imagines her family's reaction. She tries to concentrate on the kind of man she would like to marry: an engineer or technician of some sort, someone who had been to California, where the company headquarters are located and where even the grandmothers wear tight pants and lipstick—someone who had a good attitude about women. But if she ends up having to wear glasses, like her cousin who worked three years at the "scopes," she might as well forget about finding anyone to marry her.

One of the most serious occupational hazards that Julie and millions of women like her may face is the lifelong stigma of having been a "factory girl." Most of the cultures favored by multinational corporations in their search for cheap labor are patriarchal in the grand old style: any young woman who is not under the wing of a father, husband, or older brother must be "loose." High levels of unemployment among men, as in Mexico, contribute to male resentment of working women. (Ironically, in some places the multinationals have increased male unemployment—for example, by paving over fishing and farming villages to make way for industrial parks.) Add to all this the fact that certain companies—American electronics firms are in the lead—actively promote Western-style sexual objectification as a means of insuring employee loyalty: there are company-sponsored cosmetics classes, "guess whose legs these are" contests, and swim-suit-style beauty contests where the prize might be a free night *for two* in a fancy hotel. Corporate-promoted Westernization only heightens the hostility many men feel toward any independent working women—having a job is bad enough, wearing jeans and mascara to work is going too far.

Anthropologist Patricia Fernandez, who has worked in a *maquiladora* herself, believes that the stigmatization of working women serves, indirectly, to keep them in line. "You have to think of the kind of socialization that girls experience in a very Catholic—or, for that matter, Muslim—society. The fear of having a 'reputation' is enough to make a lot of women bend over backward to be 'respectable' and ladylike, which is just what management wants." She points out that in northern Mexico, the tabloids delight in playing up stories of alleged vice in the *maquiladoras*—indiscriminate sex on the job, epidemics of venereal disease, fetuses found in factory rest rooms. "I worry about this because there are those who treat you differently as soon as they know you have a job at a *maquiladora*," one woman told Fernandez. "Maybe they think that if you have to work, there is a chance you're a whore."

And there is always a chance you'll wind up as one. Probably only a small minority of Third World factory workers turn to prostitution when their working days come to an end. But it is, as for women everywhere, the employment of last resort, the only thing to do when the factories don't need you and traditional society won't—or, for economic reasons, can't—take you back. In the Philippines, the brothel business is expanding as fast as the factory system. If they can't use you one way, they can use you another.

There has been no international protest about the exploitation of Third World women by multinational corporations—no thundering denunciations from the floor of the United Nations' general assembly, no angry resolutions from the Conference of the Non-Aligned Countries. Sociologist Robert Snow, who has been tracing the multinationals on their way south and eastward for years, explained why: "The Third World governments *want* the multinationals to move in. There's cutthroat competition to attract the corporations."

The governments themselves gain little revenue from this kind of investment, though—especially since most offer tax holidays and freedom from export duties in order to attract the multinationals in the first place. Nor do the people as a whole benefit, according to a highly placed Third World woman within the UN. "The multinationals like to say they're contributing to development," she told us, "but they come into our countries for one thing—cheap labor. If the labor stops being so cheap, they can move on. So how can you call that development? It depends on the people being poor and staying poor." But there are important groups that do stand to gain when the multinationals set up shop in their countries: local entrepreneurs who subcontract to the multinationals; Harvard- or Berkeley-educated "technocrats" who become local management; and government officials who specialize in cutting red tape for an "agent's fee" or an outright bribe.

In the competition for multinational investment, local governments advertise their women shamelessly, and an investment brochure issued by the Malaysian government informs multinational executives that: "The manual dexterity of the Oriental female is famous the world over. Her hands are small, and she works fast with extreme care. . . . Who, therefore, could be better qualified by nature and inheritance, to contribute to the efficiency of a bench-assembly production line than the Oriental girl?"

The Royal Thai Embassy sends American businesses a brochure guaranteeing that in Thailand, "the relationship between the employer and employee is like that of a guardian and ward. It is easy to win and maintain the loyalty of workers as long as they are treated with kindness and courtesy." The facing page offers a highly selective photo-study of Thai womanhood: giggling shyly, bowing submissively, and working cheerfully on an assembly line.

Reckless, easily excited, ripe for labor agitators?

If you're a Korean factory worker, you wouldn't expect to get a free lunch, but you are likely to get a free book. Written by a man who is a former member of the Korean Central Intelligence Agency, the book explains why "Communists" and labor-reform religious groups "are very much more interested in getting women workers than men workers":

First, women are more susceptible than men. They are emotional and less logical. They cannot differentiate between true and false or good and bad. . . . They are easily excited and are very reckless and do things hastily. . . . Third, most women workers are sentimental young girls. Fourth, women workers are so caught by vanity that they spend much more money than men workers. . . . Sixth, management, union leaders, and city administrators find it very difficult to deal with women workers when they cause trouble. The women weep and cry and behave exaggeratedly . . . and for men this kind of behavior is very troubling.

Many "host" governments are willing to back up their advertising with whatever amount of brutality it takes to keep "their girls" just as docile as they look in the brochures. Even the most polite and orderly attempts to organize are likely to bring down overkill doses of police repression:

- In Guatemala in 1975 women workers in a North American-owned factory producing jeans and jackets drew up a list of complaints that included insults by management, piecework wages that turned out to be less than the legal minimum, no overtime pay, and "threats of death." In response, the American boss made a quick call to the local authorities to report that he was being harassed by "Communists." When the women reported for work the next day they found the factory surrounded by two fully armed contingents of military police. The "Communist" ringleaders were picked out and fired.

- In the Dominican Republic, in 1978, workers who attempted to organize at the La Romana industrial zone were first fired, then obligingly arrested by the local police. Officials from the AFL-CIO have described the zone as a "modern slave-labor camp," where workers who do not meet their production quotas during their regular shift must stay and put in unpaid overtime until they do meet them, and many women workers are routinely strip-searched at the end of the day. During the 1978 organizing attempt, the government sent in national police in full combat gear and armed with automatic weapons. Gulf & Western supplements the local law with its own company-sponsored motorcycle club, which specializes in terrorizing suspected union sympathizers.

- In Inchon, South Korea, women at the Dong-II Textile Company (which produces fabrics and yarn for export to the United States) had succeeded in gaining leadership in their union in 1972. But in 1978 the government-controlled, male-dominated Federation of Korean Trade Unions sent special "action squads" to destroy the women's union. Armed with steel bars and buckets of human excrement, the goons broke into the union office, smashed the office equipment, and smeared the excrement over the women's bodies and in their hair, ears, eyes, and mouths.

Crudely put (and incidents like this do not inspire verbal delicacy), the relationship between many Third World governments and the multinational corporations is not very different from the relationship between a pimp and his customers. The governments advertise their women, sell them, and keep them in line for the multinational "johns." But there are other parties to the growing international traffic in women—such as the United Nations' Industrial Development Organization (UNIDO), the World Bank, and the United States government itself.

UNIDO, for example, has been a major promoter of "free trade zones." These are enclaves within nations that offer multinational corporations a range of creature comforts, including: freedom from paying taxes and export duties; low-cost water, power, and buildings; exemption from whatever labor laws may apply in the country as a whole; and, in some cases, such security features as barbed-wire, guarded checkpoints, and government-paid police.

Then there is the World Bank, which over the past decade has lent several billion dollars to finance the roads, airports, power plants, and even the first-class hotels that multinational corporations need in order to set up business in Third World countries. The Sri Lankan garment industry, which like other Third World garment industries survives by subcontracting to major Western firms, was set up on the advice of the World Bank and with a $20 million World Bank loan. This particular experiment in "development" offers young women jobs at a global low of $5 for a six-day week. Gloria Scott, the head of the World Bank's Women and Development Program, sounded distinctly uncomfortable when we asked her about the bank's role in promoting the exploitation of Third World women. "Our job is to help eliminate poverty. It is not our responsibility if the multinationals come in and offer such low wages. It's the responsibility of the governments." However, the Bank's 1979 World Development Report speaks strongly of the need for "wage restraint" in poor countries.

But the most powerful promoter of exploitative conditions for Third World women workers is the United States government itself. For example, the notoriously repressive Korean textile industry was developed with the help of $400 million in aid from the U.S. State Department. Malaysia became a low-wage haven for the electronics industry, thanks to technical assistance financed by AID and to U.S. money (funneled through the Asian Development Bank) to set up free trade zones. Taiwan's status as a "showcase for the free world" and a comfortable berth for multinationals is the result of three decades of financial transfusions from the United States. On a less savory note, the U.S. funds an outfit called the Asian-American Free Labor Institute, whose ostensible purpose is to encourage "free" (i.e., non-Communist) trade unions in Asia, but whose actual mission is to discourage any truly militant union activity. AAFLI works closely with the Federation of Korean Trade Unions, which was responsible for the excrement-smearing incident described above.

But the most obvious form of United States involvement, according to Lenny Siegel, the director of the Pacific Studies Center, is through "our consistent record of military aid to Third World governments that are capitalist, politically repressive, and are not striving for economic independence." Ironically, says Siegel, there are "cases where the United States made a big investment—through groups like AAFLI or other kinds of political pressure—to make sure that any unions that formed would be pretty tame. Then we put in even more money to support some dictator who doesn't allow unions at all." And if that doesn't seem like a sufficient case of duplicate spending, the U.S. government also insures (through the Overseas Private Investment Corporation) outward-bound multinationals against any lingering possibility of insurrection or expropriation.

What does our government have to say for itself? It's hard to get a straight answer—the few parts of the bureaucracy that deal with women and development seem to have little connection with those that are concerned with larger foreign policy issues. A spokesman for the Department of State told us that if multinationals offer poor working conditions (which he questioned), this was not their fault: "There are just different standards in different countries." Offering further evidence of a sheltered life, he told us that "corporations today are generally more socially responsible than even ten years ago. . . . We can expect them to treat their employees in the best way they can." But he conceded in response to a barrage of unpleasant examples, "Of course, you're going to have problems wherever you have human beings doing things." Our next stop was the Women's Division within AID. Staffer Emmy Simmons was aware of the criticisms of the quality of employment multinationals offer, but cautioned that "we can get hung up in the idea that it's exploitation without really looking at the alternatives for women." AID's concern, she said, was with the fact that population is outgrowing the agricultural capacity of many Third World countries, dislocating millions of people. From her point of view, multinationals at least provide some sort of alternative: "These people have to go somewhere."

> *Anna, for one, has nowhere to go but the maquiladora. Her family left the farm when she was only six, and the land has long since been bought up by a large commercial agribusiness company. After her father left to find work north of the border, money was scarce in the household for years. So when the factory where she now works opened in the early 1970s, Anna felt it was "the best thing that had ever happened" to her. As a wage-earner, her status rose compared to her brothers with their on-again, off-again jobs. Partly out of her new sense of confidence, she agreed to meet with a few other women one day after work to talk about wages and health conditions. That was the way she became what management called a "labor agitator" when, six months later, 90 percent of the day shift walked out in the company's first south-of-the-border strike.*

Women like Anna—or Julie K. in Malaysia—need their jobs desperately. They know the risks of organizing. Beyond that, there's the larger risk that—if they do succeed in organizing—the company can always move on in search of a still-docile, job-hungry work force. Yet thousands of women in the Third World's industrial work force have chosen to fight for better wages and working conditions. Few of these struggles reach the North American media. We know of them from reports, often fragmentary, from church and support groups:

- Nuevo Laredo, Mexico, 1973: 2,000 workers at Transitron Electronics walked out in solidarity with a small number of workers who had been unjustly fired. Two days later, 8,000 striking workers met and elected a more militant union leadership.

- Mexicali, Mexico, 1974: 3,000 workers, locked out by Mextel (a Mattel subsidiary), set up a 24-hour guard to prevent the company from moving in search of cheaper labor. After two months of confrontations, the company moved away.

- Bangkok, Thailand, 1976: 70 young women locked their Japanese bosses out and took control of the factory. They continued to make and sell jeans and floppy hats for export, paying themselves 150 percent more than their bosses had.

- South Korea, 1977: 3,000 women at the American-owned Signetics plant went on a hunger strike for a 46.8 percent wage hike above the 39 cents an hour they were receiving. Since an actual walkout would have been illegal, they remained in the plant and held a sit-in in the cafeteria. They won a 23 percent increase.

- South Korea, 1978: 1,000 workers at the Mattel toy company in Seoul, which makes Barbie dolls and Marie Osmond dolls, staged a work slowdown to protest their 25 cents-an-hour wages and 12-hour shifts.

- South Korea, 1979: 200 young women employees of the YH textile-and-wig factory staged a peaceful vigil and fast to protest the company's threatened closing of the plant. On August 11, the fifth day of the vigil, more than 1,000 riot police, armed with clubs and steel shields, broke into the building where the women were staying and forcibly dragged the women out. Twenty-one-year-old Kim Kyong-suk was killed during the melee. It was her death that touched off widespread rioting throughout Korea that many thought led to the overthrow of President Park Chung Hee.

- Ciudad Juárez, Mexico: September, 1980: 1,000 women workers occupied an American Hospital Supply Corporation factory. They demanded better working conditions, paid vacations, and recognition of the union of their choice. The women, who are mostly in their teens and early twenties, began the occupation when 180 thugs, which the company claims were paid by a rival union, entered the factory and beat up the women's leaders. The occupation is over, but the struggle goes on.

Regarding the 1979 vigil in South Korea, Robert Snow points out: "Very few people realize that an action which began with 200 very young women factory workers led to the downfall of a government. In the 1980s Third

World factory women like this are going to be a political force to reckon with." So far, feminism, first-world style, has barely begun to acknowledge the Third World's new industrial womanpower. Jeb Mays and Kathleen Connell, co-founders of the San Francisco-based Women's Network on Global Corporations ... are two women who would like to change that. "There's still this idea of the Third World woman as 'the other'—someone exotic and totally unlike us," Mays and Connell told us. "But now we're talking about women who wear the same styles in clothes, listen to the same music, and may even work for the same corporation. That's an irony the multinationals have created. In a way, they're drawing us together as women."

Saralee Hamilton, an AFSC staff organizer of a 1978 conference on "Women and Global Corporations" (held in Des Moines, Iowa) says: "The multinational corporations have deliberately targeted women for exploitation. If feminism is going to mean anything to women all over the world, it's going to have to find new ways to resist corporate power internationally." She envisions a global network of grass-roots women capable of sharing experiences, transmitting information, and—eventually—providing direct support for each other's struggles. It's a long way off; few women anywhere have the money for intercontinental plane flights or even long-distance calls, but at least we are beginning to see the way. "We all have the same hard life," wrote Korean garment worker Min Chong Suk. "We are bound together with one string."

PART NINE

HEALTH AND WELFARE

The social stratification of health and illness is one of the most devastating inequalities in American society. Despite our enormous wealth and technological potential, the United States still lags behind most other advanced industrial societies on many measures of health and access to health care. Americans have lower life expectancies and higher rates of infant death than citizens of many other developed countries; and some groups—including the urban and rural poor—still suffer shockingly high levels of preventable diseases and inadequate health care services. In 1967 a National Advisory Commission on Health Manpower noted that the health statistics of these groups "occasionally resemble the health statistics of a developing country."[1] Unfortunately, the same statement could still be made. Almost 20 years later, another commission found growing numbers of Americans suffering from hunger, in the midst of what we were pleased to call an economic "recovery" (see Chapter 12); and rates of infant mortality began creeping upward in areas of the country hard hit by economic decline and reductions in social services.

One of the most striking differences between the United States and almost every other advanced society is our lack of any comprehensive system of national health insurance that makes adequate health care available to all citizens as a matter of right. In the early 1990s, as many as 36 million Americans lacked public or private health insurance at any given point; even more—close to 48 million—were uninsured at least part of the year. The problem was worse for the young and for minorities: about one in five Americans aged 19 to 24 were uninsured in the late 1980s, as were 30 percent of blacks and 41 percent of Hispanics. And in addition to the wholly uninsured, another 25 percent of America's nonelderly population lacked sufficient insurance to cover large medical bills.[2]

At the same time, American health care is also the most expensive in the advanced industrial world—accounting for over 12 percent of our gross national product in 1990, versus 9 percent in Canada and 6 percent in the United Kingdom. Clearly, something is very wrong with health care in America—and indeed nearly everyone, across the political spectrum, agrees that the system desperately needs fixing. But how that should be accomplished is a hotly debated issue.

As we write, a new administration plans a sweeping reform of health care in the United States, which may improve these dismal statistics. But how throughly the system will be altered in the coming years is hard to predict. Health care reform has been fiercely resisted for decades, and the obstacles to real change are formidable. Why should that be so? Why has it proven so difficult to change what most Americans agree is an ineffective and unjust system?

Part of the answer is suggested in Larry Makinson's survey of political contributions by the health and insurance industries. Between them, health professionals, hospitals, drug companies, and the health insurance industry gave over $27 million to cash-starved congressional candidates in the 1990 elections. That kind of largesse is bound to have an impact on the way Congress considers, or fails to consider, changes in our health care system. Makinson argues that the most important function of this money is not to get specific legislation passed but to *prevent* serious debate about the desirability of a national health system. As the failings of our current system become more glaring and public pressure for change more adamant, even these sums may not be enough, he argues, to keep major reform off the agenda. But they will certainly continue to influence its shape.

The resulting absence of accessible health care for all Americans, as Drs. Colin McCord and Harold P. Freeman point out in "Excess Mortality in Harlem," is one reason for the shockingly high rates of disease and death in many poor and minority communities. While health conditions have generally improved in recent years for most Americans, they have lagged behind—and sometimes deteriorated—in places like Harlem, where male life expectancy is lower than it is in Bangladesh. McCord and Freeman call for a "major commitment" to attack both the poverty and the inadequate health care that underlie these troubling statistics.

McCord and Freeman's statistics may indeed *underestimate* the amount of "excess mortality" in Harlem since they were gathered before the twin epidemics of AIDS and crack cocaine struck the inner cities. During the 1980s, the authors note, AIDS became the leading cause of death for young adults in Harlem and across New York City. That AIDS is now closely connected with intravenous drug use, especially among the minority poor, reminds us that this most frightening of modern medical problems is also, in the deepest sense, a *social* problem. In "AIDS: The Epidemic and the Society," Mary Catherine Bateson and Richard Goldsby, an anthropologist and a biologist, show some of the many ways in which the spread of AIDS has followed the "fault lines of our society." Thus, our failure to address the problems of "marginalized" people, both in the Third World and in America's inner cities, has allowed the AIDS virus to "trickle up" from the most disadvantaged; our cultural inhibition against the frank dissemination of information about sex (and drugs) has hindered our ability to control the spread of the disease by changing the behavior of those at risk. Some of the authors' specific recommendations for social policy toward AIDS are controversial, but their central point—that the AIDS epidemic forces us to examine our social institutions critically—is undeniable.

The gaps in American health care that these three articles describe are one manifestation of a broader pattern that shapes most social services in the United States. In our society, human welfare has traditionally been seen as largely dependent on individual effort. The idea that society as a whole should have responsibility for the welfare of its members is relatively undeveloped in American society. For most of us, such basic human needs as health care, shelter, and the care of children are things that we have to acquire on our own, if we can. For those who can't, government programs do exist to provide basic social services—but all too often they are provided skimpily and inhumanely. And, as we've seen so sharply in the recent past, our social services are among the first casualties of governmental budget slashing in the name of economic "renewal."

More recently, the welfare system has been increasingly blamed for the stubborn poverty and other ills of the so-called urban "underclass." That a great deal is wrong with our welfare system cannot be denied. But as Rosemary L. Bray shows in her autobiographical account of growing up on welfare, much of the newly fashionable imagery of welfare families held by more fortunate Americans is misleading and self-serving. Bray's mother, who scrambled to raise four children, send them to private schools, and ultimately turn them into "working, taxpaying adults," bears little resemblance to the stereotype of welfare women as lazy consumers of government handouts. Bray acknowledges that not all women on welfare are equally motivated. But her story of one family's successful use of the welfare system to help them move up from poverty should make us think twice about the idea that welfare's impact is uniformly negative.

References

1.   Report of the National Advisory Commission on Health Manpower, quoted in R. M. Titmuss, "Ethics and Economics of Medical Care," in *Commitment to Welfare* (New York: Pantheon, 1968), p. 268.

2.   These figures are from Emily Friedman, "The Uninsured: From Dilemma to Crisis," *Journal of the American Medical Association*, Vol. 265, No. 19 (May 15, 1991), pp. 2491–2492.

30

POLITICAL CONTRIBUTIONS FROM THE HEALTH AND INSURANCE INDUSTRIES

LARRY MAKINSON

For years, campaign dollars from medical political action committees (PACs) and from thousands of individual doctors, dentists, chiropractors, pharmacists, nursing home operators, and other medical professionals have been flowing generously toward Washington. In the 1989–1990 campaign season, the health industry provided $16.3 million in contributions to congressional candidates. Millions more—$10.9 million, to be exact—went to candidates from the insurance industry.

❖ WHERE THE MONEY CAME FROM

■ Health Professionals

Of the $16.3 million in health industry contributions during the 1989–1990 election season, the biggest portion—$11 million—came from physicians, dentists, psychologists, nurses, chiropractors, and other health professionals. The dollars came from PACs run by professional associations such as the AMA

From *Health Affairs*, Winter 1992. Reprinted by permission. Portions of the original have been omitted.

and from individuals. Physicians led the way, dispensing $5.9 million in contributions. This includes the PACs of the AMA, its state affiliates, and a handful of other PACs, such as the American College of Emergency Physicians and other similar groups. It also includes individual contributions by persons listing themselves as "doctors" or "physicians" and their immediate families. While the AMA was the dominant PAC within this group, slightly more than half of the overall dollars came from individual physicians. The money was split evenly between the two parties—Democrats got 51 percent, Republicans got 49 percent. The AMA's national PAC not only was the biggest single source of funds among physicians, it was one of the largest PACs in the nation in 1989–1990, as it has been for years. In the 1989–1990 election cycle it was second only to the Realtors' PAC in total contributions. Some 482 congressional candidates—most of them House members—received AMA donations, and the checks tended to be large. The average contribution to House candidates was $4,828; Senate candidates averaged $5,952. (PACs by law can give up to $10,000 to a single candidate during a normal election cycle. In practice, most PACs tend to give $1,000 or less to all but a few House members; Senators often receive $2,000 or more.) Money flowed equally to both sides of the aisle; Republicans had a narrow edge, receiving 50.7 percent of the dollars. Nearly 85 percent of AMA contributions went to incumbents.

Optometrists and ophthalmologists followed physicians, giving out $1.5 million—the largest contribution by a group of specialists. The biggest share of the money by far—some 89 percent—came from PACs. Overall, the eye doctors' contributions paralleled those of other physicians, by being more pragmatic than partisan—that is, the dollars tended to follow committee assignments and seniority more than party affiliation. Democrats collected 55 percent of the dollars. The next-highest group—psychiatrists and psychologists—gave $389,000, most of which (85 percent) went to Democrats. Podiatrists, orthopedists, osteopaths, pathologists, and a host of other physician specialists contributed a total of nearly $700,000 to federal candidates in the 1990 elections. Of these dollars, 71 percent came through PACs. Overall, the specialists in this group gave 60 percent of their dollars to Democratic candidates. The American Dental Association (ADA) was the primary conduit for campaign contributions from dentists (whose contributions totaled $1.1 million) in the 1990 elections. The ADA's national PAC (along with five other PACs representing state affiliates) accounted for more than $820,000. Democrats collected slightly more than half of the ADA's dollars. Some 91.5 percent went to incumbents. In all, PAC contributions accounted for 82 percent of the dentists' donations.

Nurses followed the footsteps of their physician colleagues at a slightly smaller scale, $378,000. Strictly speaking, the American Nurses Association (ANA)—whose PAC delivered nearly $290,000 of nurses' contributions in 1990—is a labor organization. But the center classifies it under health care because its primary interest is clearly tied to health legislation. Its spending patterns are typical of labor unions, however, in that 85 percent of the nurses' dollars went to Democratic candidates. Surprisingly, only 57 percent of the ANA's money went to incumbents.

A second nursing PAC, sponsored by the American Association of Nurse Anesthetists, gave $64,000 in the 1990 elections. Two dollars out of every three given by the PAC went to Democrats, but nearly all of the money (99.6 percent) went to incumbents. Individual contributions by nurses directly to candidates accounted for only 6 percent of the group's overall giving. Some 94 percent of the dollars came from PACs.

The American Chiropractic Association is the dominant source of money among chiropractors, who donated $301,000. The association's national PAC, along with nearly a dozen state affiliates, accounted for 83 percent of all contributions. Their political tilt was strongly Democratic. Pharmacists gave 88 percent of their contributions, which totaled $298,000, through PACs in the 1990 elections. The PAC of the National Association of Pharmacists was the leading provider of campaign funds, delivering almost $164,000. Democrats were the chief beneficiaries overall, drawing 68 percent of the pharmacists' dollars. The center's analysis draws a distinction between professional pharmacists and operators of drugstores; the latter were classified as retail establishments since they sell far more than prescription drugs. Drugstore PACs and individual contributors gave approximately $196,000 to federal candidates in 1989–1990. Of this, 53 percent went to Democrats. (These totals are not reflected in the $298,000 that came from pharmacists.) Physical therapists, dietitians, and a variety of other nonphysician health professionals and practitioners were the source of some $375,000 in campaign contributions to federal candidates in the 1990 elections. Ninety-four percent of their dollars came through PACs, and 73 percent went to Democratic candidates. The leading PAC contributors within this group were the American Physical Therapy Association ($150,000) and the American Occupational Therapy Association (nearly $65,000).

■ Hospitals and Nursing Homes

Hospitals, nursing homes, and other residential care facilities are another important source of campaign donations. Hospitals gave a total of $1.3 million in political contributions. The American Hospital Association (AHA) is the chief trade association for the nation's hospital administrators. Its PAC provided over $502,000 in campaign contributions in the 1990 elections; 68 percent of the dollars went to Democrats. The Federation of American Health Systems, whose PAC gave $118,000 in contributions, represents investor-owned hospitals. Many of its members, including Humana and the Hospital Corporation of America, support their own PACs. Two other hospital-related PACs gave $50,000 or more in 1989–1990: the National Association of Private Psychiatric Hospitals ($74,000) and National Medical Enterprises ($85,000). Both of these PACs followed the strong Democratic-leaning trend of their industry. Overall, hospital groups gave 70 percent of their dollars to Democrats.

PACs accounted for two-thirds of the $535,000 that came from nursing home operators and administrators. The biggest PAC was that of the American Health Care Association, which gave $263,000 to help represent the interests of its member nursing homes in all fifty states. Six other PACs, representing private nursing home operators, gave an additional $90,000 in contributions. Biggest among them were those of Manor Healthcare Corporation ($38,000) and Beverly Enterprises ($36,000). Including both PAC and individual contributions, the nursing home industry gave 72 percent of its dollars to Democrats.

■ Health Services

This broad category encompasses a variety of health care providers, from medical laboratories to home nursing services to health maintenance organizations (HMOs) and ambulance operators. Overall, contributors in this category gave $376,000 to federal candidates in the 1990 elections. HMOs were the single biggest contributors within this group, although their combined $106,000 in contributions was modest by health industry standards. Democrats collected 72 percent of the dollars from within this sector.

■ Pharmaceuticals and Health Products

Second only to health professionals, the pharmaceutical and health product industry delivered nearly $2.7 million to congressional candidates during the 1989–1990 election cycle. In contrast to all other health industry sectors, a majority of its dollars (52 percent) went to Republicans. Pharmaceutical manufacturers supplied the biggest portion of the dollars (just over $2 million), with medical supply manufacturers and distributors accounting for about half of the remaining money. Others within this group include makers of a variety of health care products and pharmaceutical wholesalers.

Nine different pharmaceutical manufacturers gave $100,000 or more in PAC contributions during the 1990 elections. The list of those top contributors is a who's who of the American pharmaceutical industry: Abbott Laboratories, Bristol-Myers Squibb, Ciba-Geigy, Eli Lilly, Glaxo, Pfizer, Schering-Plough, SmithKline Beckman, and Upjohn. By comparison, the Pharmaceutical Manufacturers Association (PMA)—the industry's chief trade association—was a relatively minor player, with just $47,000 in PAC contributions. PACs were clearly the preferred instrument for delivering political donations from the pharmaceutical industry; only 12 percent of the industry's dollars came from individuals. One notable exception to the PAC predominance was Eli Lilly. The Indianapolis-based firm delivered $51,700 in contributions to Indiana's Republican Senator Dan Coats—most of it in large individual contributions from Eli Lilly executives and their immediate families.

Among medical supply and health product manufacturers, which gave $682,000, the biggest contributor was the New Hampshire-based Henley Group, whose PAC gave nearly $99,000 in the 1990 elections. Within the category, 62 percent of the contributions came from PACs, and 55 percent went to Democrats.

In addition to all of the other health care categories, the center also identified $306,000 in contributions from individuals whose interests were clearly connected with the health industry, although their exact category could not be determined from the information provided. Two-thirds of the dollars in this catchall group went to Democrats.

■ Insurance

Insurance companies clearly are at the center of the debate on national health insurance and are a powerful lobby in their own right. The insurance industry's $10.9 million contribution puts it in the top rank of congressional contributors, ahead of commercial banks, defense contractors, oil and gas producers, and the real estate industry.

The biggest source of money within the industry came from companies or trade associations that handle multiple lines of insurance—including health, life, and property and casualty insurance. Three-quarters of this amount came from PACs. Companies dealing primarily in health insurance were comparatively modest in their contributions—giving just $887,000—but that figure represents only a fraction of companies that would be affected by universal health insurance. Even many companies whose primary product is life insurance earn a portion of their revenues from health and accident coverage. The only group of companies unlikely to be affected by national health insurance are those dealing exclusively in property and casualty insurance; they accounted for only $150,000. As in the health industry, insurance carriers spread their dollars among members of Congress on both sides of the aisle. Democrats captured a narrow majority—53 percent.

Fending off national health insurance is only one item on the insurance industry's congressional agenda. Tax legislation is another perennial concern. In fact, the tax-writing House Ways and Means Committee was the main recipient of insurance industry contributions in the 1990 elections. All told, the industry gave more than $1.7 million to members of that committee—an average of over $47,000 per member. But while many of the dollars flowing from insurance to Capitol Hill have more to do with taxation and other issues than with national health insurance, there can be no doubt that the industry's objections to a "government takeover" of health insurance will be carefully considered by politicians who have accepted those dollars over the years.

❖ WHERE THE MONEY WENT

Overall, Democratic candidates captured 57 percent of the health industry's campaign contributions in the 1990 elections and 53 percent of the money that came from the insurance industry. Hospitals and health service companies were the most likely to give to Democrats (each gave 70 percent or more). Pharmaceutical and health product manufacturers were the only group to favor Republicans.

In one respect, the health and insurance industries' preference for Democrats matches that of many other business groups—even those who may be closer philosophically to the Republican party. Without the support of Democrats, who as the majority party control the committee and subcommittee chairmanships, no legislation on Capitol Hill is likely to become law. Recognizing that political reality, many business groups—regardless of their political preferences—deliver their campaign dollars to both sides of the aisle. Overall, Democrats won a slight majority of the campaign dollars delivered by business interests in the 1990 election. They also collected 92 percent of labor dollars and about two-thirds of the money given by ideological and single-issue groups.

❖ THE WAY MONEY WORKS IN WASHINGTON

During 1989–1990, Congress tackled several important health-related measures, although consensus on the larger issue of national health insurance remained elusive. That pattern was in many ways typical of legislation debated in Washington. Most of the battles over health care in 1989 and 1990 were over relatively small-scale adjustments to current law, which may be crucial to specific industries or professional groups but generally pass unnoticed by the public. The bigger issue—solving the problem of rapidly escalating health costs and improving the plight of millions of uninsured or underinsured Americans—was never faced. The nonemergence of that underlying issue also reveals much about the way money influences legislative behavior. Disputes between competing segments of the same industry—as in the case of specialists versus primary care physicians—are the staples of Washington's legislative diet. Large-scale overhauls, such as the Clean Air Act Amendments of 1990 or the Tax Reform Act of 1986, emerge only rarely and often bear little resemblance in their final form to the original proposals.

Industry groups, including health and insurance, often contribute money not to pass legislation, but to prevent it. The deferral of serious debate over national health insurance is a prime example of what might be called "preventive medicine" by the health industry. The $16 million it spent in campaign contributions may have helped to sway a few votes in the debates between pharmaceutical companies or between specialists and primary care physicians, but its larger side effect was to dampen any legislative enthusiasm for a major health system overhaul.

The rising costs of campaigning—and in 1992, the added threat of a restive electorate and newly drawn districts—have made members of Congress more dependent than ever on raising large sums of campaign cash to fuel their reelection drives. It has also made many members even more reluctant to alienate major sources of campaign funds by taking on industries that resist what they see as legislative interference from Washington. On the other hand, campaign contributions alone are not enough to pass major new laws or to forestall forever major changes in existing laws where the public demands change. Mindful of those political realities and of the growing public intolerance of sky-high health and insurance costs, the industry is shifting its strategy from preventing national health insurance to proposing palatable alternatives.

When the 103d Congress takes office in January 1993—filled with many new faces—health care legislation is going to be near the top of the agenda. The millions of dollars that flow from the industry to the lawmakers in campaign contributions will be a powerful force in cementing friendly relationships with those lawmakers as the high-stakes debate over the future of America's health system begins in earnest.

31

EXCESS MORTALITY IN HARLEM

COLIN McCORD, M.D. AND HAROLD P. FREEMAN, M.D.

M ortality rates for white and nonwhite Americans have fallen steadily and in parallel since 1930. . . . Lower rates for nonwhites have been associated with an improved living standard, better education, and better access to health care.[1, 2] These improvements, however, have not been evenly distributed. Most health indicators, including mortality rates, are worse in the impoverished areas of this country.[3–9] It is not widely recognized just how much certain inner-city areas lag behind the rest of the United States. We used census data and data from the Bureau of Health Statistics and Analysis of the New York City Health Department to estimate the amount, distribution, and causes of excess mortality in the New York City community of Harlem.

❖ THE COMMUNITY

Harlem is a neighborhood in upper Manhattan just north of Central Park. Its population is 96 percent black and has been predominantly black since before World War I. It was the center of the Harlem Renaissance of black culture in

From *The New England Journal of Medicine*, Vol. 322, pp. 173–77, 1990. Copyright 1990 Massachusetts Medical Society. Reprinted by permission.

the 1920s, and it continues to be a cultural center for black Americans. The median family income in Harlem, according to the 1980 census, was $6,497, as compared with $16,818 in all New York City, $21,023 in the United States, and $12,674 among all blacks in the United States. The families of 40.8 percent of the people of Harlem had incomes below the government-defined poverty line in 1980. The total population of Harlem fell from 233,000 in 1960 to 121,905 in 1980. In the same 20-year period the death rate from homicide rose from 25.3 to 90.8 per 100,000.

The neighborhood is not economically homogeneous. There is a middle-to-upper-class community of about 25,000 people living in new, private apartment complexes or houses, a less affluent group of 25,000 living in public housing projects, and a third group of about 75,000 who live in substandard housing. Most of the population loss has been in the group living in substandard housing, much of it abandoned or partially occupied buildings.

The pattern of medical care in Harlem is similar to that reported for other poor and black communities.[10, 11] As compared with the per capita averages for New York City, the rate of hospital admissions is 26 percent higher, the use of emergency rooms is 73 percent higher, the use of hospital outpatient departments is 134 percent higher, and the number of primary care physicians per 1000 people is 74 percent lower.[12] . . . For our analysis, we calculated age-, sex-, and cause-specific death rates for Harlem using the recorded deaths for 1979, 1980, and 1981 and population data from the 1980 census. . . .

The reference death rates we used to calculate the standardized mortality ratios (SMRs) are those of the white population of the United States, as published in *Vital Statistics of the United States, 1980*.[13] To calculate the SMRs, the total number of observed deaths in 1979, 1980, and 1981 for each age group, sex, and cause was divided by the expected number of deaths, based on the population of each sex and age group and the reference death rate. . . .

❖ RESULTS

Since 1950, when the New York City Health Department began to keep death records according to health-center district, Central Harlem has consistently had the highest infant mortality rate and one of the highest crude death rates in the city. In 1970 and 1980, age-adjusted mortality rates for Harlem residents were the highest in New York City, much worse than the rates for nonwhites in the United States as a whole, and they had changed little since 1960. . . . This lack of improvement in the age-adjusted death rate reflected worsening mortality rates for persons between the ages of 15 and 65 that more than offset the drop in mortality among infants and young children. . . .

Figure 1 shows the survival curves for male and female residents of Harlem, as compared with those for whites in the United States and those for the residents of an area in rural Bangladesh. Bangladesh is categorized by the World Bank as one of the lowest-income countries in the world. The Matlab

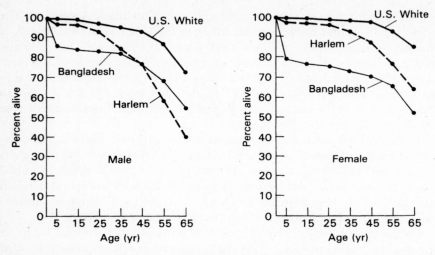

Figure 1 Survival to the Age of 65 in Harlem, Bangladesh, and among U.S. Whites in 1980.

demographic-study area is thought to have somewhat lower death rates than Bangladesh as a whole, but the rates are typical for the region. Life expectancy at birth in Matlab was 56.5 years in 1980, as compared with an estimated 49 years for Bangladesh and 57 years for India in 1986.[9, 16] For men, the rate of survival beyond the age of 40 is lower in Harlem than Bangladesh. For women, overall survival to the age of 65 is somewhat better in Harlem, but only because the death rate among girls under 5 is very high in Bangladesh.

The SMRs for Harlem . . . were high for those of all ages below 75, but they were particularly high for those between 25 and 64 years old and for children under 4. In the three years 1979 to 1981, there were 6415 deaths in Harlem. If the death rate among U.S. whites had applied to this community, there would have been 3994 deaths. Eighty-seven percent of the 2421 excess deaths were of persons under 65.

Table 1 compares the numbers of observed and expected deaths among persons under 65, according to the chief underlying causes. A large proportion of the observed excess was directly due to violence and substance abuse, but these causes did not account for most of the excess. Cirrhosis, homicide, accidents, drug dependency, and alcohol use were considered the most important underlying causes of death in 35 percent of all deaths among people under 65, and in 45 percent of the excess deaths.

For people between the ages of 65 and 74 the SMRs in Harlem were much lower than those for people younger than 65. For residents of Harlem 75 years old or older, overall death rates were essentially the same as those for U.S. whites. . . . Disease-specific SMRs for people over the age of 65 were below those of younger age groups in almost every category. In several categories (notably cardiovascular disease in Harlem residents 75 or older), they were

Table 1 CAUSES OF EXCESS MORTALITY IN HARLEM, 1979 TO 1981.*				
CAUSE	OBSERVED DEATHS (NO.)	STANDARDIZED MORTALITY RATIO	ANNUAL EXCESS DEATHS PER 100,000	% OF EXCESS DEATHS
Cardiovascular disease	880	2.23	157.5	23.5
Cirrhosis	410	10.49	120.4	17.9
Homicide	332	14.24	100.2	14.9
Neoplasm	604	1.77	84.9	12.6
Drug dependency	153	283.1	49.5	7.4
Diabetes	94	5.43	24.9	3.7
Alcoholism	73	11.33	34.6	3.2
Pneumonia and influenza	78	5.07	20.3	3.0
Disorders in newborn	64	7.24	17.9	2.7
Infection	65	5.60	17.3	2.6
Accident	155	1.17	17.2	1.1
Ill defined	44	2.07	17.4	1.1
Renal	26	4.54	6.6	0.9
Chronic obstructive pulmonary disease	35	1.29	2.6	0.4
Congenital anomalies	23	1.21	1.3	0.2
Suicide	33	0.81	− 2.5	—
All other	181	3.13	40.0	6.0
All causes	3250	2.75	671.2	100.0

*The calculations are based on the deaths of all persons—male and female under the age of 65. The reference death rates are those for U.S. whites in 1980.

lower than in whites. This may represent the survival of the fittest in this area of excess mortality.

❖ DISCUSSION

An improvement in child mortality in Harlem between 1960 and 1980 was accompanied by rising mortality rates for persons between the ages of 25 and

65. There was therefore no improvement in overall age-adjusted mortality. Death rates for those between the ages of 5 and 65 were worse in Harlem than in Bangladesh.

We have not attempted to calculate SMRs since 1981, because the 1980 census is the most recent reliable estimate of the population of New York City, but all available evidence indicates that there has been very little change since then. The total number of deaths in Harlem from 1985 through 1987 was 1.6 percent higher than from 1979 through 1981. According to the New York City Planning Department, the decline in Harlem's population stopped in 1980 and the total population has been growing at the rate of 1 percent per year since then.[18] If this estimate is accepted, there has been a slight drop in the crude death rate for Harlem since 1980, but not large enough to affect any of our conclusions. Since 1980 the number of deaths of persons 25 to 44 years of age has increased considerably (31 percent), and the acquired immunodeficiency syndrome (AIDS) has become the most common cause of death in this age group in Harlem and in all New York City. The number of deaths from AIDS is expected to continue to rise.

The situation in Harlem is extreme, but it is not an isolated phenomenon. We identified 54 health areas (of 353) in New York City, with a total population of 650,000, in which there were more than twice as many deaths among people under the age of 65 as would be expected if the death rates of U.S. whites applied. All but one of these health areas have populations more than half composed of minority members. These are areas that were left behind when the minority population of the city as a whole experienced the same improvement in life expectancy that was seen in the rest of the United States.[19] Similar pockets of high mortality have been described in other U.S. cities.[3, 20] Jenkins et al. calculated SMRs for all deaths in Roxbury and adjacent areas of Boston that were almost as high in 1972–1973 as those reported here.[20] This area of highest mortality in Boston was the area with the highest proportion of minority groups.

It will be useful to know more about the circumstances surrounding premature deaths in high-risk communities to determine the relative importance of contributing factors such as poverty, inadequate housing, psychological stress, substance abuse, malnutrition, and inadequate access to medical care.[14, 15] But action to correct the appalling health conditions reflected in these statistics need not wait for more research. The essential first steps are to identify these pockets of high mortality and to recognize the urgent severity of the problem.[17] Widespread poverty and inadequate housing are obvious in Harlem and demand a direct attack wherever they are present. . . .

Those responsible for implementing health programs must face the reality of high death rates in Harlem and the enormous burden of disease that requires treatment in the existing facilities. The health care system is overloaded with such treatment and is poorly structured to support preventive measures, detect disease early, and care for adults with chronic problems. At the same time, the population at highest risk has limited contact with the health care system except in emergencies. Brudny and Dobkyn reported that

83 percent of 181 patients discharged from Harlem Hospital with tuberculosis in 1988 were lost to follow-up and did not continue treatment.[21] New approaches must be developed to take preventive and therapeutic measures out of the hospitals, clinics, and emergency rooms and deliver them to the population at highest risk.

Intensive educational campaigns to improve nutrition and reduce the use of alcohol, drugs, and tobacco are needed and should be directed at children and adolescents, since habits are formed early and the death rates begin to rise immediately after adolescence. Education will have little effect unless it is combined with access to adequate incomes, useful employment, and decent housing for these children and their parents. Education can help in controlling epidemic drug use and associated crime only if it is combined with effective and coordinated police and public action. AIDS in Harlem is largely related to intravenous drug use and is not likely to be controlled until drugs are controlled, but effective education about this disease is also urgently needed.

Knowledge of the history of previous efforts to improve health in Harlem does not lead to optimism about the future. The Harlem Health Task Force was formed in 1976 because Harlem and the Carter administration recognized that death rates were high. An improved system of clinics, more drug-treatment centers, and active community-outreach programs were recommended. The recommendations have been implemented to varying degrees, but funding has been limited. The preventive and curative health care system is essentially unchanged today. Drug use has increased, and the proportion of the population receiving public assistance has increased. There has been no decrease in the death rates.

In 1977 Jenkins et al. pointed out that the number of excess deaths recorded each year in the areas of worst health in Boston was considerably larger than the number of deaths in places that the U.S. government had designated as natural-disaster areas. They suggested that these zones of excess mortality be declared disaster areas and that measures be implemented on this basis.[20] No such action was taken then or is planned now. If the high-mortality zones of New York City were designated a disaster area today, 650,000 people would be living in it. A major political and financial commitment will be needed to eradicate the root causes of this high mortality: vicious poverty and inadequate access to the basic health care that is the right of all Americans.

References

1. Manton KG, Patrick CH, Johnson KW. Health differentials between blacks and whites: recent trends in mortality and morbidity. Milbank Q 1987; 65:Suppl 1:125–99.

2. Davis K, Lillie-Blanton M, Lyons B, Mullan F, Powe N, Rowland D. Health care for black Americans: the public sector role. Milbank Q 1987; 65:Suppl 1:213–47.

3. Kitagawa EM, Hauser PM. Differential mortality in the United States: a study in socioeconomic epidemiology. Cambridge, Mass.: Harvard University Press, 1973.

4. Woolhandler S, Himmelstein DU, Silber R, Bader M, Harnly M, Jones A. Medical care and mortality: racial differences in preventable deaths. Int J Health Serv 1985; 15:1–22.

5. Savage D, Lindenbaum J, Van Ryzin J, Struening E, Garrett TJ. Race, poverty, and survival in multiple myeloma. Cancer 1984; 54:3085–94.

6. Black/white comparisons of premature mortality for public health program planning—District of Columbia. MMWR 1989; 38:33–7.

7. Freeman HP, Wasfie TJ. Cancer of the breast in poor black women. Cancer 1989; 63:2562–9.

8. Cancer in the economically disadvantaged: a special report prepared by the subcommittee on cancer in the economically disadvantaged. New York: American Cancer Society, 1986.

9. Demographic surveillance system—Matlab. Vital events and migration tables, 1980. Scientific report no. 58. Dhaka, Bangladesh: International Centre for Diarrheal Disease Research, 1982.

10. Davis K, Schoen C. Health and the war on poverty: a ten-year appraisal. Washington, D.C.: Brookings Institution, 1978.

11. Blendon RJ, Aiken LH, Freeman HE, Corey CR. Access to medical care for black and white Americans: a matter of continuing concern. JAMA 1989; 261:278–81.

12. Community health atlas of New York. New York: United Hospital Fund, 1986.

13. Vital statistics of the United States 1980. Hyattsville, Md.: National Center for Health Statistics, 1985. (DHHS publication no. (PHS) 85–1101.)

14. Vital statistics: instructions for classifying the underlying cause of death, 1980. Hyattsville, Md.: National Center for Health Statistics, 1980.

15. The international classification of diseases, 9th revision, clinical modification: ICD-9-CM. 2nd ed. Washington, D.C.: Department of Health and Human Services, 1980. (DHHS publication no. (PHS) 80–1260.)

16. The state of the world's children 1988 (UNICEF). New York: Oxford University Press, 1988.

17. Fay RE, Passel JS, Robinson JG. Coverage of population in the 1980 census. Washington, D.C.: Bureau of the Census, 1988. (Publication no. PHC 80-E4.)

18. Community district needs, 1989. New York: Department of City Planning, 1987. (DCP publication no. 87-10.)

19. Summary of vital statistics, 1986. New York: Bureau of Health Statistics and Analysis, 1986.

20. Jenkins CD, Tuthill RW, Tannenbaum SI, Kirby CR. Zones of excess mortality in Massachusetts. N Engl J Med 1977; 296:1354–6.

21. Brudny K, Dobkyn J. Poor compliance is the major obstacle in controlling the HIV-associated tuberculosis outbreak. Presented at the Fifth International Conference on Acquired Immune Deficiency Syndrome, Montreal, June 8, 1989.

32

AIDS: THE EPIDEMIC AND THE SOCIETY

MARY CATHERINE BATESON AND RICHARD GOLDSBY

A previously unknown life form, the virus that causes AIDS, is now making its way through the human population, spreading around the world with devastating and accelerating effects. That virus has become a part of the biological context of our lives, one of the many life forms that actually live inside of human beings rather than around them. All of these can potentially be known and at least partially controlled but the needed thinking about AIDS has just begun, and it is already clear that it raises the most basic questions about the human condition, about human biology, and about the mechanisms of social life.

The AIDS epidemic, as it moves around the planet, is posing new questions about justice and teaching us new ways of thinking about human learning and human suffering. It throws certain characteristics of society into sharp relief, just as radioisotopes, moving through the body, can be used to highlight physiological processes for diagnosis. At one level the movement of the epidemic reflects communication and travel. At another it belies out habitual self-deceptions, tracing activities that would otherwise be secret: drug addiction and sexual practices that most people have preferred not to know about—extramarital sex, homosexuality, prostitution. AIDS has made us newly aware

From Mary Catherine Bateson and Richard Goldsby, *Thinking Aids,* Menlo Park, CA, Addison-Wesley, 1989. Reprinted by permission.

of human diversity. In our own society it forces us to acknowledge bisexuality, a pattern of sexual preference that most Americans, who like their distinctions clear, have tended to ignore, and is making us more aware of middle-class intravenous drug use. It will probably increase awareness of the sexual use of children, of sex in prisons, of sex and drugs in the peacetime army.

AIDS highlights processes of social change: urbanization and monetary economies in Africa that send men to the cities for cash earnings while their wives stay in the villages to farm; changed sexual mores for heterosexuals as well as homosexuals; the economic dislocations and prejudice that are increasingly turning some minority communities in America into an underclass. The history of failure to heed the early warnings of the epidemic is a statement of our priorities as a society. Now that we know how to prevent the disease from spreading, its continued spread must advertise the ways in which, in this interconnected and interdependent world, we fail to communicate to individuals the very knowledge they need to survive. AIDS moves along the fault lines of our society and becomes a metaphor for understanding that society. . . .

Once in a while, beyond the terrifying numbers projected for the future, one hears the statement that unless there are major medical breakthroughs the AIDS epidemic could bring the end of Western civilization. This is surely an exaggeration, but it is useful to clarify exactly what it might mean. Three scenarios need to be considered.

1. *Population loss.* AIDS will cause increasing numbers of casualties until the rate of spread is reversed. In the process the death rate could theoretically come to exceed the birth rate, leading to steady population shrinkage. In the countries of Africa where prevalence is highest, the population doubles in twenty-five years or less: birth rates are so high that actual shrinkage could not become a factor unless the epidemic continued unchecked for several generations. Death rates in Africa are still shaped by a whole flock of endemic diseases, and it is projected that death from AIDS could not exceed 20 percent of the total. AIDS could not solve the African population problem—but it could subvert all regional efforts to find solutions.

The demographics are different in the industrialized countries, where general health factors probably ensure slower spread in the non-drug-using heterosexual population; but within specific communities they may be worse, and the demographic impact of AIDS will be sharpest in the great cities that are also our cultural centers. The end of civilization is not going to come about through simple loss of population due to the AIDS virus. Arguably, indeed, Europe benefited from the Black Death, which hastened the decay of medieval institutions and opened the way for the Renaissance. AIDS is similar to warfare in that the toll is highest on those in the prime of life; but functioning societies can recover remarkably quickly from massive population losses, and there are good reasons why epidemics tend to be self-limiting, as this one will surely prove to be. Diseases are rarely uniformly lethal, so the portions of the population that survive are those with natural resistance of some kind. We do not yet know for certain whether there are individuals whose own immune systems can withstand or resist HIV infection indefinitely, but there probably are. In addition, AIDS presents the possibility of behavioral immunity: anyone can make the decision to be immune by avoiding high-risk behavior, and many follow traditional patterns that already protect them. Societies have choices of how to respond, however, that may affect them long after demographic perturbations are over.

2. *Resource depletion*. AIDS will cause major economic disruption and painful choices in resource allocation which might cripple a given society or make it vulnerable to other kinds of attack. Health care costs are already a source of economic instability in the United States and the care of a single AIDS patient approaches $100,000, while the number of patients is increasing steadily. As the resources of more and more individuals are drained, more of this will become a public charge, adding to deficits. The carefully planned profitability of the health insurance industry is threatened—and so is the belief that any private industry can solve public problems like those of health care with a modicum of fairness. There will be needs for personnel and hospital facilities as well, needs that might prove to be transient. Money spent on AIDS may increase public deficits or force hard choices of taxation or reductions in other expenditures. Because the sums will be so large, major decisions of priorities will be needed. It will not be sufficient to reallocate available funds within the category of public health or human services.

This is a problem that may appear to weigh more heavily on affluent societies, where expected standards of health care are very high, than on the less developed countries, but that contrast is delusory. Officials of the United Nations Children's Fund point out that the epidemic will cause the death of more children through the diversion of resources from other public health programs than will die of AIDS. It is important to consider the cost of what does *not* happen because of the epidemic, such as the lost earnings and participation of those who die in the prime of life and opportunities missed. The AIDS epidemic may be the final straw for societies unable to establish self-sustaining economies.

In the developed world, the economic threat of AIDS will cause a certain amount of disruption in some industries and profit in others. The problem comes as always in decision making: What is the public priority on easing the pains of the dying? What are the relative values of therapy and prevention? How important is research on the immune system's defense of the body compared to research on space defense? Both will benefit basic science and have massive spinoffs, but different groups of individuals will draw the primary profit. How about drug interdiction and the immense profits of the illicit drug industry?

The concept of *triage* is a way of thinking about resource allocation on matters of life and death that originated on the battlefield. The nurse at the emergency room desk, who makes decisions about the order in which patients are seen or the need to call additional help, is called a triage nurse because of her role in sorting out need in relation to resources, but the term goes back to situations in which resources were so scarce that some patients could not be treated at all. On the battlefield, the wounded were divided into three groups:

those who were so severely wounded that they would probably die even if treatment were given, those whose wounds were so slight that they would recover without treatment, and those for whom treatment would make the difference between recovery and death. In real scarcity, the third group must take priority, but we live in an affluent society that expects to be able to provide the convenience and reassurance of care for many who probably don't need it, as well as offering heroic measures for those who are close to death. AIDS is going to put major strains on resources, however, and it seems certain that new standards of care for patients with brief life expectancies will develop, including appropriate levels of intervention that will be applied to cancer patients and to the very old.

In principle, triage is ethical when it reflects real limitations and is consistently applied, but it can easily be converted, even in the emergency room, into a form of discrimination based on ideas of differences in human worth. Still, redefinitions of appropriate care can lead to improved care as well as to the withdrawal of care. Many people with only a few months left of life would prefer to spend the time peacefully becoming used to the approach of death rather than undergoing one violation after another. The AIDS epidemic could lead to improved home care, improved hospice care, and improved psychological support for the dying. It could also confirm and extend in us habits of treating groups as expendable and callously ignoring human suffering.

The AIDS epidemic will amplify the effect of past choices and priorities, and the choices we make now will leave a continuing mark on society. The adverse effect of AIDS on the economy will be more a matter of ill-chosen priorities and bad planning than of direct costs.

3. AIDS will cause *psychological and social reactions that may change the character of human social life.* If the epidemic were to induce us to give up travel or international communication or were to sabotage our tenuous capacity for global cooperation, it would quite literally be undermining civilization. It also has the potential for creating political instability in third world societies where public order is already precarious, particularly in cities, and such instability can spread.

More narrowly, if reactions to the epidemic compromise basic values too pervasively, the epidemic could destroy the more recent and potentially more vulnerable institutions of democracy. If AIDS drives us into coercive and repressive social policies, it will have tempted us away from the basic commitments of our society. It could benefit society for individuals to become more aware and selective in their sexual practices, but a wave of puritanism or repression would work against creativity. Like the Black Death in Europe, AIDS could trigger religious movements embracing ignorance, massive scapegoating, or paranoia, a failure of hope or of compassion. It could in a generation subvert the fragile structures of dedication in the medical profession.

It is this third kind of danger, danger to the way society is organized, that is the basic threat of the AIDS epidemic. Thus it is that a consideration of how to respond to the AIDS epidemic directs us back to our own values. Our view is that many ways of reacting that might be effective would represent a compromise of those values, but that if those values were more effectively realized, our danger would be reduced. The AIDS epidemic cannot help but be a source not only of self-knowledge but also of self-determination, a way of understanding the choices that make us who we are and clarifying our priorities as a society. Just as it is possible to ask what the characteristics were of gay liberation in the 1970s that made the gay community so effective in amplifying the epidemic, so it is possible to ask about the characteristics of national policy in the 1980s that have made it so difficult to respond, and about the characteristics of a future society able to deal with the disease. The society must respond to the epidemic while maintaining basic constancies—that is, without compromising identity or fundamental value commitments. This capacity can be thought of as the immune system of society.

There are real choices to be made at a national level, choices that reflect quite different premises about human beings. So far, responses have been inconsistent, reflecting sometimes one way of thinking and sometimes another. Different national styles have been clearly visible: the Swedes displaying huge posters of condoms in the streets and the United States avoiding even the word on television, the Soviets deporting seropositive foreign students and some developing countries denying that the disease even exists. Even New York and California have shown visibly different cultural styles, while national policy has fluctuated and waffled.

It is possible to argue that there are two contrasting ways of dealing with the epidemic, each of which might be successful, each of which would leave its mark on the societies that adopted it.

On the one hand, it is possible to respond to the epidemic by reaching for a more open, just, and intercommunicating society and world in which no one is disenfranchised and individuals have the information to make appropriate decisions. Thus if we were able, as a society, to talk openly about matters related to sex and to feel compassion equally for all of our neighbors, the AIDS epidemic would probably be under control by now. Instead, we are in a situation where help has been withheld because of unstated ideas about who is and is not deserving, where essential information is not imparted to those who need it, and where many lack the trust and self-esteem needed to use the information available to them. The perennial problems of our society and of the world, which we have not had the resolution or imagination to address, are the principal source of vulnerability.

It is clear that the disease proliferated first in populations that have every reason to suspect they will be treated unfairly, and that the existence of prejudice is the main continuing barrier to communication. Homosexuality, extramarital sex, and I-V drug use are still stigmatized as antisocial or sinful behaviors by many, and the health problems that accompany them are sometimes seen as divine punishment. The same residues of prejudice give others a false sense of security. Racial and other minorities are sensitive to the possible "good riddance!" of the larger society and justifiably sensitive to the possibility that those who have discriminated against them for so long will find the epidemic a good excuse to do so again. The epidemic flourishes on discrimination and exclusion. Furthermore, stigmatized populations are burdened by a partial acceptance of external views. "Internalized homophobia" and "low self-esteem" make individuals value their own lives and health less, leave them with less hope for the future.

Internationally, the unequal distribution of resources and concern creates the setting for the proliferation of the disease. If health care in central Africa were comparable to that in industrial societies and part of a worldwide communicating network on the lines of the U.S. Centers for Disease Control, the epidemic might have been stemmed at a local level. In a genuinely interconnected and intercommunicating world, monitoring of health problems must be international. On the other hand, it is hard to imagine an effective shift in health delivery systems without substantive changes in other conditions, including the conditions that make so many people dependent on a living earned in migratory labor. There is no way of knowing for sure where the epidemic originated, but we do know that African populations suffer so many scourges that a new disease can proliferate unseen. The entire planet is vulnerable when certain areas are neglected.

Nationally and internationally, disease and drug use thrive on poverty and inequality. In America, the epidemic developed in a period when government was withdrawing from social programs, cutting budgets in all nonmilitary areas, and using the machinery of regulation to promote economic productivity rather than individual welfare. Disease also thrives on ignorance. Programs to control the spread of HIV can be blocked by unwillingness to talk candidly about sex. How many deaths will result from the refusal to use the word *condom* on television? Reluctance to use the word *semen* apparently led to the unfortunate euphemism *bodily fluids,* which escalated public anxiety by suggesting that HIV is likely to be transmitted by sweat or saliva or tears in casual and domestic contact. People have been driven from their homes as a result of such artificially maintained ignorance.

Each of the issues mentioned here is connected to other severe social problems, ranging from famine in Africa to teenage pregnancy to the increase in homelessness and malnutrition that accompanied government withdrawal from supporting social programs. The notion that affluence will spread through the society from the privileged to the underprivileged is called the "trickle-down theory." The reality that the result of allowing the AIDS epidemic to develop among marginalized groups will be its spread into the mainstream might be called the "trickle-up theory."

But this is the liberal point of view, the belief that social problems can be addressed by education and that behavior can be improved by equity. An alternative point of view would reflect other kinds of social agendas: If the society had more effective control over sexual and other private behavior, perhaps it could simply prevent promiscuity. If the concern for human rights had not been so expanded, it would be possible to deal with the epidemic by isolating it, to test everyone and intern all carriers, extruding them from society as was once done with lepers. If we were not burdened by concern for individual welfare there would be no need to struggle to prolong life for those already infected, no high insurance costs, no painful decisions about schooling. If police powers were expanded, borders could be effectively closed, drug traffic interdicted, and traffickers shot. It does indeed seem probable that the epidemic would be easier to deal with if we were a less open and caring society. Compassion can be expensive, and certainly the costs of the epidemic are increased by the desire to alleviate suffering. So far, the Soviet bloc seems to be less affected than the West, and Islamic fundamentalism does provide a model for one way of reducing homosexuality and other kinds of sexual activity: by treating them as capital crimes.

In general, there is a mirror-image quality to the costs and benefits of particular social institutions. The blood bank industry and the bathhouse industry both resist regulation within the ideology of capitalism, and the Bill of Rights protects beliefs we deplore as well as those we adhere to, allowing both information and misinformation to spread.

Against this background, we believe that policies based on openness and equity have the best chance of success, providing a framework for policy recommendations for reacting to the epidemic domestically and internationally. The proposals that will be made here are idealistic in their goals, but this is because of our conviction that survival under threat must mean the maintenance of the basic premises of the society, premises that have a certain biological as well as social logic. These proposals are not based on the assumption of universal altruism, but rather on the assumption that we as a society can recognize this as a situation in which the general welfare benefits from care for individuals and from empowering individuals to care for each other.

Policy must be thought through place by place. There are tasks to be done in every school and corporation, every town and city. AIDS policy is often treated like a hot potato, passed from person to person and from agency to agency. More painfully, individuals with AIDS are often routed from place to place or hospital to hospital, even deported from country to country. Because the private challenges of developing a personal behavioral immunity to AIDS must be faced everywhere, it is necessary that the public challenges be faced consistently, so that the visible institutions of society support molecular change. The following, then, are some of the places where change is needed.

▓ In the Schools and Communications Media

The handling of sex education represents a major philosophical inconsistency in American society: the belief that the social good is best achieved by enforcing ignorance of possible options rather than by informed choice. There are many who are more comfortable with that way of doing things. Recent lawsuits brought by some fundamentalist groups about textbooks have protested against any stimulation of the imagination through fairy tales and mythology as well as exposure to different belief systems and aspects of scientific knowledge. There is also an inconsistency in the argument that children can be exposed to violence and weapons with impunity, but will be corrupted by exposure to information about sexuality. Furthermore, the ignorance we conserve is never total. Children not taught about sex pick up misinformation from their classmates. We cannot afford to conserve ignorance about sex. The alternative is to present it so early that it is clear that the information is not an invitation to immediate action.

The management of the classroom has always been important in public health education, alongside actual lessons. Particularly in the lower grades, children pick up ideas of nutrition and sanitation from school practices like hand washing and discarding dropped food and the reactions when a child is hurt. School management should be based on the possible presence of students who are knowingly or unknowingly seropositive, and this in itself is an important lesson for adult living.

Once we manage to clarify what knowledge is necessary for a responsible adaptation to a world that contains the AIDS virus, and once a commitment is made to information in preference to ignorance, it follows that the media should provide specific and candid information and corrections to misinformation—and this should take precedence over considerations of taste. The effort will be long, and hard to maintain in focus. Much can be done by including safer sex in story lines, just as smoking has been progressively excluded and interracial casts have become routine.

■ In the Workplace

It is the task of all managers and all those making administrative decisions on the organization of work to maintain a workplace in which transmission of infection is prevented—part of a general effort to maintain health and prevent industrial accidents—and to be sure that misinformation does not lead to discrimination. No one should lose his or her job because of false beliefs about how AIDS is transmitted. Similarly, no qualified person should be denied a fair chance for a job because of the possibility of developing AIDS—this is comparable to refusing to employ women because they may eventually have children. No employer welcomes the complexities of dealing with disability but no equitable hiring policy can avoid it. An open and matter-of-fact policy toward the disease and the distribution of information are ways of promoting realistic prevention. Discrimination goes with magical thinking about one's own safety.

■ In the Streets

There are two issues here. First, America cannot afford to maintain an underclass that is chronically impoverished and alienated. The despair of unemployed youth in the ghettos often leads directly to I-V drug use, but it should be addressed in its own right, not because it promotes the spread of AIDS. Treatment should be easily available for all addicts, with the possibility of methadone support and even government-supplied heroin and hygienically run public shooting galleries. Addicts should not have to rent needles because carrying their own might lead to arrest. But these are half measures unless people are given alternatives: quality education, real access to employment, reason to aspire toward the future. Even the classic escape of the disinherited through the armed forces is now often closed, as the military services become increasingly selective. We need to offer every girl and boy a life that is more attractive than drug addiction.

Similar arguments apply to prostitution, which has been a major factor in the spread of AIDS in Africa and will probably be increasingly important elsewhere. The sex industry resembles I-V drug use in that you cannot make something safe if you pretend it isn't there. Many countries, such as the Netherlands, regulate prostitution and carefully supervise health in order to control venereal disease. Again, this is a necessary first step, but it needs to be combined with programs that will increase the options available to women in the sex industry, many of whom are also afflicted with problems of low self-esteem and many of whom have been long-term victims of exploitation and molestation. "The world's oldest profession" is not likely to go away, but women who choose to remain in it could benefit from better control of their own conditions of work, just as addicts who remain addicted are better off with safer and cheaper drugs.

Second, America cannot afford the massive enrichment of drug dealers and their destructive effect on the lives of youth. Drugs are a multimillion-dollar international industry so large that it threatens political stability in many regions of Latin America. There are estimated to be over a million intravenous drug users in the United States, which was a tragedy of major proportions before AIDS, contributing to a whole range of other social problems. In some cities, 60 to 80 percent of heroin users are already seropositive, and here the group that is perhaps hardest to contact and persuade has to be persuaded to change both sexual and needle-sharing behavior. The largest numbers of infants born with AIDS are the children of this population, largely black and Hispanic.

Many proposals to make the drug-using population more accessible involve partial decriminalization of some kinds of drug abuse. The criminalization of any behavior creates the motivation to support it and makes it difficult to reach those who are involved. Whatever hesitations we might have about the government supporting drug addiction or the sale of sexual services are minor compared to the cost of criminalization. In fact much of the pressure against partial or complete decriminalization of many crimes probably comes from those who see the connection between profitability and illegality.

■ In the Drugstore

Someone should design a hypodermic needle that cannot—mechanically—be reused, and it should be available as cheaply and easily as Kleenex. Failing that, handy portable bottles of bleach solution for cleaning needles and syringes are needed. Condoms are another product that should be available as cheaply and easily as Kleenex, not only in stores but in vending machines in multiple locations and along with the free shampoo in hotel rooms.

■ In the Marriage Office

Gay rights provide the best path to gay responsibility. We need both. We need to create an environment that is accepting and supportive of gays precisely so that they will feel like full members and participants in the society, with all the responsibilities that entails. You cannot selectively approve and disapprove aspects of someone's behavior by starting from a blanket condemnation. We cannot expect those with homosexual preferences to fit into social expectations of sustained relationships unless we treat gay and lesbian relationships as equivalent in value to heterosexual relationships. Marriage is hard enough to maintain in a society that approves of it and values it. This would mean finding ways to register and celebrate new commitments, permitting gay couples to adopt, preventing discrimination in housing, and treating same-sex companions as legal spouses. Saint Paul was speaking of heterosexual marriage when he said that it is better to marry than to burn. There seems to be no question that the voluntary concentration of gays in a few urban neighborhoods has provided a breeding ground for disease, but it would be reduced if gays were not made to feel uncomfortable elsewhere. We know that the gay community has produced many of the heroes of the epidemic so far, and men who were at one time involved in impersonal sex have nursed their loves selflessly while others have given all their resources to help the community, setting extraordinary examples for the rest of the society.

Stable relationships are valuable to society for many reasons, not just to prevent the spread of AIDS, and this means that all policies and legislation that work against them should be altered. This is especially true of welfare, since the need for welfare often forces couples to live separately and drives them apart.

■ In the Clinic and the Ward

Policy toward those who are actually sick should deal with individuals in ways that express society's value commitments and elicit their cooperation and trust. This will mean changes in society's response to illness of all kinds, not only to AIDS, which will involve public expenditures and more flexible policies. One common form of medical discrimination practiced implicitly in our society is to give more and better care to people who are felt to have no responsibility for their diseases, and this kind of inequality needs to be addressed. It will not be acceptable, however, to make massive diversions of health funding, and so it seems likely that the AIDS epidemic will cause a long-overdue rethinking of the American health system. This may involve some reductions in available health care, for there is certain to be a demand for controlling medical costs by reducing heroic medical interventions at public expense that will make no more than a few days' or weeks' difference, and if this is implemented throughout the system without discrimination, it seems reasonable. Experience in the AIDS ward of San Francisco's General Hospital suggests that when patients are in an environment where they are deeply convinced that every effort is being made to sustain quality of life, there is less insistence on futile and expensive interventions.

Although many patients live for considerable periods—even several years—after developing Kaposi sarcoma, and many recover from a bout of Pneumocystis pneumonia and are able to lead normal lives, there comes a time when multiple opportunistic infections converge and medications begin to conflict, a final slide toward death. Fortunately, there is a gradually emerging ethic, represented by the hospice and home care movements, that values making that final period as peaceful and comfortable as possible. It is not reasonable to expect the society to subsidize forms of care that are regarded as ineffectual. This applies to all patients, not just AIDS patients. It is unethical to prescribe massive doses of medication or expensive treatments to support the illusion of activity.

Individuals with full-blown AIDS will make choices that, while not putting other people at risk, are widely disapproved of, and here there seems to be a great deal to be gained from tolerance. Some will pursue therapies that the medical profession regards as valueless but that the victim experiences as helpful. Some will wish to commit suicide, and are being helped to do so responsibly in some European countries. Logically, it makes sense to try to dissuade individuals from suicide after a first diagnosis, when a considerable period of nearly normal living is still available without risk to others, but this epidemic may become the occasion for a reconsideration of the individual's right to end his or her own life. Voluntary euthanasia probably promotes more careful consideration and even postponement than the need some feel to achieve suicide before they become incapable of independent action, trapped in a hospital bed, and some suicidal improvisations are dangerous to others or lead to costly and unwanted emergency procedures. Because so many victims are at the prime of life, AIDS will probably be the focal point of thinking about death and dying over the next decade, and all Americans may be the beneficiaries of the increased sensitivity and realism it engenders.

AIDS patients also differ from other groups close to death in their concern for self-determination, including making their own decisions on treatment. Currently this is leading to a form of guerrilla medicine, unsupervised self-care and experimentation with unproved therapies. The solution is a greater partnership and respect between providers and patients, including respect of patient acceptance of experimentation and risk.

Hospital administrations will have to deal with fears of infection in their personnel. The numbers suggest that these fears are very much affected by public hysteria. There are 6.8 million people working in health care, and so far there have been nine cases of AIDS directly attributable to occupational accidents, occurring mostly when recommended precautions were not being observed. Hospital administrations have a two-sided task: at the same time that they must make sure health care workers do not neglect AIDS patients, they need to persuade workers actually to observe standard precautions. Supporting the morale of health care workers and protecting them from burnout and the impact of repeated failure will also increase willingness to work with AIDS patients.

Another kind of publicly supported medical investment is needed for better care of conditions that are not life-threatening but can be co-factors of AIDS, including all of the sexually transmitted diseases.

■ In the Research Lab

Medical research and drug approval will also call for restructuring. There is a demand for relaxing some of the restrictions on experimental drugs and permitting their use with patients who are clearly terminal. AIDS-related research is of many different kinds. The search for a vaccine has been immensely popular among drug companies but offers less promise of controlling the epidemic than do education and social change—there are huge theoretical and delivery problems to be surmounted before AIDS could go the way of smallpox and polio. The very concept of vaccine may be inapplicable because of HIV's use of the immune system itself. However, only medical research and treatment can address the problems of those actually infected with the virus, controlling or ending its ravages, treating opportunistic infections, and ultimately reconstituting the immune system. There are also issues about the coordination of research, since in some areas close coordination is most useful while in others a thousand flowers should bloom. Perhaps secrecy and duplications of effort motivated by the desire for a Nobel Prize or for huge manufacturing profits should be regarded as opportunistic infections of AIDS research, but the scientific community seems to do much of its most creative work under the spur of competition.

Implementation of policies like those just discussed is necessarily a piecemeal process, with decisions and procedures being taken at hundreds of different points. But human behavior is not generated piecemeal; rather, it expresses basic premises carried from one context to another and specifics learned by analogy. The best way to persuade individuals to behave differently in the bedroom is to create a consistent climate that is expressed in those more public places that are more easily influenced by public policy: in the classroom and in the boardroom, on the street corner and on the evening news.

Each of these proposals addresses an area where individual decisions are not likely to be adequate and public policy making is needed, but each needs to be complemented by new kinds of caution in all groups, personal decisions balanced and supported by public commitment. The same general principles hold, however, for both public and private behavior: responsible choices rest on genuine freedom; fear is a poor teacher; delay means loss of lives. If the population at large does not alter its sexual behavior until it has experienced the depth of loss and direct contact with suffering that the gay community has experienced, it will be too late to change.

Can we then visualize a society voluntarily arrived at in which all drug addicts and prostitutes are reformed and responsible members of society, all teenagers are cautious about sex, and all gays are semi-monogamous? Of course not. The vision here is of a society in which these choices are genuinely accessible, supported, and valued, and, because the choices are open, more aspects of behavior will be accessible to influence. But there is no such thing as a society in which every member is responsible.

Each of these proposals, phrased here in relation to the United States, needs rethinking and rephrasing to make it applicable in other parts of the world. It seems clear that any measures that combat ignorance and illiteracy and poverty will be helpful if the basic thrust is to give people genuine choice in protecting their own lives. AIDS drives home the message of global interdependence and demonstrates that sharp differences in quality of life are a source of instability. At the same time, rather basic information about the dangers of infection can make a difference in behavior, provided the individual has a sense of having choices. Those who are addicted to drugs feel that they have no choice; those who can barely buy food will not pay for condoms; those who do not know the alternatives cannot choose among them. The AIDS epidemic proposes a new commitment at a global level to literacy and economic opportunity.

It will not happen overnight. The first goal is a society in which the epidemic will cease to spread, and this means a society in which on the average each person infected with AIDS will transmit the disease to no more than one other person, over an apparently healthy infectious lifetime of five years or more. The next step must be to force the epidemic to recede. The number of people with full-blown AIDS will continue to rise for a decade unless there are major medical breakthroughs, and will level off five to ten years after the rate of new infection levels off. The rate of transmission per infected person has probably begun to slow, but the numbers of new infections are still rising.

What about costs? Every one of the proposals mentioned here requires social investment that will save money later. We live in a society that spends money lavishly on military preparedness under the rubric of "defense," but in this situation we should read a new meaning into that term. Talk about epidemics is always full of metaphors from warfare, metaphors of invasion and defense and infiltration, and in the area of expenditure at least, a military metaphor is useful. The most useful model for the kind of scientific mobilization needed to combat the AIDS epidemic may be the Manhattan Project. The most useful model for the social response to the epidemic is surely the response of urban Londoners to the Blitz: defense based on calm realism and mutual concern.

Outside the economic area, these warlike metaphors are flawed by the same simple assumption of competition that pervades most evolutionary discussion. Once in a while it is reasonable to speak of the total defeat of a disease, as in the eradication of smallpox. More often, the task of public health is an adjustment of mutual boundaries and niches that lowers the toll of disease. It may be that ultimately it will be possible to defeat AIDS. But in the meantime, it should be possible to learn to live with AIDS—possibly, indeed, to live better.

Warfare is an activity with only a single purpose, an activity in which priorities are simplified and energies are focused on a single goal of victory. But the proposals laid out here have multiple goals. Safer sex can control most sexual transmission of disease, and provide an effective option of family planning to whole populations. A genuine effort to improve conditions for minorities can bring all the benefits of full social participation, flowing in both directions. AIDS is a powerful reminder that ignorance and injustice are themselves insidious diseases that endanger the entire world community.

33

SO HOW DID I GET HERE? GROWING UP ON WELFARE

ROSEMARY L. BRAY

Growing up on welfare was a story I had planned to tell a long time from now, when I had children of my own. My childhood on Aid to Families with Dependent Children (A.F.D.C.) was going to be one of those stories I would tell my kids about the bad old days, an urban legend equivalent to Abe Lincoln studying by firelight. But I know now I cannot wait, because in spite of a wealth of evidence about the true nature of welfare and poverty in America, the debate has turned ugly, vicious and racist. The "welfare question" has become the race question and the woman question in disguise, and so far the answers bode well for no one.

In both blunt and coded terms, comfortable Americans more and more often bemoan the waste of their tax money on lazy black women with a love of copulation, a horror of birth control and a lack of interest in marriage. Were it not for the experiences of half my life, were I not black and female and of a certain age, perhaps I would be like so many people who blindly accept the lies and distortions, half-truths and wrongheaded notions about welfare. But for better or worse, I do know better. I know more than I want to know about being poor. I know that the welfare system is designed to be inadequate, to leave its constituents on the edge of survival. I know because I've been there.

And finally, I know that perhaps even more dependent on welfare than its

From *The New York Times Magazine*, December 1992. Reprinted by permission.

recipients are the large number of Americans who would rather accept this patchwork of economic horrors than fully address the real needs of real people.

My mother came to Chicago in 1947 with a fourth-grade education, cut short by working in the Mississippi fields. She pressed shirts in a laundry for a while and later waited tables in a restaurant, where she met my father. Mercurial and independent, with a sixth-grade education, my Arkansas-born father worked at whatever came to hand. He owned a lunch wagon for a time and prepared food for hours in our kitchen on the nights before he took the wagon out. Sometimes he hauled junk and sold it in the open-air markets of Maxwell Street on Sunday mornings. Eight years after they met—seven years after they married—I was born. My father made her quit her job; her work, he told her, was taking care of me. By the time I was 4, I had a sister, a brother and another brother on the way. My parents, like most other American couples of the 1950's, had their own American dream—a husband who worked, a wife who stayed home, a family of smiling children. But as was true for so many African-American couples, their American dream was an illusion.

The house on the corner of Berkeley Avenue and 45th Street is long gone. The other houses still stand, but today the neighborhood is an emptier, bleaker place. When we moved there, it was a street of old limestones with beveled glass windows, all falling into vague disrepair. Home was a four-room apartment on the first floor, in what must have been the public rooms of a formerly grand house. The rent was $110 a month. All of us kids slept in the big front room. Because I was the oldest, I had a bed of my own, near a big plate-glass window.

My mother and father had been married for several years before she realized he was a gambler who would never stay away from the track. By the time we moved to Berkeley Avenue, Daddy was spending more time gambling, and bringing home less and less money and more and more anger. Mama's simplest requests were met with rage. They fought once for hours when she asked for money to buy a tube of lipstick. It didn't help that I always seemed to need a doctor. I had allergies and bronchitis so severe that I nearly died one Sunday after church when I was about 3.

It was around this time that my mother decided to sign up for A.F.D.C. She explained to the caseworker that Daddy wasn't home much, and when he was he didn't have any money. Daddy was furious; Mama was adamant. "There were times when we hardly had a loaf of bread in here," she told me years later. "It was close. I wasn't going to let you all go hungry."

Going on welfare closed a door between my parents that never reopened. She joined the ranks of unskilled women who were forced to turn to the state for the security their men could not provide. In the sterile relationship between herself and the State of Illinois, Mama found an autonomy denied her by my father. It was she who could decide, at last, some part of her own fate and ours. A.F.D.C. relegated marginally productive men like my father to the ranks of failed patriarchs who no longer controlled the destiny of their families. Like so many of his peers, he could no longer afford the luxury of a woman who did as she was told because her economic life depended on it. Daddy became one of the shadow men who walked out back doors as caseworkers came in through the front. Why did he acquiesce? For all his anger, for all his frightening brutality, he loved us, so much that he swallowed his pride and periodically ceased to exist so that we might survive.

In 1960, the year my mother went on public aid, the poverty threshold for a family of five in the United States was $3,560 and the monthly payment to a family of five from the State of Illinois was $182.56, a total of $2,190.72 a year. Once the $110 rent was paid, Mama was left with $72.56 a month to take care of all the other expenses. By any standard, we were poor. All our lives were proscribed by the narrow line between not quite and just enough.

What did it take to live?

It took the kindness of friends as well as strangers, the charity of churches, low expectations, deprivation and patience. I can't begin to count the hours spent in long lines, long waits, long walks in pursuit of basic things. A visit to a local clinic (one housing doctors, a dentist and pharmacy in an incredibly crowded series of rooms) invariably took the better part of a day; I never saw the same doctor twice.

It took, as well, a turning of our collective backs on the letter of a law that required reporting even a small and important miracle like a present of $5. All families have their secrets, but I remember the weight of an extra burden. In a world where caseworkers were empowered to probe into every nook and cranny of our lives, silence became defense. Even now, there are things I will not publicly discuss because I cannot shake the fear that we might be hounded by the state, eager to prosecute us for the crime of survival.

All my memories of our years on A.F.D.C. are seasoned with unease. It's painful to remember how much every penny counted, how even a gap of 25 cents could make a difference in any given week. Few people understand how precarious life is from welfare check to welfare check, how the word "extra" has no meaning. Late mail, a bureaucratic mix-up . . . and a carefully planned method of survival lies in tatters.

What made our lives work as well as they did was my mother's genius at making do—worn into her by a childhood of rural poverty—along with her vivid imagination. She worked at home endlessly, shopped ruthlessly, bargained, cajoled, charmed. Her food store of choice was the one that stocked pork and beans, creamed corn, sardines, Vienna sausages and potted meat all at 10 cents a can. Clothing was the stuff of rummage sales, trips to Goodwill and bargain basements, where thin cotton and polyester reigned supreme. Our shoes came from a discount store that sold two pairs for $5.

It was an uphill climb, but there was no time for reflection; we were too busy with our everyday lives. Yet I remember how much it pained me to know that Mama, who recruited a neighbor to help her teach me how to read when I was 3, found herself left behind by her eldest daughter, then by each of us in turn. Her biggest worry was that we would grow up uneducated, so Mama enrolled us in parochial school.

When one caseworker angrily questioned how she could afford to send four children to St. Ambrose School, my mother, who emphatically declared "My kids need an education," told her it was none of her business. (In fact, the school had a volume discount of sorts; the price of tuition dropped with each child you sent. I still don't know quite how she managed it.) She organized our lives around church and school, including Mass every morning at 7:45. My brother was an altar boy; I laid out the vestments each afternoon for the next day's Mass. She volunteered as a chaperone for every class trip, sat with us as we did homework she did not understand herself. She and my father reminded us again and again and again that every book, every test, every page of homework was in fact a ticket out and away from the life we lived.

My life on welfare ended on June 4, 1976—a month after my 21st birthday, two weeks after I graduated from Yale. My father, eaten up with cancer and rage, lived just long enough to know the oldest two of us had graduated from college and were on our own. Before the decade ended, all of us had left the welfare rolls. The eldest of my brothers worked at the post office, assumed support of my mother (who also went to work, as a companion to an elderly woman) and earned his master's degree at night. My sister married and got a job at a bank. My baby brother parked cars and found a wife. Mama's biggest job was done at last; the investment made in our lives by the State of Illinois had come to fruition. Five people on welfare for 18 years had become five working, taxpaying adults. Three of us went to college, two of us finished; one of us has an advanced degree; all of us can take care of ourselves.

Ours was a best-case phenomenon, based on the synergy of church and state, the government and the private sector and the thousand points of light that we called friends and neighbors. But there was something more: What fueled our dreams and fired our belief that our lives could change for the better was the promise of the civil rights movement and the war on poverty—for millions of African-Americans the defining events of the 1960's. Caught up in the heady atmosphere of imminent change, our world was filled not only with issues and ideas but with amazing images of black people engaged in the struggle for long-denied rights and freedoms. We knew other people lived differently than we did, we knew we didn't have much, but we didn't mind, because we knew it wouldn't be long. My mother borrowed a phrase I had read to her once from Dick Gregory's autobiography: Not poor, just broke. She would repeat it often, as often as she sang hymns in the kitchen. She loved to sing a spiritual Mahalia Jackson had made famous: "Move On Up a Little Higher." Like so many others, Mama was singing about earth as well as heaven.

These are the things I remember every time I read another article outlining America's welfare crisis. The rage I feel about the welfare debate comes from listening to a host of lies, distortions and exaggerations—and taking them personally.

I am no fool. I know of few women—on welfare or off—with my mother's grace and courage and stamina. I know not all women on welfare are cut from the same cloth. Some are lazy; some are ground down. Some are too young; many are without husbands. A few have made welfare fraud a lucrative career; a great many more have pushed the rules on outside income to their very limits.

I also know that none of these things justify our making welfare a test of character and worthiness, rather than an acknowledgment of need. Near-sainthood should not be a requirement for financial and medical assistance.

But all manner of sociologists and policy gurus continue to equate issues that simply aren't equivalent—welfare, race, rates of poverty, crime, marriage and childbirth—and to reach conclusions that serve to demonize the poor. More than one social arbiter would have us believe that we have all been mistaken for the last 30 years—that the efforts to relieve the most severe effects of poverty have not only failed but have served instead to increase and expand the ranks of the poor. In keeping women, children and men from starvation, we are told, we have also kept them from self-sufficiency. In our zeal to do good, we have undermined the work ethic, the family and thus, by association, the country itself.

So how did I get here?

Despite attempts to misconstrue and discredit the social programs and policies that changed—even saved—my life, certain facts remain. Poverty was reduced by 39 percent between 1960 and 1990, according to the Census Bureau, from 22.2 percent to 13.5 percent of the nation's population. That is far too many poor people, but the rate is considerably lower than it might have been if we had thrown up our hands and reminded ourselves that the poor will always be with us. Of black women considered "highly dependent," that is, on welfare for more than seven years, 81 percent of their daughters grow up to live productive lives off the welfare rolls, a 1992 Congressional report stated; the 19 percent who become second-generation welfare recipients can hardly be said to constitute an epidemic of welfare dependency. The vast majority of African-Americans are now working or middle class, an achievement that occurred in the past 30 years, most specifically between 1960 and 1973, the years of expansion in the very same social programs that it is so popular now to savage. Those were the same years in which I changed from girl to woman, learned to read and think, graduated from high school and college, came to be a working woman, a taxpayer, a citizen.

In spite of all the successes we know of, in spite of the reality that the typical welfare recipient is a white woman with young children, ideologues have continued to fashion from whole cloth the specter of the mythical black welfare mother, complete with a prodigious reproductive capacity and a galling laziness, accompanied by the uncaring and equally lazy black man in her life who will not work, will not marry her and will not support his family.

Why has this myth been promoted by some of the best (and the worst) people in government, academia, journalism and industry? One explanation may be that the constant presence of poverty frustrates even the best-intentioned among us. It may also be because the myth allows for denial about who the poor in America really are and for denial about the depth and intransigence of racism regardless of economic status. And because getting tough on welfare is for some a first-class career move; what better way to win a position in the next administration than to trash those people least able to respond? And, finally, because it serves to assure white Americans that lazy black people aren't getting away with anything.

Many of these prescriptions for saving America from the welfare plague not only reflect an insistent, if sometimes unconscious, racism but rest on the bedrock of patriarchy. They are rooted in the fantasy of a male presence as a path to social and economic salvation and in its corollary—the image of woman as passive chattel, constitutionally so afflicted by her condition that the only recourse is to transfer her care from the hands of the state to the hands of a man with a job. The largely ineffectual plans to create jobs for men in communities ravaged by disinvestment, the state-sponsored dragnets for men who cannot or will not support their children, the exhortations for women on welfare to find themselves a man and get married, all are the institutional expressions of the same worn cultural illusion—that women and children without a man are fundamentally damaged goods. Men are such a boon, the reasoning goes, because they make more money than women do.

Were we truly serious about an end to poverty among women and children, we would take the logical next step. We would figure out how to make sure women who did a dollar's worth of work got a dollar's worth of pay. We would make sure that women could go to work with their minds at ease, knowing their children were well cared for. What women on welfare need, in large measure, are the things key to the life of every adult woman: economic security and autonomy. Women need the skills and the legitimate opportunity to earn a living for ourselves as well as for people who may rely on us; we need the freedom to make choices to improve our own lives and the lives of those dear to us.

"The real problem is not welfare," says Kathryn Edin, a professor of sociology at Rutgers University and a scholar in residence at the Russell Sage Foundation. "The real problem is the nature of low-wage work and lack of support for these workers—most of whom happen to be women raising their children alone."

Completing a five-year study of single mothers—some low-wage workers, some welfare recipients—Edin is quantifying what common sense and bitter experience have told millions of women who rotate off and on the welfare rolls: Women, particularly unskilled women with children, get the worst jobs available, with the least amount of health care, and are the most frequently laid off. "The workplace is not oriented toward people who have family responsibilities," she says. "Most jobs are set up assuming that someone else is minding the kids and doesn't need assistance."

But the writers and scholars and politicians who wax most rhapsodic about the need to replace welfare with work make their harsh judgments from the comfortable and supportive environs of offices and libraries and think tanks. If they need to go to the bathroom midsentence, there is no one timing their absence. If they take longer than a half-hour for lunch, there is no one waiting to dock their pay. If their baby sitter gets sick, there is no risk of someone having taken their place at work by the next morning. Yet these are conditions that low-wage women routinely face, which inevitably lead to the cyclical nature of their welfare histories. These are the realities that many of the most vocal and widely quoted critics of welfare routinely ignore. In his book "The End of Equality," for example, Mickey Kaus discusses social and economic inequity, referring to David Ellwood's study on long-term welfare dependency without ever mentioning that it counts anyone who uses the services for at least one month as having been on welfare for the entire year.

In the heated atmosphere of the welfare debate, the larger society is encouraged to believe that women on welfare have so violated the social contract that they have forfeited all rights common to those of us lucky enough not to be poor. In no area is this attitude more clearly demonstrated than in issues of sexuality and childbearing. Consider the following: A Philadelphia Inquirer editorial of Dec. 12, 1990, urges the use of Norplant contraceptive inserts for welfare recipients—in spite of repeated warnings from women's health groups of its dangerous side effects—in the belief that the drug "could be invaluable in breaking the cycle of inner-city poverty." (The newspaper apologized for the editorial after it met widespread criticism, both within and outside the paper.) A California judge orders a woman on welfare, convicted of abusing two of her four children, to use Norplant; the judge's decision was appealed. The Washington state legislature considers approving cash payments of up to $10,000 for women on welfare who agree to be sterilized. These and other proposals, all centering on women's reproductive capacities, were advanced in spite of evidence that welfare recipients have fewer children than those not on welfare.

The punitive energy behind these and so many other Draconian actions and proposals goes beyond the desire to decrease welfare costs; it cuts to the heart of the nation's racial and sexual hysteria. Generated neither by law nor by fully informed public debate, these actions amount to social control over "those people on welfare"—a control many Americans feel they have bought and paid for every April 15. The question is obvious: If citizens were really aware of who receives welfare in America, however inadequate it is, if they acknowledged that white women and children were welfare's primary beneficiaries, would most of these things be happening?

Welfare has become a code word now. One that enables white Americans to mask their sometimes malignant, sometimes benign racism behind false concerns about the suffering ghetto poor and their negative impact on the rest of us. It has become the vehicle many so-called tough thinkers use to undermine compassionate policy and engineer the reduction of social programs.

So how *did* I get here?

I kept my drawers up and my dress down, to quote my mother. I didn't end up pregnant because I had better things to do. I knew I did because my uneducated, Southern-born parents told me so. Their faith, their focus on our futures are a far cry from the thesis of Nicholas Lemann, whose widely acclaimed book "The Promised Land" perpetuates the myth of black Southern sharecropping society as a primary source of black urban malaise. Most important, my family and I had every reason to believe that I had better things to do and that when I got older I would be able to do them. I had a mission, a calling, work to do that only I could do. And that is knowledge transmitted not just by parents, or school, or churches. It is a palpable thing, available by osmosis from the culture of the neighborhood and the world at large.

Add to this formula a whopping dose of dumb luck. It was my sixth-grade teacher, Sister Maria Sarto, who identified in me the first signs of a stifling boredom and told my mother that I needed a tougher, more challenging curriculum than her school could provide. It was she who then tracked down the private Francis W. Parker School, which agreed to give me a scholarship if I passed the admissions test.

Had I been born a few years earlier, or a decade later, I might now be living on welfare in the Robert Taylor Homes or working as a hospital nurse's aide for $6.67 an hour. People who think such things could never have happened to me haven't met enough poor people to know better. The avenue of escape can be very narrow indeed. The hope and energy of the 1960's—fueled not only by a growing economy but by all the passions of a great national quest—is long gone. The sense of possibility I knew has been replaced with the popular cultural currency that money and those who have it are everything and those without are nothing.

Much has been made of the culture of the underclass, the culture of poverty, as though they were the free-floating illnesses of the African-American poor, rendering them immune to other influences: the widespread American culture of greed, for example, or of cynicism. It is a thinly veiled continuation of the endless projection of "dis-ease" onto black life, a convenient way to sidestep a more painful debate about the loss of meaning in American life that has made our entire nation depressed and dispirited. The malaise that has overtaken our country is hardly confined to African-Americans or the poor, and if both groups should disappear tomorrow, our nation would still find itself in crisis. To talk of the black "underclass threat" to the public sphere, as Mickey Kaus does, to demonize the poor among us and thus by association all of us— ultimately this does more damage to the body politic than a dozen welfare queens.

When I walk down the streets of my Harlem neighborhood, I see women like my mother, hustling, struggling, walking their children to school and walking them back home. And I also see women who have lost both energy and faith, talking loud, hanging out. I see the shadow men of a new generation, floating by with a few dollars and a toy, then drifting away to the shelters they call home. And I see, a dozen times a day, the little girls my sister and I used to be, the little boys my brothers once were.

Even the grudging, inadequate public help I once had is fading fast for them. The time and patience they will need to re-create themselves is vanishing under pressure for the big, quick fix and the crushing load of blame being heaped upon them. In the big cities and the small towns of America, we have let theory, ideology and mythology about welfare and poverty overtake these children and their parents.

PART TEN

THE SCHOOLS

Hardly a year goes by without another dire report on the sad state of America's public schools. Although they are often reasonably satisfied with the schools their own children attend, many Americans believe that the schools in general are falling apart. Bad schools are blamed for a host of our national problems, from declining economic competitiveness to the violence and drugs in our cities.

As many commentators (including Peter Schrag here) have pointed out, the popular image of the schools is more than a little misleading. *Overall,* the public schools are not necessarily as bad as they are often said to be. They are educating more children, from a wider range of backgrounds—and often with more difficult problems—than ever before. Scores on achievement tests, which fell disturbingly in the 1970s, aren't falling any more. More American students go on to college than those of most other industrial countries—and our system of higher education remains one of the best in the world, drawing students from every part of the globe.

But the problems, if sometimes exaggerated, are nevertheless very real. The three articles in this part help us to pinpoint where the schools are in the most serious trouble and help us to think critically about the possibilities for constructive change.

Jonathan Kozol's grim description of the deteriorating schools in the poverty-stricken city of East St. Louis illustrates the most dramatic of those problems: the "savage" inequalities that continue to split America's school-children into educational haves and have-nots. From backed-up sewage in the kitchen to poorly paid and overworked teachers to a gym with no heat in the winter, East St. Louis's schools, like those in poor communities across the country, are a stark reminder of how far we remain from anything approaching equal educational opportunity. Kozol's disturbing portrait reminds us, too, that inequality inside the schools can't be separated from the widening social and economic gaps outside them. As long as children are condemned by race and income to live in declining communities without jobs, public services, or futures, the schools are likely to reflect the message that as a society we regard those young people as fundamentally expendable.

As Harvey Kantor and Barbara Brenzel point out in "Urban Education and the 'Truly Disadvantaged,'" this unhappy situation isn't altogether new. The educational chasm between the impoverished inner city and the affluent suburb was well charted by critics as far back as the 1950s. Recognizing that the crisis of the inner-city schools was a "recipe for disaster," they urged a broad mix of school reforms and other help for disadvantaged children. But as Kantor and Brenzel show in troubling detail, the forces underlying the perilous condition of urban schools have generally gotten worse, not better, in the intervening years. The cities have lost jobs and income to the suburbs and, partly as a consequence, have become even more racially concentrated. Those shifts caused a steady transformation of many urban school districts, as the population of white students fell and that of heavily disadvantaged minority students rose. As the inner-city schools become more and more responsible for coping with the multiple social problems of the stricken cities, they have also become "more and more associated with educational failure." The result, according to the authors, has been a widening gap between "nationwide progress and inner-city decline" in our school systems.

The concentration of problems in the urban schools has spurred a growing movement of more affluent Americans out of the public schools altogether. As Peter Schrag points out, the sense that urban public schools are both inadequate and dangerous, along with the poor showing of American students in comparison with those from many other countries, has led to a search for strong medicine for the ailing schools. One idea—increasingly popular since the 1980s—is school "choice." In the most extreme version of this approach, parents would receive "vouchers" allowing them to send their children to any school of their choice—including private and religious ones. According to its advocates, that would not only give children and parents a wider range of choices among existing schools, but would exert pressure on the schools to improve—or lose out in the competition. Schrag, however—along with other critics—thinks otherwise. The schools, he agrees, certainly need reforming. But the "choice approach" fails to address the social and economic changes that drive the crisis of the urban schools. More likely, choice will simply allow many more affluent parents to opt out of concern for the public schools—and for other people's children—altogether, leaving poor children at the bottom of what will increasingly become a "two-tiered" school system. In place of the classic American democratic ideal of "common" school for everyone, school choice would, Schrag argues, institutionalize the trend toward a dual school system in the United States—a fairly good one for the better-off, and a second, increasingly stigmatized one for the children of the poor.

34

LIFE ON THE MISSISSIPPI: EAST ST. LOUIS, ILLINOIS

JONATHAN KOZOL

E ast of anywhere," writes a reporter for the *St. Louis Post-Dispatch*, "often evokes the other side of the tracks. But, for a first-time visitor suddenly deposited on its eerily empty streets, East St. Louis might suggest another world." The city, which is 98 percent black, has no obstetric services, no regular trash collection, and few jobs. Nearly a third of its families live on less than $7,500 a year; 75 percent of its population lives on welfare of some form. The U.S. Department of Housing and Urban Development describes it as "the most distressed small city in America."

Only three of the 13 buildings on Missouri Avenue, one of the city's major thoroughfares, are occupied. A 13-story office building, tallest in the city, has been boarded up. Outside, on the sidewalk, a pile of garbage fills a ten-foot crater.

The city, which by night and day is clouded by the fumes that pour from vents and smokestacks at the Pfizer and Monsanto chemical plants, has one of the highest rates of child asthma in America.

It is, according to a teacher at the University of Southern Illinois, "a repository for a nonwhite population that is now regarded as expendable." The *Post-Dispatch* describes it as "America's Soweto."

The problems of the streets in urban areas, as teachers often note, frequently spill over into public schools. In the public schools of East St. Louis this is literally the case.

"Martin Luther King Junior High School," notes the *Post-Dispatch* in a story published in the early spring of 1989, "was evacuated Friday afternoon after sewage flowed into the kitchen. . . . The kitchen was closed and students were sent home." On Monday, the paper continues, "East St. Louis Senior High School was awash in sewage for the second time this year." The school had to be shut because of "fumes and backed-up toilets." Sewage flowed into the basement, through the floor, then up into the kitchen and the students' bathrooms. The backup, we read, "occurred in the food preparation areas."

School is resumed the following morning at the high school, but a few days later the overflow recurs. This time the entire system is affected, since the meals distributed to every student in the city are prepared in the two schools that have been flooded. School is called off for all 16,500 students in the district. The sewage backup, caused by the failure of two pumping stations, forces officials at the high school to shut down the furnaces.

At Martin Luther King, the parking lot and gym are also flooded. "It's a disaster," says a legislator. "The streets are underwater; gaseous fumes are being emitted from the pipes under the schools," she says, "making people ill."

In the same week, the schools announce the layoff of 280 teachers, 166 cooks and cafeteria workers, 25 teacher aides, 16 custodians and 18 painters, electricians, engineers and plumbers. The president of the teachers' union says the cuts, which will bring the size of kindergarten and primary classes up to 30 students, and the size of fourth to twelfth grade classes up to 35, will have "an unimaginable impact" on the students. "If you have a high school teacher with five classes each day and between 150 and 175 students. . . , it's going to have a devastating effect." The school system, it is also noted, has been using more than 70 "permanent substitute teachers," who are paid only $10,000 yearly, as a way of saving money.

Governor Thompson, however, tells the press that he will not pour money into East St. Louis to solve long-term problems. East St. Louis residents, he says, must help themselves. "There is money in the community," the governor insists. "It's just not being spent for what it should be spent for."

The governor, while acknowledging that East St. Louis faces economic problems, nonetheless refers dismissively to those who live in East St. Louis. "What in the community," he asks, "is being done right?" He takes the opportunity of a visit to the area to announce a fiscal grant for sewer improvement to a relatively wealthy town nearby.

In East St. Louis, meanwhile, teachers are running out of chalk and paper, and their paychecks are arriving two weeks late. The city warns its teachers to expect a cut of half their pay until the fiscal crisis has been eased.

The threatened teacher layoffs are mandated by the Illinois Board of Education, which, because of the city's fiscal crisis, has been given supervisory control of the school budget. Two weeks later the state superintendent partially relents. In a tone very different from that of the governor, he notes that East

St. Louis does not have the means to solve its education problems on its own. "There is no natural way," he says, that "East St. Louis can bring itself out of this situation." Several cuts will be required in any case—one quarter of the system's teachers, 75 teacher aides, and several dozen others will be given notice—but, the state board notes, sports and music programs will not be affected.

East St. Louis, says the chairman of the state board, "is simply the worst possible place I can imagine to have a child brought up. . . . The community is in desperate circumstances." Sports and music, he observes, are, for many children here, "the only avenues of success." Sadly enough, no matter how it ratifies the stereotype, this is the truth; and there is a poignant aspect to the fact that, even with class size soaring and one quarter of the system's teachers being given their dismissal, the state board of education demonstrates its genuine but skewed compassion by attempting to leave sports and music untouched by the overall austerity.

Even sports facilities, however, are degrading by comparison with those found and expected at most high schools in America. The football field at East St. Louis High is missing almost everything—including goalposts. There are a couple of metal pipes—no crossbar, just the pipes. Bob Shannon, the football coach, who has to use his personal funds to purchase footballs and has had to cut and rake the football field himself, has dreams of having goalposts someday. He'd also like to let his students have new uniforms. The ones they wear are nine years old and held together somehow by a patchwork of repairs. Keeping them clean is a problem, too. The school cannot afford a washing machine. The uniforms are carted to a corner laundromat with fifteen dollars' worth of quarters.

Other football teams that come to play, according to the coach, are shocked to see the field and locker rooms. They want to play without a half-time break and get away. The coach reports that he's been missing paychecks, but he's trying nonetheless to raise some money to help out a member of the team whose mother has just died of cancer.

"The days of the tight money have arrived," he says. "It don't look like Moses will be coming to this school."

He tells me he has been in East St. Louis 19 years and has been the football coach for 14 years. "I was born," he says, "in Natchez, Mississippi. I stood on the courthouse steps of Natchez with Charles Evers. I was a teen-age boy when Michael Schwerner and the other boys were murdered. I've been in the struggle all along. In Mississippi, it was the fight for legal rights. This time, it's a struggle for survival.

"In certain ways," he says, "it's harder now because in those days it was a clear enemy you had to face, a man in a hood and not a statistician. No one could persuade you that you were to blame. Now the choices seem like they are left to you and, if you make the wrong choice, you are made to understand you are to blame. . . .

"Night-time in this city, hot and smoky in the summer, there are dealers standin' out on every street. Of the kids I see here, maybe 55 percent will graduate from school. Of that number, maybe one in four will go to college. How many will stay? That is a bigger question.

"The basic essentials are simply missing here. When we go to wealthier schools I look at the faces of my boys. They don't say a lot. They have their faces to the windows, lookin' out. I can't tell what they are thinking. I am hopin' they are saying, 'This is something I will give my kids someday.'"

Tall and trim, his black hair graying slightly, he is 45 years old.

"No, my wife and I don't live here. We live in a town called Ferguson, Missouri. I was born in poverty and raised in poverty. I feel that I owe it to myself to live where they pick up the garbage."

In the visitors' locker room, he shows me lockers with no locks. The weight room stinks of sweat and water-rot. "See, this ceiling is in danger of collapsing. See, this room don't have no heat in winter. But we got to come here anyway. We wear our coats while working out. I tell the boys, 'We got to get it done. Our fans don't know that we do not have heat.'"

He tells me he arrives at school at 7:45 A.M. and leaves at 6:00 P.M.—except in football season, when he leaves at 8:00 P.M. "This is my life. It isn't all I dreamed of and I tell myself sometimes that I might have accomplished more. But growing up in poverty rules out some avenues. You do the best you can."

In the wing of the school that holds vocational classes, a damp, unpleasant odor fills the halls. The school has a machine shop, which cannot be used for lack of staff, and a woodworking shop. The only shop that's occupied this morning is the auto-body class. A man with long blond hair and wearing a white sweat suit swings a paddle to get children in their chairs. "What we need the most is new equipment," he reports. "I have equipment for alignment, for example, but we don't have money to install it. We also need a better form of egress. We bring the cars in through two other classes." Computerized equipment used in most repair shops, he reports, is far beyond the high school's budget. It looks like a very old gas station in an isolated rural town.

Stopping in the doorway of a room with seven stoves and three refrigerators, I am told by a white teacher that this is a class called "Introductory Home Ec." The 15 children in the room, however, are not occupied with work. They are scattered at some antiquated tables, chatting with each other. The teacher explains that students do no work on Friday, which, she says, is "clean-up day." I ask her whether she regards this class as preparation for employment. "Not this class," she says. "The ones who move on to Advanced Home Ec. are given job instruction." When I ask her what jobs they are trained for, she says: "Fast food places—Burger King, McDonald's."

The science labs at East St. Louis High are 30 to 50 years outdated. John McMillan, a soft-spoken man, teaches physics at the school. He shows me his lab. The six lab stations in the room have empty holes where pipes were once attached. "It would be great if we had water," says McMillan.

Wiping his hand over his throat, he tells me that he cannot wear a tie or jacket in the lab. "I want you to notice the temperature," he says. "The heating system's never worked correctly. Days when it's zero outside it will be 100

Fahrenheit within this room. I will be here 25 years starting September—in the same room, teaching physics. I have no storage space. Those balance scales are trash. There are a few small windows you can open. We are on the side that gets the sun."

Stepping outside the lab, he tells me that he lives in East St. Louis, one block from the school. Balding and damp-looking in his open collar, he is a bachelor 58 years old.

The biology lab, which I visit next, has no laboratory tables. Students work at regular desks. "I need dissecting kits," the teacher says. "The few we have are incomplete." Chemical supplies, she tells me, in a city poisoned by two chemical plants, are scarce. "I need more microscopes," she adds.

The chemistry lab is the only one that's properly equipped. There are eight lab tables with gas jets and water. But the chemistry teacher says he rarely brings his students to the lab. "I have 30 children in a class and cannot supervise them safely. Chemical lab work is unsafe with more than 20 children to a teacher. If I had some lab assistants, we could make use of the lab. As it is, we have to study mainly from a text."

Even texts are scarce, however. "We were short of books for four months last semester. When we got replacement copies, they were different from the texts that we already had. So that presented a new problem. . . .

"Despite these failings, I have had two students graduate from MIT."

"In how many years?" I ask.

He tells me, "Twenty-three."

Leaving the chemistry labs, I pass a double-sized classroom in which roughly 60 kids are sitting fairly still but doing nothing. "This is supervised study hall," a teacher tells me in the corridor. But when we step inside, he finds there is no teacher. "The teacher must be out today," he says.

Irl Solomon's history classes, which I visit next, have been described by journalists who cover East St. Louis as the highlight of the school. Solomon, a man of 54 whose reddish hair is turning white, has taught in urban schools for almost 30 years. A graduate of Brandeis University in 1961, he entered law school but was drawn away by a concern with civil rights. "After one semester, I decided that the law was not for me. I said, 'Go and find the toughest place there is to teach. See if you like it.' I'm still here. . . .

"This is not by any means the worst school in the city," he reports, as we are sitting in his classroom on the first floor of the school. "But our problems are severe. I don't even know where to begin. I have no materials with the exception of a single textbook given to each child. If I bring in anything else—books or tapes or magazines—I pay for it myself. The high school has no VCRs. They are such a crucial tool. So many good things run on public television. I can't make use of anything I see unless I can unhook my VCR and bring it into school. The AV equipment in the building is so old that we are pressured not to use it."

Teachers like Mr. Solomon, working in low-income districts such as East St. Louis, often tell me that they feel cut off from educational developments in modern public schools. "Well, it's amazing," Solomon says. "I have done without so much so long that, if I were assigned to a suburban school, I'm not sure I'd recognize what they are doing. We are utterly cut off."

Of 33 children who begin the history classes in the standard track, he says, more than a quarter have dropped out by spring semester. "Maybe 24 are left by June. Mind you, this is in the junior year. We're speaking of the children who survived. Ninth and tenth grades are the more horrendous years for leaving school.

"I have four girls right now in my senior home room who are pregnant or have just had babies. When I ask them why this happens, I am told, 'Well, there's no reason not to have a baby. There's not much for me in public school.' The truth is, that's a pretty honest answer. A diploma from a ghetto high school doesn't count for much in the United States today. So, if this is really the last education that a person's going to get, she's probably perceptive in that statement. Ah, there's so much bitterness—unfairness—there, you know. Most of these pregnant girls are not the ones who have much self-esteem. . . .

"Very little education in the school would be considered academic in the suburbs. Maybe 10 to 15 percent of students are in truly academic programs. Of the 55 percent who graduate, 20 percent may go to four-year colleges: something like 10 percent of any entering class. Another 10 to 20 percent may get some other kind of higher education. An equal number join the military. . . .

"I get $38,000 after nearly 30 years of teaching. If I went across the river to one of the suburbs of St. Louis, I'd be earning $47,000, maybe more. If I taught in the Chicago suburbs, at a wealthy high school like New Trier, for example, I'd be getting close to $60,000. Money's not an issue for me, since I wouldn't want to leave; but, for new, incoming teachers, this much differential is a great deterrent. When you consider that many teachers are afraid to come here in the first place, or, if they are not afraid, are nonetheless offended by the setting or intimidated by the challenge of the job, there should be a premium and not a punishment for teaching here.

"Sometimes I get worried that I'm starting to burn out. Still, I hate to miss a day. The department frequently can't find a substitute to come here, and my kids don't like me to be absent."

Solomon's advanced class, which soon comes into the room, includes some lively students with strong views.

"I don't go to physics class, because my lab has no equipment," says one student. "The typewriters in my typing class don't work. The women's toilets . . . " She makes a sour face. "I'll be honest," she says. "I just don't use the toilets. If I do, I come back into class and I feel dirty."

"I wanted to study Latin," says another student. "But we don't have Latin in this school."

"We lost our only Latin teacher," Solomon says. . . .

Clark Junior High School is regarded as the top school in the city. I visit, in part, at the request of school officials, who would like me to see education in the city at its very best. Even here, however, there is a disturbing sense that one has entered a backwater of America.

"We spend the entire eighth grade year preparing for the state exams," a teacher tells me in a top-ranked English class. The teacher seems devoted to the children, but three students sitting near me sleep through the entire period. The teacher rouses one of them, a girl in the seat next to me, but the student promptly lays her head back on her crossed arms and is soon asleep again. Four of the 14 ceiling lights are broken. The corridor outside the room is filled with voices. Outside the window, where I see no schoolyard, is an empty lot.

In a mathematics class of 30 children packed into a space that might be adequate for 15 kids, there is one white student. The first white student I have seen in East St. Louis, she is polishing her nails with bright red polish. A tiny black girl next to her is writing with a one-inch pencil stub.

In a seventh grade social studies class, the only book that bears some relevance to black concerns—its title is *The American Negro*—bears a publication date of 1967. The teacher invites me to ask the class some questions. Uncertain where to start, I ask the students what they've learned about the civil rights campaigns of recent decades.

A 14-year-old girl with short black curly hair says this: "Every year in February we are told to read the same old speech of Martin Luther King. We read it every year. 'I have a dream. . . .' It does begin to seem—what is the word?" She hesitates and then she finds the word: "perfunctory."

I ask her what she means.

"We have a school in East St. Louis named for Dr. King," she says. "The school is full of sewer water and the doors are locked with chains. Every student in that school is black. It's like a terrible joke on history."

It startles me to hear her words, but I am startled even more to think how seldom any press reporter has observed the irony of naming segregated schools for Martin Luther King. Children reach the heart of these hypocrisies much quicker than the grown-ups and the experts do.

"I would like to comment on that," says another 14-year-old student, named Shalika. "I have had to deal with this all of my life. I started school in Fairview Heights. My mother pushes me and she had wanted me to get a chance at better education. Only one other student in my class was black. I was in the fifth grade, and at that age you don't understand the ugliness in people's hearts. They wouldn't play with me. I couldn't understand it. During recess I would stand there by myself beside the fence. Then one day I got a note: 'Go back to Africa.'

"To tell the truth, it left a sadness in my heart. Now you hear them sayin' on TV, 'What's the matter with these colored people? Don't they care about their children's education?' But my mother did the best for me she knew. It was not my mother's fault that I was not accepted by those people."

"It does not take long," says Christopher, a light-skinned boy with a faint mustache and a somewhat heated and perspiring look, "for little kids to learn they are not wanted."

Shalika is small and looks quite young for junior high. In each ear she wears a small enameled pin of Mickey Mouse. "To some degree I do believe," she says, "that this is caused by press reports. You see a lot about the crimes committed here in East St. Louis when you turn on the TV. Do they show the crimes committed by the government that *puts* black people here? Why are all the dirty businesses like chemicals and waste disposal here? This is a big country. Couldn't they find another place to put their poison?"

"Shalika," the teacher tells me afterward, "will go to college."

"Why is it this way?" asks Shalika in a softer voice again. But she doesn't ask the question as if she is waiting for an answer.

"Is it 'separate but equal,' then?" I ask. "Have we gone back a hundred years?"

"It is separate. That's for sure," the teacher says. She is a short and stocky middle-aged black woman. "Would you want to tell the children it is equal?"

Christopher approaches me at the end of class. The room is too hot. His skin looks warm and his black hair is damp. "Write this down. You asked a question about Martin Luther King. I'm going to say something. All that stuff about 'the dream' means nothing to the kids I know in East St. Louis. So far as they're concerned, he died in vain. He was famous and he lived and gave his speeches and he died and now he's gone. But we're still here. Don't tell students in this school about 'the dream.' Go and look into a toilet here if you would like to know what life is like for students in this city."

Before I leave, I do as Christopher asked and enter a boy's bathroom. Four of the six toilets do not work. The toilet stalls, which are eaten away by red and brown corrosion, have no doors. The toilets have no seats. One has a rotted wooden stump. There are no paper towels and no soap. Near the door there is a loop of wire with an empty toilet-paper roll.

"This," says Sister Julia, "is the best school that we have in East St. Louis."

URBAN EDUCATION AND THE "TRULY DISADVANTAGED": THE HISTORICAL ROOTS OF THE CONTEMPORARY CRISIS

HARVEY KANTOR AND BARBARA BRENZEL

Thirty years ago James Bryant Conant alarmed the nation by calling attention to the inadequacies of urban education. Concerned about the growing disparity between inner-city schools and schools in the suburbs, Conant pointed out that while suburban schools prospered, urban schools were in a state of crisis, plagued by insufficient funding and outdated facilities, low academic achievement, and exceedingly high dropout rates. Indeed, Conant warned the nation that the deterioration of urban schooling coupled with high levels of youth unemployment and the persistence of racial segregation was a recipe for social disaster that threatened the health of the nation's large cities and could be avoided only by improving urban schools and broadening the employment prospects of inner-city youth.

Beginning in the 1960s, the federal government launched an unprecedented series of programs to address the urban problems Conant had documented.

From Teachers College *Record*, Winter 1992. Copyright by Teachers College, Columbia University. Reprinted by permission. Portions of the original have been omitted.

Together with other initiatives begun by states and local school districts, these programs provided much-needed funding for urban schools and contributed to some measurable gains in achievement as well as an increase in educational attainment among economically disadvantaged and minority children. Despite these programs and the improvements they produced, urban schools today remain in a state of crisis. After two and a half decades of federal, state, and local efforts to improve urban education for low-income and minority children, achievement in inner-city schools continues to lag behind national norms and dropout rates in inner-city high schools (especially among African-American and Hispanic youth) remain distressingly high, while many of those who do graduate are often so poorly prepared they cannot compete successfully in the labor market. One recent report on urban education concluded that because of the continued failure to educate city children, many people now dismiss urban schools "as little more than human storehouses to keep young people off the streets."

Liberals and conservatives offer different explanations for the persistence of this crisis in urban education. The standard liberal view generally attributes the contemporary crisis in urban education to the inadequacies of the reforms instituted in the 1960s. According to this view, even though the Great Society stimulated a considerable effort at both the national and local levels to address the problems of urban education, the escalation of the war in Vietnam, the growth of inflation, and the urban riots of the 1960s eroded the country's financial and political commitment to equal opportunity and racial justice before the new school reforms could be funded sufficiently or implemented adequately. The end result has been a patchwork of new programs too marginal and too fragmented to have much impact on urban schooling and the education of poor and minority children. Many liberal observers contend that because of the constraints imposed on the social policies of the 1960s, the changes in schooling were actually much less substantial than some critics subsequently claimed.

Conservative critics also blame the crisis in urban education on the failure of the policies initiated in the 1960s, but in contrast to the liberal view, the conservative perspective maintains that the current failure of urban schooling is due to the very nature of the reforms themselves. According to this view, efforts to end school segregation, provide compensatory educational services for the poor, and expand participation in school governance, however well-intentioned, undermined academic requirements and trapped school leaders in a web of regulations that made it impossible for the schools to perform their essential educational and social functions. Conservative critics contend that schools today should return to a conventional, discipline-based approach to subject matter and a structured approach to the mastery of skills in order to restore standards of excellence undermined by the educational policies of the 1960s and 1970s.

These disagreements are hardly minor. However, because they tend to focus on matters of educational policy per se at the expense of long-term trends in the social and economic context in which schools operate, both of these perspectives on the recent history of urban education generally fail to acknowledge how fundamental changes in the society and economy—particularly changes in the social ecology of cities and the structure of urban labor markets—have shaped the development of urban education since World War II. Consequently, neither liberal nor conservative analyses of the contemporary crisis in urban education explain adequately why the educational initiatives begun in the 1960s have failed so frequently to live up to the expectations of their proponents or why conditions in urban schools have not substantially improved over the last two decades. . . .

The current condition of urban education is not of course solely a product of these changes in social geography and labor markets. Nor is it entirely new. There has never been a "golden age" when urban schools provided equal educational opportunity for the mass of students. But the postwar transformation of social space and the urban labor market has reshaped the urban landscape and changed the social and economic contours of urban education in ways that have made equal opportunity and popular control particularly difficult to secure. Without reference to these developments it is impossible to make sense of the recent history of urban schooling or to understand the constraints on the capacity of public policy to shape the development of urban education.

This article addresses these issues. It argues that the postwar transformation of American cities gave new form to longstanding racial divisions and economic inequities in American education and intensified the barriers to educational success facing low-income and minority students. At the same time, changes in the structure of urban economies pushed undereducated minority workers out of the labor market and increasingly dimmed the economic prospects for many better-educated workers as well. As a result, urban schools have been unable to expand educational and economic opportunities for inner-city children. But neither have urban schools and school systems done much to address the new problems they have faced or to counteract the inequities on which they have been based. On the contrary, largely because of the persistence of bureaucratic structures of decision making and organization, they have responded grudgingly and inadequately to their changed social and economic setting and remain nearly as unresponsive to the voices of low-income and minority students and parents as they were when Conant wrote *Slums and Suburbs* three decades ago.

❖ THE SOCIAL ECOLOGY OF AMERICAN CITIES

The most basic factor in the development of urban school systems since the end of World War II has been the spatial redistribution of the population from cities to suburbs. Though urban out-migration was hardly a new phenomenon in American life, the pace and dimensions of this postwar shift in the territorial distribution of the population and its effects on the organization of social space were unprecedented. Facilitated by public policies that encouraged home ownership in the suburbs, city dwellers in the postwar years left for the urban fringes more rapidly and in greater numbers than ever before. In the process, the nation's metropolitan areas were remade and the social and economic context of urban education was substantially transformed.

This shift in the territorial distribution of the population dwarfed prewar migration patterns and reversed long-term trends in city growth, particularly in the Northeast and the Midwest. What made this reorganization of space after World War II so significant to the history of urban education, however, is not just its magnitude but the spatial patterning of race and class that accompanied it. For what changed most dramatically with the suburbanization of the American population was not just the relative proportion of the population living in cities and suburbs, but the racial and economic distribution of the population within metropolitan areas.

Two processes were at work here: the migration of African Americans and Hispanics to northern cities and the flight of white Americans to the suburbs. Though black migration to northern cities first began during World War I, as late as 1940, nearly 80 percent of the nation's black population still lived in the South and 63 percent lived in rural areas. But the mechanization of southern agriculture and the wartime demand for labor in northern factories pushed black southerners off the land and pulled them into urban centers in the north. During the 1940s, 1.6 million African Americans migrated from the south to northern and western cities and another 1.5 million followed in the 1950s. By 1970, 47 percent of all African Americans lived outside the South and three-quarters lived in metropolitan areas.

African-American migration from the South slowed in the 1970s. At the same time, however, Hispanic immigrants from Mexico, Central America, and the Caribbean (especially from Puerto Rico) began moving to major American cities in growing numbers. Mexicans and especially Puerto Ricans had of course been present in American cities earlier, but their numbers increased especially rapidly after 1970. By 1980, the Hispanic population numbered 581,000 in Chicago, 118,000 in Philadelphia, 90,000 in Boston, and over one and a half million in New York, where nearly one-fifth of the population was Spanish-speaking. In 1985, Hispanics accounted for nearly 16 percent of the population of central cities in the Northeast compared with 11.5 percent ten years earlier.

While African Americans and then Hispanics moved into northern cities in steadily increasing numbers, first middle-class and later working-class whites moved out. As the pace of suburbanization accelerated during the 1950s, New York, Chicago, Philadelphia, Detroit, Boston, and St. Louis all suffered a net loss of white population, a trend that persisted in the 1960s and 1970s. By 1980, only 28 percent of the white population in metropolitan areas in the Northeast and the Midwest lived in central cities compared with 77 percent of blacks.

This racial division between city and suburb was not just the result of consumer preference or the chance workings of the market. In the 1940s and 1950s, white hostility toward minorities, together with the use of restrictive covenants that prohibited white homeowners from selling to minorities, Federal Housing Administration policies that discouraged loans to racially mixed neighborhoods in favor of all-white residential developments in the suburbs, and suburban zoning practices designed to preserve residential class segregation all effectively closed the suburbs to minority families. This began to change in the 1960s and 1970s when the passage of antidiscrimination legislation coupled with rising income among the black middle class helped open segments of the suburban housing market formerly off-limits to African Americans and other people of color. Even then the persistence of discrimination continued to keep the majority of African-American families in the city while the process of ghettoization in the suburbs confined most black suburbanites to areas already housing blacks or abandoned by whites. Although the pace of black suburbanization accelerated in the 1970s, the result of the reorganization of social space after the war was the racial polarization of the nation's large metropolitan areas.

The economic distinction between center and periphery that accompanied this shift in the racial distribution of the population was equally striking. Though median family income rose in cities as well as suburbs between 1950 and 1980, the income gap between city and suburban families grew wider each decade. After 1950, the suburb-to-city ratio of median family income increased in every major metropolitan area of the country. By 1980, median household income in all central cities had fallen to 74 percent of that in the suburbs compared with 80 percent in 1970, and just three years later had declined again to 72 percent.

This connection between income and location was tightened after 1970 largely because poverty was increasingly concentrated in central cities. Though poverty rates declined everywhere during the 1960s, the number of poor people living in the nation's central cities nearly doubled during the 1970s and early 1980s, and the urban poverty rate climbed while it continued to fall in the suburbs and nonmetropolitan areas. This hardly made poverty unique to the city, but as poverty rates rose in central cities and fell outside them, the proportion of all poor people in the United States living in cities increased from 27 percent in 1959 to 43 percent in 1985, and poverty came to be seen more and more as an urban phenomenon.

Urban poverty was not limited exclusively to African Americans and other people of color, but the concentration of the poverty population in central cities was strongly linked to the changing racial composition of urban areas and rising poverty rates among African Americans and Hispanics. Moreover, poor African Americans and Hispanics were also more likely than poor whites to live in low-income neighborhoods. For this reason, as the racial composition of the city shifted and as urban poverty rates rose, poverty also became concentrated in particular "poverty areas" within cities. Kathryn Neckerman and William Julius Wilson have calculated that in the nation's fifty largest cities, the number of people living in poverty areas (i.e., census tracts with a poverty rate at least 20 percent) rose by more than 20 percent between 1970 and 1980, though the total population in these cities fell 5 percent. In the nation's ten largest cities in 1970, the concentration of the poor in poverty areas was even more pronounced, especially among African Americans.

This connection between race, class, and location was of course hardly an entirely new feature of urban life in America. From the moment of the first

great black migration to northern cities during World War I, the combination
of discriminatory local real estate practices (later reinforced by federal housing
policies) and white violence segregated blacks from whites and forced African
Americans to live in the least desirable city neighborhoods, while discrimination in the labor market kept many black and other minority families locked in
poverty. Together with the fragmentation of local political jurisdictions, the
new social ecology of American cities institutionalized prewar patterns of class
and racial separation, creating geographically distinct communities with different social and economic opportunities and problems and different capacities to
meet them.

❖ THE SOCIAL TRANSFORMATION OF URBAN EDUCATION

Nowhere were the effects of these changes in the social organization of space
more evident than in the public schools. As the pace of suburbanization accelerated after 1950, distancing the white middle class from the city, the class and
racial composition of city schools was altered, and the connection between
race, income, and school location was tightened. In the process, city schools
became more and more associated with low educational achievement, and the
inequities between city and suburban schools became more clearly marked. As
Peter Schrag observed over twenty years ago, just as the Supreme Court was
mandating the dismantling of the old dual system of schooling, the transformation of space was creating two new separate and unequal systems of schooling in many metropolitan areas: one mainly for low-income children of color
in the cities, the other largely for middle-class children in the suburbs.

As white families moved out of the city and African Americans and Hispanics moved in, the racial and economic composition of the urban school
population changed dramatically. In nearly every major urban school system
in the country, the number of white students declined while the number of
minority students increased. Even in those cities where whites increased
absolutely, the proportion of whites in the school population declined because
African-American and Hispanic enrollment rose more rapidly. Whereas whites
had been a majority in all of the nation's largest school systems except Washington, D.C., in 1950, by 1968, six of the ten largest school systems in the
country were more than half minority, and by 1980 all were two-thirds and
most were at least three-fourths minority.

Indeed, because African-American and Hispanic city dwellers were
younger, had more children, and were less likely to send their children to private school than whites, city school systems enrolled a greater proportion of
minority students than the proportion of minorities in the city population as a
whole. In 1970, for example, people of color made up 31 percent of New
York's entire population but 54 percent of those enrolled in school. The pattern was the same in Chicago, Philadelphia, Detroit, and Los Angeles, and
nothing altered it in the 1970s. By 1980 the proportion of minority children
enrolled in city schools was at least one and a half times as great as the propor-

tion of minorities in the entire city population in all of the fifteen largest city school systems.

Segregated housing combined with local school attendance policies intended to separate blacks and whites in different schools meant that as the proportion of minority students increased, most found themselves in segregated schools in the North and Midwest as well as in the South. The U.S. Commission on Civil Rights reported that in seventy-five cities in 1965–1966, 75 percent of African-American elementary children were in 90 percent black schools (while 83 percent of white students were in nearly all-white schools) and nearly nine of ten African-American elementary students attended majority black schools. In Los Angeles, Detroit, Philadelphia, Chicago, Dallas, Houston, and Milwaukee, the proportion of African-American elementary students in majority black schools ranged from 87 to 97 percent. According to the commission, between 1950 and 1965 (and twelve years after the *Brown* decision), segregation actually increased in many inner-city schools, especially in the North and Midwest. In fifteen northern cities studied by the commission, 84 percent of the increase in African-American enrollment was absorbed in nearly all-black schools and 97 percent in majority black schools.

After 1968 school segregation of African Americans decreased nationwide. Largely because of increased pressure from the federal courts, the proportion of African Americans in nearly all black schools declined from 64 to 33 percent between 1968 and 1980 and the proportion in majority black schools decreased from 76 to 63 percent. But changes in segregation varied by region. Although the proportion of African-American students in all-black and majority black schools dropped substantially in the South, segregation remained above the national average in the Midwest and West and increased in the Northeast, especially in northern cities. In New York, Chicago, Philadelphia, and Detroit, African-American students actually became more isolated from white students during the 1970s, while in Chicago, Cleveland, and many other large cities the level of school segregation in 1980 was similar to what it was in many southern cities in the early 1960s.

This increase in racial segregation in northern and midwestern cities was partly attributable to tensions over court-ordered school integration. Though pressure from the courts succeeded in reducing segregation in some cities (especially small and middle-size ones), it also threatened many middle-class whites. Fearful that school integration would undermine the quality of urban education, they began sending their children to private schools or moving to suburbs where they thought schools were superior, leaving city schools to African Americans, Hispanics, and those whites too poor to leave or to opt out of the public system. But the growth of racial segregation was not due only to the escalation of white fears about the consequences of court-ordered integration. Although integration plans accelerated the movement of whites to the suburbs, especially during the first year in which a city's schools were desegregated, the decline in white enrollment due to "white flight" was relatively small compared with long-run trends such as the movement of whites away from central cities. Because suburbanization left so few whites in city schools, African-American and Hispanic students became more segregated from white students whether or not a city was under a court-ordered plan to desegregate.

In the early 1970s, civil rights groups challenged the legality of this pattern of city-suburban school segregation. In contrast to its earlier decisions in southern and urban school desegregation cases, however, the Supreme Court in 1974 for all intents and purposes ruled out legal action to remedy the effects of city-suburban segregation on the racial composition of city schools, at least in the Northeast and the Midwest. In *Milliken* v. *Bradley,* the Court reversed the lower federal courts, which had found that metropolitan school segregation in Detroit was the product of unconstitutional state and local actions and that metropolitan desegregation was required to alleviate the situation. Instead, the Court stressed the importance of "local control over the operation of schools" and held that concern for "local autonomy" must take precedence over the effort to desegregate the children of Detroit and its surrounding suburbs. In order to secure a broader remedy, the Court concluded, it must be proven that violations had occurred in suburban districts, most of which had few minority students, or that suburban district lines had been drawn with racial intent. Otherwise desegregation must proceed only within the city limits, even though, as Justice Thurgood Marshall pointed out in his dissenting opinion, this meant that because of the social ecology of American cities racial and economic segregation would only get worse.

Indeed, absent court action, the changing racial composition of the urban school population increasingly concentrated minority students in the city and intensified the racial and economic distinctions between urban and suburban schools. As whites fled city schools and the proportion of minority students grew, central city schools enrolled the vast proportion of minority students in metropolitan areas, especially in the Northeast and the Midwest, and had a much greater number of schools with a majority of minority students. At the same time, because African-American, Hispanic, and other students of color were more likely to come from poor families than their white (or minority) counterparts in the suburbs, the number of economically disadvantaged students in city schools also increased, and city schools accounted for a growing proportion of all poor students in metropolitan areas.

Nowhere did these connections between race, poverty, and location become more apparent than in Chicago, as Gary Orfield's 1984 study of the metropolitan Chicago public schools illustrated. By 1980, 60 percent of the students enrolled in Chicago's schools were African American, 18 percent were Hispanic, and 22 percent were white: 58 percent also came from low-income families. Of these low-income students, 57 percent attended all-minority schools, while 22 percent of the city's minority students attended schools that were completely low-income. By contrast, 85 percent of the students in the suburbs were white, and 9 percent came from low-income families. Only ten out of eighty-five of these suburban districts had a minority enrollment over 20 percent and a low-income enrollment above the suburban average of 9 percent; sixty-six had minority enrollments less than 10 percent, half had less than 5 percent low-income, and only six of the eighty-five districts had low-income enrollments over 20 percent.

The connections between race, poverty, and urban education are especially well documented for Chicago, but evidence from other cities makes clear that the situation in Chicago was not unique. In Milwaukee, for instance, over half of those enrolled in the city's schools in 1985 were African American, 11 percent were Hispanic and other students of color, and 35 percent were white; approximately one-third of the students were also low-income, and in some city schools over 60 percent of the students came from poor families. In the typical Milwaukee suburban high school, on the other hand, most of the students were white, and only 8 percent were low-income. Overall, 58 of 102 schools in Milwaukee but only one school in its surrounding suburbs had more than 25 percent low-income students. In Los Angeles, in contrast to Milwaukee, Hispanics were the largest group in the city schools in 1986. They made up 44 percent of the city's students (up from 15 percent in 1967), while African Americans were 15 percent (a 2 percent increase since 1967). But, as in Milwaukee, a strong connection existed between percentage of minority students and the concentration of low-income students in city schools. Of the ten lowest-income schools in metropolitan Los Angeles in 1976, six were in the city in 1976 and seven were in the city in 1986, and all ten were in Los Angeles County.

The concentration of poor and minority students in city schools thus tightened the connection between the class and racial composition of the school and its location. But this was not the only consequence of the changes in the composition of school enrollment that occurred after the war. As middle-class whites left urban schools and the proportion of poor and minority students grew, urban education also became more and more associated with educational failure. Although nationwide African-American and Hispanic students succeeded in school in greater numbers than in the past, in inner-city schools in the nation's largest metropolitan areas, educational outcomes consistently lagged behind outcomes in the suburbs, especially in those urban schools with the greatest concentrations of minority and economically disadvantaged students.

This was evident in both school achievement and school completion rates. In large northern cities in 1973, 42 percent of the children fell below the twenty-fifth percentile in reading compared with 15 percent in the suburbs; in 1977, 41 percent of big-city schools reported that half their students were reading one year or more below grade level while suburbs had only 3.5 percent of their schools in this category. In Chicago five years later, only two out of seventy high schools scored above the national average in reading whereas all of the suburban high schools had average achievement scores at or above the national norm, while in Los Angeles in 1985 the top ten scoring high schools in the metropolitan area were predominantly suburban and the bottom ten were all in the central city.

Achievement varied not only between cities and suburbs but by race and income within the city and by the proportion of low-income and minority students in different schools. Those city schools with the largest proportion of low-income and minority students generally scored the poorest on achievement tests. In Chicago in the early 1960s, for example, average sixth-grade achievement in reading and arithmetic in those districts with the most African-American students was more than a year and a half below those schools with the fewest, while average sixth-grade achievement in the "lowest socioeconomic districts" was two years below achievement in the "highest socioeconomic districts." The situation was the same in Detroit, New York, and Boston; in Pittsburgh, in June 1964, average sixth-grade achievement in the ten lowest schools (located in "deprived neighborhoods") was three years below the ten highest schools in arithmetic, four years below in reading, and one year below the national average in verbal ability, reading, and arithmetic.

Some recent evidence suggests that these patterns may have changed since the late 1960s and that achievement scores for poor and minority students in urban schools may actually have risen. According to the results of the National Assessment of Educational Progress (NAEP), for example, nationwide reading and math achievement among African-American and Hispanic students rose substantially in the late 1970s and 1980s, though both groups were still considerably behind non-Hispanic whites. Other evidence, however, suggests that these gains were not uniform and that poor and minority students in the inner city continued to lag behind their peers nationwide. According to NAEP data analyzed by Lyle Jones, for example, while reading achievement among African-American children in the elementary grades rose as fast in central cities as in the rest of the nation between 1970 and 1984, reading achievement among central-city African-American students at the high school level improved at only one-fourth to one-half the black rate nationally. Within central cities, according to Jones, except for gains among nine-year-olds, African-American students made no progress in closing the black-white achievement gap.

Evidence from individual cities confirms that low-income and minority high school students in central cities have continued to do much worse than other students on achievement tests and that especially in high schools with a large proportion of minority and low-income students achievement has improved little, if at all, over the last two decades. In Chicago in 1964, for example, eight of the top ten high schools in reading achievement were in the highest socioeconomic districts of the city, and only two had any minority students. By contrast, all ten of the poorest scoring schools were in the lowest socioeconomic districts, eight were more than 80 percent minority, and in five of these schools over 40 percent of ninth-graders were reading below sixth-grade level. Two decades later, only one of Chicago's top ten high schools in reading achievement had a minority enrollment above the city average and only one had more than 50 percent low-income students, while the ten lowest scoring schools were 98 percent minority and 92 percent low income. The same was the case in Los Angeles, where in 1986 the typical minority high school had 20 percent more low-income students than the typical white high school and scored ten to twelve points lower on citywide reading tests, which was actually worse than ten years earlier.

The recent history of school completion and dropout rates for low-income and minority students also presents a contrasting picture of nationwide progress and inner-city decline. From the end of World War II until the 1960s, for example, high school completion rates rose and dropout rates declined for African Americans, Hispanics, and other minorities. After the 1960s, minority dropout rates continued to decline in the nation as a whole, and completion rates continued to rise, but despite these gains, racial differences in dropout rates persisted, and in central cities increasingly large numbers of poor and minority students dropped out of school. Consequently, even though the overall gap between white and minority educational attainment narrowed after World War II, dropout rates remained much higher in cities than in the suburbs or in rural areas and even worsened in many inner-city high schools, especially in the Northeast and the Midwest.

These trends are evident in the statistics on school completion, attainment, and dropout rates in the nation as a whole and in individual cities. Nationwide, the percentage of African Americans age 25 to 34 who did not finish high school began to decline after World War II and between 1974 and 1986 fell even further from 32 to 19 percent, while the percentage of Hispanics without a high school diploma dropped from 51 percent in 1974 to 40 percent twelve years later. Partly as a result, average educational attainment among African Americans age 25 to 34 increased from eight years to eleven years between 1960 and 1970 and to slightly over twelve years by the early 1980s; average attainment among Hispanics was lower for Puerto Ricans than for Mexicans, but overall it too rose, though it was about one year less than that for African Americans in 1980.

This substantially reduced the racial gap in educational attainment. By the early 1980s, for example, average black attainment was less than a year behind white attainment. Yet, despite these gains in attainment, dropout rates in the 1980s as in the 1960s and 1970s continued to differ by race as well as by gender. Nationwide, in 1968 Hispanics were twice as likely to drop out as non-Hispanic whites and one and a half times as likely to drop out as African Americans. By 1984, dropout rates had declined for all racial groups and the gap between whites and African Americans and Hispanics had been reduced. But Hispanics still dropped out nearly twice as often as African Americans, who continued to leave school much more frequently than whites, except for African-American females, who dropped out at about the same rate as white females and slightly less often than white males.

In individual cities too dropout rates declined and graduation rates climbed steadily after World War II, at least until the early 1960s. In New York City, for instance, the dropout rate declined from 55 percent in 1941 to 35 percent in 1960. But, since poor and minority children were more concentrated in inner cities, dropout rates remained substantially higher in big cities than in the rest of the nation from the late 1950s on. In the early 1960s, the dropout rate in the nation's five largest cities (New York, Chicago, Los Angeles, Philadelphia, and Detroit) ranged anywhere from 10 to 21 percentage points above their respective statewide rates, and the difference persisted in the 1960s and 1970s. Of these five cities, only Philadelphia reduced its dropout rate between 1963 and 1980. Even then 40 percent of the city's high school students still left school without graduating, and the city's graduation rate continued to lag far behind the statewide graduation rate, as it did in cities in other states. Nationwide in 1980 the dropout rate in urban communities was 19 percent compared with 12 percent in the suburbs and 13 percent in rural areas.

That urban dropout rates have remained so high at the same time that African-American and Hispanic school completion rates rose and their average educational attainment increased is rather puzzling, but there are two reasons why this has been the case. One is that part of the overall gain in minority high school completion rates, at least for African Americans, reflects changes in the South. This gain was due partly to the postwar mechanization of southern agriculture, which reduced the demand for young black workers in rural labor markets, and partly to pressure from the civil rights movement, which improved black access to secondary education throughout the South. These changes did not entirely eliminate racial differences in attainment between blacks and whites in the region, but together they raised substantially the number of blacks who finished high school in the area of the country where black high school completion had historically been the lowest, and, in doing so, pushed up African-American completion rates in the nation as a whole even as minority dropout rates remained high or increased in central cities in the Northeast and the Midwest.

The second reason for the apparently paradoxical trend in minority dropout and school completion rates is that in the 1970s and 1980s many students who dropped out of high school subsequently returned or obtained a general equivalency diploma (GED). Between 1961 and 1985, for example, the number of people taking the GED examination increased tenfold, peaking in the early 1980s at just over 800,000 per year. Of these, only about 450,000 passed the exam—but together with those dropouts who returned to high school and graduated, this meant that about 30 to 40 percent of those who dropped out of high school in the 1970s and early 1980s eventually received a high school diploma or an alternative credential. The result has been the coexistence of high minority dropout rates and increased school completion.

These trends in dropout rates, school completion, and educational attainment were not, of course, characteristic of every big-city high school. Nor was the pattern of low achievement. In some central city schools in the 1960s and 1970s, achievement scores improved, dropout rates declined, and graduation rates rose. By and large, however, the nationwide rise in minority achievement and school completion has not been due to gains made by students in urban schools. Rather, by concentrating poor and minority students in the city, the postwar transformation of social space tightened the link between urban education and educational failure and intensified the educational barriers facing inner-city children. For many poor and minority students in the inner city, particularly those in schools with high poverty rates and a large proportion of minority students, the educational disaster Conant warned about thirty years ago has become a reality.

36

THE GREAT SCHOOL SELL-OFF

PETER SCHRAG

Long before Bill Clinton appeared on the presidential horizon, he had, as governor of Arkansas, established himself as one of a half-dozen national leaders in the public school reform movement of the 1980s. The movement was determinedly bipartisan, pragmatic, and nonideological. In addition to Clinton, it included Republican governors Thomas Kean of New Jersey and Lamar Alexander of Tennessee, as well as independent California State School Superintendent Bill Honig. These reformers sought, and generally achieved, tougher graduation requirements; more rigorous curricula and textbooks; competency tests for both students and teachers; merit pay or other incentives for outstanding teachers; longer school days and school years; and better funding for K-12 schools almost everywhere.

But before the decade was over, a combination of recession, budget cuts, impatience, and political expediency helped start a deep and very ideological current running in the opposite direction—a retreat from public education. With a lot of cheerleading from George Bush, the self-proclaimed education president, more people began to ask just what the country had bought with its school reform dollars. The greater the belief that the Germans and Japanese were beating us in the global economy, the greater the influence of international test results showing American students scoring behind their foreign coun-

From *The American Prospect*, Winter 1993, pp. 35–43. Reprinted by permission. Portions of the original have been omitted.

terparts. As a result, the encouraging returns from the reforms of the 1980s—they were not great, as we shall see, but they were hardly negligible—were ignored. The schools, according to the conventional wisdom, were simply failing, and stronger medicine was required.

For the Bush administration, a growing number of conservative scholars and businesspeople, and the religious right, that medicine was vouchers—tax-supported "scholarships" allowing parents to send their children to any school, public or private, in an educational free market. School choice was also one of the few issues that could replace Communism in linking the Republican Party's suburban conservatives with free-market libertarians and Christian-right fundamentalists.

❖ THE CHOICE BANDWAGON

The idea is hardly new. Milton Friedman first proposed vouchers more than 30 years ago. In the 1960s, it was taken up by liberal reformers such as Christopher Jencks and Henry M. Levin and by academics such as John E. Coons and Stephen D. Sugarman at Berkeley. In the 1980s, Ronald Reagan occasionally talked about private school tuition tax credits but paired the idea so closely with school prayer and even creationism that it looked more like an ideological crumb for Christian fundamentalists than a serious policy.

Bush had come to office declaring the country couldn't afford vouchers for private schools. But by 1991 the idea had become the centerpiece of his education policy, with the support of respected activists like the Department of Education's Alexander, former Xerox chairman David Kearns, and educational historian Diane Ravitch.

A further event that gave choice intellectual respectability was the 1990 publication by the Brookings Institution, home of Democratic brains-in-exile, of John E. Chubb and Terry M. Moe's *Politics, Markets, and America's Schools.* The book argues not only that the reforms of the 1980s were inadequate but that such reforms couldn't succeed as long as schools were run by school boards, superintendents, central offices, and departments of education—what the authors disparagingly call "direct democratic control." The only way to escape that, Chubb and Moe assert, is by letting parents choose among self-governing schools, public or private, with state tax money following their children to the schools they select, thereby building into schools a market incentive to offer better service. The authors are uncompromising. "Without being too literal about it, we think that reformers would do well to entertain the notion that choice *is* a panacea. . . . Choice is not like other reforms and should not be combined with them as part of a reformist strategy. . . . It has the capacity *all by itself* to bring about the kind of transformation that, for years, reformers have been seeking to engineer in myriad other ways" (italics original). . . .

❖ TARNISHED MYTHS

Of all the sectors of American life, none seems so driven by the myth of a lost golden age as education—time and other details unspecified—when all children went to nice bright schools, sat in orderly rows before dedicated teachers, learned what they had to know (by first learning "the basics") and then graduated, every one of them, to become productive citizens.

Just to say that, of course, is to expose its absurdity. Until the 1950s, U.S. schools were never expected to succeed with all children. Some attended only five or six months a year and quit after the fourth or fifth grade; many more left after the eighth grade to enter an economy that had plenty of unskilled and semi-skilled jobs. Schools, accordingly, were judged not by their failures—by dropout rates (a phrase that did not exist fifty years ago) or by how many did not go to college or fell below some standard test score—but by their successes. Blacks rarely figured into the education calculus at all.

One might even say that the golden age myth is itself a piece of vestigial racism—those nice orderly classrooms were predominantly, if not totally, white—but it's also important in explaining our pervasive discontent with the schools and the calls for radical "restructuring" that are based on it. No nation, Henry Commager once wrote, demands as much of its schools—expects them not only to teach reading and writing, but patriotism, morality, the evils of alcohol and tobacco (to which we have now added the dangers of drugs and AIDS), not to mention driver education, good citizenship, racial tolerance, self-esteem, and a hundred other things. And never have the schools been required to do it with a population as diverse—not to say troubled—as the schools do now. In 1970, one child in seven fell below the poverty line; now it's closer to one in five, and in the elementary grades it's closer to one in four. In 1970, 15 percent of the nation's school-age population was nonwhite; now it's well over 20 percent. In states like California, where whites are now a minority of the public school enrollment, one child in four is on welfare; one in four comes from a home where English is not the primary language. Los Angeles, the country's second largest school system, now enrolls children speaking some 80 different languages. Of the 185,000 new children who entered the state's schools in fall 1992, less than half came from homes where the primary language is English.

The facile response to such data is that American schools have always absorbed huge numbers of immigrants—Germans, Swedes, Italians, Poles, Russians, Greeks. But never have they been expected to do it as completely and against such great odds. Today there is a much smaller market for unskilled dropouts—quite the contrary in this global economy—and thus no significant possibility that the schools can forget about their failures, much less threaten to boot them out as they could a half century ago.

That's not to say that criticism of American public schools is unfounded. Many schools are mindless; many districts are paralyzed by self-serving bureaucracies; many teachers, a lot of whom came from the lowest ranks of their college classes, do as much to sabotage curiosity and thinking as they do to encourage them. Nothing that follows should be taken as an indication that things are fine in American education. But many of the common assumptions about educational performance are wrong.

Dropouts.   If one adds those who have graduated from high school (about 75 percent) and those who have a high school equivalency diploma, roughly 90 percent of young Americans are now high school graduates, the highest percentage in history. Over 20 percent are college graduates. The percentage who drop out of high school continues to decline—and that includes all races except perhaps first-generation Hispanic immigrants, who often leave for extended returns to the old country.

Academic Achievement in the "Basics."   According to the National Assessment of Education Progress, much of the decline of the 1970s, though not all, was offset by progress in the 1980s. Black students, while not yet on a par with whites in math and reading, made substantial gains through the 1970s and the 1980s.

Average SAT Scores.   Although they sank badly in the 1970s, scholastic aptitude test scores started to come back in the 1980s, particularly in math. This rebound came despite the substantial increase in the percentage of high school graduates (and thus the number of students not in the top ranks of their classes) who now take SATs. The number of students taking more intense academic programs in secondary school, like honors courses, advanced placement courses, and more serious math and science courses, has risen substantially in the past decade.

College Graduation Rates.   Roughly 26 percent of all U.S. twenty-two-year-olds obtained a bachelor's degree in 1987, according to the National Center for Education Statistics, substantially more than in Japan (21 percent), Germany (13 percent), the UK or France (14 percent each). Similarly, we outrank other major nations in the percentage of twenty-two-year-olds getting a bachelor's degree in science and engineering. And since the institutions from which they graduate continue to draw hundreds of thousands of foreign students—we are far and away the world's leading exporter of education—the complaints about curricular inadequacy need a lot of qualification.

Collectively, the data are nothing to cheer about. A lot of students don't know in what century the Civil War took place or on what continent to find Ethiopia. American thirteen-year-olds rank at or near the bottom in most international measures of math and science proficiency. The comparisons may be somewhat misleading since most of those countries begin specialized education at age fourteen, placing more emphasis on high test performance in the earlier grades, and since some teach geometry to thirteen-year-olds (usually taught to American children at fourteen or fifteen). At the same time, however, even after the reforms of the 1980s, U.S. students appear to do less homework and have less demanded of them, either by schools or parents, than their foreign peers.

It's hard to know how much of that can be controlled by the school and how much comes from our indifferent intellectual atmosphere. Given the enormous changes in the demographics of American schools and considering the idiot culture in which our students live most of the day, it's surprising the schools have done as well as they have.

❖ TICKET TO RIDE

It's precisely the demographic and social factors that are driving some middle-class Americans to buy their way out of the system. Some parents honestly perceive schools to be unsafe; the schools can't deal with the diversity of cultures; the systems are distracted by the avalanche of personal and social problems that students bring and that no other institution addresses.

More and more voters are not parents, and more parents are not voters. That's one of the reasons support for public education is eroding. In 1970, white school children, who, of course, bring the most electoral clout, were fully 21 percent of the total population. In 1990, twenty years beyond the end of the baby boom, white school children were 14 percent of the population. In the suburbs, where parents are concentrated and have political clout, communities still provide lavish support for schools, but increasingly they become islands of exception.

Those groups who vote in high numbers, older people in particular, tend not to have children in the schools, while Americans who have more children in the schools have fewer votes per child and often don't exercise them. California's Proposition 13, which was passed in 1978 and which set the tone for much of U.S. social policy in the past decade, was largely a revolt of elderly people against high property taxes at the expense of local services for children: schools, parks, libraries. (This year, about 20 percent of California voters were parents of school children, roughly half of what it was a generation ago.) Even now, when local districts attempt to pass school bonds in California, they often exempt property owned by people over sixty-five from the additional taxes.

The middle class, of course, is not alone in looking for escape or in supporting vouchers. The Catholic church, whose remaining inner-city parochial schools are struggling to survive, has been seeking government help for years. And so have many inner-city black parents who desperately want some escape from the brutal schools their children are forced to attend. With a modest voucher, they could afford to attend those parochial schools; as a result, inner-city parents lead the polls in their support for vouchers. There's also support from the parents of Christian fundamentalist school children. But it's unlikely that vouchers would enjoy their widespread attention without considerable middle-class support.

For the conservatives who are now its greatest champions, choice may well have an additional use. If the problem are the schools and not children, no one has to concern himself too much about nutrition, health and day care, decent housing, or the children's issue in general. The *Wall Street Journal* editorial page, among others, is fond of quoting UNESCO data showing that the United States spends more per child on schools than most other modern nations. But the *Journal* fails to acknowledge the universal day care in France, the German social welfare system, the homogeneity of Japanese society, or the universal health care and generous other benefits that nearly all those countries provide—social programs that relieve the burdens on schools. The blessings that the market is supposed to bestow on the schools tends to drive the rest of the problem into obscurity. If the good people can get away from the nasty kids, however defined, the conditions that shape those children's lives become practically, politically, and morally invisible.

❖ REFORM SCHOOL BOYS

Terry Moe, who teaches political science at Stanford and is a senior fellow at Brookings, says that the school market is like any other—he recently compared it to the market for candy bars. People shop around, choose what's best for them, and thus drive all competitors to improve their products. But there's no empirical evidence of that. In a study of the one public-private plan (Milwaukee's) now in operation, the Carnegie Foundation found that while the small number of students who have been enabled to leave the public schools "feel pleased with the decision they have made," more than 40 percent of those who left the public schools in 1991–92 for a private school didn't return to the private school in 1992–93. More important, there was "no evidence . . . that the participating students made significant academic advances or that either the public or the private schools have been revitalized by the transfers." Overall, Carnegie found, as have others, that "choice is a wholly unrealistic proposal for literally millions of children (because) there simply is no other school within easy reach or, if there is, the alternative school may be no better than the one close by.". . .

The voucher movement is silent about society's interest in common schooling. In the West and Southwest, where the only semblance of community is the shopping mall, the freeway, and the radio talk show, the public school is virtually the last institution that spans the entire community, bringing together not only children but their parents and often their neighbors in a common enterprise. Public schools embody the idea of community itself—the democratic ideals of a common culture that assimilates and integrates diversity even as it celebrates it. That's not an ideal that, however short of realization, can be casually abandoned.

What of children of parents who can't negotiate the market or are not interested in their schooling at all? What of the need, especially now, to acculturate immigrants? What of racial integration and understanding? One of the great ironies is to hear people like former education secretary William Bennett, who became apoplectic when Stanford University added a few nonwestern writers and a few women to its western civilization course a few years ago, defend a choice system that would feed tax money to Moonie schools, to the flat earth society, to African nationalists (the Louis Farrakhan school?), or indeed any other cultural separatist who could attract a few suckers.

Coons and Sugarman worry—with good reason—that unless voucher regulations are carefully written, the affluent will use them to supplement private school tuition while the poor will be stuck with whatever schooling the voucher will provide. While that could be fixed by limiting vouchers to schools that charge no more than the voucher is worth (which is what Chubb and Moe and Coons and Sugarman propose), no plan yet overcomes other problems in an unregulated market: that racial and ethnic segregation would rise, or that some parents would not be able to find a school that will take their children. The advocates of the California voucher argue that since they propose "scholarships" averaging only about half of what existing public schools spend per pupil, vouchers, if widely used, could save money. But since no plan that's made it to the ballot significantly limits how or where vouchers can be used, vouchers will not only become tuition supplements for private school parents but also an inducement to those schools to raise their tuition.

Nor is it likely that any radically different voucher plan would go very far. Any plan that is too restrictive about how and where a voucher can be used would immediately lose its parochial and fundamentalist school constituency; any plan that's too costly will look too blatantly like a raid on the treasury. Both the Colorado and California plans provide roughly $2,500, about half what the public schools spend. That's enough for a parish elementary school but no more than a third of the tuition at a good private day school and not remotely enough to educate a handicapped child or any other child with special needs.

Chubb and Moe would provide "add-ons" for such children, as well as a whole range of other "special educational needs ... arising from economic deprivation, physical handicaps, language difficulties, emotional problems," all of it to be determined and refereed by an oxymoronic "choice office" in each district. In addition, there would be an array of other bureaucracies—to inform parents of their options, to place children who aren't accepted by any school (which, of course, conflicts with their insistence that all schools be autonomous regarding admissions and expulsions), to organize transportation, and to monitor compliance with the health, safety, and credentialing regulations that they seem to favor. That may not restore all of the old school bureaucracy, but the groups that have put vouchers on the ballot say they'll tolerate no such restrictions. As a "market," what this most resembles is our two-tier medical system, with the assigned-risk schools the corollary of the emergency room at the county hospital.

✦ THE MARKET CANARD

The more the system becomes a "market," the more the child and her parents become customers rather than citizens. In the existing system, the public schools have to register every child who lives in the appropriate attendance area. With an unrestricted voucher plan and deregulated schools, nobody has to take (or notice) anybody. The voucherites are designing a system that will allow more people to buy their way out but that will lock the children from whom they're trying to escape not just into their third-class schools, or out of schools altogether, but into civic and political invisibility.

✦ REAL REFORM

Perhaps the greatest irony of the voucher movement is that even as it pretends to be concerned with individuals, it so thoroughly focuses on abstractions: the market, competition, the schools as institutions. But if one looks at real schools or real children, it's clear that the solutions, like the problems, are far more complicated and qualified. There are no panaceas here. The research is not even clear on how much difference money, class size, or the school themselves make. Still, there are a number of emerging conclusions.

The most successful schools are those with a clear sense of mission and shared values—schools that foster cooperative rather than bureaucratic relationships. That suggests that more school site control is preferable to more control by downtown bureaucrats and that more diversity and choice is preferable to a single model. Choice within the public system therefore makes sense, but as the Carnegie study points out, probably only as part of a plan of broader reforms; only if the schools are able to create sufficiently compelling programs; only if there is enough reliable information and quality control so that the choices can be made intelligently; and only if there are relevant programs even for marginal students.

One of the most interesting and celebrated of the public school choice programs now in operation—East Harlem's—didn't begin with choice at all. It began with attempts within a few schools to create distinctive and attractive programs—a performing arts school, among others, a math-science school, a bilingual school, a "bridge" school for tough-to-teach kids. Once these schools were established, choice was necessary to allow the children to opt for those programs. The voucherite faith has it the other way: that once there is a market, other reforms will automatically follow.

But there is no real reason to believe that. If there is any moral justification anywhere for limited vouchers, it's in the inner-city. But the better alternative is to give parents a greater voice and to make the necessary social investment—in health, in training parents to teach their preschool kids (the model is an Israeli program that Hillary Clinton brought to Arkansas), and in school-industry apprenticeship programs. The point is that real reform, particularly in the cities, requires precisely the kind of broad social concern that vouchers and an educational free market would allow the country to avoid. To address that concern, federal education policy in the next couple of years probably ought not focus on schools at all but on children. Maureen DiMarco, California secretary of education and social services, has urged that if there is more money for children, most of it should go not to the schools but to health (especially prenatal care and nutrition), Head Start, day care, counseling, housing, and recreation. Though extreme, such a focus reflects a justified sense that the needs are more urgent in, and that the money can be spent more effectively on, children's social services and parent training than on an educational system whose reform depends primarily on the states and local communities.

That's not to say the schools are well funded; many are not. But any additional money for schools (most of it no doubt state money) should be disbursed only with a quid pro quo—in curricular changes, school-site control, accountability for teachers and parents, and, where real options justify it, public school choice. Without these, little will change. Surely Bill Clinton, who was the driving force behind the school reforms in Arkansas, understands that as well as anyone. The essence of school reform during the 1980s, from Arkansas and Mississippi to New Jersey and California, was its ability to use additional funding to buy those higher standards for teachers, even a few halting steps toward merit pay, as well as tougher graduation requirements and other reforms—trading some flexibility from the unions and the bureaucrats for greater tax support. The reforms fell short largely in their failure to get enough reform for their additional tax dollars.

National performance-based testing can help. If done right—if we measure higher order skills such as problem solving, historical analysis, as well as writing and other creative work (all of which, of course, is expensive)—it may do more to generate a realistic appreciation of how the nation's schools are doing and how every particular school is doing against Shanker's world standard. It certainly could shake up those very satisfied parents; and it could shake up school boards, legislatures, and perhaps teachers colleges as well.

In the final analysis, however, the most important thing a Clinton administration—or any national administration—could do now for schools is to re-energize general confidence in government, in community, and in the efficacy of public service. Private school vouchers, after all, are not much more than the educational version of privatization in a dozen other areas. If the idea is driven by a desire to escape from the latter day (mostly social) problems of the schools, it can also be dampened by renewed confidence in government's interest in, and ability to deal with, those problems. For the most part, schools are local and state concerns anyway—the federal government funds no more than 6 percent of the total enterprise, less than it did when Reagan came to office in 1980. Though that federal contribution should be raised, what Washington mainly can do is set the climate. And in the past decade, the climate has been awful.

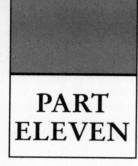

PART ELEVEN

CRIME AND JUSTICE

In recent years, crime has often been perceived by the public as America's number one social problem—closely matched, since the mid-1980s, by the deeply related problem of drugs. Violent crime, in particular, has made growing numbers of Americans afraid to walk their streets and has generally diminished the quality of urban life in the United States. Moreover, our violent crime rates remain disastrously high—far higher, in fact, than those of other advanced industrial societies—despite dramatic increases in the numbers of criminals who have been put behind bars.

What are the causes of violent crime? Is there a connection between criminal violence and unemployment, as our intuition suggests? Conservative criminologists tend to downplay such an association, arguing that there is only slight evidence linking the crime rate to economic fluctuations. They argue that America experienced relatively little crime during the 1930s Great Depression, while the crime rate rose during the more affluent 1960s and reached a peak in the 1970s. In "Crime and Work," Elliott Currie reviews the evidence and concludes that there is a strong association between unemployment and crime. He argues that those who downplay the relationship make three mistakes. First, subgroups with high crime rates—such as young, black males—do experience high unemployment rates, even when overall employment is low. Second, unemployment has a different impact when it portends a lifetime of diminished opportunity. Finally, unemployment statistics do not reflect the *quality* of available work.

Drug crime in the United States has likely risen, and quite dramatically, although it is hard to tell how much from crime statistics, as contained in the Uniform Crime Reports, since these are based on crimes reported to the police. The robbery victim is indeed likely to report the crime to the police. The rape victim may be more hesitant but may tell her story to a National Victim surveyor attempting to learn how many victims did not report crime to the police. But when a drug seller sells to a buyer, the purchaser is unlikely to report the crime either to the police or to a crime surveyor. In his article, Jerome H. Skolnick concludes that based on his recent research, drug crimes are overwhelming the American criminal justice system. He argues, moreover, that law enforcement is severely limited in its capacity to undermine the drug trade. Drugs, he argues, are a public health and social problem, and fundamental dilemmas undermine law enforcement's capacity to deal with it.

If drug crime is one part of the crime problem, corporate crime and violence is another. So argues Sierra Club author Russell Mokhiber, who asserts that we seriously undercount the tangible harm to human beings and the environment caused by the excesses of corporate power. In part, Mokhiber reminds us how harmful some of big business excesses have been; the Dalkon Shield intrauterine device, for example, seriously injured tens of thousands of women. Some of the earlier selections in this book—those dealing with the original Pintos (selection 1), hazardous chemicals (selection 25), and the tobacco companies (selection 2)—make a similar point.

Mokhiber, however, goes beyond a recounting of corporate abuses to analyze how it is that big corporations are able to engage in such destructive activity without being held responsible as *criminals,* although they may have to pay money damages as convicted defendants in civil court actions. He argues that the severe injury generated by violent corporate misconduct warrants the stigma and penalties associated with the idea of crime.

If the hazards of business dealings sometimes take years to discover, there is never any subtlety in death by gunshot. In this part's final selection, Erik Larson tells the story of the gun of Nicholas Elliot, a barely sixteen-year-old boy who fired round after round of 9-millimeter bullets in the Atlantic Shores Christian School in Virginia Beach, Virginia, from a semiautomatic weapon that had been hidden in his backpack.

Nicholas killed one teacher and severely injured another; two others narrowly escaped. That Nicholas could wind up firing away on the peaceful grounds of a suburban school, Larson maintains, tells us much about the incredible proliferation of guns in America. This has led to an unprecedented crisis that can no longer be interpreted as simply a contemporary manifestation of a pioneer spirit. Instead, Nicholas was supported by a array of institutions, norms, and laws that has made it possible for him—and other shooters—to terrorize city streets and suburban schools.

37

CRIME AND WORK

ELLIOTT CURRIE

Toward the end of the sixteenth century, Richard Hakluyt depicted the ominous consequences of England's widespread unemployment. "For all the statutes that hitherto can be devised," he wrote, "and the sharp execution of the same in punishing idle and lazy persons for want of sufficient occasion of honest employment," it had proven impossible to

> deliver our Commonwealth from multitudes of loiterers and idle vagabonds, which, having no way to be set on work . . . often fall to pilfering and thieving and other lewdness, whereby all the prisons of the land are daily pestered and stuffed full of them, where either they pitifully pine away, or else at length are miserably hanged, even twenty at a clap out of some one jail.

The same problem worried American observers three centuries later. In 1878, the economist Carroll D. Wright, Massachusetts Commissioner of Statistics, noted that more than 67 percent of convicts in that state were recorded as "having had no occupation"; of 220 men sentenced to prison one year, "147 were without a trade or any regular means of earning a living." Wright warned of the disquieting implications of this for the "reform" of prisoners:

> Will these men serve their time, and be discharged in their present unfit state to battle with the world? They may go out into society again resolved to do right;

From *Confronting Crime: An American Challenge* by Elliott Currie. Copyright © 1985 by Elliott Currie. Reprinted by permission of Pantheon Books. A division of Random House, Inc.

but without a reliable means of support they are ill-prepared to meet the
adversities of hard times, or the temptation to gain by crime what they do not
know how to obtain by honest labor.

The connection between crime and the lack of any "regular means of earning a living" has changed little since Wright's time, or even Hakluyt's. At the
close of the 1970s, nearly 40 percent of state prison inmates and 55 percent of
the inmates of local jails had not been working full-time in the months before
they went behind bars, while those who did work typically had little to show
for it. Only about half of a sample of "habitual felons" in a Rand Corporation
survey of the California prisons in the late seventies had gained their usual pre-
prison income by working; of those who had, most "had earnings that were
not much above a poverty level." Within this generally deprived sample, moreover, those prisoners who had been even slightly more successful in the labor
market—those the Rand researchers called the *better employed*—committed
crimes, while on the "street," at about one-sixth the rate of the others. This
difference is all the more remarkable given the study's extremely generous definition of what it meant to be *better employed:* earning all of $100 a week and
working at least 75 percent of their "street" time.

Nor is this all. Later Rand research . . . suggests that unemployment is one
of the most powerful predictors of which inmates among the already "hardened" prison population are most likely to go on to become *high-rate* offenders, responsible for much more than their share of serious crime even in this
rather select group.

These findings are no surprise; they fit our commonsense understanding
of who goes to prison, and they are compatible with a broad range of theories
of crime, including the "economic" approach favored by many conservatives.
In a society in which work is the indispensable key to most things—material
and otherwise—that our culture considers worth having, it's easy to see why
those without work might try other, less legitimate ways to get them. And
since work is also one of the most important ways individuals become integrated into a larger community, it isn't surprising that those excluded from the
world of work will be held less tightly by the bonds that keep a society together. On the face of it, the appropriate response seems fairly cut-and-dried; if we
want to lower the crime rate once and for all, we will have to do a much better
job of providing access to work—especially for those groups, like minorities
and the young, who have been most excluded from its benefits.

So far, all this seems fairly obvious; and it has been a staple argument of
liberal criminology for decades. But as it turns out, the relationship between
crime and unemployment is surprisingly controversial. Not everyone agrees
that unemployment has much to do with crime; and of those who do, not all
agree that there is much we can do about it.

For instance, despite the stark evidence supplied by the work histories of
those in prison, James Q. Wilson writes that "contrary to what many people
assert, very little research shows a relationship between economic factors and
crime." For most conservative writers, it follows that improving the prospects

for economic security cannot have much effect on the crime rate. More generally, the argument that unemployment is only minimally related to crime serves to focus attention on more "individual" factors—temperament, family practices, perhaps genetic abnormalities—which are presumably less amenable to social intervention. All this is confusing, to say the least, and it contributes greatly to the paralysis that afflicts our public policies toward crime.

It is also misleading. The relationships between unemployment and crime are real; we won't be able even to begin an attack on crime that is both humane and effective if we do not confront them. But these relationships are more complicated than they might seem at first glance, and they deserve careful analysis.

One line of argument dismisses the connections between unemployment and crime on the grounds that there is no good evidence that the crime rate responds strongly to economic *fluctuations.* Conservatives point especially to rising crime in the prosperity of the 1960s and its apparent decline in the Depression of the 1930s. And it's true that formal research on crime and economic fluctuations presents a mixed picture.

The connections between crime rates and the ups and downs of the economy were studied by several noted American scholars in the twenties, and the coming of the Great Depression in the thirties gave the issue new urgency. Many of these early studies were so poorly designed that, as the University of Pennsylvania criminologist Thorsten Sellin concluded in a well-known monograph for the Social Science Research Council in 1937, it was "difficult to arrive at any generalizations" from their results. But two of the most sophisticated efforts in that period—Dorothy S. Thomas's 1927 "Social Aspects of the Business Cycle" and Emma Winslow's study of crime and employment in Massachusetts, commissioned as part of the work of the National Commission on Law Observance and Enforcement in 1931—found strong associations between economic downturns and some kinds of crime, especially what Thomas called "crimes against property with violence"—robbery, housebreaking, and burglary.

Interest in the effect of "hard times" on crime waned in the prosperous postwar era; it was revived only in the gloomier seventies, most notably by the sociologist M. Harvey Brenner of Johns Hopkins University. In a series of studies covering a variety of countries and time periods, Brenner has consistently found chillingly precise correlations between changes in the overall unemployment rate and several measures of crime, including national homicide rates and admissions to state prisons. Thus in 1970, according to Brenner, an increase in the American unemployment rate of one percentage point accounted for nearly 4 percent of that year's homicides, almost 6 percent of its robberies, and close to 9 percent of narcotics arrests. Brenner attributes these tragic effects of unemployment only partly to the pressures of income loss suffered by those out of work; equally important is what Brenner calls the *compound-interest effect* of unemployment on crime rates. Unemployment aggravates two other social pathologies that everyone agrees are closely related to both violent and property crimes: drug and alcohol abuse. Losing a job leads to drug abuse, and drug abuse leads to property crime. Alcohol consumption, Brenner argues, also rises dramatically during economic slumps, and drinking in turn is closely associated with serious violent crime. Moreover, unemployment disrupts family ties by forcing the jobless to migrate in search of work; and this, too, in Brenner's view, leads to higher crime rates.

Brenner has made the strongest recent argument for a clear-cut relationship between national unemployment rates and crime. Other studies in the past two decades have been less confident. On balance, the studies provide what the economist Robert Gillespie, in a 1975 review of the evidence, called "general, if not uniform, support" for the commonsense belief that unemployment rates are related to crime. The kernel of truth in the conservative argument—and it is an important one—is that many careful scholars have found at best what the economists Thomas Orsagh and Ann Dryden Witte call "weak" associations between national-level changes in unemployment rates and crime. Why?

Part of the problem involves technical, methodological difficulties inherent in this kind of research . . . : it is very sensitive to the specific assumptions that are made about what other factors might influence crime rates. Depending on how such factors as age distribution or sentencing policies are entered into the equation, researchers of equal honesty and scrupulousness may well come up with strikingly different conclusions.

But the deeper and more crucial issues involve several ambiguities in the relationship between unemployment and crime itself. These do not disprove the importance of the connection between crime and work; indeed, they strengthen it. But they do mean that we have to view that connection through a more refined lens. The ambiguities fall under three general headings:

- Unemployment itself appears to have *contradictory* effects on crime.

- The official unemployment rate alone (on which most of this research has been based) is a poor guide to the true significance of the relationships between employment and crime.

- Those relationships are affected by a number of intervening factors, including public policies and the level of community support, that do not generally show up in quantitative research.

The first complexity is that, while unemployment tends to increase crime in some ways, it may tend to decrease it in others. In particular, it may restrict the *opportunities* for some kinds of crime, even while increasing the motivation to commit them. Thus, as Lawrence Cohen, Marcus Felson, and Kenneth Land have argued, increases in unemployment may reduce the chances of being robbed by keeping potential victims at home, out of "transit" areas—areas between home and the workplace. By the same token, the fact that unemployed workers spend more time at home restricts opportunities for residential burglary. Looking at rates of robbery, burglary, and auto theft from the late

1940s to the early 1970s, Cohen, Felson, and Land found a "modest" but noticeable association between increases in unemployment and decreases in these crimes. (A somewhat similar argument was made in the late fifties by the sociologists Daniel Glaser and Kent Rice to explain their finding that high levels of unemployment seemed to go hand in hand with increased crime among adults but decreased crime among juveniles. In times of high unemployment, they reasoned, unemployed parents would spend more time at home—and thus give more time and attention to the behavior of their children.) It follows that the same mechanisms probably work in the other direction as well: widespread economic prosperity can increase crimes like robbery and burglary by multiplying the opportunities to commit them.

Another, still more crucial, set of complications arises from the clumsiness of our standard measures of unemployment. At first glance there might seem to be few things simpler than to determine what it means to be unemployed; but in fact, as critics have long pointed out, the conventional definition of unemployment embodied in the official rates obscures more than it reveals. To begin with, it lumps together what are actually widely different experiences among people with very different propensities toward serious crime. In terms of its effects on crime rates, for example, unemployment clearly means one thing in the case of a forty-year-old machinist with three children, a mortgage, and a twenty-year work history who has just lost his job, and another if we're talking about an eighteen-year-old inner-city dropout who has never held a job for more than three months, may never in the future, and knows it. The official rate tells us nothing by itself about the differences between the pain of being out of work for six months and the demoralization of a lifetime with minimal prospects for work. Similarly, because the rate is *national,* it obscures differences at the level of local communities, where, arguably, they count the most. National changes in unemployment may have little effect on the job situation in communities that face persistently high unemployment through good times and bad. When we do focus on specific neighborhoods, the connections between crime and unemployment emerge dramatically. A recent study by Robert Sampson and Thomas Castellano, for example, found that victimization rates were 80 percent higher for crimes of theft and 40 percent higher for crimes of violence in urban neighborhoods with high unemployment than in those with low.

Most important, the strength of the unemployment-crime relationship is obscured by what the official definition of unemployment leaves out. In the first place, it omits great numbers of people who do not have jobs. We count as "unemployed" only those who describe themselves as "looking for work." But if we want to know how the lack of work affects the crime rate, this is misleading. It's logical, after all, that those of the jobless who are still sufficiently hopeful and attached to the world of legitimate work to be actually looking for jobs are *less* likely to be involved in serious crime than those uncounted others who have given up the search for a job—or who have never begun it.

Thus research that has broadened its focus to include people who are both jobless and not in search of work—those who, in economic language, are not "participating in the labor force"—has come up with stronger associations between joblessness and crime than research using the official category of "unemployment" alone. In one of the most careful of these studies, the economists Llad Phillips and Harold Votey of the University of California at Santa Barbara tried to determine how much of the dramatic rise in youth crime in the sixties could be attributed to changes in the labor-market opportunities open to youth. Much had been made (and still is) of the supposed "paradox" of increasing crime in the face of declining *overall* unemployment rates in the sixties. But Phillips and Votey pointed out that despite the *general* improvement in the national unemployment rate, another crucial trend was a simultaneous rise in the unemployment rate for youths—particularly nonwhites—and an even more precipitous drop in their labor-force participation. In 1952, for example, the official unemployment rate for nonwhite men aged eighteen and nineteen was about 10 percent; by 1967 it had reached 20 percent. This took place even though the unemployment rate for the country as a whole was about 3 percent in both years. Measured by their participation in the labor force, the position of youth was even worse; the proportion of nonwhite youths either at work or actively looking for work dropped from nearly 80 percent in 1952 to just 63 percent in 1967. Part of this shift is explainable by the fact that a greater proportion were in school, but not all of it. The harsh fact was that by the late sixties, more youths, especially blacks, were neither working, looking for work, nor pursuing an education. How did that change affect the crime rate?

According to Phillips and Votey, very strongly indeed—so strongly, in fact, that these changes in the labor market were *by themselves* "sufficient to explain increasing crime rates for youths" in the sixties. The most powerful associations between joblessness and youth crime, they found, emerged when they divided their sample into youths who were in the labor force (either working or looking for work) and those who were out of it—those who neither had jobs nor sought them. This distinction was a more accurate predictor of youth crime rates than the more conventional contrast between youths who were working and those who were not. In short, what seemed most closely related to crime among youths was not just being out of work but being so *far* out of work that they had ceased to look for it. To Philips and Votey, this suggested that what principally influenced youth crime was not the *current* state of the economy so much as the long-term experience of fundamentally constricted economic opportunities, an experience that had convinced many urban minority youths that not much was to be gained by looking for a job.

Clearly, then, we need to broaden the focus of investigation beyond the conventional measure of unemployment to include other forms of joblessness. But we need to broaden the terms of our discussion in another way as well; for what the narrow emphasis on the unemployment rate ignores is the larger, ultimately more crucial, issue of how the *quality* of work affects the crime rate. One of the most consistent findings in recent research is that *un*employment is less strongly associated with serious crime than *under*employment—the prospect of working, perhaps forever, in jobs that cannot provide a decent or stable livelihood, a sense of social purpose, or a modicum of self-esteem. As the economist Ann Dryden Witte puts it, "It is not so much individual unemployment per se which causes crime, but rather the failure to find relatively high-wage, satisfying employment." What is at issue, Witte concluded after reviewing the evidence in the late seventies, is "economic viability, rather than just employment per se."

The idea that crime might be linked with the larger problem of inadequate and unstable work, not just the absence of work altogether, is not new. "The kind of labor which requires the most skill on the part of the workman to perform," Carroll D. Wright argued in 1878, "insures the laborer most perfectly against want and crime." Furthermore, he wrote, the benefits of skilled work were passed down across the generations through their elevating effects on family life. "The occupation of the parents has a wonderful effect upon the character and tendencies of their children." The character of work, in other words, shaped the character of individuals in enduring ways; and to Wright, the implication was "so self-evident that it is to my own mind axiomatic in nature." The upgrading of labor—that "elevating process which would make self-supporting citizens out of the unfortunate and criminal classes"—would "conduce to the relief and protection of the community, the alleviation of the condition of the poor and helpless, the judicious punishment of the wicked, and the practical reformation of the vagrant and criminal." "Employers should remember," Wright insisted,

> that if conditions become ameliorated, if life becomes less of a struggle, if leisure be obtained, civilization, as a general rule, grows up. If these conditions be reversed, if the struggle for existence tends to occupy the whole attention of each man, civilization disappears in a measure, communities become dangerous. . . . The undue subjection of the laboring man must tend to make paupers and criminals, and entail a financial burden upon wealth which it would have been easier to prevent than to endure.

Wright's central point—that an economy that condemns many to "drudgery" as well as to frequent unemployment will be neither just nor safe—still holds true today. It is the condition of being locked into what some economists call the "secondary labor market"—low-level, poorly paying, unstable jobs that cannot support a family and that offer little opportunity for advancement—that is most likely to breed crime. Curiously enough, the same conservatives who continually point to the studies that suggest weaker connections between unemployment and crime rates have not usually gone on to acknowledge that the same research also confirms that *inadequate* employment does matter—and matters a lot.

Some of the most revealing findings come from research at New York's Vera Institute of Justice. In one study, the Vera researchers interviewed a sample of men released from the Riker's Island prison in New York City in the late seventies. These were mainly young, minority men who had been convicted of a variety of misdemeanors, mostly crimes against property, and had usually served time before. Most were also poorly educated: less than a third had a high-school diploma or its equivalent, another third never got past the ninth grade. Some had fairly solid job histories, but most didn't; a few had never worked in their lives. Of those who *had* worked, only about half had ever held a job for more than a year; a third had never kept a job for longer than six months. And even those who had had a reasonably solid connection with the labor market in the past had often lost it well before their current spells in prison. Only 16 percent had been working immediately before the arrest that had put them behind bars.

Not only did these men have a decidedly loose relation to the world of work, but with few exceptions the jobs they did hold were "low level and paid poorly": two-thirds of the jobs paid less than $125 a week, in a year when it took almost that amount just to reach the federal poverty level; just 14 percent paid more than $175.

The Vera researchers expected that the careers of these men would exhibit fairly clear-cut and direct connections between unemployment and crime. Instead, as interviews with the men over the space of several months revealed, things were more complicated.

For some of these offenders, work and crime seemed indeed to be, as the Vera researchers put it, mutually exclusive activities; they either worked or stole. "If you're working and you see something you want," one interviewee told them, "you wonder how you're going to save enough to buy it. If you're not working and you see something you want, you wonder how you're going to take it." Some felt that losing a job had been directly responsible for their turning to crime—either because of the loss of income or indirectly, because it led to depression, idleness, and drug use. Others both worked and stole at the same time, but stole much more when they were out of work. All these patterns fit, in one way or another, the researchers' initial expectations. But other patterns also turned up. For a few of the men, working actually *encouraged* their criminality. Some used their jobs as a cover for drug sales. One worked in order to buy enough drugs to resume a career as a dealer. Another, in a truly complex pattern, worked at casual labor in order to buy enough heroin so that he would feel well enough to go out and steal at night. Others simply stole whatever they could from the places they worked. Thus, another respondent, one of the few who had found work since release, claimed he "never had a job where he did not steal."

> When he worked in a hospital, he stole baby socks, sheets, and embalming fluid (which he sold to marijuana dealers to enhance "bad reefer"). When he worked in a bank training program, he stole $50 as soon as he had the chance. His heaviest offense, for which he served four years in an upstate prison, came when he committed an armed robbery at the office building where he worked, having observed when the greatest amount of cash would be out of the safe. He claimed to have worked thirty days since his release cleaning floors at a large discount store, where he reports stealing four television sets, ten tennis outfits, and six pairs of sneakers.

A more common pattern was to alternate between legitimate work and small-scale crime. Men would take jobs for as long as they could handle the boredom, harassment, and low pay that usually came with them, or as long as they felt constrained against replacing petty work with petty crime by the risks of arrest. But these jobs could not hold them for long, and they soon moved back into street crime. What comes out most clearly in Vera's interviews with these men is the relative attractiveness of crime—even the small-time property crimes most of them engaged in—when balanced against the inadequacy of the work available. "If the job pays good, I'll go to the job," one respondent acknowledged; "if the street is good, I'll go back to the street." Over and over, the interviews show how thoroughly the tenuous, unsatisfying work roles available to these men are simply outclassed by the potential rewards of the street. "That's one thing I don't like about jobs," another respondent told the interviewers. "Out on the street . . . I can make close to $300 a night if I were to stay out there 5 or 6 hours . . . whereas if I was working I would make close to $200 in two weeks."

Revealingly, the Vera respondents were "generally far more animated when discussing successful criminals and crime fantasies than they were when defining the kind of job they would 'most like to have'"; they "could more easily envision themselves in grander roles in crime than their daily lives in the legitimate world of work allowed." "Apparently," the Vera researchers conclude, "at least in imagination, there are fewer barriers to upward mobility in crime than in employment."*

It's understandable that these poor expectations for decent work might breed the patterns of alternating low-level work and petty property crime documented in the Vera study. But there is also considerable evidence that the same alienated relationship to productive work is deeply implicated in *violent* crime as well. This connection emerges starkly in interviews conducted by researchers at the URSA Institute in San Francisco, who were particularly interested in any characteristics that distinguished violent delinquents from other young offenders. They interviewed sixty-three youths in juvenile prisons in four cities; each was guilty of a violent felony and had been convicted of at least one similar crime in the past. They concluded that "youth employment per se does not reduce delinquency"; but that the *quality* of work—its "status, skills, promotions, wages"—strongly affects all kinds of delinquent behavior, especially serious violence. "Where working youths perceive growth, benefits, and tangible rewards from their employment," the study concludes, "they

---

*That inability even to envision clearly what kind of work they would *like* to do fits a pattern I have seen in conducting interviews with hard-core drug-addicted offenders in California. It was hard to talk with these men and women for very long without realizing that they simply did not think in positive terms, even on the level of fantasy, about what "straight" life had to offer. They could complain about the shortcomings of the jobs they sporadically held and discourse at length about both the benefits and the pains of street life, but if you asked them what they would do if they could do what they wanted—what kind of work they would like to do, what they would like to learn—they had great trouble thinking of anything and often barely understood the questions.

commit fewer of each type of offense." And "work quality" was precisely what was most lacking in the communities from which these youths came; indeed, these young men "identified few lifestyle choices in their neighborhoods other than criminal activity or idleness."

One reason why this narrowing of choices so conduces to violence is that it makes *illicit* work—like selling drugs—relatively attractive, as the comments in the Vera study suggest. And since disputes over markets or "turf" in illegal occupations cannot be resolved through legal means, force and violence are typically used instead. Deadly weapons have always been a hallmark of illegal work, a fact that helps account for the appearance of peaks in American homicide rates in the twenties—during Prohibition—and from the late sixties onward, when hard drugs spread virulently in American cities. (Close to a third of the homicides in Oakland, California, in 1983 and 1984 were related to drug dealing; most of the victims were young black men—or innocent bystanders.) Reducing the central role of drug dealing in the subterranean economy of the inner cities would surely lower the violent crime rate; but it has proven hard to do (despite heavy penalties . . .) when legitimate labor markets have offered so few attractive alternatives.

The accumulating evidence, then, tells us that it is not just the fact of having or not having a job that is most important, nor is the level of crime most strongly or consistently affected by fluctuations in the national unemployment rate. The more consistent influence is the *quality* of work—its stability, its level of pay, its capacity to give the workers a sense of dignity and participation, the esteem of peers and community. In our society these fundamental needs are virtually impossible to satisfy without a job—but they are all too often difficult even *with* a job, and nearly impossible in many of the kinds of jobs available in America today, especially to the disadvantaged young. Whether work can avert crime, in short, depends on whether it is part of a larger process through which the young are gradually integrated into a productive and valued role in a larger community. Similarly, whether unemployment leads to crime depends heavily on whether it is a temporary interruption of a longer and more hopeful trajectory into that kind of role, or represents a permanent condition of economic marginality that virtually assures a sense of purposelessness, alienation, and deprivation.

Obviously, this has more than theoretical relevance. It suggests . . . that efforts to force the young, the marginal, and the deprived into *any* kind of work, however ill rewarded and demeaning, are likely to be futile at best and destructive at worst. If we wish to build a less volatile and violent society, we will need to concentrate on improving the long-term prospects for stable and valued work for those now largely excluded from it.

38

RETHINKING THE DRUG PROBLEM

JEROME H. SKOLNICK

When first delineated in the late nineteenth century, Tourette's syndrome was regarded as a "moral" disease, an expression of deliberate mischievousness or weakness of the will. In a sudden reversal in the 1960s, when it was discovered that the drug haloperidol could suppress Tourette's symptoms, including involuntary twitching and grimacing, the disease came to be understood "as the result of an imbalance of a neurotransmitter, dopamine, in the brain." In a recent article, the neurologist Oliver Sacks discussed Tourette's as having an extraordinarily complex etiology and cure. Sacks argues, however, that no single perspective—biological, moral-social, or psychological—adequately captures the full meaning and impact of the disease.[1]

The etiology and solution to the American drug problem is possibly even more complex than that of Tourette's syndrome. Yet it has been defined at the national level as primarily a moral challenge. In September 1989, the Bush administration published its first *National Drug Control Strategy*, which set a tone and direction for drug policy which has continued throughout the Bush presidency. (Another *Strategy* was published in January 1992 with only a slightly different ordering of priorities.) The use of any drug, in whatever quantity, was attributed to the deficient moral character of individuals, or

Jerome H. Skolnick is Claire Clements Dean's Professor of Law, Jurisprudence and Social Policy Program, University of California, Berkeley.

weakness of will. Drug use was said to "degrade human character," while a good society "ignores its people's character at its peril."

The high priority accorded repressive law enforcement seemed to flow naturally from the moralistic attitudes toward drug use and the role of government as expressed in the 1989 *Strategy*. Adopting the "war on drugs" as its overriding metaphor, the 1989 *Strategy* fulfilled the metaphor's promise by advocating a vast expansion of the apparatus of social control—particularly of law enforcement and prisons—into what resembles a semimartial state. Introducing the 1989 *Strategy* to America on national television, President Bush proposed that the federal government increase spending to combat drugs by $1.5 billion for enforcement and $1.5 billion for interdiction, but only by $321 million for treatment and $250 million for education. The *Strategy* advocated that billions more be spent by the states, particularly to expand the criminal justice system.

While acknowledging that there is no easy, or even difficult, solution to the American drug problem, I shall argue that, like the shift in understanding Tourette's syndrome, we need a sharp reversal in our thinking regarding drugs, from a perspective centered on moral failure to a broader and more complex etiology highlighting public health and underlying social issues. The militaristic approach is, in any case, programmed to fail. Persistent dilemmas and paradoxes will undermine the capacity of law enforcement officers, at any level, to solve the drug problem.

Working narcotic police understand the limitations of law enforcement, perhaps more than anyone. I asked an experienced New York narcotics officer, a trainer of undercover operatives, whom I accompanied in 1990 to observe the drug dealing scene in New York City's Washington Heights (a major marketing center for crack cocaine), how effective narcotics enforcement was in interfering with cocaine trafficking. His succinct and evocative reply: "We're like a gnat biting on a horse's ass."

The drug problem has two facets: one is abuse and addiction of both legal and illegal drugs; the second is the crime and violence connected to illegal drug use and sale. The administration's approach to expand law enforcement in an unprecedented way has had little impact on either of these problems—except to worsen street violence—because it ignores or does not appreciate the imperatives driving people to use and sell illegal drugs; it underestimates the dilemmas faced by law enforcement in controlling the distribution and use of drugs; it is insensitive to the social and economic underpinnings of drug marketing and use in the United States; and it is oblivious to the implications of a war on drugs for the character of the nation.

❖ DRUGS: NATURAL CRIME OR VICE?

The Bush administration's approach is built on the premise that drug dealing and use is something morally repugnant in and of itself; the solutions that flow from this premise treat people's involvement in drugs as major crimes which must be punished severely. This vision has, of course, serious implications for the workings of our criminal justice system at every level, for the police, the courts, and the prisons. Criminological theorists classically distinguish between "natural" and "regulatory" conceptions of crime. A "natural" conception of crime "embodies a sense of an act that is deeply wrong, that evokes strong communal disapproval, and that is thought to deserve, indeed to call for, a punitive sanction.[2] Ordinarily then, when we think of crime we think of homicide, rape, and assault. We think of these because all are "natural" wrongs, *mala in se,* acts that we understand, almost intuitively, to be wrong in themselves.

By contrast, under a "regulatory" conception, crime is not grounded in moral intuition. It is simply conduct prohibited by a legislature to which penalties are attached. For example, in England the law requires automobiles to drive on the left, while in the United States we drive on the right. Similarly, it might be considered *mala prohibitum* to accept bets on horse racing in a city where off-track betting is illegal (for example, New York) because accepting these bets does not conform to the regulations under which legal horse race betting is permitted. In neither of these cases, however, could the conduct that is prohibited be considered *mala in se.*

A key question that any drug strategy must address is whether the sale or use of drugs is more comparable to illegal betting (use) and bookmaking (sale) or to armed robbery and homicide. How one answers that question will in large part determine one's assessment of the nation's drug control policy. The *Strategy* rests on the moral vision that not only the sale but also the use of illegal drugs is *mala in se.* The *Strategy* accordingly advocates expanding and reshaping the criminal justice system "in an unprecedented way" with not only more police, but more "jails, prosecutors, judges, courtrooms, prisons and administrative staff."[3] The criminal justice system has, in fact, become a growth industry, yet with not nearly enough capacity to contain the more than one million inmates already incarcerated.

From the perspective of the *mala in se* theorist, environmental causes of crime and drug use are largely irrelevant, practically invisible. Since individual moral failure, or the failure of will, activates the drug problem, environmental or medical causes—poverty, unemployment, family breakdown, addiction—need not be given high priority. Punishment thus becomes the primary and preferred response. From this perspective it makes sense to stigmatize the casual user as the root villain of the drug problem, since without the casual user, the seller would presumably disappear.[4]

But is the casual user the root of the drug problem? The 1989 *Strategy's* statistical analysis suggests that attributing the drug problem to the casual user rather than the addict is a moral judgement, not an analytical one. The *Strategy* itself begins with good news. Citing a July 1989 survey by the National Institute on Drug Abuse (NIDA), the *Strategy* reports that "current use of the two most common illegal substances—marijuana and cocaine—is down 36 and 48 percent respectively."[5] But it quickly moves to the bad news. Drug related crime and violence continue to rise, the *Strategy* points out, and the threat drugs pose to public health has never been greater because drugs are cheap and "available to almost everyone who wants them."[6]

Who wants drugs? The 1992 *Strategy* acknowledges that the "drug war" is a "two-front" affair.[7] It takes credit for declining use by casual and younger users but sadly reports increasing use by addicted users and those over 35. In actuality, this pattern occurred in 1989 as well. According to an earlier self-report study, casual users never did use much of the total cocaine consumed in the United States. The National Narcotics Intelligence Consumer Committee found that "heavy users" comprised 6.9 percent of the user population, yet consumed 63 percent of the cocaine in this country.[8]

This pattern is probably true of most drugs, including alcohol. One report, for example, shows that 10 percent of the population uses 57 percent of the alcohol, 20 percent of the population uses 78 percent.[9] Moreover, if as the *Strategy* reports, casual use is declining while demand for drugs rises or remains about the same, it seems clear that the addict, not the casual user, is the chief source of demand for cocaine.

Nevertheless, casual use rather than addiction is the focal point of the *Strategy*. The theory plays out something like this: addicts need treatment, but they do not contribute much to the spread of drug use. An addict is a "bottomed-out mess" and his or her drug use is therefore "not very contagious."[10] But the casual user is an attractive person "likely to have a still-intact family, social and work life."[11] More attractive than the addict, the casual user sets a bad and appealing example; therefore, his drug use "is *highly* contagious."[12]

Since, however, casual use seems to be declining, and since addicts consume most of the drugs consumed, including alcohol, a focus on the casual, more moderate, user can scarcely be justified. How can we account for it? Three possible reasons come to mind. First, it virtually insures a measure of success, since casual drug use seems to be flagging anyhow. Second, denunciation of the casual user, who is more likely to be white and middle class, relieves the administration of accusations that the law enforcement side of the war on drugs will surely turn out to be disproportionately a war on minority sellers and users, which it surely will be. Finally, a focus on the addict would shift the priorities of drug policy away from police and punishment to treatment, rehabilitation, AIDS research, and the social and economic conditions under which treatment is most likely to work.

Yet casual use of drugs and alcohol is fairly commonplace in American society—enough so that there is almost intuitive agreement that these acts should be heavily punished. If casual use can be shown to have a practical, harmful effect, however, even if not a direct one—i.e., the "contagious" spread of the drug "disease"—the more persuasive is the justification for cracking down on an activity considered to be immoral.

The disease metaphor implies such a justification, although scarcely a compelling one. The casual user's supposed propensity to "infect" others becomes the reason for cracking down. Use, it is assumed, must inevitably lead to abuse. In actuality, the relation between use and abuse depends on the drug, the nature of the user, and the circumstances under which it is consumed. But a moralistic stance easily escalates into a legalistic one collapsing "use" with "abuse." Thus, all marijuana users become, by that definition, immoral abusers who deserve punishment.

■ Alternative Views: *Mala Prohibitum*

Those who believe that drug use is *mala prohibitum* fall into two basic camps. One regards drug use in classic libertarian terms, as a private matter. This view is grounded in John Stuart Mill's theory of individual liberty. Mill feared the tyranny of the majority which he described as "the tyranny of the prevailing opinion and feeling."[13] He argued that society has a "tendency to impose, by other means than civil penalties, its own ideas and practices as rules of conduct on those who dissent from them." Mill believed in the sanctity of the individual, in individual independence. Most of all he feared the tendency of collective opinion to *compel* others "to fashion themselves upon the model of its own."

Mill did not deny that collective opinion had a legitimate need to interfere with individual independence. He believed that unless society found the proper limit and maintained it against encroachment, the result would be a form of political despotism. This limit is widely known among philosophers as the "harm principle." The enduring influence of *On Liberty* and its harm principle is derived less from some exquisite utilitarian summation than from Mill's intuitions about the despotic potential of government. "The only purpose for which power can be rightfully exercised over any member of a civilized community, against his will," Mill says, "is to prevent harm to others."[14] Mill did not oppose persuading, entreating, or remonstrating with people who engage in admittedly self-destructive conduct. He believed that the criminal law, the power of government, should not be used to deter and to punish individuals in that part of conduct which "merely concerns himself."

Assuming the validity of the harm principle, what standard or principle should we employ to decide whether a particular line of potentially harmful conduct—smoking cigarettes, snorting cocaine, eating to obesity—is of sufficient concern to others to warrant the imposition of a criminal penalty? Mill is himself not entirely clear on this point, but he does make two observations which suggest how it is that such political opposites as William Buckley, Milton Friedman, and the American Civil Liberties Union can agree that drug use ought to be decriminalized.

Mill strongly opposed government interference. He believed in competition, and in competitive examinations, even though the losers might be hurt. In general, he believed in free trade and opposed governmental regulation of advertising. Nor could he be considered a powerful advocate of consumer protection. Indeed, the harm principle was for him not an invitation for the government to act when conduct is harmful; rather, it is a limiting principle—the government should not act unless there is demonstrable harm to others.

Nevertheless, Mill did not oppose and even encouraged government regulation where appropriate. The state of Maine had passed a 19th-century prohibition statute, and the "Maine Law" figures prominently in Mill's discussion of liberty. He recognized that those who sold alcoholic beverages—"strong drink" as he called it—had an interest in promoting sales and, contrary to popular assumptions about Mill, he was not at all opposed to regulating them. On the contrary, he saw their interest in promoting intemperance as a "real evil," justifying State restrictions.[15]

Mill, furthermore, uses the example of drunkenness to illustrate the boundaries of the harm principle. Whether someone becomes drunk or not is their business. When, however, under the influence of alcohol, the drunken person commits an act of violence against another, it becomes the government's business. Then, Mill writes:

> I should deem it perfectly legitimate that a person, who had once been convicted of any act of violence to others under the influence of drink, should be placed under a special legal restriction, personal to himself; that if he were afterwards found drunk, he should be liable to a penalty, and that if when in that state he committed another offense, the punishment to which he would be liable for that other offense should be increased in severity.[16]

In sum, the key distinction for those who stand by the harm principle is between private and public space. Mill believed that individuals should be free to gamble in their own homes or private clubs, but that public gambling should not at all be permitted.[17] A Millian liberal distinguishes between being in a state of intoxication in the privacy of one's home, thereby doing whatever harm intoxication does to oneself; and driving on public roads under the influence of drugs or alcohol. A liberal opposes, on principle, as "legal paternalism" any form of coercive legislation that seeks to protect individuals from self-inflicted harm.

A second *mala prohibitum* view regards drug use as at worst undesirable, unfortunate, even deviant, but not necessarily so socially harmful as to justify its characterization as a crime. How we should deal with it is less a matter of the principled relationship between the government and the individual than a weighing of the costs and benefits of one policy over another. In this view, drug use should be regulated, not because it is a serious criminal offense, but because drug use entails external costs that society must bear. This position could be termed "post-Millian" in that it calculates the interests of society rather than the individual. This pragmatic position balances the costs against the benefits of a proposed policy. The Millian vision is broadened to include a plurality of others, including costs to community and public safety. Since the morality of a line of conduct is not dispositive, proponents might *entertain* legalization of drugs, as does George P. Schultz, who as Secretary of State led the Reagan Administration's overseas crop eradication program.[18] Even Milton Friedman and William Buckley increasingly make their arguments based on the social consequences of criminalization rather than on individual freedom alone.

■ The Consequential Critique

How should we think about drugs? If one accepts the underlying assumptions of the Bush administration's *Strategy,* it is difficult to argue with its combination of unprecedented punishment and moral regeneration. But if one rejects, or is even unsure of, the underlying assumptions and perceptions of the problem, we need to ask how well its proposals will work and whether alternative policies might work better, and at less cost to the values of a free society.

There is much disagreement, especially within the policy-making and academic communities, over the appropriate definition of and response to the drug problem. Advocates of repression have gained their share of supporters as the social acceptability of drug use has shifted dramatically toward moral intolerance over the past twenty years. In an anticrime climate, politicians are responding to an electorate demanding higher penalties for drug dealing and use. However, these views, while increasingly popular, by no means represent a consensus.

Many people maintain quite different attitudes toward drug use, depending on the levels, time, place, and occasion for intoxication. They are ambivalent about the moral blameworthiness of private drug use and even of addiction, should it occur. As Herbert Packer once observed:

> The extent of disagreement about moral judgements is an obvious reason for hesitancy about an automatic enforcement of morals. There have been monolithic societies in which a static and homogeneous ethnic, religious, and class structure conduces to widely shared acceptance of a value system. But that is hardly a description of the reality of twentieth-century American society, or of its pluralistic and liberal aspirations. . . . We don't begin to agree about the "morality" of smoking, drinking, gambling, fornicating, or drug-taking, for example, quite apart from the gap between what we say and what we do. The more heterogeneous the society, the more repressive the enforcement of morals must be.[19]

If, as Packer suggests, there is no consensus that intoxication—absent tangible harm to others—is inherently despicable, then we have no intuitive sense of deserved retribution. This does not imply that drug use should never be penalized, but rather that consequentialist arguments stressing the impact of deterrence, incarceration, and rehabilitation will make more sense than moralistic ones. People will ask, "What works and what doesn't work and why?"—rather than assuming that drug use of any kind, by any consenting adult, is inherently evil. So the question becomes, how well do the law enforcement forces arrayed against drug use and dealing work in practice?

❖ THE DILEMMAS OF LAW ENFORCEMENT

One would think that the heightened penalties and huge infusions of resources we have devoted to drug enforcement at the state and national levels would long ago have dried up the drug trade. Yet that did not happen during the 1980s and early 1990s. New York City arrest statistics tell the story. Despite efforts by dedicated and resourceful police officers, the New York narcotics scene seemed impervious to their intervention. Arrests increased every year in New York City following the introduction of crack cocaine in 1984. There were 45,000 arrests in that year, rising to 58,000 in 1986, 79,000 a year later, 89,000 in 1988 and more than 100,000 by the end of the decade. I asked then New York narcotics Chief John Hill whether these increasing arrests have been effective in stopping the problem. Chief Hill was less colorful in his language than the street detectives with whom I had been riding, but equally pessimistic. "The easiest thing to do is make an arrest," he said to me. "The hardest thing is to stop it. Enforcement will never stop it."

The "get tough" approach is essentially based on a theory of deterrence that sounds superficially persuasive. If we raise the cost of selling and using drugs by increasing penalties, it is assumed, we will drive out dealers and sellers. In the abstract, the theory seems to make sense. In practice, when we delve more deeply into its workings, we can understand how and why it works far less efficiently than assumed, or, paradoxically, may even worsen the drug problem.

■ Supply and Demand

The sale of drugs is economically motivated, and is thus responsive to market incentives and disincentives. The question remains as to how these operate in the context of the drug trade. The 1989 *Strategy* acknowledges that "despite interdiction's successful disruptions of trafficking patterns, the supply of illegal drugs entering the United States has, by all estimates, continued to grow."[20] Why should that have happened? One reason is that demand generates supply for drugs. Demand for drugs in the United States and Europe contributed to the growth of the cocaine business in Colombia and Peru, the world's main growers of coca.[21] A rise in production increases supply, which causes a drop in price. Price reduction in turn further invigorates demand, which stimulates the whole cycle again.

■ Efficient Suppliers: Survival of the Fittest

"As we have expanded our interdiction efforts," the 1989 *Strategy* states, "we have seized increasing amounts of illegal drugs. Stepped up interdiction has also forced drug traffickers to make significant operational changes.... Every time we disrupt or close a particular trafficking route, we have found that traffickers resort to other smuggling tactics that are even more difficult to detect."[22] This is undoubtedly true, but it argues as well against, rather than for, stepped-up interdiction.

More recently, the 1992 *Strategy* took pride in record drug seizures. It reported that in May 1991, US Customs inspectors seized a record 1,080 pounds of heroin in a cargo container arriving at San Francisco. In July 1991, the US Navy intercepted the *Lucky Star* in the Pacific. The ship was escorted to Pearl Harbor, where Customs agents seized a record 73 tons of hashish. In

November 1991, US Customs and DEA agents seized, in the second largest cocaine seizure in US history, 23,641 pounds of cocaine concealed in concrete fence posts that were being delivered from Venezuela to Miami.

Should record seizures be considered an accomplishment or a concern? If we interpret the record seizures as a cutoff of the drug supply to the United States, then they are a triumph. If we believe, however, as most observers of the drug trade do, including law enforcement observers, that we interdict around 10 percent to, at most, 20 percent of the shipments of drugs to the United States, these record seizures suggest the enormity of the drug supply and the relatively efficient organization of the suppliers.

As these more efficient producers exercise greater control over markets, they may exercise monopolistic control to raise prices. Law enforcement officials may mistakenly assume that rises in the street price of drugs are a result of efficient interdiction strategies. In actuality, higher prices may bring greater profits to efficient suppliers.

Approximately 60 percent of the world's cocaine is grown in the Peruvian Andes and processed in Columbia. Late in 1991, the United States assisted the Peruvian government in asserting control over airspace by introducing and manning new radar stations at airfields at Andoas and Iquitos, two river towns in the vast Amazonian region. In the first three months of 1992, nine planes were intercepted, forcing six to land and three to crash. Yet an estimated six planes a day leave Peru carrying coca base north.[23] Thus, only nine planes out of more than 1,000, approximately 1 percent, were intercepted. Even if ten or fifteen times that number were to be intercepted, there would be minor interference with the overall enterprise. Practically, interdiction is said to "introduce another level of risk to the individual drug smuggler."[24] Yet, while defending interdiction, the 1989 *Strategy* concedes that "interdiction alone cannot prevent the entry of drugs or fully deter traffickers and their organizations."[25]

Quite an understatement. In reality, interdiction efforts face what might be called "the Darwinian Trafficker Dilemma." Interdiction undercuts the marginally efficient drug traffickers and their operations, while the fittest—the best organized, the most corrupting of authorities, the most ruthless and efficient—survive. As Stephen G. Trujillo, a former Army Ranger, Green Beret, and enforcement specialist with the Drug Enforcement Administration's Operation Snowcap wrote of his experiences the day after President Alberto Fujimori suspended the Peruvian Constitution with the army's backing, in effect, a right wing military coup: Paradoxically, the destruction of dozens of cocaine labs by US and Peruvian forces has only encouraged the coca processors to be more efficient. Smaller, more decentralized labs are processing purer cocaine in the impenetrable jungles.[26]

■ The Permeability of Borders

Rand Corporation economist Peter Reuter, who studied the question of border permeability for the Department of Defense, concluded that "the U.S.-Mexico border can be crossed at many points . . . and a high value crossing can be accomplished very suddenly by a single individual in a large crowd of similar individuals. . . ."[27] Thus, the sheer number of people who make border crossings each year aggravates the problem of penetrable borders.

When the Reagan Administration's war on drugs cracked down on Florida as the main entry point for cocaine, drug smugglers moved the main supply route of the product from Florida to California. I spent four days reviewing the border situation in California with the assistance of the California State Narcotics Agency. They assigned a Mexican-American agent to me in Los Angeles, to help me understand the drug scene in southern California. Through his assistance, I was able to observe DEA operations, and to interview local and federal police. As with most narcotics police, they seemed to be intelligent, energetic, and well supplied with equipment. I was told that 60 percent of the narcotics entering the United States passed through California. The Mexican border posed a major, and virtually insolvable problem, however. The Mexican-American state narcotics agent who was my guide, and who had been raised in a Los Angeles gang neighborhood, took me to a Mexican restaurant for lunch, told me about his childhood, his entry into the police, looked at me earnestly, and said with some exasperation: "Look professor, 400,000 of my people cross the border illegally every year. How can you stop a much smaller number who carry a kilo or two of cocaine on their back?"[28] None of the record seizures reported in the 1992 *Strategy*, it might be noted, were at the Mexican border.

What is the administration's justification for interdiction efforts? The 1989 *Strategy* claims that interdiction "has major symbolic and practical value."[29] The symbolic value is gained from showing foreign governments and trafficking organizations our commitment to combating the drug trade. But symbolism seems an odd reason for policy, resting neither on practical achievement nor on canons of justice. Still, much of the proposal is grounded on symbolic themes and on the appearance of determination, rather than on a careful assessment of short and long range outcomes.

Interdiction advocates vastly overestimate the costs that interdiction imposes on drug trafficking. Interdiction is supposed to reduce street sales by increasing smuggling costs—in effect, taxing smuggling—and thus raising the street price. This assumes that smuggling costs constitute a significant percentage of street price. But that simply is not true. It is relatively cheap to produce and refine a kilo of cocaine, perhaps around $1,000 for a kilo that might eventually retail for $250,000 when broken down into quarter or even eight gram units. Smuggling costs might amount to an additional few percent of the retail price. In actuality, most of the retail price of cocaine is divided among those who distribute it on this side of the border. Rand economist Peter Reuter writes, "Fully 99 percent of the price of the drug when sold on the streets in the United States is accounted for by payments to people who distribute it."[30]

Thus, if a kilo of cocaine retails for $250,000, smuggling costs account for around $2,500. A doubling or tripling of smuggling costs accordingly has a negligible impact on street price. Combined with the vastly increased production which has driven prices down, interdiction has had little, if any, positive effects—and these can be outweighed by the unanticipated side effect of strengthening drug marketing organizations.

▉ Drug Hardening and Demand Substitution

When the Nixon administration succeeded in reducing the supply of low potency Mexican marijuana to California in the early 1970s, agriculturally skilled drug entrepreneurs developed a high potency marijuana (sensimilla) industry in Northern California, generating a market for a drug five or more times as potent. This example is illustrative of what might be called "The Drug Hardening Paradox." The more successful law enforcement is at cutting off supply, the more incentive drug dealers have for hardening drugs—i.e., developing varieties that are more potent, portable, and dangerous. Thus, the recent crackdown by state narcotics agents on the California marijuana market has reduced its supply, but crack cocaine has now emerged to replace marijuana. My colleagues and I have interviewed Oakland and south central Los Angeles youngsters who have never used marijuana, but who have used crack cocaine, which has for several years been less expensive and more available on California streets. In sum, law enforcement tactics may create more severe public health problems by generating demand for and production of more potent and dangerous drugs.

A paradox closely related to drug hardening, might be called "The Demand Substitution Paradox." Those who are interested in faster living through chemistry often find it possible to substitute one drug for another. (Most drug abusers usually ingest more than one drug.) Thus, price increases or lack of availability of one drug may activate consumers to seek out cheaper alternative drugs.

In the 1970s, marijuana was the popular drug among students. Today, it is alcohol. Thirty percent of high school seniors reported in 1991 that they had drunk heavily (five or more drinks in a row) at least once in the previous two weeks. Since alcohol is illegal for those under 21, all of this drinking was in violation of the law.

Twenty or thirty years ago, heroin was the "problem" drug in American society.[31] More recently, it has been crack cocaine, which is becoming less popular. At the same time, according to the 1992 *Strategy*, "the price of heroin has dropped, the purity has increased, seizures by law enforcement officials have increased, and there has been an upsurge in heroin emergency room mentions in the first two quarters of 1991—all, it would seem, indicative of a resurgence in drug use."[32] Although heroin users tend to be older, they are also more dangerous to the public health. Heroin is consumed intravenously, and its users are thus more likely to spread the HIV virus.

If we succeed in destroying agricultural drugs through crop destruction efforts in Peru, Bolivia, and Columbia, we could find an increase in the use of alternate drugs and in the supply of synthetic, designer drugs that are more potent and destructive than anything we have yet seen. These include fentanyl, for example, which is around 100 times as powerful as morphine and 20 times stronger than heroin. Fentanyl's medicinal analogs, sufentanyl and alfentanyl, are 2,000 to 6,000 times stronger than morphine. These drugs can produce bizarre, destructive, and unpredictable toxic effects. Fentanyl may be more widely used than we now know, since it cannot be detected by drug tests.[33]

As demand for particular drugs waxes and wanes based either on fashion or on interdiction, new drugs will be demanded by consumers and supplied by innovative entrepreneurs.

■ Corruption

Whatever the latest trend in drug use, manufacturers, smugglers, and distributors can operate more efficiently by corrupting public officials. Neither the 1989 nor 1992 *Strategy* discuss corruption, another dilemma confronting law enforcement efforts in the war on drugs, although it discusses "turf battles" among federal enforcement agencies.[34] A discussion of interagency rivalry is acceptable because it is a normal and acceptable aspect of bureaucratic processes.[35]

Corruption, on the other hand, is unmentionable. Any strategy, however, which fails to consider the possibility and ramifications of increased corruption in the wake of expanded law enforcement is seriously flawed.[36]

As we attempt to pressure foreign producers, we will have to work with authorities in such countries as Colombia, Bolivia, Panama, and Peru, countries where the bribe is a familiar part of law enforcement. Thus, the State Department's Bureau of International Narcotics Matters found that Jorge Luis Ochoa, a major Colombian drug trafficker, "was able to buy his freedom through the intimidated and vulnerable Colombian judicial system."[37] Concerning Colombia, journalist Tina Rosenberg observed:

> *In general, the closer an institution gets to the traffickers, the more corrupt it becomes. Cocaine's new income opportunities for judges have been well documented. Prosecutors are less corrupt, but it is a matter of logistics, not morals: it is simply easier to win cases by bribing judges, or the police. . . . Policemen, the infantry in the war on drugs, are usually young men from slum neighborhoods with third grade educations—exactly the profile of a drug dealer, and the line between the two tends to blur on the job.[38]*

No matter how honest US drug enforcement agents operating abroad are, they may find themselves operating in a climate of official corruption. In Peru, police officers bribe their superiors to be transferred to interdiction zones, where illegal landing fees can bring $5,000. Peru's Attorney General said in March 1992, "Many policemen, instead of fighting against drug trafficking . . . are involved in it."[39]

Indeed, in Peru, the corruption is so pervasive, and so sinister—the military are also in league with and protective of the drug dealers—as to endanger the safety of American advisers and DEA agents. Stephen Trujullo describes one of several threatening incidents:

> On June 15, 1990, three other DEA advisers and I accompanied the drug police to Tocache, north of the Santa Lucia base. Hovering over the municipal airfield in our helicopters, we caught soldiers red-handed as they transferred a load of cocaine base to a stash house. We landed and chased the fleeing soldiers back to their barracks, only to be surrounded by the remainder of the garrison. The soldiers raised their assault rifles, and their commander ordered us to surrender our weapons. Only the adroit diplomacy of the senior DEA agent saved us.[40]

Domestic police officers are equally susceptible to the temptations of drug money. Unfortunately, we are all too familiar with the legendary narcotics scandals which have plagued police departments in various cities. Perhaps the most famous have occurred in New York City where the Knapp Commission investigations reached both narcotics and other forms of vice. Patrick V. Murphy, a man with a reputation for reform, was recruited as Police Commissioner in New York in the wake of the scandal uncovered by the Knapp Commission. In his autobiography, he writes, "We ultimately discovered that the narcotics units under the previous police administration had made major contributions to the city's drug traffic. It was this area of corruption more than anything else which most shocked me."[41]

Narcotics corruption is not confined to New York City. Deputies in the Los Angeles County Sheriff's Department were recently involved in what *The Los Angeles Times* called "one of the worst corruption cases" in the department's history. Videotapes revealed one deputy hurriedly taking three $10,000 bundles of $100 bills from a dealer's shoulder bag and putting them into his partner's leather briefcase.[42]

Although the possibilities of corruption exist in any form of enforcement against criminal activity, it is particularly in drug enforcement that agents and officers encounter large sums of cash and drugs with great market value. In short, corruption must be counted as one of the anticipated costs of an unprecedented expansion of drug law enforcement. As Peter Reuter recently summed up the dilemma of corruption, "The incentive to bribe criminal justice officials is positively related to the intensity of enforcement."[43]

■ The Explosion of Imprisonment

The "unprecedented" expansion of police, prosecutors, and prisons implicates a third set of problems related to imprisonment. Attempting to solve the drug problem by imprisoning more drug users and sellers may, paradoxically, worsen the problem at the street level. State and federal prison populations have virtually doubled in the 1980s[44] and the rate of our prison population per 100,000 of total resident population has increased from 96 in 1970 to 228 in

1987.[45] Overcrowded jails and prisons are bulging with newly convicted criminals, and also with criminals whose probation and parole were revoked. In California, for example, the number of parole violators returned to prison between 1978 and 1988 increased by about eleven times.[46]

A likely reason for this rise is the increased frequency with which drug tests are being required of parolees.[47] Revised estimates by the California Department of Corrections project that the state's prison population will grow by more than 50 percent by the year 1994, and that the state will need to build up to twenty prisons to house the expected growth in inmate population.[48] As our advanced drug testing technology consigns more parolees and probationers to prison, we cannot continue to convict and impose longer sentences without building many new prisons.

The Bush administration's drug policy acknowledges this critical lack of prison space. It appreciates that "most state prisons are already operating far above their designed capacity."[49] It also recognizes that "many states have been forced under court order to release prisoners before their terms have been served whenever a court-established prison population limit has been exceeded."[50] The solution, however, is to encourage state governments to persuade their citizens to support new prisons. "The task of building [prisons], remains with state governments, who poorly serve their constituents when prison construction is stalled or resisted."[51]

Yet not a word appears about how to persuade citizens to pay for the continuing and rising expense of maintaining prisons, without raising state taxes to support prison construction. Furthermore, even those citizens who demand longer and more certain prison sentences are reluctant to live next door to prisons, which are being built in increasingly remote areas. Highly publicized plans for a 700 bed prison to house convicted Washington, D.C. drug dealers at Fort Meade, Maryland were embarrassingly withdrawn the day after they were announced because "there was too much public resistance,"[52] as there is near urban areas whenever a new prison site is proposed.

■ Ineffective Criminal Sanctions

Even if new prisons could be constructed over financial and community objections, a more fundamental problem is the failure of criminal sanctions to achieve purported goals. One of these is the reform and correction of inmates. Imprisonment is not necessarily stigmatic, nor entirely foreboding for those who sell drugs. My students and I have been interviewing imprisoned drug dealers in California since 1989, and learned that imprisonment may bring a certain elevated "home boy" status, especially for gang youths for whom prison, and prison gangs can become an alternative site of loyalty.[53]

Moreover, imprisonment often reinforces prisoners in their troublesome behavior. Already consigned to the margins of society, prisoners join gangs, use drugs, and make useful connections for buying and selling drugs. Perhaps the penitentiary was once a place for experiencing penance. However, today's correctional institutions, overcrowded with short-term parole violators who have failed their court-mandated drug tests, often serve purposes similar to those advanced by academic and business conventions—as an opportunity for "networking."[54] A recent newspaper survey of prison drug use found that it has become a "major problem," and it cited "threats to prison order, violence among inmates and corruption of guards and other employees" as among the most serious.[55]

President Bush and others have made the incarceration and execution of "drug kingpins" a focus of the drug war. When we succeed in incarcerating drug dealers in prisons, however, we encounter what I think of as the Felix Mitchell Paradox, named in honor of the West Coast's formerly most infamous drug distributor. In the mid-1980s, a federal strike force, with considerable assistance and dogged investigation by an Oakland Police vice squad, succeeded in convicting and imprisoning the East Bay's three leading drug dealers. Among these was the legendary Felix Mitchell, who, the prosecution charged, was largely responsible for Oakland's becoming a major drug dispensary, and who received a life sentence without possibility of parole in a federal district court for his drug related convictions.[56] One would expect that confining three leading drug dealers to prison would reduce the violence and other crimes related to narcotics. On the contrary, Oakland has since then experienced a continued increase in narcotics crimes and the absence of any indication that the Oakland residents perceive the community to be safer.[57] The post Felix Mitchell drug related homicide rate has proved especially vexing. Gangs competing for the Mitchell territory accounted for multiple murders, high speed chases, daytime assassinations, four assaults on police officers, and scores of other shootings. It is likely that, for the drug gangs, whatever deterrent value the criminal law has can be outweighed by the profits to be gained through expanding into the market vacuum created by the withdrawal of imprisoned suppliers.

Peter Reuter makes a similar observation about the relationship between violence and market share as an explanation for the District of Columbia's soaring homicide rate. He argues that when the supply of drug dealers exceeds the demand for drugs, "one obvious way to raise earnings is to eliminate the competition through violence."[58] The District of Columbia's soaring homicide rate cannot be attributed to inactivity of the District's police during the 1980s. Only 58 juveniles had been arrested for drug dealing offenses in 1981; by 1987 that figure had reached 1550.[59] In 1981, adult arrests—usually men in their early twenties—totalled 408; by 1987 it was 5,297.[60]

However notorious for drugs and homicides, Oakland, California and Washington, D.C. are scarcely unrepresentative. One can pick up almost any major metropolitan newspaper on any given day and read of drugs and homicide. Drugs and violence have in the 1980s and 1990s become as institutionalized a part of American life and journalism as the Vietnam War was in the 1960s, and as much of a quagmire. Thus, on April 2, 1992, the front page of *The New York Times* carried an article titled "From Queens to Rochester: Adrift in a World of Violence," about an 18-year-old who was arrested in a church, where he had sought sanctuary as a suspect who had killed eight people in four days. The author, Alison Mitchell, had interviewed the suspect's friends and neighbors who spoke to her of "a land in which a teen-ager sold cocaine like candy, putting an 'out' sign in his apartment window when he had run out of supplies." Increased criminal sanctions, as in the war on drugs, have had little impact in the cities of America against either drug kingpins and lower level dealers. Stepped-up enforcement has usually encouraged other suppliers to enter the market or amplify their activities through the violent elimination of competitors. It is time to face reality. The drug war has failed.

■ What Is to Be Done?

It is easier to say what is *not* to be done than what is to be. To be avoided are the ineffectual and costly policies and the misinformation of previous decades. When we educate about drugs we need to stress reality and health values. Drug education often poses false polarities. Drugs are either harmless or will "fry your brain." The dangers of marijuana were overstated in the 1950s and 1960s. The absurd overstatements (that marijuana use leads to violent assaults) instead of discouraging use, encouraged false inferences in the opposite direction— that marijuana use posed no dangers. In fact, drug effects and side effects are complex and vary according to the chemical properties of the drug; the setting in which it used; the potency (unfortified wine vs. distilled spirits), the quantity used, the frequency of use, and the biological, psychological, and social circumstances of the user. Many people can control their use of alcohol, cocaine, and marijuana. Others cannot.

Legalization has often been proposed as an alternative to the vast expansion of law enforcement that we witnessed during the Reagan-Bush years. Legalization is no panacea either, however. Questions to be asked about it are: what form would legalization take; are all or only some drugs to be legalized; what would be the costs and benefits and to which groups; and can legalization be reconciled with a positive moral message?

Essentially, legalization implies four models. Under the least restrictive free-market model, every drug, even cocaine and heroin, could be sold as we do aspirin, over-the-counter. The free-market model offers the strongest argument for legalizing. At one stroke, the free market would wipe out smuggling (drugs could be taxed), organized drug syndicates, street sales, and street violence. Scarcely less restrictive is the cigarette paradigm, regulating only as to age of purchaser. Alcohol offers a third, slightly more regulated model, while the most restrictive of the legalization models is the prescription drug paradigm, which is already employed for methadone treatment, and for treatment accorded to a vast patient population of users of tranquilizers and sleeping pills.

Marijuana offers the most plausible case for nonprohibition. Were we to regulate marijuana more tightly than we do alcohol, we would end half or more of our current drug arrests without a significant impact on public health.

We would expect that more people would use marijuana, but not so many more, given the increasing concern for health and sobriety between the 1960s and the 1990s. None of this will perfectly succeed. The more controls government imposes, the greater the incentives to develop illegal markets. If we allow the sale and use of low potency marijuana, we will stimulate illegal markets in the high potency stuff. If we control sales to youngsters, some will surely buy on the black market, as they already do.

If Cocaine HCL (powder cocaine) were to be legalized, we would generate incentives for producing crack cocaine, that is, purified, heat stable cocaine, suitable for smoking. "Absorbed across the pulmonary vascular bed," explain the neurologists Golbe and Merkin, "it produces a more intense euphoria and more precipitous withdrawal than Cocaine HCL and is therefore more addictive."[61]

There is thus no perfect legalization solution, but the benefits of marijuana legalization seem to outweigh the costs of enforcement. On the other hand, since crack cocaine, heroin, and phencyclidine (PCP) remain inner-city favorites, the actual and symbolic consequences of legalizing these drugs may prove disastrous, possibly generating a sharp rise in use among the truly disadvantaged, especially among teenagers already inclined to use these drugs. To be sure, these drugs are already easily obtainable, though not as easily as they would be under a legalization regime. Reasonable prudence demands that these drugs remain illegal. As John Kaplan observed in opposing cocaine legalization: "If we legalize cocaine now, how long should we wait before deciding whether we made a mistake? And if we decided that we had, how would we go about recriminalizing the drug?"[62]

The issue, however, is not only whether to legalize a drug, but how to influence the message accompanying legalization. Legalization of a vice does not necessarily connote approval or promotion of the activity, although it so often has in the United States. When Prohibition was repealed, the saloon doors were thrown open. We not only legalized distilled spirits, but the cocktail lounge and a culture of drinking along with it. When our state governments have legalized gambling—lotteries, casinos, and off-track betting—they have also, and shamelessly, promoted gambling. However, it is possible to reconcile legalization with a strong public health message. When the British legalized casinos in 1968, the purpose was to control organized crime. They did not permit casinos to advertise at all, not even with matchbooks or advertisements in the telephone directory.

Similarly, if we eliminated criminal penalties for possession of marijuana, and strictly regulated its sale, such decriminalization would need to be accompanied by a larger moral purpose—to reduce crime and violence, to enhance public health and safety through drug education and treatment, and to invigorate a sense of community. Legalization of marijuana, in sum, need not and should not imply advocacy. On the contrary, the taxed proceeds from such legalization should discourage, even while permitting, use of the drug. A slogan for legal drugs might be: "Never use cigarettes; and if you must use alcohol and marijuana, use moderately."

❖ A PUBLIC HEALTH/SOCIAL PROBLEMS STRATEGY

On March 12, 1992, *The San Francisco Examiner,* a Hearst newspaper critical of the Bush Administration's war on drugs strategy, praised Dr. Andrew Mecca, director of California's Department of Alcohol and Drug Programs, for his new ideas. What are these? Presently, two-thirds of the nearly 13 billion dollars the United States spends waging a war on drugs is allocated to interdiction and law enforcement. Only one-third goes to prevention and treatment. In the *Examiner's* view, and in my own, these priorities should be reversed. Dr. Mecca is taking the right course but is not there yet. With a $1 billion budget to fight drugs, California is allocating 50 percent for enforcement, and 50 percent for treatment and prevention. Nevertheless, this recognition that priorities need to be shifted is the sensible direction in which to move.

I would add, however, that the public health approach needs to be supplemented by a "social problems" dimension critical to understanding the etiology of drug use and the obstacles to successful treatment and prevention. The moralistic stance adopted by the Bush administration in its *Strategy* assumes a single minded moral paradigm—drug users and sellers are evil and they must be punished. But it ignores key issues: why do some communities produce street drug dealers and street violence, while others do not? How do social, economic, and psychological conditions affect drug use and sale? Why do users ingest crack cocaine? What does it mean to say that it is "addicting"?

Here are some answers: Crack cocaine, like Cocaine HCL, but unlike heroin, is psychologically, but not physiologically addicting. A drug dealer (and former user) whom I interviewed communicated the distinction vividly and clearly in nonmedical terminology:

> *It's not addicting like your body craves it. You're not going to get sick . . . by not smoking. Only thing that craves crack is your mind. It's like an illusion. You hit the pipe you are whatever you want to be. . . . Say you're into music and you're basing (using crack or its chemical equivalent). You feel like you are James Brown or Stevie Wonder or Michael Jackson.*

The above description suggests that users ingest drugs to feel euphoric, to take one out of life's circumstances, to overcome despair, hopelessness, and low self-esteem. Such feeling states can occur to individuals within any social group, but they are heightened by joblessness, poverty, and neglect. Thus, the more satisfied and engaged people are with their lives and themselves, the less likely are they to be drawn—regardless of the consequences—to the euphoric feeling states of crack cocaine. A clean and sober addict with a job will be less likely to relapse than one who is unemployed.

Total abstinence—being clean and sober—should be the treatment goal for cocaine and alcohol addictions. Oral methadone maintenance is a less desirable, but necessary, alternative for heroin addicts, especially since heroin addicts, who are physically addicted, typically ingest intravenously, and therefore are at risk for contracting and spreading the HIV virus. Whatever the treatment modality, the more an addict can count on social support through family, friends, a therapy group such as Alcoholics Anonymous, the more likely will the goal of total abstinence be achieved.

The "truly disadvantaged" are less likely to enjoy this sort of social and economic support. Such addicts live in a world—often a housing project—which cues craving as they see drugs being sold and used all around them. Treatment is often unavailable as there are no Betty Ford clinics for the desperately poor. It is in this setting, through foot patrol, community policing and community organization, that law enforcement enjoys perhaps its greatest potential.

But even the best organized and most thoughtful local law enforcement strategies are constrained, since those who sell, as well as those who buy, are also responding to underlying economic and social conditions. Terry Williams, a sociologist who spent more than 1,200 hours studying a primarily Dominican drug gang in Washington Heights, whom he called "The Cocaine Kids," portrays them as both antisocial criminals and "struggling young people trying to make a place for themselves in a world few care to understand and many wish would go away." The kids have learned a trade. They know how to buy cocaine, cook it into crack, distribute, and sell it. Williams portrays them as entrepreneurs, interested not only in making money, but also in showing their families and friends that they can succeed at something.[63] And Phillipe Bourgeois, who studied crack dealers in New York's Spanish Harlem, challenges the assertion of culture-of-poverty theorists that the poor are socialized out of the mainstream and have different values. He concludes that:

> On the contrary, ambitious, energetic, inner-city youths are attracted to the underground economy precisely because they believe in the rags-to-riches American dream. . . . Without stretching the point too much, they can be seen in conventional terms as rugged individualists on an unpredictable frontier where fortune, fame and destruction are all just around the corner.[64]

Neither moral exhortation nor an unprecedented expansion of law enforcement, or military intervention can or should be used to address what is essentially a health and social problem. These hard edged responses are costly to our pocketbooks and, worse, are largely counterproductive. Until we redefine the drug problem as a public health and social problem rather than as a moral failure, we will make little headway in promoting the health and public safety of our citizens.

Endnotes

1. Oliver Sacks, "A Neurologist's Notebook," *The New Yorker,* 16 March 1992, 85.

2. Hughes, *The Concept of Crime,* in S. Kadish, ed., *Encyclopedia of Crime and Justice* (1983), 294–95. This excellent essay goes on to develop the distinction.

3. See the first *National Drug Control Strategy* issued by the Office of National Drug Control Policy, Executive Office of the President (Washington, D.C.: US Government Printing Office, 1989), 24 [hereinafter *Strategy*].

4. Jaynes and Williams, eds., *A Common Destiny: Blacks and American Society* (Washington, D.C.: National Academy Press, 1989), 398.

5. Sacks, "A Neurologist's Notebook."

6. *Strategy*, 2.

7. *National Drug Control Strategy: A Nation Responds to Drug Use* (Washington, D.C.: US Government Printing Office, 1992).

8. These data are cited in Cloud, "Cocaine, Demand, and Addiction: A Study of the Possible Convergence of Rational Theory and National Policy," *Vanderbilt University Law Review* 42 (1989): 725, 752.

9. Dean R. Gerstein, "Alcohol Use and Consequences," in Mark H. Moore and Dean Gerstein, eds., *Alcohol and Public Policy: Beyond the Shadow of Prohibition* (Washington, D.C.: National Academy Press, 1981).

10. *Strategy*, 11.

11. Ibid.

12. Ibid.

13. John Stuart Mill, *On Liberty* (London: Penguin, 1974), 9. (First published in 1859).

14. Ibid.

15. Ibid., 170.

16. Ibid., 167.

17. Ibid., 170.

18. Even conservative policy analyst Charles Murray thinks legalization might be the answer to the drug problem. *The New York Times,* 27 November 1989, A15, C14.

19. H. Packer, *The Limits of the Criminal Sanction* (1968), 265.

20. *Strategy*, 73.

21. The notorious Peruvian guerrilla organization, the Shining Path, has become deeply involved in the narcotics business. It serves as a broker for coca growers, collects taxes from traffickers, and protects both from security sources. See, for example, *The New York Times,* 6 December 1989.

22. *Strategy*, 73.

23. James Brown, "Fighting the Drug War in the Skies Over Peru," *The New York Times,* 28 March 1992.

24. *Strategy*, 74.

25. *Strategy*, 73.

26. Stephen G. Trujillo, "Corruption and Cocaine in Peru," *The New York Times,* 7 April 1992, Op-Ed.

27. P. Reuter, G. Crawford, and J. Cave, "Sealing the Borders: The Effects of Military Participation," in *Drug Interdiction* 18 (1988).

28. Skolnick, Correl, Navarro, and Raab, *The Social Structure of Street Drug Dealing,* California Bureau of Criminal Statistics Forum (Office of the Attorney General, 1988) [hereinafter *Social Structure*].

29. *Strategy,* 74.

30. Peter Reuter, "Can The Borders Be Sealed?" *The Public Interest* (Summer 1988): 56.

31. For a thorough analysis of the problems posed to American society by heroin, see J. Kaplan, *Heroin: The Hardest Drug* (1983).

32. *Strategy* (1992), 11.

33. *Journal of the American Medical Association,* 12 December 1986, 3061.

34. *Strategy* (1992), 11.

35. The *Strategy* suggests that "we should be extremely reluctant to restrict within formal and arbitrary lines" the extent of bureaucratic bickering when it is attributable to the "overriding spirit and energy of our front-line drug enforcement officers . . . " *Strategy,* 8.

36. For an account of rampant corruption in the Drug Enforcement Agency, see *The New York Times,* 17 December 1989.

37. US Department of State, Bureau of International Narcotics Matters, *International Narcotics Strategy,* Report 86 (March 1988).

38. Rosenberg, "The Kingdom of Cocaine: A Report from Colombia," *New Republic,* 27 November 1989, 28.

39. Brown, "Fighting the Drug War in the Skies Over Peru."

40. Trujillo, "Corruption and Cocaine in Peru."

41. P. Murphy and T. Plate, "Commissioner: A View From the Top of the American Law Enforcement" (1977), 245.

42. *The Los Angeles Times,* 24 October 1989.

43. Peter Reuter, *On the Consequences of Toughness,* RAND Note 3347 (Santa Monica, Calif.: Drug Policy Research Center, 1991), 147.

44. At year end 1988, the number of prisoners under the jurisdiction of federal or state correctional authorities reached 627,402, compared to 329,821 in 1980. This amounts to an increase of approximately 90 percent in eight years. Bureau of Justice Statistics, US Department of Justice, Bulletin, Prisoners in 1988 (1989).

45. Bureau of Justice Statistics, US Department of Justice, Sourcebook of Criminal Justice Statistics—1988, 612 (Table 6.31) (1988).

46. See Messinger, Berecochea, Berk, and Rauma, "Parolees Returned to Prison and the California Prison Population" 13 (Table 5) (California Bureau of Criminal Statistics and Special Services Collaborative Report, 1988). In 1988, about 43 percent of the admissions to California state prisons were parole violators returned to prison by the Parole Board without a conviction for a new charge. Sourcebook 612, 11 (Table 3).

47. Messinger, et al., 5.

48. *San Francisco Chronicle,* 18 May 1989.

49. *Strategy,* 26.

50. Ibid.

51. Ibid.

52. *The New York Times,* 18 April 1989. Mr. Bennett has attributed the halting progress of the war on drugs to state officials who are reluctant to use state funding for new prison construction. *The Wall Street Journal,* 30 November 1989.

53. *Social Structure,* 13.

54. Ibid.

55. *The New York Times,* 30 December 1989, 1.

56. See Covino, *How the 69th Mob Maximized Earnings in East Oakland* (California: November 1985), 83.

57. Center for the Study of Law and Society, *Courts, Probation, and Street Drug Crime: Executive Summary and Conclusions* (Final report on the Targeting Urban Crime Narcotics Task Force, 1988), 4–5, 9 [hereinafter *Executive Summary*].

58. Peter Reuter, "The D.C. Crime Surge: An Economist Looks at the Carnage," *The Washington Post,* 26 March 1989.

59. Ibid.

60. Ibid.

61. Lawrence I. Golbe and Michael D. Merkin, "Cerebral Infarction in a User of Free-Base ("Crack")," *Neurology* 36 (1986): 1602.

62. John Kaplan, "Taking Drugs Seriously," *The Public Interest* 42 (Summer 1988).

63. Terry Williams, *The Cocaine Kids: The Inside Story of a Teenage Drug Ring* (Reading, Mass.: Addison-Wesley, 1989).

64. Phillipe Bourgeois, "Just Another Night on Crack Street," *The New York Times Magazine,* 12 November 1989, 63.

39

CORPORATE CRIME AND VIOLENCE

RUSSELL MOKHIBER

Name a crime.

Outside of the context of this book, many would respond "burglary" or "robbery" or "murder." Few would respond "monopoly" or "knowingly marketing unsafe pharmaceuticals" or "dumping of toxic wastes."

Name an act of violence.

Similarly, many would respond with examples of violent street crimes, such as assault. Few would respond with examples of violent corporate crime, such as the marketing of a dangerous automobile or the pollution of a community's water supply.

People respond this way despite a near universal consensus that all corporate crime and violence combined, both detected and undetected, prosecuted and not prosecuted, is more pervasive and more damaging than all street crime. The electrical price fixing conspiracy of the early 1960s alone cost American consumers $2 billion, more than all the burglaries in America in one year. According to the Federal Bureau of Investigation, there were 19,000 victims of street murder and manslaughter in 1985. Compare that one-year total with the numbers of victims of corporate crime and violence in the United States today:

- One hundred and thirty Americans die every day in automobile crashes. Many of those deaths are either caused by vehicle defects or preventable by available vehicle crashworthiness designs.

From Russell Mokhiber, *Corporate Crime and Violence,* San Francisco, Sierra Club Books, 1988. Reprinted by permission.

- Almost 800 Americans die every day from cigarette-induced disease.

- Over the next 30 years, 240,000 people—8,000 per year, one every hour—will die from asbestos-related cancer.

- The Dalkon Shield intrauterine device seriously injured tens of thousands of women who used it.

- An estimated 85,000 American cotton textile workers suffer breathing impairments due to cotton dust (brown lung) disease.

- 100,000 miners have been killed and 265,000 disabled due to coal dust (black lung) disease.

- One million infants worldwide died in 1986 because they were bottle-fed instead of breast-fed.

- In 1984, 2,000 to 5,000 persons were killed and 200,000 injured, 30,000 to 40,000 of them seriously, after a Union Carbide affiliate's factory in Bhopal, India, released a deadly gas over the town. . . .

Why is it that despite the high numbers of victims, when people think of crime, they think of burglary before they think of monopoly (if they think of monopoly at all), of assault before they think of the marketing of harmful pharmaceuticals, of street crime before they think of corporate crime? And what can be done to curb corporate crime and violence?

❖ WHY DO PEOPLE THINK OF STREET CRIME BEFORE THEY THINK OF CORPORATE CRIME?

Many corporate executives assume that preventable violence is a cost of doing business, a cost that we as a society must accept as the price of living in an industrial America. With advertising campaigns aimed at molding public opinion and policy, some corporations have covered their violent behavior with a veneer of misinformation and distortion in an attempt to make acceptable what in any other context would be morally repugnant. A case in point is the advertisement run by Monsanto on the heels of many chemical disasters during the late 1970s with the theme "Without Chemicals, Life Itself Would Be Impossible."

Furthermore, in the United States, corporate lawbreakers double as corporate lawmakers. Corporate America has saturated the legislatures with dollars in order to promote laws making legal or non-criminal what by any common standard of justice would be considered illegal and criminal, and to obstruct legislation that would outlaw the violent activity. For example, the tobacco and automobile industries have, over the years, blocked attempts to ban or curb the marketing of tobacco, and to require that automobiles be manufactured with life-saving passive restraints.

When public pressure does produce legislation curbing corporate excesses, corporations then lobby, often successfully, to weaken the constraint. When

Congress passed the auto safety law, for example, auto industry lobbyists on Capitol Hill defeated an effort to add criminal sanctions to the bill for knowing or willful violations.

The result is a legal system biased in favor of the corporate violator and against its victims. Because the higher standards of proof in criminal trials are more difficult to meet, and because of finely tuned corporate methods of delay and obfuscation most federal prosecutions of corporations seek civil, not criminal, sanctions; few serious acts of corporate violence are criminally prosecuted. Moreover, most of the penalties that are imposed in civil cases are mere slap-on-the-wrist settlements known as consent decrees.

Even when the criminal prosecution of a corporation is successful, the imposed sanctions are rarely effective. When, for example, General Motors was convicted in 1949 of conspiracy to destroy the nation's mass transit systems, surely one of the more egregious corporate crimes in U.S. economic history, the judge fined the company $5,000.

There are many corporate wrongdoers allowed to go free and many street criminals punished harshly for minor violations. Not one corporate executive went to jail, nor was any corporation criminally convicted for the marketing of thalidomide, a drug that caused severe birth defects in 8,000 babies during the early 1960s, but Wallace Richard Stewart of Kentucky was sentenced in July 1983 to ten years in prison for stealing a pizza. No Ford Motor Company executive went to jail for marketing the Pinto automobile, with its deadly fuel tank, nor was the company convicted of criminal charges (although in one case it was indicted, tried, and found not guilty of reckless homicide). Not one Hooker Chemical executive went to jail, nor was Hooker charged with a criminal offense, after the company exposed its workers and Love Canal neighbors to toxics, but under a Texas habitual offenders statute William Rummel was given life in prison for stealing a total of $229.11 over a period of nine years.

"Crime is a sociopolitical artifact, not a natural phenomenon," Herbert L. Packer wrote in 1968 in *The Limits of the Criminal Sanction*. "We can have as much or as little crime as we please, depending on what we choose to count as criminal." By setting up a system of civil fines, consent decrees, recalls, and other non-criminal controls on corporations, we have chosen to have very little corporate "crime," in Professor Packer's sense of the word, and by so choosing, we have insulated the corporation from the effective sanctions and stigma of the criminal process. In addition, we have sent the outnumbered and underfunded police who investigate corporate crime—euphemistically known as regulators—up against some of the most powerful lawbreakers in society without access to meaningful sanctions. . . .

❖ SIDESTEPPING THE CRIMINAL JUSTICE SYSTEM

Professor Christopher Stone, of the University of Southern California Law School, has observed that up until the nineteenth century, the law was paying increasing attention to the individual, and less to the group. During this period, according to Stone, laws, rules, and concepts were being developed to deal with what motivated, what steered, and what was "possible, just and appropriate in the case of individual human beings." Corporations did not move to center stage until late in the nineteenth century, and when they did, the criminal law, developed to bring justice to individuals, was not equipped to answer the question: what motivated, what steered, and what was possible, just, and appropriate in the case of corporations?

At the turn of the century, as corporations became increasingly wealthy and powerful, legislatures moved to protect the public from corporate abuses. In 1890, Congress passed the Sherman Antitrust Act, which forbade monopolizing or attempting to monopolize trade and made illegal "every contract, combination . . . or conspiracy in restraint of trade." The act was aimed at busting the corporate monopoly makers that were threatening the competitive economic system. Violation of the act was a criminal offense, punishable by a fine not exceeding $5,000 or by imprisonment up to a year, or both.

But the Sherman Act and a host of subsequent laws aimed at controlling corporate wrongdoing were different in one crucial respect from the criminal laws that governed the noncorporate citizenry. In a radical departure from the historical development of criminal law, legislatures gave prosecutors of corporate crime the option of seeking a *civil injunction* to enforce a law with *criminal sanctions.*

Rather than charging the corporation with a criminal violation and then prosecuting the case in open court before a jury of citizens who would determine guilt or innocence, prosecutors choose instead, in the overwhelming number of cases, to go to civil court and seek to enjoin the corporation from further violations of law. Today, this civil injunction against crime has become the option of choice for federal "regulators."

By relying on the civil injunction, federal police avoid branding the defendant corporation with the symbols of crime, thus crippling the intended punitive and deterrent effects of the criminal sanction. "The violations of these laws are crimes," commented Edwin Sutherland, who formulated this concept of corporate crime, in his ground-breaking 1949 book *White-Collar Crime,* ". . . but they are treated as though they were not crimes, with the effect and probably the intention of eliminating the stigma of crime."

A second radical departure—or "clever invention," to use a Sutherland phrase—from the traditional criminal procedure came in the guise of the abovementioned consent decree. A consent decree is essentially a compromise between two parties in a civil suit, the exact terms of which are fixed by negotiation between the parties and formalized by the signature of a judge.

Thus while the civil injunction against crime removed the corporate defendant from the criminal sphere, the consent decree provided further insulation by moving the legal process from the open courtroom to behind closed doors. Although the defendant corporation invariably emerged from behind those closed doors consenting to an injunction against further violations of the law, it did so without admitting or denying the allegations.

Most federal cases brought against corporations are settled in this manner.

The "neither admit nor deny" clause is understandably relished by corporate defendants because it precludes the use of the decree as an admission of guilt in subsequent court proceedings, be they civil or criminal. In many cases, this clause is worth millions of dollars to corporations; without it, private plaintiffs could use the decree as evidence of law violation in private damage actions. Corporate defendants cite numerous other reasons for agreeing to consent decrees (prompt resolution of the case to avoid expensive and protracted litigation, and opportunity to negotiate the language of the consent decree and of the allegations of the complaint), but the "neither admit nor deny" clause is itself the primary motivation for a defendant to settle a case. Once the consent is signed, the public perception is that the corporate defendant is not a lawbreaker, not a criminal, not a crook. The defendant is merely "enjoined."

Sutherland proffered three reasons for this "differential implementation of the law as it applied to large corporations." Most important was the status of businessmen in the United States. According to Sutherland,

> Those who are responsible for the system of criminal justice are afraid to antagonize businessmen; among other consequences, such antagonism may result in a reduction in contributions to the campaign funds needed to win the next election. . . . Probably much more important than fear, however, is the cultural homogeneity of legislators, judges, and administrators with businessmen. Legislators admire and respect businessmen and cannot conceive of them as criminals; businessmen do not conform to the popular stereotype of "the criminal." The legislators are confident that these respectable gentlemen will conform to the law as a result of very mild pressures. The most powerful group in medieval society secured relative immunity by "benefit of clergy" and now our most powerful group secures immunity by "benefit of business," or more generally, "high social status."

Secondly, Sutherland recognized a shift away from implementation of penal sanctions in general, with the shift occurring "more rapidly in the area of white collar crimes than of other crimes." And finally, Sutherland believed that the more gentle treatment of corporate criminals was due in part to "the relatively unorganized resentment of the public toward white collar crimes." This, he explained, was because the violations of laws by businessmen are "complex and their effects diffused," and because

> [T]he public agencies of communication do not express the organized moral sentiments of the community as to white collar crimes, in part because the crimes are complicated and not easily presented as news, but probably in the greater part because these agencies of communication are owned or controlled by businessmen and because these agencies are themselves involved in the violations of many of these laws.

This two-track prosecutorial setup—a criminal system for individuals and a civil system for corporations—works to undermine the effectiveness of the criminal justice system. Individuals convicted by the criminal justice system must carry not only the burden of the penal sanction, but also the stigma of crime. The corporation is relieved of both. When a corporation signs a consent decree, little public shame attaches because the corporation "neither admits nor denies" violating the law. . . .

❖ CRIMINALS IN THE USUAL SENSE: LAYING THE GROUNDWORK FOR DECRIMINALIZATION OF CORPORATE LAW

"Most criminals in antitrust cases are not criminals in the usual sense." That statement, quoted above, of Wendell Berge, who was assistant to the head of the Justice Department's Antitrust Division in 1940, epitomizes the view of a group of academics, including the likes of Richard Posner and Sanford Kadish, and politicians, such as Ronald Reagan, who believe that criminal sanctions should not be applied to corporate wrongdoing, or should be applied only as a last resort. Many in this camp are adherents to the view that a corporate polluter is not a criminal in the sense that an individual burglar is a criminal, that a corporate price fixer is not a criminal in the sense that an individual robber is a criminal, and that a white-collar criminal is not a criminal in the sense that a street criminal is a criminal.

The academic who argues for decriminalization is not as direct as . . . Mr. Berge, in arguing that price fixers are not "criminals in the usual sense." Instead, the academics present a utilitarian argument for decriminalization that goes something like this:

Because of the heavy reliance on civil remedies and the complementary disuse of the criminal remedies, the criminal law governing corporations is in such an underdeveloped state that corporate criminal sanctions should be effectively scrapped in favor of exclusive reliance on civil monetary penalties, supplemented by equitable remedies such as injunctions and consent decrees. Furthermore, the only significant goal of corporate criminal law is deterrence, and deterrence can be adequately attained through civil monetary penalties and other civil sanctions without reliance on criminal sanctions.

Thus, this school advocates the effective crippling of corporate criminal law, the moral equivalent of throwing the baby out with the bathwater. Brent Fisse, a noted Australian legal scholar, has powerfully argued against such abolition and for a reconstruction of the corporate criminal law to control socially harmful corporate behavior. Fisse notes that "modern corporate criminal law owes its origin and design more to crude borrowings from individual criminal and civil law than to any coherent assessment of the objectives of corporate criminal law and of how those objectives might be attained."

Embarking on such an assessment, a growing number of legal scholars have joined Fisse in reacting strongly against those who would prefer to condemn corporate criminal law to windowdressing in perpetuity. The academic dispute intensified when the *Harvard Law Review*, one of the most respected law journals, published a commentary by its editors in 1979 titled "Developments in the Law—Corporate Crime," which came down on the side of decriminalization by advocating a civil-fine model to control corporate wrongdoing. The Harvard commentary rested on the proposition that although deterrence, rehabilitation, and incapacitation are the traditional aims of the criminal law as applied to individuals, deterrence is the only aim that is important in the realm of the corporate criminal law. From this proposition, the Harvard commentary suggested that since successful deterrence of corporate crime requires the threat of substantial monetary penalties, "one must wonder whether the same or a higher level of deterrence could be better achieved through civil [as opposed to criminal] penalties."

That suggestion takes insufficient account of the deterrent value resulting from the stigma of criminal conviction and punishment. Herbert Packer argued that "there is very little evidence to suggest that the stigma of criminality means anything very substantial in the life of the corporation. John Doe has friends and neighbors; a corporation has none. And the argument that the fact of criminal conviction may have an adverse effect on a corporation's economic position seems fanciful." Millions of dollars spent since then on corporate image advertising by large multinationals argue against Packer's view. A recent study of the effects of adverse publicity on 17 corporations found the loss of corporate prestige was a significant concern of executives in 15 of the cases.

The laissez faire school focuses on the financial motives of corporate executives, ignores other well-documented motivations. A strictly monetary scheme to control corporate wrongdoing addresses the corporation's drive for profits, not a corporate executive's urge for power, nor his or her desire for prestige, creative urge, need to identify with the group, desire for security, urge for adventure, or desire to serve others. As Fisse has noted, "deterring unwanted corporate behavior may require sanctions which, unlike monetary exactions, would be unconstitutional if characterized as civil. Preventive orders and formal publicity orders would be needed to inflict loss of corporate power and prestige directly." . . .

❖ SANCTIONS AGAINST THE INDIVIDUAL WHITE-COLLAR CRIMINAL

If a corporation engages in socially undesirable behavior, the odds are that neither the corporation nor its executives will ever face a sentencing judge. In some cases, the law will not prohibit the corporation's antisocial behavior, as when auto manufacturers knowingly market dangerously constructed or designed vehicles. If such behavior is covered, law enforcement officials may be looking the other way, as with many Reagan administration "regulators." If laws cover such behavior and law enforcement agencies are conscientious about their enforcement responsibilities, corporation-induced political pressures may force a cut of monetary or political support to hamper those agencies.

If an unlucky corporation makes it to the sanctioning stage, the chances are that the corporation and its executives will be treated with kid gloves, especially when compared with individual street criminals.

Street criminals, mostly poor and black, get long prison terms for minor property crimes, yet corporate and white-collar criminals, in the words of Braithwaite, "can fix prices, defraud consumers of millions, and kill and maim workers with impunity, without prison." When General Electric was convicted of price fixing in the early 1960s, the company was fined $437,000. As Lee Loevinger, former chief of the Justice Department's Antitrust Division, put it, the fine was no more severe than "a three-dollar ticket for overtime parking for a man with a $15,000 a year income."

In 1978, the Olin Corporation was convicted of false filings to conceal illegal shipments of arms to South Africa. The company was fined $40,000 and no Olin executive went to jail. In July 1984, Elizabeth McAllister, a peace activist, was sentenced to three years in jail for participating in an antinuclear demonstration at an upstate New York U.S. Air Force Base.

The Clinard corporate crime study found that serious violations by corporations generally receive minor sanctions, with only administrative penalties given in approximately two-thirds of the cases identified as serious violations. The Clinard study also found that 16 executives of 582 companies studied were sentenced to a total of 594 days of actual imprisonment. Three hundred and sixty of those days were accounted for by two officers who received six months each in the same case.

Professor Stone alleges that jailings do not guarantee significant changes in corporate direction since "the very nature of bureaucracy is to make the individual dispensable." But prison sentences for corporate executives are an efficient deterrent mechanism, in terms of both specific deterrence (against the convicted individual) and general deterrence (against those other executives observing the proceedings), available to sentencing judges. Jail sentences in the electrical equipment conspiracy cases had both specific and general deterrent effects. Clarence Burke, a former GE general manager, told a congressional committee after the convictions, "I would starve before I'd do it again." A second GE manager told a senator, "the way my family and myself have been suffering, if I see a competitor on one side of the street, I will walk on the other side, sir."

Gordon Spivack, former assistant chief in charge of field operations for the Justice Department's Antitrust Division, discussing the general deterrent effect of the electrical price fixing prison sanctions, believed that "similar sentences in a few cases each decade would almost completely cleanse our economy of the cancer of collusive price fixing, and the mere threat of such sentences is itself the strongest available deterrent to such activity."

However, there appears to be a general belief among judges that white-collar criminals, no matter what the crime, don't deserve prison. This despite the fact that judges believe in the deterrent effect of imprisonment and have no confidence that fines or other nonincarcerative sanctions would be as effective. One federal judge is quoted as saying that he would not "penalize a businessman trying to make a living when there are felons out on the street." A second judge is of the opinion that "all people don't need to be sent to prison. For white-collar criminals, the mere fact of prosecution, pleading guilty—the psychological trauma of that is punishment enough. They've received the full benefit of punishment."

In one of the few empirical studies of sentencing judges' attitudes toward white-collar criminals, Yale Law School's research program on white-collar crime found that although judges take a serious view of white-collar crime, several factors lead them to find what the authors of the study call "a non-incarcerative disposition," that is, judges don't like to throw white-collar criminals in jail. The authors attribute judges' reluctance to imprison white-collar criminals partly to their belief that such defendants are "more sensitive to the impact of the prison environment than are non-white-collar defendants." One judge put it this way:

> I think the first sentence to a prison term for a person who up to now has lived and has surrounded himself with a family, that lives in terms of great respectability and community respect and so on, whether one likes to say this or not I think a term of imprisonment for such a person is probably a harsher, more painful sanction than it is for someone who grows up somewhere where people are always in and out of prison. There may be something racist about saying that, but I am saying what I think is true or perhaps needs to be laid out on the table and faced.

The Yale study also found judges wanting to avoid eliminating the contribution to community and family that white-collar offenders make in the normal course of their lives. One judge described this feeling in the following manner:

> Usually the defendant is one who looks as though he can resume his place, if indeed not just continue on his place, in society, as a valuable and contributing member of society. Almost always he is a husband and a father. Almost always he has children who are in the process of becoming what we like to think children ought to be—well brought up, well educated, nurtured, cared for—usually he is a member of the kinds of civic organizations in the community who value his services and derive value from his services. . . . As a result you are up against this more difficult problem in degree in the so called white-collar criminals as to whether you are not going to inflict a hurt on society by putting such person in a prison and making him cease to be a good father and a good husband and a good worker in the community.

Finally, the judges felt that white-collar defendants' ability to make restitution to their victims militated against the argument for prison sentences. The judges also felt that community service orders were better suited to white-collar prisoners than was prison.

If judges are not throwing convicted corporate executives in jail, then how are they punishing them? With fines and community service orders whose deterrent effect is questionable. The Clinard study found that the average fine levied against individual officers was $18,250, a pittance compared with the large salaries and bonuses granted corporate executives. In addition to inadequacy, other factors mitigate the effectiveness of the fine as a sanction against criminal activity. First, many corporations indemnify an executive who is found to be acting for the benefit of the corporation if he had no reasonable cause to believe that what he was doing was criminal. Secondly, in some states, notably Delaware, a corporation can take out insurance against fines levied against its executives. One federal judge complained that "one jail sentence is worth 100 consent decrees and that fines are meaningless because the defendant in the end is always reimbursed by the proceeds of his wrongdoing or by his company down the line."

Community service orders, which have grown in popularity over the years, can be seen as a mechanism by which judges try to "do something" to fill the void created by the widespread reluctance to throw white-collar criminals in jail. The most notable of the recent community service orders was U.S. District Court Judge Charles Renfrew's order in the paper label price fixing case. Five individuals defendants convicted of price fixing were fined between $5,000 and $15,000 apiece and were put on probation. As a condition of their probation, each was ordered to "make an oral presentation before twelve civic or other groups about the circumstances of his case and his participation therein. . . ." Robert Herbst has labeled Renfrew's sentence "a joke . . . no deterrent threat at all."

In other cases, convicted white-collar criminals have been ordered to:

- give speeches about their violations to business and civic groups;

- work in programs designed to aid the poor;

- help former street criminals participate in community groups and secure job pledges for them from business concerns;

- work 40 hours a week in a drug treatment center for five months and eight hours a week for one additional year;

- work 25 hours a week for five months and 10 hours a week for an additional year in an agricultural school that he had founded;

- make a community service film. The film, about the dangers of PCP, so impressed the judges that he reduced the conviction to a misdemeanor.

There is little evidence that these community service orders have any deterrent effect, either against the individual convicted criminal or generally against those observing the sanctioning process. Judges imposing these sentences further undermine the nation's system of justice. "To keep coming up with alternative sentences," charged Thomas Cahill, former Chief Assistant U.S. Attorney, "in the public's image makes it look like it's a technical violation. It's not. . . . It's a crime and should be treated as a crime." Second, if community service orders are going to be used to displace prison sentences, they should be used to displace prison sentences across the board, for street as well as for corporate criminals. The current system of jail for street thugs and speeches for corporate thugs creates an inequality of justice that undermines respect for the law.

❖ SANCTIONS AGAINST THE CORPORATION

The *Harvard Law Review* commentary on corporate crime rejected retribution as a goal of corporate criminal sanctions, and focused on deterrence as the sole goal. It concluded that corporations cannot be punished in a stigmatic manner; that if stronger deterrents are needed, they should come in the form of heavier fines; and that since criminal fines have no advantage over civil fines, they should come in the form of heavier civil fines.

But the overwhelming evidence from scholars, prosecutors, and judges is that fines, often small and well below authorized ceilings, do not deter corporate crime. Criminologist John Braithwaite has called them "license fees to break the law." Fines in the typical antitrust case rarely reach the authorized ceiling. W. Breit and K. Elzinger, in a study of antitrust violations between 1967 and 1970, found that the Justice Department recommended imposing the maximum fine in less than one-third of the cases where it obtained convictions. Braithwaite, in a recent study of law enforcement in the mine safety area, found that about 90 percent of the mine operators stated that civil penalties assessed or paid did not affect their production or safety activities. "Penalty dollar amounts were not considered of sufficient magnitude to warrant avoidance of future penalties and improvements in safety procedure," he observed. Operators contemptuously classified the fines as a "cost of doing business" or as a royalty paid to the government to continue in business. Producers who were fined saw no connection between penalties and safety.

Christopher Stone's study of laws governing corporations, *Where the Law Ends,* came to similar conclusions. "The overall picture," according to Stone, "is that our strategies aimed to control corporations by threatening their profits are a very limited way of bringing about the internal changes that are necessary if the policies behind the law are to be effectuated." The trouble with using fines to control corporate crime, according to Clinard, is that the amount paid is more than offset by the financial gain from the offense. In his study of more than 500 major U.S. corporations, Clinard found that four-fifths of the penalties levied against corporations were $5,000 or less, 11.6 percent were between $5,000 and $50,000, 3.7 percent were between $50,000 and $1,000,000, and 0.9 percent were over $1,000,000.

A major criticism of using fines to control corporate crime has been described by New York University Law School Professor John C. Coffee, Jr. and others as "the deterrence trap." The corporation contemplating the commitment of a crime will be deterred only if the expected punishment cost of the illegal activity exceeds the expected gain. Coffee gives the following example: If the expected gain were $1 million and the risk of arrest were 25 percent, then the penalty would have to be $4 million in order to make the expected punishment cost equal to the expected gain. Coffee observes that "the maximum meaningful fine that can be levied against any corporate offender is necessarily bound by its wealth." For example,

> *if a corporation having $10 million of wealth were faced with an opportunity to gain $1 million through some criminal act or omission, such conduct could not logically be deterred by monetary penalties directed at the corporation if the risk of apprehension were below 10%. That is, if the likelihood of apprehension were 8%, the necessary penalty would have to be $12.5 million (i.e., $1 million times 12.5, the reciprocal of 8%). Yet such a fine exceeds the corporation's ability to pay. In short, our ability to deter the corporation may be confounded by our inability to set an adequate punishment cost which does not exceed the corporation's resources.*

Since corporate crimes are easy to conceal and all indications are that rates of apprehension are exceedingly low, most major corporations will not be deterred by the types of fines that federal sentencing officials currently are imposing.

A second practical objection to using fines to control corporate crime is that the costs of any given corporate crime and the corresponding retributive fine may be far larger than the amount a corporation is able to pay. This "retribution trap" is a barrier to effective control of corporate crime. Braithwaite makes the point by asking:

> *[C]an we imagine any penalty short of revoking the corporation's right to sell drugs which would be commensurate to the harm caused by the fraud and deceit of a thalidomide disaster? Given what we know about how disapproving the community feels toward corporate crime, there may be many situations where the deserved monetary or other punishments bankrupt the company. The community then cuts its nose to spite its face.*

In addition, threatening the corporation as a monolithic "black box" ignores the possible role of individual motivations in directing corporate actions. Stone and others have observed that there may be a fundamental lack of congruence between the aims of the individual and the aims of the firm. A corporate executive may engage in criminal activity to further his own ends, not necessarily those of the firm. Coffee gives the hypothetical example of an executive vice president who is a candidate for promotion to president and may be willing to run risks that are counterproductive to the firm as a whole because he is eager to make a record profit for his division or to hide an error of judgment. In such situation a fine aimed at the corporation won't deter the perpetrator and will probably fail in controlling illegal conduct. Thus when a criminal sanctioning system aims at the "black box" of the corporation instead of the individual decision makers within the black box, it may prove irrelevant to certain kinds of misconduct. Coffee argues that

> *the most shocking safety and environmental violations are almost exclusively the product of decisions at lower managerial levels. . . . The directive from the top of the organization is to increase profits by fifteen percent but the means are left to the managerial discretion of the middle manager who is in operational control of the division. . . . The results of such a structure are predictable: when pressure is intensified, illegal or irresponsible means become attractive to a desperate middle manager who has no recourse against a stern but myopic notion of accountability that looks only to the bottom line of the income statement.*

Thus in firms where there is a strong "bottom line" ethic, one that loosens legal, moral, and ethical constraints, fines against the organization will fail to have the deterrent effect upon which the entire structure of fines is premised.

Even when fined, criminals tend not to pay. From 1977 to 1983 the federal government collected only about 55 percent of all criminal fines imposed. Since 1968, the dollar volume of criminal fines has increased by a factor of twelve; at the same time, collection rates have fallen from around 80 percent to less than 40 percent. At the end of fiscal year 1982, the amount of delinquent debt owed to the federal government was a staggering $38 billion. This failure to pay fines has the effect of severely undercutting the deterrent and punitive effects of the sanction. As Senator Charles Percy stated in opening Senate hearings in 1983 on the subject, "the collection of criminal fines goes beyond mere fiscal responsibility. Five of every six fines are levied on criminals who do *not* go to prison. Half of the time, they are not even on probation. Therefore, in many cases, when these fines are not paid, these criminals go unpunished. It is as simple as that."

Braithwaite, in his study of coal mine safety enforcement, found that at the time of the Buffalo Creek waste tip disaster, in which over 125 people lost their lives, the operator had been assessed fines exceeding $1.5 million, "not a cent of which was paid." In another case, a coal company had been assessed fines totaling $76,330 for 379 violations, 178 of them for electrical or trolley wire standards. Less than half of the amount had been paid at the time of a coal disaster at the company's Blacksville mine, in which a fire triggered by a trolley wire ignition caused the death of nine men.

The failure of fines as deterrents of corporate crime has led to a call for the imposition of more effective and varied criminal sanctions. Discussions of sanctions against the corporation have traditionally focused on a narrow field of civil sanctions, specifically fines and injunctive orders. This focus has been broadened in recent years by a number of Australian corporate criminologists who seek to expand the goals of criminal law and to elevate retribution as a legitimate goal of corporate criminal law. This broadened perspective brings into play sanctions that many consider inappropriate or ineffective in punishing or deterring street crime—such as incapacitation and execution—but may work well in the corporate criminal context.

Although individual corporate executives can be incapacitated for crimes against society, corporations willing to continue to flout the laws will merely substitute one executive for another. Thus, if a product safety control manager comes under an incapacitative order forbidding him or her from serving in such a position for three years, the corporation may merely substitute a manager of like mind in place of the exiled manager.

To overcome this substitution problem, legislatures and courts may turn to issuing incapacitation orders against the corporate entity. Courts may order companies to cease operating in areas where the company has shown repeated criminal conduct. In extreme cases, courts may impose an execution order, or death sentence. Since a corporation is a creation of the state, there is no reason why, in cases of egregious conduct, courts may not order the dissolution of the corporate entity. In 1983, for example, the Attorney General of Virginia asked the state's Corporation Commission to dissolve the charter of Croatan Books Inc., a firm reportedly convicted 69 times in five years for possessing obscene films or magazines. The dissolution was moved for on the grounds that the corporation had "continued to exceed or abuse the authority conferred upon it by law."

It is generally agreed that rehabilitation has failed as an approach to controlling street crime. However, there is a growing consensus that it must be examined carefully as a way of gaining control of the corporate crime problem. As Fisse and Braithwaite have observed, it may be difficult to reorganize or rehabilitate a human psyche, but it is much easier to rearrange a corporation's standard operating procedures, defective control systems, inadequate communication mechanisms, and in general its internal structure. Australian investigators who have conducted most of the empirical research in this area conclude that rehabilitation works in the corporate sphere. Hopkins's study of the rehabilitation of corporate criminals in Australia found that most companies prosecuted under the consumer protection provisions of the Australian Trade Practices Act introduced at least some measures to ensure that the offense did not recur. And Fisse and Braithwaite found similar patterns in their study of adverse publicity. Rehabilitation can be demanded by police agencies, through consent decrees and probation orders, as a condition of a suspended sentence or as a contingency of settlement. The police or the courts may thereby order a number of changes within the corporate organization, including changes in how information is exchanged and how decisions are made, as well as the creation of an internal ombudsman and accounting groups.

Court-sanctioned adverse publicity has great potential for bringing corporate criminal conduct under control. The recent quantitative study by Fisse and Braithwaite of 17 corporations involved in publicity crises found that large corporations care greatly about their reputations. The study concluded that corporations fear the sting of adverse publicity more than they fear the law itself.

Corporate antisocial conduct is brought to the attention of the public through a number of channels, including consumer activist groups, investigative reporters, federal police agency enforcement actions, official inquiries, governmentally mandated disclosures, and international boycotts. In some instances a corporation is ordered to publicize its misdeeds as part of the sanction for a violation of law. In the J.P. Stevens case, for example, the company was ordered to give notice of anti-union violations by mail to its employees in North and South Carolina. In a securities case, a defendant was required to send its shareholders copies of the court's decision against it. And, in an FTC case against ITT Continental Baking, in which the company was accused of deceptive advertising for its Profile brand bread, the company agreed to a consent decree that required it to allocate 25 percent of its advertising budget for one year to a disclosure stating that "Profile is not effective for weight reduction."

These instances involved civil and administrative proceedings, but there is a strong case to be made for court-ordered use of formal publicity orders as a sanction for convicted corporations. A 1970 draft of the U.S. National Commission on Reform of Federal Criminal Law (the Brown Commission) recommended:

> When an organization is convicted of an offense, the court may, in addition to or in lieu of imposing other authorized sanctions . . . require the organization to give appropriate publicity to the conviction by notice to the class or classes of persons or sector of the public interested in or affected by the conviction, by advertising in designated areas or by designated media, or otherwise. . . .

Fisse and Braithwaite suggest two ways of implementing this recommendation: first, that publication of the details of an offense be made available as a court-ordered sentence against corporate offenders, and second, that pre-sentence or probation orders against corporate offenders should be used to require disclosure of organizational reforms and disciplinary action undertaken as a result of the offense.

Still, some argue that corporations cannot be stigmatized by adverse publicity despite strong evidence and common sense suggesting the opposite. Surely corporate heads would turn and listen more attentively to law enforcement agents if, for example, Hooker Chemical Company were required to buy television ads to tell the nation about its pollution activities, or if the Ford Motor Company were required to run television ads informing the nation about how it marketed the unsafe Pinto, or if Grunenthal were required to tell the world about how it marketed thalidomide and how thalidomide affected its consumers. To use adverse publicity sanctions not just in remedial orders, but as punitive and educational measures, is one of the more effective and efficient ways of shaming corporate America out of its antisocial behavior and bringing it back within the bounds of legal commerce.

Another alternative corporate sentence is the equity fine. Professor John Coffee, dismayed by the failure of cash fines to effectively sanction corporate wrongdoing, has suggested that the corporation be fined not in cash, but in the equity securities of the corporation. Under Coffee's equity fine proposal, the convicted corporation would be required to authorize and issue such number of shares to a state's victim compensation fund as would have an expected market value equal to the cash fine necessary to deter illegal activity. The fund would then be able to liquidate the securities in whatever manner best maximized its return.

Coffee's equity fine proposal overcomes a number of the problems associated with cash fines. First, the equity fine better aligns the self-interest of managers with the interests of the corporation. When the corporation issues the shares designated for the victims' compensation fund, the per share market value would decline, thus reducing the value of stock options and other compensation available to the executives. Second, Coffee argues that a large block of marketable securities would make the corporation an inviting target for a takeover. Third, stockholders would have greater incentive to take a longer term view of the profit goals of the corporation and to insist on keeping operations within legal bounds. Fourth, the equity fine proposal overcomes the unfairness of cash fines in that the corporation would be less able to pass on the cost of the equity fine to workers and consumers. Finally, the deterrence trap problem associated with cash fines is overcome since the market value of the corporation exceeds its cash reserves. Under equity fines, much larger fines can be levied, fines large enough to deter giant companies from illegal behavior.

Although community service orders against individual white-collar violators have attracted widespread attention and condemnation, little attention has been paid to the potential of community service orders in controlling corporate crime. As Fisse has observed, community service orders against the corporation can be invoked in a wide variety of legal settings: as a condition of probation, as a condition of mitigation of sentence, and as a condition of non-prosecution.

In the Allied Chemical/Kepone case, U.S. District Court Judge Robert Merhige fined Allied $13.24 million after the company pleaded no contest to 940 counts of water pollution. The amount of the fine was reduced to $5 million when the company agreed to spend $8,356,202 to establish the Virginia Environmental Endowment, a nonprofit group that would "fund scientific research projects and implement remedial projects and other programs to help alleviate problems that Kepone has created . . . and . . . enhance and improve the overall quality of the environment in Virginia."

In *United States v. Olin Mathieson,* the corporate defendant, Olin, pleaded no contest to a charge of conspiring to ship 3,200 rifles to South Africa in violation of the trade embargo. U.S. District Court Judge Robert Zampano fined Olin Mathieson $45,000 after the company agreed to give $500,000 to set up the New Haven Community Betterment Fund, a nonprofit group "to promote the general welfare of the greater New Haven area with gifts or grants to charitable organizations."

Another notable example came in 1980, when FMC Corporation pleaded guilty to lying to the federal police (EPA) in 1975 and 1976 by reporting that it was discharging about 200 pounds per day of carbon tetrachloride into the Kanawha River in West Virginia when in reality it knew that the actual discharge was ten times that amount. As part of the plea agreement with U.S. police agents, FMC agreed to pay $1 million into the Virginia Environmental Endowment that had been created by the court order in the Allied/Kepone case.

The community service sanctions in the Allied, Olin, and FMC cases were deductible, whereas fines are not—an advantage regarded favorably by corporate criminals. Fisse suggests making these sanctions expressly a sentence of punishment, thus disallowing tax deductibility and any patent or copyright protection from any product of a project of the community service. But, by redirecting money fines to environmental, consumer, and other community and citizen action groups, judges can leverage the money, money usually lost in the shuffle at state and federal treasury departments, to assist the victims of the corporate criminal activity. Automobile corporate criminals could be directed to pay money to the auto safety groups, pharmaceutical corporate criminals could be directed to pay money to support health groups, and chemical corporate criminals could be directed to support environmental action groups. The deterrent and punitive effects of forcing companies to support their public policy adversaries cannot be overestimated.

And judges need not be limited to redirecting money fines to citizen groups. In the thalidomide case, Fisse suggests that the German manufacturer Grunenthal could have been required to set up production facilities to produce and supply artificial limbs, robotic devices, and other special aids. In the Pinto case, Ford could have been required to set up regional burn treatment centers. Ralph Nader has suggested that "making a coal executive work in a coal mine for two years is better than putting him in a cushy jail." The only limits to imaginative and effective community service orders are those binding the minds of legislators and sentencing judges.

THE STORY OF A GUN

ERIK LARSON

O n December 16, 1988, Nicholas Elliot, barely sixteen, walked into the Atlantic Shores Christian School, in Virginia Beach, Virginia, with a semi-automatic handgun hidden in his backpack. By midmorning a forty-one-year-old teacher had been shot dead, and another teacher, struck by two nine-millimeter bullets, was extraordinarily lucky to be alive. Two other teachers narrowly escaped Nicholas Elliot's bullets. One found herself running a zigzag pattern through the school yard as Nicholas fired round after round at her back. The other, a man who tackled Nicholas and in the process saved the lives of a roomful of crying and praying teenagers, felt a bullet breeze past his head.

In a nation accustomed to multiple murders, the shootings received little out-of-state coverage. But the story of how Nicholas wound up firing away on the grounds of a peaceful suburban school says a great deal about America's gun crisis. Nicholas in effect carried with him the good wishes of a gun culture whose institutions and mores have helped make commonplace in America the things he did that morning.

A none-of-my-business attitude permeates the firearms distribution chain from production to final sale, allowing gunmakers and gun marketers to pro-

Erik Larson, "The Story of a Gun," from the *Atlantic Monthly,* January 1993. Reprinted by permission. Portions of the original have been omitted.

mote the killing power of their weapons while disavowing any responsibility for their use in crime. Nicholas carried a gun that should never by any reasonable standard have been a mass-market product. He acquired the gun from a federally licensed dealer, using a means that puts thousands of guns into the hands of illegal users each year, yet that existing federal gun-trade regulations do much to encourage. His story describes a de facto conspiracy of gun dealers, manufacturers, marketers, writers, and federal regulators which makes guns—ever more powerful guns, and laser sights, silencer-ready barrels, folding stocks, exploding bullets, and flame-thrower shotgun rounds—all too easy to come by and virtually assures their eventual use in the bedrooms, alleys, and school yards of America.

America is currently in the midst of a gun crisis that can no longer be considered just a manifestation of the pioneer spirit; instead, it has become a costly global embarrassment. That a crisis does exist should be well beyond dispute by now, given the bleak statistics on gunshot death and damage—yet these statistics, capable of kindling outrage in a stone, have failed to impress America's gun industry and the gun culture that supports it.

Over the past two years firearms have killed 60,000 Americans, more than the number of U.S. soldiers killed in the Vietnam War. Handguns account for 22,000 deaths a year. In 1991, well before the Los Angeles riots, the guns of Los Angeles County alone killed or wounded 8,050—thirteen times the number of U.S. casualties in the Persian Gulf War, according to a survey by the *Los Angeles Times.* Handguns terrorize far more people than they kill: Department of Justice statistics show that every twenty-four hours handgun-wielding assailants rape thirty-three women, rob 575 people, and assault another 1,116.

A relatively new phenomenon, originating in the 1980s, is the appearance of young children on the list of urban gunshot casualties. In 1987 a team of researchers from the UCLA School of Medicine and King/Drew Medical Center in Los Angeles found that King/Drew hadn't admitted a single child under ten for gunshot wounds before 1980. From 1980 to 1987 the center admitted thirty-four. The study, published in the *American Journal of Diseases of Children,* included a macabre table of wounds and complications which hinted at the true horror of gunshot injuries—a horror spared us in daily news coverage, which devotes little space to the merely wounded. A five-year-old lost a hand. A three-year-old, shot in the rectum, endured a colostomy. Other children on the list lost fingers, eyes, and brain tissue; at least one—an eight-year-old girl— was consigned to an institution for the rest of her life. These children were shot by grandfathers, cousins, friends, robbers, snipers, and—in a particularly cruel twist—by gang members seeking only to exact revenge on an elder sibling.

Despite the carnage, guns continue to proliferate. The nation began arming itself in earnest in the roaring sixties, amid race riots and assassinations. From 1967 to 1968, the two most tumultuous years, the number of handguns made available for sale to civilians in the United States rose by 50 percent—some 802,000 pistols and revolvers—to 2.4 million, the greatest single annual leap in

American history. As of 1989 there were 66.7 million handguns (and 200 million firearms of all kinds) in circulation in the United States.

If these guns were controlled by a legion of sober adults, we'd have far less to worry about. One study of 11,000 teenagers in ten states found that 41 percent of the boys and 21 percent of the girls said they could obtain a handgun whenever they wished. A University of North Carolina study of adolescents in suburban and rural communities in the Southeast found that nine percent of the boys actually owned a handgun, despite federal laws prohibiting anyone under twenty-one from buying one. Boys typically received their first firearm—usually a shotgun or a rifle, but seven percent of the time a handgun—at the age of twelve and a half, but more than a fifth of this juvenile militia received their first guns around the age of ten.

Increasingly, you don't need to own a gun or be the intended target of someone else's gun to get shot. As guns have proliferated, the rate at which bystanders are wounded and killed has soared. In 1985 stray bullets killed four New Yorkers; in 1990 they killed forty.

Gun merchants and hobbyists steadfastly protest that guns aren't the problem and that even if they were, gun ownership is explicitly endorsed by the Second Amendment to the Constitution—the much cited right-to-bear-arms clause—and is therefore as much a part of the American way as, say, voting. A comparison of international homicide statistics proves that guns do indeed set America apart from the rest of the developed world.

In 1987 America's civilian guns were used to murder 3,187 young men aged fifteen to twenty-four, accounting for three fourths of the annual homicide rate of 21.9 per 100,000 people.

In Canada only seventeen young men were murdered with firearms, for an overall rate of 2.9 per 100,000.

In Japan, with 0.5 homicides per 100,000 people, gunshot homicides totaled eight—as many as New York City police officers encounter on a single robust weekend.

Mounting evidence suggests that the mere presence of a gun can lead to injury or death. An especially damning kind of data is just now becoming available and is certain to make its way into some of the growing number of lawsuits that seek to make the gun industry accountable for firearms injuries and deaths. In 1989, rather late in the computer revolution, the Bureau of Alcohol, Tobacco, and Firearms (ATF) was finally able to say which gun manufacturers turned up most often in trace requests. The company whose handguns were traced most often from January of 1990 to December of 1991 was the giant Smith & Wesson.

However, when the frequency of traces is considered in proportion to each company's production, a tiny Atlanta company, S. W. Daniel, Inc., shows a tracing rate far higher. By 1989 S. W. Daniel had produced some 60,500 handguns and an untold number of accessories, including silencers and machine-gun kits. Among the guns it produced was Nicholas Elliot's weapon, the Cobray M-11/9, which it fondly advertised as "The gun that made the 80s roar."

Condemned by the police, reviled even by those who sell it, the gun has been remarkably controversial ever since its creation as a cheap, reliable submachine gun meant specifically for close military combat. How that gun went on to become a readily available consumer product—something S. W. Daniel once even gave away free in a monthly contest—provides a clear example of the culture of nonresponsibility prevailing in America's firearms industry; it is but one example of how this commercial ethos governed the gun's progress from conception to its use as a murder weapon in a Virginia Beach classroom.

"The reality that bothers me is there is no self-control, no self-policing, in the gun industry itself," says Colonel Leonard Supenski, of the Baltimore County Police Department, a nationally recognized firearms expert who early last year testified in a pathbreaking liability suit stemming from Nicholas Elliot's rampage. "The premise seems to be that if they've got the right to do something then that's the right thing to do."

❖ THE DEALER

To be a gun dealer in America is to occupy a strange and dangerous outpost on the moral frontier. Every storefront gun dealer winds up at some point in his career selling weapons to killers, drug addicts, psychos, and felons; likewise, every storefront dealer can expect to be visited by ATF agents and other lawmen tracing weapons backward from their use in crime to their origins in the gun-distribution network. One must be a cool customer to stay in business knowing that the products one sells are likely to be used to kill adults and children or to serve as a terroristic tool in robberies, rapes, and violent assaults. Yet gun dealers deny at every step of the way the true nature of the products they sell and absolve themselves of responsibility for their role in the resulting mayhem. Guns used in crime are commonly thought to have originated in some mythic inner-city black market. Such markets do exist, of course, but they are kept well supplied by the licensed gun-distribution network, where responsibility is defined as whatever the law allows.

Guns Unlimited demonstrates the kind of position every legitimate gun shop must eventually find itself in. Guns Unlimited considers itself a "good" dealer. Indeed, in the view of Mike Dick, the general manager of the company and the son of its founder, Guns Unlimited is not just a sterling corporate citizen but also a de facto deputy of the ATF and a vital bulwark in the fight against crime and civil-rights abuse.

Nonetheless, Guns Unlimited sold Nicholas Elliot a gun under circumstances that led, early last year, to a jury verdict against the dealer in a civil suit, brought by the husband of the slain teacher, which charged the dealer with negligence.

Federal law bars anyone under twenty-one from buying a handgun, but Nicholas acquired his with ease through a "straw-man" purchase three months before the shootings, when he was fifteen years old. Straw-man purchases, in which a qualified buyer buys a handgun for an unqualified person, are the primary means by which America's bad guys acquire their weapons, and one the ATF cannot hope to put an end to, given the implicit and explicit restraints on its law-enforcement activities.

One peaceful September weekend Nicholas Elliot, apparently at loose ends, asked his second cousin, Curtis Williams, a truck driver in his thirties, to take him to look at guns in a gun store. Nicholas had pestered Williams before, calling "all the time," as Williams remembered it. Williams didn't want to go— he was busy stripping wax off a floor in his home and wanted to finish the job that day—but he felt guilty. Williams decided that he could be back in plenty of time to finish stripping the floor. He suggested Bob's Guns, a few minutes away.

When he arrived at Nicholas's house, however, he learned that the boy had other ideas. He didn't want to visit just any gun store, according to William's court testimony. He wanted to go to Guns Unlimited, in Carrollton. Williams didn't know the store, but he did know Carrollton. It was little more than a wide space on Route 17 in Isle of Wight County, a rural wedge of land bordered on the north by the James River and on the east by the Portsmouth-Norfolk metropolitan area. It was a long drive from Nicholas's house, on Colon Avenue in Norfolk's Campostella neighborhood: a round trip of ninety minutes minimum, and that was just travel time. Williams told Nicholas he didn't have enough gas for the trip. Nicholas passed him $20.

On the way the boy talked about a gun he'd come to appreciate, the Cobray M-11/9 made by S. W. Daniel. "Man," Williams recalled Nicholas's saying, "you've got to see that; it's a nice gun."

The easy, fluid commerce of guns embraced them the moment they entered the shop. An elderly couple browsing in the store approached almost immediately and offered to sell Williams a gun in a private sale. "My husband has plenty of guns," the man's wife said. "He'll sell you a gun, if you want to buy one." Williams declined.

With the help of Tony Massengill, a firefighter and former policeman now moonlighting as a gun salesman, Williams and Nicholas looked at numerous guns, Nicholas acting more and more like an earnest shopper, not some kid infatuated with guns. Soon, Williams testified, Nicholas was asking to see particular guns and peppering Massengill with detailed questions about muzzle velocity and comparative power. When Nicholas asked to see the Cobray, Massengill obliged. "They got in such a lengthy conversation about that," Williams recalled, "I just kind of moved away from them a little bit, looking around on my own."

Williams returned, and he and Nicholas browsed until they reached the far end of the store, where Nicholas peeled off $300 and gave the money, from his savings, to Williams, instructing him to buy the Cobray. This did not surprise Williams. He knew a lot of adults who had bought guns for their kids; he knew a lot of kids who had guns.

The store was larger then, and configured a bit differently from the way it is now, but it was still small enough that anyone watching would have been aware of the exchange. What Massengill did see, however, became a matter of debate. He claimed he did not remember the sale at all, although, curiously, another employee, present in the store at the time but not actually involved in the transaction, testified later that he remembered seeing the buyers in the store. This clerk, Christopher Hartwig, also testified that he and Massengill had discussed the purchase after the shootings.

Williams testified in court that when the money changed hands, Massengill was still behind the counter at the place where he had last talked with Nicholas, some eight or nine feet away. "He was still standing there, waiting to wait on us, looking at us."

Nicholas and Williams returned to the counter to buy the Cobray. Massengill passed Williams a copy of Form 4473. Everyone who buys a gun from a federally licensed firearms dealer must fill out this two-page form, which, among other things, asks the would-be purchaser if he is a drug addict, is a convicted felon, is mentally ill, or is an illegal alien; if he has renounced his U.S. citizenship; whether he has been dishonorably discharged from the armed forces. The form goes nowhere. It is kept in the dealer's files (provided the dealer in fact keeps such files, and keeps them accurately) for later reference should the gun be used in a crime and traced by the ATF. By federal law, the buyer need present only enough identification to prove that he is twenty-one or older and resides in the state in which the dealer is located. (State and local laws may add requirements.)

Williams testified that as he began filling out the form, Massengill told him, "The only thing that will keep you from buying this gun here in this store is you put a 'yes' answer to these questions. Everything should be marked no. If you put a yes up there, that will stop you from getting the gun." Williams completed the form and concluded the purchase.

Nicholas, meanwhile, had taken the gun from the counter and begun looking it over. He left the store carrying the gun.

Immediately after the Atlantic Shores shootings ATF agents arrested Williams and charged him with making a straw-man purchase. He was tried promptly and served thirteen months in prison. During the trial the federal prosecutor asked him, "What would ever possess someone who's thirty-six, thirty-seven, years old to arrange for a fifteen-year-old young man to get a weapon like that?"

What no federal authority ever bothered to ask, however, is what would possess Guns Unlimited to allow this sale to be made, given the apparent level of Nicholas's involvement. . . .

❖ THE REGULATORS

Gun aficionados may liken the Bureau of Alcohol, Tobacco, and Firearms to the Gestapo, but in its relationship with America's gun dealers the ATF behaves more like an indulgent parent. This is partly the result of restrictions imposed by budget and statute, and partly an institutional reluctance to offend its primary source of investigative leads or to provoke the cantankerous gun lobby. The ATF is in the business not of seeking to prevent the migration of weapons, a spokesman told me, but of building and preserving a paper trail for the day when those weapons will be used to commit major crimes.

In fairness, the ATF, like the dealers it monitors, is in an almost untenable position. It must police the nation's 245,000 licensed firearms dealers with only 400 inspectors, each of whom must also conduct inspections of wineries, breweries, distillers, liquor distributors, tobacco producers, and the country's 10,500 explosives users and manufacturers.

At the same time, the agency is obliged by law to grant a firearms license to virtually anyone who asks for one, provided that the applicant has never been convicted of a felony and has $30 to cover the minimum licensing fee. In 1990, of the 34,336 Americans who applied for a license, only seventy-five had their applications denied.

Depending on one's stance in the gun debate, the application process is either too stringent or appallingly easy. An applicant doesn't have to demonstrate any knowledge of firearms, not even whether he knows the difference between a pistol and a revolver. It is much harder to get a license to operate a powerboat on Chesapeake Bay, to become a substitute teacher in New Jersey, or to get a California driver's license—and *far, far* harder to get a Maryland permit to carry a single handgun—than it is to get a license that enables you to acquire at wholesale prices thousands of varieties of weapons and have them shipped right to your home. Roughly half of federal firearms licensees don't maintain bona fide stores, according to the ATF, but operate instead out of their homes. Many sell guns at gun shows; many don't deal guns at all but hold a license simply in order to buy their guns at wholesale prices. A small but obviously important proportion use their licenses to buy guns wholesale for distribution to inner-city arms traffickers.

My neighbors may not want to hear this, but last May 15 I applied for a federal firearms license as part of an effort to inject myself as deeply as possible into America's gun culture. The two-page application, ATF Form 7, asked which grade of license I wanted. I could choose among nine levels, costing from $30 to $3,000, the most expensive qualifying the holder to import "destructive devices" such as mortars, bazookas, and other weapons with a barrel-bore diameter of half an inch or more. The form asked the same eight questions about a person's criminal past and mental health which appear on Form 4473.

I received my license on June 22, well within the forty-five days in which the ATF is required to accept or deny an application. No one called to verify my application. No one interviewed me to see if in fact I planned to sell weapons. And I was not required by federal law to check with authorities in Maryland and Baltimore about specific local statutes that might affect my ability to peddle guns in the heart of my manicured, upscale, utterly established Baltimore neighborhood. As far as the federal government was concerned, I was in business, and could begin placing orders for as many weapons as I choose.

If the current rate of licensing continues, the number of federal firearms licensees will double in the next decade, to well over half a million—even though the fortunes of domestic arms manufacturers are likely to continue their current decline. With more-intense competition for the shrinking gun-consumer dollar will come far greater incentive to do only the minimum required by law to keep guns out of the wrong hands.

Dealers who violate the law *will* get caught, the ATF is fond of saying. And that's largely true. When law-enforcement officials actually request a federal trace, the ATF tracing network often proves a very effective investigative tool, both in solving crimes and in identifying renegade dealers. A fundamental problem with this approach, however, is that by the time the ATF tracing network gets involved, the guns in question have been used in crime, typically serious crime involving homicide, assault, or narcotics peddling.

Current statistics suggest that the ATF is reluctant to police the vast dealer network. From 1975 through 1990 the ATF revoked an average of ten licenses a year. The low was in 1978, with none, and the high in 1986, with twenty-seven. This rate seems low given the sheer numbers of licenses and the rate of violations discovered whenever the ATF's skeleton crew of inspectors does routine compliance audits. In 1990, for example, inspectors conducted 8,471 of these routine inspections; they found violations in 90 percent of them.

The ATF publicly argues that the vast majority of licensees are honest, law-abiding citizens, and that only "one or two" go bad. Even if true, this argument would hardly be comforting, given the speed with which guns migrate. A single illicit dealer can put hundreds, perhaps thousands, of weapons into the hands of would-be killers and felons before a sufficient number of his weapons are used in crimes, and enough of these are traced, to raise the ATF's suspicions. The fact is, many dealers do operate illegally, as the ATF discovers on those rare occasions when it takes a preventive approach to firearms-law enforcement. A classic example of such enforcement, and the kind that ought to be pursued as a matter of routine, is Project Detroit, an ongoing effort by the ATF and the Detroit police to trace as many guns confiscated in that city as possible.

In its report on the first phase of Project Detroit, covering guns confiscated by the Detroit police from January of 1989 to April of 1990, the ATF, typically, was careful to note, "just because [a federal firearms licensee] has sold a large number of weapons that were subsequently used in crimes does not necessarily indicate the [licensee] is intentionally diverting weapons to the criminal element." Large-volume dealers, the report explained, would necessarily experience more traces.

Yet of the five licensed dealers who turned up most often in Project Detroit traces, four became the targets of full-scale ATF investigations. The worst offender was Sherman Butler, of Sterling Heights, Michigan, near Detroit, whose Sherm's Guns accounted for twenty-nine traces stemming from a range of crimes that included at least two homicides. Butler's specialty was the sale of S. W. Daniel semiautomatics modified to include a sixteen-inch barrel and shoulder stock, thus qualifying them as long rifles and allowing customers to avoid more stringent federal and state rules governing handgun sales, such as Michigan's requirement that anyone buying a handgun must first have a state license to purchase. For $125 extra, however, Butler threw in a pistol-length barrel and enough of a pistol frame—a pistol "upper receiver"—to allow buyers quickly to turn their carbines into semi-automatic pistols.

In all, this first phase of Project Detroit involved the tracing of 1,226 weapons, leading to investigations of thirteen licensed dealers and successful prosecutions against ten. Two suspects died. One case is pending. The ATF discovered that three of these dealers had, as a routine business practice, obliterated the serial number on every gun they received from wholesalers. "We estimate," the report said, "that over 3,000 firearms were sold by these dealers, and that law enforcement officers will be recovering them in various crimes for years to come."

The Project Detroit report failed to note what ought to be the most troubling finding of its investigations: that apparently honest dealers accounted for the remaining 1,000 traces, a fact that testifies again to the high costs imposed on the rest of us by even legitimate gun shops. Indeed, of the top ten dealers, four weren't investigated by the ATF but nonetheless accounted for ten to twenty traces each, including traces involving at least four homicides. In all, Project Detroit traced guns sold by legitimate dealers from New York to Alaska and used subsequently in *at least* two kidnappings, thirty-four homicides, and scores of narcotics offenses—again, from only 1,226 traced weapons.

In his introduction to the report, Bernard La Forest, the special agent in charge, wrote, "What would the results indicate if we had the capability of successfully tracing 10,000 to 15,000 weapons seized by all law enforcement agencies in this metropolitan area?"

Raymond Rowley, the Norfolk ATF agent, initiated the ATF's search for the source of Nicholas Elliot's gun. He heard about the shooting on the news and quickly volunteered his help to Detective Donald Adams, the Virginia Beach homicide investigator. Rowley ordered a trace. The serial number was relayed to Tom Stokes, the special agent in charge in Atlanta, who managed after considerable effort to reach Sylvia Daniel by phone. In a departure from the usual frosty relations between her company and the ATF, Daniel agreed to stop by her office on the way to her company Christmas party to look up the serial number herself.

The number led to a distributor, who in turn said he had shipped the pistol to Guns Unlimited. By eleven o'clock that evening Rowley, another agent, and Adams were at Curtis William's door.

As noted, Williams went to jail. As far as federal law was concerned, however, Guns Unlimited did nothing wrong when it sold the Cobray to Williams, even under such obviously suspicious circumstances. Williams had shown the appropriate identification and had filled out Form 4473 properly, dutifully writing "no" after every background question on the form.

No one thought to investigate Guns Unlimited, not even after the suit for negligence yielded a judgment against the company.

"We're always looking for, and sensitive to, violations of federal law, regardless of who may be the individual or entity involved," Rowley told me. "In this case, no, we did not go back and reinvestigate. Nothing that came up during the investigation of Williams pointed to wrongdoing on the part of Guns Unlimited."

PART TWELVE

EPILOGUE: OPTIONS AND STRATEGIES

Between World War II and the 1960s, the United States enjoyed a period that the sociologist C. Wright Mills called the "American celebration"—a time when the stability of American institutions seemed assured, prosperity was virtually taken for granted, and the American way of life was held up as a shining example for other, less fortunate countries to follow.

As we've seen throughout this book, all of that seems very distant now. American society is changing rapidly—not always for the better—and those changes are, in turn, reflections of our changing role in the wider world. One result is that many of our traditional approaches to social problems have outlived their usefulness. What worked in the rapidly expanding economy of the past—and in a world where American economic and political dominance was virtually unchallenged—no longer works today.

On that point, there would be little disagreement. But exactly what new strategies we should put into place instead is another, much more controversial question. Each of the articles in this part takes up that question, exploring some alternative social and economic options open to us as we move toward the twenty-first century. The specifics vary considerably, but there are common themes.

Some of those themes are set out in the statement on economic justice by the bishops of the Catholic church in the United States. The bishops find much that is inspiring and encouraging in contemporary America, but also much "unfinished business." In particular, they find it both irrational and unjust that millions of Americans are unable to be fully "active and productive participants in the life of society." One of the most formidable barriers to that participation is unemployment, and in the excerpt in this part the bishops outline strategies to move us closer to full employment—strategies based on the fundamental moral principle that all citizens have a *right* to decent work.

The bishops argue that the challenge of building an economy that is more just, more equitable, and more productive is as important and as difficult as the political challenge faced by America's founders. To make such a reformed economy possible, we will need the coordination of all sectors of society—business, labor, the general public, and government. As we noted in the introduction to this book, there has been much recent criticism of what many people see as government's excessive role in American society. The bishops reject the argument that government intervention to serve social goals is necessarily a bad thing, and so do Gar Alperovitz and Jeff Faux, who tackle that argument head-on. They note that government has always been involved in the American economy, often in productive and indeed indispensable ways. And, contrary to what many believe, for several years we have been allowing government's role in American society to expand—but often in destructive or unproductive ways and rarely with a clear sense of what we want government to do. Alperovitz and Faux call for a more conscious use of government to guide economic activity, especially in directions that strengthen local communities and build full employment.

As we saw in Part Nine, health care is one of the areas in which a more active role for government has been most strongly resisted in the United States. But our extreme reliance on the private market to deliver medical care sets us apart from virtually every other advanced society—including our northern neighbor, Canada. Many people have argued that Canada's universal health care system should be a model for the United States; others criticize it as a cumbersome example of heavy-handed government control. As the selection from *Consumer Reports* magazine illustrates, Canada's system isn't what some of its American opponents claim. It is not "socialized medicine": Most doctors work for themselves, not for the government, and Canadians can pick any doctor they choose. And it is *less* bureaucratic than the U.S. system, not more. Meanwhile, it has managed to keep Canadians' health costs relatively low compared to ours, while assuring access to care for everyone.

Since the close of World War II, many of the kinds of social and economic initiatives suggested by the bishops and by Alperovitz and Faux have been put on hold, in part because of the diversion of American resources to support an enormous military. In "Planning for Economic Conversion," Seymour Melman and Lloyd J. Dumas argue that the lessening of the threat of war between the United States and the Soviet Union has now made it both possible and urgently necessary to carry out long-delayed civilian agendas for economic and social reconstruction. They stress that shifting our economy from military to civilian purposes won't happen automatically; it will require careful planning. Huge sections of the American economy, from the defense industries themselves to the universities, are now dependent wholly or partly on military spending, and the transition will not be easy. But a rationally planned conversion of resources now absorbed by defense is, they argue, the best hope for reversing America's domestic and international economic decline.

Robert Heilbroner's article takes up one aspect of that decline more specifically: the erosion of America's infrastructure—the roads and bridges, research centers, airports, and other public facilities that undergird our economic and social life. The steady deterioration of that foundation, resulting from our commitment to military spending, our reluctance to raise taxes, and our fear that the necessary public spending will increase the deficit, has contributed importantly to our economic decline relative to more farsighted industrial societies. Rebuilding the infrastructure will cost vast amounts of money, but the costs of *not* doing so are much greater, and Heilbroner, like Melman and Dumas, argues that reduced superpower tensions now allow us to shift resources from the military to this most urgent civilian priority.

ECONOMIC JUSTICE FOR ALL

CATHOLIC BISHOPS OF THE UNITED STATES

❖ THE U.S. ECONOMY TODAY: MEMORY AND HOPE

6. The United States is among the most economically powerful nations on earth. In its short history the U.S. economy has grown to provide an unprecedented standard of living for most of its people. The nation has created productive work for millions of immigrants and enabled them to broaden their freedoms, improve their families' quality of life and contribute to the building of a great nation. Those who came to this country from other lands often understood their new lives in the light of biblical faith. They thought of themselves as entering a promised land of political freedom and economic opportunity. The United States *is* a land of vast natural resources and fertile soil. It *has* encouraged citizens to undertake bold ventures. Through hard work, self-sacrifice and cooperation, families have flourished; towns, cities and a powerful nation have been created.

7. But we should recall this history with sober humility. The American experiment in social, political and economic life has involved serious conflict

and suffering. Our nation was born in the face of injustice to native Americans, and its independence was paid for with the blood of revolution. Slavery stained the commercial life of the land through its first 250 years and was ended only by a violent civil war. The establishment of women's suffrage, the protection of industrial workers, the elimination of child labor, the response to the Great Depression of the 1930s and the civil rights movement of the 1960s all involved a sustained struggle to transform the political and economic institutions of the nation.

8. The U.S. value system emphasizes economic freedom. It also recognizes that the market is limited by fundamental human rights. Some things are never to be bought or sold. This conviction has prompted positive steps to modify the operation of the market when it harms vulnerable members of society. Labor unions help workers resist exploitation. Through their government the people of the United States have provided support for education, access to food, unemployment compensation, security in old age and protection of the environment. The market system contributes to the success of the U.S. economy, but so do many efforts to forge economic institutions and public policies that enable *all* to share in the riches of the nation. The country's economy has been built through a creative struggle; entrepreneurs, business people, workers, unions, consumers and government have all played essential roles.

9. The task of the United States today is as demanding as that faced by our forebears. Abraham Lincoln's words at Gettysburg are a reminder that complacency today would be a betrayal of our nation's history: "It is for us, the living, rather to be dedicated here to the unfinished work they have thus far nobly advanced." There is unfinished business in the American experiment in freedom and justice for all. . . .

15. Several areas of U.S. economic life demand special attention. Unemployment is the most basic. Despite the large number of new jobs the U.S. economy has generated in the past decade, approximately 8 million people seeking work in this country are unable to find it and many more are so discouraged they have stopped looking. Over the past two decades the nation has come to tolerate an increasing level of unemployment. The 6 percent to 7 percent rate deemed acceptable today would have been intolerable 20 years ago. Among the unemployed are a disproportionate number of blacks, Hispanics, young people, or women who are the sole support of their families. Some cities and states have many more unemployed persons than others as a result of economic forces that have little to do with people's desire to work. Unemployment is a tragedy no matter whom it strikes, but the tragedy is compounded by the unequal and unfair way it is distributed in our society.

16. Harsh poverty plagues our country despite its great wealth. More than 33 million Americans are poor; by any reasonable standard another 20 million to 30 million are needy. Poverty is increasing in the United States, not decreasing. For a people who believe in "progress," this should be cause for alarm. These burdens fall most heavily on blacks, Hispanics and native Americans. Even more disturbing is the large increase in the number of women and children living in poverty. Today children are the largest single group among the

poor. This tragic fact seriously threatens the nation's future. That so many people are poor in a nation as rich as ours is a social and moral scandal that we cannot ignore.

17. Many working people and middle-class Americans live dangerously close to poverty. A rising number of families must rely on the wages of two or even three members just to get by. From 1968 to 1978 nearly a quarter of the U.S. population was in poverty part of the time and received welfare benefits in at least one year. The loss of a job, illness or the breakup of a marriage may be all it takes to push people into poverty.

18. The lack of a mutually supportive relation between family life and economic life is one of the most serious problems facing the United States today. The economic and cultural strength of the nation is directly linked to the stability and health of its families. When families thrive, spouses contribute to the common good through their work at home, in the community and in their jobs, and children develop a sense of their own worth and of their responsibility to serve others. When families are weak or break down entirely, the dignity of parents and children is threatened. High cultural and economic costs are inflicted on society at large.

19. The precarious economic situation of so many people and so many families calls for examination of U.S. economic arrangements. Christian conviction and the American promise of liberty and justice for all give the poor and the vulnerable a special claim on the nation's concern. They also challenge all members of the church to help build a more just society. . . .

70. *Distributive justice requires that the allocation of income, wealth and power in society be evaluated in light of its effects on persons whose basic material needs are unmet.* The Second Vatican Council stated: "The right to have a share of earthly goods sufficient for oneself and one's family belongs to everyone. The fathers and doctors of the church held this view, teaching that we are obliged to come to the relief of the poor and to do so not merely out of our superfluous goods." Minimum material resources are an absolute necessity for human life. If persons are to be recognized as members of the human community, then the community has an obligation to help fulfill these basic needs unless an absolute scarcity of resources makes this strictly impossible. No such scarcity exists in the United States today.

71. Justice also has implications for the way the larger social, economic and political institutions of society are organized. *Social justice implies that persons have an obligation to be active and productive participants in the life of society and that society has a duty to enable them to participate in this way.* This form of justice can also be called "contributive," for it stresses the duty of all who are able to help create the goods, services and other nonmaterial or spiritual values necessary for the welfare of the whole community. In the words of Pius XI, "It is of the very essence of social justice to demand from each individual all that is necessary for the common good." Productivity is essential if the community is to have the resources to serve the well-being of all. Productivity, however, cannot be measured solely by its output in goods and services. Patterns of production must also be measured in light of their

impact on the fulfillment of basic needs, employment levels, patterns of discrimination, environmental quality and sense of community.

72. The meaning of social justice also includes a duty to organize economic and social institutions so that people can contribute to society in ways that respect their freedom and the dignity of their labor. Work should enable the working person to become "more a human being," more capable of acting intelligently, freely and in ways that lead to self-realization.

73. Economic conditions that leave large numbers of able people unemployed, underemployed or employed in dehumanizing conditions fail to meet the converging demands of these three forms of basic justice. Work with adequate pay for all who seek it is the primary means for achieving basic justice in our society. Discrimination in job opportunities or income levels on the basis of race, sex or other arbitrary standard can never be justified. It is a scandal that such discrimination continues in the United States today. Where the effects of past discrimination persist, society has the obligation to take positive steps to overcome the legacy of injustice. Judiciously administered affirmative-action programs in education and employment can be important expressions of the drive for solidarity and participation that is at the heart of true justice. Social harm calls for social relief.

74. Basic justice also calls for the establishment of a floor of material well-being on which all can stand. This is a duty of the whole of society, and it creates particular obligations for those with greater resources. This duty calls into question extreme inequalities of income and consumption when so many lack basic necessities. Catholic social teaching does not maintain that a flat, arithmetical equality of income and wealth is a demand of justice, but it does challenge economic arrangements that leave large numbers of people impoverished. Further, it sees extreme inequality as a threat to the solidarity of the human community, for great disparities lead to deep social divisions and conflict.

75. This means that all of us must examine our way of living in light of the needs of the poor. Christian faith and the norms of justice impose distinct limits on what we consume and how we view material goods. The great wealth of the United States can easily blind us to the poverty that exists in this nation and the destitution of hundreds of millions of people in other parts of the world. Americans are challenged today as never before to develop the inner freedom to resist the temptation constantly to seek more. Only in this way will the nation avoid what Paul VI called "the most evident form of moral underdevelopment," namely greed.

76. These duties call not only for individual charitable giving but also for a more systematic approach by businesses, labor unions and the many other groups that shape economic life—as well as government. The concentration of privilege that exists today results far more from institutional relationships that distribute power and wealth inequitably than from differences in talent or lack of desire to work. These institutional patterns must be examined and revised if we are to meet the demands of basic justice. . . .

❖ OVERCOMING MARGINALIZATION AND POWERLESSNESS

77. These fundamental duties can be summarized this way: *Basic justice demands the establishment of minimum levels of participation in the life of the human community for all persons.* The ultimate injustice is for a person or group to be actively treated or passively abandoned as if they were non-members of the human race. To treat people this way is effectively to say that they simply do not count as human beings. This can take many forms, all of which can be described as varieties of marginalization or exclusion from social life. This exclusion can occur in the political sphere: restriction of free speech, concentration of power in the hands of a few or outright repression by the state. It can also take economic forms that are equally harmful. Within the United States, individuals, families and local communities fall victim to a downward cycle of poverty generated by economic forces they are powerless to influence. The poor, the disabled and the unemployed too often are simply left behind. This pattern is even more severe beyond our borders in the least-developed countries. Whole nations are prevented from fully participating in the international economic order because they lack the power to change their disadvantaged position. Many people within the less-developed countries are excluded from sharing in the meager resources available in their homelands by unjust elites and unjust governments. These patterns of exclusion are created by free human beings. In this sense they can be called forms of social sin. . . .

95. The economic challenge of today has many parallels with the political challenge that confronted the founders of our nation. In order to create a new form of political democracy they were compelled to develop ways of thinking and political institutions that had never existed before. Their efforts were arduous and their goals imperfectly realized, but they launched an experiment in the protection of civil and political rights that has prospered through the efforts of those who came after them. *We believe the time has come for a similar experiment in securing economic rights: the creation of an order that guarantees the minimum conditions of human dignity in the economic sphere for every person.* . . .

136. Full employment is the foundation of a just economy. The most urgent priority for domestic economic policy is the creation of new jobs with adequate pay and decent working conditions. We must make it possible as a nation for everyone who is seeking a job to find employment within a reasonable amount of time. Our emphasis on this goal is based on the conviction that human work has a special dignity and is a key to achieving justice in society.

137. Employment is a basic right, a right which protects the freedom of all to participate in the economic life of society. It is a right which flows from the principles of justice which we have outlined above. Corresponding to this right is the duty on the part of society to ensure that the right is protected. The importance of this right is evident in the fact that for most people employment

is crucial to self-realization and essential to the fulfillment of material needs. Since so few in our economy own productive property, employment also forms the first line of defense against poverty. Jobs benefit society as well as workers, for they enable more people to contribute to the common good and to the productivity required for a healthy economy.

138. Joblessness is becoming a more widespread and deep-seated problem in our nation. There are about 8 million people in the United States looking for a job who cannot find one. They represent about 7 percent of the labor force. The official rate of unemployment does not include those who have given up looking for work or those who are working part time but want to work full time. When these categories are added, it becomes clear that about one-eighth of the work force is directly affected by unemployment. The severity of the unemployment problem is compounded by the fact that almost three-fourths of those who are unemployed receive no unemployment insurance benefits.

139. In recent years there has been a steady trend toward higher and higher levels of unemployment, even in good times. Between 1950 and 1980 the annual unemployment rate exceeded current levels only during the recession years of 1975 and 1976. Periods of economic recovery during these three decades brought unemployment rates down to 3 percent and 4 percent. Since 1979, however, the rate has generally been above 7 percent.

140. Who are the unemployed? Blacks, Hispanics, native Americans, young adults, female heads of households and those who are inadequately educated are represented disproportionately among the ranks of the unemployed. The unemployment rate among minorities is almost twice as high as the rate among whites. For female heads of households, the unemployment rate is over 10 percent. Among black teen-agers unemployment reaches the scandalous rate of more than one in three.

141. The severe human costs of high unemployment levels become vividly clear when we examine the impact of joblessness on human lives and human dignity. It is a deep conviction of American culture that work is central to the freedom and well-being of people. The unemployed often come to feel they are worthless and without a productive role in society. Each day they are unemployed our society tells them: We don't need your talent. We don't need your initiative. We don't need *you.* Unemployment takes a terrible toll on the health and stability of both individuals and families. It gives rise to family quarrels, greater consumption of alcohol, child abuse, spouse abuse, divorce and higher rates of infant mortality. People who are unemployed often feel that society blames them for being unemployed. Very few people survive long periods of unemployment without some psychological damage even if they have sufficient funds to meet their needs. At the extreme, the strains of job loss may drive individuals to suicide.

142. In addition to the terrible waste of individual talent and creativity, unemployment also harms society at large. Jobless people pay little or no taxes, thus lowering the revenues for cities, states and the federal government. At the same time, rising unemployment requires greater expenditures for unemploy-

ment compensation, food stamps, welfare and other assistance. It is estimated that in 1986, for every one percentage-point increase in the rate of unemployment, there will be roughly a $40 billion increase in the federal deficit. The costs to society are also evident in the rise in crime associated with joblessness. The Federal Bureau of Prisons reports that increases in unemployment have been followed by increases in the prison population. Other studies have shown links between the rate of joblessness and the frequency of homicides, robberies, larcenies, narcotics arrests and youth crimes.

143. Our own experiences with the individuals, families and communities that suffer the burdens of unemployment compel us to the conviction that as a nation we simply cannot afford to have millions of able-bodied men and women unemployed. We cannot afford the economic costs, the social dislocation and the enormous human tragedies caused by unemployment. In the end, however, what we can least afford is the assault on human dignity that occurs when millions are left without adequate employment. Therefore, we cannot but conclude that current levels of unemployment are intolerable, and they impose on us a moral obligation to work for policies that will reduce joblessness.

❖ UNEMPLOYMENT IN A CHANGING ECONOMY

144. The structure of the U.S. economy is undergoing a transformation that affects both the quantity and the quality of jobs in our nation. The size and makeup of the work force, for example, have changed markedly in recent years. For a number of reasons, there are now more people in the labor market than ever before in our history. Population growth has pushed up the supply of potential workers. In addition, large numbers of women have entered the labor force in order to put their talents and education to greater use and out of economic necessity. Many families need two salaries if they are to live in a decently human fashion. Female-headed households often depend heavily on the mother's income to stay off the welfare rolls. Immigrants seeking a better existence in the United States have also added to the size of the labor force. These demographic changes, however, cannot fully explain the higher levels of unemployment.

145. Technological changes are also having dramatic impacts on the employment picture in the United States. Advancing technology brings many benefits, but it can also bring social and economic costs, including the downgrading and displacement of workers. High technology and advanced automation are changing the very face of our nation's industries and occupations. In the 1970s, about 90 percent of all new jobs were in service occupations. By 1990, service industries are expected to employ 72 percent of the labor force. Much of the job growth in the 1980s is expected to be in traditionally low-paying, high-turnover jobs such as sales, clerical, janitorial and food service. Too often these jobs do not have career ladders leading to high-

er-skilled, higher-paying jobs. Thus the changing industrial and occupational mix in the U.S. economy could result in a shift toward lower-paying and lower-skilled jobs.

146. Increased competition in world markets is another factor influencing the rate of joblessness in our nation. Many other exporting nations have acquired and developed up-to-the-minute technology, enabling them to increase productivity dramatically. Combined with very low wages in many nations, this has allowed them to gain a larger share of the U.S. market and to cut into U.S. export markets. At the same time many corporations have closed plants in the United States and moved their capital, technology and jobs to foreign affiliates.

147. Discrimination in employment is one of the causes for high rates of joblessness and low pay among racial minorities and women. Beyond the normal problems of locating a job, blacks, Hispanics, native Americans, immigrants and other minorities bear this added burden of discrimination. Discrimination against women is compounded by the lack of adequate childcare services and by the unwillingness of many employers to provide flexible employment or extend fringe benefits to part-time employees.

148. High levels of defense spending also have an effect on the number of jobs in our economy. In our pastoral letter "The Challenge of Peace," we noted the serious economic distortions caused by the arms race and the disastrous effects that it has on society's ability to care for the poor and the needy. Employment is one area in which this interconnection is very evident. The hundreds of billions of dollars spent by our nation each year on the arms race create a massive drain on the U.S. economy as well as a very serious "brain drain." Such spending on the arms race means a net loss in the number of jobs created in the economy, because defense industries are less labor-intensive than other major sectors of the economy. Moreover, nearly half of the American scientific and engineering force works in defense-related programs, and over 60 percent of the entire federal research and development budget goes to the military. We must ask whether our nation will ever be able to modernize our economy and achieve full employment if we continue to devote so much of our financial and human resources to defense-related activities.

149. These are some of the factors that have driven up the rate of unemployment in recent years. Although our economy has created more than 20 million new jobs since 1970, there continues to be a chronic and growing job shortage. In the face of this challenge, our nation's economic institutions have failed to adapt adequately and rapidly enough. For example, failure to invest sufficiently in certain industries and regions, inadequate education and training for new workers and insufficient mechanisms to assist workers displaced by new technology have added to the unemployment problem.

150. Generating an adequate number of jobs in our economy is a complex task in view of the changing and diverse nature of the problem. It involves numerous tradeoffs and substantial costs. Nevertheless, it is not an impossible task. Achieving the goal of full employment may require major adjustments

and creative strategies that go beyond the limits of existing policies and institutions, but it is a task we must undertake.

❖ GUIDELINES FOR ACTION

151. We recommend that the nation make a major new commitment to achieve full employment. At present there is nominal endorsement of the full-employment ideal, but no firm commitment to bringing it about. If every effort were now being made to create the jobs required, one might argue that the situation today is the best we can do. But such is not the case. The country is doing far less than it might to generate employment.

152. Over the last decade, economists, policy-makers and the general public have shown greater willingness to tolerate unemployment levels of 6 percent to 7 percent or even more. Although we recognize the complexities and tradeoffs involved in reducing unemployment, we believe that 6 percent to 7 percent unemployment is neither inevitable nor acceptable. While a zero unemployment rate is clearly impossible in an economy where people are constantly entering the job market and others are changing jobs, appropriate policies and concerted private and public action can improve the situation considerably, if we have the will to do so. No economy can be considered truly healthy when so many millions of people are denied jobs by forces outside their control. The acceptance of present unemployment rates would have been unthinkable 20 years ago. It should be regarded as intolerable today.

153. We must first establish a consensus that everyone has a right to employment. Then the burden of securing full employment falls on all of us—policy-makers, business, labor and the general public—to create and implement the mechanisms to protect that right. We must work for the formation of a new national consensus and mobilize the necessary political will at all levels to make the goal of full employment a reality.

154. Expanding employment in our nation will require significant steps in both the private and public sectors, as well as joint action between them. Private initiative and entrepreneurship are essential to this task, for the private sector accounts for about 80 percent of the jobs in the United States, and most new jobs are being created there. Thus a viable strategy for employment generation must assume that a large part of the solution will be with private firms and small businesses. At the same time, it must be recognized that government has a prominent and indispensable role to play in addressing the problem of unemployment. The market alone will not automatically produce full employment. Therefore, the government must act to ensure that this goal is achieved by coordinating general economic policies, by job creation programs and by other appropriate policy measures.

155. Effective action against unemployment will require a careful mix of general economic policies and targeted employment programs. Taken together, these policies and programs should have full employment as their No. 1 goal.

■ General Economic Policies

156. The general or macro-economic policies of the federal government are essential tools for encouraging the steady economic growth that produces more and better jobs in the economy. *We recommend that the fiscal and monetary policies of the nation—such as federal spending, tax and interest-rate policies—should be coordinated so as to achieve the goal of full employment.*

157. General economic policies that attempt to expand employment must also deal with the problem of inflation. The risk of inflationary pressures resulting from such expansionary policies is very real. Our response to this risk, however, must not be to abandon the goal of full employment, but to develop effective policies that keep inflation under control.

158. While economic growth is an important and necessary condition for the reduction of unemployment, it is not sufficient in and of itself. In order to work for full employment and restrain inflation, it is also necessary to adopt more specific programs and policies targeted toward particular aspects of the unemployment problem.

■ Targeted Employment Programs

159. *(1) We recommend expansion of job-training and apprenticeship programs in the private sector administered and supported jointly by business, labor unions and government.* Any comprehensive employment strategy must include systematic means of developing the technical and professional skills needed for a dynamic and productive economy. Investment in a skilled work force is a prerequisite both for sustaining economic growth and achieving greater justice in the United States. The obligation to contribute to this investment falls on both the private and public sectors. Today business, labor and government need to coordinate their efforts and pool their resources to promote a substantial increase in the number of apprenticeship programs and to expand on-the-job training programs. We recommend a national commitment to eradicate illiteracy and to provide people with skills necessary to adapt to the changing demands of employment.

160. With the rapid pace of technological change, continuing education and training are even more important today than in the past. Businesses have a stake in providing it, for skilled workers are essential to increased productivity. Labor unions should support it, for their members are increasingly vulnerable to displacement and job loss unless they continue to develop their skills and their flexibility on the job. Local communities have a stake as well, for their economic well-being will suffer serious harm if local industries fail to develop and are forced to shut down.

161. The best medicine for the disease of plant closings is prevention. Prevention depends not only on sustained capital investment to enhance productivity through advanced technology, but also on the training and retraining of

workers within the private sector. In circumstances where plants are forced to shut down, management, labor unions and local communities must see to it that workers are not simply cast aside. Retraining programs will be even more urgently needed in these circumstances.

162. *(2) We recommend increased support for direct job-creation programs targeted on the long-term unemployed and those with special needs.* Such programs can take the form of direct public-service employment and also of public subsidies for employment in the private sector. Both approaches would provide jobs for those with low skills less expensively and with less inflation than would general stimulation of the economy. The cost of providing jobs must also be balanced against the savings realized by the government through decreased welfare and unemployment-insurance expenditures and increased revenues from the taxes paid by the newly employed.

163. Government funds, if used effectively, can also stimulate private sector jobs for the long-term unemployed and for groups particularly hard to employ. Experiments need to be conducted on the precise ways such subsidies would most successfully attract business participation and ensure the generation of permanent jobs.

164. These job-generation efforts should aim specifically at bringing marginalized persons into the labor force. They should produce a net increase in the number of jobs rather than displacing the burden of unemployment from one group of persons to another. They should also be aimed at long-term jobs and should include the necessary supportive services to assist the unemployed in finding and keeping jobs.

165. Jobs that are created should produce goods and services needed and valued by society. It is both good common sense and sound economics to create jobs directly for the purpose of meeting society's unmet needs. Across the nation, in every state and locality, there is ample evidence of social needs that are going unmet. Many of our parks and recreation facilities are in need of maintenance and repair. Many of the nation's bridges and highways are in disrepair. We have a desperate need for more low-income housing. Our educational systems, day-care services, senior-citizen services and other community programs need to be expanded. These and many other elements of our national life are areas of unmet need. At the same time, there are more than 8 million Americans looking for productive and useful work. Surely we have the capacity to match these needs by giving Americans who are anxious to work a chance for productive employment in jobs that are waiting to be done. The overriding moral value of enabling jobless persons to achieve a new sense of dignity and personal worth through employment also strongly recommends these programs.

166. These job-creation efforts will require increased collaboration and fresh alliances between the private and public sectors at all levels. There are already a number of examples of how such efforts can be successful. We believe that the potential of these kinds of partnerships has only begun to be tapped.

■ Examining New Strategies

167. In addition to the actions suggested above, we believe there is also a need for careful examination and experimentation with alternative approaches that might improve both the quantity and quality of jobs. More extensive use of job sharing, flex time and a reduced work week are among the topics that should continue to be on the agenda of public discussion. Consideration should also be given to the possibility of limiting or abolishing compulsory overtime work. Similarly, methods might be examined to discourage the overuse of part-time workers who do not receive fringe benefits. New strategies also need to be explored in the area of education and training for the hard-to-employ displaced workers, the handicapped and others with special needs. Particular attention is needed to achieve pay equity between men and women, as well as upgrading the pay scale and working conditions of traditionally low-paying jobs. The nation should renew its effort to develop effective affirmative-action policies that assist those who have been excluded by racial or sexual discrimination in the past. New strategies for improving job-placement services at the national and local levels are also needed. Improving occupational safety is another important concern that deserves increased attention.

168. Much greater attention also needs to be devoted to the long-term task of converting some of the nation's military production to more peaceful and socially productive purposes. The nation needs to seek more effective ways to retool industries, to retrain workers and to provide the necessary adjustment assistance for communities affected by this kind of economic conversion.

169. These are among the avenues that need to be explored in the search for just employment policies. A belief in the inherent dignity of human work and in the right to employment should motivate people in all sectors of society to carry on that search in new and creative ways. . . .

363. Confronted by this economic complexity and seeking clarity for the future, we can rightly ask ourselves one single question: How does our economic system affect the lives of people—*all* people? Part of the American dream has been to make this world a better place for people to live in; at this moment of history that dream must include everyone on this globe. Since we profess to be members of a "catholic" or universal church, we all must raise our sights to a concern for the well-being of everyone in the world. Third World debt becomes our problem. Famine and starvation in sub-Saharan Africa become our concern. Rising military expenditures everywhere in the world become part of our fears for the future of this planet. We cannot be content if we see ecological neglect or the squandering of natural resources. In this letter we bishops have spoken often of economic interdependence; now is the moment when all of us must confront the reality of such economic bonding and its consequences, and see it as a moment of grace—a *kairos*—that can unite all of us in a common community of the human family. We commit ourselves to this global vision.

42

MORE GOVERNMENT, NOT LESS

GAR ALPEROVITZ AND JEFF FAUX

I s government inherently bureaucratic, wasteful, clumsy and burdened by red tape? Do private corporations automatically develop and manage a nation's resources better than public enterprises? Is the free market invariably more efficient than careful planning in guiding and directing a nation's economic destiny?

Unfashionable as it is to say so in the midst of the "Reagan revolution," the answer to all these questions is an emphatic no. In fact, it is almost certain that we will one day look back on the current period of anti-government sentiment in the United States as a brief interlude before a new era of efficient, enlightened and—yes—expanded involvement of federal, state and local government in the economy.

It is pure nostalgia to think that our post-industrial society will be run in the future as if it were a semi-developed, agricultural nation in mid-19th century. There is a worldwide trend toward more government, and not even America under Ronald Reagan has been immune to it.

Contrary to common opinion, federal spending as a percentage of Gross National Product has risen, not fallen, during the Reagan administration. In the Jimmy Carter years, federal spending averaged just over 22 percent of GNP; under Reagan it has averaged 24.2 percent.

This president, like others before him, has openly used the power of government to manage the economy. He continued the Chrysler bailout. His Agriculture Department handed over $21 billion of surplus commodities to farmers as part of a Payment-in-Kind program. His administration "informally" limited imports of Japanese automobiles and restricted imports of steel, sugar and motorcycles. Not only has the government taken over Continental Illinois National Bank—the nation's eighth largest—but it has virtually guaranteed all large banks that it will not permit them to fail.

The Reagan administration has supported government programs that aid the defense and nuclear power industries. And that is to say nothing of indirect government action, such as the 1981 tax bill that heavily favored big manufacturing industries over small business and the service sector.

The administration's actual record, if not its rhetoric, is part of a trend with a long history. Over the years, the federal government has subsidized regions of the United States with military bases and aerospace projects; an interstate highway system; billion-dollar water projects; rural electrification; ports and waterways. It has promoted American agriculture with price supports for corn, export subsidies for wheat and an elaborate system of allotments, quotas and marketing orders that help growers of tobacco, cotton, sugar, peanuts, oranges, apples and dozens of other commodities.

Federal investment in canals and turnpikes, and vast subsidies to railroads, helped "open the West." Government policies that subsidized the development of new labor-saving technologies in agriculture encouraged the mass migration of rural blacks to northern and midwestern cities after World War II.

There is nothing unusual about any of this, much as it goes against the grain of America "free enterprise" mythology. In every nation in the world, governments are deeply involved in planning, subsidizing, financing and in some cases operating major sectors of the economy. Such private-public cooperation helps countries compete internationally, avoids wasteful duplication of research efforts, safeguards employment and maintains the stability of communities.

The expansion of the Japanese steel industry, which contributed to the devastation of U.S. steel companies, was the result of an economic strategy designed by the Japanese government.

There is no iron law of economics that says private enterprise is innately superior to public enterprise. Big corporations are as vulnerable as big government to the ills of size, bureaucracy and monopoly.

Real conservatives are the first to acknowledge this. The late Henry C. Simons, founder of the Chicago school of economics, came to believe that many corporations (as opposed to individual entrepreneurs) had outlived their usefulness.

Simons recognized the need for restraints on corporate practices. He advocated strong antitrust laws and federal chartering of corporations. He favored public ownership of utilities, railroads, and other industries that were not competitive. This highly respected conservative teacher of Milton Friedman declared that "every industry should be either effectively competitive or socialized."

Government-owned, or partially owned, railroad, airline, aircraft, electrical, and automobile companies have been responsible for good deal of France's industrial innovation and, in the case of aircraft and autos, for a significant part of her manufacturing exports. Government-owned Renault, for example, has been highly successful in competition with private firms. And European governments, working together, built the successful commercial aircraft Airbus.

In Western Europe public enterprises account for 8 to 12 percent of total employment and 15 to 30 percent of total capital investment. Six of the largest 12, and 15 of the largest 50, Western European industrial firms are wholly or substantially owned by governments. For example, West German, Canadian, French, Italian and British governments are major shareholders in their respective oil and gas industries.

Current economic difficulties in Europe have aroused new interest in U.S.-style free enterprise and entrepreneurism. In England, some public enterprises have been sold back to the private sector. However, on balance, the changes in Europe as a whole have been relatively modest. French President Francois Mitterand has brought more banks into the public sector.

Despite our anti-government ideology, the record of public agencies in this country is quite different from what the conventional wisdom holds. During World War II the federal government created a variety of efficient businesses—aluminum industries on the West Coast, steel mills and an oil pipeline from Texas to the East Coast, all of which were later purchased by the private sector. The federal government currently operates civilian airports, builds ships in Navy shipyards, manages a third of the nation's land and administers the world's largest pension system, Social Security.

The state of Wisconsin runs the State Life Insurance Fund, created by Republican populist Gov. Robert LaFollette in 1917. State Life is solvent and unsubsidized. Moreover, it sells life insurance for 10 to 40 percent less than its private competitors.

State governments operate liquor stores, hotels, resorts and lotteries. South Dakota makes and sells cement, and Nebraska produces and sells hog cholera serum. Hundreds of localities efficiently run their own water companies.

Comparing the efficiency of public and private enterprises is no easy matter. Public utility companies, for example, often have the disadvantage of serving unprofitable rural areas. On the other hand, they don't pay taxes and can offer investors tax-free bonds. Several studies have found public utilities to be more efficient producers and distributors of electric power, even when their tax advantages are eliminated.

A Twentieth Century Fund study of public authorities in states and cities found that, with some exceptions, "the present system . . . has been generally successful at producing good management and effective operations." The major criticism was that public organizations were too conservative in their operations and tended to reflect the interest and biases of businessmen who dominate their boards.

To be sure, during the recent slowdown in economic growth there is some evidence that the relative productivity of public enterprises in Western Europe declined in late 1970s. But that seems, in large part, to have resulted from the greater freedom of private managers to lay off workers in recessions. In effect, private companies shifted the costs of unemployment to the public (which paid increased welfare and unemployment costs), while public firms tended to absorb these costs themselves.

This is a point that is too often side-stepped by enthusiastic supporters of the free market and the private sector. While it is all very well to extol the efficiency of private enterprise, it is easy to ignore the costs of this efficiency to taxpayers and communities. In our current, relatively unplanned economy, taxpayers subsidize major corporate investment decisions, which, in turn, often wreak havoc on communities and their tax bases.

Any accountant looking at the overall costs from the taxpayers' point of view of a company's decision to pull up stakes and move would evaluate the "efficiency" of such a move very differently from the company's own bookkeepers.

At present, communities have little power to control the flight of companies and capital. They are caught up in a competition for capital that is ultimately destructive to all. The Sunbelt may be benefiting temporarily from a wave of business investment at the expense of the North and Midwest, but the benefits may only be shortlived. At some point, companies are likely to shut down and move elsewhere to take advantage of cheaper labor, more ample water and other factors, leaving communities to pick up the tab for schools, highways and other services.

This is where planning comes in. Only a comprehensive approach at both the national and local level can define investment goals that protect communities, jobs and, ultimately, taxpayers.

Since 1978, legislation has been introduced at the local, state, and federal level to require advance notice of plant closings and to aid firms owned by their workers or their communities.

A serious strategy for safeguarding local economic stability would include technical assistance, loans and loan guarantees to build up community-based enterprises. The federal government has a role to play here. A firm should always be free to move if it so desires; but there is no reason for it to receive tax incentives, grants for training programs and research and development funds from federal, state and local governments if its move throws excessive numbers of people out of work and makes them dependent on public welfare and unemployment funds. In that case, the total costs far outweigh the total benefits.

The closing of a plant by an absentee conglomerate does not necessarily mean that the plant is unprofitable. Rather, it means that the plant is not profitable enough for the liking of the conglomerate. Local owners however, might be willing to settle for a smaller profit, because of the jobs and other economic benefits from keeping the plant running.

The experience of Herkimer, N.Y., a small city not far from Syracuse, illustrates the broader returns that are possible from emphasizing economic stability strategies.

The nation's largest manufacturer of library furniture, a Sperry Rand subsidiary named the Library Bureau, was located in Herkimer. In 1975 the parent company decided to close the plant because it was not producing the 22 percent return on investment that Sperry Rand required of its subsidiaries. Closing the 250-worker plant would have devastated the little community, so after several futile efforts to change Sperry Rand's mind, the workers and small businessmen in the town decided to buy the firm and run it themselves.

A group headed by John Ladd, a local businessman with a flair for politics, formed a corporation and sold $1.5 million worth of stock in $1 and $2 shares to workers and local residents. They borrowed $2 million from local banks, another $2 million from the U.S. Department of Commerce, and bought the plant. When the dust settled, the employees owned some 30 to 40 percent of the shares, and their neighbors in Herkimer owned the rest.

During the first full year of operation, the worker- and community-owned company earned 17 percent on its investment—not enough for the multinational Sperry Rand Corp., but plenty for the people and workers of Herkimer, who saved their jobs and their town.

The impact on local communities of unexpected new investment is not always positive, either. In California's "Silicon Valley," the cost of an average house has jumped dramatically, and large numbers of new houses are awaiting basic service hookups. By the year 2000, Houston's population is expected to have grown sixfold from its 1950 level, resulting in congestion, pollution, water shortages, overcrowded schools and hospitals and a huge run-up in real estate values. Because of excessively rapid growth, a city industrial and real estate commission took the almost unheard-of step of recommending that large industrial corporations be encouraged to locate outside the county, since new tax revenue from industry was not adequate to offset the costs of growth.

If we are to reduce these costly and inefficient patterns of boom and bust, we must face up to the need for a comprehensive assessment of the cost and benefits of corporate investment decisions. This requires increasing the scope and competence of government planning.

Arguments have been made that a more coherently planned economy would make it harder for this country to compete internationally. In fact, the opposite is the case.

As things now stand, the closing of out-moded factories in declining industries is so threatening to jobs and community welfare that corporations, communities and unions all team together to fight for protection. This only postpones the day of reckoning, perpetuating inefficiency and lack of competitiveness.

But if communities and workers were assured alternative jobs, the impasse could be broken, allowing the modernization to go forward more rapidly.

Planning does not do away with politics; it puts politics out in the open. It forces special-interest groups to stand up and be counted. Cozy alliances between political leaders and economics interests are brought to light. In a more planned economy, there are still deals and compromises, but they can be labeled and evaluated openly.

At present, the expansion of government is carried on behind a smoke-screen of free-enterprise rhetoric that confuses the public and makes rational decision-making impossible. A sensible U.S. economic policy would recognize the need to build up a coherent planning capacity at both the national and local level. It would accept the fact that only government is capable of assessing the total costs and benefits of economic decisions to the taxpayer and the nation. It would put community well-being at the center of national planning for full employment. And it would reap the benefits of an economy that mixed public and private enterprises in ways that took advantage of the special contributions of each.

Only such an economic policy allows a satisfactory answer to the question, "What's in it for me?" The answer cannot be that we will beat the Japanese to 40 percent of the world's computer business, but you will lose your job or your business in the process.

43

HEALTH CARE IN CRISIS: DOES CANADA HAVE THE ANSWER?

CONSUMER REPORTS

More than 30 years ago Canada enacted a program to bring health care within reach of all its citizens. By 1971, Canada's provincial governments were paying the medical bills for everyone in Canada, and few people outside Canada were paying much attention.

As the U.S. health-care system began to creak and groan under the weight of its runaway costs—and as its inability to serve every citizen became increasingly apparent—Americans started to look seriously at Canada's health-care system as a model for reform. At the same time, Canada's system started to come under concerted attack from those special-interest groups—health-insurance companies, medical associations, and hospitals—that profit most from the present nonsystem of health care. This report examines the strengths and weaknesses of the Canadian system and evaluates the criticisms leveled against it.

❖ HOW THE SYSTEM WORKS

Contrary to what some in the U.S. health-care industry would have you believe, Canada does not have "socialized medicine." Medicare, as Canada's

From *Consumer Reports*, September 1992. Reprinted by permission.

health-care system is called, is simply a social insurance plan, much like Social Security and Medicare for older people in the U.S. Canada's doctors do not work on salary for the government.

Canadians pay for health care through a variety of federal and provincial taxes, just as Americans pay for Social Security and Medicare through payroll taxes. The government of each province pays the medical bills for its citizens. Because the government is the primary payer of medical bills, Canada's health-care system is referred to as a "single-payer" arrangement. Benefits vary somewhat among the provinces, but most cover, in addition to medical and hospital care, long-term care, mental-health services, and prescription drugs for people over 65. Private insurance exists only for those services the provincial plans don't cover.

Although each province runs its own insurance program as it sees fit, all are guided by the five principles of the Canada Health Act:

1. Universality. Everyone in the nation is covered.

2. Portability. People can move from province to province and from job to job (or onto the unemployment rolls) and still retain their health coverage.

3. Accessibility. Everyone has access to the system's health-care providers.

4. Comprehensiveness. Provincial plans cover all medically necessary treatment.

5.   Public administration. The system is publicly run and publicly accountable.

❖ WHERE DOCTORS FIT IN

The role of doctors in the Canadian system is little understood in the U.S. and frequently distorted by the foes of a single-payer system. For example, in announcing his plan for health reform last winter, President Bush declared: "We don't need to put Government between patients and their doctors and create another wasteful federal bureaucracy." Nor should the Government tell doctors how to practice medicine, other opponents of Canadian-style health care often add.

Canada's health-care system does neither. "In the U.S. there's a myth that Canadians have an awful government bureaucracy that tells doctors how to practice medicine," says Dr. Michael Rachlis, a Toronto physician and health-policy consultant. "There's much more interference from third parties [such as insurance companies and utilization-review firms] in the U.S. than from the government in Canada."

Canada's physicians practice in their own offices and work for themselves, just as most U.S. doctors do. The main difference: Canadian doctors may not charge whatever they wish. Their fees are set according to a schedule negotiated by the ministry of health in each province and the provincial medical association. Canadian doctors cannot engage in the common American practice of "balance billing"—billing the patient the difference between what an insurer will pay and what the doctor wishes to charge.

The negotiation process has managed to keep fee inflation in Canada at least modestly in check. Fees tend to be much lower than those commanded by American doctors for the same service. In British Columbia, for example, doctors receive about $349 to remove a gallbladder, in Manitoba, $354; and in Ontario, $348. But in New York City, the customary fee paid by insurance carriers averages about $2700: in Buffalo, N.Y., $945. (All figures are in U.S. dollars.)

Despite the lower fees, physicians in Canada, like those in the U.S., enjoy high incomes. In British Columbia, the average payment (before overhead) made by the health ministry to cardiologists last year was $290,500; to ophthalmologists, $240,500; to dermatologists, $200,500; and to general practitioners, $128,000.

❖ WHERE PATIENTS FIT IN

Canadians, like U.S. citizens, can select any doctor they like. Those doctors bill the provincial insurance plans directly and are usually paid within two to four weeks. For patients, there are no bills, claim forms, out-of-pocket costs, or waits for reimbursement from insurance carriers, all common complaints in the U.S.

Roughly half of all Canadian physicians are family practitioners (compared with 13 percent in the U.S.), and Canadians go to them for treatment that Americans might seek from costlier specialists. Most Canadians, for instance, take their children to family practitioners instead of to pediatricians for common childhood illnesses. Most children see pediatricians only for serious problems.

The provinces encourage people who need a specialist's care to obtain a referral from a family doctor, much the way HMOs and other managed-care plans do in the U.S. If a specialist sees a patient who has not obtained a referral, that specialist can bill the Government only the fee that would ordinarily have been paid to a general practitioner.

Those rules, aimed at controlling costs by preventing the overuse of high-priced specialists, do not always have their intended effect. If a patient shows up at a specialist's office without a referral, the specialist need only call the family practitioner, obtain a referral number, and bill the Government the higher fee. Many family doctors are only too glad to send any complicated or time-consuming case to a specialist so they can see more patients and earn more fees. The increased use of medical services is a major reason costs are escalating there as they are here.

❖ NOT ENOUGH HOSPITAL BEDS?

Canada's rising health-care costs are a favorite target of U.S. critics, who have also made much of the fact that Canadian hospitals have reduced their number of beds in recent months. The implication is that the Canadian health-care system is collapsing and that Canadians now suffer from insufficient hospital facilities. Actually, Canada has too many hospital beds, which is also the case in the U.S. Hospitals proliferated in both countries during the last two decades. Money flowed freely, building new hospitals was good politics, and the public as well as the government came to believe that another hospital bed meant better health.

As health-care costs in Canada rise, the provinces are being forced to rethink how best to spend their health dollars. Most bed closings stem from deliberate government strategies to eliminate waste and duplication of services. In Toronto, for example, where a total of 2200 beds have been permanently closed, the city's 45 hospitals still have 1000 beds empty on any given day.

Provincial governments can implement such cost-cutting measures because they control how much money a hospital receives. Every year they negotiate a "global budget" with each hospital in the province. That budget includes money to cover operating costs, increases for inflation and greater utilization, and any special services the ministry wants the hospital to offer. The global budgets set by the provincial governments comprise about 95 percent of a hospital's total funds. Any other money must come from fund-raising and investment earnings. Within the global budgets, hospitals are free to move money around. If, say, a hospital finds the costs of running the emergency room are lower than expected, it can redirect some of the money to increase the number of cataract surgeries, if it chooses to. Canadian hospitals, however, are not allowed to run deficits.

❖ LONG WAITS FOR CARE?

Perhaps the most frequently heard charge against the Canadian system is that it rations care, and people don't get the treatment they need. *The New York Times* told readers of its editorial page last November that as a result of "rationing," Canadian "women must wait months for a simple Pap smear."

In reality, women in Canada routinely have Pap smears done by their family doctors, who perform them the same way U.S. doctors do. Canada's ambassador to the U.S. traced the tale of Pap smear waits to a brief delay in laboratory processing in Newfoundland some years ago—a problem long since corrected.

Canadian men and women routinely have general surgery, diagnostic ultrasound, X-rays, thyroid tests, amniocentesis, EKGs, and hundreds of other procedures and treatments without delay. But Canadians may not have immediate access to the latest technological innovations, such as lithotripters (machines that crush kidney stones with sound waves) and magnetic resonance imagers (MRIs), or to such surgical procedures as a coronary-artery bypass or hip replacement. Someone who pulls a knee muscle playing soccer isn't likely to get an MRI scan the day after the accident. And those who want bypass surgery to relieve angina symptoms won't be wheeled into the operating room right away. However, anyone requiring emergency care gets it immediately.

Because provincial governments control hospital budgets, they also control the introduction and use of technology. In some cases, they have kept a tight lid on that technology to restrain the high costs associated with overuse, inappropriate use, or duplication. Hospitals denied some piece of equipment by the provincial health ministry are free to buy it with money raised from private contributions, but they can't look to the ministry for funds to operate it.

In Winnipeg, Manitoba, for example, Seven Oaks Hospital purchased a CT scanner with its own funds and is already operating it. The Ministry of Health maintains that the province doesn't need another CT scanner, that the six scanners available at other provincial hospitals are enough to serve the province's needs. The ministry has hinted that it may not cover the $1-million operating and depreciation expenses for the machine.

The ministry has taken a hard line on MRIs as well. The province has just one, and the hospital operating it must follow strict guidelines in deciding when it should be used. The province probably could use another MRI machine, says Dr. Cam Mustard, an assistant professor of community health sciences at the University of Manitoba. But, he adds, "it's not such a scarce resource that people are coming to harm because they can't get on it. Doctors are very satisfied with the quality of service, and the waiting times are not seen as obstructing their ability to care for patients."

"The alternative [to having such waiting times]," says Dr. Charles Wright, a vice president for medicine at Vancouver General Hospital, "is to have a grossly overbuilt system as in the U.S. If you build for the peaks, you have a hell of a lot of wasted resources."

The published figures on the number of Canadians on waiting lists probably exaggerate the actual delays in receiving care. For the most part, doctors manage the lists, putting people on one or more of them as they deem appropriate. Sometimes doctors put a patient on a list to give him or her hope when a condition is actually hopeless. Sometimes they put patients on just in case their condition worsens and a procedure not now necessary becomes necessary. Queues shift constantly as those needing care immediately move ahead of those whose conditions are less serious. Sometimes queues develop and then disappear. At Wellesley Hospital in Toronto, for example, kidney patients once faced a three-month wait for lithotripsy. Now there's virtually no wait, and the machine doesn't always run at capacity.

When St. Boniface Hospital in Winnipeg investigated its waiting list of 143 people for cardiac angiography, a radiological examination of the arteries surrounding the heart, it found that only 56 people were really candidates for the procedure. Some didn't need it, some didn't want it, and some had already had the procedure done at another hospital. One doctor was accused of packing the list for his own political reasons.

In 1991, a British Columbia Royal Commission on health care investigated all the well-publicized cases of people who claimed to have been harmed by delays in the queue for heart surgery. "When we tracked them down, almost all of the cases crumbled," says Appeals Court Justice Peter Seaton, who chaired the commission.

That finding hasn't stopped opponents of Canadian-style health care from citing waiting lists in British Columbia as evidence that the system is grinding to a halt. "A waiting list of 700 to 800 people for heart surgery is not uncommon," a vice president of the National Center for Public Policy Research, a conservative think tank, wrote in a 1992 *New York Times* column.

A waiting list of that length did exist, but only for a short time. When researchers looked into it, they found that two-thirds of the people on the list were waiting not for the procedure, but for three particular surgeons.

When waiting lists have grown too long, provincial governments have in some instances offered patients the option of going to the U.S. for treatment. The British Columbia Ministry of Health, for example, contracted with hospitals in Seattle to provide 200 heart surgeries. It took more than a year before Canadians filled all 200 slots, raising the question of whether the delays were indeed life-threatening.

Critics like to portray the availability of treatment in the U.S. as a safety valve for Canadians. However, that says as much about the overcapacity of the American system as it does about poor planning on the part of Canada. The British Columbia Health Ministry received many calls from U.S. hospitals eagerly soliciting its heart-surgery business.

❖ UNAVAILABLE OPERATIONS?

When he was running for the Democratic presidential nomination, Paul Tsongas said that if he had lived in Canada, he would be dead by now. The procedure that arrested his cancer, Tsongas said, was not available there. In fact, the procedure that saved Tsongas' life, autologous bone-marrow transplantation, was indeed available in Canada in 1986 when Tsongas had his operation. In fact, the pioneering research that led to bone-marrow transplants took place at a Toronto hospital 30 years ago.

In making his charge, Tsongas joined the long list of critics of the Canadian health-care system who contend that it denies its citizens appropriate care. The National Center for Public Policy Research, for example, has asserted that "Canadians do not have enough surgery, at least not enough of the surgery they need the most." and Newt Gingrich, the Republican whip in the House of Representatives, has contended that "it is illegal in Canada to get a whole series of operations."

If anything, Canadians are probably getting too much care, just as Americans are. A report prepared for the Conference of Deputy Ministers of Health last year found that a "nontrivial" amount of the medical services Canadians receive are ineffective and inappropriate. The report blamed fee-for-service reimbursements to doctors for much of the problem. The same criticism applies to the U.S. . . .

Surgery rates for some procedures are actually higher in Canada than elsewhere. Canada is a world leader in the number of gallbladder surgeries and is second only to the U.S. in heart bypass operations. Each year, the French perform 15 to 20 bypass surgeries per 100,000 people; the British, 20 to 30; the Canadians, 50; and the Americans, about 100.

❖ NEEDLESS DEATHS?

In its health-care reform proposals put forward earlier this year, the Bush Administration asserted that "post-operative mortality is 44 percent higher in Canada than in the U.S. for high-risk procedures, including heart surgery." Dr. Leslie Roos, a professor of community health sciences at the University of Manitoba and one of the authors of the study to which the Administration referred, told CU that the statement "seriously distorts our overall findings."

For one thing, the study compared only Manitoba and New England, not the U.S. and Canada. For another, it compared a number of low-risk and moderately risky procedures and only two that were high-risk—repair of hip fracture and concurrent valve replacement with bypass (one kind of heart surgery). The study showed that for the low- and moderate-risk procedures, the number of people who died shortly after surgery was similar in the two regions. The mortality rates for hip-fracture repair in New England were lower than in Manitoba, primarily because many Manitoba patients had to be transported long distances from remote, northern parts of the province.

Roos told CU that later research is showing Manitoba's heart-surgery results "to be fully comparable with those of the leading American centers." He added that three-year survival rates for cardiovascular surgery are better in Manitoba than they are in the U.S.

❖ HOW COSTS COMPARE

Opponents of a single-payer system also like to claim that health-care costs are rising faster in Canada than in the U.S. A study by the Health Insurance Association of America (HIAA), the insurance companies' trade organization, reported that per capita spending in the U.S. rose, on average, 4.38 percent per year from 1967 to 1987, compared with 4.58 percent in Canada. But Canada's single-payer system wasn't even completely in place until 1971. Although other researchers have refuted the HIAA's findings, the numbers live on in propaganda against the Canadian system. . . .

Health-care costs are lower in Canada than in the U.S., whether measured by per capita spending or as a percentage of gross national product. In 1989, the U.S. spent $2450 per person on health care, while the Canadians spent $1800. In 1990, the U.S. spent 12.2 percent of its GNP on health care; Canada spent 9.5 percent.

Before Canada fully implemented its Medicare system in 1971, both it and the U.S. were spending comparable amounts of their respective GNPs on health care. But as Canada's system of universal coverage took hold in all the provinces, spending by the two countries sharply diverged.

Canadian researchers believe that 25 to 35 percent of the difference may be due to Canada's controls on hospitals. One study found that in the early 1980s, for instance, the U.S. spent as much as 50 percent more per person on hospital services, even though Canadians stayed in the hospital longer, on average.

But perhaps the most striking differences are in administrative costs. In 1987, researchers have estimated, the U.S. spent between 19 and 24 percent of its health-care dollars on administrative expenses; the Canadians spent between 8 and 11 percent.

❖ PLAYING POLITICS

Much of the ammunition fired at the Canadian system has inadvertently been supplied by the Canadians themselves. When it comes time to negotiate fees or new budgets, doctors and other providers there often assert that the Canadian system is underfunded.

Providers don't hesitate to make waiting lists a political issue or to put their case before the public by writing letters and running advertisements that take their health-care system to task. This spring, a Manitoba Medical Association newsletter featured an open letter to the minister of health headlined "Rationing eye surgery impairs patients' quality of life, MMA President tells Minister." The publication also ran letters from a doctor and a patient's relative pleading for more money for hip-replacement surgery. The British Columbia Medical Association ran newspaper ads warning of the harm that could come from placing a cap on the fees earned by its highest-paid members, such as ophthalmologists, dermatologists, and cardiologists—a strategy the ministry was pursuing to reduce health-care expenditures.

Conflicts between Canada's health-care providers and the government, however, are often overblown in the U.S. Not long ago, Dr. Gur S. Singh, then president of the British Columbia Medical Association, sent a letter to provincial newspapers arguing that Americans should keep their system basically unchanged. Singh said he wanted the U.S. to "continue to provide the necessary safety valve to an overly restrictive Canadian system which will only get worse as further bureaucratic controls are adopted." Health Insurance Association of America president Carl Schramm quoted from Singh's letter in testimony to the U.S. Senate.

At the end of his letter, however, Singh said the Canadian system was "one of the best, and perhaps it still is the best health-care system in the world." That point didn't make it into Schramm's testimony.

An astute Canadian observer would have known that Singh's letter was simply a "piece of negotiating rhetoric intended to bat the minister [of health] over the head," says Dr. Hedy Fry, Singh's predecessor at the medical group. "That letter was for public consumption in B.C."

❖ WHAT AILS THE SYSTEM?

The Canadian health-care system, like every health-care system in the world, has problems, though they're not of the scary sort usually cited by U.S. critics. There is a more-than-adequate supply of doctors in Canada, but there is a shortage of physicians in the remote, northern areas of the country, where few want to practice. The U.S. has the same problem, of course; few doctors care to practice in rural or poverty-stricken areas.

Even though Canada has a greater proportion of family doctors than the U.S., medical-school incentives have steered doctors-in-training to specialities that command higher fees and result in higher costs to the system. . . . A report presented to Canada's deputy ministers of health last year blamed at least part of this trend on the bad example of the U.S., where 87 percent of all physicians are specialists.

A more fundamental flaw is that through the years, provincial governments have acted more like check-writers than health-care managers. As in the U.S., hospitals and doctors often received generous increases simply by asking for them. In Ontario, for instance, hospital spending has increased 10 percent or more each year for the last 10 years. But that is changing. This year Ontario hospitals are getting just a 1 percent increase in their global budgets, and the ministry is redirecting money to other types of health care.

Canadian patients also may have stayed in hospitals longer than was necessary. In 1989, the average length of stay was 10.5 days, compared to 7.2 days in the U.S. In Canada, patients are still entering hospitals a day or two before their surgeries for preoperative workups, a practice that utilization firms in the U.S. are rapidly putting an end to.

Since 1984, health-care spending by the provinces has increased 80 percent, to about $44-billion. At the same time, the economy that funds that spending has grown less than 20 percent. The Canadian federal government, which once provided about 50 percent of the funding for the provincial health budgets, now supplies only about 35 percent. Eventually it may leave the funding solely to the provinces.

Pushed by rising costs and by pressures on funding, the provinces are redirecting money and starting programs to make better use of their dollars. "We're afraid we're going to lose our system if we don't change it," says Lin Grist, a special assistant to Ontario's minister of health. "It's really quite precious to us."

The U.S. faces similar problems, but Canada is in a better position to solve

A MODEL OF SIMPLICITY
Long-Term Care in Canada

All Canadians are eligible for government-paid long-term care no matter how high their incomes or how much money they have in the bank. They are not forced to "spend down" their assets or impoverish themselves before the government will pay for their care, as many Americans are.

Canadians who use long-term-care services must pay a modest amount for them, currently between $17 and $21 a day. In British Columbia, for instance, residents in long-term-care facilities pay about $19 toward the typical $67 daily charge for nursing-home care. The Ministry of Health pays the rest. That payment is adjusted periodically, based on changes in the cost of living and in government-financed pensions.

If someone also receives welfare or old-age assistance from the government, the government deducts the amount it pays toward nursing-home care from those payments. But a person in that situation is still left with more disposable income than nursing-home residents in the U.S. who receive Medicaid benefits. In Canada, patients can keep between $84 and $143 each month for incidental expenses. A nursing-home resident in New York City who receives Medicaid can keep only $50.

Provinces differ in the long-term-care services they provide and in how people gain access to them. British Columbia and Manitoba are the most advanced, allowing residents to enter their long-term-care systems through a "single entry point." If people in British Columbia, for example, need long-term care, they or their families contact one of the health ministry's 90 offices. The Health Ministry then dispatches case managers who direct patients to appropriate services, such as medical treatment, home care, day-care centers, or nursing-home care. In the U.S., people needing long-term care have no one entry point. They must first get a doctor to certify they need nursing-home care and then shop around for a facility willing to take them.

The ministry also has created 15 quick-response teams that go into action when an older person seeks treatment in a hospital emergency room. The teams identify people who can be helped with early intervention, such as patients who have broken hips. The idea is to get them the right kind of treatment immediately, rather than let them languish in costly hospital rooms.

Other provinces are beginning to follow the lead of Manitoba and British Columbia in establishing a single-entry system for their citizens' long-term care. Each province is also trying to move long-term-care patients who do not need to be hospitalized out of hospitals and into less expensive community and home-care settings. The single-payer system is well suited for that task, since it allows the health ministries to decide where to direct their money. In British Columbia, for example, the ministry has increased by 9 percent the number of hours of homemaker care it will pay for, while increasing the number of nursing-home beds only by about 2 percent. "You can create incentives to direct people to community-based services," says Paul Pallan, an assistant deputy minister in the province's Ministry of Health.

them. For one thing, it long ago answered the question of whether everyone in the country should be entitled to health care—a question the U.S. seems incapable of resolving. For another, Canada's single-payer system is better suited to the task of redeploying resources as needed. It can decide where to spend its budget for the good of all citizens.

In the U.S., the rhetoric of the day is to contain costs. But few, if any, doctors or other providers embrace limits on their own incomes. And there's no single payer with enough influence to impose the controls necessary to squeeze the billions of dollars of waste out of the system.

One option Canadians are not considering is a move back to a system like the one in the U.S. Of the 1503 people who testified before the British Columbia Royal Commission in its hearings on health reform, only one favored adopting the American way of paying for health care.

Canadians like their health-care system and expect their government to fix its current problems. But a government that tried to tinker with the basic principles of the Canada Health Act would be a government out of power very soon.

44

PLANNING FOR ECONOMIC CONVERSION

SEYMOUR MELMAN AND LLOYD J. DUMAS

It's time to start planning the conversion of America's defense economy to civilian work. By conversion we mean political, economic and technical measures for assuring the orderly transformation of labor, machinery and other economic resources now being used for military purposes to alternative civilian uses. The political impetus for conversion is gaining momentum as a result of the relaxation of cold war tensions. Another stimulus to action is America's deteriorating competitive position in the world economy.

A major factor in America's decline to the status of a second-class industrial power has been the voracious appetite of the military-industrial complex, which employs 6.5 million civilian and military personnel in more than 135,000 factories, laboratories and bases. From 1947 to 1989 this country diverted to military purposes resources whose value exceeded the fixed reproducible, tangible wealth of the entire civilian economy. Tens of thousands of factories became virtual wards of the Pentagon; sheltered from the discipline of the marketplace, they adopted inefficient and costly methods. An indirect consequence of the larger share of tax dollars funneled into the military establishment was a diminution of public investment in the infrastructure and its resulting decay. The debilitating effect of all those developments on American industrial strength is readily apparent.

Labor productivity, a key indicator of long-term efficiency, has signifi-cantly declined. Between 1968 and 1988 labor productivity (measured by the dollar value of output per hour of workers in the nonagricultural business sec-tor) rose by 24 percent, approximately one-third of the gain between 1948 and 1968.

In every year between 1894 and 1970 the United States ran a trade sur-plus—exporting more goods than it imported. In 1971 these surpluses turned into deficits. By 1987 the foreign trade deficit hit a peak of $170 billion, more than 160 percent above the record level set only four years earlier. "Made in the U.S.A." once meant well-made, high-quality, reasonably priced goods pro-duced by industrial workers earning the highest wages in the world. Now U.S. trade deficits reflect in part a decline in quality and productive efficiency.

In 1982 the American economy plunged into its worst economic down-turn since the Great Depression. By the end of the 1980s, however, the unem-ployment rate fell to more tolerable levels. Inflation remained well below the double-digit rates of the late 1970s. And the real gross national product grew more than 25 percent between 1982 and the third quarter of 1988, when it passed the $4 trillion mark. Supposedly, the country is in the midst of the strongest economic recovery since World War II.

But that is an illusion. We have merely pumped up the economy with a huge infusion of public and private debt. This facade of prosperity is not based on the efficient production that drove the economy's remarkable growth throughout much of America's industrial history—an expansion whose bene-fits were spread among the population rather than going to one small segment of it at the expense of all the rest.

Between fiscal 1980 and fiscal 1989 the national debt more than tripled, from $914 billion to $2.8 trillion. In less than three years after 1985, the federal government added nearly $780 billion in debt, an amount equal to more than 85 percent of the *total* national debt as of 1980. State and local government debt, and the private debt of households and nonfinancial institutions, soared from nearly $3 trillion in 1980 to more than $6 trillion by September 1988. Between 1980 and 1987 the United States went from being the world's largest creditor nation, to whom $106 billion was owed, to being the world's largest debtor nation, with a net international debt approaching $400 billion.

All that borrowing served temporarily to paper over deep-seated econom-ic problems, giving us a fleeting reprieve. But it has also created a "bubble of debt" on top of a steadily eroding economic base, adding the possibility of a sudden collapse to the continuing long-term deterioration in American eco-nomic performance.

❖ THE FORCES OF REAL RECOVERY

Despite these very serious problems, the end of the 1980s has brought some cause for optimism. Three powerful political forces have begun to develop that may just push the United States in the direction it needs to go to turn this downbeat picture around: the growing pressure to balance the federal budget, the increasing prominence of the competitiveness issue and the extraordinary opportunities created by *perestroika* and *glasnost* in the Soviet Union and Eastern Europe.

■ Balancing the Budget

The enormous increase in the national debt between 1980 and 1989 was clearly the result of the Reagan Administration's tax cuts combined with a military spending binge. Had the borrowing been in support of a major program of public investment in infrastructure, education and the like, it would not have been a great problem. Productive investment would have eventually generated more than enough additional wealth to pay back the borrowed money with interest. But unproductive use of the money for military expansion means that it must now be paid back out of existing wealth—and that will be painful.

Annual military budgets more than doubled during that period, and this accelerated spending accounted for more than 50 percent of the increase in national debt. The military-driven debt, in turn, led to a near tripling of the annual net interest on that debt, from $53 billion to $152 billion. Looked at differently, without this explosive increase in the national debt, the interest savings alone would have taken us two-thirds of the way to balancing the federal budget.

In the 1987 fiscal year, spending on the military and interest on the national debt accounted for almost 90 percent of all the federal income tax revenues collected from both individuals and corporations. . . . In the absence of draconian tax increases or slashes in social programs greater than the public was willing to accept from the previous administration, significant cuts in the military budget are highly likely. Without them it will be impossible to balance the federal budget in the foreseeable future. This is not a question of ideology or political preference. It is simply a matter of fiscal reality.

■ Competitiveness

The fiscal pressures for cutbacks in military spending reinforce demands for the changes that are needed to rebuild American industrial competitiveness. More than forty years of high military spending has diverted from civilian industry the resources that are critical to efficient, competitive production, including roughly 30 percent of the nation's engineers and scientists and a comparable portion of its capital. Engineers and scientists trained to design and produce for cost-minimizing in civilian industry are the key to developing technology for better product designs and more efficient methods of production; capital allows these innovations to be put into use on the factory floor. The long-term drain of these resources has undermined the ability of U.S.-

based factories to maintain competitive position, especially relative to those nations (Japan and Germany, for example) whose commercial industries are only lightly burdened by that drain.

To revitalize the competitiveness of American industry we must attack the structural causes of inefficiency. This can be accomplished in a solid, long-term way only by an infusion of capital and technical talent. That means redirecting a significant fraction of these critical resources from military to civilian research and production.

▣ Perestroika and Glasnost

The remarkable changes in the Soviet Union and Eastern Europe offer great promise of substantial arms reduction. We have seen only a beginning, but it is a hopeful one. The prospect of a 50 percent reduction in strategic nuclear arsenals—even talk of the total elimination of nuclear weapons within a decade or two—has moved from the realm of an impossible dream to the real world of negotiations. Progress toward reduction of conventional forces has begun.

Each of the three forces we have been discussing has its counterpart in the Soviet Union, which has finally admitted that it too is plagued by out-of-control budget deficits. The military's diversion of critical resources from the country's civilian industrial base has played no small part in rendering those industries hopelessly inefficient. At the same time, the attention of the nations of Western Europe has turned increasingly to economic integration rather than military adventurism. As far as the Soviet Union is concerned, this surely diminishes the threat to their security.

The convergence of these three forces in both the United States and the Soviet Union has made large-scale demilitarization an increasingly practical, attainable goal. And large-scale demilitarization is just what is needed to free sufficient resources for building healthy, growing economies in both nations.

❖ OBSTACLES TO CONVERSION

Nevertheless, there are strong institutional and ideological barriers to implementation of economic conversion. The most prominent of these are the managements in central government offices and the private firms that are dependent on the military economy. Government departments are ordinarily viewed as "bureaucracies"; however, the central management in the Defense Department that controls the operations of 35,000 prime contracting establishments is, functionally, a central administrative office. This central administrative office is probably the largest such entity in the world and performs the same functions as similar offices in large corporations.

Furthermore, the management of the Pentagon's central office controls the largest block of finance capital in the hands of any single American management. Every year since 1951 the new capital made available to the Defense Department has exceeded the combined net profits of all U.S. corporations. The top managers in the Pentagon and their subordinates are endowed with the usual managerial imperative to maintain and enlarge their decision-making power. Accordingly, they have consistently opposed all proposals for economic conversion planning in the United States.

This managerial opposition to conversion planning is not specific to any particular social structure, political ideology or management technique. Thus the managers of the U.S. military economy perform their command function via allocation of money resources, while those of the Soviet Union perform the command function by direct physical resource preemption and allocation. The results in each case are similar: pre-emption of major resources from civilian production and powerful pressures for operating in an unproductive, cost-maximizing way.

The work force and surrounding communities of factories, bases and laboratories that serve the military are another institutional barrier to economic conversion. In the United States 3.5 million men and women work in the military industry. An additional 1 million are employees of the Pentagon, including civilian workers on bases, and there are 2 million in the armed forces. For these 6.5 million people and their families and surrounding communities, the military-serving facilities have been the principal sources of jobs for most of their lives. The skills they have developed and the relationships with which they are familiar are powerful incentives to continue working for the military. The people in such enterprises know that even the appearance of an interest in the idea of economic conversion would bring the disfavor of the Pentagon's top managers.

The nation's organized engineering societies include large numbers of engineers beholden to the military economy. This has a significant effect on the contents of society meetings, the subject matter of journals and learned papers, and the network of contacts available for employment opportunity. At this writing no single engineering society has ventured to propose contingent conversion planning for its members as a way of coping with the possible reversal of military budget growth. In its November 1989 issue *Spectrum,* a journal of the Institute of Electrical and Electronics Engineers, published a special report titled "Preparing for Peace," a serious, courageous attempt to survey the military engineers' prospects during a subsiding cold war.

Finally, there are the universities, particularly the larger ones, which have grown accustomed to receiving major R&D grants from the Defense Department and to administering major research institutions, like the Lawrence Livermore and Los Alamos nuclear weapons laboratories, for the Pentagon. At the same time the departments of universities that might be expected to have some connection with civilian production, the engineering and business schools, have become less production-oriented during the long cold war period. Some schools are beginning to make an effort to reestablish the importance of civilian production in their curriculums, but the emphasis is small compared with the military-oriented research activities. The universities also contain large departments and schools—such as political science and international relations—whose faculties and curriculums have focused on training cold war technicians, researchers and administrators.

For all the personnel of the military-serving institutions it is significant that the knowledge for performing their tasks comprises their intellectual capital and work skills. Therefore a change to a civilian economy entails the obsolescence of intellectual capital and the necessity for learning new skills.

Alongside these direct economic ties to the military at the universities there are a number of ideological commitments that play an important part in sustaining support for military institutions. Among economists, for example, it is generally accepted that money equals wealth, that the proper measure of economic product is in money terms, that the money value of an economic activity denotes its value independent of the usefulness of the product. Military goods and services are thus counted as additions to real wealth despite the fact that they do not contribute to the central purpose of the economy—to provide the material standard of living. They add neither to the present standard of living (as do ordinary consumer goods) nor to the future standard of living by increasing the economy's capacity to produce (as do industrial machinery, equipment and the like).

Since the Great Depression, economists, and indeed the larger society, have defined the central problem of the U.S. economy as the maintenance of proper levels of market demand, and thereby of income and employment. From this perspective, expenditures that generate market demand are critical, regardless of the nature of the product. A consensus formed that military spending is the best way to accomplish this effect. Thus, most economics textbooks do not differentiate between firms producing military goods and civilian enterprises.

From these assumptions it is a short step to the idea that the United States is uniquely capable of affording guns *and* butter for an indefinite period of time. This belief has facilitated the acceptance of sustained negative trade balances and spreading incompetence in U.S. manufacturing. Large subsidies to the American standard of living in the form of trade imbalances are therefore considered normal, while the role of the military economy in causing a collapse of production competence is ignored. Nevertheless, domestic economic problems and international political changes compel attention to the feasibility of economic conversion.

❖ THE PROCESS OF ECONOMIC CONVERSION

The ideology of the free-market economy argues that the labor and facilities no longer needed in the military-serving sector will flow smoothly and efficiently toward an expanding civilian sector once military spending is cut. The market will take care of the transition. There is no need for special attention and certainly no need for advance preparation.

But this isn't true. The world of military industry is very different from the world of commercial industry. For one thing, military-serving firms do not operate in anything like a free-market environment. In the military production system, the nature, quantity and price of output are not determined by impersonal market forces. They are set by the interaction of the Pentagon's central planners and the managers of the military-industrial firms. Military industry, unlike any civilian industry, has only one customer—the Defense Department. Even when military firms sell to other nations, they typically sell products initially designed and produced to satisfy the needs of the Defense Department and can sell abroad only with its permission. Furthermore, the vast majority of defense contracts are negotiated rather than awarded through true price-competitive bidding.

More important, competition in the civilian commercial marketplace provides a crucial element of cost discipline that is largely absent in military industry. In practice, most major military contractors operate on a cost-plus basis, being reimbursed for whatever they have spent plus a guaranteed profit. In such an environment, there are no real penalties for inefficient production. In fact, company revenues can be increased by jacking up costs. Such cost escalation would spell bankruptcy for firms operating in a free market.

The sales function of a typical civilian company involves dealing with large numbers of potential customers, ranging from perhaps a few dozen for firms purveying industrial products to millions for consumer goods producers. For military firms the sales function means knowing the Armed Service Procurement Regulations, developing contacts within the Defense Department and being adept at lobbying. The most crucial job of managers in civilian industries is keeping costs down while producing good quality products. Managers in defense firms need pay relatively little attention to cost, but they must try to manufacture products capable of operating under extreme conditions while delivering every possible increment of performance.

It is not a question of one kind of management being easier or harder than the other. The point is that they are very different. It is simply not reasonable to expect a manager used to operating in one of these worlds to perform efficiently in the other without undergoing substantial retraining and reorientation. That takes time and will not happen automatically. Civilian firms may well prefer to hire inexperienced civilian managers instead of facing the costs involved in retraining an experienced military manager for civilian work. The same consideration holds for engineers and scientists—the other main component of the military-serving labor force—who would require substantial retraining and reorientation.

The products of military industry are notorious for their poor reliability, despite requirements that only components meeting stringent military specifications be used. These components are not only remarkably costly but also certified to withstand extraordinary extremes of shock, temperature and so on. Poor reliability is an unavoidable consequence of the increasing complexity of military weaponry. Thus sophisticated military aircraft have been in repair a third or more of the time. That's bearable when the cost of maintenance is not a limiting factor. But city transportation systems cannot accept vehicles that are "not mission capable" a third of the time. Hence, the retraining of military-experienced engineers and managers is an essential aspect of economic conversion. Of course, the physical facilities and equipment of military industry will require modification as well.

❖ PLANNING FOR CONVERSION

Advanced contingency plans for moving into alternative civilian-oriented activity could help carry the nation smoothly through the transition to a demilitarized economy and protect militarily dependent communities against the considerable economic disruption they will otherwise experience. The transformation of a facility and its work force to civilian production must be planned locally, by those who know them best—not by distant "experts." Even at its best such a planning process will be lengthy. A great many details must be worked through to insure that the transition is smooth and that the resulting facility and work force are properly restructured to be an efficient civilian producer, able to operate profitably without continuing subsidies. It is long past time to get this process under way.

A bill now before Congress, House Resolution 101, would institutionalize a nationwide system of highly decentralized contingency planning for economic conversion at every military facility in the United States. The resolution, called the Defense Economic Adjustment Act, sponsored by Representative Ted Weiss, would require the establishment of labor-management Alternative Use Committees at every military facility with 100 or more people. These local committees would be empowered to draw up detailed technical and economic plans for shifting to viable alternative civilian activity. Funds would be provided for services such as income support, continued health insurance and pension benefits during any actual transition resulting from military cutbacks.

There are two reasons why military-industry workers should be specially protected, even though workers in other industries are not. First, such protection is vital to breaking the hold of the politically powerful "jobs" argument, which raises the specter of lost jobs to constituents and thus damage to the political careers of representatives who vote against any military programs. The second is that the special obstacles to conversion of military industry must be overcome to allow the infusion of resources into civilian activity that will ultimately revitalize the whole of U.S. industry, and not just the prospects of converted defense workers and firms.

By moving military-sector resources into profitable civilian activity through a carefully planned process of economic conversion, the nation can break its decades-long addiction to military spending and build a stronger and more secure economic base. Without such a revitalization of civilian production, it is difficult to see how America can climb out of the deep hole of production incompetence, deficit and debt it dug for itself in the 1980s and reverse the deterioration of its economic performance and competitive position in the global marketplace.

❖ CONVERSION TO WHAT?

What could the 6.5 million employees of the military-serving institutions do for a living beyond their work for the Pentagon? There are three major areas of work that could be done by these people. The first is repairing the American infrastructure. This includes building and repairing roads, railroads and bridges; constructing waste disposal plants; cleaning up toxic and nuclear wastes; erecting new housing to make up for the enormous shortfall in construction and repair during the past decades; refurbishing libraries, public school buildings, university facilities and so on. In New York City alone there are 1,000 public school buildings, of which 83 percent require major repairs. Bridges and highways have been crumbling for want of proper maintenance, and the country's railroads are more like the Toonerville Trolley of cartoon fame than modern high-speed facilities. The cost of repairing the infrastructure could amount to more than $5 trillion. The work to be done would surely extend over several decades.

House Resolution 101 includes a provision for a Cabinet-level council that would be charged with encouraging state, city and county governments to prepare capital budgets for renovating the public works and services under their jurisdiction. If carried out, this would set in motion a thoroughly decentralized set of nationwide planning operations for projects that would have employment needs beyond the size and capabilities of the existing work force.

The second area of new work for the converted military labor force would involve producing in the United States many of the products that are now imported. There is no law of nature or economics that prevents factories in the United States from once again becoming competent producers of shoes, for example; we now import 80 percent of our supply. An infusion of fresh investment and talent into the machine-tool industry could restore our former ability to produce high-quality machinery. The United States now buys 50 percent of its new machine tools from Japan, Germany and South Korea.

The third area is new ideas, a sphere in which American engineers and technicians once excelled.

A uniquely large proportion of engineers and administrators are employed in the military-serving industries. For those occupations some special conversion prospects will surely be in order. Teachers of mathematics and the sciences are in notoriously short supply in American high schools and junior colleges. The major teachers colleges could design appropriate programs for training some of these men and women to teach the young, an activity that would have long-range benefits for society. Many engineers could be retrained as civil engineers to work in American communities. The addition of an engineer to a city's or a town's staff would mean a substantial improvement in the ability of local governments to cope with the array of public works that are their responsibility.

❖ COLLECTING THE PEACE DIVIDEND

Apart from the planning of economic conversion, its actual execution will be heavily dependent on the timing and the size of the peace dividend that would result from the reduction of military budgets. Savings can be expected from two sources: first, and early on, reduction of certain military activities (such as base closings and elimination of marginal weapons programs) at the initiative of the federal government; second, de-escalation of military spending and the size of the military-serving institutions as a result of international agreements setting in motion a programmed reduction of the arms race. The first of these approaches could yield possible savings of several billion dollars annually. *The New York Times* editorialized on March 8 in favor of weapons and force cuts starting with $20 billion per year and reaching $150 billion annually after ten years. That would bring down annual military spending to a level comparable to that in President Carter's budgets. But a thoroughgoing military de-escalation would require international disarmament agreements.

A program for reversing the arms race was laid out by President Kennedy in April 1962 in a document called "Outline of Basic Provisions of a Treaty on General and Complete Disarmament in a Peaceful World." This plan called for a ten-year period to accomplish a significant reversal of the arms race among nations and the parallel establishment of international institutions for inspecting the disarmament process, for coping with international conflict by nonmilitary means and for developing an international peacekeeping force. If this blueprint is implemented, a ten-year cumulative peace dividend of $1.5 trillion is within reach. That is the magnitude of resources needed to start serious economic conversion and to rebuild the infrastructure and industry of the country.

45

SEIZE THE DAY

ROBERT HEILBRONER

A merica is falling behind. I do not mean only that we are losing ground against Europe and Japan. I mean that we are falling behind with respect to our own capacities. We are not the country we once were, or the country we could be.

I do not need to document this sorry assertion. I want to write about what I think we can do to catch up. For we now have a unique chance to become the country we could be if we lived up to our possibilities. It lies within our grasp to overcome the single most difficult obstacle we face in trying to recover our momentum. That obstacle is the inadequacy of our infrastructure, the public underpinnings without which a society cannot be healthy or an economy prosperous.

Infrastructure is the public capital of a nation—the network of roads and water mains, harbors and air navigation systems, public health research facilities and public waste disposal facilities, on which we all depend for much of the quality of our individual lives. We also depend on it for much of our collective efficiency. Just as a train cannot exceed the limits of its roadbed, an economy cannot exceed those of its infrastructure.

From *New York Review of Books*, February 15, 1990. Reprinted with permission from the *New York Review of Books*. Copyright © 1990, Nyrev, Inc.

American infrastructure is in a state of near collapse. For nearly twenty-five years we have virtually ceased to improve our public capital. Following World War II, we set out to build up interstate highways, airports, research and development laboratories and the like, until by 1952 spending on infrastructure absorbed 6.9 percent of the nonmilitary federal budget. Irregularly, but with increasing momentum, this share has been declining ever since. During the 1970s it plummeted to an average of 1.5 percent. During the 1980s the share dropped still further to 1.2 percent. Thus a smaller and smaller fraction of government spending has gone into reinforcing or extending the public foundation of the economy. To drive across the Queensboro Bridge in New York is to know at first hand the meaning of allowing our infrastructure to decay.

Where there is longstanding current neglect, catch-up costs become large. The United States Department of Transportation tells us that it will now take $50 billion to repair the nation's 240,000 bridges. To bring our highways up to their condition in 1983 will take ten years and $315 billion in current dollars. Air traffic control is in desperate need of funds for expansion and modernization—at least $25 billion by the year 2000. According to the Department of Housing and Urban Development, it will cost $20 billion to rehabilitate the nation's stock of public housing, and rehabilitation does not mean adding to the current, shamefully inadequate stock. There is no official tally of the total expenditures needed to repair and maintain the infrastructure over the next ten years. The Congressional Budget Office estimates the amount at about $60 billion per year. The Association of Public Contractors puts it at $118 billion per year. The nation's contractors are hardly a disinterested source, but in this case their estimates may be closer to reality.

These totals, moreover, include only "hard" investment—the public counterpart of private spending for plant and equipment. But some public spending for "soft" purposes is also properly included in infrastructure because it contributes to economic growth. One obvious such candidate is expenditure on education, whose economic consequence is the improvement of the skills and productivity of our citizenry.

This "soft" portion of our infrastructure is also badly neglected. Spending on elementary and secondary education reached 4.4 percent of GNP in the 1970s. It has fallen by 10 percent during the present decade. At the same time, investment in higher education has not risen since the 1970s. This is an important part of the reason that the quality of our labor force is deteriorating both at the bottom and at the top—and thus part of the reason that we are falling behind.

Economists of all political colorations agree that our ramshackle and rotting infrastructure constitutes a serious obstacle to vigorous economic growth. For example, David Aschauer of the Chicago Federal Reserve Bank has calculated that a dollar of public investment is today productive of more output than a dollar of private investment, and that private profitability would rise by two percentage points—that is, from, say 10 to 12 percent—if infrastructure investment were merely brought back to its 1981 levels. The final report of

President Reagan's Council of Economic Advisers also notes the fall in federal investment spending as "a matter for concern" because it can adversely affect the growth of the private sector.

Thus the neglect of the national infrastructure has been an unmitigated disaster. No one has gained: all have lost. That is why I argue that of all the means of reestablishing our place, the most important is to rebuild the embankment on which the economy runs—indeed to expand it to the size consonant with our present-day social and economic needs. Paradoxically, this is also the cheapest way of regaining our momentum—indeed, as we shall see, it could be thought of as costing nothing.

I will turn in a moment to that opportunity. First, however, it is important to understand how we got where we are. How could a state of disrepair clearly injurious to our individual as well as our national interests have been permitted to come about?

There are three reasons, and everyone knows the first. We have been unwilling to impose the taxes—on income, consumption, or even on sin—to pay for public improvements. This is not because our tax structure is so high: in 1985 Sweden's tax revenues amounted to 51 percent of its gross domestic product, France's came to 46 percent, Germany's and England's each to 38 percent. Our revenue—federal plus state and local—was 29 percent of our gross product. Among advanced industrial capitalisms only Japan's was lower—28 percent.

I do not point this out to deplore (although I do deplore it), but to locate the first reason for our inadequate stock of public capital. It has simply been our refusal to pay for a more adequate one—a refusal as evident in the state legislatures as it is on Capitol Hill. The American public has made clear its distaste for taxes, even though opinion polls have again and again indicated the public's dissatisfaction with the existing state of the environment, public facilities, the schools, and the like. However self-defeating and paradoxical this frame of mind, it is a fact of political life that must be reckoned with.

The second reason that we have allowed our infrastructural base to erode has been our fear of deficits. Even though adamantly opposed to paying more taxes, we could still have built roads and bridges, financed education, undertaken housing programs or carried on bold programs of public research and development, if we had been willing to pay for them by borrowing. That is, after all, the way in which the private sector typically finances its capital undertakings. Corporate America does not pay for its own infrastructure— that is, for its investment outlays—by writing checks against its earnings. It finances capital expenditures by issuing new bonds or new stock, which it will "service" from the enhanced earnings that its new capital projects are expected to produce.

Precisely such an avenue of finance is open to the government. Public investment, like private investment, typically yields its payback over a number of years, which is the rationale behind borrowing to pay for it, rather than paying the bill immediately. Moreover, just as private investment brings added earnings, so public investment brings a larger national income. The private corporation uses its additional earnings to pay the dividends or interest on its newly issued securities; the government uses the enhanced tax revenues that flow from a larger national income to pay interest on its new debts.

So why have we not used government borrowing to build public capital, as we have so often done in the past? Part of the answer is that, at least during the last few years, the opposition of the public to more taxes seems to have been matched by its opposition to more deficits. In late 1988, 44 percent of a nation-wide poll of voters chose "reducing the deficit" as the single most pressing issue facing the incoming Bush administration—more than twice the percentage of the next most worrisome issue (protecting U.S. workers against foreign competition). Perhaps the fear of deficits reflects the failure of politicians to explain the resemblance of government borrowing for infrastructure to corporate borrowing for plant and equipment. Perhaps it reflects the failure of economists to explain the similarity to politicians. Whatever the explanation, the fear of deficits is clearly another reason why infrastructure did not get built. We were afraid that we might bankrupt ourselves if we built it. That, too, is a state of mind not likely to change in the near future.

There is one last reason why we have so neglected our public capital. It is that while our public capital expenditures for roads and housing and transportation and education have been declining, our spending for military purposes has been growing. Between 1980 and 1989, military spending doubled from $143 billion to over $300 billion. If we had managed to reduce military spending in 1989 to its inflation-corrected level in 1980, we would have been able to "find" some $50 to $60 billion for infrastructural repairs. But that option was not open to us. As long as the existence of a Soviet threat was the unchallengeable assumption on which American foreign policy was based, the claims of the military might have been whittled away, but could not be radically slashed.

The extraordinary events in Europe have challenged this assumption. There is no longer any question that the Pentagon budget will be sharply cut. Savings on the order of $50 billion ought to be visible within a year or two. If military spending decreases over the next three to five years to perhaps half its present level, which seems possible, $150 billion or more will be pared from the Pentagon budget. Moreover, these are annual savings, available each year from the budgets of the future.

Applied to the improvement of our infrastructure, these funds would approximately restore its level to that of the 1960s. Moreover, that tremendous restoration could take place without incurring a penny of new taxes or a dime of new borrowing. History does not offer many such opportunities. If we let this one slip through our fingers, we will have passed over the greatest and most nourishing free lunch we are likely ever to enjoy.

Of course that lunch is not really free. It is true that we can rebuild our infrastructure without either paying added taxes or suffering the consequences of additional borrowing, but it is also true that we could use the cut in military spending to reduce our taxes or to cut back the amount that the government borrows. Thus the real cost of taking advantage of the chance to rebuild the country's infrastructure is the private gain we will have to forgo—lower taxes, less public borrowing, with its interest costs—in order to achieve a long-denied public gain.

Nevertheless, if the money is spent effectively, it will feel like a free lunch. The proviso is important. The Pentagon has no monopoly on waste. Free or not, the lunch will not be nourishing if we use the peace dividend to buy ourselves a gigantic pork barrel.

That sobering consideration does not argue against seizing the unique chance to make up for past neglect. Rather, it alerts us to the need to find appropriate ways to monitor an opportunity of such extraordinary importance. Perhaps a newly organized bipartisan committee, along the lines of the much respected Congressional Budget Office, or entirely outside the structure of government, should watch over the performance of our public investment effort as we bring it up to the level that will be necessary.

In that case, we would see a change in the quality of life, as the numbers of school dropouts decline, the air gets cleaner, and the economy becomes more productive, the society more decent. We may even remember with disbelief what a ride across the old Queensboro bridge was like. Some may still declare that they would rather have had a tax cut, or a reduction in the national debt, but I suspect that most of us will simply be thankful that America has finally stopped falling behind and has begun to ready itself for whatever place it deserves in the scheme of things.